Microprocessor Architecture, Programming, and Applications

with the 8085/8080A

Merrill's International Series in Electrical and Electronics Technology

Microprocessor Architecture, Programming, and Applications

with the 8085/8080A

Ramesh S. Gaonkar
ONONDAGA COMMUNITY COLLEGE
STATE UNIVERSITY OF NEW YORK

Charles E. Merrill Publishing Company
A Bell & Howell Company
Columbus   Toronto   London   Sydney

To Shivram K. Gaokar—
my father, my teacher, my inspiration

Published by Charles E. Merrill Publishing Company
A Bell & Howell Company
Columbus, Ohio 43216

Production Coordinator: Gnomi Schrift Gouldin
Cover Design: Tony Faiola
Cover Image: Courtesy of Intel Corporation
This book was set in Times Roman and Lubalin

Library of Congress Catalog Card Number: 84-60073
International Standard Book Number: 0-675-20159-4

Printed in the United States of America
        5 6 7 8 9 10—91 90 89 88 87 86

Preface

This text is intended primarily for undergraduate students in technology and engineering curricula. The treatment of the microprocessor is comprehensive, covering both theoretical concepts and practical applications using the 8085/8080A microprocessor family for illustrations. The text assumes that the student has completed a course in digital logic; however, it does not assume any background in programming.

The microprocessor is a general purpose programmable logic device. The thorough understanding of the microprocessor demands the concepts and skills from two different disciplines: hardware concepts from electronics and programming skills from computer science. Hardware is the physical structure of the microprocessor and programming makes it come alive—one without the other is meaningless. Therefore, in this text, the contents are presented with an integrated approach to hardware and software in the context of 8085/8080A microprocessor. Part I focuses on the microprocessor architecture and related hardware; Part II introduces programming; and Part III integrates hardware and software in interfacing and designing microprocessor-based products. Each topic is covered in depth from basic concepts to industrial applications and the topics are illustrated by numerous examples with complete schematics. The material is supported by assignments using practical applications.

Part I, dealing with the hardware of the microcomputer as a system, has four chapters presented with the spiral approach, in a format similar to the view from an airplane that is getting ready to land. As the plane circles around, one observes a view without any details. As the plane descends, the view begins to include more details. This approach allows the students to use a microcomputer as a system in their laboratory work during the early stages of the course, before they have an understanding of all aspects of the system. Chapter 1 presents an overview of the computer systems and discusses the microcomputer and its assembly language in the context of the entire spectrum of computers and computer languages. Chapters 2, 3, and 4 examine microprocessor architecture, memory, and I/O, each chapter increases in depth—from registers to instruction timing.

Part II has six chapters dealing with 8085/8080A instructions, programming techniques, program development, and software development systems. The contents are presented in a step-by-step format. A few instructions that can perform a simple task are selected. Each instruction is described fully with illustrations of its operations and its effects on the selected flags. Then, these instructions are used to write programs, along with programming techniques and troubleshooting hints. Each illustrative program begins with a problem statement, provides the analysis of the problem, illustrates the program, and explains the programming steps. The chapters conclude by reviewing all the instructions discussed within them. The contents of Part II are presented in such a way that, in a course with heavy emphasis on hardware, students can teach themselves assembly language programming if necessary.

Part III synthesizes the hardware concepts of Part I and the software techniques of Part II. It deals with the interfacing of I/Os and contains numerous examples from industry and other practical applications. Each illustration analyzes the hardware and software and describes how the two work together to accomplish a given objective. Chapters 11 through 16 include various types of data transfer between the microprocessor and its peripherals such as simple I/O, interrupts, interfacing of data converters, I/O with handshake signals using programmable devices, and serial I/O. Chapter 14 discusses programmable devices used in the Intel SDK-85 system (such as 8155, 8755, and 8279), while Chapter 15 discusses general purpose programmable devices (such as 8255A, 8253, 8259A, and 8257). Chapter 17 deals primarily with the project design of a single-board microcomputer that brings together all the concepts discussed previously in the text.

A WORD WITH FACULTY MEMBERS

This text is based on my teaching experience, my development of courses, and my association with industry engineers and programmers during the past five years; it is an attempt to share these experiences in and out of the classroom. Some of my assumptions and observations are as follows:

1. Software (instructions) is an integral part of the microprocessor and demands the emphasis equal to that of the hardware.

2. In industry, for the development of microprocessor-based projects, 70 percent of the effort is devoted to software and 30 percent to hardware.
3. Technology and engineering students tend to be hardware oriented and have considerable difficulty learning programming.
4. Students have difficulty in understanding mnemonics and realizing the critical importance of flags.
5. Introductory microprocessor courses should be based on a specific microprocessor. It is irrelevant which microprocessor is selected as an illustration; the concepts transfer easily from one device to another device.

This text is written with the concerns and assumptions stated above. The text should be able to meet the objectives of undergraduate courses with various areas of emphasis. For a one-semester course whose emphasis is evenly divided between hardware and software, the following chapters are recommended: Chapters 1 through 4 for hardware lectures and Chapters 5 through 8 and selected sections of Chapter 9 for software laboratory sessions. For an emphasis on interfacing, initial sections of Chapters 11, 12, and 16 (concepts in peripheral and memory-mapped I/O, and introduction to interrupts and serial I/O) are recommended. If the course is heavily oriented towards hardware, Chapters 1 through 4 and Chapters 11 through 16 are recommended and the necessary programs selected from Chapters 5 through 9. Interfacing laboratory sessions can be designed around the illustrations in those chapters or the experimental assignments given at the end of the chapters. If the course is heavily oriented towards software, Chapters 1 through 10 and selected portions of 11 and 12 can be used. The entire text can be covered in a two-semester course. The instructor's manual includes course designs, a suggested weekly lecture and laboratory schedule, solutions, and selected figures to produce transparencies.

A WORD WITH STUDENTS

Microprocessors are exciting and challenging, and the field is growing. These microcomputers will pervade industry for decades to come. To meet the challenges of this growing technology, you will have to be well conversant with microprocessor programming. Programming is a process of problem solving and communication through the strange language of mnemonics. Most often, hardware oriented students find this communication process very difficult. One of the questions, frequently asked by a student is, How do I get started on a given programming assignment? One approach to learning programming is to examine various types of programs and imitate them. You can begin by studying the illustrative program relevant to an assignment, its flowchart, its analysis, program description and, particularly, the comments. Read the instructions from Appendix F when you need to and pay attention to the flags. This text is written in such way that simple programming of the microprocessor can be self-taught. Once you master the elementary programming techniques, interfacing and design will become exciting and fun.

ACKNOWLEDGMENTS

My students provided the primary incentive for writing this text. Their difficulties, questions, and frustrations shaped the book's design and its development; however, several individuals have made valuable contributions to this text. I would like to extend my sincere appreciation to James Delaney, a colleague who made valuable contributions to the book throughout its various phases. I would also like to thank two other colleagues, Charles Abate and John Merrill, and Dr. Jack Williams of General Electric, who offered many suggestions throughout the project. Similarly, I appreciate the efforts and numerous suggestions of my principal reviewers: John Morgan from DeVry Institute of Technology — Dallas, Peter Holsberg of Mercer County Community College, (N.J.), David M. Hata of Portland Community College (Ore.). Other reviewers were Leslie Sheets of Southern Illinois University at Carbondale — School of Technical Careers, William B. Oltman of Atlas Electric Devices Co., Richard T. Burchell of Riverside City College (Calif.) Jon LeGro of S.U.N.Y. Agricultural and Technical College at Alfred, and Manuel Lizarzaburu of Suffolk County Community College. If this text reads well, the credit goes to Dr. Kathy Forrest of the English Department, who devoted painstaking hours editing the rough draft. Finally, I would like to thank Chris Conty for undertaking and coordinating this project through all its phases and Gnomi Schrift Gouldin for all her efforts through the production process; she made this project more enjoyable than I imagined.

Contents

Part I of this book deals primarily with the microcomputer as a system. The system is discussed in terms of the four components — microprocessor, memory, input, and output — and their communication process. The role of the programming languages, from machine language to higher-level languages, is presented in the context of the system.

The material is presented in a format similar to the view from an airplane that is getting ready to land. As the plane circles around, a passenger observes a view without any details. As the plane starts descending, the passenger begins to see the same view but with more details. In the same way, Chapter 1 presents a general computer as a system, various types of computers (from large computers to microcomputers), and their processes of communication. Chapter 2 provides a closer look at a microcomputer system in relation to the 8085/8080A microprocessor, while Chapter 3 examines the details of the components of the system and their interfacing. Chapter 4 provides an overview of the instructions — the tasks the microprocessor can perform — and their timing relationship. (Chapters 2 and 3 focus on the hardware aspect of the 8085/8080A microcomputer system; Chapter 4, on the other hand, focuses on the 8085/8080A's software capability.)

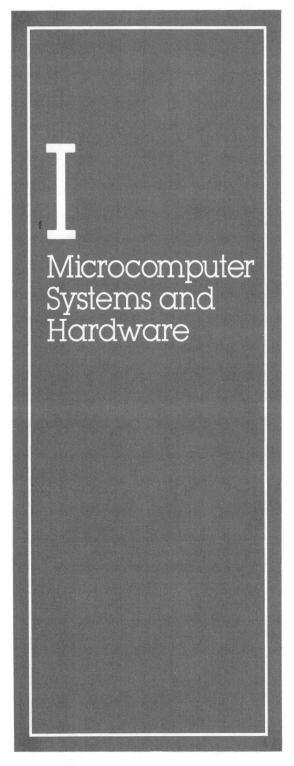

I
Microcomputer Systems and Hardware

PREREQUISITES

The reader is expected to know the following concepts:

☐ Number systems (binary, octal and hexadecimal) and their conversions.
☐ Boolean algebra, logic gates, flip-flops, and registers.
☐ Concepts in combinational and sequential logic.

Microcomputers, Microprocessors, and Assembly Language

The microcomputer is making an impact on every aspect of our lives; and soon it will play a significant role in the daily functioning of all industrialized societies. The basic structure of the microcomputer is no different from any other computer. In the 1960s, computers were accessible and affordable only to large corporations, big universities, and government agencies. Because of advances in semiconductor technology, the million-dollar computing capacity of the 1960s is now available for less than ten dollars in an integrated circuit called the **microprocessor**. A computer designed using the microprocessor is called a **microcomputer**. This chapter introduces the basic structure of a computer and shows how the same structure is applicable to the microcomputer.

Computers communicate and operate in the binary numbers 0 and 1, called **bits**. Each computer has a fixed set of instructions in the form of binary patterns called a **machine language**. Since it is difficult for people to communicate with computers in the language of 0s and 1s, the binary instructions are given abbreviated names, called mnemonics, which form the **assembly language** for a given computer. This chapter provides an explanation of both the machine language and the assembly language of a microcomputer designed with the microprocessor known as the 8085 (or the 8080A — the 8085 is the enhanced version of the 8080A). In addition, the advantages of assembly language in comparison with such English-like languages as BASIC and FORTRAN are discussed. Later in the chapter, microcomputer applications in an industrial environment are presented in the context of the entire spectrum of computer applications.

OBJECTIVES

☐ Draw a block diagram of a computer and explain the functions of each component.
☐ Explain the functions of each component of a microcomputer: microprocessor, memory, and I/O, and their lines of communication, called the bus.
☐ Explain the terms SSI, MSI, and LSI.

☐ Define the terms bit, byte, word, instruction, software, and hardware.
☐ Explain the difference between the machine language and the assembly language of a computer.
☐ Explain the terms low-level and high-level languages.
☐ Explain the advantages of assembly language over high-level languages.

1.1 DIGITAL COMPUTERS

A digital computer is a multipurpose, *programmable* machine that reads *binary* instructions from its *memory,* accepts binary data as *input* and processes data according to those instructions, and provides results as *output*. The physical components of the computer are called **hardware**. A set of instructions written for the computer to perform a task is called a **program**, and a group of programs is called **software**. (This definition of the computer includes several new concepts and technical terms that will be explained in the following paragraphs.)

BINARY

The computer recognizes and operates in binary digits, 0 and 1, also known as bits. A bit is the abbreviated form of the term **binary digit**. These digits are represented in terms of electrical voltages in the machine: generally, 0 represents one voltage level and 1 represents another. The digits 0 and 1 are also synonymous to **low** and **high**, respectively.

PROGRAMMABLE

The computer is **programmable**; that is, it can be instructed to perform tasks within its capability. A toaster can be cited as an example of an elementary programmable machine. It can be programmed to remain on for a given time period by adjusting the setting to "light" or "dark." The toaster is designed to understand and execute one instruction given through a mechanical lever. On the other hand, digital computers are designed to understand and execute many binary instructions. A computer is a much more sophisticated machine than a toaster. It is a multipurpose machine that can be used to perform sophisticated computing functions, as well as to perform such simple control tasks as turning devices on and off. One of the primary differences between a toaster and a computer is that a toaster executes only one function, and that function cannot be changed. On the other hand, the person using a computer can select appropriate instructions and ask the computer to perform various tasks on a given set of data.

The engineer who designs a toaster determines the timing for light and dark toast, and the manufacturer of the toaster provides the necessary instructions to operate the toaster. Similarly, the design engineers of a computer determine a set of tasks the computer should perform, and design the necessary logic circuits. The manufacturer of the computer provides the user with a list of the instructions the computer will understand. Typically, an instruction for adding two numbers may look like a group of eight binary digits, such as 1 0 0 0 0 0 0 1. These instructions are simply a pattern of 0s and 1s. Now, the question is: Where does one write those instructions and enter data? The answer is *memory*.

MEMORY

Memory is like the page of a notebook with space for a fixed number of binary numbers on each line; however, these pages are generally made of semiconductor material. Typically, each line has space for eight binary bits. In reality, a line is an 8-bit register that can store eight binary bits; several of these registers are arranged in a sequence called memory. These registers are always grouped together in powers of two. For example, a group of 1024 (2^{10}) 8-bit registers on a semiconductor chip is known as 1K byte of memory; 1K is the closest approximation in thousands. The user writes the necessary instructions and data in memory, and asks the computer to perform the given task and find an answer. This statement raises several questions: How does one enter those instructions and data in the computer's memory? And where does one look for the answer? The answers are *input* and *output* (I/O) devices.

INPUT/OUTPUT

The user can enter instructions and data in memory through such devices as a keyboard or simple switches, which are called input devices. The computer reads the instructions from the memory and processes the data according to those instructions. The result can be displayed in several ways, such as by seven-segment LEDs (Light Emitting Diodes) or printed by a printer. These devices are called output devices.

This still does not explain how and where the computer processes data. It processes data by using the group of logic circuits called its Central Processing Unit (CPU).

THE CPU

The central processing unit of the computer consists of various registers to store data, the arithmetic/logic unit (ALU) to perform arithmetic and logical operations, instruction decoders, counters, and control lines. The CPU reads instructions from the memory and performs the tasks specified. The CPU communicates with input/output devices to accept or to send data. The input and output devices are known also as **peripherals**. The CPU is the primary and central player in communicating with various devices such as memory, input, and output; however, the timing of the communication process is controlled by the group of circuits called the **control unit**.

The description of a computer given here is traditionally represented by the block diagram shown in Figure 1.1. The block diagram shows that the computer has five components: ALU, control unit, memory, input, and output. The combination of the ALU and the control unit is known as the CPU. Before exploring the details of these components of the computer, we should examine what changes have occurred in semiconductor technology and how those changes have affected computers.

FIGURE 1.1
Traditional Block Diagram of
a Computer

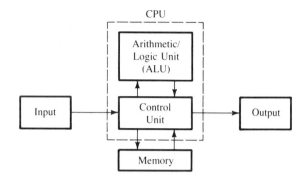

1.11   Computer Technology

In the last twenty-five years, semiconductor technology has undergone unprecedented changes. Integrated circuits (ICs) appeared on the scene at the end of the 1950s, following the invention of the transistor. In an integrated circuit, an entire circuit consisting of several transistors, diodes, and resistors is contained on a single chip. In the early 1960s, logic gates known as the 7400 series were commonly available as ICs, and the technology of integrating the circuits of a logic gate on a single chip became known as Small-Scale Integration (SSI). As semiconductor technology advanced, more than a hundred gates were fabricated on one chip; this was called Medium-Scale Integration (MSI). A typical example of MSI is a decade counter (7490). Within a few years, it was possible to fabricate more than a thousand gates on a single chip; this came to be known as Large-Scale Integration (LSI). Now we are in the era of Very-Large-Scale Integration (VLSI) and Super-Large-Scale Integration (SLSI). The lines of demarcation between these different scales of integration are ill-defined and arbitrary.

    As the technology moved from SSI to SLSI, the face of the computer changed. Initially, computers were built with discrete logic gates (SSI). As more and more logic circuits were built on one chip using LSI technology, it became possible to build the whole CPU with its related timing function on a single chip. This came to be known as the **microprocessor**, and a computer built with a microprocessor is known as a **micro-computer**. This distinction may soon disappear, however, as the computing power of the microprocessor approaches that of the CPUs of the traditional large computers. Early microcomputers were built with a 4-bit microprocessor. Now a 64-bit microprocessor is being used in some prototype computers. Even if they are built with a microprocessor, it is meaningless to classify them as microcomputers.

1.12   Microcomputer Organization

Figure 1.2 shows a simplified but formal structure of a microcomputer. It includes four components: microprocessor, input, output, and memory (read/write memory and read-only memory). These components are organized around a common communication path called a *bus*. The entire group of components is called a *system* or a *microcomputer system,* while the components are called *subsystems.*

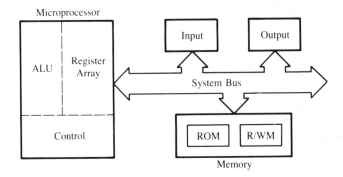

FIGURE 1.2
Block Diagram of a Microcomputer

At the outset, we will differentiate between the terms **microprocessor** and **micro-computer** because of the common misuse of these terms in popular literature. The microprocessor is one component of the microcomputer. On the other hand, the micro-computer is a complete computer similar to any other computer, except that the CPU functions of the microcomputer are performed by the microprocessor. Similarly, the term **peripheral** is used for input/output devices; however, occasionally memory is also included in this term. The various components of the microcomputer shown in Figure 1.2 and their functions are described in the following paragraphs.

MICROPROCESSOR

The microprocessor is a semiconductor device consisting of electronic logic circuits manufactured by using either a large-scale (LSI) or very-large-scale integration (VLSI) technique. The microprocessor is capable of performing computing functions and making decisions to change the sequence of program execution. In large computers, the CPU performs these computing functions and it is implemented on one or more circuit boards. The microprocessor is in many ways similar to the CPU; however, the microprocessor includes all the logic circuitry (including the control unit) on one chip. For clarity, the microprocessor can be divided into three segments, as shown in Figure 1.2: arithmetic/logic unit (ALU), register unit, and control unit.

☐ **Arithmetic/Logic Unit.** In this area of the microprocessor, computing functions are performed on data. The ALU performs arithmetic operations such as addition and subtraction, and logic operations such as AND, OR, and exclusive OR. Results are stored *either* in registers or in memory or sent to output devices.
☐ **Register Unit.** This area of the microprocessor consists of various registers. The registers are used primarily to store data temporarily during the execution of a program. Some of the registers are accessible to the user through instructions.
☐ **Control Unit.** The control unit provides the necessary timing and control signals to all the operations in the microcomputer. It controls the flow of data between the micro-processor and peripherals (including memory).

At present, microprocessors are available from many manufacturers. Examples of widely used microprocessors include the Intel 8080A and 8085, Zilog Z80, Motorola 6800 and 6809, and MOS Technology 6500 series. Microcomputers such as the Radio Shack TRS-80 and the TeleVideo 802 are designed around the Z80 microprocessor. The design of the IBM Personal Computer is based on the Intel 8088 microprocessor. Single-board microcomputers such as the Intel SDK-85 (see Figure 1.5), the Motorola MEK-6800-D2, and the Rockwell Aim 65 are commonly used in college laboratories. The SDK-85 is based on the 8085 microprocessor, the MEK-6800-D2 is based on the 6800 microprocessor, and the Aim 65 is based on the 6502 microprocessor.

INPUT

The input section transfers data and instructions in binary from the outside world to the microprocessor. It includes devices such as keyboards, teletypes, and analog-to-digital converters. Typically, a microcomputer used in college laboratories includes either a hexadecimal keyboard or an ASCII keyboard as an input device. The hexadecimal keyboard has sixteen data keys (0 to 9 and A to F) and some additional function keys to perform operations such as storing data and executing programs. The ASCII keyboard is similar to a typewriter keyboard, and it is used to enter programs in an English-like language. Although the ASCII keyboard is found in most microcomputers, single-board microcomputers generally have a Hex keyboard.

OUTPUT

The output section transfers data from the microprocessor to output devices such as light emitting diodes (LEDs), cathode-ray-tubes (CRTs), printers, magnetic tape, or another computer. Typically, single-board computers include LEDs and seven-segment LEDs as output devices.

MEMORY

Memory stores binary information such as instructions and data, and provides that information to the microprocessor whenever necessary. To execute programs, the microprocessor reads instructions and data from memory and performs the computing operations in its ALU section. Results are either transferred to the output section for display or stored in memory for later use. The memory block (Figure 1.2) has two sections: Read-Only Memory (ROM) and Read/Write Memory (R/WM), popularly known as Random-Access Memory (RAM).

The ROM is used to store programs that do not need alterations. The **monitor program** of a single-board microcomputer is generally stored in the ROM. This program interprets the information entered through a keyboard and provides equivalent binary digits to the microprocessor. Programs stored in the ROM can only be read; they cannot be altered.

The Read/Write memory (R/WM) is also known as **user memory**. It is used to store user programs and data. In single-board microcomputers, in which instructions and data are entered through a Hex keyboard, the monitor program monitors the keys and stores those instructions and data in the R/W memory. The information stored in this memory can be read and altered easily.

SYSTEM BUS

The system bus is a communication path between the microprocessor and the peripherals; it is nothing but a group of wires that carries bits. (In fact, there are several buses in the system; we will discuss them in the next chapter.) The microcomputer bus is in many ways similar to a one-track, express subway: the bus carries bits, just as the subway carries people. The analogy of an express subway with only one destination is more appropriate than that of a regular subway, because the microcomputer bus carries bits between the microprocessor and only one peripheral at a time. The same bus is time-shared to communicate with various peripherals, with the timing provided by the control section of the microprocessor.

1.13   How Does the Microcomputer Work?

Assume that a program and data are already entered in the R/W memory (writing and executing a program will be explained later). The program includes binary instructions to add given data and to display the answer at the seven-segment LEDs. When the microcomputer is given a command to execute the program, it reads and executes one instruction at a time and finally sends the result to the seven-segment LEDs for display.

This process of program execution can best be described by comparing it to the process of assembling a radio kit. The instructions for assembling the radio are printed on a sheet of paper in sequence. One reads the first instruction, then picks up the necessary components of the radio and performs the task. The sequence is this: read, interpret, and perform. The microprocessor performs in the same way. The instructions are stored sequentially in the memory. The microprocessor fetches the first instruction from its memory sheet, decodes it, and executes that instruction. The sequence of fetch, decode, and execute is continued until the microprocessor comes across the instruction, Stop. During the entire process, the microprocessor uses the system bus to fetch the binary instructions and data from the memory. It uses registers from the register section to store data temporarily, and it performs the computing function in the ALU section. Finally, it sends out the result in binary, using the same bus lines, to the seven-segment LEDs.

1.14   Review of Important Concepts

The functions of various components of a microcomputer can be summarized as follows:

1. The microprocessor
   □ communicates with all peripherals (memory and I/Os) using the system bus.
   □ controls timing of information flow.
   □ performs the computing tasks specified in a program.
2. The memory
   □ stores binary instructions and data, called programs.
   □ provides the instructions and data to the microprocessor on request.
   □ stores results and data for the microprocessor.

3. The Input Device
    ☐ enters data and instructions under the control of a program such as a monitor program.

4. The Output Device
    ☐ accepts data from the microprocessor as specified in a program.

5. The Bus
    ☐ carries bits between the microprocessor and the peripherals.

1.2   COMPUTER LANGUAGES

Computers recognize and operate in binary numbers. However, each computer has its own binary words, meanings, and language. The words are formed by combining a number of bits for a given machine. The **word** (or word length) is defined as the number of bits the computer recognizes and processes at a time. The word length ranges from 4 bits for small, microprocessor-based computers to 32 bits for such large computers as the IBM 370. Another term commonly used to express word length is byte. A **byte** is defined as a group of 8 bits. For example, a 16-bit microprocessor has a word length equal to 2 bytes. The term **nibble**, which stands for a group of 4 bits, is found also in popular computer magazines and books. A byte has two nibbles.

Each machine has its own set of instructions based on the design of its CPU or of its microprocessor. To communicate with the computer, one must give instructions in binary language (**machine language**). Since it is difficult for most people to write programs in sets of 0s and 1s, computer manufacturers have devised English-like words to represent the binary instructions of a machine. Programmers can write programs, called **assembly language** programs, using these words. Because an assembly language is specific to a given machine, programs written in assembly language are not transferable from one machine to another. To circumvent this limitation, such general-purpose languages as BASIC and FORTRAN have been devised, a program written in these languages can be machine-independent. These languages are called **high-level languages**. This section deals with various aspects of these three types of languages: machine, assembly, and high-level. The machine and assembly languages are discussed in the context of the 8085/8080A microprocessor.

1.21   Machine Language

The number of bits in a word for a given machine is fixed, and words are formed through various combinations of these bits. For example, a machine with a word length of 8 bits can have 256 (2^8) combinations of 8 bits — thus a language of 256 words. However, not all of these words need be used in the machine. The microprocessor design engineer selects combinations of bit patterns and gives a specific meaning to each combination by using electronic logic circuits; this is called an **instruction**. Instructions are made up of one word or several words. The set of instructions designed into the machine makes up its machine language, a binary language, composed of 0s and 1s, that is specific to each computer. In this book, we are concerned with the language of microcomputers designed with the widely used microprocessors (the 8085 or the 8080A) manufactured by Intel Corporation. The primary focus here is on the microprocessor, because the microprocessor determines the machine language and the operations of a microcomputer.

1.22   8085/8080A Machine Language

The 8085 (or 8080A) is a microprocessor with 8-bit word length: its **instruction set** (or language) is designed by using various combinations of these 8 bits. The 8085 is an improved version of the 8080A; programs written for microcomputers designed with the 8080A can be executed on 8085 microcomputers.

An instruction is a binary pattern entered through an input device to command the microprocessor to perform that specific function.

For example:

0011   1100   is an instruction that increments the number in the register
                 called the **accumulator** by one.

1000   0000   is an instruction that adds the number in the register called
                 B to the number in the accumulator, and keeps the sum in the
                 accumulator.

The 8085 microprocessor has 246 such bit patterns, amounting to 74 different instructions for performing various operations. These 74 different instructions are called its **instruction set**. In addition to the instruction set, the microprocessor also accepts data in eight bits as input from input devices, and sends out data in eight bits to output devices. This binary language of communication with a predetermined instruction set is called the 8085/8080A machine language.

Since it is tedious and error-prone for people to recognize and write instructions in binary language, for convenience, these instructions are written in hexadecimal (or octal) code and entered in a single-board microcomputer by using Hex keys. For example, the binary instruction 0011 1100 (mentioned previously) is equivalent to 3C in hexadecimal. This instruction can be entered in a single-board microcomputer system with a Hex keyboard by pressing two keys: 3 and C. The monitor program of the system translates these keys into their equivalent binary pattern.

1.23   8085/8080A Assembly Language

Even though the instructions can be written in hexadecimal code, it is still difficult to understand a program written in hexadecimal numbers. Therefore, each manufacturer of microprocessors has devised a symbolic code for each instruction, called a **mnemonic**. (The word *mnemonic* is based on the Greek word meaning *mindful*, that is a memory aid.) The mnemonic for a particular instruction consists of letters which suggest the operation to be performed by that instruction.

For example, the binary code 0011 1100 ($3C_{16}$ or 3CH* in hexadecimal) of the 8085/8080A microprocessor is represented by the mnemonic INR A:

---

*Hexadecimal numbers are shown either with the subscript $_{16}$, or as a number followed by the letter *H*.

INR A   INR stands for increment, and A represents the accumulator. This symbol suggests the operation of incrementing the accumulator contents by one.

Similarly, the binary code 1000 0000   (80_{16} or 80H) is represented as

ADD B   ADD stands for addition, and B represents the contents in register B. This symbol suggests the addition of the contents in register B and the contents in the accumulator.

Although these symbols do not specify the complete operations, they suggest its significant part. The complete description of each instruction must be supplied by the manufacturer. The complete set of 8085/8080A mnemonics is called the 8085/8080A assembly language, and a program written in these mnemonics is called an assembly language program. (Again, the assembly language or mnemonics are specific to each microprocessor. For example, the Motorola 6800 microprocessor has an entirely different set of binary codes and mnemonics than the 8085/8080A. Therefore, the assembly language of the 6800 is far different from that of the 8085/8080A.) An assembly language program written for one microprocessor is not transferable to a computer with another microprocessor unless the two microprocessors are compatible in their machine codes.

Machine language and assembly language are microprocessor-specific, and are both considered **low-level languages**. The machine language is in binary, and the assembly language is in English-like words; however, the microprocessor understands only the binary. How, then, do the assembly language mnemonics get translated into binary code? The translation is performed either manually, called **hand assembly**, or by a program, called an **assembler**. These topics are discussed in the next section.

1.24 Writing and Executing an Assembly Language Program

As we explained earlier, a program is a set of logically related instructions written in a specific sequence to accomplish a task. To manually write and execute an assembly language program on a single-board computer, with a Hex keyboard for input and LEDs for output, the following steps are necessary:

1. Write the instructions in mnemonics obtained from the instruction set supplied by the manufacturer.
2. Find the hexadecimal machine code for each instruction by searching through the set of instructions.
3. Enter (load) the program in the user memory in a sequential order by using the Hex keyboard as the input device.
4. Execute the program by pressing the *Execute* key. The answer will be displayed by the LEDs.

This procedure is called either **manual** or **hand assembly**.

When the user program is entered by the keys, each entry is interpreted and converted into its binary equivalent by the monitor program, and the machine code is stored as eight bits in each memory location in a sequence. When the *Execute* command is given, the microprocessor fetches each instruction, decodes it, and executes it in a sequence until the end of the program.

The manual assembly procedure is commonly used in single-board microcomputers and is suited for small programs; however, looking up the machine codes and entering the program is tedious and subject to errors. This process can be avoided if an assembler and an ASCII keyboard are available on the system.

The **assembler** is a program that translates the mnemonics entered by the ASCII keyboard into the corresponding binary machine codes of the microprocessor. Each microprocessor has its own assembler because the mnemonics and machine codes are specific to the microprocessor being used, and each assembler has rules that must be learned by the programmer. (Assemblers are discussed in detail in Chapter 10.)

1.25 High-Level Languages

Programming languages that are intended to be machine-independent are called **high-level languages**. These include such languages as FORTRAN, BASIC, PASCAL and COBOL, all of which have certain sets of rules and draw on symbols and conventions from English. Instructions written in these languages are known as **statements** rather than mnemonics. A program written in BASIC for a microcomputer with the 8085 microprocessor can generally be run on another microcomputer with a different microprocessor.

Now the question is: How are words in English converted into the binary languages of different microprocessors? The answer is: Through another program called either a **compiler** or an **interpreter**. These programs accept English-like statements as their input, called the *source code*. The compiler or interpreter then translates the source code into the machine language compatible with the microprocessor being used in the system. This translation in the machine language is called the object code (Figure 1.3). Each microprocessor needs its own compiler or an interpreter for each high-level language. The primary difference between a compiler and an interpreter lies in the process of generating machine code. The compiler reads the entire program first and then generates the object code. On the other hand, the interpreter reads one instruction at a time, produces its object code, and executes the instruction before reading the next instruction. M-Basic is a common example of an interpreter for the BASIC language. Compilers are generally used in languages such as FORTRAN, COBOL, and PASCAL.

FIGURE 1.3
Block Diagram: Translation of
High-Level Language Program
into Machine Code

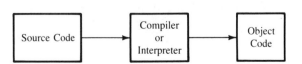

Compilers and interpreters require large memory space because each instruction in English requires several machine codes to translate it into binary. On the other hand, there is one-to-one correspondence between the assembly language mnemonics and the machine code. Thus, assembly language programs are compact and require less memory space. They are more efficient than the high-level language programs. The primary advantage of high-level languages is in troubleshooting (**debugging**) programs. It is much easier to find errors in a program written in a high-level language than to find them in a program written in the assembly language.

In certain applications such as traffic control and appliance control, where programs are small and compact, assembly language is suitable. Similarly, in such real-time applications as converting a high frequency waveform into digital data, program efficiency is critical. In real-time applications, events and time should closely match each other without significant delay; therefore, assembly language is highly desirable in these applications. On the other hand, for applications in which programs are large and memory is not a limitation, high-level languages may be desirable. The advantage of time saved in debugging a large program in a high-level language may outweigh its disadvantages of memory requirements and inefficiency.

1.3 FROM LARGE COMPUTERS TO SINGLE-CHIP MICROCOMPUTERS

In the last quarter century, advances in semiconductor technology have had an unprecedented impact on computer designs. Twenty-five years ago, computers were accessible only to big corporations, universities, and government agencies. Now, "computer" is becoming a common word. The range of computers available extends from such sophisticated, multimillion-dollar machines as the IBM 4300 to the less than fifty-dollar Sinclair Timex home computer. Although all the computers now on the market include the same basic components (shown in Figure 1.1), they are obviously very different.

Different types of computers are designed to serve different purposes. Some are suitable for scientific calculations, while others are used simply for turning appliances on or off. Thus, it is necessary to have an overview of the entire spectrum of computer applications in order to appreciate the topics and applications discussed in this text.

Until five years ago, computers were broadly classified in three categories: main frame, mini, and microcomputers. Since then, technology has changed considerably, and the distinctions between these categories have been blurred. Initially, the microcomputer was defined as a computer with a microprocessor as its CPU. Now practically all computers have various types of microprocessors performing different functions within the large CPU. For the sake of convenience, computers are classified here as large computers, medium-sized computers, and microcomputers.

1.31 Large Computers

Large, general-purpose computers are designed to perform data processing tasks such as complex scientific and engineering calculations and record-handling for large corporations or government agencies. The price is generally beyond a million dollars and can go as high as $6 million. Typical examples of these computers include: IBM 370, IBM 4300 or IBM 3000 series, Burroughs B 7900, and Univac 1180.

These high speed computers have word lengths ranging from 32 to 64 bits. They are capable of addressing megabytes of memory and handling all types of peripherals. At the high end of the range, the CPU alone may cost more than a million dollars. For example, the IBM 3000/81 CPU, capable of addressing 32 megabytes of memory, may cost more than $3 million; the price of the total system may go as high as $6 million. On the other hand, IBM also has medium-sized systems called the 4300 series costing around $100 thousand, and they are known also as **main frame computers**.

1.32 Medium-Sized Computers

In the late 1960s, medium-sized computers were designed to meet the instructional needs of small colleges, the manufacturing problems of small factories, and the data processing tasks of medium-sized businesses, such as payroll and accounting. They were called **minicomputers**. The price range used to be anywhere from $25,000 to $100,000. Typical examples include computers such as Digital Equipment PDP 11/45 and Data General Nova.

These computers were slower than the large computers, and their word length generally ranged from 12 to 32 bits. They were capable of addressing 64K to 256K bytes of memory. At the high end were minicomputers known as midicomputers. However, these classifications are no longer valid. Digital Equipment's new VAX 11 system is a 32-bit machine with the memory addressing capacity of 5 megabytes. The price ranges from $50,000 to $450,000. The high end of the VAX 11 system is almost in the territory of the large computers.

1.33 Microcomputers

The 4-bit and 8-bit microprocessors became available in the mid-1970s, with initial applications primarily in machine control and instrumentation. As the price of the micro-processors and memory declined, the applications mushroomed into video games, word processing, and small business applications. Early arrivals in the microcomputer market, such as Cromemco, North Star Horizon, Radio Shack TRS-80, and Apple, were designed around 8-bit microprocessors. Since then, 16-bit microprocessors, such as Intel 8086/88, Motorola 68000, and Zilog Z8000, have been introduced, and recent microcomputers are being designed around 16-bit microprocessors. Today's microcomputers can be classified into four groups: business (or personal), home, single-board, and single-chip microcomputers.

BUSINESS OR PERSONAL MICROCOMPUTERS

Business microcomputers are being used for a variety of purposes, such as payroll, business accounts, word processing, legal and medical recordkeeping, personal finance, and instruction. They are known also as **personal computers**. Typically, the price ranges from $2,000 to $8,000 for a single-user system, and it can go higher for a multi-user system. Examples include microcomputers such as the IBM Personal Computer, Televideo TS 802, Apple IIe, Radio Shack TRS-80, Intertec Superbrain, and Morrow Design Microdecision (Figure 1.4).

At the low end of the microcomputer spectrum, a typical configuration includes an 8-bit microprocessor, 64K bytes of memory, a CRT terminal, a printer, and dual disk drive for 5¼-inch floppy disks. The **floppy disk** is a magnetic medium similar to a cassette tape except that it is round in shape, like a record. Information recorded on these disks can be accessed randomly using disk drives, while information stored on a cassette tape is accessed serially. In order to read information at the end of the tape, the user must run the entire tape through the machine. Floppy disks are used to store programs such as compilers, interpreters, system programs, user programs, and data. Whenever the user needs to write a program, the necessary software is transferred from the floppy disk to the system's memory. At the high end of the microcomputer spectrum, the basic configuration remains essentially similar. It may include a 16-bit microprocessor, a hard disk with megabytes of storage or an 8-inch disk, an expensive terminal, and a printer.

HOME COMPUTERS

Home computers are differentiated from business microcomputers in terms of their memory storage. Typically, these computers have an 8-bit microprocessor, a CRT terminal with an ASCII typewriter, 16K to 64K memory, and a cassette tape as a storage medium. Some of these computers can be used with television as a video monitor. The

FIGURE 1.4
Microcomputer with Disk Storage
SOURCE: Photograph courtesy of Morrow Designs.

prices of these computers may range from less than $50 to $1,000. Typical examples include the Sinclair TS1000, Commodore 64, and Adam. These microcomputers are used primarily for playing video games, learning simple programming, and running some instructional programs.

SINGLE-BOARD MICROCOMPUTERS

These microcomputers are used primarily in college laboratories and industries for instruction or to evaluate the performance of a given microprocessor. They can also be part of some larger systems. These microcomputers typically include an 8-bit microprocessor, from 256 bytes to 2K bytes of user memory, a Hex keyboard, and seven-segment LEDs for display. The system monitor programs of these computers are generally small, and can be stored in less than 2K bytes of ROM. The prices of these single-board computers range from $100 to $800, with the average price around $300.

Examples of these computers include systems such as Intel SDK-85 (Figure 1.5), Rockwell Aim 65, Motorola Evaluation Kit, E&L Instrument MMD1-Microdesigner, and SD Systems Starter Kit. These single-board microcomputers are used generally to write and execute assembly language programs and to perform interfacing experiments. Aim 65 is an exception to the typical single-board computer, since it has an ASCII keyboard, a BASIC interpreter, and a small printer.

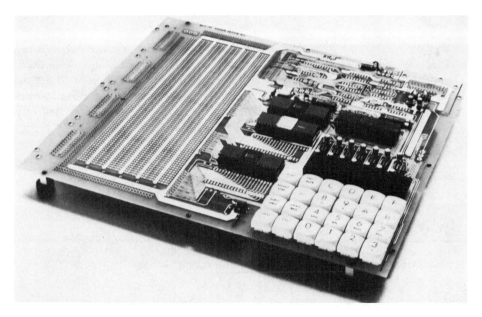

FIGURE 1.5
SDK-85 System
SOURCE: Photograph courtesy of Intel Corporation.

TABLE 1.1
Microcomputer Applications

Characteristics	Types			
	Microcomputer with Disk Storage	Microcomputer with Cassette Tape Storage	Single-Board Microcomputer	Single-Chip Microcomputer
Price range	$2,000–8,000	$50–1000	$100–800	<$100
Memory size (R/WM and ROM)	48K–128K	4K–64K	256 bytes–2K	64–128 bytes
I/O	ASCII keyboard CRT	ASCII keyboard CRT	Hex keyboard (Rarely ASCII) LEDs	Keyboard LEDs
Languages used	Various types of high level languages, assembly	High level, generally BASIC	Assembly	Assembly
Applications	Small business applications, word processing, instructional applications	Entertainment (video games), personal computing	Evaluation of microprocessors, assembly language instruction; as a subsystem	Industrial control

SINGLE-CHIP MICROCOMPUTERS

These microcomputers are designed on a single chip, which typically includes a microprocessor, 64 bytes of R/W memory, from 1K to 2K bytes of ROM, and several signal lines to connect I/Os. These are complete microcomputers on a chip, and are known also as **microcontrollers**. They are used primarily for functions such as controlling appliances and traffic lights. Typical examples of these microcomputers include the Intel 8048 series, Fairchild F8, Motorola 6802, and Zilog Z8.

Various applications and categories of microcomputers are listed in Table 1.1, and the entire spectrum of computer applications is shown in Figure 1.6.

SUMMARY

The various concepts and terms discussed in this chapter are summarized here:

Computer Structure

☐ **Digital Computer**—a programmable machine that processes binary data. It includes five components: CPU (ALU plus control unit), memory, input, and output.

☐ **CPU**—the central processing unit. The group of circuits that processes data and provides control signals and timing. It includes the arithmetic logic unit, registers, instruction decoder, and the control unit.

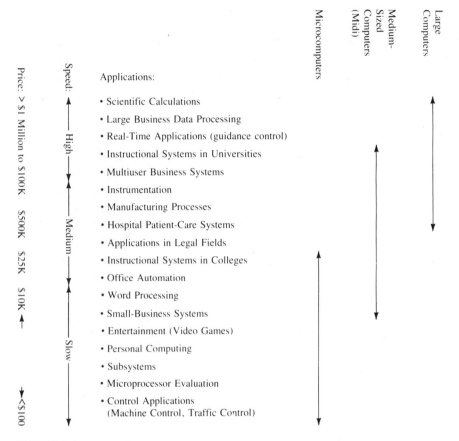

FIGURE 1.6
Applications: From Large Computers to Single-Chip Microcomputers

☐ **ALU**—the group of circuits that performs arithmetic and logic operations. The ALU is a part of the CPU.

☐ **Control Unit**—the group of circuits that provides timing and signals to all operations in the computer and controls data flow.

☐ **Memory**—a medium that stores binary information (instructions and data).

☐ **Input**—a device that transfers information from the outside world to the computer.

☐ **Output**—a device that transfers information from the computer to the outside world.

Scale of Integration

☐ **SSI**—Small-Scale Integration. The process of designing a few circuits on a single chip. The term refers to the technology used to fabricate discrete logic gates on a chip.

☐ **MSI** — Medium-Scale Integration. The process of designing more than a hundred gates on a single chip.

☐ **LSI** — Large-Scale Integration. The process of designing more than a thousand gates on a single chip. Similarly, the terms VLSI (Very-Large-Scale Integration) and SLSI (Super-Large-Scale Integration) are used to indicate the scale of integration.

Microcomputers

☐ **Microprocessor** — a semiconductor device (integrated circuit) manufactured by using the Large-Scale Integration technique. It includes the ALU, register arrays, and control circuits on a single chip.

☐ **Microcomputer** — a computer that is designed using a microprocessor as its CPU. It includes four components: microprocessor, memory, input, and output.

☐ **Bus** — a group of lines used to transfer bits between the microprocessor and other components of the computer system.

☐ **ROM** — (Read-Only Memory) A memory that stores binary information permanently. The information can be read from this memory but cannot be altered.

☐ **R/WM** — (Read/Write Memory) A memory that stores binary information during the operation of the computer. This memory is used as a writing pad to write user programs and data. The information stored in this memory can be read and altered easily.

Computer Languages

☐ **Bit** — a binary digit, 0 or 1.

☐ **Byte** — a group of eight bits.

☐ **Nibble** — a group of four bits.

☐ **Word** — a group of bits the computer recognizes and processes at a time.

☐ **Instruction** — a command in binary that is recognized and executed by the computer in order to accomplish a task. Some instructions are designed with one word, and some require multiple words.

☐ **Mnemonic** — a combination of letters to suggest the operation of an instruction.

☐ **Program** — a set of instructions written in a specific sequence for the computer to accomplish a given task.

☐ **Machine Language** — the binary medium of communication with a computer through a designed set of instructions specific to each computer.

☐ **Assembly Language** — a medium of communication with a computer in which programs are written in mnemonics. An assembly language is specific to a given computer.

☐ **Low-Level Language** — a medium of communication that is machine-dependent or specific to a given computer. The machine and the assembly languages of a computer are considered low-level languages. Programs written in these languages are not transferrable to different types of machines.

☐ **High-Level Language** — a medium of communication that is independent of a given computer. Programs are written in English-like words, and they can be executed on a machine using a translator (a compiler or an interpreter).

☐ **Compiler** — a program that translates English-like words of a high-level language into the machine language of a computer. A compiler reads a given program, called a source code, in its entirety, and then translates the program into the machine language, which is called an object code.

☐ **Interpreter** — a program that translates the English-like statements of a high-level language into the machine language of a computer. An interpreter translates one statement at a time from a source code to an object code.

☐ **Assembler** — a computer program that translates an assembly language program from mnemonics to the binary machine code of a computer.

☐ **Manual Assembly** — a procedure of looking up the machine codes manually from the instruction set of a computer and entering those codes into the computer through a keyboard.

☐ **Monitor Program** — a program that interprets the input from a keyboard and converts the input into its binary equivalent.

LOOKING AHEAD

This chapter has given a brief introduction to computer organization and computer languages, with emphasis on the 8085/8080A microprocessor and its assembly language. The last section has provided an overview of the entire spectrum of computers, including their salient features and applications. The primary focus of this book is on the architectural details of the 8085/8080A microprocessor and its industrial applications. Heavy emphasis also is put on assembly language programming in the context of these applications. In the microcomputer field, little separation is made between hardware and software, especially in applications where assembly language is necessary. In designing a microprocessor-based product, hardware and software tasks are carried out concurrently because a decision in one area affects the planning of the other area. Some functions can be performed either through hardware or software, and a designer needs to consider both approaches. This book focuses on the trade-offs between the two approaches as a design philosophy.

Laboratory experience is a vital part of learning about microprocessors. We assume that single-board microcomputers, such as the Intel SDK-85 or the E&L Instrument Microdesigner, will be available to students for verifying assembly language programs and performing hardware experiments.

Chapter 2 expands on the architectural concepts of microcomputers introduced in this chapter; it deals in detail with each component of the block diagram shown in Figure 1.2. Chapter 3 describes a complete microcomputer system similar to the single-board microcomputer that might be available in college laboratories.

ASSIGNMENTS

1. List the components of a computer.
2. Explain the functions of each component of a computer.
3. What is a microprocessor? What is the difference between a microprocessor and a CPU?
4. Explain the difference between a microprocessor and a microcomputer.
5. Explain these terms: SSI, MSI, and LSI.
6. Define bit, byte, word, instruction.
7. How many bytes make a word of 32 bits?
8. Explain the difference between the machine language and the assembly language of the 8085/8080A microprocessor.
9. What is an assembler?
10. What are low- and high-level languages?
11. Explain the difference between a compiler and an interpreter.
12. What are the advantages of an assembly language in comparison with high-level languages?

Microprocessor Architecture and Microcomputer Systems

A microcomputer system consists primarily of four components — the microprocessor, memory, input, and output — as discussed in the previous chapter. The microprocessor manipulates data, controls timing of various operations, and communicates with such peripherals (devices) as memory and I/O. The internal logic design of the microprocessor, called its **architecture**, determines how and what various operations are performed by the microprocessor. The system bus provides paths for data flow.

This chapter expands on the bus concept discussed in the previous chapter and shows how data flow externally among the components of the system. The chapter deals with the internal architecture and various operations of the microprocessor in the context of the 8085/8080A. It also expands on topics such as memory and I/O, and reviews interfacing devices such as buffers, decoders, and latches, in a microcomputer system more detailed than the one presented in the last chapter.

OBJECTIVES

☐ List the four operations commonly performed by the microprocessor or the MPU.

☐ Define the **address bus,** the **data bus,** and the **control bus,** and explain their functions in reference to the 8085/8080A microprocessor.

☐ List the registers in the 8085/8080A microprocessor, and explain their functions.

☐ Explain the functions: **Reset, Interrupt, Wait,** and **Hold**.

☐ Explain memory organization and memory map, and explain how memory addresses are assigned to a memory chip.
☐ List the types of memory and their functions.
☐ Explain the difference between the peripheral I/O and the memory-mapped I/O.

☐ Describe the steps in executing an instruction in a bus-oriented system.
☐ Define **tri-state logic** and explain the functions of such MSI devices as buffer, decoder, encoder, and latch.

2.1 MICROPROCESSOR ARCHITECTURE AND ITS OPERATIONS

The microprocessor is a programmable logic device, designed with registers, flip-flops, and timing elements. The microprocessor has a set of instructions designed internally, to manipulate data and communicate with peripherals. This process of data manipulation and communication is determined by the logic design of the microprocessor, called the **architecture**.

The microprocessor can be programmed to perform functions on given data by selecting necessary instructions from its set. These instructions are given to the microprocessor by writing them into its memory. Writing (or entering) instructions and data is done through an input device such as a keyboard. The microprocessor reads or transfers each instruction one at a time, matches it with its instruction set, and performs the data manipulation indicated by the instruction. The result can be stored in memory or sent to such output devices as LEDs or a CRT terminal. In addition, the microprocessor can respond to external signals. It can be interrupted, reset, or asked to wait to synchronize with slower peripherals. All the various functions performed by the microprocessor can be classified in three general categories:

☐ Microprocessor-initiated operations
☐ Internal data operations
☐ Peripheral (or externally) initiated operations

To perform these functions, the microprocessor requires a group of logic circuits and a set of signals called control signals. However, early processors do not have the necessary circuitry on one chip; the complete units are made up of more than one chip. Therefore, the term Micro Processing Unit (MPU) is defined here as a group of devices that can perform these functions with the necessary set of control signals. This term is similar to the term Central Processing Unit (CPU). However, later microprocessors include most of the necessary circuitry to perform these operations on a single chip. Therefore, the terms *MPU* and *microprocessor* often are used synonymously.

The microprocessor functions listed above are explained here in relation to the 8085 or 8080A MPU. The explanation does not include either the details of the MPUs or the differences between the 8085 and 8080A microprocessors. The devices necessary to make up the 8085 and the 8080A MPUs will be discussed in the next chapter.

2.11 Microprocessor-Initiated Operations and 8085/8080A Bus Organization

The MPU performs primarily four operations:*

1. Memory Read: Reads data from memory.
2. Memory Write: Writes data into memory.
3. I/O Read: Accepts data from input devices.
4. I/O Write: Sends data to output devices.

All these operations are part of the communication process between the MPU and peripheral devices (including memory). To communicate with a peripheral (or a memory location), the MPU needs to perform the following steps:

☐ Step 1: Identify the peripheral or the memory location (with its address).
☐ Step 2: Transfer data.
☐ Step 3: Provide timing or synchronization signals.

The 8085/8080A MPU performs these functions using three sets of communication lines called buses: the address bus, the data bus, and the control bus (Figure 2.1). In Chapter 1, these buses are shown as one group, called the system bus.

ADDRESS BUS

The address bus is a group of sixteen lines generally identified as A_0 to A_{15}. The address bus is **unidirectional**: bits flow in one direction—from the MPU to peripheral devices. The MPU uses the address bus to perform the first function: identifying a peripheral or a memory location (Step 1).

In a computer system, each peripheral or memory location is identified with a binary number, called an **address**, and the address bus is used to carry a 16-bit address. This is similar to the postal address of a house. The number of a house can be identified with various number schemes. For example, the forty-fifth house in a lane can be identified with the two-digit number 45, or with the four-digit number 0045. The two-digit numbering scheme can identify only a hundred houses, from 00 to 99. On the other hand, the four-digit scheme can identify ten thousand houses, from 0000 to 9999. Similarly, the number of address lines of the MPU determines its capacity to identify different memory locations (or peripherals). The 8085/8080A MPU with its sixteen address lines is capable of addressing $2^{16} = 65536$ (generally known as 64K) memory locations. As explained in Chapter 1, 1K memory is determined by rounding off 1024 to the nearest thousand; similarly, 65536 is rounded off to 64000 as a multiple of 1K.

Most 8-bit microprocessors have sixteen address lines. This may explain why most microcomputer systems have 64K memory—however, not every microcomputer system

---

*Other operations are omitted here for clarity and discussed in the next chapter.

has 64K memory. In fact, most single-board microcomputers have memory less than 2K, even if the MPU is capable of addressing 64K memory. The number of address lines is arbitrary; it is determined by the designer of a microprocessor based on such considerations as availability of pins and intended applications of the processor. For example, the MOS Technology MCS 6515 microprocessor has twelve address lines and is capable of addressing 4K ($2^{12} = 4096$) memory. Another example is the Motorola 68000, which has 23 address lines.

DATA BUS

The data bus is a group of eight lines used for data flow (Figure 2.1). These lines are **bidirectional** — data flow in both directions between the MPU and peripheral devices. The MPU uses the data bus to perform the second function: transferring data (Step 2).

The eight data lines enable the MPU to manipulate 8-bit data ranging from 00 to FF ($2^8 = 256$ numbers). The largest number that can appear on the data bus is 11111111 (255_{10}). The data bus influences the microprocessor architecture considerably. It determines the word length and the register size of a microprocessor; thus the 8085/8080A microprocessor is called an 8-bit microprocessor. Microprocessors such as the Intel 8086, Zilog Z8000, and Motorola 68000 have sixteen data lines; thus they are known as 16-bit microprocessors.

CONTROL BUS

The control bus is comprised of various single lines that carry synchronization signals. The MPU uses such lines to perform the third function: providing timing signals (Step 3).

The term **bus**, in relation to the control signals, is somewhat confusing. These are individual lines that provide a pulse to indicate an MPU operation. The MPU generates specific control signals for every operation (such as Memory Read or I/O Write) it performs. These signals are used to identify a device type with which the MPU intends to communicate.

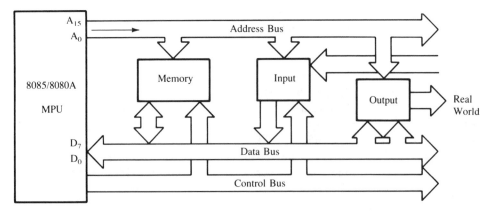

FIGURE 2.1
The 8085/8080A Bus Structure

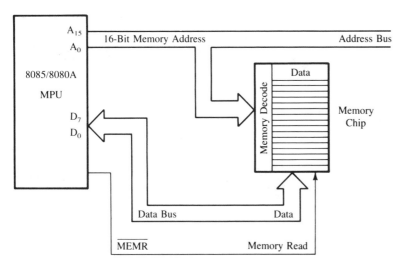

FIGURE 2.2
Memory Read Operation

To communicate with a memory—for example, to read an instruction from a memory location—the MPU places the 16-bit address on the address bus (Figure 2.2). The address on the bus is decoded by an external logic circuit, which will be explained later, and the memory location is identified. The MPU sends a pulse called Memory Read as the control signal. The pulse activates the memory chip, and the contents of the memory location (8-bit data) are placed on the data bus and brought inside the microprocessor.

What happens to the data byte brought into the MPU depends on the internal architecture of the microprocessor, which we will describe in the next section.

2.12   Internal Data Operations and the 8085/8080A Registers

The internal architecture of the 8085/8080A microprocessor determines how and what operations can be performed with the data. These operations are

1. Store 8-bit data.
2. Perform arithmetic and logical operations.
3. Test for conditions.
4. Sequence the execution of instructions.
5. Store data temporarily during execution in the defined R/W memory locations called the stack.

To perform these operations, the microprocessor requires registers, an arithmetic logic unit (ALU) and control logic, and internal buses (paths for information flow). Figure 2.3 is a simplified representation of the 8085/8080A internal architecture; it shows only those registers which are programmable, meaning those registers that can be used for

FIGURE 2.3
The 8085/8080A Programmable
Registers

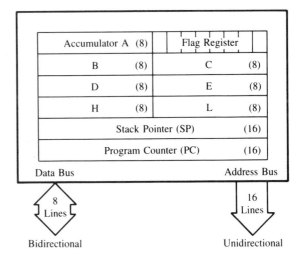

data manipulation by writing instructions. These registers are described in reference to the five operations previously listed.

REGISTERS

The 8085/8080A has six general-purpose registers to perform the first operation listed above; that is, to store 8-bit data during a program execution. These registers are identified as B, C, D, E, H, and L, as shown in Figure 2.3. They can be combined as register pairs — BC, DE, and HL — to perform some 16-bit operations.

These registers are **programmable**, meaning that a programmer can use them to load or transfer data from the registers by using instructions. For example, the instruction MOV B,C transfers the data from register C to register B. Conceptually, the registers can be viewed as memory locations, except they are built inside the microprocessor and identified by specific names. Some microprocessors do not have these types of registers; instead, they use memory space as their registers.

ACCUMULATOR

The accumulator is an 8-bit register that is part of the arithmetic logic unit (ALU). This register is used to store 8-bit data and to perform arithmetic and logical operations. The result of an operation is stored in the accumulator. The accumulator is also identified as register A.

FLAGS

The ALU includes five fip-flops that are set or reset according to data conditions in the accumulator and other registers. The microprocessor uses them to perform the third operation; namely, testing for data conditions.

For example, after an addition of two numbers, if the sum in the accumulator is larger than eight bits, the flip-flop that is used to indicate a carry, called the **Carry flag**

(CY), is set to one. When an arithmetic operation results in zero, the flip-flop called the **Zero flag** (Z) is set to one. The 8085/8080A has five flags to indicate five different types of data conditions. They are called Zero (Z), Carry (CY), Sign (S), Parity (P), and Auxiliary Carry (AC) flags. The most commonly used flags are Zero and Carry; the others will be explained as necessary.

Figure 2.3 shows an 8-bit register, called the **flag register**, adjacent to the accumulator. It is not really a register; five bit positions, out of eight, are used to store the outputs of the five flip-flops. The flags are stored in the 8-bit register so that the programmer can examine these flags (data conditions) by accessing the register through an instruction. In the instruction set, the term PSW (Program Status Word) refers to the accumulator and the flag register. This term will be discussed again in Chapter 8: Stack and Subroutines.

These flags have critical importance in the decision-making process of the microprocessor. The conditions (set or reset) of the flags are tested through software instructions. For example, the instruction JC (Jump On Carry) is implemented to change the sequence of a program when the CY flag is set. The importance of the flags cannot be emphasized enough; they will be discussed again in applications of conditional jump instructions.

PROGRAM COUNTER (PC)

This 16-bit register deals with the fourth operation, sequencing the execution of instructions. This register is a **memory pointer**. Memory locations have 16-bit address, and that is why this is a 16-bit register (see section 2.22 for memory address).

The microprocessor uses this register to sequence the execution of instructions. The function of the program counter is to point to the memory address from which the next byte is to be fetched. When a byte (machine code) is being fetched the program counter is incremented by one to point to the next memory location.

STACK POINTER (SP)

The stack pointer is also a 16-bit register used as a memory pointer; initially, it will be called the stack pointer register to emphasize that it is a register. It points to a memory location in R/W memory, called the **stack**. The beginning of the stack is defined by loading a 16-bit address in the stack pointer (register).*

2.13 Peripheral or Externally Initiated Operations

External devices (or signals) can initiate the following operations, for which individual pins on the microprocessor chip are assigned: *Reset, Interrupt, Ready, Hold.*

☐ *Reset:* When the reset is activated, all internal operations are suspended and the program counter is cleared (it holds 0000H). Now the program execution can again begin at the zero memory address.

---

*The concept of the stack memory is difficult to explain at this time; it is not necessary for the reader to understand the stack memory until the topic called Subroutines is discussed. It is included here only to provide continuity to the description of programmable registers and microprocessor operations. This concept will be explained more fully in Chapter 8.

☐ *Interrupt:* The microprocessor can be interrupted from the normal execution of instructions and asked to execute some other instructions called **service routine** (for example, emergency procedures). The microprocessor resumes its operation after completing the service routine.

☐ *Ready:* The 8085/8080A has a pin called READY. If the signal at this READY pin is low, the microprocessor enters into a Wait state. This signal is used primarily to synchronize slower peripherals with the microprocessor.

☐ *Hold:* When the HOLD pin is activated by an external signal, the microprocessor relinquishes control of buses and allows the external peripheral to use them. For example, the HOLD signal is used in Direct Memory Access (DMA) data transfer.

These operations are listed here to provide an overview of capabilities of the 8085/8080A. They will be discussed again in Part III, Interfacing Peripherals (I/Os) and Applications.

2.2   MEMORY

Memory is an essential component of a microcomputer system. It stores binary instructions and data for the microprocessor. Two types of memory were identified in the last chapter: Read/Write Memory (R/WM) and Read-Only Memory (ROM). The R/W Memory is made of registers, and each register has a group of flip-flops that stores bits of information. The number of bits stored in a register is called a **memory word**; memory devices (chips) are available in various word sizes. The MPU can read from or write into this memory. The second type of memory, the ROM, stores information permanently in the form of diodes; a group of diodes can be viewed as a register. The MPU can only read information from the ROM; it cannot write into this memory.

In a memory chip, all registers are arranged in a sequence and identified by binary numbers called memory addresses. The assignment of memory addresses to various registers in a memory chip and the process of communication between the MPU and the memory are described below. The following discussion is equally applicable to R/WM and ROM except for slight differences in Read/Write control signals.

2.21   Memory Organization (R/W Memory)

For an 8-bit microprocessor, memory is required to store eight bits of information as a group; thus, the memory word length should be eight bits. To communicate with memory, the MPU should be able to

☐ Select the chip
☐ Identify the register
☐ Read from or write into the register

Figure 2.4 shows a hypothetical memory chip of eight registers with three address lines, one chip select ($\overline{\text{CS}}$) line, one read/write (R/$\overline{\text{W}}$) line, and eight I/O lines. The MPU uses the $\overline{\text{CS}}$ line to select the chip, and the R/$\overline{\text{W}}$ line to control data flow. The registers

FIGURE 2.4
A Memory Chip with
Eight Registers

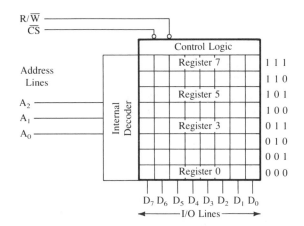

are arranged sequentially and numbered 000_2 to 111_2. These numbers are called **memory addresses**, identifying each register as a memory location. To identify each register, the MPU would require three address lines to place eight different addresses from 000_2 to 111_2. The 8085/8080A MPU with its sixteen address lines is capable of identifying or addressing 65,536 (64K) such memory registers or locations.

The size of this hypothetical chip can be specified either as 8 byte, 8×8 bit, or 64 bit. A memory chip with 256 registers (or locations) with 4 I/O lines is specified as 256×4 bit or 1024 bit. For an 8-bit microprocessor, two such memory chips (256×4) would be necessary to form the 8-bit memory word size, resulting in 256 bytes of memory.

To read from or write into a memory location (e.g., register 5 in Figure 2.4), the microprocessor places the address (1 0 1) on the address bus. The decoder decodes the address and identifies the register. (The decoder and its decoding function are explained in Section 2.53.) The control signal $R/\overline{W}$ enables the I/O lines, and the data byte is either read from or stored in the memory location. The Chip Select $\overline{CS}$ line, also known as Chip Enable ($\overline{CE}$), is necessary to select one particular memory chip from among several memory chips in a system. The 8085/8080A microprocessor has sixteen address lines, and this hypothetical chip (Figure 2.4) requires only three address lines. The question of what to do with the other thirteen lines and the Chip Select ($\overline{CS}$) line is still unresolved. This question is answered in the next section.

2.22   Memory Map

Memory map is defined as the assignment of addresses to memory registers in various memory chips in a system. In a system based on the 8085/8080A microprocessor, the entire memory map can range from 0000H to FFFFH ($2^{16} = 65,536$). This memory map can be illustrated with an analogy of identical houses built in a sequence and their postal addresses or numbers.

Let us assume that houses are given four-digit decimal numbers, which will enable us to number ten thousand houses from 0000 to 9999. Since it is cumbersome to direct someone to houses with large numbers, the numbering scheme can be devised with the concept of a row or block. Each block will have a hundred houses to be numbered with the last two digits from 00 to 99. Similarly, the blocks are also identified by the first two decimal digits. For example, a house with the number 0247 is house number 47 in block 2. With this scheme, all the houses in block 0 will be identified from 0000 to 0099, in block 20 from 2000 to 2099, and in block 99 from 9900 to 9999. This numbering scheme with four decimal digits is capable of giving addresses to ten thousand houses from 0000 to 9999 (100 blocks of 100 houses each). A new area under development may have only two blocks completed — block 0 and block 20 — the houses on these blocks can have addresses 0000 to 0099 and 2000 to 2099, even if other blocks are still empty. Let us also assume that all houses are identical, and have eight rooms.

The example of numbering the houses is directly applicable to assigning addresses to memory registers. In the binary number system, sixteen binary digits can have 65,536 (2^{16}) different combinations. In the hexadecimal number system, sixteen binary bits are equivalent to four Hex digits that can be used to assign addresses to 65,536 memory registers from 0000H to FFFFH; however, it is easier to think in terms of two Hex digits than four Hex digits. Therefore, the concept of memory page, similar to the concept of block, can be devised, as explained below.

In a memory system, memory registers can be conceptually organized in a group to be numbered with low-order two hexadecimal digits, similar to the last two digits of the house address. With two Hex digits, 256 registers can be numbered from 00H to FFH; this is known as a page with 256 lines to read from or write on. Although the number FFH is equal to 255, the total number of lines is equal to 256 because the first line is numbered 0. Similarly, the high-order (first) two Hex digits can be used to number the pages from 00H to FFH. For example, the memory address 020FH represents line 15 (register) on page 2, the address 07FFH represents line 255 on page 7, and the address 1064H represents line 100 on page 16 ($64H = 100_{10}$ and $10H = 16_{10}$). The total memory address will range from 0000H to FFFFH — 256 pages with 256 lines each ($256 \times 256 = 65,536$, known as 64K). To complete the analogy, a line (register) is equivalent to a house, a page is equivalent to a block, and eight flip-flops in a register are equivalent to eight rooms in a house. These concepts are further illustrated by the following example of a memory chip with 256 bytes of memory.

Example 2.1	Illustrate the memory map of the chip with 256 bytes of memory, shown in Figure 2.5(a), and explain how the memory map can be changed by modifying the hardware of the Chip Select ($\overline{CS}$) line in Figure 2.5(b).
Solution	Figure 2.5(a) shows a memory chip with 256 registers and 8 I/O lines; the memory size of this chip is expressed as 256×8. It has eight address lines, one Chip Select ($\overline{CS}$) line (active low), and one Read/Write (R/$\overline{W}$) line. The eight address lines (A_7–A_0) of the microprocessor are required to identify 256 (2^8) memory registers. Eight other address lines (A_{15}–A_8) are connected to the Chip Select ($\overline{CS}$) line through inverters* and the NAND gate. The memory chip is enabled or selected when the $\overline{CS}$ goes low. Therefore, to select the memory chip, the address lines A_{15}–A_8 should be at logic 0, which will cause the output

---

*See Appendix C, Preferred Logic Symbols, for the explanation of the inverter symbol.

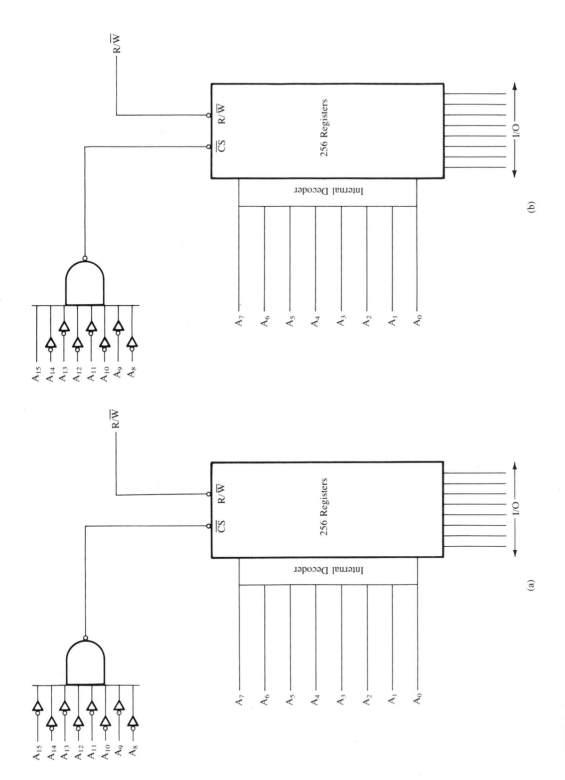

FIGURE 2.5
Memory Map: 256 Bytes of Memory

of the NAND gate to go low. No other logic levels on the lines A_{15}–A_8 can select the chip. Once the chip is selected (enabled), the address lines A_7–A_0 can assume any combination from 00H to FFH, and identify any one of the 256 memory locations through its decoder. The control signal $R/\overline{W}$ enables data flow. Therefore, the memory addresses of the chip in Figure 2.5(a) will range from 0000H to 00FFH as shown below.

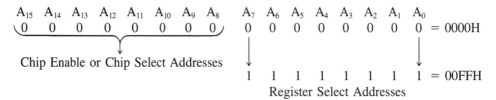

The entire range of the memory addresses from 0000 to 00FFH is known as the memory map of the chip in Figure 2.5(a). The Chip Select addresses are determined by the hardware (the inverters and NAND gate); therefore, the memory map of the chip can be changed by modifying the hardware. For example, if the inverter on line A_{15} is removed as shown in Figure 2.5(b), the address required on A_{15}–A_8 to enable the chip will be as follows:

$$A_{15} \quad A_{14} \quad A_{13} \quad A_{12} \quad A_{11} \quad A_{10} \quad A_9 \quad A_8$$
$$1 \qquad 0 \qquad 0 \qquad 0 \qquad 0 \qquad 0 \qquad 0 \qquad 0 \ = 80H$$

Therefore, the memory map of the chip (Figure 2.5(b)) ranges from 8000H to 80FFH. By eliminating all the inverters of the NAND gate in Figure 2.5(a), the memory map will be from FF00H to FFFFH. The memory chips in Figure 2.5(a) and (b) are the same chips. However, by changing the hardware of the Chip Select logic, the memory map can be changed, and memory can be assigned addresses in various locations over the entire map (of 64K).

After reviewing the example and the previous explanation of the memory map, we can summarize the following points.

1. In a numbering system, the number of digits used determines the maximum addressing capacity of the system. Sixteen address lines (16 bits) of the 8085/8080A micro-processor can address 65,536 memory registers; this is similar to four decimal digits providing the postal addresses for ten thousand houses.
2. In a numbering system, the number of digits used can be conceptually divided in groups. In memory addressing, low-order addresses from 00H to FFH are viewed as line numbers, and high-order addresses are viewed as page numbers.
3. For a given memory chip, the number of address lines required to identify the registers is determined by the number of registers in the chip. The remaining address lines can be used for selecting the chip.
4. The memory map of a given chip can be changed by changing the hardware of the Chip Select ($\overline{CS}$) line. This line is also known as the Chip Enable ($\overline{CE}$) line.

2.23 Memory Map of a 1K Memory Chip

The analogy of line and page number is ideally suited to explain the memory map of a chip with 256 registers. However, if a chip includes more than 256 registers (e.g., 512 or 1024 registers), the analogy requires some elaboration as shown in the following example.

Explain the memory map of 1K (1024×8) memory shown in Figure 2.6, and explain the changes in the memory map if the hardware of the $\overline{\text{CS}}$ line is modified.

Example 2.2

The memory chip has 1024 registers; therefore, 10 address lines (A_9-A_0) are required to identify the registers. The remaining six address lines ($A_{15}-A_{10}$) of the microprocessor are used for the Chip Select ($\overline{\text{CS}}$) signal. In Figure 2.6, the memory chip is enabled when the address lines $A_{15}-A_{10}$ are at logic 0. The address lines A_9-A_0 can assume any address of the 1024 registers starting from all 0s to all 1s as shown below.

Solution

A_{15}	A_{14}	A_{13}	A_{12}	A_{11}	A_{10}	A_9	A_8	A_7	A_6	A_5	A_4	A_3	A_2	A_1	A_0	
0	0	0	0	0	0	0	0	0	0	0	0	0	0	0	0	= 0000H

Chip Select Logic

0	0	0	0	0	0	1	1	1	1	1	1	1	1	1	1	= 03FFH

FIGURE 2.6
Memory Map: 1024 Bytes of Memory

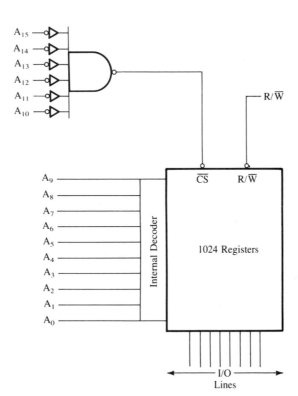

The memory map ranges from 0000H to 03FFH. In terms of the page analogy, this can be interpreted as the memory having four pages as shown below:

00	00	Page 0 with 256 lines.
00	FF	
01	00	Page 1 with 256 lines.
01	FF	
02	00	Page 2 with 256 lines.
02	FF	
03	00	Page 3 with 256 lines.
03	FF	

As explained in the previous example, the memory map of the 1K chip in Figure 2.6 can be changed to any other location by changing the hardware of the $\overline{\text{CS}}$ line. For example, if the inverter of the line A_{15} is removed, the memory map will range from 8000H to 83FFH.

In the preceding example, the memory map can be viewed as four pages; in reality, all the registers are on one chip. This concept is similar to building four hundred houses in one block, but conceptually viewing them as four blocks with one hundred houses in each block. The house numbers will range from 0000 to 0399 in decimal (assuming the first house has the number 0000).

The preceding discussion concerning the memory map is equally applicable to the Read-Only Memory (ROM). The ROM is in many ways organized the same as the R/W memory. The primary difference between the organization of the two memories is in the control signals. The ROM requires the *Read* signal from the MPU.

This section has been concerned primarily with assigning addresses using the address lines; the next section describes how the microprocessor communicates with memory using the address lines and control signals.

2.24 Memory and Instruction Fetch

The primary function of memory is to store instructions and data and to provide that information to the MPU whenever the MPU requests it. The MPU requests the information by sending the address of a specific memory register on the address bus and enables the data flow by sending the control signal — as illustrated in the next example.

Example 2.3	The instruction code 0100 1111 (4FH) is stored in memory location 2005H. Illustrate the data flow and list the sequence of events when the instruction code is fetched by the MPU.
Solution	To fetch the instruction located in memory location 2005H, the following steps are performed:

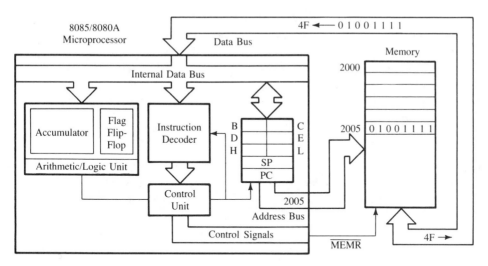

FIGURE 2.7
Instruction Fetch Operation

1. The program counter places the 16-bit address 2005H of the memory location on the address bus (Figure 2.7).
2. The control unit sends the Memory Read control signal ($\overline{\text{MEMR}}$, active low) to enable the memory chip.
3. The instruction (4F) stored in the memory location is placed on the data bus and transferred (copied) to the microprocessor. (The execution of the instruction will be discussed in the next chapter.)

Figure 2.7 shows how the 8085/8080A MPU fetches the instruction using the address, the data, and the control buses. Figure 2.7 is similar to Figure 2.2, Memory Read Operation, except that Figure 2.7 shows additional details.

2.25 Types of Memory

Memory can be classified into two groups: **prime** (or **main memory**) and **storage memory**. The R/WM and ROM discussed in the last section are examples of prime memory; this is the memory the microcomputer uses in executing and storing programs. The storage memory includes cassette tape, magnetic tape, floppy disk, and hard disk (see Chapter 10). The R/WM and ROM are general categories of the prime memory; they include several types of memory listed below.

R/WM

As mentioned previously, this is a read/write memory popularly known as Random Access Memory (RAM). This memory is **volatile**, meaning that when the power is turned off, all the contents are destroyed. Two types of R/W memories are available, static and dynamic.

Static memory is made up of flip-flops, and it stores a bit as a voltage. **Dynamic memory** is made up of MOS transistor gates, and it stores a bit as a charge. The advantage of dynamic memory is that a large number of transistor gates can be placed on a memory chip; thus it has high density and is faster than static memory. The disadvantage is that the charge (bit information) leaks; therefore, information needs to be read and written again every few milliseconds. This is called **refreshing** the memory, and it requires additional circuitry.

ROM

The ROM is a **nonvolatile** memory, meaning that it retains the stored information even if the power is turned off. The concept underlying the ROM memory can be explained with the diodes arranged in a matrix format as shown in Figure 2.8. The horizontal lines are connected to vertical lines only through the diodes; they are not connected where they appear to cross in the diagram. Each of the eight horizontal rows can be viewed as a register with binary addresses ranging from 000 to 111; information is stored by the diodes in the register as 0s or 1s. The presence of a diode stores 1, and its absence stores 0. When a register is selected, the voltage of that line goes high, and the output lines, where diodes are connected, go high. For example, when the memory register 1 1 1 is selected, the data byte 0 1 1 1   1 0 0 0 (78H) can be read at the data lines D_7 to D_0.

The diode representation is a simplified version of the actual MOS FET memory cell. The manufacturer of the ROM designs the MOS FET matrix according to the

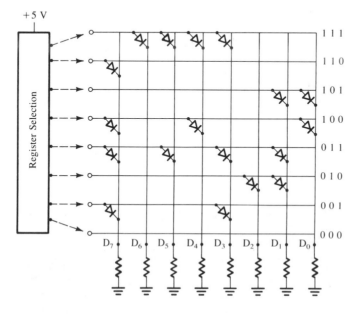

FIGURE 2.8
Functional Representation of ROM Memory Cell

information to be stored; therefore, information is permanently recorded in the ROM, as a song is recorded on a record. Four types of ROM are presently available: Masked ROM, PROM, EPROM, and EE-PROM.

MASKED ROM

In this ROM, a bit pattern is permanently recorded by the masking and metalization process, an expensive and specialized process. Memory manufacturers are generally equipped to do this process, but it is economical only for production quantities in the thousands.

PROM (PROGRAMMABLE READ-ONLY MEMORY)

This memory has nichrome or polysilicon wires arranged in a matrix as shown in Figure 2.8. The wires can be functionally viewed as diodes or fuses. This memory can be programmed by the user with a special PROM programmer that selectively burns the fuses according to the bit pattern required to be stored. The process is known as "burning the prom," and the information stored is permanent.

EPROM (ERASABLE PROGRAMMABLE READ-ONLY MEMORY)

The information stored in this memory is semipermanent. All the information can be erased by exposing the memory to ultraviolet light through a quartz window installed on the chip. Then the memory chip can be reprogrammed again and again. This memory is commonly used in product development and experimental projects.

EE-PROM (ELECTRICALLY ERASABLE PROM)

This memory is functionally similar to EPROM, except that information can be altered by using electrical signals at the register level rather than erasing all the information. However, the manufacturing process is quite complex, and some of the technical problems are yet to be resolved. At present, it is expensive and not in common use.

In a microprocessor-based product, programs are generally written in ROM, and data that are likely to vary are stored in R/WM. For example, in a microprocessor-controlled oven, programs that run the oven are permanently stored in ROM, and data such as baking period, starting time, and temperature are entered in R/W memory through the keyboard. On the other hand, when microcomputers are used for developing software or for learning purposes, programs are first written in R/W memory, and then stored on a storage memory such as cassette tape or a floppy disk.

INPUT/OUTPUT (I/O)   2.3

The remaining components of the microcomputer system are Input/Output devices. The MPU communicates with the "the outside world" through such devices. The MPU accepts binary data as input from devices such as keyboards or floppy disks, and sends data to output devices such as LEDs or printers. There are two different methods by which the

MPU identifies and communicates with the I/O devices. These methods are known as **Peripheral** (or **Direct**) **I/O** and **Memory-Mapped I/O**. The methods differ in terms of the number of address lines used in identifing an I/O device, the type of control lines used to enable the device, and the instructions used for data transfer. The 8085/8080A MPU can use either eight address lines or sixteen address lines to identify an I/O device, as discussed below.

2.31   Peripheral or Direct I/O

In peripheral or direct I/O (also known as accumulator I/O) two instructions (IN and OUT) are used for data transfer. The MPU uses eight address lines to send the address of an I/O device. (Recall the analogy of postal addresses. The eight address lines are capable of identifying 256 input devices and 256 output devices.) The input and output devices are differentiated by the control signals I/O Read ($\overline{\text{IOR}}$) and I/O Write ($\overline{\text{IOW}}$). Thus, in this method, I/O addresses range from 00 to FF. These addresses are known as either **I/O device addresses** or **I/O port numbers**.

   The steps in communicating with an I/O device are similar to those in communicating with memory and can be summarized as follows:

1. The MPU places an 8-bit device address on the address bus, which is decoded by the external decode logic (explained in Chapter 11).
2. The MPU sends a control signal (I/O Read or I/O Write) and enables the I/O device.
3. Data are placed on the data bus for transfer.

2.32   Memory-Mapped I/O

In memory-mapped I/O, the MPU uses sixteen address lines to identify an I/O device. This process is similar to communicating with a memory location. The memory-mapped I/O technique uses the same control signals ($\overline{\text{MEMR}}$ or $\overline{\text{MEMW}}$) and instructions as those of memory. The memory map (64K) is shared between memory and I/O devices. The MPU views these I/O devices as if they were memory locations. In such microprocessors as the Motorola 6800, there are no special I/O instructions; all I/Os are part of the memory map.

   The peripheral and the memory-mapped I/O techniques will be discussed in detail in Chapter 11.

2.4   EXAMPLE OF A MICROCOMPUTER SYSTEM

Based on the discussion in the previous sections, we can expand the microcomputer system shown in Figure 2.1 to include additional details. Figure 2.9 illustrates such a system. It shows the 8085/8080A MPU, two types of memory (EPROM and R/WM), input and output, and the buses linking all peripherals (memory and I/Os) to the MPU.

   The address lines A_{15} to A_0 are used to address memory, and the low-order address bus A_7 to A_0 is used to identify the input and the output. The data bus D_7 to D_0 is bidirectional and common to all the devices. The four control signals generated by the MPU are connected to different peripheral devices, as shown in Figure 2.9.

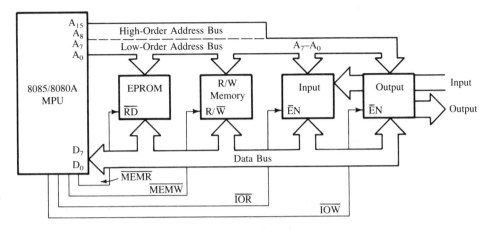

FIGURE 2.9
Example of an 8085/8080A Microcomputer System

The MPU communicates with only one peripheral at a time by enabling the peripheral through its control signal. For example, to send data to the output device, the MPU places the device address (output port number) on the address bus, data on the data bus, and enables the output device using the control signal $\overline{IOW}$ (I/O Write). The output device latches and displays data if the output device happens to be LEDs. The other peripherals that are not enabled remain in a high impedance state called tri-state (explained later), similar to being disconnected from the system.

The preceding description mentions two new concepts: tri-state and data latching. It suggests that the tri-state is a high impedance state. The concept of data latching suggests the need for a device in addition to the output device. Figure 2.9 is a simplified block diagram of the system; it does not show such details as data latching and tri-state devices (see Section 2.5 — Interfacing Devices).

Figure 2.10 shows an expanded version of the output section and the buses of Figure 2.9. The block diagram includes tri-state bus drivers, a decoder, and a latch. The bus drivers increase the current driving capacity of the buses, the decoder decodes the address to identify the output port, and the latch holds data output for display. These devices are called **interfacing devices**. The interfacing devices are semiconductor chips that are needed to connect peripherals to the bus system. Before we discuss interfacing concepts, we will review these interfacing devices.

INTERFACING DEVICES 2.5

Several types of interfacing devices are necessary to interconnect the components of a bus-oriented system. The devices used in today's microcomputer systems are designed using Medium-Scale Integration (MSI) technology. In addition, tri-state logic devices are essential to proper functioning of the bus-oriented system, in which the same bus lines are

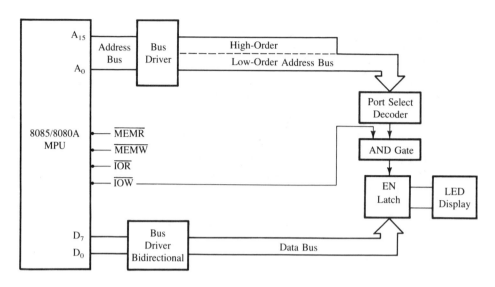

FIGURE 2.10
The Output Section of the Microcomputer System Illustrated in Figure 2.9

shared by several components. The concept underlying the tri-state logic, as well as commonly used interfacing devices, will be reviewed in the following section.

2.51   Tri-State Devices

Tri-state logic devices have three states: logic 1, logic 0, and high impedance. The term TRI-STATE is a trade mark of National Semiconductor and is used to represent three logic states. A tri-state logic device has a third line called Enable as shown in Figure 2.11. When this line is activated, the tri-state device functions the same way as ordinary logic devices. When the third line is disabled, the logic device goes into a high impedance state — as if it were disconnected from the system. Ordinarily, current is required to drive a device in logic 0 and logic 1 states. In the high impedance state, practically no current is drawn from the system. Figure 2.11(a) shows a tri-state inverter. When the Enable is high the circuit functions as an ordinary inverter; and when the Enable line is low, the inverter stays in the high impedance state. Figure 2.11(b) also shows a tri-state inverter with active low Enable line — notice the bubble. When the Enable line is high, the inverter stays in the high impedance state.

FIGURE 2.11
Tri-State Inverters with
Active High and Active Low
Enable Lines

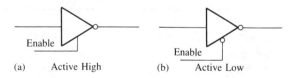

FIGURE 2.12
A Buffer and a Tri-State Buffer

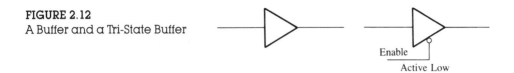

Enable

Active Low

In microcomputer systems, peripherals are connected in parallel between the address bus and the data bus. However, because of the tri-state interfacing devices, peripherals do not load the system buses. The microprocessor communicates with one device at a time by enabling the tri-state line of the interfacing device. Tri-state logic is critical to proper functioning of the microcomputer.

2.52 Buffer

The **buffer** is a logic circuit which amplifies the current or power. It has one input line and one output line (a simple buffer is shown in the first drawing of Figure 2.12). The logic level of the output is the same as that of the input; logic 1 input provides logic 1 output (the opposite of an inverter). The buffer is used primarily to increase the driving capability of a logic circuit. It is also known as a driver.

Figure 2.12 also shows a tri-state buffer. When the Enable line is low, the circuit functions as a buffer; otherwise it stays in high impedance state. The buffer is commonly used to increase the driving capability of the data bus and the address bus.

EXAMPLES OF TRI-STATE BUFFERS

The octal buffer 74LS244 shown in Figure 2.13 is a typical example of a tri-state buffer. It is also known as a **line driver** or **line receiver**. This device is commonly used as a driver for the address bus in a bus-oriented system.

FIGURE 2.13
Logic Diagram of the 74LS244
Octal Buffer

SOURCE: Courtesy of Texas Instruments Incorporated.

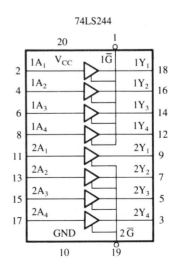

Figure 2.13 shows two groups of four buffers with noninverted tri-state output. The buffers are controlled by two active low Enable lines ($\overline{1G}$ and $\overline{2G}$). Until these lines are enabled, the output of the drivers remains in the high impedance state. Each buffer is capable of sinking 24 mA and sourcing −15 mA of current. The 74LS240 is another example of a tri-state buffer; it has tri-state inverted output.

BIDIRECTIONAL BUFFER

The data bus of a microcomputer system is bidirectional; therefore, it requires a buffer that allows data to flow in both directions. Figure 2.14 shows the logic diagram of the bidirectional buffer 74LS245, also called an **octal bus transceiver**. This is commonly used as a driver for the data bus.

The 74LS245 includes sixteen bus drivers, eight for each direction, with tri-state output. The direction of data flow is controlled by the pin DIR. When DIR is high, data flow from the A bus to the B bus; and when it is low, data flow from B to A. The schematic also includes an Enable signal ($\overline{G}$), which is active low. The Enable signal and the DIR signal are ANDed to activate the bus lines. The device is designed to sink 24 mA and source −15 mA of current.

Another example of a bidirectional buffer is shown in Figure 2.15, the Intel 8286 octal bus transceiver. It is functionally similar to the 74LS245 with slightly higher driving capacity. However, the two buffers are not pin compatible.

2.53 Decoder

The decoder is a logic circuit that identifies each combination of the signals present at its input. For example, if the input to a decoder has two binary lines, the decoder will have

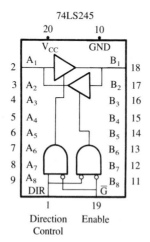

Enable $\overline{G}$	Direction Control DIR	Operation
L	L	B Data to A Bus
L	H	A Data to B Bus
H	X	Isolation

Function Table

H = high level, L = low level, X = irrelevant

FIGURE 2.14

Logic Diagram of the 74LS245 Bidirectional Buffer

SOURCE: Courtesy of Texas Instruments Incorporated.

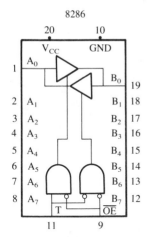

Function Table		
Output Enable $\overline{OE}$	Transmit T	Operation
L	L	Data Flow from B to A
L	H	Data Flow from A to B
H	X	High Impedance

FIGURE 2.15

Logic Diagram of the 8286 Bidirectional Buffer

SOURCE: Adapted from Intel Corporation, *MCS — 80/85 Family User's Manual* (Santa Clara, Calif.: Author, 1979) p. 6-154.

FIGURE 2.16

2-to-4 (1-out-of-4) Decoder
Logic Symbol

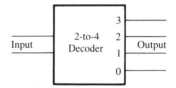

four output lines (Figure 2.16). The two lines can assume four combinations of input signals — 00, 01, 10, 11 — with each combination identified by the output lines 0 to 3. If the input is 11_2, the output line 3 will be at logic 1, and the others will remain at logic 0. This is called **decoding**. Figure 2.16 shows a symbolic representation for a hypothetical 2:4 decoder. It is also called a 1-out-of-4 decoder. Various types of decoders are available; for example, 3-to-8, 4-to-16 (to decode binary inputs), and 4-to-10 (to decode BCD input). In addition, some decoders have active low output lines as well as Enable lines, as shown in Figure 2.17. The decoder shown in Figure 2.17(b) will not function unless it is enabled by a low signal. The internal logic of these decoders is discussed using the example of a 2-to-4 decoder.

Figure 2.18 shows the internal gates of a 2-to-4 decoder with low active output. The decoder has four NAND gates and two inverters. For each combination of the input, only one output line goes low and the others remain high.

A 2-to-4 decoder with an Enable line can be implemented as shown in Figure 2.19. The schematic shows that each NAND gate has three inputs, and the third input is from the Enable line through an inverter. When the Enable line is inactive (high), the circuit does not function as a decoder; all output lines remain high despite any input signals. When the Enable is low, the output of the decoder changes according to the input.

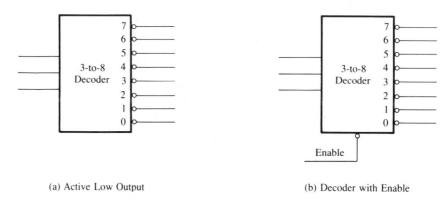

(a) Active Low Output   (b) Decoder with Enable

FIGURE 2.17
3-to-8 (1-out-of-8) Decoder Logic Symbol

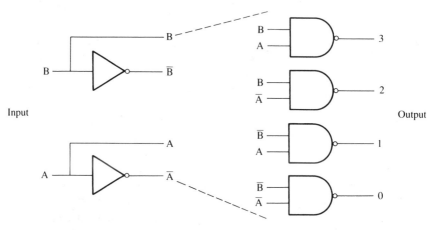

FIGURE 2.18
Internal Logic of a 2-to-4 Decoder with Active Low Output

A decoder is a commonly used device in interfacing I/O peripherals and memory. In Figure 2.10 the decoder (Port Select Decoder) is used to decode an address bus to identify the output device. Decoders are built also internal to a memory chip to identify individual memory locations.

EXAMPLES OF DECODERS

Figure 2.20 shows the block diagrams of two 3-to-8 decoders, the 74LS138 and the Intel 8205. These are pin compatible with slight differences in their switching response and current capacity. They are also called **1-out-of-8 binary decoders** or **demultiplexers**.

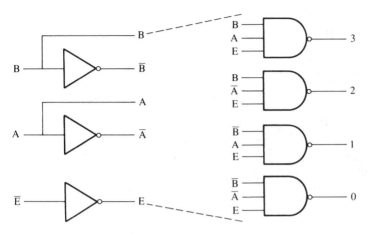

FIGURE 2.19
Internal Logic of 2-to-4 Decoder with Enable and Active Low Output

The 74LS138 has three input lines and eight active low output lines. It requires three enable inputs: two are active low and one is active high; these three enable inputs are ANDed together internally, generating a single enable signal for the decoder. Thus, all three enable lines should be activated so that the device can function as a decoder. For example, if the 74LS138 is enabled ($\overline{G2A} = \overline{G2B} = 0$ and $G1 = 1$) and if the input is 1 0 1, the output line Y_5 will go low; others will remain high.

2.54 Encoder

The encoder is a logic circuit that provides the appropriate code (binary, BCD, etc.) as output for each input signal. The process is the reverse of decoding. Figure 2.21 shows an 8-to-3 encoder; it has eight active low inputs and three output lines. When the input line 0 goes low, the output is 000; and when the input line 5 goes low, the output is 101. However, this encoder is unable to provide an appropriate output code if two or more input lines are activated simultaneously. Encoders called priority encoders can resolve the problem of simultaneous inputs.

Figure 2.22 shows the logic symbol of the 74LS148, an 8-to-3 **priority encoder**. It has eight inputs and one active low enable signal. It has five output signals—three are encoding lines and two are output-enable indicators. The output lines GS and EO can be used to encode more than eight inputs by cascading these devices. When the encoder is enabled and two or more input signals are activated simultaneously, it ignores the low priority inputs and encodes the highest priority input.

Encoders are commonly used with keyboards. For each key pressed, the corresponding binary code is placed on the data bus.

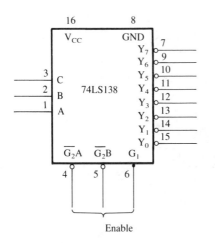

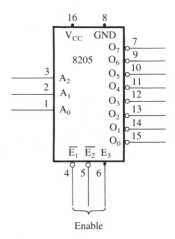

LS138, S138
Function Table

Inputs				Outputs							
Enable		Select									
G_1	G_2	C	B	A	Y_0	Y_1	Y_2	Y_3	Y_4	Y_5	Y_6	Y_7
X	H	X	X	X	H	H	H	H	H	H	H	H
L	X	X	X	X	H	H	H	H	H	H	H	H
H	L	L	L	L	L	H	H	H	H	H	H	H
H	L	L	L	H	H	L	H	H	H	H	H	H
H	L	L	H	L	H	H	L	H	H	H	H	H
H	L	L	H	H	H	H	H	L	H	H	H	H
H	L	H	L	L	H	H	H	H	L	H	H	H
H	L	H	L	H	H	H	H	H	H	L	H	H
H	L	H	H	L	H	H	H	H	H	H	L	H
H	L	H	H	H	H	H	H	H	H	H	H	L

H = high level, L = low level, X = irrelevant

Address			Enable			Outputs							
A_0	A_1	A_2	E_1	E_2	E_3	0	1	2	3	4	5	6	7
L	L	L	L	L	H	L	H	H	H	H	H	H	H
H	L	L	L	L	H	H	L	H	H	H	H	H	H
L	H	L	L	L	H	H	H	L	H	H	H	H	H
H	H	L	L	L	H	H	H	H	L	H	H	H	H
L	L	H	L	L	H	H	H	H	H	L	H	H	H
H	L	H	L	L	H	H	H	H	H	H	L	H	H
L	H	H	L	L	H	H	H	H	H	H	H	L	H
H	H	H	L	L	H	H	H	H	H	H	H	H	L
X	X	X	L	L	L	H	H	H	H	H	H	H	H
X	X	X	H	L	L	H	H	H	H	H	H	H	H
X	X	X	L	H	L	H	H	H	H	H	H	H	H
X	X	X	H	H	L	H	H	H	H	H	H	H	H
X	X	X	L	L	H	H	H	H	H	H	H	H	H
X	X	X	H	L	H	H	H	H	H	H	H	H	H
X	X	X	L	H	H	H	H	H	H	H	H	H	H
X	X	X	H	H	H	H	H	H	H	H	H	H	H

(a) 74LS138

(b) 8205

FIGURE 2.20

Logic Diagram: 3-to-8 Decoder

SOURCE: (a) Courtesy of Texas Instruments Incorporated. (b) Intel Corporation, *MCS — 80/85 Family User's Manual* (Santa Clara, Calif.: Author, 1979), p. 6-74.

FIGURE 2.21

Logic Symbols: 8-to-3 Encoder

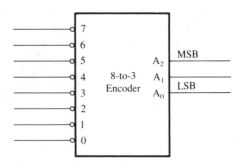

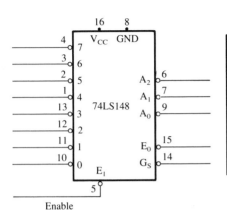

'148, 'LS148
Function Table

	Inputs									Outputs				
E_I	0	1	2	3	4	5	6	7	A_2	A_1	A_0	G_S	E_0
H	X	X	X	X	X	X	X	X	H	H	H	H	H
L	H	H	H	H	H	H	H	H	H	H	H	H	L
L	X	X	X	X	X	X	X	L	L	L	L	L	H
L	X	X	X	X	X	X	L	H	L	L	H	L	H
L	X	X	X	X	X	L	H	H	L	H	L	L	H
L	X	X	X	X	L	H	H	H	L	H	H	L	H
L	X	X	X	L	H	H	H	H	H	L	L	L	H
L	X	X	L	H	H	H	H	H	H	L	H	L	H
L	X	L	H	H	H	H	H	H	H	H	L	L	H
L	L	H	H	H	H	H	H	H	H	H	H	L	H

FIGURE 2.22
8-to-3 Priority Encoder — 74LS148: Logic Symbol and Function Table

SOURCE: Function table courtesy of Texas Instruments, Incorporated.

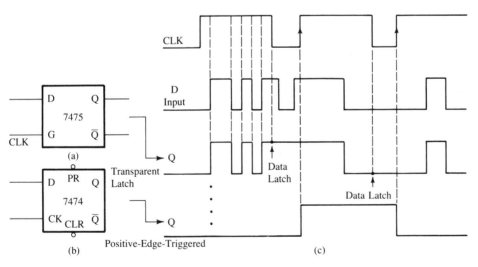

FIGURE 2.23
D Flip-Flops and Output Waveforms

2.55 Latch

In its simplest form, a latch is a D flip-flop. Two types of D flip-flops are available, as shown in Figure 2.23; a **transparent latch** (a), and a **positive-edge-triggered flip-flop** (b). In a transparent latch, when the clock signal is high, the output Q changes according to the input D. When the clock signal goes low, the output Q will latch (hold) the last value of the input D (Figure 2.23(c)). A typical example of a latch is the 7475 D flip-flop. In a positive-edge-triggered flip-flop, the output changes with the positive edge of the clock. The 7474 is a positive edge-triggered flip-flop.

A latch is used commonly to interface output devices. When the MPU sends an output, data are available on the data bus for only a few microseconds, and therefore, a latch is used to hold data for display.

EXAMPLES OF LATCHES

Typical examples of transparent latches are the 74LS373 and the Intel 8282, shown in Figure 2.24. Both are functionally similar; however, they are not pin compatible. These octal latches are suitable to latch 8-bit data.

The devices include eight D latches with tri-state buffers. They require two input signals, Enable (G) and Output Control ($\overline{OC}$) for the 74LS373, which are synonomous to the Strobe (STB) and Output Enable ($\overline{OE}$) for the 8282. The Enable (or the Strobe) is an active high signal connected to the clock input of the flip-flop. When this signal goes low, data are latched from the data bus. The Output Control (or the Output Enable) signal is active low, and it enables the tri-state buffers to output data to display devices.

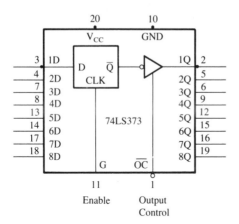

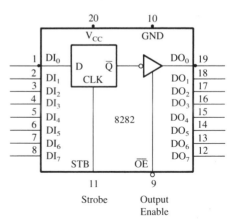

	Function Table		
Output Control	Enable G	D	Output
L	H	H	H
L	H	L	L
L	L	X	Q_0
H	X	X	Z

(a)

	Function Table		
Output Enable	STB	Input DI	Output DO
L	H	H	H
L	H	L	L
L	L	X	Data Latch
H	X	X	Z

(b)

FIGURE 2.24
Logic Symbols: D Latches

These interfacing devices are discussed briefly here as a review to explain why they are needed and how they are used in microcomputer systems. The next section will explain how some of them are used in a memory device, and they will be discussed again in Chapter 11, Parallel I/O and Interfacing Applications.

2.56 Inside Look at a Memory Device

An inside look at a memory chip can illustrate an application of devices discussed in the previous section. Figure 2.25 shows the internal organization of an 8×8 memory device. It includes eight memory registers, a 3-to-8 decoder, an input buffer, and an output buffer. The device has three input address lines, eight input and eight output lines for data flow, and two control lines: Read/Write ($R/\overline{W}$) and Chip Select ($\overline{CS}$).

To write an 8-bit word, the MPU places the register address on the three address lines. For example, to write in the register No. 7 (see Figure 2.25), the MPU places 111 on the address lines. The decoder decodes the address and selects the register No. 7. Next, the MPU places the data on the data bus and sends the active low $R/\overline{W}$ control signal. The control signal enables the input buffer, and data are placed in the selected register. To read from this memory, the process is similar to that of the write operation except that the output buffer is enabled with the $R/\overline{W}$ active high signal. The remaining address lines of the MPU address bus can be used to select the chip ($\overline{CS}$).

The address decoding scheme shown in Figure 2.25 is conceptually easy to understand. However, as the memory size increases, this decoding scheme becomes impractical.

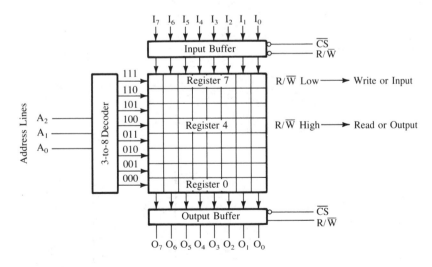

FIGURE 2.25
Block Diagram of a Memory Chip

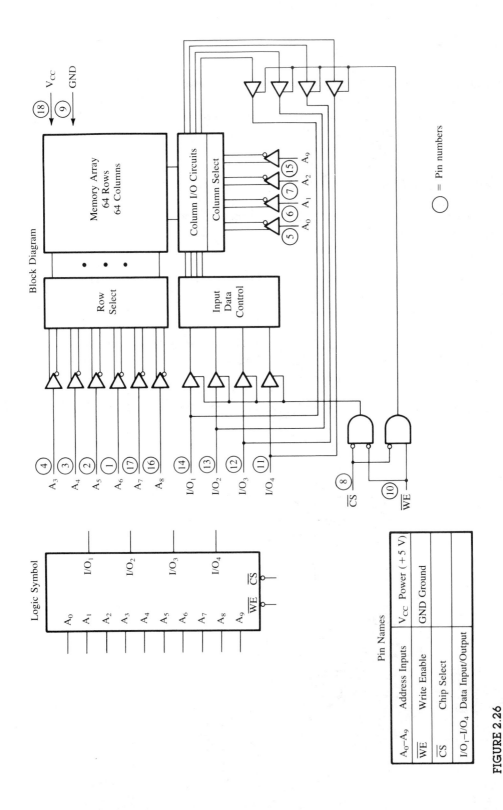

FIGURE 2.26

Logic Diagram of the 2114 Memory Device

SOURCE: Intel Corporation, *MCS — 80/85 Family User's Manual* (Santa Clara, Calif.: Author, 1979), p. 6-173.

Figure 2.26 shows the block diagram of the 2114 memory device. This device has a 1024×4 memory size, with the memory registers arranged in rows and columns. The decoding scheme uses row select and column select circuits. It does not have separate external data lines for input and output; however, it has two different internal I/O buffers. The control logic shows that both signals $\overline{CS}$ and $\overline{WE}$ (Write Enable) are required to enable the device. When the $\overline{WE}$ is low, the input buffers are enabled; when the $\overline{WE}$ is high, the output buffers are enabled.

This example illustrates how interfacing devices are used internally in memory chips. The next chapter will show how interfacing devices are used to interconnect peripherals and memory with the 8085 MPU.

SUMMARY

☐ The microprocessor (MPU) primarily performs four operations: Memory Read, Memory Write, I/O Read, and I/O Write. For each operation, it generates the appropriate control signal.

☐ To communicate with a peripheral (and memory), the MPU identifies the peripheral or the memory location by its address, transfers data, and provides timing signals.

☐ **Address Bus** — a group of lines that are used to send a memory address or a device address from the MPU to the memory location or the peripheral. The 8085/8080A microprocessor has sixteen address lines.

☐ **Data Bus** — a group of bidirectional lines which are used to transfer data between the MPU and peripherals (or memory). The 8085/8080A microprocessor has eight data lines.

☐ **Control Bus** — single lines that are generated by the MPU to provide timing of various operations.

☐ The 8085/8080A microprocessor has six general-purpose 8-bit registers to store data, and an accumulator to perform arithmetic and logical operations.

☐ The data conditions, after an arithmetic or logical operation, are indicated by setting or resetting the flip-flops called flags. The 8085/8080A includes five flags: Sign, Zero, Auxiliary Carry, Parity, and Carry.

☐ The 8085/8080A has two 16-bit registers: the program counter and the stack pointer. The program counter is used to sequence the execution of a program, and the stack pointer is used as a memory pointer for the stack memory.

☐ The 8085/8080A has four signals to respond to externally initiated operations: Reset, Interrupt, Ready, and Hold.

☐ Memory is a group of registers, arranged in a sequence, to store bits. The 8085/8080A MPU requires an 8-bit-wide memory word and uses the 16-bit address to select a register called a memory location.

☐ The memory addresses assigned to a memory chip in a system are called the memory map. The assignment of memory addresses is done through the chip-select logic.

☐ Memory can be classified primarily into two groups, Read/Write Memory (R/WM) and Read-Only Memory (ROM). The R/W memory is volatile and can be used to read and write information. This is also called the user memory. The ROM is a nonvolatile memory and the information written into this memory is permanent.

☐ Input/Output devices or peripherals can be interfaced with the 8085/8080A MPU in two ways, peripheral I/O and memory-mapped I/O. In peripheral I/O, the MPU uses an 8-bit address to identify an I/O, and IN and OUT instructions for data transfer. In memory-mapped I/O, the MPU uses a 16-bit address to identify an I/O, and memory-related instructions for data transfer.

☐ To execute an instruction, the MPU places the 16-bit address on the address bus, sends the control signal to enable the memory chip, and fetches the instruction. The instruction is then decoded and executed.

☐ To interconnect peripherals with the 8085/8080A MPU, additional logic circuits, called interfacing devices, are necessary. These circuits include devices such as buffers, decoders, encoders, and latches.

☐ A tri-state logic device has three states: two logic states and one high impedance state. When the device is not enabled, it remains in high impedance and does not draw any current from the system.

ASSIGNMENTS

1. What is a bus?
2. Specify the direction of the information flow on the address bus.
3. How many memory locations can be addressed by a microprocessor with fourteen address lines?
4. How many address lines are necessary to address two megabytes (2048K) of memory?
5. Why is the data bus bidirectional?
6. How many data lines are necessary in a 16-bit microprocessor, and what is the magnitude of the largest number that can be placed on its data bus?
7. Specify the four control signals commonly used by the 8085/8080A MPU.
8. Specify the control signal and the direction of the data flow on the data bus in a memory-write operation.
9. What is the function of the accumulator?
10. What is a flag?
11. Why are the program counter and the stack pointer 16-bit registers?
12. While executing a program, if the 8085/8080A MPU fetches the machine code located at the memory address 2057H, what is the content of the program counter?
13. What is the memory word size required in an 8085/8080A system?
14. If the memory chip size is 1024 × 4 bits, how many chips are required to make up 2K (2048) bytes of memory?
15. If the memory chip size is 256 × 1 bits, how many chips are required to make up 1K (1024) bytes of memory?

16. How many address lines are necessary on the chip of 2K (2048) byte memory?

17. The memory map of a 4K (4096) byte memory chip begins at the location 2000H. Specify the address of the last location on the chip and the number of pages in the chip.

18. The memory address of the last location of a 1K byte memory chip is given as FBFFH. Specify the memory map.

19. How many address lines are used to identify an I/O port in the peripheral I/O and in the memory-mapped I/O methods?

20. What are tri-state devices and why are they essential in a bus-oriented system?

21. In Figure 2.13, if the input to the octal buffer is 4FH and the enable lines $1\overline{G}$ and $2\overline{G}$ are high, what is the output of the buffer?

22. In Figure 2.15, if signals $\overline{OE}$ (Output Enable) and T (Transmit) are low, specify the direction of data flow.

23. Specify the output line of the 4-to-16 decoder that goes low if the input to the decoder is as shown in Figure 2.27.

24. In Figure 2.28, specify the output line that goes low if the input (including the enable lines) to the 3-to-8 decoder (74LS138) is:

A_7	A_6	A_5	A_4	A_3	A_2	A_1	A_0
1	1	1	1	0	1	1	1

FIGURE 2.27

Logic Diagram of a
4-to-16 Decoder

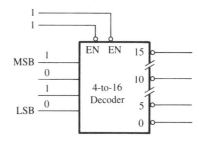

FIGURE 2.28

The 3-to-8 Decoder (74LS138)

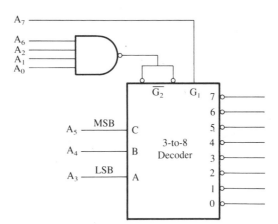

25. What is the output of the encoder (Figure 2.29) if the key K_6 is pushed? (See Figure 2.22 for the function table.)

26. What is a transparent latch, and why is it necessary to use a latch with output devices such as LEDs?

27. Specify the memory map of the schematic shown in Figure 2.30.

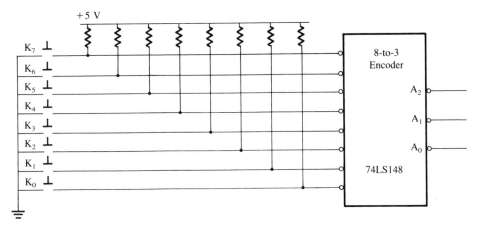

FIGURE 2.29
The 8-to-3 Encoder (74LS148)

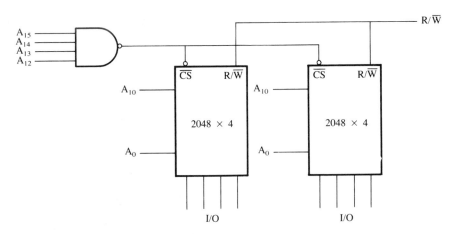

FIGURE 2.30
Memory Schematic

8085/8080A-Based Microcomputer Systems

The 8085 microprocessor is a much improved version of its predecessor, the 8080A. The 8085 includes on its chip most of the logic circuitry for performing computing tasks and for communicating with peripherals. However, eight of its bus lines are **multiplexed**; that is, they are time shared by the low-order address and data. This chapter discusses the 8085 architecture in detail and illustrates techniques for demultiplexing the bus and generating the necessary control signals.

Later, the chapter describes a typical 8085-based microcomputer designed with general purpose memory and I/O devices; it also illustrates the bus timing signals in executing an instruction. In addition, the chapter includes illustrations of special-purpose devices such as the 8155 and 8755/8355, and their memory maps in the Intel SDK-85 system. Finally, the chapter includes a discussion of the 8080A microprocessor and related devices, and compares the 8080A with the 8085.

OBJECTIVES

- ☐ Recognize the functions of various pins of the 8085 microprocessor.
- ☐ Explain the bus timings in fetching an instruction from memory.
- ☐ Explain how to demultiplex the AD_7–AD_0 bus using a latch.

- ☐ Draw a logic schematic to generate four control signals, using the 8085 IO/$\overline{M}$, $\overline{RD}$ and $\overline{WR}$ signals: (1) $\overline{MEMR}$, (2) $\overline{MEMW}$, (3) $\overline{IOR}$, and (4) $\overline{IOW}$. Explain the functions of these control signals.
- ☐ List the various internal units that make up the 8085 architecture, and explain their functions in decoding and executing an instruction.
- ☐ Draw the block diagram of an 8085-based microcomputer.

☐ Analyze a memory interfacing circuit, and specify the memory map of a given memory device.

☐ Recognize the port address of a given I/O device.

☐ List additional signals found in such specially designed devices as the 8155 and the 8755/8355, and analyze the interfacing circuit of the SDK-85 memory sections.

☐ Describe the 8080A MPU in terms of its component devices: the 8080A microprocessor, the 8228 system controller, and the 8224 oscillator.

☐ List the features of the 8085 microprocessor and compare them with those of the 8080A microprocessor.

3.1 THE 8085 MPU

The term **Micro Processing Unit** (MPU) is similar to the term Central Processing Unit (CPU) used in traditional computers. We define the MPU as a device or a group of devices (as a unit) that can communicate with peripherals, provide timing signals, direct data flow, and perform computing tasks as specified by the instructions in memory. The unit will have the necessary lines for the address bus, the data bus, and the control signals, and would require only a power supply and a crystal (or equivalent frequency-determining components) to be completely functional.

Using this description, the 8085 microprocessor can almost qualify as an MPU, but with the following two limitations.

1. The low-order address bus of the 8085 microprocessor is **multiplexed** (time shared) with the data bus. The buses need to be demultiplexed.

2. Appropriate control signals need to be generated to interface memory and I/O with the 8085. (Intel has some specialized memory and I/O devices that do not require such control signals).

This section shows how to demultiplex the bus and generate the control signals after describing the 8085 microprocessor and illustrates the bus timings.

3.11 The 8085 Microprocessor

The 8085 is an 8-bit general purpose microprocessor capable of addressing 64K of memory. The device has forty pins, requires a +5 V single power supply, and can operate with a 3-MHz single-phase clock. The 8085 is an enhanced version of its predecessor, the 8080A; its instruction set is upward-compatible with that of the 8080A, meaning that the 8085 instruction set includes all the 8080A instructions plus some additional ones. Programs written for the 8080A will be executed by the 8085, but the 8085 and the 8080A are not pin compatible.

Figure 3.1 shows the logic pinout of the 8085 microprocessor. All the signals can be classified into six groups: (1) address bus, (2) data bus, (3) control and status signals, (4) power supply and frequency signals, (5) interrupts and peripheral initiated signals, and (6) serial I/O ports.

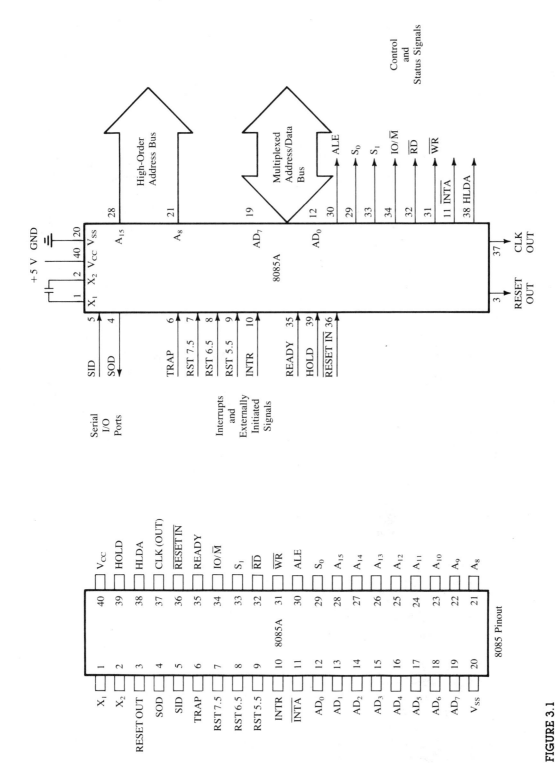

FIGURE 3.1

The 8085 Microprocessor Pinout and Signals

NOTE: The 8085A is commonly known as the 8085.
SOURCE (Pinout): Intel Corporation, *MCS — 80/85 Family User's Manual* (Santa Clara, Calif.: Author, 1979), p. 6-2.

ADDRESS BUS

The 8085 has eight signal lines, A_{15}–A_8, which are unidirectional and used as the high-order address bus.

MULTIPLEXED ADDRESS/DATA BUS

The signal lines AD_7 to AD_0 are bidirectional, they serve a dual purpose. They are used as the low-order address bus as well as the data bus. In executing an instruction, during the earlier part of the cycle, these lines are used as the low-order address bus. During the later part of the cycle, these lines are used as the data bus. (This is also known as multiplexing the bus.) However, the low-order address bus can be separated from these signals by using a latch.

CONTROL AND STATUS SIGNALS

This group of signals includes two control signals ($\overline{RD}$ and $\overline{WR}$), three status signals ($IO/\overline{M}$, S_1 and S_0) to identify the nature of the operation, and one special signal (ALE) to indicate the beginning of the operation. These signals are as follows.

☐ ALE—Address Latch Enable: This is a positive going pulse generated every time the 8085 begins an operation (machine cycle); it indicates that the bits on AD_7–AD_0 are address bits. This signal is used primarily to latch the low-order address from the multiplexed bus and generate a separate set of eight address lines, A_7 to A_0.
☐ $\overline{RD}$—Read: This is a Read control signal (active low). This signal indicates that the selected I/O or memory device is to be read and data are available on the data bus.
☐ $\overline{WR}$—Write: This is a Write control signal (active low). This signal indicates that the data on the data bus are to be written into a selected memory or I/O location.
☐ $IO/\overline{M}$: This is a status signal used to differentiate between I/O and memory operations. When it is high, it indicates an I/O operation; when it is low, it indicates a memory operation. This signal is combined with $\overline{RD}$ (Read) and $\overline{WR}$ (Write) to generate I/O and memory control signals.
☐ S_1 and S_0: These status signals, similar to $IO/\overline{M}$, can identify various operations, but they are rarely used in small systems. (All the operations and their associated status signals are listed in Table 3.1 for reference.)

POWER SUPPLY AND CLOCK FREQUENCY

The power supply and frequency signals are as follows.

☐ V_{CC}: +5 volt power supply.
☐ V_{SS}: Ground Reference.
☐ X_1, X_2: A crystal (or RC, LC network) is connected at these two pins. The frequency is internally divided by two; therefore, to operate a system at 3 MHz, the crystal should have frequency of 6 MHz.
☐ CLK (OUT)—Clock Output: This signal can be used as the system clock for other devices.

TABLE 3.1
8085 Machine Cycle Status and Control Signals

		Status		
Machine Cycle	**IO/$\overline{\text{M}}$**	**S_1**	**S_0**	**Control Signals**
Opcode Fetch	0	1	1	$\overline{\text{RD}} = 0$
Memory Read	0	1	0	$\overline{\text{RD}} = 0$
Memory Write	0	0	1	$\overline{\text{WR}} = 0$
I/O Read	1	1	0	$\overline{\text{RD}} = 0$
I/O Write	1	0	1	$\overline{\text{WR}} = 0$
Interrupt Acknowledge	1	1	1	$\overline{\text{INTA}} = 0$
Halt	Z	0	0 ⎫	
Hold	Z	X	X ⎬	$\overline{\text{RD}}, \overline{\text{WR}} = Z$ and $\overline{\text{INTA}} = 1$
Reset	Z	X	X ⎭	

NOTE: Z = Tri-state (high impedance)
     X = Unspecified

INTERRUPTS AND EXTERNALLY INITIATED OPERATIONS

The 8085 has five interrupt signals that can be used to interrupt a program execution. One of the signals, INTR (Interrupt Request), is identical to the 8080A microprocessor interrupt signal (INT); the others are enhancements to the 8080A. The microprocessor acknowledges an interrupt by the $\overline{\text{INTA}}$ (Interrupt Acknowledge) signal. (The interrupt process is discussed in Chapter 12.)

In addition to the interrupts, three pins — RESET, HOLD, and READY — accept the externally initiated signals as inputs. To respond to the HOLD request, it has one signal called HLDA (Hold Acknowledge). The functions of these signals were previously discussed in Section 2.13. The RESET is again described below, and others are listed in Table 3.2 for reference.

☐ $\overline{\text{RESET IN}}$: When the signal on this pin goes low, the program counter is set to zero, the buses are tri-stated, and the MPU is reset.
☐ RESET OUT: This signal indicates that the MPU is being reset. The signal can be used to reset other devices.

SERIAL I/O PORTS

The 8085 has two signals to implement the serial transmission: SID (Serial Input Data) and SOD (Serial Output Data). They will be discussed in Chapter 16 on Serial I/O.

In this chapter, we will focus on the first three groups of signals, while others will be discussed in later chapters.

3.12   Bus Timings

To understand the functions of various signals of the 8085, we must examine the timings of these signals in relation to the system clock. The best way to illustrate the timing is through an example.

TABLE 3.2
8085 Interrupts and Externally Initiated Signals

• INTR (Input)	Interrupt Request: This is used as a general-purpose interrupt; it is similar to the INT signal of the 8080A.
• $\overline{\text{INTA}}$ (Output)	Interrupt Acknowledge: This is used to acknowledge an interrupt.
• RST 7.5 (Inputs) RST 6.5 RST 5.5	Restart Interrupts: These are vectored interrupts and transfer the program control to specific memory locations. They have higher priorities than the INTR interrupt. Among these three, the priority order is 7.5, 6.5, and 5.5.
• TRAP (Input)	This is a nonmaskable interrupt and has the highest priority.
• HOLD (Input)	This signal indicates that a peripheral such as a DMA (Direct Memory Access) controller is requesting the use of the address and data buses.
• HLDA (Output)	Hold Acknowledge: This signal acknowledges the HOLD request.
• READY (Input)	This signal is used to delay the microprocessor Read or Write cycles until a slow responding peripheral is ready to send or accept data. When this signal goes low, the microprocessor waits for an integral number of clock cycles until it goes high.

Example 3.1	Refer to the example in the last chapter (2.24): Illustrate the timing of data flow when the instruction code 0 1 0 0 1 1 1 1 (4FH — MOV C,A), stored in location 2005H, is being fetched.
Solution	To fetch the byte (4FH), the MPU needs to identify the memory location 2005H and enable the data flow from memory. This is called the Fetch cycle. The data flow is shown in Figure 3.2; the timings (Figure 3.3) are explained below.

Figure 3.3 shows the timing of how a data byte is transferred from memory to the MPU; it shows five different groups of signals in relation to the system clock. To fetch the byte, the MPU performs the following steps:

☐ Step 1: The program counter places the 16-bit memory address on the address bus (Figure 3.2).

Figure 3.3 shows that at T_1 the high-order memory address 20H is placed on the address lines A_{15} to A_8, the low-order memory address 05H is placed on the bus AD_7 to AD_0, and the ALE signal goes high. Similarly, the status signal $IO/\overline{M}$ goes low, indicating that this is a memory related operation. (For the sake of clarity, the other two status signals, S_1 and S_0, are not shown in Figure 3.3; they will be discussed in the next chapter).

☐ Step 2: The control unit sends the control signal $\overline{\text{RD}}$ to enable the memory chip (Figure 3.2).

The control signal $\overline{\text{RD}}$ is sent out during the clock period T_2, thus enabling the memory chip (Figure 3.3). The $\overline{\text{RD}}$ signal is active during two clock periods.

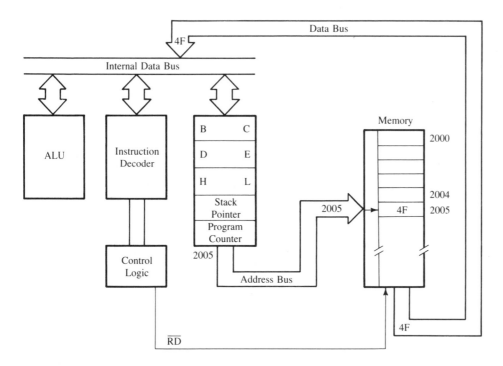

FIGURE 3.2
Data Flow from Memory to the MPU

☐ Step 3: The byte from the memory location is placed on the data bus.

When the memory is enabled, the instruction byte (4FH) is placed on the bus AD_7–AD_0 and transferred to the microprocessor. The $\overline{RD}$ signal causes 4FH to be placed on bus AD_7–AD_0 (shown by the arrow), and when $\overline{RD}$ goes high, it causes the bus to go in high impedance. (Figure 3.3 shows only three T-states; the complete cycle is shown in Figure 4.1).

3.13 Demultiplexing the Bus AD_7–AD_0

The need for demultiplexing the bus AD_7–AD_0 becomes easier to understand after examining Figure 3.3. This figure shows that the address on the high-order bus (20H) remains on the bus for three clock periods. However, the low-order address (05H) is lost after the first clock period. This address needs to be latched and used for identifying the memory address. If the bus AD_7–AD_0 is used to identify the memory location (2005H), the address will change to 204FH after the first clock period.

Figure 3.4 shows a schematic that uses a latch and the ALE signal to demultiplex the bus. The bus AD_7–AD_0 is connected as the input to the latch 74LS373. The ALE signal

FIGURE 3.3
Timing: Transfer of Byte from
Memory to MPU

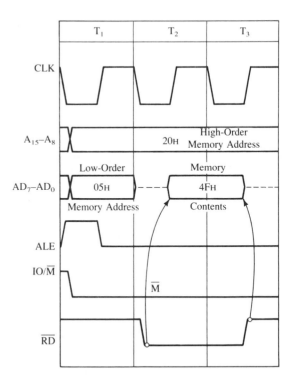

is connected to the Enable (G) pin of the latch, and the Output control ($\overline{OC}$) signal of the latch is grounded.

Figure 3.3 shows that the ALE goes high during T_1. When the ALE is high, the latch is transparent; this means that the output changes according to input data. During T_1, the output of the latch is 05H. When the ALE goes low, the data byte 05H is latched until the next ALE, and the output of the latch represents the low-order address bus A_7–A_0 for the 8085. Figure 3.4 shows the entire address bus A_{15}–A_0 after the latching operation.

Intel has circumvented the problem of demultiplexing the low-order bus by designing special devices such as the 8155 (256 bytes of R/W memory + I/Os) and 8355 (2K ROM + I/Os), which are compatible with the 8085 multiplexed bus. These devices internally demultiplex the bus using the ALE signal (see Figure 3.14 and 3.15).

3.14 Generating Control Signals

Figure 3.3 shows the $\overline{RD}$ (Read) as a control signal. Since this signal is used both for reading memory and for reading an input device, it is necessary to generate two different Read signals: one for memory and another for input. Similarly, two separate Write signals must be generated.

Figure 3.5 shows that four different control signals are generated by combining the signals $\overline{RD}$, $\overline{WR}$, and IO/$\overline{M}$. The signal IO/$\overline{M}$ goes low for the memory operation. This

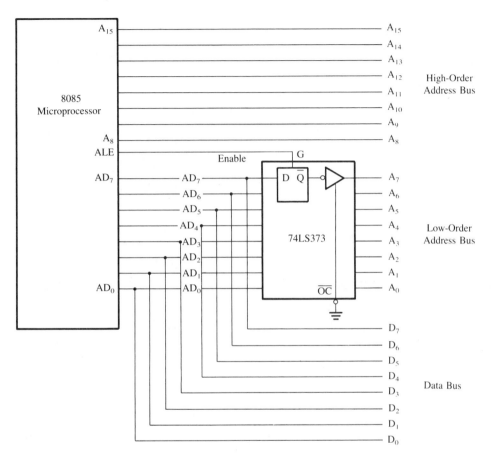

FIGURE 3.4
Schematic of Latching Low-Order Address Bus

signal is ANDed with $\overline{RD}$ and $\overline{WR}$ signals by using the 74LS32 quadruple two-input OR gates, as shown in Figure 3.5. The OR gates are functionally connected as negative NAND gates (see Appendix C, Preferred Logic Symbols). When both input signals go low, the outputs of the gates go low and generate $\overline{MEMR}$ (Memory Read) and $\overline{MEMW}$ (Memory Write) control signals. When the IO/$\overline{M}$ signal goes high, it indicates the peripheral I/O operation. Figure 3.5 shows that this signal is complemented using the Hex inverter 74LS04 and ANDed with the $\overline{RD}$ and $\overline{WR}$ signals to generate $\overline{IOR}$ (I/O Read) and $\overline{IOW}$ (I/O Write) control signals. These control signals are unnecessary for Intel's 8155 and 8355 devices because these signals are generated internally using $\overline{RD}$, $\overline{WR}$, and IO/$\overline{M}$ signals.

To demultiplex the bus and to generate the necessary control signals, the 8085 microprocessor requires a latch and logic gates to build the MPU, as shown in Figure 3.6. This MPU can be interfaced with any memory or I/O.

FIGURE 3.5
Schematic to Generate
Read/Write Control Signals
for Memory and I/O

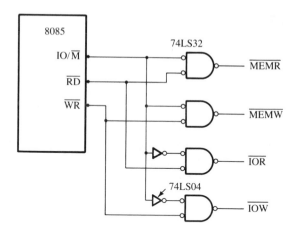

3.15   A Detailed Look at the 8085 MPU and Its Architecture

Figure 3.7 shows the internal architecture of the 8085 beyond the programmable registers
we discussed previously. It includes the ALU (Arithmetic and Logic Unit), Timing and
Control Unit, Instruction Register and Decoder, Register Array, Interrupt Control, and
Serial I/O Control. We will discuss the first four units below, while the last two will be
discussed later in the book.

FIGURE 3.6
8085 Demultiplexed
Address and Data Bus
with Control Signals

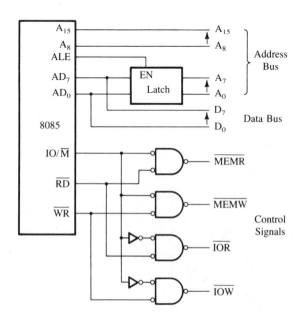

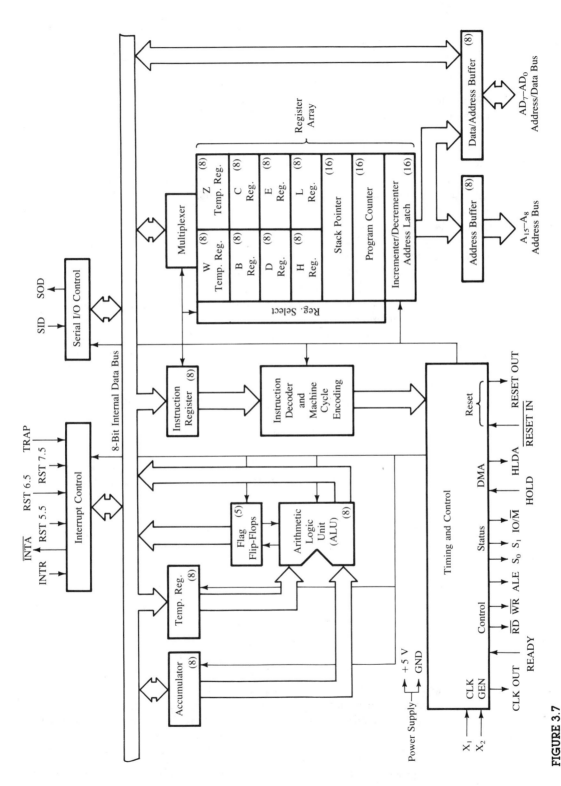

FIGURE 3.7

The 8085A Microprocessor: Functional Block Diagram

NOTE: The 8085A microprocessor is commonly known as the 8085.
SOURCE: Intel Corporation, *MCS — 80/85 Family User's Manual* (Santa Clara, Calif.: Author, 1979), p. 6-1.

The ALU

The arithmetic logic unit performs the computing functions; it includes the accumulator, the temporary register, the arithmetic and logic circuits, and five flags. The temporary register is used to hold data during an arithmetic and logic operation. The result is stored in the accumulator, and the flags (flip-flops) are set or reset according to the result of the operation.

The flags are affected by the arithmetic and logic operations in the ALU. In most of these operations, the result is stored in the accumulator. Therefore, the flags generally reflect data conditions in the accumulator — with some exceptions. The descriptions and conditions of the flags are as follows:

- ☐ **S — Sign Flag:** After the execution of an arithmetic or logic operation, if bit D_7 of the result (usually in the accumulator) is 1, the Sign flag is set. This flag is used with signed numbers. In a given byte, if D_7 is 1, the number will be viewed as a negative number; if it is 0, the number will be considered positive. In arithmetic operations with signed numbers, bit D_7 is reserved for indicating the sign, and the remaining seven bits are used to represent the magnitude of a number.
- ☐ **Z — Zero Flag:** The Zero flag is set if the ALU operation results in 0, and the flag is reset if the result is not 0. This flag is modified by the results in the accumulator as well as in the other registers.
- ☐ **AC — Auxiliary Carry Flag:** In an arithmetic operation, when a carry is generated by digit D_3 and passed on to digit D_4, the AC flag is set. The flag is used only internally for BCD (Binary Coded Decimal) operations, and is not available for the programmer to change the sequence of a program with a jump instruction.
- ☐ **P — Parity Flag:** After an arithmetic or logical operation, if the result has an even number of 1s, the flag is set. If it has an odd number of 1s, the flag is reset. (For example, the data byte 0 0 0 0 0 0 1 1 has even parity even if the magnitude of the number is odd).
- ☐ **CY — Carry Flag:** If an arithmetic operation results in a carry, the Carry flag is set; otherwise it is reset. The Carry flag also serves as a borrow flag for subtraction.

The bit positions reserved for these flags in the flag register are as follows:

D_7	D_6	D_5	D_4	D_3	D_2	D_1	D_0
S	Z		AC		P		CY

Among the five flags, the AC flag is used internally for BCD arithmetic; the instruction set does not include any conditional jump instructions based on the AC flag. Of the remaining four flags, the Z and CY flags are those most commonly used.

TIMING AND CONTROL UNIT

This unit synchronizes all the microprocessor operations with the clock, and generates the control signals necessary for communication between the microprocessor and peripherals.

The control signals are similar to a sync pulse in an oscilloscope. The $\overline{RD}$ and $\overline{WR}$ signals are sync pulses indicating the availability of data on the data bus.

INSTRUCTION REGISTER AND DECODER

The instruction register and the decoder are part of the ALU. When an instruction is fetched from memory, it is loaded in the instruction register. The decoder decodes the instruction and establishes the sequence of events to follow. The instruction register is not programmable and cannot be accessed through any instruction.

REGISTER ARRAY

The programmable registers have been discussed in the last chapter. Two additional registers, called temporary registers W and Z, are included in the register array. These registers are used to hold 8-bit data during the execution of some instructions. However, since they are used internally, they are not available to the programmer.

3.16   Decoding and Executing an Instruction

Decoding and executing an instruction after it has been fetched can be illustrated with the example from Section 3.12.

Assume that the accumulator contains data byte 82H, and the instruction MOV C, A (4FH) is fetched. List the steps in decoding and executing the instruction.

Example
3.2

This example is similar to the example in Section 3.12, except that the contents of the accumulator are specified. To decode and execute the instruction, the following steps are performed.

Solution

1. The contents of the data bus (4F) are placed in the instruction register and decoded (Figure 3.8).

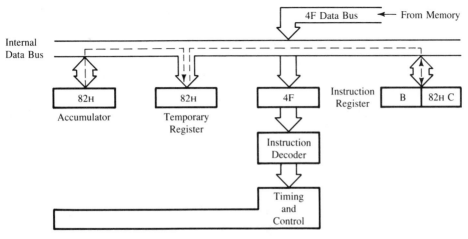

FIGURE 3.8
Instruction Decoding and Execution

2. The contents of the accumulator (82H) are transferred to the temporary register in the ALU.

3. The contents of the temporary register are transferred to register C.

3.17   Review of Important Concepts

1. The 8085 microprocessor has a multiplexed bus AD_7–AD_0 used as the low-order address bus and the data bus.

2. The bus AD_7–AD_0 can be demultiplexed by using a latch and the ALE signal.

3. The 8085 has a status signal IO/$\overline{M}$ and two control signals $\overline{RD}$ and $\overline{WR}$. By ANDing these signals, four control signals can be generated: $\overline{MEMR}$, $\overline{MEMW}$, $\overline{IOR}$ and $\overline{IOW}$.

4. The 8085 MPU

☐ transfers data from a memory location to the microprocessor by using the control signal Memory Read ($\overline{MEMR}$ — Active Low). This is also called **reading from memory**.

☐ transfers data from the microprocessor to memory by using the control signal Memory Write ($\overline{MEMW}$ — Active Low). This is also called **writing into memory**.

☐ accepts data from input devices by using the control signal I/O Read ($\overline{IOR}$ — Active Low). This is also known as **reading from an input port**.

☐ sends data to output devices by using the control signal I/O Write ($\overline{IOW}$ — Active Low). This is also known as **writing to an output port**.

5. To execute an instruction, the MPU

☐ places the memory address of the instruction on the address bus.

☐ indicates the operation status on the status lines.

☐ sends the $\overline{MEMR}$ control signal to enable the memory, fetches the instruction byte, and places it in the instruction decoder.

☐ executes the instruction.

3.2   EXAMPLE OF AN 8085-BASED MICROCOMPUTER

A general microcomputer system was illustrated in Figure 2.9, in the last chapter. After our discussion of the 8085 microprocessor and the interfacing devices, we can expand the system to include more details, as shown in Figure 3.9. The system includes interfacing devices such as buffers, decoders, and latches. This system is discussed below in three sections: the 8085 MPU, memory, and I/Os.

3.21   The 8085 MPU

The 8085 MPU module (Figure 3.9) includes devices such as the 8085 microprocessor, an octal latch, and logic gates as shown previously in Figure 3.6. The octal latch demultiplexes the bus AD_7–AD_0 using the signal ALE, and the logic gates generate the

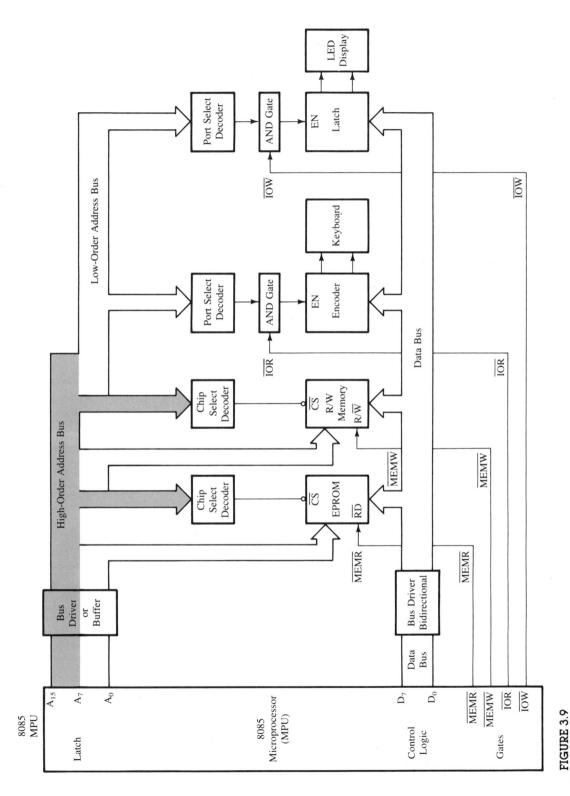

FIGURE 3.9

8085 Single-Board Microcomputer System

NOTE: The bus AD_7–AD_0 is demultiplexed using a latch and memory, and I/O control signals are generated using gates. Figure 3.6 is included in the MPU.

necessary control signals. Figure 3.9 shows the demultiplexed address bus, the data bus, and the four active low control signals: $\overline{\text{MEMR}}$, $\overline{\text{MEMW}}$, $\overline{\text{IOR}}$, and $\overline{\text{IOW}}$. In addition, to increase the driving capacity of the buses, a unidirectional bus driver is used for the address bus and a bidirectional bus driver is used for the data bus.

3.22 Memory

The 8085 microcomputer shown in Figure 3.9 has two types of memory chips — R/WM (Read/Write Memory) and EPROM (Erasable Programmable Read-Only Memory) — both with 256 bytes. The memory section of Figure 3.9 is expanded in Figure 3.10 to show a few more details. The aim of this discussion is to identify the memory map by analyzing the associated circuits, and to recognize the functions of two control signals: $\overline{\text{MEMR}}$ and $\overline{\text{MEMW}}$. To simplify the presentation, details concerning the memory chips and the memory timing are excluded here. Intel's special-purpose memory chips — the 8155 and the 8755 — and their memory maps in the SDK-85 system are described in section 3.24.

R/W MEMORY

Figure 3.10 shows that the eight address lines A_7–A_0 are connected directly to the address lines on the memory chip to identify 256 memory locations. The address lines A_{15} to A_8 are used to select the memory chip through a 3-to-8 decoder and logic gates.

Identifying the memory map is a two-step process. The first step is to recognize the logic levels required on the address lines A_{15}–A_8 to select the memory chip. The second step is to examine the possible logic level combinations that can be assumed by the address lines A_7–A_0.

When the R/WM memory chip is selected, the logic levels on the address lines A_{15}–A_8 should be as follows:

A_{15}	A_{14}	A_{13}	A_{12}	A_{11}	A_{10}	A_9	A_8	
0	0	0	0	0	1	1	1	= 07H

The address line A_{15} is connected to the active high enable line of the decoder through an inverter; therefore, it should be at logic 0. The address lines A_{14}–A_{11} should also be at logic 0 to activate the other two enable lines (active low) of the decoder. The gates G_1 and G_2 are OR gates, functionally connected as negative NAND gates (see Appendix C, Preferred Logic Symbols) When the input address lines A_{10}–A_8 to the decoder assume the logic levels 1 1 1, the output line 7 of the decoder goes low and selects the R/W memory chip.

The memory chip has eight address lines that can assume 256 different combinations from 00H to FFH. Therefore, the memory map of this chip ranges from 0700H to 07FFH, as shown below.

A_{15}	A_{14}	A_{13}	A_{12}	A_{11}	A_{10}	A_9	A_8	A_7	A_6	A_5	A_4	A_3	A_2	A_1	A_0	
0	0	0	0	0	1	1	1	0	0	0	0	0	0	0	0	= 0700H
			07H													
		Chip Select Address						1	1	1	1	1	1	1	1	= 07FFH

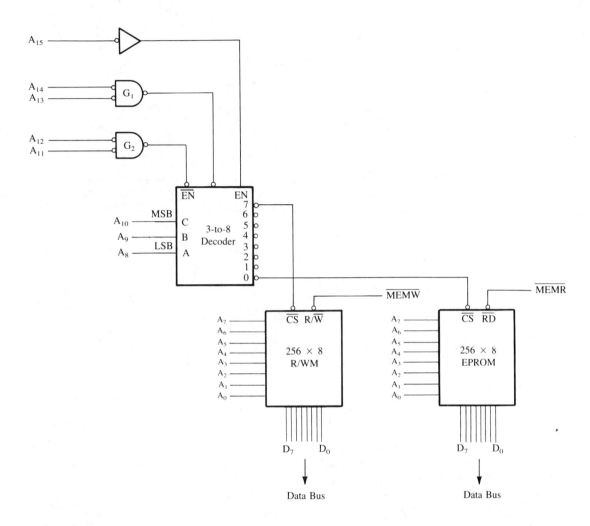

FIGURE 3.10
Schematic: Memory Interfacing

To read from and write into this memory, one control signal — $\overline{\text{MEMW}}$ — is necessary. When the $\overline{\text{MEMW}}$ is high, data can be read just by selecting the chip. The timing of the memory write cycle is shown in Figure 3.11. The 8085 places the address of the memory location into which it intends to write on the address bus at T_1, and causes the IO/$\overline{\text{M}}$ signal to go low at the same time. At period T_2, it places the data on the data bus and sends the $\overline{\text{WR}}$ signal ($\overline{\text{MEMW}}$ shown in Figure 3.11 is generated from the $\overline{\text{WR}}$ and IO/$\overline{\text{M}}$ signals). During T_2 and T_3, the memory location is identified, and the data are written into the location. The Memory Write cycle is in many ways similar to the Memory Read cycle.

FIGURE 3.11
Timing of the Memory
Write Cycle

*Demultiplexed address bus

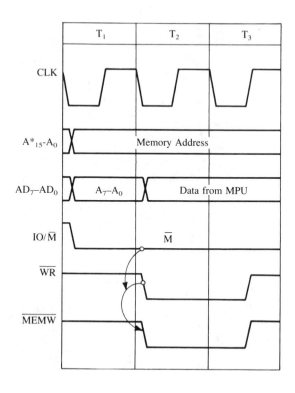

EPROM

Like the R/W memory chip, the EPROM also has 256 bytes of memory and requires eight address lines, A_7–A_0, to identify 256 locations. However, its memory map ranges from 0000H to 00FFH, as shown below.

$$A_{15} \quad A_{14} \quad A_{13} \quad A_{12} \quad A_{11} \quad A_{10} \quad A_9 \quad A_8 \qquad A_7 \quad A_6 \quad A_5 \quad A_4 \quad A_3 \quad A_2 \quad A_1 \quad A_0$$

$$\underbrace{0 \quad\; 0 \quad\; 0 \quad\; 0 \quad\; 0 \quad\; 0 \quad\; 0 \quad\; 0}_{\substack{\text{00H} \\ \text{Chip Select Address}}} \qquad 0 \quad\; 0 \quad\; 0 \quad\; 0 \quad\; 0 \quad\; 0 \quad\; 0 \quad\; 0 = \text{0000H}$$

$$\qquad\qquad\qquad\qquad\qquad\qquad\qquad 1 \quad\; 1 \quad\; 1 \quad\; 1 \quad\; 1 \quad\; 1 \quad\; 1 \quad\; 1 = \text{00FFH}$$

In this memory circuit, the only difference from the R/W memory circuit is that the Chip Select line goes low when the input to the decoder is 0 0 0. Thus, the high-order address becomes 00H.

This memory chip requires the control signal $\overline{\text{MEMR}}$. It is a Read-Only Memory; information can not be written into it. The timing diagram, shown in Figure 3.12, is similar to that of Figure 3.3, except that Figure 3.12 shows $\overline{\text{MEMR}}$ control signal and the demultiplexed buses.

FIGURE 3.12
Timing of the Memory
Read Cycle

*Demultiplexed address bus

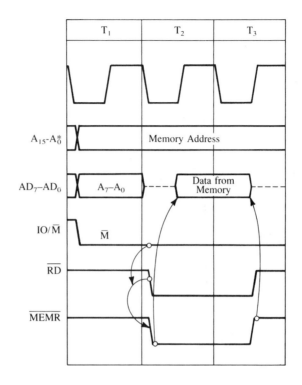

3.23 Input/Output

Although this topic belongs more appropriately to the discussion of I/O interfacing and will be examined in detail in Chapter 11, it is included briefly here to introduce the concept of I/O port addresses.

Figure 3.13 shows an expanded version of the I/O section of Figure 3.9. In Figure 3.13, the eight address lines A_7-A_0 are connected to the decoder; the output line 2 of the decoder is ANDed with the control signal $\overline{IOW}$; and the output of the AND signal is used to enable the latch. But the question remains: What logic levels are required on the address lines A_7-A_0 for the output line 2 to go low? The required logic levels are as follows:

$$
\begin{array}{cccccccc}
A_7 & A_6 & A_5 & A_4 & A_3 & A_2 & A_1 & A_0 \\
1 & 0 & 0 & 0 & 0 & 0 & 1 & 0 = 82H
\end{array}
$$

When the microprocessor places the address 82H on the bus and sends the control signal $\overline{IOW}$, the latch is enabled and the data on the bus are latched.

Similarly, the input port in Figure 3.13 can be accessed with the port address 82H. The output line 2 of the decoder is ANDed with the control signal $\overline{IOR}$ to enable the input key board. An input and an output port can have the same port address; however, they are enabled by different control signals.

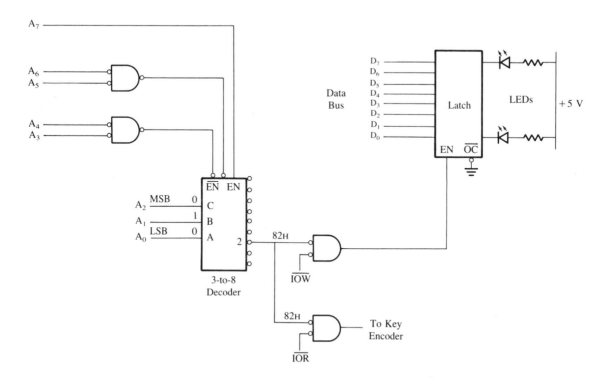

FIGURE 3.13
Interfacing I/O Ports

3.24 The SDK-85 Memory

The SDK-85 is a single-board microcomputer designed by Intel and widely used in college laboratories. The system is designed using the 8085 microprocessor and specially compatible devices, such as the 8155/8156 and the 8355/8755.

The 8155/8156 and the 8355/8755 include multiple devices on the same chip. The 8155 has 256 bytes of R/W memory, two programmable I/O ports, and a timer. The 8156 is identical to the 8155, except that its Chip Enable (CE) signal is active high. The 8355 is a ROM with two programmable I/O ports, and the 8755 is an EPROM, pin compatible with the 8355. The programmable I/O ports of these devices are discussed in Chapter 14. The memory section of these chips and their memory maps in the SDK-85 system will now be disccused.

THE 8155 MEMORY SECTION

Figure 3.14 shows the block diagram of the 8155 memory section. It has eight address lines and six lines compatible with the control and status signals of the 8085: $\overline{CE}$ (Chip Enable), IO/$\overline{M}$, ALE, $\overline{RD}$, $\overline{WR}$, and RESET. These control and status lines are not found in the general-purpose memory devices shown in the previous section. These lines elimi-

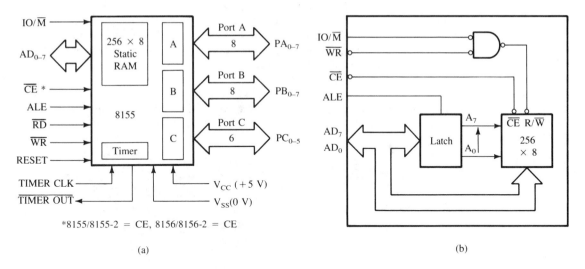

*8155/8155-2 = CE, 8156/8156-2 = CE

(a)

(b)

FIGURE 3.14

The 8155 Memory Section: The Block Diagram (a) and the Internal Structure (b)

SOURCE: A: Intel Corporation, *MCS—80/85 Family User's Manual* (Santa Clara, Calif.: Author, 1979), p. 6-17.

nate the need for external demultiplexing the bus AD_7–AD_0 and generating separate control signals for memory and I/O.

Figure 3.14 also shows the internal structure of the 8155 memory section. The memory section includes 256×8 memory locations and an internal latch to demultiplex the bus lines AD_7–AD_0. The memory section also requires a Chip Enable ($\overline{CE}$) signal and a Memory Write ($\overline{MEMW}$) control signal, generated internally by combining the IO/$\overline{M}$ and $\overline{WR}$ signals

Figure 3.15 shows a schematic of the SDK-85 system of interfacing the 8155 memory section with the 8085. The 8205, a 3-to-8 decoder, decodes the address lines

FIGURE 3.15

Interfacing the 8155 Memory Schematic from the SDK-85 System

SOURCE: Intel Corporation, *SDK—85 User's Manual* (Santa Clara, Calif.: Author, 1978), Appendix B.

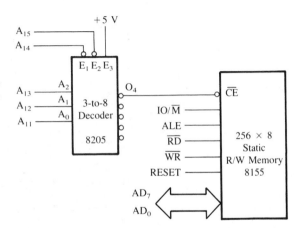

A_{15}–A_{11} and the output line 4 of the decoder enables the memory chip. The control and the status signals from the 8085 are connected directly to the respective signals on the memory chip. Similarly, the bus lines AD_7–A_0 are also connected directly to the memory chip to address any one of the 256 memory locations.

Example 3.3

Explain the decoding logic and the memory map of the 8155 shown in Figure 3.15.

Solution

The interfacing logic shows the 3-to-8 decoder; its output line 4 (O_4) is used to select the 8155. The address lines A_{11} to A_{13} are connected as input to the decoder, and the lines A_{15} and A_{14} are used as active low Enable lines. The third Enable line (active high) is permanently enabled by tying it to +5V. Therefore, output line 4 of the decoder goes low when the address lines have the following address:

A_{15}	A_{14}	A_{13}	A_{12}	A_{11}	A_{10}	A_9	A_8
0	0	1	0	0	X	X	X

= 20H (Assuming the don't care lines are at logic 0)

Thus, the memory map of the 8155 memory will range from 2000H to 20FFH. In reality, the memory section of this 8155 uses the memory space from 2000H to 27FFH. The SDK-85 manual refers to the memory space from 2100H to 27FFH as "foldback space," which means it is not being used, but neither is it available for any expansion because of multiple addresses (as explained below).

In Figure 3.15, the address lines A_{10}, A_9, and A_8 are don't care and can assume logic states 0 or 1. If these three lines assume logic 1 state, the memory map will range from 2700H to 27FFH. Attempting to store a program in locations on page 27H is the same as entering the program in locations on page 20H. The memory addresses from 2100H to 2700H will access the memory registers from 2000H to 20FFH. Therefore, the memory space from 2100H to 27FFH, called foldback memory, cannot be used.

THE 8755 MEMORY SECTION

Figure 3.16 shows the interfacing of the 8755 EPROM from the SDK-85 system. The circuit uses the same decoder, 8205, as the 8155 interfacing (Figure 3.15). The 8755 has 2048 bytes of memory and requires 11 address lines from the microprocessor. The rest of the address lines are used to select the chip. The output line 0 of the decoder selects the chip. Therefore, the memory map ranges from 0000H to 07FFH, as shown below.

A_{15}	A_{14}	A_{13}	A_{12}	A_{11}	A_{10}	A_9	A_8	A_7	A_6	A_5	A_4	A_3	A_2	A_1	A_0	
0	0	0	0	0	0	0	0	0	0	0	0	0	0	0	0	= 0000H
		00H														
0	0	0	0	0	1	1	1	1	1	1	1	1	1	1	1	= 07FFH
	0					7			F				F			

FIGURE 3.16

Interfacing the 8755 Memory—
Schematic from SDK-85
System

SOURCE: Intel Corporation, *SDK—85 User's Manual* (Santa Clara, Calif.: Author, 1978), Appendix B.

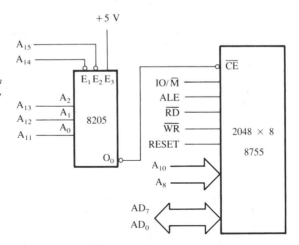

3.25 How Does an 8085-Based Single-Board Microcomputer Work?

Hardware is the skeleton of the computer; software is its life. The software (programs) makes the computer live; without it, the hardware is a dead piece of semiconductor material. Single-board microcomputers, such as the one shown in Figure 3.9 or the SDK-85, have a program called "Key Monitor" or "Key Executive" permanently stored in memory. This program is stored either in EPROM or in ROM beginning at the memory location 0000H.

When the power is turned on, the monitor program comes alive. Initially, the program counter has a random address. When the system is reset, the program counter in the 8085 is cleared, and it holds the address 0000H. The SDK-85 system includes a "power on" reset circuit, which resets the system and clears the program counter when the system is turned on. The MPU places the address 0000H on the address bus. The instruction code stored in location 0000H is fetched and executed, and the execution continues according to the instructions in the monitor program. The primary functions of the monitor program are as follows:

1. Reading the Hex keyboard and checking for a key closure. Continuing to check the keyboard until a key is pressed.
2. Displaying the Hex equivalent of the key pressed at the output port, such as the seven-segment LEDs.
3. Identifying the key pressed and storing its binary equivalent in memory, if necessary.
4. Transferring the program execution sequence to the user program when the *Execute* key is pressed.

The programmer enters a program in R/W memory in sequential memory locations by using the data keys (0 to F) and the function key called *Store* or *Next*. When the system is reset, the program counter is cleared, and the monitor program begins to check a key closure again. By using the keyboard, the programmer enters the first memory address where the user program is stored in R/W memory and directs the MPU to execute the program by pressing the *Execute* or *Go* key. The MPU fetches, decodes, and executes one instruction code at a time and continues to do so until it fetches the *Halt* instruction.

The key monitor program is a critical element in entering, storing, and executing a program. Until the *Execute* key is pushed, the monitor program in the EPROM (or ROM) directs all the operations of the MPU. After the *Execute* key is pushed, the user program directs the MPU to perform the functions written in the program.

3.3   THE 8080A MPU

The 8080A microprocessor is the predecessor of the 8085 and the descendant of the first 8-bit processor, the 8008. The instruction set of the 8080A and the 8085 is practically the same. Programs written for 8080A systems can be executed in 8085 systems without modifications. The primary improvement of the 8085 is in the area of hardware. The 8080A is not in itself a complete functional unit as a processor; it requires two additional chips; the 8224 clock generator driver, and the 8228 system controller and bus driver. The 8080A does not have all the necessary control signals (such as Memory Read/Write and I/O Read/Write); these signals are generated by using the 8228 system controller.

Figure 3.17 shows the complete, three-chip, functional Micro Processing Unit (MPU). The functional details of these chips are described below.

3.31   The 8080A Microprocessor

Manufactured on a single LSI chip using an *n*-channel silicon-gate MOS process, this microprocessor is housed in a 40-pin DIP (dual-in-line package). The 8080A is an improved version of Intel's first 8-bit microprocessor, the 8008. Figure 3.18 shows the pin connections grouped in functional units (see Figure 3.1 for pin configuration).

The 8080A has sixteen address lines and eight data lines, and requires three power supplies (+5 V, −5 V and +12 V) and a clock with two phases (ϕ_1 and ϕ_2). It has ten control signals not including such control signals as Memory Read/Write and I/O Read/Write discussed before. These are generated using the system controller. For the sake of clarity, the functional details of each control signal are omitted here.

THE 8224 CLOCK GENERATOR DRIVER (FIGURE 3.17)

This is a clock generator chip designed to provide a two-phase clock, ϕ_1 and ϕ_2, to the 8080A. The crystal oscillator provides the basic frequency divided by nine inside the chip, and two phases — ϕ_1 and ϕ_2 — are generated for the 8080A. In addition, the 8224 generates the RESET and READY signals for the 8080A, and the $\overline{\text{STSTB}}$ (Status Strobe signal) for the system controller, the 8228.

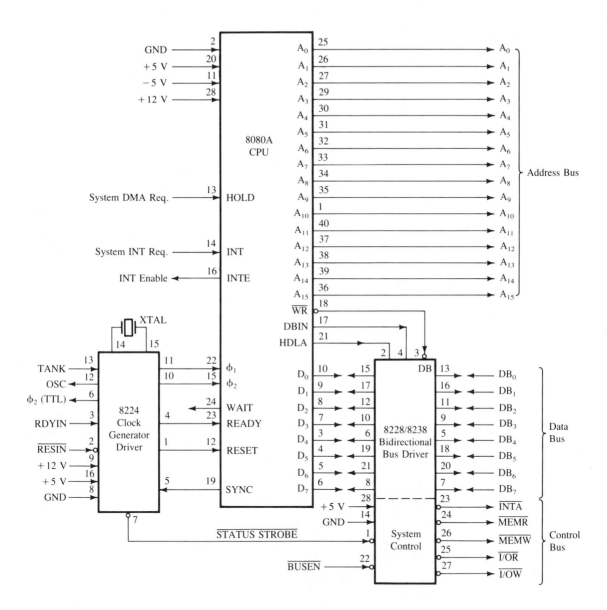

FIGURE 3.17

The 8080A MPU: The 8080A Microprocessor, the 8224 Clock Generator and the 8228
System Controller

SOURCE: Intel Corporation, *MCS — 80/85 Family User's Manual* (Santa Clara, Calif.: Author, 1979), p. 6-71.

FIGURE 3.18

The 8080A Microprocessor

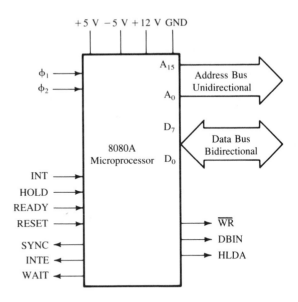

THE 8228 SYSTEM CONTROLLER AND BUS DRIVER (FIGURE 3.17)

This single-chip integrated circuit is employed for two purposes: (1) as a bidirectional bus driver for the data bus, to provide additional current capability to drive peripherals; and (2) as a controller, to generate the necessary control signals.

The eight data lines of the 8080A are connected to the chip to generate a buffered data bus. Three signals from the 8080A — DBIN (Data Bus In), $\overline{WR}$ (Write), and HLDA (Hold Acknowledge) and $\overline{STSTB}$ (Status Strobe Signal) from the clock are used as input to generate five control signals: Memory Read ($\overline{MEMR}$), Memory Write ($\overline{MEMW}$), I/O Read ($\overline{I/OR}$), I/O Write ($\overline{I/OW}$), and Interrupt Acknowledge ($\overline{INTA}$). For future discussion, all three chips will be viewed as the MPU. The control signals $\overline{I/OR}$ and $\overline{I/OW}$ are functionally similar to the 8085 control signals $\overline{IOR}$ and $\overline{IOW}$, respectively; they just have different names in the 8080A and 8085 manuals.

3.32   The 8080A Bus Timings

Figure 3.19 shows the timing of the 8080A Memory Read cycle. It is in many ways similar to the Memory Read cycle of the 8085; however, there are some differences.

The 8080A data bus is used for the status identification of an operation and for data transfer. The MPU places the status of the operation on the data bus during the earlier part of the cycle, and places data on the bus during the later part of the cycle. While the 8080A uses an 8-bit status format to identify various MPU operations, the 8085 uses three separate lines (IO/$\overline{M}$, S_1, and S_0) to identify an operation. Furthermore, all the necessary control signals can be generated in an 8085 system by using the status line IO/$\overline{M}$ and two control signals.

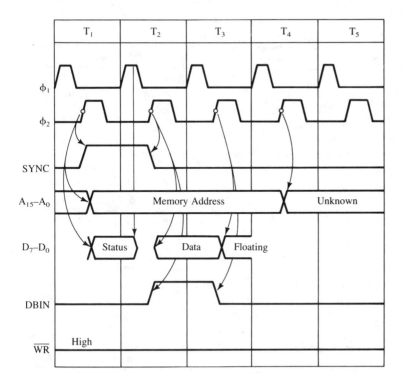

FIGURE 3.19

The 8080A Bus Timings for the Instruction Fetch

SOURCE: Adapted from Intel Corporation, *8080 Microcomputer Systems User's Manual* (Santa Clara, Calif.: Author, 1975), p. 2-8.

The MPU control signals in the 8080A are generated in the fashion similar to that in the 8085, by combining the microprocessor control signals and the status. However, in the 8080A, the status is identified using eight data lines, and the MPU operations are classified in ten different categories. Therefore, the system controller (the 8228) is required to latch the status and generate the necessary control signals (Figure 3.17). These control signals can be generated by using the discrete logic to point out the conceptual similarity between the 8085 and the 8080A.

SUMMARY

This chapter described the architecture of the 8085 microprocessor and illustrated the techniques for demultiplexing the bus AD_7-AD_0 and generating the control signals.

TABLE 3.3
Comparison of the 8085 and the 8080A Microprocessors

	8080A	**8085**
1. Power Supplies	Three: $+5$ V, -5 V, $+12$ V	One: $+5$ V
2. Functional MPU	Three chips: 8080A, 8224 and 8228	One chip: 8085 plus latch and gates.
3. Clock Phases	Two: ϕ_1 and ϕ_2	One: ϕ
4. Clock Frequency	2 MHz	3 MHz
5. Address Bus	16 Address lines	16 Address lines Low-order address bus is multiplexed with the data bus.
6. Data Bus	8 Data lines Data and status information are multiplexed.	8 Data lines Multiplexed with the low-order address bus.
7. Interrupt	One line	Five lines One is same as 8080A.
8. Extra Features	—	Serial I/O lines.
9. Status	Complex procedure to generate status information. Needs extra chip. Information is multiplexed with data bus.	Simpler procedure. The lines S_0, S_1, and IO/$\overline{\text{M}}$ indicate operation status.
10. Instruction Set	72 instructions	74 instructions: 72 instructions are same as in the 8080A.

Important concepts related to the 8085 architecture and the execution of an instruction were reviewed in Section 3.17.

The chapter illustrated an 8085-based microcomputer system and analyzed the memory map of the devices 8155 and 8755/8355 used in the SDK-85 system. In addition, the architecture of the 8080A and the necessary devices to design an 8080A MPU were discussed.

Table 3.3 compares the 8080A with the 8085, its improved version. In addition to the obvious enhancements in the area of chip count, power supply, and frequency, the 8085 has a much simpler way of generating status information and control signals. The 8085 includes all the 8080A instructions plus two more instructions related to serial I/O and additional interrupt lines.

ASSIGNMENTS

1. Explain the functions of ALE and IO/$\overline{\text{M}}$ signals of the 8085 microprocessor.
2. Draw a schematic to demultiplex the bus AD_7–AD_0 using the 8282 octal latch.
3. Figure 3.20 shows the 8205 (3-to-8) decoder with the three input signals: IO/$\overline{\text{M}}$, $\overline{\text{RD}}$, and $\overline{\text{WR}}$ from the 8085 microprocessor. Specify and name the valid output signals.

FIGURE 3.20

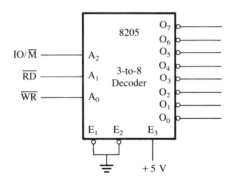

4. Explain why four output signals are invalid in Fig. 3.20.
5. Specify the crystal frequency required for an 8085 system to operate at 1.1 MHz.
6. What are Zero (Z) and Carry (CY) flags, and when are they set?
7. List the sequence of events that occurs when the 8085 MPU reads from memory.
8. Assume that memory location 2075H has a data byte 47H. Specify the contents of the address bus A_{15}–A_8 and the multiplexed bus AD_7–AD_0 when the MPU reads that location. Specify the contents of the program counter when the MPU is reading location 2075H.
9. In question 8, when does the $\overline{RD}$ signal go low if the system's frequency is 1 MHz?
10. In Figure 3.10, specify the memory maps of the R/WM and the EPROM chips if the inverter of the address line A_{15} is eliminated.
11. In the SDK-85 system, the specified map of the 8155 memory is 2000H to 20FFH (see Figure 3.15). If you enter a data byte at the location 2100H, will the system accept the data byte? If it accepts it, where will it store the data byte? Explain your answer.
12. In Figure 3.15, specify the memory map if output line O_1 of the decoder 8205 is connected to the $\overline{CE}$ signal. Specify the range of the foldback memory.
13. In Figure 3.16, specify the memory map if output line O_7 of the decoder 8205 is connected to the $\overline{CE}$ signal.
14. List three improved features of the 8085 over the 8080A microprocessor.
15. Explain the function of the system controller in the 8080A MPU.

Instructions and Timings

This chapter provides an overview of the instruction set of the 8085/8080A microprocessor. The instruction set determines the operations the microprocessor can perform. Examples are given to illustrate how the 8085 and the 8080A microprocessors execute instructions, and terms such as *instruction cycle, machine cycle,* and *T-states* are defined.

OBJECTIVES

☐ List the four data-manipulation functions that can be performed by the microprocessor.

☐ List the five major groups of instructions in the 8085/8080A instruction set.

☐ Explain the terms **operation code** (opcode) and **operand**, and illustrate these terms by writing an instruction.

☐ Define: **instruction cycle**, **machine cycle**, and **T-state**.

☐ List the 8085 operations that occur frequently in executing a program and the associated status and control signals.

☐ List the steps in executing 8085 1-byte and 2-byte instructions, and explain the associated signal timings.

☐ Explain the timings and the contents of the 8080A address and data buses during the execution of an instruction.

4.1 INSTRUCTION CLASSIFICATION

An **instruction** is a binary pattern designed inside a microprocessor to perform a specific function. The entire group of instructions, called the **instruction set**, determines what functions the microprocessor can perform. The 8085 microprocessor includes the 8080A instruction set plus two additional instructions. These instructions can be classified into the following five functional categories: data transfer (copy) operations, arithmetic operations, logical operations, branching operations, and machine-control operations.

DATA TRANSFER (COPY) OPERATIONS

This group of instructions copies data from a location called a source to another location, called a destination, without modifying the contents of the source. In technical manuals, the term *data transfer* is used for this copying function. However, the term *transfer* is misleading; it creates the impression that the contents of a source are destroyed when, in fact, the contents are retained without any modification. The various types of data transfer (copy) are listed below together with examples of each type:

Types	**Examples**
Between registers	Copy the content of register B into register D.
Specific data byte to register or a memory location	Load register B with the data byte 32H.
Between a memory location and a register	From the memory location 2000H to register B.
Between an I/O device and the accumulator	From an input keyboard to the accumulator.
Between a register pair and the stack	From register pair BC to two memory locations defined as the stack. (See Chapter 8 for details.)

ARITHMETIC OPERATIONS

These instructions perform arithmetic operations such as addition, subtraction, increment, and decrement.

☐ **Addition** — Any 8-bit number, or the contents of a register, or the contents of a memory location can be added to the contents of the accumulator and the sum is stored in the accumulator. No two other 8-bit registers can be added directly (e.g., the contents of register B cannot be added directly to the contents of register C). The instruction DAD is an exception; it adds 16-bit data directly in register pairs.

☐ **Subtraction** — Any 8-bit number, or the contents of a register, or the contents of a memory location, can be subtracted from the contents of the accumulator and the results stored in the accumulator. The subtraction is performed in 2's complement, and the results, if negative, are expressed in 2's complement. No two other registers can be subtracted directly.

☐ **Increment/Decrement** — The 8-bit contents of a register or a memory location can be incremented or decremented by 1. Similarly, the 16-bit contents of a register pair (such as *BC*) can be incremented or decremented by 1. These increment and decrement operations differ from addition and subtraction in an important way; i.e., they can be performed in any one of the registers or in a memory location.

LOGICAL OPERATIONS

These instructions perform various logical operations with the contents of the accumulator.

☐ **AND, OR, Exclusive-OR** — Any 8-bit number, or the contents of a register, or of a memory location can be logically ANDed, ORed, or Exclusive-ORed with the contents of the accumulator. The results are stored in the accumulator.

☐ **Rotate** — Each bit in the accumulator can be shifted either left or right to the next position.

☐ **Compare** — Any 8-bit number, or the contents of a register, or a memory location can be compared for equality, greater than, or less than, with the contents of the accumulator.

☐ **Complement** — The contents of the accumulator can be complemented; all 0s are replaced by 1s and all 1s are replaced by 0s.

BRANCHING OPERATIONS

This group of instructions alters the sequence of program execution either conditionally or unconditionally.

☐ **Jump** — Conditional jumps are an important aspect of the decision-making process in programming. These instructions test for a certain condition (e.g., Zero or Carry flag) and alter the program sequence when the condition is met. In addition, the instruction set includes an instruction called *unconditional jump*.

☐ **Call, Return, and Restart** — These instructions change the sequence of a program either by calling a subroutine or returning from a subroutine. The conditional Call and Return instructions also can test condition flags.

MACHINE CONTROL OPERATIONS

These instructions control machine functions such as Halt, Interrupt, or do nothing.

4.11 Review of the 8085/8080A Operations

The microprocessor operations related to data manipulation can be summarized in four functions:

1. copying data
2. performing arithmetic operations
3. performing logical operations
4. testing for a given condition and altering the program sequence

Some important aspects of the instruction set are noted below:

1. In data transfer, the contents of the source are not destroyed; only the contents of the destination are changed.
2. An I/O device can transfer or receive data from the accumulator but not from other registers (except for the memory-mapped I/O device).
3. Arithmetic and logical operations are performed with the contents of the accumulator, and the results are stored in the accumulator (with some exceptions).
4. Any register including memory can be used for increment and decrement.
5. A program sequence can be changed either conditionally or by testing for a given data condition.

4.2   INSTRUCTION FORMAT

An **instruction** is a command to the microprocessor to perform a given task on specified data. Each instruction has two parts: one is the task to be performed, called the **operation code** (Opcode), and the second is the data to be operated on, called the **operand**. The operand (or data) can be specified in various ways. It may include 8-bit (or 16-bit) data, an internal register, a memory location, or 8-bit (or 16-bit) address. In some instructions, the operand is implicit.

4.21   Instruction Word Size

The 8085/8080A instruction set is classified into the following three groups according to word size:

1. One-word or 1-byte instructions
2. Two-word or 2-byte instructions
3. Three-word or 3-byte instructions

In the 8085/8080A, "byte" and "word" are synonymous because it is an 8-bit microprocessor. However, instructions are commonly referred to in terms of bytes rather than words.

ONE-BYTE INSTRUCTIONS

A 1-byte instruction includes the opcode and the operand in the same byte. For example:

Task	Opcode	Operand	Binary Code	Hex Code
Copy the contents of the accumulator in register C.	MOV	C, A	0100 1111	4FH

| Add the contents of register B to the contents of the accumulator. | ADD | B | 1000 0000 | 80H |
| Invert (complement) each bit in the accumulator. | CMA | | 0010 1111 | 2FH |

These instructions are 1-byte instructions performing three different tasks. In the first instruction, both operand registers are specified. In the second instruction, the operand *B* is specified and the accumulator is assumed. Similarly, in the third instruction, the accumulator is assumed to be the implicit operand. These instructions are stored in 8-bit binary format in memory; each requires one memory location.

TWO-BYTE INSTRUCTIONS

In a 2-byte instruction, the first byte specifies the operation code and the second byte specifies the operand. For example:

Task	Opcode	Operand	Binary Code	Hex Code	
Load an 8-bit data byte in the accumulator.	MVI	A, Data	0011 1110	3E	First Byte
			DATA	Data	Second Byte

Assume the data byte is 32H. The assembly language instruction is written as:

Mnemonics	Hex Code	
MVI A,32H	3E	32H

This instruction would require two memory locations to store in memory.

THREE-BYTE INSTRUCTIONS

In a 3-byte instruction, the first byte specifies the opcode, and the following two bytes specify the 16-bit address. Note that the second byte is the low-order address and the third byte is the high-order address. For example:

Task	Opcode	Operand	Binary Code	Hex Code	
Transfer the program sequence to the memory location 2085H.	JMP	2085H	1100 0011	C3	First Byte
			1000 0101	85	Second Byte
			0010 0000	20	Third Byte

This instruction would require three memory locations to store in memory.

These commands are in many ways similar to our everyday conversation. For example, while eating in a restaurant, we may make the following requests and orders:

1. Pass (the) butter.   **4.** I will have combination 17 (on the menu).
2. Pass (the) bowl.   **5.** I will have what Susie ordered.
3. (Let us) eat.

The first request specifies the exact item, it is similar to the instruction for loading a specific data byte in a register. The second request mentions the bowl rather than the contents, even though one is interested in the contents of the bowl. It is similar to the instruction MOV C,A where registers (bowls) are specified rather than data. The third suggestion (let us eat) assumes that one knows what to eat. It is similar to the instruction Complement, which implicitly assumes that the operand is the accumulator. In the fourth sentence, the location of the item on the menu is specified and not the actual item. It is similar to the instruction: transfer the data byte from the location 2050H. The last order (what Susie ordered) is specified indirectly. It is similar to an instruction that specifies a memory location through the contents of a register pair. (Examples of the last two types of instruction are illustrated in later chapters.)

These various ways of specifying data are called the **addressing modes**. Although microprocessor instructions require one or more words to specify the operands, the notations and conventions used in specifying the operands have very little to do with the operation of the microprocessor. The mnemonic letters used to specify a command are chosen (somewhat arbitrarily) by the manufacturer. When an instruction is stored in memory, it is stored in binary code, the only code the microprocessor is capable of reading and understanding. The conventions used in specifying the instructions are valuable in terms of keeping uniformity in different programs and in writing assemblers. The important point to remember is that the microprocessor neither reads nor understands mnemonics nor hexadecimal numbers.

4.22 Opcode Format

In order to understand operation codes, we need to examine how an instruction is designed into the microprocessor. This information will be useful in reading a user's manual, in which operation codes are specified in binary format and 8-bits are divided in various groups.

In the design of the 8085/8080A microprocessor chip, all operations, registers, and status flags are identified with a specific code. For example, all internal registers are identified as follows:

Code	Registers	Code	Register Pairs
000	B	00	BC
001	C	01	DE

010	D	10	HL
011	E	11	AF OR SP
100	H		
101	L		
111	A		
110	Reserved for		

Memory Related Operation

Some of the operation codes are identified as follows:

Function	**Operation Code**
1. Rotate each bit of the accumulator to the left by one position.	00000111 = 07H (8-bit opcode)
2. Add the contents of a register to the accumulator.	10000 SSS (5-bit opcode — 3 bits are reserved for a register)

This instruction is completed by adding the code of the register. For example,

Add	:	10000
Register B	:	000
to A	:	Implicit
Binary Instruction:		10000000 = 80H

Add Reg. B

In assembly language, this is expressed as:

Opcode	**Operand**	**Hex Code**
ADD	B	80H

3. MOVE (Copy) the content of register Rs (source) to register Rd (destination)

01   *ddd*   *sss*
2-bit Opcode   Reg. Rd   Reg. Rs
for MOVE

This instruction is completed by adding the codes of two registers. For example,

Move (copy) the content:		0 1	
To register C	:	0 0 1	(ddd)
From register A	:	1 1 1	(sss)
Binary Instruction	:	0 1 0 0 1 1 1 1 → 4FH	

Opcode   Operand

In assembly language, this is expressed as:

Opcode	Operand	Hex Code
MOV	C, A	4F

Please note that the first register is the destination and the second register is the source—from A to C—which appears reversed for a general pattern from left to right. Typically, in the 8085/8080A user's manual the data transfer (copy) instruction is shown as follows:

MOV   r1,   r2*

0	1	D	D	D	S	S	S

4.3   HOW TO WRITE AND EXECUTE A SIMPLE PROGRAM

A program is a sequence of instructions written to tell a computer to perform a specific function. The instructions are selected from the instruction set of the microprocessor. To write a program, divide a given problem in small steps in terms of the operations the 8085/8080A can perform, then translate these steps into instructions. Writing a simple program of adding two numbers in the 8085/8080A language is illustrated below.

4.31   Illustrative Program: Add Two Hexadecimal Numbers

Problem Statement   Write instructions to add two hexadecimal numbers, 32H and 48H, and save the answer in register C.

Problem Analysis   The program to add two numbers can be written in various ways by selecting different internal registers and instructions related to these registers. However, the logical approach will more or less remain the same. It is described below in English, followed by a translation of these steps into the 8085/8080A assembly and machine languages.

The steps needed to add two numbers are as follows:

1. Load the number 32H in one register.
2. Load the number 48H in another register.
3. ADD the contents of the two registers.

4. Save the sum in register C.
5. End the program.

To translate these steps into assembly and machine languages, you should be familiar with the instruction set of the 8085/8080A or at least with the general classification of instructions described earlier.

---

*In this text, r1 is specified as Rd and r2 is specified as Rs to indicate destination and source.

Program in 8085/8080A Assembly Language   After reviewing the instruction set, we can translate the logical steps into assembly language as follows:

Opcode	Operand	Comments
1. MVI	A, 32H	;Load the number 32H in the accumulator
2. MVI	B, 48H	;Load the number 48H in register B
3. ADD	B	;Add the content of register B to the content of the accumulator. The sum is stored in the accumulator.
4. MOV	C, A	;Copy the sum from the accumulator to register C
5. HLT		;End of the program

Program in Machine Language   By looking up the machine code for each instruction in the instruction set, we can translate the program into machine language as follows:

Mnemonics	Machine Code (Hex)	
1. MVI A, 32H	3E 32	2-byte instruction
2. MVI B, 48H	06 48	2-byte instruction
3. ADD B	80	1-byte instruction
4. MOV C, A	4F	1-byte instruction
5. HLT	76	1-byte instruction

How to Enter and Execute a Program in a Single-Board Microcomputer   We assume that you have a single-board microcomputer equipped with a Hex keyboard and R/W memory. To enter the program, select a memory location — preferably, the first memory location of the user R/W memory — and enter the program sequentially. For example, the above program is stored as follows:

Memory Location	Memory Contents in Binary	Hex Code
2000	0 0 1 1 1 1 1 0	3E
2001	0 0 1 1 0 0 1 0	32
2002	0 0 0 0 0 1 1 0	06
2003	0 1 0 0 1 0 0 0	48
2004	1 0 0 0 0 0 0 0	80
2005	0 1 0 0 1 1 1 1	4F
2006	0 1 1 1 0 1 1 0	76

☐ Reset the system.
☐ Direct the microprocessor where your program begins by pushing the appropriate keys.
☐ Execute the program.

Program Execution   When the microprocessor is directed to the memory location 2000H, it begins the program execution by fetching the first machine code. The processor decodes the code by matching it with its predesigned set of instructions, and performs the function specified in the code. The microprocessor continues this process sequentially, one memory location to the next, until it is directed to halt. The timing details of the execution of an instruction are described later.

Result   The answer of your addition (32 + 48 = 7AH) is found in two registers — the accumulator and register C. Even if the sum is transferred from the accumulator to register C, the contents of the accumulator are not destroyed. (Remember, in data transfer, the source is not destroyed). However, the answer will not be displayed automatically because the program does not include an OUT instruction.

4.4   INSTRUCTION TIMINGS AND OPERATION STATUS

A program or instructions are stored in the memory of a microcomputer. To execute an instruction, the MPU must locate the memory location, fetch the code via the data bus, decode it in the instruction register, and perform the function specified in the code. These steps were described in the last chapter as "Fetch, Decode, and Execute." In 2- and 3-byte instructions, the subsequent codes are fetched, decoded, and executed in the same way as the first code. All these operations are performed at a given moment and within a given period. The timing is provided by the clock of the system, and the sequencing is done by the control unit of the microprocessor.

4.41   Execution of an Instruction (8085)

The 8085 identifies its various operations, called **machine cycles**, through the three status signals $IO/\overline{M}$, S_0, and S_1, as follows:

		Status		Control	
The 8085 Operations	$IO/\overline{M}$	S_1	S_0	$\overline{RD}$	$\overline{WR}$
1. Opcode Fetch (OF)	0	1	1	0	1
2. Memory Read (MR)	0	1	0	0	1
3. Memory Write (MW)	0	0	1	1	0
4. I/O Read (IOR)	1	1	0	0	1
5. I/O Write (IOW)	1	0	1	1	0

In addition to these operations, the 8085 performs other operations, such as Interrupt Acknowledge (see Table 3.1), which are ommitted here for the sake of clarity. Before discussing the timing and the execution of these five operations we need to define three terms: instruction cycle, machine cycle, and T-state.

Instruction cycle is defined as the time required to complete the execution of an instruction. The 8085/8080A instruction cycle consists of one to five machine cycles or one to five operations.

Machine cycle is defined as the time required to complete the operation of accessing either memory or I/O. In the 8085, the machine cycle may consist of three to six T-states, and in the 8080A, three to five T-states.

T-state is defined as one subdivision of the operation performed in one clock period. These subdivisions are internal states synchronized with the system clock.

The following examples illustrate these concepts.

The instruction MOV C, A (Code 4FH) is stored at memory location 2005H (refer to Section 4.31, Illustrative Program). The accumulator has data byte 7AH. Illustrate the execution of the instruction and calculate the execution time if the system clock frequency is 2 MHz.

Example
4.1

Memory Location (H)	Machine Code (H)
2005	4F

The execution of all instructions is sequenced by the program counter. Before the execution of an instruction, its memory address must be in the program counter. It is assumed here that the instruction located at the previous memory location 2004H is already executed, and that the program counter has the address 2005H.

Solution

To execute the instruction located at 2005H, the following sequence takes place (see Figure 4.1):

1. The MPU places the contents of the program counter (2005H) on the address bus, 20H on the high-order bus and 05H on the low-order bus AD_7–AD_0.
2. The MPU causes the ALE signal to go high; that can be used to demultiplex the bus.
3. The MPU indentifies the nature of the machine cycle — Opcode Fetch (Instruction Fetch) — by using the status signals ($IO/\overline{M} = 0$, $S_1 = 1$, $S_0 = 1$).
4. During T_2, the MPU sends the control signal $\overline{RD}$ to enable memory and increment the program counter by 1 to 2006H. The contents of the memory location — 4FH (MOV C, A) — are placed on the data bus.
5. The MPU reads the byte 4FH, and places it in the instruction register (T_3).
6. The MPU decodes the instruction, places the accumulator content (7AH) in the temporary register, and then transfers it to register C (T_4).

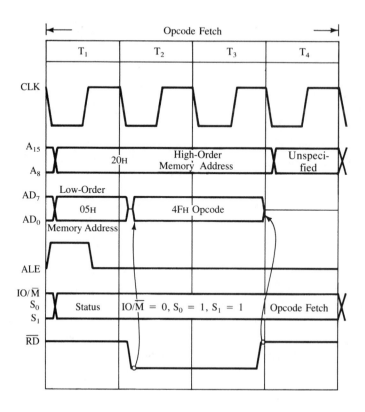

FIGURE 4.1
8085 Timing for Execution of the Instruction (MOV C, A)

Figure 4.1 shows the complete machine cycle of four T-states; it is the extension of Figure 3.3.

These operations require four clock periods. If the clock frequency is 2 MHz, the clock period is

$$T = 1/F = 1/2 \text{ MHz} = 0.5 \ \mu s$$
$$\text{Execution Time} = (\text{T-states} \times \text{clock period})$$
$$= (4 \text{ Ts} \times 0.5 \times 10^{-6})$$
$$= 2.0 \ \mu s$$

Example 4.2

Illustrate the execution of the 2-byte instruction MVI A, 32H (load the accumulator with the data 32H) stored in location as shown below. (Refer to the Illustrative Program in Section 4.31.)

Memory Location	Machine Code	Mnemonics
2000	3E	MVI A, 32H
2001	32	

This instruction requires two machine cycles with a total of seven T-states. The first machine cycle, M_1, has four T-states, and the second cycle, M_2, has three T-states (Figure 4.2).

The machine cycle M_1 is identified as the Opcode Fetch cycle by the signals $IO/\overline{M} = 0$, $S_1 = 1$, and $S_0 = 1$. During the state T_1, the high-order address (20H) is placed on the bus $A_{15}-A_8$, the low-order address (00H) is placed on the bus AD_7-AD_0, and the ALE (Address Latch Enable) signal is made to go high. In the state T_2, the control signal $\overline{RD}$ goes low, and the data (3EH) from the memory location 2000H are placed on the data bus. The fetch cycle is completed in the state T_3, and the instruction is decoded in the state T_4. During the state T_4, the contents of the bus are unknown.

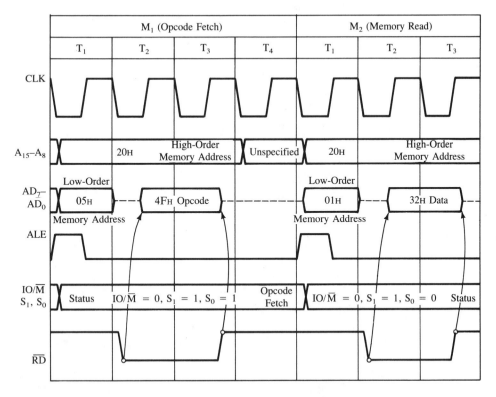

FIGURE 4.2
8085 Timing for Execution of the Instruction (MVI A, 32 H)

The machine cycle M_2, which is identified as a Memory Read cycle ($IO/\overline{M} = 0$, $S_1 = 1$, $S_0 = 0$), is similar to the M_1 cycle. In this cycle, the address 2001H is placed on the bus as in M_1, the data byte (32H) is fetched via the data bus, and the instruction is executed during the T_3 state. Machine cycles M_1 and M_2 are similar; they both perform the Memory Read function. However, the first machine cycle of each instruction is identified as the Opcode Fetch cycle rather than the Memory Read cycle.

From the two examples above, we can summarize the following points:

1. The instruction cycle consists of the execution of one or more machine cycles, and the execution time is determined by the T-states. (Please note that a 1-byte instruction does not mean one machine cycle. The 1-byte instruction XTHL has five machine cycles.)
2. The machine cycle is defined as the sequence of operations required to complete one of the functions.
3. The T-state is an internally defined operation and is synchronized with the system clock.
4. The type of operation is identified at the beginning of a machine cycle by the status signals.
5. The control signal identifies the timing of the operation.

4.42 Execution of an Instruction (8080A)

The execution of an instruction in the 8080A is somewhat more complex than in the 8085. The 8080A has a 2-phase clock, and its operations are identified by the 8-bit status on the data bus. The status codes are as follows :

Operations	Status Code
1. Opcode Fetch	A2H
2. Memory Read	82H
3. Memory Write	00H
4. I/O Read	42H
5. I/O Write	10H

Example
4.3

Illustrate the execution of the 2-byte instruction MVI A, 32H stored in memory locations 2000H and 2001H as in Example 4.2.

Solution

The execution of this instruction is in many ways similar to the execution of the instruction shown in Example 4.2. It requires two machine cycles with a total of seven T-states.

Figure 4.3 shows that the beginning of a machine cycle is indicated by the sync pulse, similar to the ALE signal in the 8085. At T_1, the microprocessor places the address (2000H) on the address bus and the operation status (Opcode Fetch — A2H) on the data bus. The 8228 controller uses the sync pulse to latch the status.

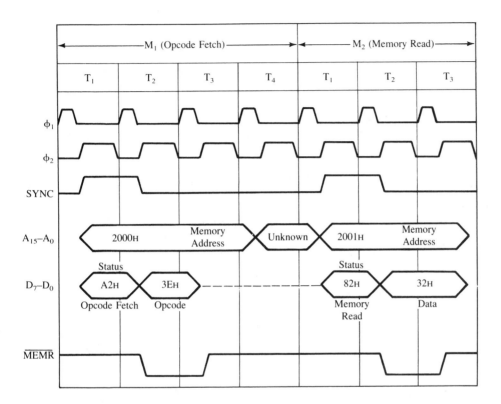

FIGURE 4.3
8080A Timing for Execution of the Instruction (MVI A, 32 H)

At T_2, the control signal $\overline{MEMR}$ is sent to enable the memory chip, and the instruction byte (3EH) is placed on the data bus. After decoding the instruction during T_3 and T_4, the 8080A starts the machine cycle M_2 to fetch the second byte located at the location 2001H. The M_2 cycle is identified with the status 82H as a Memory Read cycle. In the M_2 cycle, the data byte 32H is fetched and placed in the accumulator.

4.43 Comparison of the 8085 and the 8080A Instruction Cycles

Figure 4.4 shows the clock signals (T-states), labelled as T_1–T_6, and the machine cycles, labelled as M_1–M_5 for the 8085 and the 8080A microprocessors. The optional machine cycles and T-states are shown in the shaded portion. The instruction cycles of both processors are compared as follows:

1. The 8085 has a 1-phase clock, and the 8080A has a 2-phase clock.

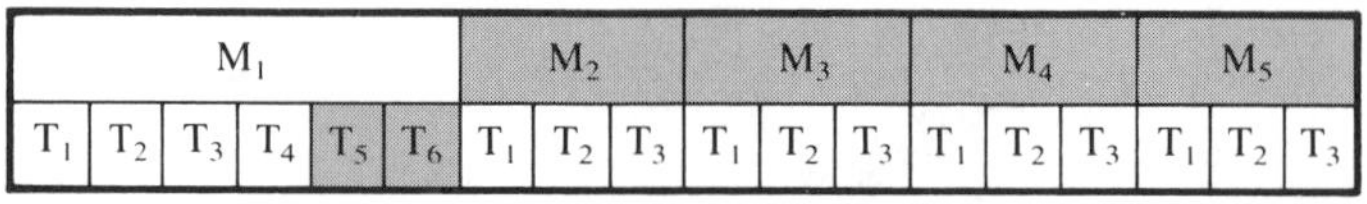

(a) 8085 Machine Cycles

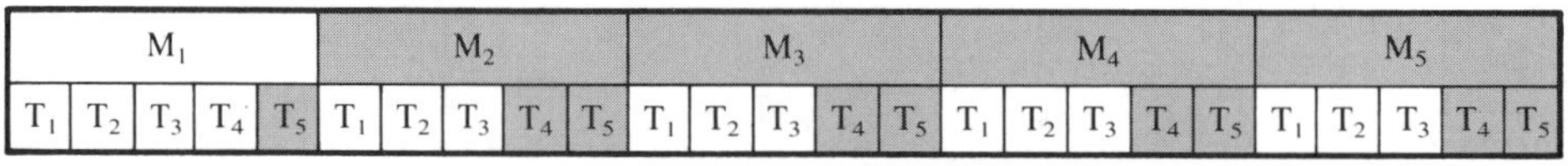

(b) 8080A Machine Cycles

FIGURE 4.4

Comparison of the 8085 and the 8080A Instruction Cycles

SOURCE: Adam Osborne and Gerry Kane, *4- & 8-Bit Microprocessor Handbook* (Berkeley, Calif.: Osborne/McGraw-Hill, 1981), pp. 4-7, 5-7. Reprinted with permission.

2. Both processors require one to five machine cycles to execute an instruction; M_1 is necessary for all instructions.

3. The 8085 M_1 cycle has four to six T-states, and the 8080A M_1 cycle has four to five T-states.

4. In the subsequent machine cycles, the 8085 requires only three T-states; the 8080A, on the other hand, requires four to five T-states.

4.5   OVERVIEW OF THE 8085/8080A INSTRUCTION SET

The 8085 microprocessor instruction set has 74 operation codes that result in 246 instructions. The set includes all the 8080A instructions plus two additional instructions (SIM and RIM, related to serial I/O). It is an overwhelming experience for a beginner to study these instructions. You are strongly advised not to attempt to read all these instructions at one time. However, you should be able to grasp an overview of the set by examining the frequently used instructions listed below.*

The following notations are used in the description of the instructions.

$$\begin{array}{ll}
R & = \text{8085/8080A 8-bit Register} \\
M & = \text{Memory register (location)} \\
Rs & = \text{Register source} \\
Rd & = \text{Register destination} \\
Rp & = \text{Register pair} \\
(\ ) & = \text{Contents of}
\end{array}$$

---

*These instructions are explained and illustrated in the next two chapters. The complete instruction set is explained alphabetically in Appendix F for easy reference; the appendix also includes three lists of instruction summaries arranged according to the functions, hexadecimal sequence of machine codes, and alphabetical order.

1. Data transfer (copy) instructions:

From register to register.
Load an 8-bit number in a register.
Between memory and register.
Between I/O and accumulator.
Load 16-bit number in a register pair.

Mnemonics	**Tasks**
MOV Rd, Rs	Copy data from source register Rs into destination register Rd.
MVI Rd, 8-bit	Load 8-bit data in a register.
OUT 8-bit (Port Address)	Send (write) data byte from the accumulator to an output device.
IN 8-bit (Port Address)	Accept (read) data byte from an input device and place it in the accumulator.
LXI Rp, 16-bit	Load 16-bit in a register pair.
MOV R, M	Copy the data byte from a memory location (source) into a register.
LDAX Rp	Copy the data byte into the accumulator from the memory location indicated by a register pair.
LDA 16-bit	Copy the data byte into the accumulator from the memory location specified by 16-bit address.
MOV M, R	Copy the data byte from register into memory location.
STAX Rp	Copy the data byte from the accumulator into the memory location indicated by a register pair.
STA 16-bit	Copy the data byte from the accumulator in the memory location specified by 16-bit address.

2. Arithmetic instructions:

Add
Subtract
Increment (Add 1)
Decrement (Subtract 1)

ADD R	Add the contents of the register to the contents of the accumulator.
ADI 8-bit	Add 8-bit data to the contents of the accumulator.
SUB R	Subtract the contents of register from the contents of the accumulator.

SUI 8-bit	Subtract 8-bit data from the contents of the accumulator.
INR R	Increment the contents of a register.
DCR R	Decrement the contents of a register.
INX Rp	Increment the contents of a register pair.
DCX Rp	Decrement the contents of a register pair.
ADD M	Add the contents of a memory location to the contents of the accumulator.
SUB M	Subtract the contents of a memory location from the contents of the accumulator.
INR M	Increment the contents of a memory location.
DCR M	Decrement the contents of a memory location.

3. Logical instructions:

AND
OR
X-OR
Compare
Rotate

ANA R/M	Logically AND the contents of register/memory with the contents of the accumulator.
ANI 8-bit	Logically AND the 8-bit data with the contents of the accumulator.
ORA R/M	Logically OR the contents of register/memory with the contents of the accumulator.
ORI 8-bit	Logically OR the 8-bit data with the contents of the accumulator.
XRA R/M	Exclusive-OR the contents of register/memory with the contents of the accumulator.
XRI 8-bit	Exclusive-OR the 8-bit data with the contents of the accumulator.
CMA	Complement the contents of the accumulator.
RLC	Rotate each bit in the accumulator to the left position.
RAL	Rotate each bit in the accumulator including the carry to the left position.
RRC	Rotate each bit in the accumulator to the right position.
RAR	Rotate each bit in the accumulator including the carry to the right position.

CMP R/M	Compare the contents of register/memory with the contents of the accumulator for less than, equal to, or more than.
CPI 8-bit	Compare 8-bit data with the contents of the accumulator for less than, equal to, or more than.
4. Branch instructions:	Change the program sequence unconditionally. Change the program sequence if specified data conditions are met.
JMP 16-bit Address	Change the program sequence to the location specified by the 16-bit address.
JZ 16-bit Address	Change the program sequence to the location specified by the 16-bit address if the Zero flag is set.
JNZ 16-bit Address	Change the program sequence to the location specified by the 16-bit address if the Zero flag is reset.
JC 16-bit Address	Change the program sequence to the location specified by the 16-bit address if the Carry flag is set.
JNC 16-bit Address	Change the program sequence to the location specified by the 16-bit address if the Carry flag is reset.
CALL 16-bit Address	Change the program sequence to the location of a subroutine.
RET	Return to the calling program after completing the subroutine sequence.

5. Machine control instructions:	
HLT	Stop processing and wait.
NOP	Do not perform any operation.

This set of instructions is a representative sample; it does not include various instructions related to 16-bit data operations, additional Jump instructions, and conditional Call and Return instructions.

4.51 How to Recognize Number of Bytes in an Instruction

As we become familiar with instructions and begin to use them in writing programs to be assembled manually, we need to know the number of bytes required for a given instruction. It is easy to write programs if we can find a way to recognize the number of bytes in an instruction without looking up the instruction list.

There are no hard and fast rules to identify the number of bytes in an instruction, but some clues can be found by examining the instruction set.

ONE-BYTE INSTRUCTIONS

1. Data transfer instructions that copy the contents from one register (or memory) into another register (or memory) are 1-byte instructions.
Example: MOV
2. Arithmetic/Logic instructions without the ending letter I are 1-byte instructions.
Examples: ADD, SUB, ORA, ANA, INR, DCR

TWO-BYTE INSTRUCTIONS

1. Instructions that load or manipulate 8-bit data directly are 2-byte instructions.
2. These instructions are generally represented by three letters with the ending letter I.
Examples: MVI, ADI, ANI, ORI (Exception: the LXI instructions)

THREE-BYTE INSTRUCTIONS

1. Instructions that load 16 bits or refer to memory addresses are 3-byte instructions.
Examples: LXI, JMP, Conditional Jumps, CALL

Although these statements are generally applicable, they may not apply to all the instructions in the set. However, these rules of thumb will be useful in the initial stages of writing programs. After writing a few programs, you will begin to see the pattern and will be able to recognize the number of bytes required for an instruction.

SUMMARY

This chapter described the data manipulation functions of the 8085/8080A microprocessor, provided an overview of the instruction set, and illustrated the execution of instructions in relation to the system's clock. The important concepts in this chapter can be summarized as follows.

☐ The 8085/8080A microprocessor operations are classified into five major groups: data transfer (copy), arithmetic, logic, branch, and machine control.
☐ An instruction has two parts: opcode (operation to be performed) and operand (data to be operated on). The operand can be data (8- or 16-bit), address, register, or it can be implicit. The method of specifying an operand (directly, indirectly, etc.) is called the addressing mode.
☐ The instruction set is classified in three groups according to the word size: 1-, 2-, or 3-byte instructions.

☐ To write an assembly language program, divide given problem into small steps in terms of the microprocessor operations, translate these steps into assembly language instructions, and then translate them into the 8085/8080A machine code.

☐ The instruction cycle is defined as the time required to complete the execution of an instruction; it consists of various machine cycles. Each machine cycle is a micro-processor operation made up of various T-states (equivalent to the clock period).

☐ The machine cycles—Opcode Fetch, Memory Read, Memory Write, I/O Read, and I/O Write—are frequently used by the microprocessor. In the 8085, the machine cycles are identified by the status signals IO/$\overline{M}$, S_0, and S_1. In the 8080A, the machine cycles are identified by placing the 8-bit status code on the data bus at the beginning of the machine cycle.

☐ The microprocessor sends out an appropriate control signal to identify the timing of each machine cycle.

ASSIGNMENTS

1. List the four categories of 8085/8080A instructions that manipulate data.
2. Define opcode and operand, and specify the opcode and the operand in the instruction MOV H, L.
3. Write the machine code for the instruction MOV H, A if the opcode = 01, the register code for H = 100_2, and the register code for A = 111.
4. Write the 8085/8080A mnemonics and the machine code to transfer the program sequence to the location 0155H.
5. Define: instruction cycle, machine cycle, and T-state.
6. Calculate the time required to execute the following two instructions if the system clock frequency is 750 kHz:

$$\text{MOV C, B} \qquad \text{5 T-states}$$
$$\text{JMP 2050H} \qquad \text{10 T-states}$$

7. Illustrate the contents of the address bus and the data bus with respect to the system clock in an 8080A system when the following instruction is executed. Show the appropriate control signals.

Memory Address	Machine Code	Mnemonics	Comment
0051	C6	ADI, F2H	Add F2H to the contents of
0052	F2		the accumulator

8. Illustrate the contents of the address bus and the data bus, and the timing of the control signals in an 8085 system when the instruction in Question 7 is executed. Show the logic levels of the signals IO/$\overline{\text{M}}$, S_0 and S_1.

9. Write logical steps to add the following two Hex numbers. Both the numbers should be saved for future use. Save the sum in the accumulator.

   Numbers: A2H and 18H

10. Translate the program in Question 9 into the 8085/8080A assembly language.

11. Data byte 28H is stored in register B and data byte 97H is stored in the accumulator. Show the contents of registers B, C, and the accumulator after the execution of the following two instructions:

   MOV A, B
   MOV C, A

II
Programming the 8085/8080A

Part II of this book is an introduction to assembly language programming for the 8085/8080A. It explains commonly used instructions, elementary programming techniques, and their applications.

The content is presented in a format as if for teaching a foreign language. One approach to learning a foreign language is to begin with a few words that can form simple, meaningful, and interactive sentences. After learning a few sentences, the student begins to write a paragraph that can convey an idea in a coherent fashion; then, by sequencing a few paragraphs, begins to compose a letter. Chapters 5 to 10 are arranged in similar fashion — from simple instructions to applications.

Chapters 5 and 6 are concerned primarily with the instructions that occur most frequently. The instructions are not introduced according to the five groups as classified in Chapter 4; instead, a few instructions that can perform a simple task are selected from each group. Chapter 5 includes the discussion of instructions from each group — from data copy to branch instructions. Chapter 6 introduces elementary programming techniques such as looping and indexing. Chapter 7 uses the instructions and techniques presented in these chapters to design software delays and counters.

Chapter 8 introduces the concepts of subroutine and stack, which provide flexibility and variety for program design. Chapter 9 includes applications of the concepts presented in Chapter 8, presenting techniques for writing programs concerned with code conversions and arithmetic routines. Chapter 10 deals with the uses of assemblers in disk-based software development systems.

PREREQUISITES

The reader is expected to know the following topics:

☐ The 8085/8080A architecture, especially the programming registers.
☐ The concepts related to memory and I/Os.
☐ Logic operations, and binary and hexadecimal arithmetic.

Introduction to 8085/8080A Basic Instructions

A microcomputer performs a task by reading and executing the set of instructions written in its memory. This set of instructions, written in a sequence, is called a **program**. Each instruction in the program is a command, in binary, to the microprocessor to perform an operation. This chapter introduces 8085/8080A basic instructions, their operations, and their applications.

Chapters 2 and 3 described the architecture of the 8085/8080A microprocessor and Chapter 4 provided an overview of the instruction set and the tasks the 8085/8080A can perform. This chapter is concerned with using instructions within the constraints and capabilities of its registers and the bus system. A few instructions are introduced from each of the five groups (Data Transfer, Arithmetic, Logical, Branch, and Machine Control) and are used to write simple programs to perform specific tasks.

The simple illustrative programs given in this chapter can be entered and executed on the single-board microcomputers used commonly in college laboratories.

OBJECTIVES

☐ Explain the functions of data transfer (copy) instructions and how the contents of the source register and the destination register are affected.

☐ Explain the Input/Output instructions and port addresses.

☐ Explain the functions of the machine control instructions HLT and NOP.

☐ Recognize the addressing modes of the instructions.

☐ Draw a flowchart of a simple program.

☐ Write a program in 8085/8080A mnemonics to illustrate an application of data copy instructions, and translate those mnemonics manually into their Hex codes.

□ Write a program in the proper format showing memory addresses, Hex machine codes, mnemonics, and comments.

□ Explain the arithmetic instructions, and recognize the flags that are set or reset for given data conditions.

□ Write a set of instructions to perform an addition and a subtraction (in 2's complement).

□ Explain the logic instructions, and recognize the flags that are set or reset for given data conditions.

□ Write a set of instructions to illustrate logic operations.

□ Explain the use of logic instructions in masking, setting, and resetting individual bits.

□ Explain the unconditional and conditional Jump instructions and how flags are used by the conditional Jump instructions to change the sequence of a program.

□ Write a program to illustrate an application of Jump instructions.

□ List the important steps in writing and troubleshooting a simple program.

5.1   DATA TRANSFER (COPY) OPERATIONS

One of the primary functions of the microprocessor is copying data, from a register (or I/O or memory) called the source, to another register (or I/O or memory) called the destination. In technical literature, the copying function is frequently labelled as the **data transfer function**, which is somewhat misleading. In fact, the contents of the source are not transferred, but are copied into the destination register without modifying the contents of the source.

Several instructions are used to copy data (as listed in Chapter 4). This section is concerned with the following operations.

MOV	: Move	Copy a data byte.
MVI	: Move Immediate	Load a data byte directly.
OUT	: Output to Port	Send a data byte to an output device.
IN	: Input from Port	Read a data byte from an input device.

The term *copy* is equally valid for input/output functions because the contents of the source are not altered. However, the term *data transfer* is used so commonly to indicate the data copy function that, in this book, these terms are used interchangeably when the meaning is not ambiguous.

In addition to data copy instructions, it is necessary to introduce two machine-control operations to execute programs.

HLT	: Halt	Stop processing and wait.
NOP	: No Operation	Do not perform any operation.

These operations (opcodes) are explained and illustrated below with examples.

Instructions   The data transfer instructions copy data from a source into a destination without modifying the contents of the source. The previous contents of the destination are replaced by the contents of the source.

Important Note: Data transfer instructions do not affect the flags.

Opcode	Operand	Description
MOV	Rd, Rs	Move This is a 1-byte instruction Copies data from source register Rs to destination register Rd
MVI	Rd, 8-Bit	Move Immediate This is a 2-byte instruction Loads the 8 bits of the second byte into the register specified
OUT	8-Bit Port Address	Output to Port This is a 2-byte instruction Sends (copies) the contents of the accumulator (A) to the output port specified in the second byte
IN	8-Bit Port Address	Input from Port This is a 2-byte instruction Accepts (reads) data from the input port specified in the second byte, and loads into the accumulator
HLT		Halt This is a 1-byte instruction The processor stops executing and enters wait state The address bus and data bus are placed in high impedance state. No register contents are affected
NOP		No Operation This is a 1-byte instruction No operation is performed Generally used to increase processing time or substitute in place of an instruction. When an error occurs in a program and an instruction needs to be eliminated, it is more convenient to substitute NOP than to reassemble the whole program.

Load the accumulator A with the data byte 82H (the letter H indicates hexadecimal number), and save the data in register B.

Example 5.1

Instructions   MVI A, 82H,
MOV B, A

The first instruction is a 2-byte instruction that loads the accumulator with the data byte 82H, and the second instruction MOV B, A copies the contents of the accumulator in register B without changing the contents of the accumulator.

Example 5.2

Write instructions to read eight ON/OFF switches connected to the input port with the address 00H, and turn on the devices connected to the output port with the address 01H, as shown in Figure 5.1. (I/O port addresses are given in hexadecimal.)

Solution

The input has eight switches that are connected to the data bus through the tri-state buffer. Any one of the switches can be connected to +5 V (logic 1) or to ground (logic 0), and each switch controls the corresponding device at the output port. The microprocessor needs to read the bit pattern on the switches and send the same bit pattern to the output port to turn on the corresponding devices.

Instructions IN   00H
                 OUT   01H
                 HLT

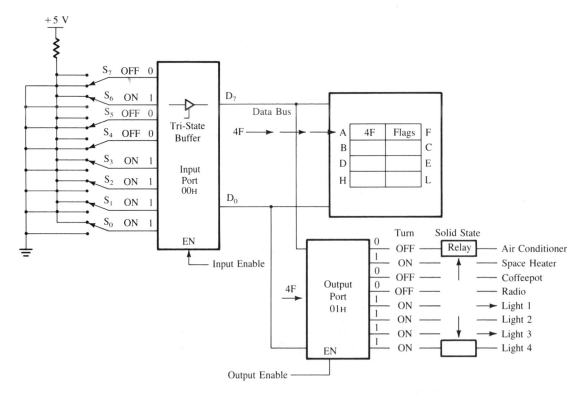

FIGURE 5.1
Reading Data at Input Port and Sending Data to Output Port

When the microprocessor executes the instruction IN 00H, it enables the tri-state buffer. The bit pattern 4FH formed by the switch positions is placed on the data bus and transferred to the accumulator. This is called reading an input port.

When the microprocessor executes the next instruction OUT 01H, it places the contents of the accumulator on the data bus, and enables the output port 01H. (This is also called writing data to an output port.) The output port latches the bit pattern and turns ON/OFF the devices connected to the port according to the bit pattern. In Figure 5.1, the bit pattern 4FH will turn on the devices connected to the output port data lines D_6, D_3, D_2, D_1, and D_0: the space heater and four light bulbs. To turn off some of the devices and turn on other devices, the bit pattern can be modified by changing the switch positions. For example, to turn on the radio and the coffee pot and turn off all other devices, the switches S_4 and S_5 should be on and the others should be off. The microprocessor will read the bit pattern 0 0 1 1 0 0 0 0, and this bit pattern will turn on the radio and the coffee pot and turn off other devices.

The preceding explanation raises two questions:

1. What are the second bytes in the instructions IN and OUT?
2. How are they determined?

In answer to the first question, the second bytes are I/O port addresses. Each I/O port is identified with a number or an address similar to the postal address of a house. The second byte has 8 bits meaning $256(2^8)$ combinations; thus 256 input ports and 256 output ports with addresses from 00H to FFH can be connected to the system.

The answer to the second question depends on the logic circuit (called interfacing) used to connect and identify a port by the system designer (see Chapter 11).

ADDRESSING MODES

The above instructions are commands to the microprocessor to copy 8-bit data from a source into a destination. In these instructions, the source can be a register, an input port, or an 8-bit number (00H to FFH). Similarly, a destination can be a register or an output port. The sources and destinations are, in fact, operands. The various formats of specifying the operands are called the addressing modes. The 8085/8080A instruction set has the following addressing modes. (Each mode is followed by an example and by the corresponding piece of restaurant conversation from the analogy discussed in Chapter 4.)

1. Immediate Addressing — MVI Rs, Data (Pass the butter)
2. Register Addressing — MOV Rd, Rs (Pass the bowl)
3. Direct Addressing — IN/OUT Port # (Combination number 17 on the menu)
4. Indirect Addressing — Illustrated in the next chapter (I will have what Susie has)

This classification of the addressing modes is unimportant, except that it provides some clues in understanding mnemonics. For example, in case of the MVI opcode, the letter *I* suggests that the second byte is data and not a register. What is important is to become familiar with the instructions. After you study the examples given in this chapter, a pattern will begin to emerge.

5.11 Illustrative Program: Data Transfer—From Register to Output Port

PROBLEM STATEMENT

Load the hexadecimal number 37H in register B, and display the number at the output port labelled as PORT1.

PROBLEM ANALYSIS

Even though this is a very simple problem it is necessary to break the problem into small steps and to outline the thinking process in terms of the tasks described in Section 5.1.

STEPS

Step 1: Load register B with a number.
Step 2: Send the number to the output port.

QUESTIONS TO BE ASKED

☐ Is there an instruction to load the register B? YES—MVI B.
☐ Is there an instruction to send the data from register B to the output port? NO.
  Review the instruction OUT. This instruction sends data from the accumulator to an output port.
  The solution appears to be as follows: copy the number from register B into accumulator A.
☐ Is there an instruction to copy data from one register to another register? YES—MOV Rd, Rs

FLOWCHART

The thinking process described here and the steps necessary to write the program can be represented in a pictorial format, called a **flowchart**. Figure 5.2 describes the preceding steps in a flowchart.

Flowcharting is an art. The flowchart in Figure 5.2 does not include all the steps described earlier. Although the number of steps that should be represented in a flowchart is ambiguous, not all of them should be included. That would defeat the purpose of the flowchart. It should represent a logical approach and sequence of steps in solving the problem. A flowchart is similar to the block diagram of a hardware system or to the outline of a chapter. Information in each block of the flowchart should be similar to the heading of a paragraph. Generally, a flowchart is used for two purposes: to assist and clarify the thinking process and to communicate the programmer's thoughts or logic to others.

Symbols commonly used in flowcharting are shown in Table 5.1. Two types of symbols—rectangles and ovals—are already illustrated in Figure 5.2. The diamond is

FIGURE 5.2
Flowchart

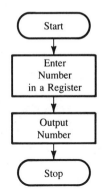

TABLE 5.1
Flowcharting Symbols .

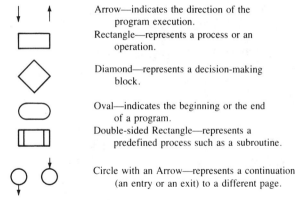

Arrow—indicates the direction of the
    program execution.
Rectangle—represents a process or an
    operation.

Diamond—represents a decision-making
    block.

Oval—indicates the beginning or the end
    of a program.
Double-sided Rectangle—represents a
    predefined process such as a subroutine.

Circle with an Arrow—represents a continuation
    (an entry or an exit) to a different page.

used with Jump instructions for decision making (see Figure 5.9), and the double-sided rectangle is used for subroutines (see Chapter 8).

The flowchart in Figure 5.2 includes what steps to do and in what sequence. As a rule, a general flowchart does not include how to perform these steps nor what registers are being used. The steps described in the flowchart are translated into an assembly language program in the next section.

ASSEMBLY LANGUAGE PROGRAM

Tasks	**8085/8080A Mnemonics**
1. Load register B with 37H.	MVI B, 37H*
2. Copy the number from B to A.	MOV A, B
3. Send the number to the output — port 01H.	OUT, PORT1
4. End of the program.	HLT

*A number followed by the letter *H* represents a hexadecimal number.

TRANSLATION FROM ASSEMBLY LANGUAGE TO
MACHINE LANGUAGE

Now, to translate the assembly language program into machine language, look up the hexadecimal machine codes for each instruction in the 8085/8080A instruction set and write each machine code in the sequence, as follows:

8085/8080A Mnemonics	Hex Machine Code
1. MVI B, 37H	06
	37
2. MOV A, B	78
3. OUT, PORT1	D3
	01
4. HLT	76

This program has six machine codes and will require six bytes of memory to enter the program into your system. If your single-board microcomputer has R/W memory starting at the address 2000H, this program can be enetered in the memory locations 2000H to 2005H. The format generally used to write an assembly language program is shown below.

PROGRAM FORMAT

Memory Address (Hex)	Machine Code (Hex)	Instruction Opcode	Instruction Operand	Comments
XX00*	06	MVI	B, 37H	;Load register B with data 37H
XX01	37			
XX02	78	MOV	A, B	;Copy (B) into (A)
XX03	D3	OUT	PORT1	;Display accumulator contents
XX04	PORT1†			(37H) at Port1
XX05	76	HLT		;End of the program

This program has five columns: Memory Address, Machine Code, Opcode, Operand, and Comments. Each is described in the context of a single-board microcomputer.

Memory Address   These are 16-bit addresses of the user (R/W) memory in the system, where the machine code of the program is stored. The beginning address is shown as XX00; the symbol XX represents the page number of the available R/W memory in the microcomputer, and 00 represents the line number. For example, if the microcomputer has the user memory at 2000H, the symbol XX represents page number 20H; if the user

---

*Enter high-order address (page number) of your R/W memory in place of XX.

†Enter the output port address of your system. If an output port is not available on your system, see "How to Execute a Program Without an Output Port" later in this section.

memory begins at 0300H, the symbol XX represents page 03H. Substitute the appropriate page when entering the machine code of a program.

Machine Code   These are the hexadecimal numbers (instruction codes) that are entered (or stored) in the respective memory addresses through the hexadecimal keyboard of the microcomputer. The monitor program, which is stored in Read-Only Memory (ROM) of the microcomputer, translates the Hex numbers into binary digits and stores the binary digits in the R/W memory.

If the system has R/W memory with the starting address at 2000H and the output port address 01H, the program will be stored as follows:

Memory Address	Memory Contents									Hex Code
2000	0	0	0	0	0	1	1	0	$\longrightarrow$	06
2001	0	0	1	1	0	1	1	1	$\longrightarrow$	37
2002	0	1	1	1	1	0	0	0	$\longrightarrow$	78
2003	1	1	0	1	0	0	1	1	$\longrightarrow$	D3
2004	0	0	0	0	0	0	0	1	$\longrightarrow$	01
2005	0	1	1	1	0	1	1	0	$\longrightarrow$	76

Opcode   (Operation Code)   An instruction is divided into two parts: Opcode and Operand. Opcodes are the abbreviated symbols specified by the manufacturer (Intel) to indicate the type of operation or function that will be performed by the machine code.

Operand   The operand part of an instruction specifies the item to be processed; it can be 8- or 16-bit data, a register, or a memory address.

An instruction, called a mnemonic or mnemonic instruction, is formed by combining an opcode and an operand. The mnemonics are used to write programs in the 8085/8080A assembly language; and then the mnemonics in these programs are translated manually into the binary machine code by looking them up in the instruction set.

Comments   The comments are written as a part of the proper documentation of a program to explain or elaborate the purpose of the instructions used. These are separated by a semicolon (;) from the instruction on the same line. They play a critical role in the user's understanding of the logic behind a program. Since the illustrative programs in the early part of this chapter are simple, most of the comments are either redundant or trivial. The purpose of the comments in these programs is to reinforce the meaning of the instructions. In actual usage, the comments should not just describe the operation of an instruction.

HOW TO ENTER AND EXECUTE THE PROGRAM

This program assumes that one output port is available on your microcomputer system. The program cannot be executed without modification if your microcomputer has no independent output ports other than the system display of memory address and data or if it has programmable I/O ports. (See Chapter 14.) To enter the program*

1. Push *Reset* key.
2. Enter the 16-bit memory address of the first machine code of your program. (Substitute the page number of your R/W memory for the letters XX and the output port address for the label PORT1.)
3. Enter and store all the machine codes sequentially, using the hexadecimal keyboard on your system.
4. Reset the system.
5. Enter the memory address where the program begins and push the *Execute* key.

If the program is properly entered and executed, the data byte 37H will be displayed at the output port.

HOW TO EXECUTE A PROGRAM WITHOUT AN OUTPUT PORT

If your system does not have an output port, either eliminate the instruction OUT PORT1, or substitute NOP (No Operation) in place of the OUT instruction. Assuming your system has R/W memory starting at 2000H, you can enter the program as follows:

Memory Address	Machine Code	Mnemonic Instruction
2000	06	MVI B, 37H
2001	37	
2002	78	MOV A, B
2003	00	NOP
2004	00	NOP
2005	76	HLT

After you have executed this program, you can find the answer in the accumulator by pushing the *Examine Register* key (see your user's manual).

The program also can be executed by entering the machine code 76 in location 2003H, thus eliminating the OUT instruction.

5.12   Illustrative Program: Data Transfer to Control Output Devices

PROBLEM STATEMENT

A microcomputer is designed to control various appliances and lights in your house. The system has an output port with the address 01H, and various units are connected to the bits D_7 to D_0 as shown in Figure 5.3. For a cool morning you want to turn on the radio, the

*Refer to the user's manual of your microcomputer for details. If you have an Intel SDK-85 system, refer to Appendix B.

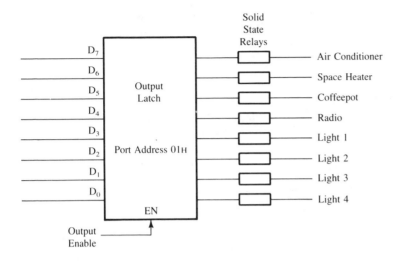

FIGURE 5.3
Output Port to Control Devices

coffee pot, and the space heater. Write appropriate instructions for the microcomputer. Assume the R/W memory in your system begins at 0300H.

PROBLEM ANALYSIS

The output port in Figure 5.3 is a latch (D flip-flop). When data bits are sent to the output port they are latched by the D flip-flop. A data bit at logic 1 supplies approximately 5 V as output and can turn on solid-state relays.

To turn on the radio, the coffeepot, and the space heater, set D_6, D_5, and D_4 at logic 1, and the other bits at logic 0.

$$\begin{array}{cccccccc} D_7 & D_6 & D_5 & D_4 & D_3 & D_2 & D_1 & D_0 \\ 0 & 1 & 1 & 1 & 0 & 0 & 0 & 0 \end{array} = 70H$$

The output port requires 70H, and it can be sent to the port by loading the accumulator with 70H.

PROGRAM

Memory Address	Machine Code	Mnemonic Instruction	Comments
HI-LO*			
0300	3E	MVI A, 70H	;Load the accumulator with the bit pattern
0301	70		necessary to turn on the devices

*Change the high-order memory address 03 to the appropriate address for your system.

0302	D3	OUT 01H	;Send the bit pattern to the port 01H, and
0303	01†		turn on the devices
0304	76	HLT	;End of the program

PROGRAM OUTPUT

This program simulates controlling of the devices connected to the output port by displaying 70H on a seven-segment LED display. If your system has individual LEDs, the binary pattern—0 1 1 1 0 0 0 0—will be displayed.

5.13 Review of Important Concepts

1. Registers are used to load data directly or to save data bytes.
2. In data transfer (copying), the destination register is modified but the source register retains its data.
3. The 8085/8080A transfers data from an input port to the accumulator (IN) and from the accumulator to an output port (OUT). The instruction OUT cannot send data from any other register.

See Assignments 1–4 at the end of this chapter.

5.2 ARITHMETIC OPERATIONS

The 8085/8080A microprocessor performs various arithmetic operations, such as addition, subtraction, increment, and decrement. These arithmetic operations have the following mnemonics.

ADD: Add	Add the contents of a register.*
ADI : Add Immediate	Add 8-bit data.
SUB : Subtract	Subtract the contents of a register.
SUI : Subtract Immediate	Subtract 8-bit data.
INR : Increment	Increase the contents of a register by 1.
DCR: Decrement	Decrease the contents of a register by 1.

These arithmetic operations are performed in relation to the contents of the accumulator. However, the Increment or the Decrement operations can be performed in any register. The instructions for these operations are explained below.

INSTRUCTIONS

These arithmetic instructions (except INR and DCR)

---

†Substitute the appropriate port address.
*Memory-related arithmetic operations are excluded here; they are discussed in Chapter 6.

1. assume implicitly that the accumulator is one of the operands.
2. modify all the flags according to the data conditions in the accumulator.
3. place the result in the accumulator.
4. do not affect the contents of the operand register.

The descriptions of the instructions (including INR and DCR) are as follows:

Opcode	Operand	Description
ADD	R	Add This is a 1-byte instruction Adds the contents of register R to the contents of the accumulator
ADI	8-bit	Add Immediate This is a 2-byte instruction Adds the second byte to the contents of the accumulator
SUB	R	Subtract This is a 1-byte instruction Subtracts the contents of register R from the contents of the accumulator
SUI	8-bit	Subtract Immediate This is a 2-byte instruction Subtracts the second byte from the contents of the accumulator
INR	R	Increment This is a 1-byte instruction Increases the contents of register R by 1 *Caution:* All flags except the CY are affected
DCR	R	Decrement This is a 1-byte instruction Decreases the contents of register R by 1 *Caution:* All flags except the CY are affected

5.21 Addition

The 8085/8080A performs addition with 8-bit binary numbers and stores the sum in the accumulator. If the sum is larger than eight bits (FFH), it sets the Carry flag. Addition can be performed either by adding the contents of a source register (B, C, D, E, H, L, or memory) to the contents of the accumulator (ADD) or by adding the second byte directly to the contents of the accumulator (ADI).

The contents of the accumulator are 93H and the contents of register C are B7H. Add both contents.

Example
5.3

Instruction   ADD C

$$
\begin{array}{lllllllllll}
 & & & CY & D_7 & D_6 & D_5 & D_4 & D_3 & D_2 & D_1 & D_0 \\
(A) & : & 93H = & & 1 & 0 & 0 & 1 & 0 & 0 & 1 & 1 \\
 & + & & & & & & & & & & \\
(C) & : & B7H = & & 1 & 0 & 1 & 1 & 0 & 1 & 1 & 1 \\
 & & & 1 & & 1 & 1 & & 1 & 1 & 1 & & \text{Carry}
\end{array}
$$

SUM (A) : $\boxed{1}$4AH = $\boxed{1}$ 0 1 0 0   1 0 1 0
         CY

Flag Status:* $S = 0, Z = 0, CY = 1$

When the 8085/8080A adds these two numbers, the accumulator will have 4AH in binary, and the Carry flag will be set.

Example 5.4

Add the number 35H directly to the sum in the previous example when CY flag is set.

Instruction   ADI 35H

$$
\begin{array}{llll}
 & & & CY \\
(A) & : & 4AH = & \boxed{1} \; 0 \; 1 \; 0 \; 0 \quad 1 \; 0 \; 1 \; 0 \\
 & + & & \\
(Data) & : & 35H = & \phantom{\boxed{1}} 0 \; 0 \; 1 \; 1 \quad 0 \; 1 \; 0 \; 1 \\
\hline
(A) & : & 7FH = & \boxed{0} \; 0 \; 1 \; 1 \; 1 \quad 1 \; 1 \; 1 \; 1
\end{array}
$$

Flag Status: $S = 0, Z = 0, CY = 0$

The addition of 4AH and 35H does not generate a carry and will reset the previous Carry flag. Therefore, in adding numbers, it is necessary to count how many times CY flag is set by using some other programming techniques (see Section 6.32).

Example 5.5

Assume the accumulator holds the data byte FFH. Illustrate the differences in the flags set by adding 01H and by incrementing the accumulator contents.

Instruction   ADI 01H

$$
\begin{array}{llll}
 & & & CY \\
(A) & : & FFH = & 1 \; 1 \; 1 \; 1 \quad 1 \; 1 \; 1 \; 1 \\
 & + & & \\
(Data) & : & 01H = & 0 \; 0 \; 0 \; 0 \quad 0 \; 0 \; 0 \; 1 \\
 & & & 1 \; 1 \; 1 \; 1 \; 1 \quad 1 \; 1 \; 1 \quad \text{Carry}
\end{array}
$$

(A) : $\boxed{1}$00H = $\boxed{1}$ 0 0 0 0   0 0 0 0
      CY

Flag Status: $S = 0, Z = 1, CY = 1$

*P and AC flags are not shown here. In this chapter, the focus will be on the Sign, Zero, and Carry flags.

Instruction INR A

The accumulator contents will be 00H, same as before. However, the instruction INR will not set the Carry flag.

Flag Status: S = 0, Z = 1 and CY = 0

5.22 Illustrative Program: Arithmetic Operations— Addition and Increment

PROBLEM STATEMENT

Write a program to perform the following functions, and verify the output.

1. Load the number 8BH in register D.
2. Load the number 6FH in register C.
3. Increment the contents of register C by one.
4. Add the contents of registers C and D and display the sum at the output PORT1.

PROGRAM

The illustrative program for arithmetic operations using addition and increment is presented as Figure 5.4 in order to show the register contents during some of the steps.

PROGRAM DESCRIPTION

1. The first four machine codes load 8BH in register D and 6FH in register C. See the register contents in Figure 5.4.

Memory Address (H)	Machine Code	Instruction Opcode	Operand	Comments and Register Contents
HI-LO				
XX00	16	MVI	D.8BH	
01	8B			
02	0E	MVI	C, 6FH	
03	6F			
04	0C	INR	C	
05	79	MOV	A, C	
06	82	ADD	D	
07	D3	OUT	PORT1	
08	PORT #	PORT1		
09	76	HLT		

The first four machine codes load the registers as

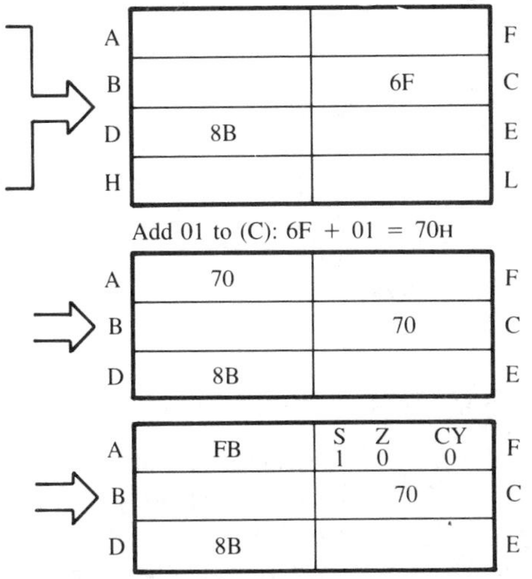

A			F
B		6F	C
D	8B		E
H			L

Add 01 to (C): 6F + 01 = 70H

A	70		F
B		70	C
D	8B		E

		S Z CY	
A	FB	1 0 0	F
B		70	C
D	8B		E

End of the program

FIGURE 5.4

Illustrative Program for Arithmetic Operations—Using Addition and Increment

2. Instruction INR C adds 1 to 6FH and changes the contents of C to 70H.

3. To add (C) to (D), the contents of one of the registers must be transferred to the accumulator because the 8085/8080A cannot add two registers directly. Review the ADD instruction. The instruction MOV A, C copies 70H from register C into the accumulator without affecting (C). See the register contents.

4. Instruction ADD D adds (D) to (A), stores the sum in A, and sets the Sign flag as shown below.

$$
\begin{array}{llll}
\text{(A)} & : & 70\text{H} = & 0\ 1\ 1\ 1 \quad 0\ 0\ 0\ 0 \\
& + & & \\
\text{(D)} & : & 8\text{BH} = & 1\ 0\ 0\ 0 \quad 1\ 0\ 1\ 1 \\
\hline
\text{(A)} & : & \text{FBH} = \boxed{0} & 1\ 1\ 1\ 1 \quad 1\ 0\ 1\ 1 \quad \text{(see Figure 5.4)}
\end{array}
$$

CY

Flag Status: S = 1, Z = 0, CY = 0

5. The sum FBH is displayed by the OUT instruction.

PROGRAM OUTPUT

This program will display FBH at the output port. If an output port is not available, the program can be executed by entering NOP instructions in place of the OUT instruction and the answer FBH can be verified by examining the accumulator A. (Most systems have Examine-Register operation.) Similarly, the contents of registers C, D and the flags can also be verified.

By examining the contents of the registers, the following points can be confirmed.

1. The sum is stored in the accumulator.

2. The contents of the source registers are not changed.

3. The Sign (S) flag is set.

Even though the Sign (S) flag is set this is not a negative sum. The microprocessor sets the Sign flag whenever an operation results in $D_7 = 1$. The microprocessor cannot recognize whether FBH is a sum, a negative number, or a bit pattern. It is your responsibility to interpret and use the flags. (See Flag Concepts and Cautions in Section 5.25.) In this example, the addition is not concerned with the signed numbers. With the signed numbers, bit D_7 is reserved for a sign by the programmer (not by the microprocessor), and no number larger than $+127_{10}$ can be entered.

5.23 Subtraction

The 8085/8080A performs subtraction by using the method of 2's complement. (If you are not familiar with the method of 2's complement, review Appendix A2.)

Subtraction can be performed either by using the instruction SUB to subtract the contents of a source register or the instruction SUI to subtract an 8-bit number from the contents of the accumulator. In either case, the accumulator contents are regarded as the minuend (the number from which to subtract).

The 8085/8080A performs the following steps internally to execute the instruction SUB (or SUI).

Step 1: Converts subtrahend (the number to be subtracted) into its 1's complement.

Step 2: Adds 1 to 1's complement to obtain 2's complement of the subtrahend.

Step 3: Adds 2's complement to the minuend (the contents of the accumulator).

Step 4: Complements the Carry flag.

These steps are illustrated in the following example.

Register B has 65H and the accumulator has 97H. Subtract the contents of register B from the contents of the accumulator.

Example 5.6

Instruction   SUB B

Subtrahend (B) : 65H =	0	1	1	0		0	1	0	1	

Step 1:   1's complement of 65H = 1 0 0 1   1 0 1 0
(Substitute 0 for 1 and 1 for 0)

$+$

Step 2:   Add 01 to obtain   0 0 0 0   0 0 0 1
2's complement of 65H $=$ 1 0 0 1   1 0 1 1

$+$

To subtract: 97H − 65H,
Add 97H to 2's complement of 65H = 1 0 0 1   0 1 1 1
                                    1 1   1 1 1   Carry

Step 3:   CY $\boxed{1}$ 0 0 1 1   0 0 1 0

Step 4: Complement Carry $\boxed{0}$ 0 0 1 1   0 0 1 0
Result (A)   :   32H

Flag Status: S = 0, Z = 0, CY = 0

If the answer is negative, it will be shown in 2's complement of the actual magnitude. For example, if the above subtraction is performed as 65H − 97H, the answer will be the 2's complement of 32H with the Carry (Borrow) flag set.

5.24 Illustrative Program: Subtraction of Two Unsigned Numbers

PROBLEM STATEMENT

Write a program to do the following:

1. Load the number 30H in register B and 39H in register C.
2. Subtract 39H from 30H.   **3.** Display the answer at PORT1.

Memory Address (H)	Machine Code	Opcode	Operand	Comments and Register Contents
HI-LO				
XX00	06	MVI	B,30H	Load the minuend in register B
01	30			Load the subtrahend in register C
02	0E	MVI	C,39H	The register contents:
03	39			
04	78	MOV	A,B	

A | 30 | | F
B | 30 | 39 | C

| 05 | 91 | SUB | C | |

A | F7 | S Z 1 0 | CY 1 | F
B | 30 | 39 | C

06	D3	OUT	PORT 1	
07	PORT#			
08	76	HLT		

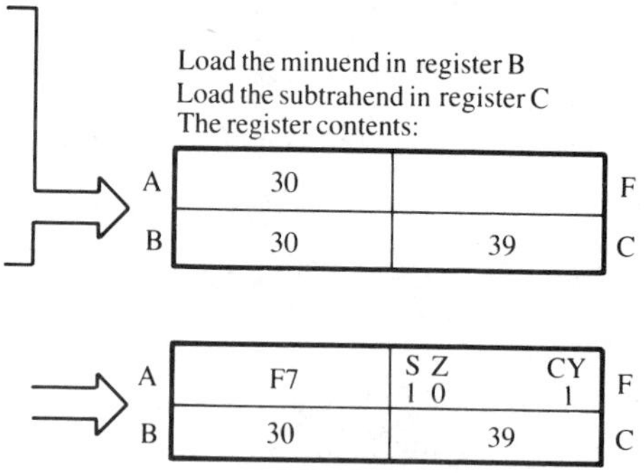

FIGURE 5.5
Illustrative Program for Subtraction of Two Unsigned Numbers

PROGRAM

The illustrative program for subtraction of two unsigned numbers is presented as Figure 5.5 in order to show the register contents during some of the steps.

PROGRAM DESCRIPTION

1. Registers B and C are loaded with 30H and 39H, respectively. The instruction MOV A,B copies 30H into the accumulator (shown as register contents). This is an essential step because the contents of a register can only be subtracted from the contents of the accumulator and not from any other register.
2. To execute the instruction SUB C the microprocessor performs the following steps internally:

Step 1:

$$39H = 0\ 0\ 1\ 1\quad 1\ 0\ 0\ 1$$
$$1\text{'s complement of }39H = 1\ 1\ 0\ 0\quad 0\ 1\ 1\ 0$$
$$+$$

Step 2:

$$\text{Add }01 = 0\ 0\ 0\ 0\quad 0\ 0\ 0\ 1$$
$$2\text{'s complement of }39H = 1\ 1\ 0\ 0\quad 0\ 1\ 1\ 1$$
$$+$$

Step 3: Add 30H to 2's complement of $39H = 0\ 0\ 1\ 1\quad 0\ 0\ 0\ 0$

$$CY\ \boxed{0}\quad 1\ 1\ 1\ 1\quad 0\ 1\ 1\ 1$$

Step 4: Complement carry $\boxed{1}\quad 1\ 1\ 1\ 1\quad 0\ 1\ 1\ 1 = F7H$

Flag Status: S = 1, Z = 0, CY = 1

3. The number F7H is a 2's complement of the magnitude (39H − 30H) = 09H.
4. The instruction OUT displays F7H at PORT1.

PROGRAM OUTPUT

This program will display F7H as the output. In this program, the unsigned numbers were used to perform the subtraction. Now, the question is: How do you recognize that the answer F7H is really a 2's complement of 09H and not a straight binary F7H?

The answer lies with the Carry flag. If the Carry flag (also known as Borrow flag in subtraction) is set, the answer is in 2's complement. The Carry flag raises a second question: Why isn't it a positive sum with a carry? The answer is implied by the instruction SUB (it is a subtraction).

There is no way to differentiate between a straight binary number and 2's complement by examining the answer at the output port. The flags are internal and not easily displayed. However, a programmer can test the Carry flag by using the instruction Jump On Carry (JC) and can find a way to indicate that the answer is in 2's complement. (This is discussed in Branch instructions.)

5.25 Review of Important Concepts

1. The arithmetic operations implicitly assume that the contents of the accumulator are one of the operands.
2. The results of the arithmetic operations are stored in the accumulator; thus, the previous contents of the accumulator are altered.
3. The flags are modified to reflect the data conditions of an operation.
4. The contents of a register are not changed as a result of an arithmetic operation.
5. In the *add* operation, if the sum is larger than 8-bit, CY is set.
6. The *subtract* operation is performed by using the 2's complement method, and CY is complemented after the subtraction.
7. If a subtraction results in a negative number, the answer is in 2's complement and CY (the Borrow flag) is set.
8. In unsigned arithmetic operations, the Sign flag (S) should be ignored.
9. The instructions INR (Increment) and DCR (Decrement) are special cases of the arithmetic operations. These instructions can be used for any one of the registers, and they do not set CY, even if the result is larger than 8-bit.

FLAG CONCEPTS AND CAUTIONS

As described in the previous chapter, the flags are flip-flops that are set or reset after the execution of arithmetic and logic operations, with some exceptions. In many ways, the flags are like signs on an interstate highway that help drivers find their destinations. Drivers may see one or more signs at a time. They may take the exit when they find the sign they are looking for, or they may continue along the interstate and ignore the signs.

Similarly, flags are signs of data conditions. After an operation, one or more flags may be set, and they can be used to change the direction of the program sequence by using Jump instructions, which will be described later. However, the programmer should be alert for them to make a decision. If the flags are not appropriate for the tasks, the programmer can ignore them.

Caution #1   In Example 5.3, the CY flag is set, and in Example 5.4, the CY flag is reset. The critical concept here is that if the programmer ignores the flag, it can be lost after the subsequent instructions. However, the flag can be ignored when the programmer is not interested in using it.

Caution #2   In Example 5.5, two flags are set. The programmer may use one or more flags to make decisions or may ignore them if they are irrelevant.

Caution #3   The CY flag has a dual function; it is used as a carry in addition and as a borrow in subtraction.

Caution #4   If the Sign flag is set, it indicates that bit D_7 in the accumulator (or in the result) is 1; this does not necessarily imply a negative number in the accumulator or the negative result.

See Assignments 5–10 at the end of this chapter.

5.3   LOGIC OPERATIONS

A microprocessor is basically a programmable logic chip. It can perform all the logic functions of the hard-wired logic through its instruction set. The 8085/8080A instruction set includes such logic functions as AND, OR, Ex OR, and NOT (complement). The opcodes of these operations are as follows:*

ANA	: AND	Logically AND the contents of a register.
ANI	: AND Immediate	Logically AND 8-bit data.
ORA	: OR	Logically OR the contents of a register.
ORI	: OR Immediate	Logically OR 8-bit data.
XRA	: X-OR	Exclusive-OR the contents of a register.
XRI	: X-OR Immediate	Exclusive-OR 8-bit data.

All logic operations are performed in relation to the contents of the accumulator. The instructions of these logic operations are described below.

INSTRUCTIONS

The logic instructions

1. implicitly assume that the accumulator is one of the operands.
2. reset (clear) CY and AC flags. The instructions ANA and ANI in the 8085 and CMA are exceptions to this.
3. modify Z, P, and S flags according to the data conditions of the result.

---

*Memory-related logic operations are excluded here; they will be discussed in the next chapter.

4. place the result in the accumulator.

5. do not affect the contents of the operand register.

Opcode	Operand	Description
ANA	R	Logical AND with Accumulator This is a 1-byte instruction Logically ANDs the contents of the register R with the contents of the accumulator 8085: CY is reset and AC is set
ANI	8-bit	AND Immediate with Accumulator This is a 2-byte instruction Logically ANDs the second byte with the contents of the accumulator 8085: CY is reset and AC is set
ORA	R	Logically OR with Accumulator This is a 1-byte instruction Logically ORs the contents of the register R with the contents of the accumulator
ORI	8-bit	OR Immediate with Accumulator This is a 2-byte instruction Logically ORs the second byte with the contents of the accumulator
XRA	R	Logically Exclusive-OR with Accumulator This is a 1-byte instruction Exclusive-ORs the contents of register R with the contents of the accumulator
XRI	8-bit	Exclusive-OR Immediate with Accumulator This is a 2-byte instruction Exclusive-ORs the second byte with the contents of the accumulator
CMA		Complement Accumulator This is a 1-byte instruction that complements the contents of the accumulator No flags are affected

5.31 Logic AND

The process of performing logic operations through the software instructions is slightly different from the hardwired logic. The AND gate shown in Figure 5.6(a) has two inputs and one output. On the other hand, the instruction ANA simulates eight AND gates (Figure 5.6(b)). For example, assume that register B holds 77H and the accumulator A holds 81H. The result of the instruction ANA B is 01H and is placed in the accumulator replacing the previous contents as shown in Figure 5.6(b).

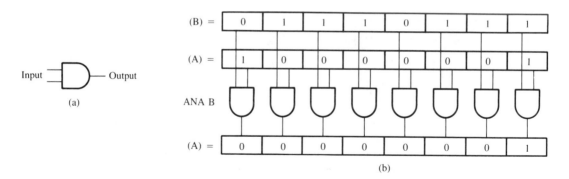

FIGURE 5.6
AND Gate (a) and a Simulated ANA Instruction (b)

Figure 5.6(b) shows that each bit of register B is independently ANDed with each bit of the accumulator, thus simulating eight 2-input AND gates. To simulate one 2-input AND gate, all other bits can be masked or eliminated, as illustrated in the next program.

5.32   Illustrative Program: Data Masking with Logic AND

PROBLEM STATEMENT

To conserve energy and to avoid an electrical overload on a hot afternoon, implement the following procedures to control the appliances throughout the house (Figure 5.7). Assume that the control switches are located in the kitchen, and they are available to anyone in the house. Write a set of instructions to

1. turn on the air conditioner if switch S_7 of the input port 00H is on.
2. ignore all other switches of the input port even if someone attempts to turn on other appliances.

(To perform this experiment on your single-board microcomputer, simulate the reading of the input port 00H with the instruction MVI A, 8-bit data.)

PROBLEM ANALYSIS

In this problem you are interested in only one switch position, S_7, which is connected to data line D_7. Assume that various persons in the family have turned on the switches of the air conditioner (S_7), the radio (S_4), and the lights (S_3, S_2, S_1, S_0).

If the microprocessor reads the input port (IN 00H), the accumulator will have data byte 9FH. This can be simulated by using the instruction MVI A, 9FH. However, if you are interested in knowing only whether switch S_7 is on, you can mask bits D_6 through D_0

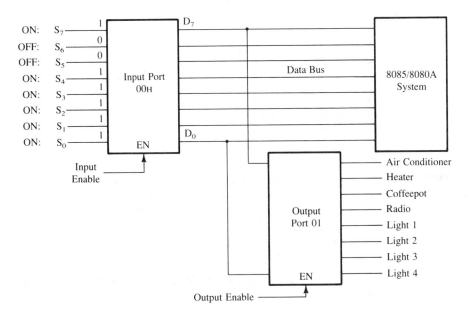

FIGURE 5.7
Input Port to Control Appliances

by ANDing the input data with a byte that has 0 in bit positions D_6 through D_0 and 1 in bit position D_7.

$$
\begin{array}{cccccccc}
D_7 & D_6 & D_5 & D_4 & D_3 & D_2 & D_1 & D_0 \\
1 & 0 & 0 & 0 & 0 & 0 & 0 & 0 = 80H
\end{array}
$$

After bits D_6 through D_0 have been masked, the remaining byte can be sent to the output port to simulate turning on the air conditioner.

PROGRAM

Memory Address	Machine Code	Instruction Opcode	Operand	Comments
HI-LO				
XX00	3E	MVI	A, Data	;This instruction simulates the
01	9F			instruction IN 00H
02	E6	ANI	80H	;Mask all the bits except D_7
03	80			
04	D3	OUT	01H	;Turn on the air conditioner if
05	01			S_7 is on
06	76	HLT		;End of the program

PROGRAM OUTPUT

The instruction ANI 80H ANDs the accumulator data as follows.

$$
\begin{array}{llllllllll}
 & (A) & = & 1 & 0 & 0 & 1 & 1 & 1 & 1 & 1 & (9FH) \\
AND & & & & & & & & & & & \\
 & (Masking\ Byte) & = & 1 & 0 & 0 & 0 & 0 & 0 & 0 & 0 & (80H) \\
\hline
 & (A) & = & 1 & 0 & 0 & 0 & 0 & 0 & 0 & 0 & (80H)
\end{array}
$$

Flag Status: $S = 1$, $Z = 0$, $CY = 0$

The ANDing operation always resets the CY flag. The result (80H) will be placed in the accumulator and then sent to the output port, and logic 1 of data bit D_7 turns on the air conditioner. In this example, the output (80H) is the same as the masking data byte (80H) because switch S_7 (or data bit D_7) is on. If S_7 is off, the output will be zero.

5.33   OR, Exclusive-OR, and NOT

The instruction ORA (and ORI) simulates logic ORing with eight 2-input OR gates; this process is similar to that of ANDing, explained in the previous section. The instruction XRA (and XRI) performs Exclusive-ORing of eight bits, and the instruction CMA inverts the bits of the accumulator.

Example 5.7

Assume register B holds 93H and the accumulator holds 15H. Illustrate the results of the instructions ORA B, XRA B and CMA.

1. The instruction ORA B will perform the following operation:

$$
\begin{array}{llllllllll}
 & (B) & = & 1 & 0 & 0 & 1 & 0 & 0 & 1 & 1 & (93H) \\
OR & & & & & & & & & & & \\
 & (A) & = & 0 & 0 & 0 & 1 & 0 & 1 & 0 & 1 & (15H) \\
\hline
 & (A) & = & 1 & 0 & 0 & 1 & 0 & 1 & 1 & 1 & (97H)
\end{array}
$$

Flag Status: $S = 1$, $Z = 0$, $CY = 0$

The result 97H will be placed in the accumulator, the CY flag will be reset, and the other flags will be modified to reflect the data conditions in the accumulator.

2. The instruction XRA B will perform the following operation.

$$
\begin{array}{llllllllll}
 & (B) & = & 1 & 0 & 0 & 1 & 0 & 0 & 1 & 1 & (93H) \\
X\text{-}OR & & & & & & & & & & & \\
 & (A) & = & 0 & 0 & 0 & 1 & 0 & 1 & 0 & 1 & (15H) \\
\hline
 & (A) & = & 1 & 0 & 0 & 0 & 0 & 1 & 1 & 0 & (86H)
\end{array}
$$

Flag Status: $S = 1$, $Z = 0$, $CY = 0$

The result 86H will be placed in the accumulator, and the flags will be modified as shown.

3. The instruction CMA will result in

$$(A) = 0 \ 0 \ 0 \ 1 \quad 0 \ 1 \ 0 \ 1 \quad (15H)$$

CMA

$$(A) = 1 \ 1 \ 1 \ 0 \quad 1 \ 0 \ 1 \ 0 \quad (EAH)$$

The result EAH will be placed in the accumulator and no flags will be modified.

5.34 Setting and Resetting Specific Bits

At various times, we may want to set or reset a specific bit without affecting the other bits. OR logic can be used to set the bit, and AND logic can be used to reset the bit.

In Figure 5.7, keep the radio on (D_4) continuously without affecting the functions of other appliances, even if someone turns off the switch S_4.

Example 5.8

To keep the radio on without affecting the other appliances, the bit D_4 should be set by ORing the reading of the input port with the data byte 10H as follows:

Solution

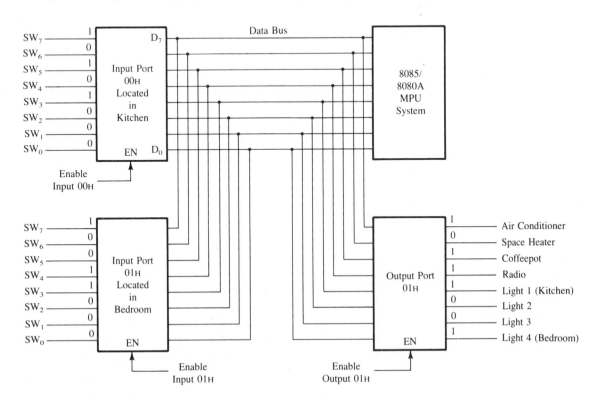

FIGURE 5.8
Two Input Ports to Control Output Devices

$$
\begin{array}{llllllllllll}
\text{IN} & \text{00H} & : & \text{(A)} & = & D_7 & D_6 & D_5 & D_4 & D_3 & D_2 & D_1 & D_0 \\
\text{ORI} & \text{10H} & : & & = & 0 & 0 & 0 & 1 & 0 & 0 & 0 & 0 \\
\hline
& & & \text{(A)} & = & D_7 & D_6 & D_5 & 1 & D_3 & D_2 & D_1 & D_0
\end{array}
$$

Flag Status: $CY = 0$; others will depend on data.

The instruction IN reads the switch positions shown as D_7–D_0 and the instruction ORI sets the bit D_4 without affecting any other bits.

Example 5.9

In Figure 5.7, assume it is winter, and turn off the air conditioner without affecting the other appliances.

Solution

To turn off the air conditioner, reset bit D_7 by ANDing the reading of the input port with the data byte 7FH as follows:

$$
\begin{array}{llllllllllll}
\text{IN} & \text{00H} & : & \text{(A)} & = & D_7 & D_6 & D_5 & D_4 & & D_3 & D_2 & D_1 & D_0 \\
\text{ANI} & \text{7FH} & : & & = & 0 & 1 & 1 & 1 & & 1 & 1 & 1 & 1 \\
\hline
& & & & & 0 & D_6 & D_5 & D_4 & & D_3 & D_2 & D_1 & D_0
\end{array}
$$

Flag Status: $CY = 0$; others will depend on the data bits.

The ANI instruction resets bit D_7 without affecting the other bits.

5.35 Illustrative Program: ORing Data from Two Input Ports

PROBLEM STATEMENT

An additional input port with eight switches and the address 01H (Figure 5.8) is connected to the microcomputer shown in Figure 5.7 to control the same appliances and lights from the bedroom as well as from the kitchen. Write instructions to turn on the devices from any of the input ports.

PROBLEM ANALYSIS

To turn on the appliances from any one of the input ports, the microprocessor needs to read the switches at both ports and logically OR the switch positions.

Assume that the switch positions in one input port (located in the bedroom) correspond to the data byte 91H and the switch positions in the second port (located in the kitchen) correspond to the data byte A8H. The person in the bedroom wants to turn on the air conditioner, the radio, and the bedroom light; and the person in the kitchen wants to turn on the air conditioner, the coffee pot, and the kitchen light. By ORing these two data bytes the microprocessor can turn on the necessary appliances.

To test this program, we must simulate the readings of the input port by loading the data into registers — for example, into B and C.

PROGRAM

Memory Address	Machine Code	Instructions Opcode	Instructions Operand	Comments
HI-LO				
XX00	06	MVI	B, 91H	;This instruction simulates reading input port 01H
01	91			
02	0E	MVI	C, A8H	;This instruction simulates reading input port 00H
03	A8			
04	78	MOV	A, B	;It is necessary to transfer data byte from B to A to OR with C. B and C cannot be ORed directly
05	B1	ORA	C	;Combine the switch positions from registers B and C in the accumulator
06	D3	OUT	PORT1	;Turn on the appliance
07	PORT1			
08	76	HLT		;End of the program

PROGRAM OUTPUT

By logically ORing the data bytes in registers B and C

$$(B) \rightarrow (A) \ = \ 1 \ 0 \ 0 \ 1 \quad 0 \ 0 \ 0 \ 1 \quad (91H)$$
$$(C) \ = \ 1 \ 0 \ 1 \ 0 \quad 1 \ 0 \ 0 \ 0 \quad (A8H)$$
$$(A) \ = \ 1 \ 0 \ 1 \ 1 \quad 1 \ 0 \ 0 \ 1 \quad (B9H)$$

Flag Status: $S = 1, Z = 0, CY = 0$

Data byte B9H is placed in the accumulator that turns on the air conditioner, radio, coffee pot, and bedroom and kitchen lights.

5.36 Review of Important Concepts

1. Logic operations are performed in relation to the contents of the accumulator.
2. Logic operations simulate eight 2-input gates (or inverters).
3. The Sign, Zero (and Parity) flags are modified to reflect the status of the operation. The Carry flag is reset. However, the NOT operation does not affect any flags.
4. After a logic operation has been performed, the answer is placed in the accumulator replacing the original contents of the accumulator.
5. The logic operations cannot be performed directly with the contents of two registers.
6. The individual bits in the accumulator can be set or reset using logic instructions.

See Assignments 11–16 at the end of this chapter.

5.4   BRANCH OPERATIONS

The **branch instructions** are the most powerful instructions because they allow the microprocessor to change the sequence of a program, either unconditionally or under certain test conditions. These instructions are the key to the flexibility and versatility of a computer.

The microprocessor is a sequential machine; it executes machine codes from one memory location to the next. Branch instructions instruct the microprocessor to go to a different memory location, and the microprocessor continues executing machine codes from that new location. The address of the new memory location is either specified explicitly or supplied by the microprocessor or by extra hardware. The branch instructions are classified in three categories.

1. Jump instructions
2. Call and Return instructions
3. Restart instructions

This section is concerned with applications of Jump instructions. The Call and Return instructions are associated with the subroutine technique and will be discussed in Chapter 8, while Restart instructions are associated with the interrupt technique and will be discussed in Chapter 12.

The Jump instructions specify the memory location explicitly. They are 3-byte instructions: one byte for the operation code, followed by a 16-bit memory address. Jump instructions are classified into two categories: Unconditional Jump and Conditional Jump.

5.41   Unconditional Jump

The 8085/8080A instruction set includes one unconditional Jump instruction. The unconditional Jump instruction enables the programmer to set up continuous loops.

INSTRUCTION

Opcode	Operand	Description
JMP	16-bit	Jump
		This is a 3-byte instruction
		The second and third bytes specify the 16-bit memory address. However, the second byte specifies the low-order and the third byte specifies the high-order memory address

For example, to instruct the microprocessor to go to the memory location 2000H, the mnemonics and the machine code entered will be as follows:

Machine Code	Mnemonics
C3	JMP 2000H
00	
20	

Note the sequence of the machine code. The 16-bit memory address of the jump location is entered in the reverse order, the low-order byte (00H) first followed by the high-order byte (20H). The 8085/8080A is designed for such a reverse sequence. The jump location can also be specified using a label. While writing a program, you may not know the exact memory location to which a program sequence should be directed. In that case, the memory address can be specified with a label (or a name). This is particularly useful and necessary for an assembler. However, you should not specify both a label and its 16-bit address in a Jump instruction. Furthermore, you cannot use the same label for different memory locations. The next illustrative program shows use of the Jump instruction.

5.42 Illustrative Program: Unconditional Jump to Set Up a Continuous Loop

PROBLEM STATEMENT

Modify the program in Example 5.2 to read the switch positions continuously and turn on the appliances accordingly.

PROBLEM ANALYSIS

One of the major drawbacks of the program in Example 5.2 is that the program reads switch positions once and then stops. Therefore, if you want to turn on/off different appliances, you have to reset the system and start all over again. This is impractical in real-life situations. However, the unconditional Jump instruction, in place of the HLT instruction, will allow the microcomputer to monitor the swtich positions continuously.

PROGRAM

Memory Address	Machine Code	Label	Mnemonics	Comments
2000	DB	START:	IN 00H	;Read input switches
2001	00			
2002	D3		OUT 01H	;Turn on devices according to
2003	01			to switch positions
2004	C3		JMP START	;Go back to beginning and
2005	00			read the switches again
2006	20			

PROGRAM FORMAT

The program includes one more column called *label*. The memory location 2000H is defined with a label *START;* therefore, the operand of the Jump instruction can be specified by the label START. The program sets up the endless loop, and the microprocessor monitors the input port continuously. The output will reflect any change in the switch positions.

5.43 Conditional Jumps

Conditional Jump instructions allow the microprocessor to make decisions based on certain conditions indicated by the flags. After logic and arithmetic operations, flip-flops (flags) are set or reset to reflect data conditions. The conditional Jump instructions check the flag conditions and make decisions to change or not to change the sequence of a program.

Flags   The 8085/8080A status register has five flags, one of which (Auxiliary Carry) is used internally. The other four flags used by the Jump instructions are

1. Carry flag
2. Zero flag
3. Sign flag
4. Parity flag

Two Jump instructions are associated with each flag. The sequence of a program can be changed either because the condition is present or because the condition is absent. For example, while adding the numbers you can change the program sequence either because the carry is present (JC = Jump On Carry) or because the carry is absent (JNC = Jump On No Carry).

Instructions   All conditional Jump instructions in the 8085/8080A are 3-byte instructions; the second byte specifies the low-order (line number) memory address, and the third byte specifies the high-order (page number) memory address. The following instructions transfer the program sequence to the memory location specified under the given conditions:

Opcode	Operand	Description
JC	16-bit	Jump On Carry (If result generates carry and CY = 1)
JNC	16-bit	Jump On No Carry (CY = 0)
JZ	16-bit	Jump On Zero (If result is zero and Z = 1)
JNZ	16-bit	Jump On No Zero (Z = 0)
JP	16-bit	Jump On Plus (If D_7 = 0, and S = 0)
JM	16-bit	Jump On Minus (If D_7 = 1, and S = 1)
JPE	16-bit	Jump On Even Parity (P = 1)
JPO	16-bit	Jump On Odd Parity (P = 0)

All the Jump instructions are listed here for an overview. The Zero and Carry flags and related Jump instructions are used frequently. They are illustrated in the following examples.

5.44 Illustrative Program: Testing of the Carry Flag

PROBLEM STATEMENT

Load the two hexadecimal numbers 9BH and A7H in registers D and E respectively, and add the numbers. If the sum is greater than FFH, display 01H at output PORT0; otherwise, display the sum.

PROBLEM ANALYSIS AND FLOWCHART

The problem can be divided into the following steps:

1. Load the numbers in the registers.
2. Add the numbers.
3. Check the sum.
   Is the sum > FFH?

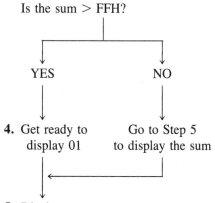

4. Get ready to   Go to Step 5
   display 01   to display the sum

5. Display.
6. End.

FLOWCHART AND ASSEMBLY LANGUAGE PROGRAM

The six steps listed above can be converted into a flowchart and assembly language program as shown in Figure 5.9.

Step 3 is a decision-making block. In a flowchart, the decision-making process is represented by a diamond shape. It is important to understand how this block is translated into the assembly language program. By examining the block carefully you will notice that

1. The question is: Is there a Carry?
2. If no, change the sequence of the program.   In the assembly language this is equivalent to Jump On No Carry — JNC.

FIGURE 5.9
Flowchart and Assembly
Language Program to Test
Carry Flag

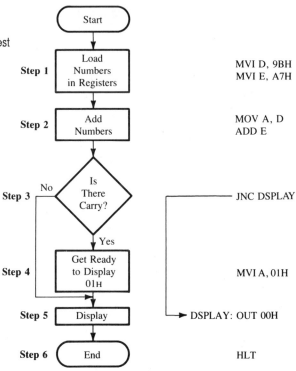

Step 1 Load Numbers in Registers	MVI D, 9BH MVI E, A7H
Step 2 Add Numbers	MOV A, D ADD E
Step 3 Is There Carry? — No	JNC DSPLAY
Yes	
Step 4 Get Ready to Display 01H	MVI A, 01H
Step 5 Display	DSPLAY: OUT 00H
Step 6 End	HLT

3. Now the next question is where to change the sequence?
To Step 5.
4. The next step in the sequence is 4.
5. After completing the straight line sequence, translate Step 5 and Step 6.

At this point the exact location is not known.
Label DSPLAY.
Get ready to display byte 01H.
Display at the port and halt.

MACHINE CODE WITH MEMORY ADDRESSES

Assuming your R/W memory begins at 2000H, the preceding assembly language program can be translated as follows:

Memory Address	Machine Code	Label	Mnemonics
2000	16	START:	MVI D, 9BH
2001	9B		
2002	1E		MVI E, A7H
2003	A7		
2004	7A		MOV A, D

2005	83		ADD E
2006	D2		JNC DSPLAY
2007	X		
2008	X		
2009	3E		MVI A, 01H
200A	01		
200B	D3	DSPLAY:	OUT 00H
200C	00		
200D	76		HLT

While translating into the machine code, we leave memory locations 2007H and 2008H blank because the exact location of the transfer is not known. What is known is that two bytes should be reserved for the 16-bit address. After completing the straight line sequence, we know the memory address of the label DSPLAY; i.e., 200BH. This address must be placed in the reversed order as shown:

| 2007 | 0B | Low-order: Line Number |
| 2008 | 20 | High-order: Page Number |

USING THE INSTRUCTION JUMP ON CARRY (JC)

Now the question remains: Can the same problem be solved by using the instruction Jump On Carry (JC)? To use instruction JC, exchange the places of the answers YES and NO to the question: Is there a Carry? The flowchart will be as in Figure 5.10, and it shows that the program sequence is changed if there is a Carry. This flowchart has two end points; thus it will require a few more instructions than that of Figure 5.9. In this particular example, it is unimportant whether to use instruction JC or JNC, but in most cases the choice is made by the logic of a problem.

FIGURE 5.10
Flowchart for the Instruction
Jump On Carry

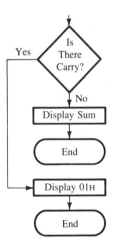

5.45   Review of Important Concepts

1. The Jump instructions change program execution from its sequential order to a different memory location.
2. The Jump instructions can transfer program execution ahead of the sequence (Jump Forward) or behind the sequence (Jump Backward).
3. The unconditional Jump is, generally, used to set up continuous loops.
4. The conditional Jumps are used for the decision-making process based on the data conditions in the accumulator (or of the result), reflected by the flags.
5. Arithmetic and logic instructions modify the flags according to the data in the accumulator (or of the result), and the conditional branch instructions use them to make decisions. However, the branch instructions do not affect the flags.

CAUTION

The conditional Jump instructions will not function properly unless the preceding instruction sets the necessary flag. Data Copy instructions do not affect the flags; furthermore, some arithmetic and logic instructions either do not affect the flags or affect only certain flags.

See Assignments 17–20 at the end of this chapter.

5.5   WRITING ASSEMBLY LANGUAGE PROGRAMS

Communicating with a microcomputer — giving it commands to perform a task and watching it perform them — is exciting. However, one can be uneasy communicating in strange mnemonics and hexadecimal machine codes. This feeling is like the uneasiness one has when beginning to speak a foreign language. How do we learn to communicate with a microcomputer in its assembly language? By using a few mnemonics at a time such as the mnemonics for Read the switches and Display the data. This chapter has introduced a group of basic instructions that can command the 8085/8080A microprocessor to perform simple tasks.

After we know a few instructions, how do we begin to write a program? Any program, no matter how large it may appear, begins with mnemonics. And, just as several persons contribute to the construction of a hundred-story building, so the writing of a large program is usually the work of a team. In addition, the 8085 instruction set contains only 74 different instructions, some of them used quite frequently.

In a hundred-story building, most of the rooms are similar. If one knows the basic fundamentals of constructing a room, one can learn how to tie these rooms together in a coherent structure. However, planning and forethought are critical. Before beginning to build a structure, an architectural plan must be drawn. Similarly, to write a program, one needs to draw up a plan of logical thoughts. A given task should be broken down into small units that can be built independently. This is called the **modular design approach**.

5.51 Getting Started

Writing a program is equivalent to giving specific *commands* to the microprocessor in a *sequence* to *perform a task*. The italicized words provide clues to writing a program. Let us examine these terms.

☐ *Perform a Task.* What is the task you are asking it to do?
☐ *Sequence.* What is the sequence you want it to follow?
☐ *Commands.* What are the commands (instruction set) it can understand?

These terms can be translated into steps as follows:

Step 1: Read the problem carefully.

Step 2: Break it down into small steps.

Step 3: Represent these small steps in a possible sequence with a flowchart — a plan of attack.

Step 4: Translate each block of the flowchart into appropriate mnemonic instructions.

Step 5: Translate mnemonics into the machine code.

Step 6: Enter the machine code in memory and execute. Only on rare occasions is a program successfully executed on the first attempt.

Step 7: Start troubleshooting (see Section 5.6, Debugging a Program).

These steps are illustrated in the next section.

5.52 Illustrative Program: Microprocessor-Controlled Manufacturing Process

PROBLEM STATEMENT

A microcomputer is designed to monitor various processes (conveyer belts) on the floor of a manufacturing plant, presented schematically in Figure 5.11. The microcomputer has two input ports with the addresses F1H and F2H, and an output port with the address F3H. Input port F1H has six switches, five of which (corresponding to data lines D_4–D_0) control the conveyer belts through the output port F3H. Switch S_7, corresponding to the data line D_7, is reserved to indicate an emergency on the floor. As a precautionary measure, input port F2H is controlled by the foreman and its switch, S_7', is also used to indicate an emergency. Output line D_6 of port F3H is connected to the emergency alarm.

Write a program to

1. Turn on the five conveyer belts according to the ON/OFF positions of switches S_4–S_0 at port F1H.
2. Turn off the conveyer belts and turn on the emergency alarm only when both switches — S_7 from port F1H and S_7' from port F2H — are triggered.
3. Monitor the switches continuously.

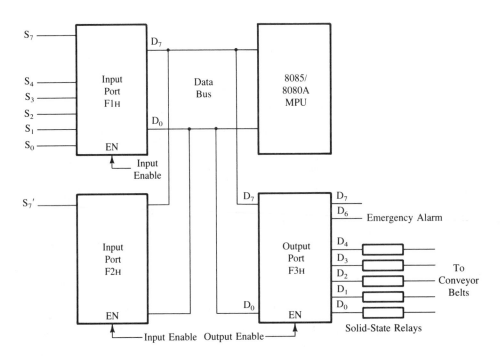

FIGURE 5.11
Input/Output Ports to Control Manufacturing Processes

PROBLEM ANALYSIS

To perform the tasks specified in the problem, the microprocessor needs to

1. Read the switch positions.
2. Check whether switches S_7 and S_7' from the ports F1H and F2H are on.
3. Turn on the emergency signal if both switches are on, and turn off all the conveyer belts.
4. If both switches, S_7 and S_7', are not on simultaneously, turn on the conveyer belts according to the switch positions S_0 through S_4 at input port F1H.
5. Continue checking the switch positions.

FLOWCHART AND PROGRAM

The five steps listed above can be translated into a flowchart and an assembly language program as shown in Figure 5.12.

5.53   Documentation

A program is similar to a circuit diagram. Its purpose is to communicate to others what the program does and how it does it. Appropriate comments are critical for conveying the logic behind a program. The program as a whole should be self-documented.

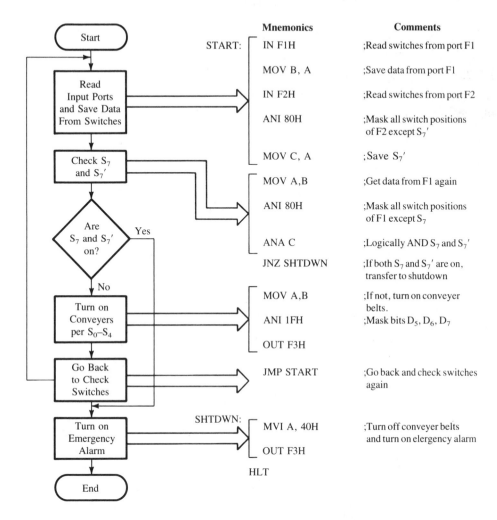

	Mnemonics	Comments
START:	IN F1H	;Read switches from port F1
	MOV B, A	;Save data from port F1
	IN F2H	;Read switches from port F2
	ANI 80H	;Mask all switch positions of F2 except S_7'
	MOV C, A	;Save S_7'
	MOV A,B	;Get data from F1 again
	ANI 80H	;Mask all switch positions of F1 except S_7
	ANA C	;Logically AND S_7 and S_7'
	JNZ SHTDWN	;If both S_7 and S_7' are on, transfer to shutdown
	MOV A,B	;If not, turn on conveyer belts.
	ANI 1FH	;Mask bits D_5, D_6, D_7
	OUT F3H	
	JMP START	;Go back and check switches again
SHTDWN:	MVI A, 40H	;Turn off conveyer belts and turn on elergency alarm
	OUT F3H	
	HLT	

FIGURE 5.12
Flowchart and Program for Controlling Manufacturing Processes

The comments should explain what is intended; they should not explain the mnemonics. For example, the first comment in Figure 5.12 indicates that the switch positions are being read at the input port and that the reading is saved. There is no point in writing: MOV B, A means transfer the contents of the accumulator to register B. Similarly, in a schematic, one does not write the word resistor once a resistor is represented by a symbol. A comment can be omitted if it does not say anything more than repeat a mnemonic.

The labels START and SHTDWN indicate what actions are being taken. These are the landmarks in a program. Avoid "cute" labels. Using cute labels in a program is similar to representing a power supply in a schematic by a picture of the sun, or a ground with the digit zero.

FROM ASSEMBLY LANGUAGE TO MACHINE CODE

Illustrative Program 5.52 is translated into its machine code, together with the corresponding suggested memory addresses, as follows:

Mnemonics		Machine Code	Memory Addresses
1. START:	IN F1H	DB	2000
		F1	2001
2.	MOV B, A	78①	2002
3.	IN F2H	DB	2003
		F2	2004
4.	ANI 80H	E6	2005
		80	2006
5.	MOV C, A	4F	2007
6.	MOV A, B	78	2008
7.	ANI 80H	E6②	2009
8.	ANA C	A1	200A
9.	JNZ SHTDWN	C2③	200B
		20	200C
		14	200D
10.	MOV A, B	78	200E
11.	ANI 1FH	E6	200F
		1F	2010
12.	OUT F3H	D3	2011
		01	2012
13.	JMP START	C3④	2013
14. SHTDWN:	MVI A, 40H	3E	2014
		40	2015
15.	OUT F3H	D3⑤	2016
16.	HLT	76	2017

This program includes several errors, indicated by the circled numbers beside the codes. (See Assignment 21 for the debugging of this program.)

5.6   DEBUGGING A PROGRAM

Debugging a program is similar to troubleshooting hardware, but it is much more difficult and cumbersome. It is easy to poke and pinch at the components in a circuit, but, in a program, the result is generally binary: Either it works or it does not work. When it does not work, very few clues alert you to what exactly went wrong. Therefore, it is essential to search carefully for the errors in the program logic, machine codes, and execution.

The debugging process can be divided into two parts, static debugging and dynamic debugging.

Static debugging is similar to visual inspection of a circuit board; it is the paper-and-pencil check of a flowchart and machine code. **Dynamic debugging** involves observing the output, or register contents, following the execution of each instruction (the single step technique) or of a group of instructions (the breakpoint technique). Dynamic debugging will be discussed in the next chapter.

5.61 Debugging Machine Code

Translating the assembly language to the machine code is similar to building a circuit from a schematic diagram; the machine code will have errors just as would the circuit board. The following errors are common:

1. Selecting a wrong code.
2. Forgetting the second or third byte of an instruction.
3. Specifying the wrong jump location.
4. Not reversing the order of high and low bytes in a Jump instruction.
5. Writing memory addresses in decimal, thus specifying wrong jump locations.

The program for controlling manufacturing processes listed in Section 5.53 has several of these errors. These errors must be corrected before entering the machine code in the R/W memory of your system.

See Assignments 21–23 at the end of this chapter.

SOME PUZZLING QUESTIONS AND THEIR ANSWERS   5.7

After one learns something about the microprocessor architecture, memory, I/O, the instruction set, and simple programming, a few questions still remain unanswered. These questions do not fit into any particular discussion. They just lurk in the corners of one's mind to reappear once in a while when one is in a contemplative mood. This section attempts to answer some of these unasked questions.

1. *What happens in a single-board microcomputer when the power is turned on and the* Reset *key is pushed?*

When the power is turned on, the monitor program stored either in EPROM or ROM comes alive. The *Reset* key clears the program counter, and the program counter holds the memory address 0000H. Some systems are automatically reset when the power is turned on (called power-on reset).

2. *How does the microprocessor know how and when to start?*

As soon as the *Reset* key is pushed, the program counter places the memory address 0000H on the address bus, the instruction at that location is fetched, and the execution of the Key Monitor program begins. Therefore, the Key Monitor program is stored on page 00H.

3. *What is a monitor program?*

In a single-board microcomputer with a Hex keyboard, the instructions are entered in R/W memory through the keyboard. The Key Monitor program is a set of instructions that continuously checks whether a key is pressed and stores the binary equivalent of a pressed key in a memory location.

4. *What is an assembler?*

An assembler is a program that translates the mnemonics into their machine code. It is generally not available on a single-board microcomputer.

A program can be entered in mnemonics in a microcomputer equipped with an ASCII keyboard (e.g., TRS-80 by Radio Shack and Micro Decision by Morrow Designs). The assembler will translate mnemonics into the 8085/8080A machine code, and assign memory locations to each machine code, thus avoiding the manual assembly and the errors associated with it. Additional instructions can be inserted anywhere in the program, and the assembler will reassign all the new memory locations and jump locations.

5. *How does the microprocessor know what operation to perform first (Read/Write Memory or Read/Write I/O)?*

The first operation is always a Fetch instruction.

6. *How does the microprocessor differentiate between data and instruction?*

When the first machine code of an instruction is fetched and decoded in the instruction register, the microprocessor recognizes the number of bytes required to fetch the entire instruction. For example, in the case of the instruction MVI A, Data (3E Data), the second byte is always considered data. If that data byte is omitted by mistake, whatever is in that memory location will be considered data. The byte after "Data" will be treated as the next instruction.

7. *How does the microprocessor differentiate between a positive number, a negative number, or a bit pattern?*

It does not know the difference. The microprocessor views any data byte as eight binary digits. The programmer is responsible for providing the interpretation.

For example, after an arithmetic or logic operation, if the bits in the accumulator are

$$1 \quad 1 \quad 1 \quad 1 \quad 0 \quad 0 \quad 1 \quad 0 \quad = \quad F2H$$

the Sign flag is set because $D_7 = 1$. This does not mean it is a negative number, even if the Sign flag is set. The Sign flag indicates only that $D_7 = 1$. The eight bits in the accumulator could be a bit pattern, or a positive number larger than 127_{10}, or the 2's complement of a number.

8. *If flags are individual flip-flops, can they be observed on an oscilloscope?*

No, they cannot be observed on an oscilloscope. The flag register is internal to the microprocessor. However, they can be tested through conditional branch instructions, and they can be examined by storing them on the stack memory location (see Chapter 8).

9. *If the program counter is always one count ahead of the memory location from which the machine code is being fetched, how does the microprocessor change the sequence of program execution with a Jump instruction?*

When a Jump instruction is fetched, its second and third bytes (a new memory location) are placed in the W and Z registers of the microprocessor. After the execution of the Jump instruction, the contents of the W and Z registers are placed on the address bus to fetch the instruction from a new memory location, and the program counter is loaded by updating the contents of the W and Z registers.

SUMMARY

The instructions from the 8085/8080A instruction set introduced in this chapter are summarized below to provide an overview. After careful examination of these instructions, you will begin to see a pattern emerge from the mnemonics, the number of bytes required for the various instructions, and the tasks the 8085/8080A can perform. Read the notations (Rs) as the contents of the source register, (Rd) as the contents of the destination register, (A) as the contents of the accumulator, and (R) as the contents of the register R.*

Instructions		Tasks	Addressing Mode
Data Transfer (Copy) Instructions			
1. MOV	Rd, Rs	Copy (Rs) into (Rd).	Register
2. MVI	Rs, 8-bit	Load the source register Rs with the 8-bit data.	Immediate
3. IN	8-bit Port Address	Read data from the input port.	Direct
4. OUT	8-bit Port Address	Write data in the output port.	Direct
Arithmetic Instructions			
1. ADD	R	Add (R) to (A).	Register
2. ADI	8-bit	Add 8-bit data to (A).	Immediate
3. SUB	R	Subtract (R) from (A).	Register
4. SUI	8-bit	Subtract 8-bit data from (A).	Immediate
5. INR	R	Increment (R)	Register
6. DCR	R	Decrement (R)	Register

*R, Rs, and Rd represent any one of the 8-bit registers—A, B, C, D, E, H, and L.

Logic Instructions

1. ANA	R	Logically AND (R) with (A).	Register
2. ANI	8-bit	Logically AND 8-bit data with (A).	Immediate
3. ORA	R	Logically OR (R) with (A).	Register
4. ORI	8-bit	Logically OR 8-bit data with (A).	Immediate
5. XRA	R	Logically Exclusive-OR (R) with (A).	Register
6. XRI	8-bit	Logically Exclusive-OR 8-bit data with (A).	Immediate
7. CMA		Complement (A).	

Branch Instructions

1. JMP	16-bit	Jump to 16-bit address unconditionally.	Immediate
2. JC	16-bit	Jump to 16-bit address if the CY flag is set.	Immediate
3. JNC	16-bit	Jump to 16-bit address if the CY flag is reset.	Immediate
4. JZ	16-bit	Jump to 16-bit address if the Zero flag is set.	Immediate
5. JNZ	16-bit	Jump to 16-bit address if the Zero flag is reset.	Immediate
6. JP	16-bit	Jump to 16-bit address if the Sign flag is reset.	Immediate
7. JM	16-bit	Jump to 16-bit address if the Sign flag is set.	Immediate
8. JPE	16-bit	Jump to 16-bit address if the Parity flag is set.	Immediate
9. JPO	16-bit	Jump to 16-bit address if the Parity flag is reset.	Immediate

Machine Control Instructions

1. NOP	No operation.	
2. HLT	Stop processing and wait.	

The set of instructions listed here (except the shaded portion) is used frequently in writing assembly language programs. The important points to be remembered about these instructions are as follows:

1. The data transfer (copy) instructions copy the contents of the source into the destination without affecting the source contents.

2. The results of the arithmetic and logic operations are usually placed in the accumulator.

3. The conditional Jump Instructions are executed according to the flags set after an operation. Not all instructions set the flags; in particular, the data transfer instructions do not set the flags.

ASSIGNMENTS

Section 5.1: Data Transfer (Copy) Operations

1. Load the hexadecimal number 65H in register C, and 92H in the accumulator A. Display the number 65H at PORT0 and 92H at PORT1.
2. Read the data at input PORT 07H and at PORT 08H. Display the input data from PORT 07H at output PORT 00H, and store the input data from PORT 08H in register B.
3. Specify the output at PORT1 if the following program is executed.

```
MVI   B,  82H
MOV   A,  B
MOV   C,  A
MVI   D,  37H
OUT   PORT1
HLT
```

4. If the switch S_7 of the input PORT0 (see Figure 5.13) connected to the data line D_7 is at logic 1 and other switches are at logic 0, specify the output at PORT1 and the contents of register B after executing the following instructions.

```
MVI   A,  9FH
IN    PORT0
MOV   B,  A
OUT   PORT1
HLT
```

FIGURE 5.13
Input Port with Switches

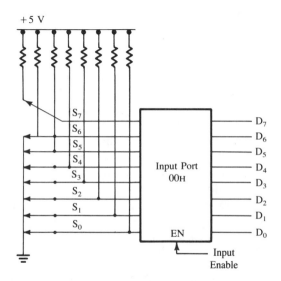

Section 5.2: Arithmetic Operations

5. What operation can be performed by using the instruction ADD A?
6. What operation can be performed by using the instruction SUB A? Specify the status of Z and CY.
7. Write a program using the ADI instruction to add the two hexadecimal numbers 3AH and 48H, and to display the answer at an output port.
8. Write instructions to
   a. Load 00H in the accumulator
   b. Decrement the accumulator
   c. Display the answer
   Specify the answer you would expect at the output port.
9. Write a program to
   a. Clear the accumulator
   b. Add 47H (use ADI instruction)
   c. Subtract 92H
   d. Add 64H
   e. Display the results after subtracting 92H and after adding 64H.
      Specify the answers you would expect at the output ports.
10. Specify the reason for clearing the accumulator before adding the number 47H directly to the accumulator in question 9.

Section 5.3: Logic Operations

11. What operation can be performed by using the instruction XRA A (Exclusive-OR the contents of the accumulator with itself)? Specify the status of Z and CY.
12. When the microprocessor reads an input port, the instruction IN does not set any flag. If the input reading is zero, what logic instruction can be used to set the Zero flag without affecting the contents of the accumulator?
13. Load the data byte A8H in register C. Mask the high-order bits (D_7–D_4), and display the low-order bits (D_3–D_0) at an output port.
14. Load the data byte 8EH in register D and F7H in register E. Mask the high-order bits (D_7–D_4) from both the data bytes, Exclusive OR the low-order bits (D_3–D_0), and display the answer.
15. Load the bit pattern 91H in register B and 87H in register C. Mask all the bits except D_0 from registers B and C.
    If D_0 is at logic 1 in both registers, turn on the light connected to the D_0 position of output port 01H; otherwise, turn off the light.
16. Figure 5.14 shows an input port with an 8-key DIP switch. When all switches are off, the microprocessor reads the data FFH. When a switch is turned on (closed), it goes to logic 0 (for all switches ON, the data will be 00H). Write instructions to read the input port and, if all switches are open, set the Zero flag. (Use the instruction CMA to complement the input reading and ORA A to set the Zero flag.)

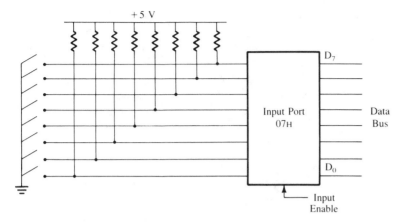

FIGURE 5.14
DIP Switch Input Port with Address 07H

Section 5.4: Branch Operations

17. Rewrite the Section 5.44 illustrative program for testing the Carry flag using the instruction JC (Jump On Carry).

18. Write instructions to clear the CY flag, to load number FFH in register B, and increment (B). If the CY flag is set, display 01 at the output port; otherwise, display the contents of register B. Explain your results.

19. Write instructions to clear the CY flag, to load number FFH in register C, and to add 01 to (C). If the CY flag is set, display 01 at an output port; otherwise, display the contents of register C. Explain your results. Are they the same as in Question 18?

20. Write instructions to load two unsigned numbers in register B and register C, respectively. Subtract (C) from (B). If the result is in 2's complement, convert the result in absolute magnitude and display it at PORT1; otherwise, display the positive result. Execute the program with the following sets of data.

Set 1	:	(B)	=	42H,	(C)	=	69H
Set 2	:	(B)	=	69H,	(C)	=	42H
Set 3	:	(B)	=	F8H,	(C)	=	23H

Section 5.6: Debugging a Program

21. In Section 5.53, a program for controlling manufacturing processes is examined, all the errors are marked as 1 through 5. Rewrite the program with the errors corrected.

22. To test this program, substitute the instructions IN F1H and IN F2H by loading the two data bytes 97H and 85H in registers D and E. Rewrite the program to include other appropriate changes. Enter and execute the program on your system.

23. In the program presented in Section 5.53, assume that a LED indicator is connected to the output line D_7 of the port F3. Modify the program to turn on the LED when switch S_7 from port F1 is turned on, even if switch S_7' is off.

24. Read the following instructions and specify register contents and the status of S, Z, and CY after the execution of each instruction (assume all flags are cleared initially).

```
MVI  A, 00H
ORA  A
SUI  01H
HLT
```

Programming Techniques with Additional Instructions

A computer is at its best, surpassing human capability, when it is asked to repeat such simple tasks as adding thousands of numbers. It does this accurately with electronic speed and without showing any signs of boredom. The programming techniques — such as looping, counting, and indexing — required for repetitious tasks are introduced in this chapter.

Data needed for repetitious tasks generally are stored in the system's R/W memory. The data must be transferred from memory to the microprocessor for manipulation (processing). The instructions related to data manipulations and data transfer (copy) between memory and the microprocessor are introduced in this chapter, as well as instructions related to 16-bit data and additional logic operations. Applications of these instructions are shown in four illustrative programs. The chapter concludes with a discussion of dynamic debugging techniques.

OBJECTIVES

☐ Draw a flowchart of a conditional loop illustrating indexing and counting.

☐ List the seven blocks of a generalized flowchart illustrating data acquisitions and data processing.

☐ Explain the functions of the 16-bit data transfer instructions LXI, and of the arithmetic instructions INX and DCX.

☐ Explain the functions of memory-related data transfer instructions, and illustrate how a memory location is specified using the indirect and the direct addressing modes.

☐ Write a program to illustrate an application of instructions related to memory data transfer and 16-bit data.

☐ Explain the functions of arithmetic instructions related to data in memory: ADD/SUB M. Write a program to perform arithmetic operations that generate carry.

□ Explain the functions and the difference between the four instructions: RLC, RAL, RRC, and RAR. Write a program to illustrate uses of these instructions.

□ Explain the functions of the Compare instructions: CMP and CPI and the flags set under various conditions. Write a program to illustrate uses of the Compare instructions.

□ Explain the term *Dynamic Debugging* and the debugging techniques: Single Step and Breakpoint.

6.1 PROGRAMMING TECHNIQUES: LOOPING, COUNTING, AND INDEXING

The programming examples illustrated in previous chapters are simple and can be solved manually. However, the computer surpasses manual efficiency when tasks must be repeated, such as adding a hundred numbers or transferring a thousand bytes of data. It is fast and accurate.

The programming technique used to instruct the microprocessor to repeat tasks is called **looping**. A loop is set up by instructing the microprocessor to change the sequence of execution and perform the task again. This process is accomplished by using Jump instructions. In addition, techniques such as counting and indexing (described below) are used in setting up a loop.

Loops can be classified into two groups:

□ Continuous Loop — repeats a task continuously
□ Conditional Loop — repeats a task until certain data conditions are met

They are described in the next two sections.

6.11 Continuous Loop

A continuous loop is set up by using the unconditional Jump instruction shown in the flowchart (Figure 6.1).

A program with a continuous loop does not stop repeating the tasks until the system is reset. Typical examples of such a program include a continuous counter (see Chapter 7, Section 7.2) or a continuous monitor system.

FIGURE 6.1
Flowchart of a Continuous Loop

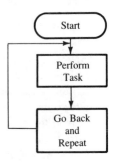

6.12 Conditional Loop

A conditional loop is set up by the conditional Jump instructions. These instructions check flags (Zero, Carry, etc.) and repeat the specified tasks if the conditions are satisfied. These loops usually include counting and indexing.

CONDITIONAL LOOP AND COUNTER

A counter is a typical application of the conditional loop. For example, how does the microprocessor repeat a task five times? The process is similar to that of a car racer in the Indy 500 going around the track 500 times. How does the racer know when 500 laps have been completed? The racing team manager sets up a counting and flagging method for the racer. This can be symbolically represented as in Figure 6.2(a). A similar approach is needed for the microprocessor to repeat the task five times. The microprocessor needs a counter; and when the counting is completed, it needs a flag. This can be accomplished with the conditional loop, as illustrated in the flowchart in Figure 6.2(b).

The computer flowchart (Figure 6.2(b)) is translated into a program as follows:

1. *Counter* is set up by loading an appropriate count in a register.
2. *Counting* is performed by either incrementing or decrementing the counter.
3. *Loop* is set up by a conditional Jump instruction.
4. *End of Counting* is indicated by a flag.

FIGURE 6.2
Flowcharts to Indicate Number of Repetitions Completed

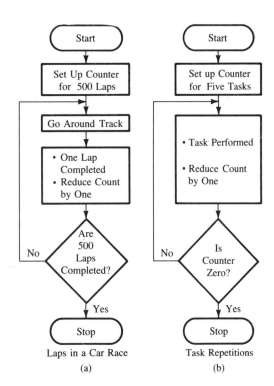

It is easier to count down to zero than to count up because the Zero flag is set when the register becomes zero. (Counting up requires the Compare instruction, which is introduced later.)

Conditional Loop, Counter, and Indexing Another type of loop includes indexing along with a counter. (*Indexing* means pointing or referencing objects with sequential numbers. In a library, books are arranged according to numbers, and they are referred to or sorted by numbers. This is called indexing.) Similarly, data bytes are stored in memory locations, and those data bytes are referred to by their memory locations.

Example 6.1

Illustrate the steps necessary to add ten bytes of data stored in memory locations starting at a given location, and display the sum. Draw a flowchart.

Procedure The microprocessor needs

a. a counter to count 10 data bytes
b. an index or a pointer to locate where data bytes are stored
c. to transfer data from a memory location to the microprocessor (ALU)
d. to perform addition
e. registers for temporary storage of partial answers
f. a flag to indicate the completion of the task
g. to store or output the result

These steps can be represented in the form of a flowchart as in Figure 6.3.

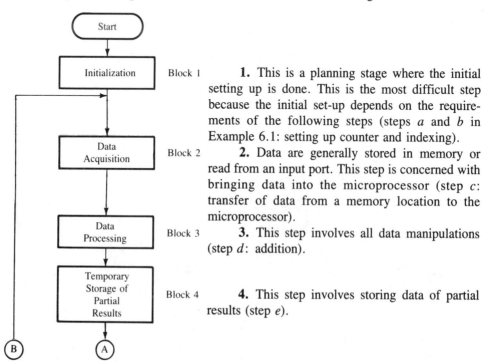

1. This is a planning stage where the initial setting up is done. This is the most difficult step because the initial set-up depends on the requirements of the following steps (steps *a* and *b* in Example 6.1: setting up counter and indexing).

2. Data are generally stored in memory or read from an input port. This step is concerned with bringing data into the microprocessor (step *c*: transfer of data from a memory location to the microprocessor).

3. This step involves all data manipulations (step *d*: addition).

4. This step involves storing data of partial results (step *e*).

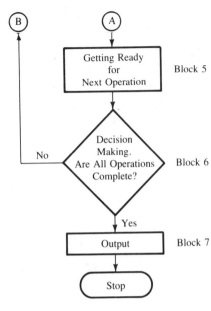

FIGURE 6.3
Generalized Programming
Flowchart

Block 5   **5.** At this point, the microprocessor does not know whether it has completed all the operations. Before it can repeat the task, it needs to get ready for the next operation; for example, go to next index or count.

Block 6   **6.** This is a decision making step; it decides whether to change the sequence of execution and repeat, or to go to the next instruction (step f: a flag check).

Block 7   **7.** This step involves either sending the result to an output port or storing in memory (step g).

This generalized flowchart can be used in solving many problems. Some blocks may have to be expanded with additional loops, or some blocks may need to interchange their positions.

6.13 Review of Important Concepts

1. Programming is a logical approach to instruct the microprocessor to perform operations in a given sequence.
2. The computer is at its best in repeating tasks. It is fast and accurate.
3. Loops are set up by using the looping technique along with counting and indexing.
4. The computer is a versatile and powerful computing tool because of its capability to set up loops and to make decisions based on data conditions.

LOOKING AHEAD

The programming techniques and the flowcharting introduced in this section will be illustrated with various applications throughout the chapter. Additional instructions necessary for these applications will be introduced first. The primary focus here is to analyze a given programming problem in terms of the basic building blocks of the flowchart shown in Figure 6.3.

6.2 ADDITIONAL DATA TRANSFER AND 16-BIT ARITHMETIC INSTRUCTIONS

While the instructions related to the data transfer among microprocessor registers and the I/O instructions were introduced in the last chapter, this section introduces the instructions related to the data transfer between the microprocessor and memory. In addition, instructions for some 16-bit arithmetic operations are included because they are necessary for using the programming techniques introduced earlier in this chapter. The opcodes are as follows:

1. Loading 16-bit data in register pairs.
   LXI :Load Register Pair Immediate
2. Data transfer (copy) from the microprocessor to memory.
   MOV M, R :Move (from register to memory)
   LDAX   :Load Accumulator Indirect
   LDA   :Load Accumulator Direct
3. Data transfer (copy) from memory to the microprocessor.
   MOV R, M :Move (from memory to register)
   STAX   :Store Accumulator Indirect
   STA   :Store Accumulator Direct
4. Incrementing/Decrementing Register Pair.
   INX :Increment Register Pair
   DCX :Decrement Register Pair

The instructions related to these operations are illustrated with examples in the following sections.

6.21 16-Bit Data Transfer to Register Pairs (LXI)

The LXI instructions perform functions similar to those of the MVI instructions, except that the LXI instructions load 16-bit data in register pairs and the stack pointer register. These instructions do not affect the flags.

INSTRUCTIONS

Opcode	Operand	
LXI	Rp, 16-Bit	:Load Register Pair
		This is a 3-byte instruction
		The second byte is loaded in the low-order register of the
LXI	B, 16-Bit	register pair (e.g., register C)
LXI	D, 16-Bit	The third byte is loaded in the high-order register of the
LXI	H, 16-Bit	register pair (e.g., register B)
LXI	SP, 16-Bit	There are four such instructions in the set as shown
		The operands B, D, and H represent BC, DE, and HL
		registers, and SP represents the stack pointer register

Example
6.2

Write instructions to load the 16-bit number 2050H in the register pair HL using LXI and MVI opcodes, and explain the difference between the two instructions.

Instructions: Figure 6.4 shows the register contents and the instructions required for Example 6.2.

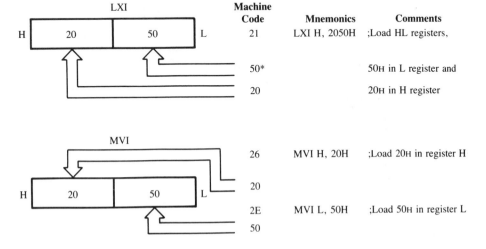

		Machine Code	Mnemonics	Comments
		21	LXI H, 2050H	;Load HL registers,
		50*		50H in L register and
		20		20H in H register
		26	MVI H, 20H	;Load 20H in register H
		20		
		2E	MVI L, 50H	;Load 50H in register L
		50		

FIGURE 6.4
Instructions and Register Contents for Example 6.2

*NOTE: The order of the LXI machine code is reversed in relation to the mnemonics; low-order byte first followed by the high-order byte. This is similar to Jump instructions.

The LXI instruction is functionally similar to two MVI instructions. The LXI instruction takes three bytes of memory and requires ten clock periods (T-states). On the other hand, two MVI instructions take four bytes of memory and require fourteen clock periods (T-states).

6.22 Data Transfer (Copy) from Memory to the Microprocessor

The 8085/8080A instruction set includes three types of memory transfer instructions; two use the indirect addressing mode and one uses the direct addressing mode. These instructions do not affect the flags.

1. MOV R, M: Move (from Memory to Register)
        This is a 1-byte instruction
        It copies the data byte from the memory location into a register
        The memory location is specified by the contents of the HL register
        This specification of the memory location is indirect; it is called the indirect addressing mode

2. LDAX Rp: Load Accumulator Indirect

This is a 1-byte instruction

LDAX B It copies the data byte from the memory location into the accumulator

LDAX D The instruction set includes two instructions as shown

The memory location is specified by the contents of the registers BC or DE

The addressing mode is indirect

3. LDA 16-bit: Load Accumulator Direct

This is a 3-byte instruction

It copies the data byte from the memory location specified by the 16-bit address in the second and third byte

The second byte is a line number (low-order memory address)

The third byte is a page number (high-order memory address)

The addressing mode is direct

Example 6.3

The memory location 2050H holds the data byte F7H. Write instructions to transfer the data byte to the accumulator using three different opcodes: MOV, LDAX, and LDA.

Instructions Figure 6.5 shows the register contents and the instructions required for Example 6.3. All of these three instructions copy the data byte F7H from the memory location 2050H to the accumulator.

After examining all three methods, you may notice that the indirect addressing mode takes four bytes and the direct addressing mode takes three bytes. The question is: Why not just use the direct addressing mode?

If only one byte is to be transferred, the LDA instruction is more efficient. But for a block of memory transfer, the instruction LDA (three bytes) will have to be repeated for each memory. On the other hand, a loop can be set up with two other instructions, and the contents of a register pair can be incremented or decremented. This is further illustrated in Section 6.25.

6.23 Data Transfer (Copy) from the Microprocessor to Memory

The instructions for copying data from the microprocessor to a memory location are similar to those described in the previous section. These instructions are

1. MOV M, R :Move (from Register to Memory).

This is a 1-byte instruction that copies data from a register, R, into the memory location specified by the contents of HL registers.

2. STAX Rp :Store Accumulator Indirect

This is a 1-byte instruction that copies data from the accumulator into

STAX B the memory location specified by the contents of either BC or DE

STAX D registers.

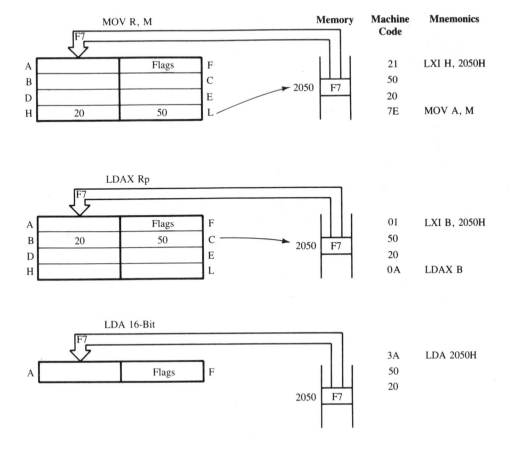

FIGURE 6.5
Instructions and Register Contents for Example 6.3

3. STA 16-Bit :Store Accumulator Direct
> This is a 3-byte instruction that copies data from the accumulator into the memory location specified by the 16-bit operand.

Write instructions to store the contents of register B (32H) in the memory location 8000H using the opcodes: MOV, STAX, and STA.	Example 6.4

Instructions Figure 6.6 shows the register contents and the instructions for Example 6.4.

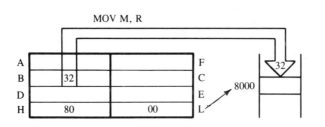

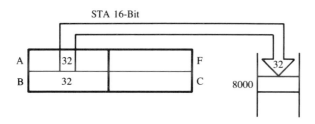

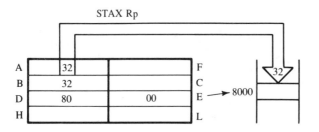

Machine Code	Mnemonics
21	LXI H, 8000H
00	
80	
70	MOV M, B

This instruction copies the contents of the accumulator into memory. Therefore, it is necessary first to copy (B) into A.

11	LXI D, 8000H
00	
80	
78	MOV A, B
12	STAX D

This also requires the transfer of (B) to A.

78	MOV A, B
32	STA 8000H
00	
80	

FIGURE 6.6
Instructions and Register Contents for Example 6.4

6.24 Arithmetic Operations Related to Sixteen Bits or Register Pairs

The instructions related to incrementing/decrementing 16-bit contents in a register pair are introduced below. These instructions do not affect flags.

1. INX Rp :Increment Register Pair

          This is a 1-byte instruction

    INX B   It treats the contents of two registers as one 16-bit number and increases
    INX D   the contents by 1
    INX H   The instruction set includes four instructions, as shown
    INX SP

2. DCX Rp :Decrement Register Pair

          This is a 1-byte instruction

DCX B   It decreases the 16-bit contents of a register pair by 1
DCX D   The instruction set includes four instructions, as shown
DCX H
DCX SP

Write the instruction to load the number 2050H in the register pair BC. Increment the number using the instruction INX B and illustrate whether the INX B instruction is equivalent to the instructions INR B and INR C.

Example 6.5

FIGURE 6.7
Instructions and Register
Contents for Example 6.5

Machine Code	Mnemonic
01	LXI B, 2050H
50	
20	
03	INX B

B | 20 | 50 | C

B | 20 | 51 | C

Instructions Figure 6.7 shows the instructions and register contents for Example 6.5. The instruction INX B views 2050H as one 16-bit number and increases the number to 2051H. On the other hand, the instructions INR B and INR C will increase (B) and (C) separately and the contents of the BC register pair will be 2151H.

6.25 Illustrative Program: Block Transfer of Data Bytes

PROBLEM STATEMENT

Sixteen bytes of data are stored in memory locations at XX50H to XX5FH. Transfer the entire block of data bytes to new memory locations starting at XX70H.

Data (H)   37, A2, F2, 82, 57, 5A, 7F, DA, E5, 8B, A7, C2, B8, 10, 19, and 98.

PROBLEM ANALYSIS

The problem can be analyzed in terms of the blocks suggested in the flowchart (Figure 6.8). The steps are as follows:

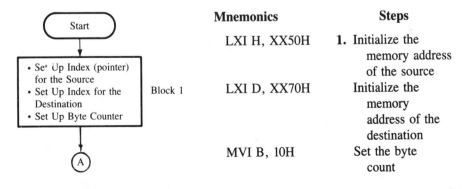

	Mnemonics	**Steps**
	LXI H, XX50H	**1.** Initialize the memory address of the source
Block 1	LXI D, XX70H	Initialize the memory address of the destination
	MVI B, 10H	Set the byte count

Start

• Set Up Index (pointer) for the Source
• Set Up Index for the Destination
• Set Up Byte Counter

Ⓐ

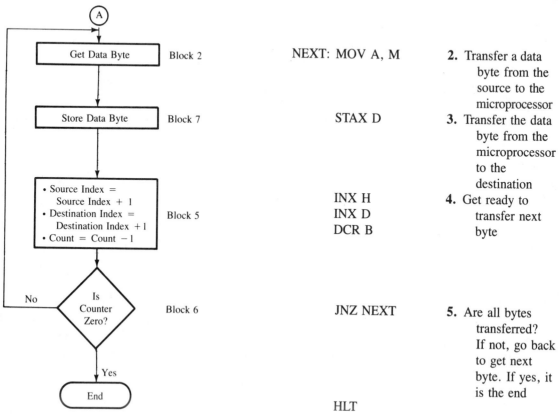

FIGURE 6.8
Flowchart for Block Transfer of Data Bytes

The flowchart in Figure 6.8 includes five blocks; these blocks are identified with numbers referring to the blocks in the generalized flowchart in Figure 6.3. This problem is not concerned with data manipulation (processing); therefore, the flowchart does not require Blocks 3 and 4 (data processing and temporary storage of partial results). The problem simply deals with the transferring of the data bytes from one location to another location in memory; therefore, the Store Data Byte block is equivalent to the Output block in the generalized flowchart.

Block 1 is the initialization block; this block sets up two memory pointers and one counter. The term *index* is synonymous to the pointer. Block 5 is concerned with updating the memory indexes and the counter. The statements shown in the block appear strange if they are read as algebraic equations; however, they are not algebraic equations. The statement, Index = Index + 1, means the new value is obtained by incrementing the previous value by one.

The statements in the flowchart correspond one-to-one with the mnemonics. In large programs, such details in the flowchart are impractical as well as undesirable. However, these details are included here to show the logic flow in writing programs. In Figure 6.8, some of the details can very easily be eliminated from the flowchart. For example, Blocks 2 and 7 can be combined in one statement; such as, Transfer Data Byte from Source to Destination. Similarly, Block 5 can be reduced to one statement; such as, Update Memory Indexes and Counter.

PROGRAM

Memory Address HI-LO	Hex Code	Label	Instructions Opcode	Operand	Comments
XX00	21	START:	LXI	H, XX50H	;Set up HL as an
01	50				index for source
02	XX				memory
03	11		LXI	D, XX70H	;Set up DE as
04	70				an index for
05	XX				destination
06	06		MVI	B, 10H	;Set up B to count
07	10				16 bytes
08	7E	NEXT:	MOV	A, M	;Get data byte from source memory
09	12		STAX	D	;Store data byte at destination
0A	23		INX	H	;Point HL to next source location
0B	13		INX	D	;Point DE index to next destination
0C	05		DCR	B	;One transfer is complete, decrement count
0D	C2		JNZ	NEXT	;If counter is not 0,
0E	08				go back to transfer
0F	XX				next byte
10	76		HLT		;End of program
XX50	37				;Data
↓	↓				
XX5F	98				

PROGRAM EXECUTION AND OUTPUT

To execute the program, substitute the page number of your system's R/W memory in place of XX, enter the program and the data, and execute it. To verify the proper execution, check the memory locations from XX70H to XX7FH.

FIGURE 6.9
Data Transfer from Memory to
Accumulator (a) then to New
Memory Location (b)

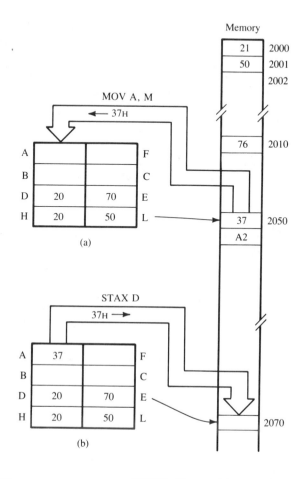

Let us assume the system R/W user memory starts at 2000H. Figure 6.9(a) shows how the contents of the memory location 2050H are copied into the accumulator by the instruction MOV A, M; the HL register points to location 2050 and instruction MOV A, M copies 37H into A. Figure 6.9(b) shows that the DE register points to the location 2070H and the instruction STAX D copies (A) into the location 2070H.

See Assignments 1 to 6 at the end of this chapter.

6.3 ARITHMETIC OPERATIONS RELATED TO MEMORY

In the last chapter, the arithmetic instructions concerning three arithmetic tasks—Add, Subtract, and Increment/Decrement—were introduced. These instructions dealt with microprocessor register contents or numbers. In this chapter, instructions concerning the arithmetic tasks related to memory will be introduced.

ADD M/SUB M: Add/Subtract the contents of a memory location to/from
                     the contents of the accumulator.
INR M/DCR M: Increment/Decrement the contents of a memory location.

6.31 Instructions

The arithmetic instructions referenced to memory perform two tasks: one is to copy a byte from a memory location to the microprocessor, and the other is to perform the arithmetic operation. These instructions (other than INR and DCR) implicitly assume that one of the operands is (A); after an operation, the previous contents of the accumulator are replaced by the result. All flags are modified to reflect the data conditions (see the exceptions: INR and DCR).

Opcode	Operand	
ADD	M:	Add Memory
		This is a 1-byte instruction
		It adds (M) to (A)
		The memory location is specified by the contents of HL register
SUB	M:	Subtract Memory
		This is a 1-byte instruction
		It subtracts (M) from (A)
		The memory location is specified by (HL)
INR	M	This is a 1-byte instruction
		It increments the contents of a memory location by 1, not the memory address
		The memory location is specified by (HL)
		All flags except the Carry flag are affected
DCR	M	This is a 1-byte instruction
		It decrements (M) by 1
		The memory location is specified by (HL)
		All flags except the Carry flag are affected

Write instructions to add the contents of the memory location 2040H to (A), and subtract the contents of the memory location 2041H from the first sum. Assume the accumulator has 30H, the memory location 2040H has 68H, and the location 2041H has 7FH.

Example 6.6

Instructions Before asking the microprocessor to perform any memory related operations, we must specify the memory location by loading the HL register pair. In the example illustrated in Figure 6.10, the contents of the HL pair 2040H specify the memory location. The instruction ADD M adds 68H, the contents of memory location 2040H, to the contents of the accumulator (30H). The instruction INX H points to the next memory location, 2041H, and the instruction SUB M subtracts the contents (7FH) of memory location 2041H from the previous sum.

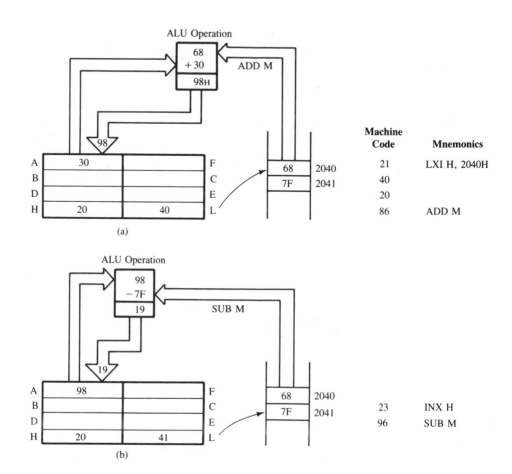

FIGURE 6.10
Register and Memory Contents and Instructions for Example 6.6

Example
6.7

Write instructions to

1. Load 59H in memory location 2040H and increment the contents of the memory location.
2. Load 90H in memory location 2041H, and decrement the contents of the memory location.

Instructions   Figure 6.11 shows register contents and the instructions required for Example 6.7. The instruction MVI M loads 59H in the memory location indicated by (HL). The instruction INR M increases the contents, 59H, of the memory location to 5AH. The instruction INX H increases (HL) to 2041H. The next two instructions load and decrement 90H.

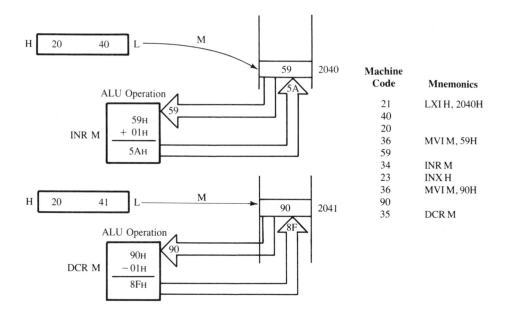

FIGURE 6.11
Register, Memory Contents, and Instructions for Example 6.7

6.32 Illustrative Program: Addition with Carry

PROBLEM STATEMENT

Six bytes of data are stored in memory locations starting at XX50H. Add all the data bytes. Use register B to save any carries generated, while adding the data bytes. Display the entire sum at two output ports, or store the sum at two consecutive memory locations, XX70H and XX71H.

Data(H)   A2, FA, DF, E5, 98, 8B

PROBLEM ANALYSIS

This problem can be analyzed in relation to the general flowchart in Figure 6.3 as follows:

1. Because of the memory-related arithmetic instructions just introduced in this section, two blocks in the general flowchart — data acquisition and data processing — can be combined in one instruction.
2. The fourth block — temporary storage of partial results — is unnecessary because the sum can be stored in the accumulator.
3. The data processing block needs to be expanded to account for carry.

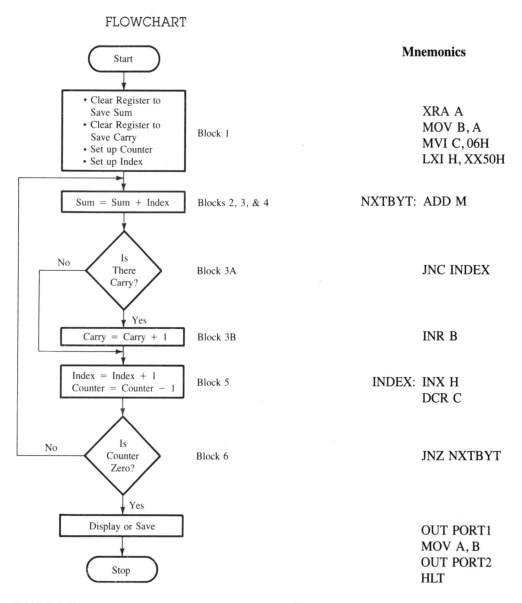

FIGURE 6.12
Flowchart for Addition
with Carry

In the first block (Block 1) of the flowchart, the accumulator and the carry register (for example, register B) must be cleared in order to use them for arithmetic operations; otherwise, residual data will cause erroneous results.

After the addition, it is necessary to check whether that operation has generated a carry (Block 3A). If a carry is generated, the carry register is incremented by one (Block 3B); otherwise, it is bypassed. The instruction ADC (Add with Carry) is inappropriate for this operation. (See Appendix F for the description of the instruction ADC.)

PROGRAM

Memory Address HI-LO	Machine Code	Label	Opcode	Operand	Comments
XX00	AF		XRA	A	;Clear (A) to save sum
01	47		MOV	B, A	;Clear (B) to save carry
02	0E		MVI	C, 06H	;Set up register C as a counter
03	06				
04	21		LXI	H, XX50H	;Set up HL register as memory
05	50				index
06	XX				
07	86	NXTBYT:	ADD	M	;Add (M) to (A)
08	D2		JNC	NXTMEM	;If no carry, do not increment
09	0C				carry register
0A	XX				Jump to increment the index
0B	04		INR	B	;If carry, save carry bit
0C	23	NXTMEM:	INX	H	;Point to next memory location
0D	0D		DCR	C	;One addition is completed;
					decrement counter
0E	C2		JNZ	NXTBYT	;If all bytes are not yet added,
0F	07				go back to get next byte
10	XX				
		;Output Display			
11	D3		OUT	PORT1	;Display low-order byte of the
12	PORT1				sum at PORT1
13	78		MOV	A, B	;Transfer carry to accumulator
14	D3		OUT	PORT2	;Display carry digits
15	PORT2				
16	76		HLT		;End of program

;Storing in Memory — Alternative to Output Display					
11	21		LXI	H, XX70H	;Point index to the memory
12	70				location to store answer
13	XX				
14	77		MOV	M, A	;Store low-order byte at XX70H
15	23		INX	H	;Point to location XX71H
16	70		MOV	M, B	;Store carry bits
17	76		HLT		;End of program

50	A2	;Data Bytes
51	FA	
52	DF	
53	E5	
54	98	
55	8B	

PROGRAM DESCRIPTION AND OUTPUT

In this program, register B is used as a carry register, register C as a counter to count six data bytes, and the accumulator to add the data bytes and save the partial sum.

After the completion of the summation, the high-order byte (bits higher than eight bits) of the sum is saved in register B and the low-order byte is in the accumulator. Both are displayed at two different ports, or they can be stored at the memory locations XX70H and 71H.

See Assignments 7 to 9 at the end of this chapter.

6.4 LOGIC OPERATIONS: ROTATE

In the last chapter, the logic instructions concerning the four operations — AND, OR, EX-OR, and NOT — were introduced. This chapter introduces instructions related to rotating the accumulator bits. The opcodes are as follows:

- □ RLC : Rotate Accumulator Left
- □ RAL : Rotate Accumulator Left Through Carry
- □ RRC : Rotate Accumulator Right
- □ RAR : Rotate Accumulator Right Through Carry

6.41 Instructions

This group has four instructions; two are for rotating left and two are for rotating right. The differences between these instructions are illustrated in the following examples.

1. RLC: Rotate Accumulator Left

- □ Each bit is shifted to the adjacent left position. Bit D_7 becomes D_0.
- □ CY flag is modified according to bit D_7.

Example 6.8

Assume the accumulator contents are AAH and CY = 0. Illustrate the accumulator contents after the execution of the RLC instruction twice.

Illustration   Figure 6.13 illustrates Example 6.8.

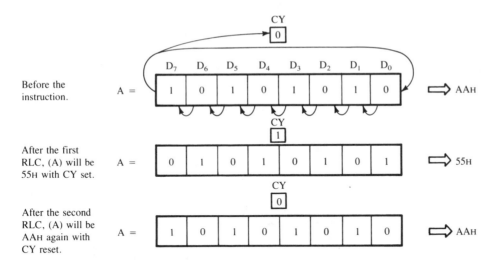

FIGURE 6.13
Accumulator Contents After RLC

2. RAL: Rotate Accumulator Left Through Carry.

☐ Each bit is shifted to the adjacent left position. Bit D_7 becomes a carry bit and the carry bit is shifted into D_0.
☐ The Carry flag is modified according to bit D_7.

Assume the accumulator contents are AAH and $CY = 0$. Illustrate the accumulator contents after the execution of the instruction RAL twice.

Example
6.9

Illustration   Figure 6.14 illustrates Example 6.9.

Examining these two examples, you may notice that the primary difference between these two instructions is that (1) the instruction RLC rotates through eight bits, and (2) the instruction RAL rotates through nine bits.

3. RRC: Rotate Accumulator Right.

☐ Each bit is shifted right to the adjacent position. Bit D_0 becomes D_7.
☐ The Carry flag is modified according to bit D_0.

RAR: Rotate Accumulator Right Through Carry

☐ Each bit is shifted right to the adjacent position. Bit D_0 becomes the carry bit, and the carry bit is shifted into D_7.

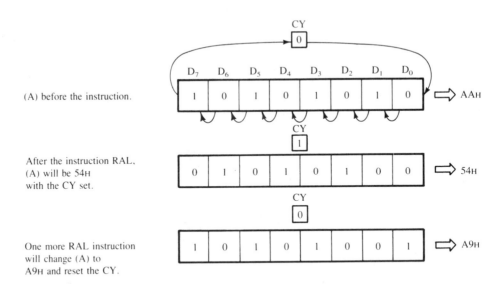

FIGURE 6.14
Accumulator Contents After RAL

Example
6.10

Assume the contents of the accumulator are 81H and CY = 0. Illustrate the accumulator contents after the RAR and RRC instructions.

Illustration   Figure 6.15 illustrates Example 6.10.

The rotate instructions are primarily used in bit manipulation and arithmetic multiply and divide operations. For example, if (A) is 0 0 0 0 1 0 0 0 = 08H,

☐ By rotating right: (A) = 0 0 0 0   0 1 0 0 = 04H
☐ This is equivalent to dividing by 2
☐ By rotating left: (A) = 0 0 0 1   0 0 0 0 = 10H
☐ This is equivalent to multiplying by 2 (10H = 16_{10})

However, these procedures are invalid when logic 1 is rotated left from D_7 to D_0 or vice versa. For example, if 80H is rotated left, it becomes 01H.

6.42   Illustrative Program: Checking Sign with Rotate Instructions

PROBLEM STATEMENT

A set of ten current readings is stored in memory locations starting at XX60H. The readings are expected to be positive ($<127_{10}$). Write a program to

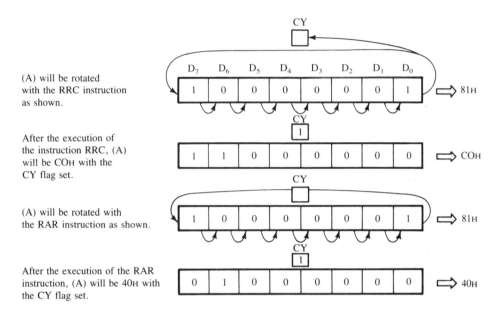

(A) will be rotated
with the RRC instruction
as shown.

After the execution of
the instruction RRC, (A)
will be C0H with the
CY flag set.

(A) will be rotated with
the RAR instruction as shown.

After the execution of the RAR
instruction, (A) will be 40H with
the CY flag set.

FIGURE 6.15
Rotate Right Instructions

1. Check each reading to determine whether it is positive or negative.
2. Reject all negative readings.
3. Add all positive readings.
4. Output FFH to PORT1 at any time when the sum exceeds eight bits to indicate overload; otherwise, display the sum. If no output port is available in the system, go to step 5.
5. Store FFH in the memory location XX70H when the sum exceeds eight bits; otherwise, store the sum.

Data (H)   28, D8, C2, 21, 24, 30, 2F, 19, F2 and 9F

PROBLEM ANALYSIS

This problem can be divided into the following steps:

1. Transfer a data byte from the memory location to the microprocessor, and check whether it is a negative number. The sign of the number can be verified by rotating bit D_7 into the Carry position and checking for CY. (See Assignment 10 at the end of this chapter to verify the sign of a number with the Sign flag.)
2. If it is negative, reject the data and get the next data byte.
3. If it is positive, add the data byte.
4. Check the sum for a carry and display an appropriate output.

The steps are shown in the flowchart in Figure 6.16.

FLOWCHART

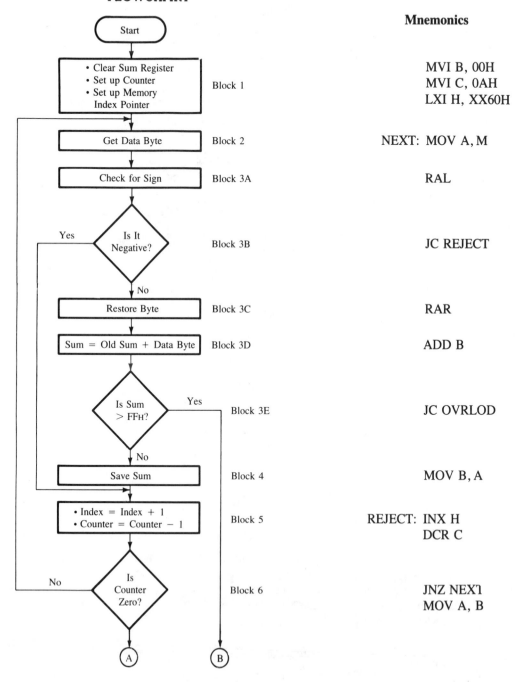

Mnemonics

Block	Mnemonic
Block 1	MVI B, 00H
	MVI C, 0AH
	LXI H, XX60H
Block 2	NEXT: MOV A, M
Block 3A	RAL
Block 3B	JC REJECT
Block 3C	RAR
Block 3D	ADD B
Block 3E	JC OVRLOD
Block 4	MOV B, A
Block 5	REJECT: INX H
	DCR C
Block 6	JNZ NEXT
	MOV A, B

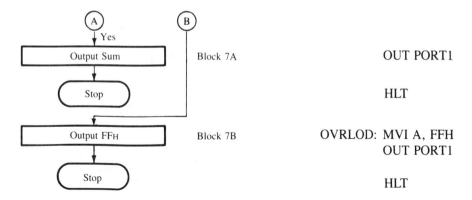

FIGURE 6.16
Flowchart for Checking Sign
with Rotate Instructions

In this flowchart, Blocks 1, 2, 4, 5, and 6 are similar to those in the generalized flowchart. Block 3 — data processing — is substantially expanded by adding two decision-making blocks. This flowchart is first drawn with decision-making answers that do not change the sequence. For example, in Blocks 3B and 3E, the flowchart should first be continued with the answers "NO." Then find appropriate locations where the program should be directed to the answers "YES."

In this program, the sign of a data byte cannot be checked with the instruction JM (Jump on Minus) because the instruction MOV A, M does not set any flags. (However, the flags can be set by ORing the accumulator contents with itself.)

Similarly, in Block 3C, the instruction RRC (Rotate Right) cannot be used when the instruction RAL is used to rotate left. However, the program can be written using RLC and RRC in both places (3A and 3C).

PROGRAM

Memory Address HI-LO	Machine Code	Label	Opcode	Operand	Comments
XX00	06		MVI	B, 00H	;Clear (B) to save sum
01	00				
02	0E		MVI	C, 0AH	;Set up register C as a counter
03	0A				
04	21		LXI	H, XX60H	;Set up HL register as memory
05	60				index
06	XX				
07	7E	NEXT:	MOV	A, M	;Transfer (M) to (A)
08	17		RAL		;Shift D_7 into CY

09	DA		JC	REJECT	;If $D_7 = 1$, reject byte and go
0A	12				to increment index
0B	XX				
0C	1F		RAR		;If byte is positive, restore it
0D	80		ADD	B	;Add previous sum to (A)
0E	DA		JC	OVRLOD	;If sum >FFH, it is overload;
0F	1C				turn on emergency
10	XX				
11	47		MOV	B, A	;Save sum
12	23	REJECT	:INX	H	;Point to next reading
13	0D		DCR	C	;One reading is checked;
					decrement counter
14	C2		JNZ	NEXT	;If all readings are not checked,
15	07				go back to transfer next byte
16	XX				
		;Output Display			
17	78		MOV	A,B	
18	D3		OUT	PORT1	;Display sum
19	PORT1				
1A	76		HLT		;End of program
1B	00		NOP		;To match Jump location,
					OVRLOD in memory storage
1C	3E	OVRLOD:	MVI	A, FFH	;It is an overload
1D	FF				
1E	D3		OUT	PORT1	;Display overload signal at
1F	PORT1				PORT1
20	76		HLT		

;Storing Result in Memory — Alternative to Output Display					
18	32		STA	XX70H	;Store sum in memory XX70H
19	70				
1A	XX				
1B	76				
1C	3E	OVRLOD:	MVI	A, FFH	;Store overload signal in
1D	FF				memory XX70
1E	32		STA	XX70H	
1F	70				
20	XX				
21	76		HLT		

XX60	28	;Current Readings
61	D8	
62	C2	
63	21	
64	24	

65	30
66	2F
67	19
68	F2
69	9F

PROGRAM DESCRIPTION AND OUTPUT

In this program, register C is used as a counter to count ten bytes. Register B is used to save the sum. The sign of the number is checked by verifying whether D_7 is 1 or 0. If the Carry flag is set to indicate the negative sign, the program rejects the number and goes to Block 5, Getting-Ready for Next Operation.

The program should reject the data bytes D8, C2, F2 and 9F, and should add the rest. The answer displayed should be E5.

See Assignments 10–12 at the end of this chapter.

LOGIC OPERATIONS: COMPARE 6.5

The 8085/8080A instruction set has two types of Compare operations: CMP and CPI.

☐ CMP: Compare with Accumulator
☐ CPI: Compare Immediate (with Accumulator)

The microprocessor compares a data byte (or register/memory contents) with the contents of the accumulator by subtracting the data byte from (A), and indicates whether the data byte is $\leqq$ (A) by modifying the flags. However, the contents are not modified.

6.51 Instructions

1. CMP R/M: Compare (Register or Memory) with Accumulator

☐ This is a 1-byte instruction.
☐ It compares the data byte in register or memory with the contents of the accumulator.
☐ If (A) < (R/M), the CY flag is set.
☐ If (A) = (R/M), the Zero flag is set.
☐ If (A) > (R/M), the CY flag is reset.
☐ When memory is an operand, its address is specified by (HL).
☐ No contents are modified; however, all remaining flags are affected.

2. CPI 8-Bit: Compare Immediate with Accumulator

☐ This is a 2-byte instruction, the second byte being an 8-bit data.
☐ It compares the second byte with (A).
☐ If (A) < 8-bit data, the CY flag is set.

☐ If (A) = 8-bit data, the Zero flag is set.
☐ If (A) > 8-bit data, the CY flag is reset.
☐ No contents are modified; however, all remaining flags are affected.

**Example
6.11**

Write an instruction to load the accumulator with the data byte 64H, and verify whether the data byte in memory location 2050H is equal to the accumulator contents. If both data bytes are equal, jump to location OUT1.

Instructions   Figure 6.17 illustrates Example 6.11.

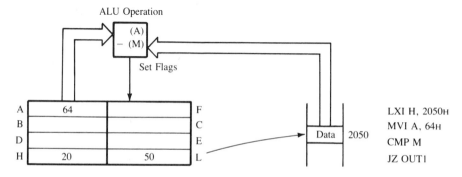

FIGURE 6.17
Compare Instructions

In these instructions, the instruction CMP M selects the memory location pointed out by the HL register (2050H) and compares the contents of that location with (A). If they are equal, the Zero flag is set, and the program jumps to location OUT1.

6.52   Illustrative Program: Use of Compare Instruction to Indicate End of Data String

PROBLEM STATEMENT

A set of current readings is stored in memory locations starting at XX50H. The end of the data string is indicated by the data byte 00H. Add the set of readings. The answer may be larger than FFH. Display the entire sum at PORT1 and PORT2 or store the answer in the memory locations XX70 and XX71H.

Data(H)   32, 52, F2, A5, 00

PROBLEM ANALYSIS

In this problem, the number of data bytes is variable, and the end of the data string is indicated by loading 00H. Therefore, the counter technique will not be useful to indicate the end of the readings. However, by comparing each data byte with 00H, the end of the data can be determined. This is shown in the following flowchart.

FLOWCHART

The flowchart shows that after a data byte is transferred, it is first checked for 00H (Block 6). This operation is similar to checking for a negative number in the previous problem. However, this is also an exit point. If the byte is zero, the program goes to the output Block 7. The other significant change is the Block 5 where the unconditional Jump brings the sequence back into the program.

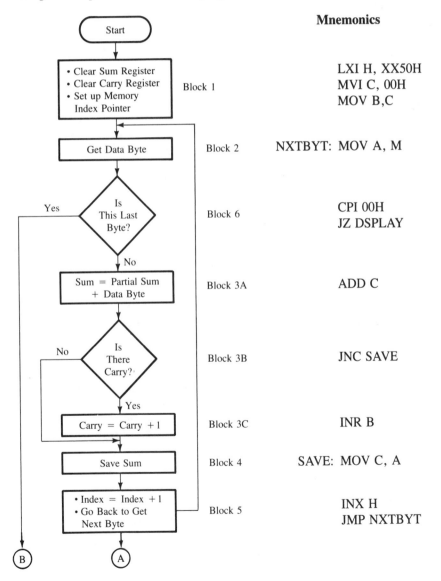

Mnemonics

Block	Description	Mnemonics
Block 1	• Clear Sum Register • Clear Carry Register • Set up Memory Index Pointer	LXI H, XX50H MVI C, 00H MOV B,C
Block 2	Get Data Byte	NXTBYT: MOV A, M
Block 6	Is This Last Byte?	CPI 00H JZ DSPLAY
Block 3A	Sum = Partial Sum + Data Byte	ADD C
Block 3B	Is There Carry?	JNC SAVE
Block 3C	Carry = Carry + 1	INR B
Block 4	Save Sum	SAVE: MOV C, A
Block 5	• Index = Index + 1 • Go Back to Get Next Byte	INX H JMP NXTBYT

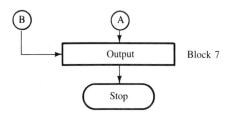

DSPLAY: MOV A, C
        OUT PORT1
        MOV A, B
        OUT PORT2

        HLT

FIGURE 6.18
Flowchart for Compare Instruction to Check
End of Data String

PROGRAM

Memory Address HI-LO	Machine Code	Label	Opcode	Operand	Comments
XX00	21	START:	LXI	H, XX50H	;Set up HL register as memory index
01	50				
02	XX				
03	0E		MVI	C, 00H	;Clear (C) to save sum
04	00				
05	41		MOV	B, C	;Clear (B) to save carry
06	7E	NXTBYT:	MOV	A, M	;Transfer current reading to (A)
07	FE		CPI	00H	;Is this the last reading?
08	00				
09	CA		JZ	DSPLAY	;Yes; go to display section
0A	16				
0B	XX				
0C	81		ADD	C	;Add previous sum to accumulator
0D	D2		JNC	SAVE	;Is there carry? If no, do not increment
0E	11				
0F	XX				
10	04		INR	B	;Update carry register
11	4F	SAVE:	MOV	C, A	;Save sum
12	23		INX	H	;Point to next reading
13	C3		JMP	NXTBYT	;Go back to get next reading
14	06				
15	XX				
		;Output Display			
16	79	DSPLAY:	MOV	A, C	
17	D3		OUT	PORT1	;Display low-order byte of sum at PORT1
18	PORT1				
19	78		MOV	A, B	;Transfer carry bits to accumulator

1A	D3		OUT	PORT2	;Display high-order byte of sum
1B	PORT2				at PORT2
1C	76		HLT		;End of program

;Storing Result In Memory — Alternative to Output Display					
16	21	DSPLAY:	LXI	H, XX70	;Point index to XX70H location
17	70				
18	XX				
19	71		MOV	M, C	;Store low-order byte of sum in XX70H
1A	23		INX	H	;Point index to XX71H
1B	70		MOV	M, B	;Store high-order byte
1C	76		HLT		;End of program

50	32	;Data — Current Readings
51	52	
52	F2	
53	A5	
54	00	

PROGRAM DESCRIPTION AND OUTPUT

This program adds the first four readings, which results in the sum 21BH. The low-order byte 1BH is saved in register C, and the high-order byte 02H is stored in the carry register B. These are each displayed at different output ports by the OUT instruction or stored in the memory locations XX70 and XX71.

See Assignments 13–16 at the end of the chapter.

DYNAMIC DEBUGGING 6.6

After you have completed the steps in the process of static debugging (described in the previous chapter) if the program still does not produce the expected output, you can attempt to debug the program by observing the execution of instructions. This is called **dynamic debugging**. In a single-board microcomputer, techniques and tools commonly used in dynamic debugging are

☐ Single Step
☐ Register Examine
☐ Breakpoint

Each will be discussed briefly below.

SINGLE STEP

The *Single-Step* key on a keyboard allows you to execute one instruction at a time, and to observe the results following each instruction. Generally, a single step facility is built with a hard-wired logic circuit. As you push the *Single-Step* key, you will be able to observe addresses and codes as they are executed. With the single step technique you will be able to spot

☐ Incorrect addresses
☐ Incorrect jump locations for loops
☐ Incorrect data or missing codes

To use this technique effectively, you will have to reduce loop and delay counts to a minimum number. For example, in a program which transfers 100 bytes, it is meaningless to set the count to 100 and single step the program 100 times. By reducing the count to two bytes, you will be able to observe the execution of the loop. (If you reduce the count to one byte, you may not be able to observe the execution of the loop.) By single stepping the program, you will be able to infer the flag status by observing the execution of Jump instructions. The single-step technique is very useful for short programs.

REGISTER EXAMINE

The *Register Examine* key allows you to examine the contents of the microprocessor register. When appropriate keys are pressed, the monitor program can display the contents of the registers. This technique is used in conjunction either with the single-step or the breakpoint facilities discussed below.

After executing a block of instructions, you can examine the register contents at a critical juncture of the program and compare these contents with the expected outcomes.

BREAKPOINT

In a single-board computer, the breakpoint facility is, generally, a software routine that allows you to execute a program in sections. The breakpoint can be set in your program by using RST instructions. (See Interrupts, Chapter 12.) When you push the *Execute* key, your program will be executed until the breakpoint, where the monitor takes over again. The registers can be examined for expected results. If the segment of the program is found satisfactory, a second breakpoint can be set at a subsequent memory address to debug the next segment of the program. With the breakpoint facility you can isolate the segment of the program with errors. Then that segment of the program can be debugged with the single-step facility. The breakpoint technique can be used to check out the timing loop, I/O section, and interrupts. (See Chapter 12, Interrupts, for how to write a breakpoint routine.)

COMMON SOURCES OF ERRORS

Common sources of errors in the instructions and programs illustrated in this chapter are as follows:

1. Failure to clear the accumulator when it is used to add numbers.
2. Failure to clear the carry registers or keep track of a carry.

3. Failure to update an index or a counter.
4. Failure to set a flag before using a conditional Jump instruction.
5. Inadvertently clearing the flag before using a Jump instruction.
6. Specification of wrong memory address for a Jump instruction.
7. Use of improper combination of Rotate instructions.
8. Specifying Jump instruction on a wrong flag. This is a very common error with the Compare instructions.

SUMMARY

In this chapter, programming techniques—such as looping, counting, and indexing—were illustrated using memory-related data transfer instructions, 16-bit arithmetic instructions, and logic instructions. Techniques used commonly in debugging a program—single step, register examine, and breakpoint—were discussed; and common sources of errors were listed.

Review of Instructions

The instructions introduced and illustrated in this chapter are summarized below for an overview.

Instructions	Task	Addressing Mode
Data Transfer (Copy) Instructions		
1. LXI Rp, 16-bit	Load 16-bit data in a register pair.	Immediate
2. MOV R, M	Copy (M) into (R).	Indirect
3. MOV M, R	Copy (R) into (M).	Indirect
4. LDAX Rp	Copy the contents of the memory, indicated by the register pair, into the accumulator.	Indirect
5. STAX Rp	Copy (A) into the memory, indicated by the register pair.	Indirect
6. LDA 16-bit	Copy (M) into (A), memory specified by the 16-bit address.	Direct
7. STA 16-bit	Copy (A) into memory, specified by the 16-bit address.	Direct
Arithmetic Instructions		
1. ADD M	Add (M) to (A).	Indirect
2. SUB M	Subtract (M) from (A).	Indirect
3. INR M	Increment the contents of M by 1.	Indirect
4. DCR M	Decrement the contents of M by 1.	Indirect
Logic Instructions		
1. RLC	Rotate each bit in the accumulator to the left.	
2. RAL	Rotate each bit in the accumulator to the left through the Carry.	

3. RRC   Rotate each bit in the accumulator to the right.

4. RAR   Rotate each bit in the accumulator to the right
                       through the Carry.

5. CMP R   Compare (R) with (A).   Register

6. CMP M   Compare (M) with (A).   Indirect

7. CPI 8-bit   Compare 8-bit data with (A).   Immediate

LOOKING AHEAD

The instructions that have been introduced in this and the previous chapter make up the major segment of the instruction set. Applications of these instructions in designing counters and time delays are illustrated in the next chapter. The other group of instructions critical for assembly language programming is related to the subroutine technique, illustrated in Chapter 8.

ASSIGNMENTS

In the following assignments, enter data manually in the respective memory locations before executing your program. If an assignment calls for an output port and your microcomputer does not have an independent output port, store the results in memory.

Section 6.2

1. The following block of data is stored in the memory locations from XX55H to XX5AH. Transfer the data to the locations XX80H to XX85H in the reverse order (e.g., the data byte 22H should be stored at XX85H and 37H at XX80H).
   Data(H)   22, A5, B2, 99, 7F, 37

2. Data bytes are stored in memory locations from XX50H to XX5FH. To insert an additional five bytes of data, it is necessary to shift the data string by five memory locations. Write a program to store the data string from XX55H to XX64H. Use any sixteen bytes of data to verify your program.
   Hint: This is a block transfer of data bytes with overlapping memory locations. If the data transfer begins at location XX50H, a segment of the data string will be destroyed.

3. A system is designed to monitor the temperature of a furnace. Temperature readings are recorded in sixteen bits and stored in memory locations starting at XX60H. The high-order byte is stored first and the low-order byte is stored in the next consecutive memory location. However, the high-order byte of all the temperature readings is constant.

   Write a program to transfer low-order readings to consecutive memory locations starting at XX80H and discard the high-order bytes.
   Temperature Readings(H)   0581, 0595, 0578, 057A, 0598

4. Add the following five data bytes stored in memory locations starting at 2060H and display the sum. (The sum is less than FF. Use register B to store the partial sum. Write the program without using ADD M, which is introduced in Section 6.3.)

   Data(H) 38, 12, 08, 41, and 5A

5. Write a program to add the following five data bytes stored in memory locations starting at 2060H. If the sum generates a carry, stop the addition, and display 01H at the output port. Otherwise, continue adding and display the sum.

   Data(H) 98, A2, 39, 22, 42

6. In Assignment 5, modify the program to count how many data bytes have been added and also to display the count at the second output port.

Section 6.3

7. Repeat the Illustrative Program for addition with carry (Section 6.32) using the DE register as an index pointer and memory location XX40H as a counter.

   Hints:

   Use the instruction MVI M to load the memory location XX40H with a count, and DCR M to decrement the counter.

8. The temperatures of two furnaces are being monitored by a microcomputer. A set of five readings of the first furnace, recorded by five thermal sensors, is stored at the memory location starting at XX50H. A corresponding set of five readings from the second furnace is stored at the memory location starting at XX60H. Each reading from the first set is expected to be higher than the corresponding reading from the second set. For example, the temperature reading at the location 54H (T_{54}) is expected to be higher than the temperature reading at the location 64H (T_{64}).

   Write a program to check whether each reading from the first set is higher than the corresponding reading from the second set. If all readings from the first set are higher than the corresponding readings from the second set, turn on the bit D_0 of the output PORT1. If any one of the readings of the first set is lower than the corresponding reading of the second set, stop the process and output FF as an emergency signal to the output PORT1.

   Data(H) First Set: 82, 89, 78, 8A, 8F

   Second Set: 71, 78, 79, 82, 7F

9. Repeat Assignment 8 with the following modification. Check whether any two readings are equal, and if they are equal, turn on bit D_7 of PORT1 and continue checking. (*Hint:* Check for the Zero flag when two readings are equal.)

   Data(H) First Set: 80, 85, 8F, 82, 87

   Second Set: 71, 74, 7A, 82, 77

Section 6.4

10. Repeat the Illustrative Program for checking the sign with Rotate instructions (Section 6.42) but include the following modifications:

a. Check the sign of a number by using the instruction JM—Jump on Minus. (*Hint:* Set the flags by using the instruction ORA A.)

b. If the sum of the positive readings exceeds eight bits, continue the addition, save generated carry, and display the total sum at two different ports.

   Data(H)   38, 78, 75, 7A, F1, 85, 98, 6F, 7C, 69

11. In Assignment 10, in addition to modifications a and b, count the number of positive readings in the set and display the count at port 3.

12. A set of eight data bytes is stored in the memory location starting at XX50H. Check each data byte for bits D_7 and D_0. If D_7 or D_0 is 1, reject the data byte; otherwise, store the data bytes at memory locations starting at XX60H.

   Data(H)   80, 52, E8, 78, F2, 67, 35, 62

Section 6.5

13. Repeat the Illustrative Program for use of the Compare instruction to indicate the end of a data string (Section 6.52), but include the following modificatons: Clear register D and use CMP D to check a byte in the memory location. If a byte is not zero, add the byte and continue processing; otherwise, go to the output.

14. A set of eight readings is stored in memory starting at location XX50H. Write a program to check whether a byte 40H exists in the set. If it does, stop checking, and display its memory location; otherwise output FFH.

   Data(H)   48, 32, F2, 38, 37, 40, 82, 8A

15. Refer to Assignment 14. Write a program to find the highest reading in the set, and display the reading at an output port.

16. Refer to Assignment 8. The program should meet the following conditions: Each temperature reading in the second set is expected to be half of each corresponding reading in the first set.

   Rewrite the program:

   a. To check whether each reading in the second set is less than half of the corresponding reading in the first set.

   b. If all readings satisfy this condition, turn on bit D_0; otherwise output FF to PORT1.

   Data(H)   First Set: 82, 88, 78, 8A, 8E
              Second Set: 40, 43, 40, 42, 45

Counter and Timing Delays

This chapter deals with the designing of counters and timing delays through software (programming). Two of the programming techniques discussed in the last chapter—looping and counting—are used to design counters and time delays. The necessary instructions have already been introduced in the previous two chapters.

A counter is designed by loading an appropriate count in a register. A loop is set up to decrement the count for a down-counter* or to increment the count for an up-counter.† Similarly, a timing delay is designed by loading a register with a delay count, and setting up a loop to decrement the count until zero. The delay is determined by the clock period of the system and the time required to execute the instructions in the loop.

Counters and time delays are important techniques. They are commonly used in applications such as traffic signals, digital clocks, process control, and serial data transfer.

OBJECTIVES

☐ Write instructions to set up time delays, using one register and a register pair.

☐ Calculate the time delay in a given loop.
☐ Draw a flowchart for a counter with a delay.
☐ Design an up/down counter for a given delay.
☐ Write a program to turn on/off specific bits at a given interval.

---

*A Down-Counter counts in the descending order.
†An Up-Counter counts in the ascending order.

7.1   COUNTERS AND TIME DELAYS

Designing a counter is a frequent programming application. Counters are used primarily to keep track of events, while time delays are important in setting up reasonably accurate timing between two events. The process of designing counters and time delays using software instructions is far more flexible and less time consuming than the design process using hardware.

COUNTER

A counter is designed simply by loading an appropriate number into one of the registers and using the INR (Increment by One) or the DCR (Decrement by One) instructions. A loop is established to update the count, and each count is checked to determine whether it has reached the final number; if not, the loop is repeated.

The flowchart shown in Figure 7.1 illustrates these steps. However, this counter has one major drawback; the counting is performed at such high speed that only the last count can be observed. To observe counting, there must be an appropriate time delay between counts.

TIME DELAY

The procedure used to design a specific delay is similar to that used to set up a counter. A register is loaded with a number, depending on the time delay required, and then the register is decremented until it reaches zero by setting up a loop with a conditional Jump instruction. The loop causes the delay, depending upon the clock period of the system, as illustrated in the next sections.

7.11   Time Delay Using One Register

The flowchart in Figure 7.2 shows a time-delay loop. A count is loaded in a register, and the loop is executed until the count reaches zero. The set of instructions necessary to set up the loop is also shown in Figure 7.2.

FIGURE 7.1
Flowchart of a Counter

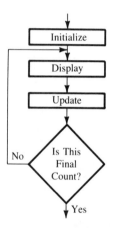

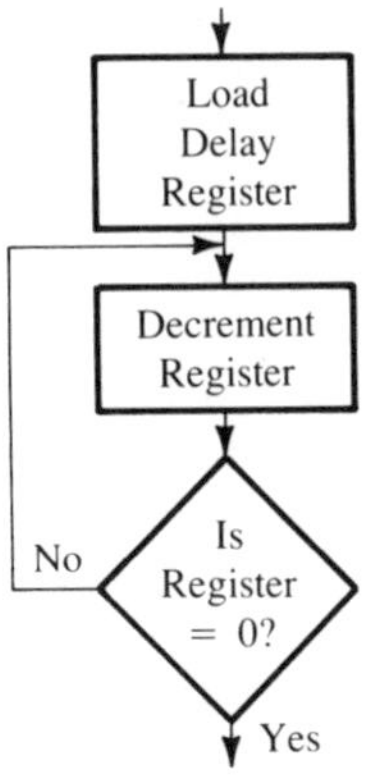

Label	Opcode	Operand	Comments	T-states (8080A)
	MVI	C, FFH	;Load register C	7
LOOP:	DCR	C	;Decrement C	5
	JNZ	LOOP	;Jump back to decrement C	10

FIGURE 7.2
Time Delay Loop: Flowchart and Instructions

The last column in the instructions shows the T-states (clock periods) required by the 8080A microprocessor to execute each instruction. (See Appendix F for the list of the 8085/8080A instructions and their T-states.) For some instructions, the 8080A requires a different number of T-states than does the 8085. For example, the 8085 executes the instruction DCR in four T-states whereas the 8080A takes five T-states. The calculations shown here are based on the 8080A instructions.

Figure 7.2 shows that instruction MVI requires seven clock periods. An 8080A-based microcomputer with 2 MHz clock frequency will execute the instruction MVI in 3.5 μs as follows:

Clock frequency of the system f = 2 MHz
Clock period T = $1/f = 1/2 \times 10^{-6}$ = 0.5 μs
Time to execute MVI = 7 T-states $\times$ 0.5
$\qquad\qquad\qquad\quad$ = 3.5 μs

However, if the clock frequency of the system is 1 MHz, the microprocessor will require 7 μs to execute the same instruction. To calculate the time delay in a loop, we must account for the T-states required for each instruction, and for the number of times the instructions are executed in the loop.

In Figure 7.2, register C is loaded with the count FFH(255_{10}) by the instruction MVI, which is executed once and takes seven T-states. The next two instructions, DCR and JNZ, form a loop with a total of fifteen (5 + 10) T-states. The loop is repeated 255 times until register C = 0.

The time delay in the loop T_L with 2 MHz clock frequency is calculated as

$$T_L = (T \times \text{Loop T-states} \times N_{10})$$

where T_L = Time delay in the loop
$\qquad$ T = System clock period

N_{10} = Equivalent decimal number of the hexadecimal count loaded in the delay register

$$= (0.5 \times 10^{-6} \times 15 \times 255)$$
$$= 1912.5 \ \mu s$$
$$\approx 1.9 \ ms$$

In most applications, this approximate calculation of the time delay is considered reasonably accurate. However, to calculate the time delay more accurately, the time for the execution of the initial instruction MVI should be included in the total time delay T_D as

Delay T_D = Time to Execute + Time to Execute
Instructions Outside Loop   Loop Instructions
$$= T_O + T_L$$
$$= (7 \times 0.5 \ \mu s) + 1912.5 \ \mu s$$
$$= 1916 \ \mu s$$
$$\approx 1.9 \ ms$$

The difference between the two calculations is only 3.5 μs and can be ignored in most instances.

The time delay can be varied by changing the count number FF; however, to increase the time delay beyond 1.9 ms in 2 MHz microcomputer systems, you must use either additional instructions or a register pair.

7.12   Time Delay Using a Register Pair

The time delay can be considerably increased by setting a loop and using a register pair with a 16-bit number (maximum FFFFH). The 16-bit number is decremented by using the instruction DCX. However, the instruction DCX does not set the Zero flag and, without the test flags, Jump instructions cannot be executed. Additional techniques, therefore, must be used to set the Zero flag.

The following set of instructions uses a register pair to set up a time delay.

Label	Opcode	Operand	Comments	T-states (8080A)
	LXI	B,208FH	;Load register pair BC with 16-bit count	10
LOOP:	DCX	B	;Decrement (BC) by one	5
	MOV	A,C	;Load accumulator with contents of register C	5
	ORA	B	;OR (B) with (C) to set Zero flag	4
	JNZ	LOOP	;If result $\neq$ 0, jump back to LOOP	10

In this set of instructions, the instruction LXI B, 208FH loads register B with the number 20H, and register C with the number 8FH. The instruction DCX decrements the entire number by one (e.g., 208FH becomes 208EH). The next two instructions are used only to set the Zero flag; otherwise, they have no function in this problem. The OR instruction sets the Zero flag only when the contents of B and C are simultaneously zero. Therefore, the loop is repeated 208FH times, equal to the count set in the register pair.

TIME DELAY

The time delay in the loop is calculated as in the previous example. The loop includes four instructions: DCX, MOV, ORA, and JNZ, and takes 24 clock periods for execution. The loop is repeated 208FH times, which is converted to decimals as

$$208FH = 2 \times (16)^3 + 0 \times (16)^2 + 8 \times (16)^1 + 15(16^0)$$
$$= 8335_{10}$$

If the clock period of the system $= 0.5~\mu s$, the delay in the Loop T_L

$$T_L = (0.5 \times 24 \times 8335_{10})$$
$$= 100~ms$$
$$\text{Total Delay } T_D = 100~ms + T_O$$
$$\approx 100~ms \text{ (The instruction LXI adds only 5 } \mu s.)$$

A similar time delay can also be achieved by using the technique of two loops. For example, register C is used in the inner loop and register B is used in the outer loop (Figure 7.3).

FIGURE 7.3
Flowchart for Time Delay with
Two Loops

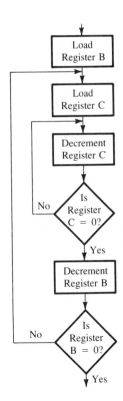

Furthermore, the time delay within a loop can be increased by using instructions that will not affect the program except to increase the delay. For example, the instruction NOP (No Operation) can add four T-states in the delay loop. The desired time delay can be obtained by using any or all available registers.

The procedure for calculating time delays in an 8085 system is the same as explained for the 8080A except that appropriate T-states should be used in the delay calculations. However, the execution of a conditional Jump instruction adds a few complications to the calculations. The 8085 requires ten T-states to execute a conditional Jump instruction when it changes the sequence of the program, and seven T-states when the program continues in the same sequence. For example, the JNZ instruction in the last loop of Figure 7.2 is executed in seven T-states. This means the number of T-states in the loop will be reduced by three T-states, which can be easily ignored.

7.13   Additional Techniques for Time Delay

The disadvantages in using software delay techniques for real-time applications in which the demand for time accuracy is high, such as digital clocks, are as follows:

1. The accuracy of the time delay depends on the accuracy of the system's clock.
2. The microprocessor is occupied simply in a waiting loop; otherwise it could be employed to perform other functions.
3. The task of calculating accurate time delays is tedious.

In real-time applications, timers (integrated timer circuits) are commonly used. The Intel 8253 (described in Chapter 15) is a programmable timer chip that can be interfaced with the microprocessor and programmed to provide timings with considerable accuracy. The disadvantages of using the hardware chip include the additional expense and the need for an extra chip in the system.

7.14   Counter Design with Time Delay

To design a counter with a time delay, the techniques illustrated in Figures 7.1 and 7.2 can be combined. The combined flowchart is shown in Figure 7.4.

The blocks shown in the flowchart are similar to those in the generalized flowchart in Figure 6.3. The block numbers shown in Figure 7.4 correspond to the block numbers in the generalized flowchart. Compare Figure 7.4 with Figure 6.3 and note the following points about the counter flowchart (Figure 7.4):

1. The output (or display) block is a part of the counting loop.
2. The data processing block is replaced by the time-delay block.
3. The save-the-partial-answer block is eliminated because the count is saved in a counter register, and a register can be incremented or decremented without transferring the count to the accumulator.

The flowchart in Figure 7.4 shows the basic building blocks. However, the sequence can be changed, depending upon the nature of the problem, as shown in Figure 7.5a and b.

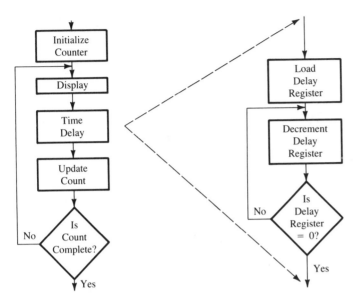

FIGURE 7.4
Flowchart of a Counter with a Time Delay

The flowchart in Figure 7.4 displays the count after initialization. For example, an up-counter starting at zero can be initialized at 00H using the logic shown in Figure 7.4. However, the flowchart in Figure 7.5(a) updates the counter immediately after the initialization. In this case, an up-counter should be initialized at FFH in order to display the count 00H.

Similarly, the decision-making block differs slightly in these flowcharts. For example, if a counter was counting up to 9, the question in Figure 7.4 would be: Is the count 10? In Figure 7.5(a) the question would be: Is the count 9? The flowchart in Figure 7.5(b) illustrates another way of designing a counter.

ILLUSTRATIVE PROGRAM: HEXADECIMAL COUNTER 7.2

PROBLEM STATEMENT

Write a program to count continuously in hexadecimal from FFH to 00H in a system with a 0.5 μs clock period. Use register C to set up a one millisecond (ms) delay between each count and display the numbers at one of the output ports.

PROBLEM ANALYSIS

The problem has two parts; the first is to set up a continuous down-counter, and the second is to design a given delay between two counts.

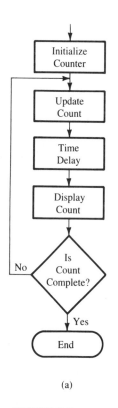

(a)

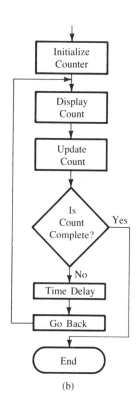

(b)

FIGURE 7.5
Variations of Counter Flowchart

1. The hexadecimal counter is set up by loading a register with an appropriate starting number and decrementing it until it becomes zero (shown by the outer loop in the flowchart, Figure 7.6). After the zero count, the register goes back to FF because decrementing zero results in a (-1), which is FF in 2's complement.
2. The one millisecond (ms) delay between each count is set up by using the procedure explained previously in Section 7.11 — Time-Delay Using One Register. Figure 7.2 is identical with the inner loop of the flowchart shown in Figure 7.6. The delay calculations are shown later.

FLOWCHART AND PROGRAM

The flowchart in Figure 7.6 shows the two loops discussed earlier — one for the counter and another for the delay. The counter is initialized in the first block, and the count is displayed in the outer loop. The delay is accomplished in the inner loop. This flowchart in Figure 7.6 is similar to that in Figure 7.5(a). You should study the flowchart carefully to differentiate between the counter loop and the delay loop because they may at first appear to be similar.

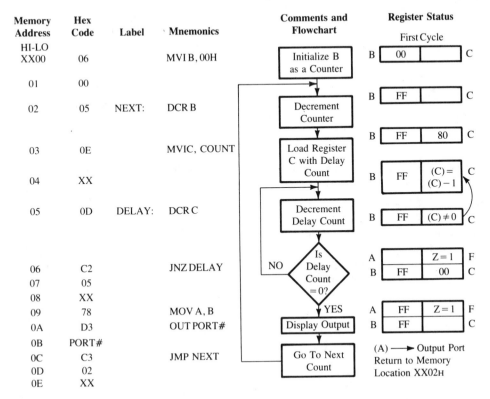

Memory Address	Hex Code	Label	Mnemonics
HI-LO			
XX00	06		MVI B, 00H
01	00		
02	05	NEXT:	DCR B
03	0E		MVI C, COUNT
04	XX		
05	0D	DELAY:	DCR C
06	C2		JNZ DELAY
07	05		
08	XX		
09	78		MOV A, B
0A	D3		OUT PORT#
0B	PORT#		
0C	C3		JMP NEXT
0D	02		
0E	XX		

FIGURE 7.6
Program and Flowchart for a Hexadecimal Counter

Delay Calculations The delay loop includes two instructions: DCR C and JNZ with 15 T-states. Therefore, the time delay T_L in the loop:

$$T_L = 15 \text{ T-states} \times T \text{ (Clock period)} \times \text{Count}$$
$$= 15 \times (0.5 \times 10^{-6}) \times \text{Count}$$
$$= (7.5 \times 10^{-6}) \times \text{Count}$$

The delay outside the loop includes the following instructions:

DCR B	5 T	Delay Outside = 40 T-states × T
MVI C, COUNT	10 T	the loop: T_O
MOV A, B	5 T	$= 40 \times (0.5 \times 10^{-6})$
OUT PORT	10 T	$= 20 \ \mu s$
JMP	10 T	
	40 T-states	

Total Time Delay $T_D = T_O + T_L$

$$1 \text{ ms} = 20 \times 10^{-6} + (7.5 \times 10^{-6}) \times \text{Count}$$
$$\text{Count} = \frac{1 \times 10^{-3} - 20 \times 10^{-6}}{7.5 \times 10^{-6}} = 128_{10}$$

Therefore, the delay count 80H (128_{10}) must be loaded in register C to obtain 1 ms delay between each count.

PROGRAM DESCRIPTION

Register B is used as a counter, and register C is used for delay. Register B initially starts with number 00H; when it is decremented by the instruction DCR, the number becomes FFH. (Verify this by subtracting one from zero in 2's complement.) Register C is loaded with the delay count 80H to provide a 1 ms delay in the loop. The instruction DCR C decrements the count and the instruction JNZ (Jump On No Zero) checks the Zero flag to see if the number in register C has reached zero. If the number is not zero, instruction JNZ causes a jump back to the instruction labelled "DELAY" in order to decrement (C) and, thus, the loop is repeated 128_{10} times.

The count is displayed by moving (B) to the accumulator, and then to the output port. The instruction JMP causes an unconditional jump for the next count in register B, forming a continuous loop to count from FFH to 00H. After the count reaches zero, (B) is decremented, becoming FFH, and the counting cycle is repeated.

PROGRAM OUTPUT

When the program is executed, the actual output seen may vary according to the device used as the output for the display. The eye cannot see the changes in a count with a 1 ms delay. If the output port has eight LEDs, the LEDs representing the low-order bits will appear to be on continuously, and the LEDs with high-order bits will go on and off according to the count. If the output port is a seven-segment display, all segments will appear to be on; a slight flicker in the display can be noticed. However, the count and the delay can be measured on an oscilloscope. (See Appendix B2 to run this program without an external port on the SDK-85 system.)

7.3   ILLUSTRATIVE PROGRAM: ZERO-TO-NINE (MODULO TEN)* COUNTER

PROBLEM STATEMENT

Write a program to count from 0 to 9 with a one-second delay between each count. At the count of 9, the counter should reset itself to 0 and repeat the sequence continuously. Use register pair HL to set up the delay, and display each count at one of the output ports. Assume the clock frequency of the microcomputer is 1 MHz.

---

*The counter goes through ten different states (0 to 9) and is called a *modulo ten* counter.

Instructions   Review the following instructions.

☐ LXI: Load Register Pair Immediate
☐ DCX: Decrement Register Pair
☐ INX: Increment Register Pair

These instructions manipulate 16-bit data by using registers in pairs (BC, DE, and HL). However, the instructions DCX and INX do not set flags to reflect the outcome of the operation. Therefore, additional instructions must be used to set the flags.

PROBLEM ANALYSIS

The problem is similar to that in the Illustrative Program for a hexadecimal counter (Section 7.2) except in two respects: the counter is an up-counter (counts *up* to the digit 9), and the delay is too long to use just one register.

1. The counter is set up by loading a register with the appropriate number and incrementing it until it reaches the digit 9. When the counter register reaches the final count, it is reset to zero. This is an additional step compared to the Illustrative Program of Section 7.2 in which the counter resets itself. (Refer to the flowchart in Figure 7.7 to see how each count is checked against the final count.)
2. The 1-second delay between each count is set up by using a register pair, as explained in Section 7.12. The delay calculations are shown later.

FLOWCHART AND PROGRAM

The flowchart in Figure 7.7 shows three loops: one for the counter (outer) loop on the left, the second for the delay (inner) loop on the left, and the third to reset the counter (the loop on the right). This flowchart is similar to the flowchart in Figure 7.4. The flowchart indicates that the number is displayed immediately after the initialization; this is different from the flowchart of Figure 7.6, in which the number is displayed at the end of the program.

The counter is incremented at the end of the program and checked against count 0AH (final count +1). If the counter has not reached number 0AH, the count is displayed (outer loop on the left); otherwise, it is reset by the loop on the right (Figure 7.7).

PROGRAM DESCRIPTION

Register B is used as a counter, and register pair HL is used for the delay. The significant differences between this program and the Illustrative Program for a hexadecimal counter (Section 7.2) are as follows:

1. Register pair HL contains a 16-bit number that can be manipulated in two ways: first, as a 16-bit number, and second, as two 8-bit numbers. The instruction DCX views the HL register as one register with a 16-bit number. On the other hand, the instructions MOV A, L and ORA H treat the contents of the HL registers as two separate 8-bit numbers.

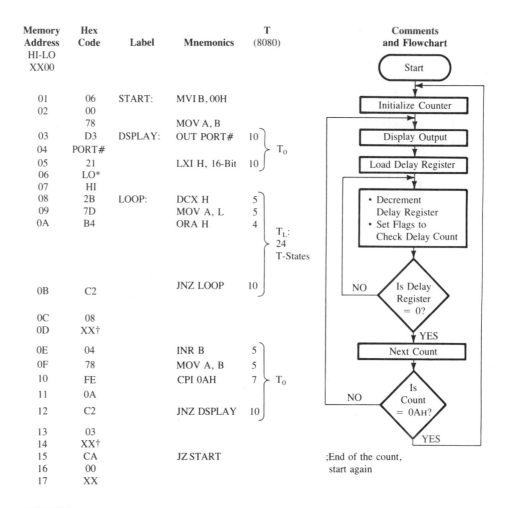

Memory Address HI-LO XX00	Hex Code	Label	Mnemonics	T (8080)	Comments and Flowchart
01	06	START:	MVI B, 00H		
02	00				
	78		MOV A, B		
03	D3	DSPLAY:	OUT PORT#	10 ⎫	
04	PORT#			⎬ T₀	
05	21		LXI H, 16-Bit	10 ⎭	
06	LO*				
07	HI				
08	2B	LOOP:	DCX H	5 ⎫	
09	7D		MOV A, L	5	
0A	B4		ORA H	4 ⎬ Tʟ: 24 T-States	
0B	C2		JNZ LOOP	10 ⎭	
0C	08				
0D	XX†				
0E	04		INR B	5 ⎫	
0F	78		MOV A, B	5	
10	FE		CPI 0AH	7 ⎬ T₀	
11	0A				
12	C2		JNZ DSPLAY	10 ⎭	
13	03				
14	XX†				
15	CA		JZ START		;End of the count,
16	00				start again
17	XX				

FIGURE 7.7
Program and Flowchart for a Zero-to-Nine Counter

NOTES: *Enter 16-bit delay count in place of LO and HI, appropriate to the clock period in your system.
          †Enter high-order address (page number) of your R/W memory.

2. In the delay loop, the sequence is repeated by the instruction JNZ (Jump on No Zero) until the count becomes zero, thus providing a delay of 1 second. However, the instruction DCX does not set the Zero flag. Therefore, the instruction JNZ would be unable to recognize when the count has reached zero, and the program would remain in a continuous loop.

In this program, the instruction ORA is used to set the Zero flag. The purpose here is to check when the 16-bit number in register pair HL has reached zero. This is accomplished by ORing the contents of register L with the contents of register H. However, the contents of two registers cannot be ORed directly. The instruction MOV A,L loads the accumulator with (L), which is then ORed with (H) by the instruction ORA H. The Zero flag is set only when both registers are zero.

3. The instruction CPI, 0AH (Compare Immediate with 0AH) checks the contents of the counter (register B) in every cycle. When register B reaches the number 0AH, the program sequence is redirected to reset the counter without displaying the number 0AH.

4. The time required to reset the counter to zero, indicated by the right-hand loop in the flowchart, is slightly different from the time delay between each count set by the left-hand outer loop.

Delay Calculations   The major delay between two counts is provided by the 16-bit number in the delay register HL (the inner loop in the flowchart). This delay is set up by using a register pair, as explained in Section 7.12.

$$\text{Loop Delay } T_L = 24 \text{ T-states} \times T \times \text{Count}$$
$$1 \text{ second} = 24 \times 1.0 \times 10^{-6} \times \text{Count}$$
$$\text{Count} = \frac{1}{24 \times 10^{-6}} = 41666 = 802FH$$

The delay count 802FH in register HL would provide approximately a 1-second delay between two counts. To achieve higher accuracy in the delay, the instructions outside the loop starting from OUT PORT# to JNZ DSPLAY must be accounted for in the delay calculations.

The instructions outside the loop are: OUT, LXI, INR, MOV, CPI, and JNZ (DSPLAY). These instructions require 47 T-states; therefore, the delay count is calculated as follows:

$$\text{Total Delay } T_D = T_O + T_L$$
$$1 \text{ second} = (47 \times 1.0 \times 10^{-6}) + (24 \times 1.0 \times 10^{-6} \times \text{Count})$$
$$\text{Count} = 41664$$

The difference between the two delay counts calculated above is of very little significance in many applications.

PROGRAM OUTPUT

In an LED output port, each LED will be lit according to the binary count representing 0 to 9. In a seven-segment display, the continuous sequence of the numbers from 0 to 9 can be very easily observed because of the 1-second delay between each count. However, it will be difficult to observe a steady pattern on the oscilloscope (except on a storage scope) because the reset cycle time is slightly different from the delay time. (See Assignment 3 at the end of this chapter to run this program on your system.)

7.4   ILLUSTRATIVE PROGRAM: PULSE TIMING FOR FLASHING LIGHTS

PROBLEM STATEMENT

A railway crossing signal has two flashing lights run by a microcomputer. One light is connected to data bit D_0, and the second light is connected to data bit D_1. Write a program to turn each signal light alternately on and off at an interval of 1 second if the clock period of the microcomputer is 0.5 μs.

Instructions   The following instructions should be reviewed and the differences between various rotate instructions observed:

☐ RAL: Rotate Accumulator Left Through Carry
☐ RAR: Rotate Accumulator Right Through Carry
☐ RLC: Rotate Accumulator Left
☐ RRC: Rotate Accumulator Right

The first two instructions, RAL and RAR, use the Carry flag as the ninth bit, and the accumulator can be viewed as a 9-bit register. The last two instructions, RLC and RRC, rotate the accumulator contents through eight positions.

In addition to using these instructions, you should review the concept of masking with the ANI instruction.

PROBLEM ANALYSIS

In this problem the two least-significant positions are used to activate the two lights. To display a flashing light, the output port should provide 0 and 1 signals alternately with the given delay. The logic 0 turns the light off, and the logic 1 turns the light on. The delay loop uses a register pair, as in the Illustrative Program for a zero-to-nine counter (Section 7.3).

The alternate pattern of 0/1 bits is provided by loading the accumulator with the number AAH (10101010) and rotating the pattern once through each delay loop. Only two positions are used. Therefore, all other bits can be masked by ANDing the accumulator with the appropriate number.

PROGRAM

Memory Address HI-LO	Hex Code	Label	Mnemonics	Comments	Register Status First Cycle	
XX00	16		MVI D, AA	;Load bit pattern	D 10101010	E
01	AA			AAH	↓	
02	7A	ROTATE:	MOV A, D	;Load bit pattern in A	A 10101010	F

03	07		RLC		;Rotate to change data from AAH to 55H and vice versa	A `01010101` `         ` F
04	57		MOV	D, A	;Save (A)	D `01010101` `         ` E
05	E6		ANI	03	;Mask bits D_7–D_2	A = 01010101
06	03					AND 00000011
						A = 00000001
07	D3		OUT	PORT1	;Turn on or off the lights	(A) → OUTPUT PORT
08	PORT1					
09	01		LXI	B, COUNT	;Load delay count for one second	B `  (HI)  ` `  (LO)  ` C
0A	LO				;Low-order byte	
0B	HI				;High-order byte	
0C	0B	DELAY:	DCX	B	;Decrement count	B `    (BC) − 1    ` C
0D	00		NOP		;Add T-states to increase delay	
0E	00		NOP			
0F	79		MOV	A, C		A `   (C)   ` `      ` F
10	B0		ORA	B	;OR register B to set Zero flag	A = (C)
11	C2					OR = (B)
12	0C		JNZ	DELAY	;Jump to location DELAY if register pair ≠ 0	(A) = Result of ORing
13	XX					
14	C3					
15	02		JMP	ROTATE	;Jump to location: ROTATE to start next sequence	
16	XX					

PROGRAM DESCRIPTION

Register D is loaded with the bit pattern AAH (10101010), and the bit pattern is moved into the accumulator. The bit pattern is rotated left once and saved again in register D. The accumulator contents must be saved because the accumulator is used later in the program.

The next instruction, ANI, ANDs (A) to mask all but the two least-significant positions (D_0 and D_1), as illustrated below.

```
(A)                 → 1  0  1  0  1  0  1  0
                       ↙  ↙  ↙  ↙  ↙  ↙  ↙
After RLC           → 0  1  0  1  0  1  0  1
AND with 03H        → 0  0  0  0  0  0  1  1
Remaining contents  → 0  0  0  0  0  0  0  1
```

This shows that 1 in D_0 turns on one light, and 0 in D_1 turns off the other light. In the next cycle of the loop, bits in D_0 and D_1 are interchanged because of the Rotate instruction. In the delay loop, two NOP instructions are used to increase the delay.

PROGRAM OUTPUT

In an LED output port, the LEDs in D_0 and D_1 positions will be alternately lit for an interval of one second. In a seven-segment LED output port, the numbers 0 and 1 can be observed every one second. (See Assignment 4 at the end of this chapter.)

7.5 DEBUGGING COUNTER AND TIME-DELAY PROGRAMS

The debugging techniques discussed in Chapters 5 and 6 can be used to check errors in a counter program. The following is a list of common errors in programs similar to those illustrated in this chapter.

1. Errors in counting T-states in a delay loop. Typically, the first instruction — to load a delay register — is mistakenly included in the loop.
2. Errors in recognizing how many times a loop is repeated.
3. Failure to convert a delay count from a decimal number into its hexadecimal equivalent.
4. Conversion error in converting a delay count from decimal to hexadecimal number or vice versa.
5. Specifying a wrong Jump location.
6. Failure to set a flag, especially with 16-bit Decrement/Increment instructions.
7. Using a wrong Jump instruction.
8. Failure to display either the first or the last count.
9. Failure to provide a delay between the last and the last-but-one count.

Some of these errors are illustrated in the following program.

7.51 Illustrative Program for Debugging

The following program is designed to count from 100_{10} to 0 in Hex continuously with a 1-second delay between each count. The delay is set up by using two loops — a loop within a loop. The inner loop is expected to provide approximately 100 ms delay, and it is repeated ten times, using the outer loop to provide a total delay of 1 second. The clock period of the system is 330 ns. The program includes several deliberate errors. Recognize the errors as specified in the following assignment.

	Mnemonics	T-states
1.	MVI A, 64H	7
2. DSPLAY:	OUT PORT1	10
3. LOOP2:	MVI B, 10H	7

```
4. LOOP1:   LXI   D, DELAY      10
5.          DCX   D             5
6.          NOP                 4
7.          NOP                 4
8.          MOV   A,D           5 (4/8085)
9.          ORA   E             4
10.         JNZ   LOOP1         10 (10/7 — 8085)
11.         DCR   B             5
12.         JZ    LOOP2         10 (10/7 — 8085)
13.         DCR   A             5
14.         CPI   00H           7
15.         JNZ   DSPLAY        10 (10/7 — 8085)
```

DELAY CALCULATIONS (8085)

Delay in LOOP1 = Loop T-states $\times$ COUNT $\times$ Clock Period (330×10^{-9})
100 ms $= 31$ T $\times$ COUNT $\times 330 \times 10^{-9}$

$$\text{DELAY COUNT} = \frac{100 \times 10^{-3}}{31 \times 330 \times 10^{-9}}$$
$$= 9775_{10}$$

This delay calculation ignores the initial T-states in loading the count and the difference of T-states in the last execution of the conditional Jump instruction.

DEBUGGING QUESTIONS

1. Examine LOOP1. Is the label LOOP1 at the appropriate location? What is the effect of the present location on the program?
2. What is the appropriate place for the label LOOP1?
3. Is the delay count accurate?
4. What is the effect of instruction 8 (MOV A, D) on the count?
5. Should instruction 3 be part of LOOP2?
6. Is the byte in register B (instruction 3) accurate?
7. Calculate T-states in the outer loop using the appropriate place for the label LOOP2. (Do not include the T-states of LOOP1.)
8. Is there any need for instruction 14 (CPI)?
9. Is there any need for an additional instruction, such as number 16?
10. What is the effect of instruction 12 (JZ) on the program?
11. Calculate the total delay in LOOP2 inclusive of LOOP1 if the byte in register B = 0AH.
12. Assuming instruction 8 is necessary, make appropriate changes in instructions 1 and 13.
13. Calculate the time delay between the display of two consecutive counts.
14. Will this program display the last count, assuming the other errors are corrected?

SUMMARY

☐ Counters and time delays can be designed using software.

☐ Time delays are designed simply by loading a count in a register or a register pair and decrementing the count by setting a loop until the count reaches zero. Time delay is determined by the number of T-states in a delay loop, the clock frequency, and the number of times the loop is repeated.

☐ Counters are designed using techniques similar to those used for time delays. A counter design generally includes a delay loop.

☐ In the 8085/8080A microprocessor, 8-bit registers can be combined as register pairs (B and C, D and E, and H and L) to manipulate 16-bit data. Furthermore, the contents of each register can be examined separately even if registers are being used as register pairs.

☐ Sixteen-bit instructions such as DCX and INX do not affect flags; therefore, some other technique must be used to set flags.

ASSIGNMENTS

1. Calculate the time delay in the Illustrative Program for a hexadecimal counter (Section 7.2), assuming a count of CFH in register C.

2. Calculate the delay in the following loop, assuming the system clock period is 0.33 μs:

Label	Mnemonics		8085 T-states
	LXI	B, 12FFH	10
DELAY:	DCX	B	6
	XTHL		16
	XTHL		16
	NOP		4
	NOP		4
	MOV	A, C	4
	ORA	B	4
	JNZ	DELAY	10/7

3. Recalculate the delay in the Illustrative Program for a zero-to-nine counter (Section 7.3) using the clock frequency of your system, and execute the program.

4. Rewrite the Illustrative Program for the pulse timing of flashing lights (Section 7.4) using a register pair and the loop within the loop technique (Section 7.5) to design the delay.

Use clock frequency of your system in the following assignments.

5. Write a program to count from 0 to 20H with a delay of 100 ms between each count. After the count 20H, the counter should reset itself and repeat the sequence. Use register pair DE as a delay register. Draw a flowchart and show your calculations to set up the 100 ms delay.

6. Design an up-down counter to count form 0 to 9 and 9 to 0 continuously with a 1.5-second delay between each count, and display the count at one of the output ports. Draw a flowchart and show the delay calculations.

7. Write a program to turn a light on and off every 5 seconds. Use data bit D_7 to operate the light.

8. Write a program to generate a square wave with period of 400 μs. Use bit D_0 to output the square wave.

9. Write a program to generate a rectangular wave with 200 μs on-period and 400 μs off-period.

---

*The illustrative programs shown in this chapter and these assignments can be verified on a single-board microcomputer with a display output port. Appendix B shows how to run these programs on the SDK-85 system without a separate output port as well as how to connect an additional output port.

Stack and Subroutines

The **stack** is a group of memory locations in the R/W memory that is used for temporary storage of binary information during the execution of a program. The starting memory location of the stack is defined in the main program, and space is reserved, usually at the high end of the memory map. The method of information storage resembles a stack of books. The contents of each memory location are, in a sense, "stacked" — one memory location above another — and information is retrieved starting from the top. Hence, this particular group of memory locations is called the *stack*. Chapter 8 introduces the stack instructions in the 8085/8080A set.

The latter part of this chapter deals with the subroutine technique, which is frequently used in programs. A **subroutine** is a group of instructions that performs a subtask (e.g., time delay or arithmetic operation) of repeated occurrence. The subroutine is written as a separate unit, apart from the main program, and the microprocessor transfers the program execution from the main program to the subroutine whenever it is called to perform the task. After the completion of the subroutine task, the microprocessor returns to the main program. The subroutine technique eliminates the need to write a subtask repeatedly; thus, it uses memory more efficiently. Before implementing the subroutine technique, the stack must be defined; the stack is used to

store the memory address of the instruction in the main program that follows the subroutine call.

The stack and the subroutine offer a great deal of flexibility in writing programs. A large software project is usually divided into subtasks called **modules**. These modules are developed independently as subroutines by different programmers. Each programmer can use all the microprocessor registers to write a subroutine without affecting the other parts of the program. At the beginning of the subroutine module, the register contents of the main program are stored on the stack, and these register contents are retrieved before returning to the main program.

This chapter includes two illustrative programs: The first illustrates the use of the stack-related instructions to examine and manipulate the flags; and the second illustrates the subroutine technique in a traffic-signal controller.

OBJECTIVES

☐ Define the stack, the stack pointer (register), and the program counter, and describe their uses.

☐ Explain how information is stored and retrieved from the stack using the instructions PUSH and POP and the stack pointer register.

☐ Demonstrate how the contents of the flag register can be displayed and how a given flag can be set or reset.

☐ Define a subroutine and explain its uses.

☐ Explain the sequence of a program when a subroutine is called and executed.

☐ Explain how information is exchanged between the program counter and the stack, and identify the contents of the stack pointer register when a subroutine is called.

☐ List and explain conditional Call and Return instructions.

☐ Illustrate the concepts in the following subroutines: nesting, multiple ending, and common ending.

☐ Compare similarities and differences between PUSH/POP and CALL/RET instructions.

8.1   STACK

The **stack** in an 8085/8080A microcomputer system can be described as a set of memory locations in the R/W memory, specified by a programmer in a main program. These memory locations are used to store binary information (bytes) temporarily during the execution of a program.

The beginning of the stack is defined in the program by using the instruction LXI SP, which loads a 16-bit memory address in the stack pointer register of the microprocessor. Once the stack location is defined, storing of data bytes begins at the memory address that is one less than the address in the stack pointer register. For example, if the stack pointer register is loaded with the memory address 2099H (LXI SP, 2099H), the storing of data bytes begins at 2098H and continues in reversed numerical order (decreasing memory addresses such as 2098H, 2097H, etc.). Therefore, as a general practice, the stack is initialized at the highest available memory location to prevent the program from being destroyed by the stack information. The size of the stack is limited only by the available memory.

Data bytes in the register pairs of the microprocessor can be stored on the stack (two at a time) in reverse order (decreasing memory address) by using the instruction PUSH. Data bytes can be transferred from the stack to respective registers by using the instruction POP. The stack pointer register tracks the storage and retrieval of the information. Since two data bytes are being stored at a time, the 16-bit memory address in the stack pointer register is decremented by two; when data bytes are retrieved, the address is incremented by two. An address in the stack pointer register indicates that the next two memory locations (in descending numerical order) can be used for storage.

The stack is shared by the programmer and the microprocessor. The programmer can store the contents of a register pair by using PUSH and POP instructions. Similarly, the microprocessor automatically stores the contents of the program counter when a subroutine is called (to be discussed in the next section). The instructions necessary for using the stack are explained below.

INSTRUCTIONS

Opcode	Operand	
LXI	SP, 16-bit	Load the stack pointer register with a 16-bit address. The LXI instructions were discussed in Chapter 6
PUSH	Rp	
PUSH	B	This is a 1-byte instruction
PUSH	D	It copies the contents of the specified register pair on the
PUSH	H	stack as described below
PUSH	PSW	The stack pointer register is decremented, and the contents of the high-order register (e.g., register B) are copied in the location shown by the stack pointer register
		The stack pointer register is again decremented, and the contents of the low-order register (e.g., register C) are copied in that location
		The operands B, D, and H represent register pairs BC, DE, and HL, respectively
		The operand PSW represents Program Status Word, meaning the contents of the accumulator and the flags
POP	Rp	This is a 1-byte instruction
POP	B	It copies the contents of the top two memory locations of
POP	D	the stack into the specified register pair
POP	H	First, the contents of the memory location indicated by the
POP	PSW	stack pointer register are copied into the low-order register (e.g., register L), and then the stack pointer register is incremented by 1
		The contents of the next memory location are copied into the high-order register (e.g., register H), and the stack pointer register is again incremented by 1

All three of these instructions belong to the data transfer (copy) group; thus, the contents of the source are not modified, and no flags are affected.

In the following set of instructions (illustrated in Figure 8.1), the stack pointer is initialized, and the contents of register pair HL are stored on the stack by using the PUSH instruction. Register pair HL is used for the delay counter (actual instructions are not shown); and at the end of the delay counter, the contents of HL are retrieved by using the instruction POP. Assuming the available user memory ranges from 2000H to 20FFH, illustrate the contents of various registers when PUSH and POP instructions are executed.

Example
8.1

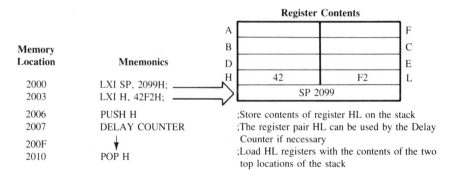

FIGURE 8.1
Instructions and Register Contents in Example 8.1

Solution

In this example, the first instruction—LXI SP, 2099H—loads the stack pointer register with the address 2099H (Figure 8.1). This instruction indicates to the microprocessor that memory space is reserved in the R/W memory as the stack, and that the locations beginning at 2098H and moving upward can be used for temporary storage. This instruction also suggests that the stack can be initialized anywhere in the memory; however, the stack location should not interfere with a program. The next instruction—LXI H—loads data in the HL register pair, as shown in Figure 8.1.

When instruction PUSH H is executed, the following sequence of data transfer takes place. After the execution, the contents of the stack and the register are as shown in Figure 8.2.

1. The stack pointer register is decremented by one to 2098H, and the contents of the H register are transferred to memory location 2098H.
2. The stack pointer register is again decremented by one to 2097H, and the contents of the L register are transferred to memory location 2097H.
3. The contents of the register pair HL are not destroyed; however, HL is made available for the delay counter.

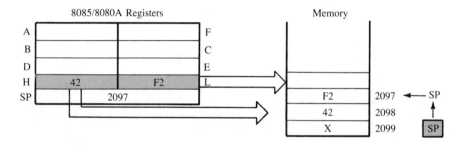

FIGURE 8.2
Contents on the Stack and in the Registers After the PUSH Instruction

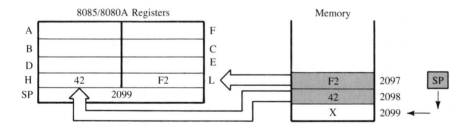

FIGURE 8.3
Contents on the Stack and in the Registers After the POP Instruction

After the delay counter, the instruction POP H restores the original contents of the register pair HL, as follows. Figure 8.3 illustrates the contents of the stack and the registers following the POP instruction.

1. The contents of the top of the stack location shown by the stack pointer are transferred to the L register, and the stack pointer register is incremented by one to 2098H.
2. The contents of the top of the stack (now it is 2098H) are transferred to the H register, and the stack pointer is incremented by one.
3. The contents of memory locations 2097H and 2098H are not destroyed until some other data bytes are stored in these locations.

The available user memory ranges from 2000H to 23FFH. A program of data transfer and arithmetic operations is stored in memory locations from 2000H to 2050H, and the stack pointer is initialized at location 2400H. Two sets of data are stored, starting at locations 2150H and 2280H. Registers HL and BC are used as memory pointers to the data locations. A segment of the program is shown below in Figure 8.4.

Example
8.2

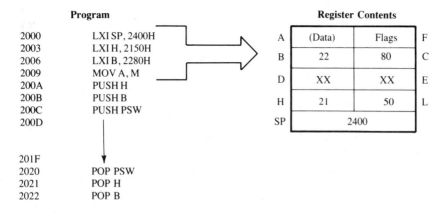

FIGURE 8.4
Instructions and Register Contents in Example 8.2

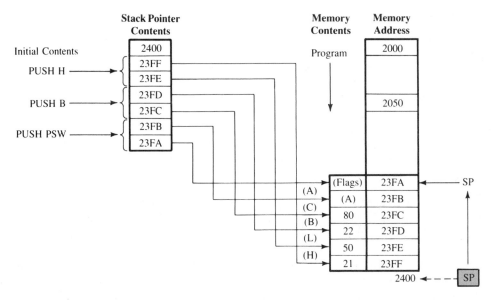

FIGURE 8.5
Stack Contents After the Execution of PUSH Instructions

1. Explain how the stack pointer can be initialized at one memory location beyond the available user memory.
2. Illustrate the contents of the stack memory and registers when PUSH and POP instructions are executed, and explain how memory pointers are exchanged.
3. Explain the various contents of the user memory.

Solution

1. The program initializes the stack pointer register at location 2400H, one location beyond the user memory (Figure 8.4). This procedure is valid because the initialized location is never used for storing information. The instruction PUSH first decrements the stack pointer register, and then stores a data byte.
2. Figure 8.5 shows the contents of the stack pointer register and the contents of the stack locations after the three PUSH instructions are executed. After the execution of the PUSH (H, B, and PSW) instructions, the stack pointer moves upward (decreasing memory locations) as the information is stored. Thus the stack can grow upward in the user memory, even to the extent of destroying the program.

   Figure 8.6 shows how the contents of various register pairs are retrieved. To restore the original contents in the respective registers, follow the sequence Last-In–First-Out (LIFO). In the example, the register contents were pushed on the stack in the order of HL, BC, and PSW. The contents should have been restored in the order of PSW, BC, and HL. However, the order is altered in this example to demonstrate how register contents are exchanged.

   The instruction POP PSW transfers the contents of the two top locations to the flag register and the accumulator, respectively, and increments the stack pointer by two

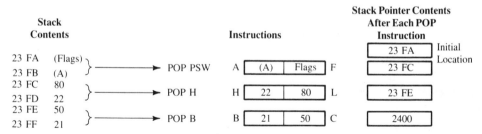

FIGURE 8.6
Register Contents After the Execution of POP Instructions

to 23FCH. The next instruction, POP H, takes the contents of the top two locations (23FC and 23FD), transfers them to registers L and H, respectively, while incrementing the stack pointer by two, to 23FEH. The instruction POP B transfers the contents of the next two locations to registers C and B, incrementing the stack pointer to 2400H. By reversing the positions of two instructions, POP H and POP B, the contents of the BC pair are exchanged with those of the HL pair. It is important to remember that the instruction POP H does not restore the original contents of the HL pair; instead it transfers the contents of the top two locations shown by the stack pointer to the HL pair.

3. Figure 8.7 shows the sketch of the memory map. The R/W memory includes three types of information. The user program is stored from 2000H to 2050H. The data are stored, starting at locations 2150H and 2280H. The last section of the user memory is initialized as the stack where register contents are stored as necessary, using the PUSH instructions. In this example, the memory locations from 23FFH to 23FAH are used as the stack, which can be extended up to the locations of the second data set.

FIGURE 8.7
R/W Memory Contents

8.11   Review of Important Concepts

The following points can be summarized from the preceding examples:

1. Memory locations in R/W memory can be employed as temporary storage for information by initializing (loading) a 16-bit address in the stack pointer register.
2. Read/Write memory generally is used for three different purposes:
   a. to write programs or some temporary instructions;
   b. to store data;
   c. to store information temporarily in defined memory locations called the stack during the execution of the program.
3. The stack space grows upward in the numerically decreasing order of memory addresses.
4. The stack can be initialized anywhere in the user memory map. However, as a general practice, the stack is initialized at the highest user memory location so that it will be less likely to interfere with a program.
5. A programmer can employ the stack to store contents of register pairs by using the instruction PUSH and can restore the contents of register pairs by using the instruction POP. The address in the stack pointer register always points to the top of the stack, and the address is decremented or incremented as information is stored or retrieved.
6. The storage and retrieval of data bytes on the stacks should follow the LIFO (Last-In–First-Out) sequence. Information in stack locations is not destroyed until new information is stored in those locations.

8.12   Illustrative Program: Resetting
and Displaying Flags

PROBLEM STATEMENT

Write a program to perform the following functions:

1. Clear all the flags.
2. Load 00H in the accumulator, and demonstrate that the Zero flag is not affected by the data transfer instruction.
3. Logically OR the accumulator with itself to set the Zero flag, and display the flag at PORT1 or store all the flags on the stack.

PROBLEM ANALYSIS

The problem concerns examining the Zero flag after instructions have been executed. There is no direct way of observing the flags; however, they can be stored on the stack by using the instruction PUSH PSW. The contents of the flag register can be retrieved in any one of the registers by using the instruction POP, and the flags can be displayed at an output port. In this example, the result to be displayed is different from the result to be stored on the stack memory. To display only the Zero flag, all other flags should be masked; however, the masking is not necessary in order to store all the flags.

PROGRAM

Memory Address	Machine Code	Instructions	Comments
XX00	31	LXI SP, XX99H	;Initialize the stack
01	99		
02	XX		
03	F5	PUSH PSW	;Save (A) and flags on the stack
04	E1	POP H	;Retrieve flags in L
05	2E	MVI L, 00H	;Clear flag contents in L
06	00		
07	E5	PUSH H	;Place (L) on stack
08	F1	POP PSW	;Clear flags
09	3E	MVI A, 00H	
0A	00		
0B	F5	PUSH PSW	;Save flags on stack
0C	E1	POP H	;Retrieve flags in L
0D	7D	MOV A,L	
0E	D3	OUT PORT0	;Display flags
0F	PORT0		
10	B7	ORA A	;Set flags and reset CY, AC
11	F5	PUSH PSW	;Save flags on stack
12	E1	POP H	;Retrieve flags in L
13	7D	MOV A,L	
14	E6	ANI 40H	;Mask all flags except Z
15	40		
16	D3	OUT PORT1	
17	PORT1		
18	76	HLT	;End of program

Storing in Memory: Alternative to Output Display

XX0C	B7	ORA A	;Set flags and reset CY and AC
0D	F5	PUSH PSW	;Save flags on stack
0E	76	HLT	;End of program

Program Description The stack pointer register is initialized at XX99H, and the instruction PUSH PSW stores (A) at XX98H and the flags (F) at XX97H. The next instruction, POP H, places (copies) the (F) into register L and (A) into register H. The instruction MVI L clears (L), and (L) is placed back on the stack, which is subsequently placed into the flag register to clear all the flags.

To verify the flags after the execution of the MVI A instruction, the PUSH and POP instructions are used in the same way as these instructions were used to clear the flags, and the flags are displayed at PORT0. Similarly, the Zero flag is displayed at PORT1 after the instruction ORA.

Program Output   Data transfer (copy) instructions do not affect the flags; therefore, no flags should be set after the instruction MVI A, even if (A) is equal to zero. PORT0 should display 00H. However, the instruction ORA will set the Zero and the Parity flags to reflect the data conditions in the accumulator, and it also resets the CY and AC flags. In the flag register, bit D_6 represents the Z flag, and the ANI instruction masks all flags except the Z flag. PORT1 should display 40H as shown below.

D_7	D_6	D_5	D_4	D_3	D_2	D_1	D_0	
0	1	0	0	0	1	0	0	= 40H
S	Z		AC		P		CY	

Storing Output in Memory   If output ports are not available, the results can be stored in the stack memory. The machine code (F5) at memory location XX0BH saves the flags affected by the instruction MVI A,00H. Then the instructions can be modified starting from memory location XX0CH. The alternative set of instructions is shown above; it sets the flags (using ORA instruction), and saves them on the stack without masking. The result (44H) includes the parity flag. The contents of the stack locations should be as shown in Figure 8.8.

8.2   SUBROUTINE

A **subroutine** is a group of instructions written separately from the main program to perform a function that occurs repeatedly in the main program. For example, if a time delay is required between three successive events, three delays can be written in the main program. To avoid repetition of the same delay instructions, the subroutine technique is used. Delay instructions are written once, separately from the main program, and are called by the main program when needed.

The 8085/8080A microprocessor has two instructions to implement subroutines: CALL (call a subroutine), and RET (return to main program from a subroutine). The CALL instruction is used in the main program to call a subroutine, and the RET instruction is used at the end of the subroutine to return to the main program. When a subroutine is called, the contents of the program counter, which is the address of the instruction

Instructions	Stack Memory	Contents	
	XX99 ◄───		Stack Pointer Initialization
XX0B PUSH PSW:	XX98	(A) = 00H	
	XX97	(F) = 00H	
XX0D PUSH PSW:	XX96	(A) = 00H	
	XX95	(F) = 44H	

FIGURE 8.8
Output Stored in Stack Memory

following the CALL instruction, is stored on the stack and the program execution is transferred to the subroutine address. When the RET instruction is executed at the end of the subroutine, the memory address stored on the stack is retrieved, and the sequence of execution is resumed in the main program. This sequence of events is illustrated in Example 8.3.

INSTRUCTIONS

Opcode	**Operand**	
CALL	16-Bit Memory Address of a Subroutine	Call Subroutine Unconditionally This is a 3-byte instruction that transfers the program sequence to a subroutine address. Saves the contents of the program counter (the address of the next instruction) on the stack. Decrements the stack pointer register by two. Jumps unconditionally to the memory location specified by the second and third bytes. The second byte specifies a line number and the third byte specifies a page number. This instruction is accompanied by a return instruction in the subroutine.
RET		Return from Subroutine Unconditionally This is a 1-byte instruction. Inserts the two bytes from the top of the stack into the program counter and increments the stack pointer register by two. Unconditionally returns from a subroutine.

The conditional Call and Return instructions will be described later in the chapter.

Illustrate the exchange of information between the stack and the program counter for the following program if the available user memory ranges from 2000H to 23FFH.

Example 8.3

Memory Address

2000 ↓ 2040 2041 2042 2043 ↓	LXI SP, 2400H ↓ CALL 2070H NEXT INSTRUCTION ↓	;Initialize the stack pointer at 2400H ;Call the subroutine located at 2070H. This is a 3-byte instruction ;The address of the next instruction following the CALL instruction

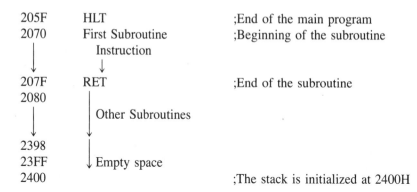

205F	HLT	;End of the main program
2070	First Subroutine	;Beginning of the subroutine
	Instruction	
207F	RET	;End of the subroutine
2080		
	Other Subroutines	
2398		
23FF	Empty space	
2400		;The stack is initialized at 2400H

Solution

After reviewing the above program note the following points:

1. The available user memory is from 2000H to 23FFH (1024 or 1K bytes); however, the stack pointer register is initialized at 2400H, one location beyond the user memory. This allows maximum use of the memory because the actual stack begins at 23FFH. The stack can expand up to the location 2398H without overlapping with the program.
2. The main program is stored at memory locations from 2000H to 205FH.
3. The CALL instruction is located at 2040H to 2042H (3-byte instruction). The next instruction is at 2043H.
4. The subroutine begins at the address 2070H and ends at 207FH.

PROGRAM EXECUTION

The sequence of the program execution and the events in the execution of the CALL and subroutine are shown in Figures 8.9 and 8.10.

CALL EXECUTION

Memory Address	Machine Code	Mnemonics	Comments
2040	CD	CALL 2070H	;Call subroutine located at the memory
2041	70		location 2070H
2042	20		
2043	NEXT	INSTRUCTION	

The sequence of events in the execution of the CALL instruction by the 8085 is shown in Figure 8.10. The instruction requires five machine cycles and eighteen T-states (seventeen T-states for the 8080A). The sequence of events in each machine cycle is as follows.

1. M_1—*Opcode Fetch:* In this machine cycle, the contents of the program counter (2040H) are placed on the address bus, and the instruction code CD is fetched using the data bus. At the same time, the program counter is upgraded to the next memory

FIGURE 8.9
Subroutine Call and
Program Transfer

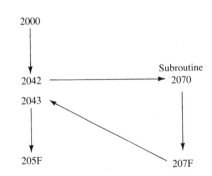

The program execution begins at 2000H, continues until
the end of CALL 2042H, and transfers to the subroutine
at 2070H. At the end of the subroutine, after executing
the RET instruction, it comes back to the main program
at 2043H and continues.

Instruction: CALL 2070H

Memory Address	Code (H)
2040	CD
2041	70
2042	20

Machine Cycles	Stack Pointer (SP) 2400	Address Bus (AB)	Program Counter (PCH) (PCL)	Data Bus (DB)	Internal Registers (W) (Z)
M₁ Opcode Fetch	23FF (SP-1)	2040	20 41	CD Opcode	—
M₂ Memory Read		2041	20 42	70 Operand	70
M₃ Memory Read	23FF	2042	20 43	20 Operand	20
M₄ Memory Write	23FE (SP-2)	23FF	20 43	20 (PCH)	
M₅ Memory Write	23FE	23FE	20 43	43 (PCL)	(20) (70)
M₁ Opcode Fetch of Next Instruction		20 70 → 2071 (W)(Z)			(2070) (W)(Z)

FIGURE 8.10
Data Transfer During the Execution of the CALL Instruction

address, 2041H. After the instruction is decoded and executed, the stack pointer
register is decremented by one to 23FFH.

2. *M₂ and M₃—Memory Read:* These are two Memory Read cycles during which the
16-bit address (2070H) of the CALL instruction is fetched. The low-order address 70H
is fetched first and placed in the internal register Z. The high-order address 20H is

fetched next, and placed in register W. During M_3, the program counter is upgraded to 2043H, pointing to the next instruction.

3. *M_4 and M_5 — Storing of Program Counter:* At the beginning of the M_4 cycle, the normal operation of placing the contents of the program counter on the address bus is suspended, instead the contents of the stack pointer register 23FFH are placed on the address bus. The high-order byte of the program counter (PCH = 20H) is placed on the data bus and stored in the stack location 23FFH. At the same time, the stack pointer register is decremented to 23FEH.

During machine cycle M_5, the contents of the stack pointer 23FEH are placed on the address bus. The low-order byte of the program counter (PCL = 43H) is placed on the data bus and stored in stack location 23FEH.

4. *Next Instruction Cycle:* In the next instruction cycle, the program execution sequence is transferred to the CALL location 2070H by placing the contents of W and Z registers (2070H) on the address bus. During M_1 of the next instruction cycle, the program counter is upgraded to location 2071 (W, Z + 1).

In summary: After the CALL instruction is fetched, the 16-bit address (the operand) is read during M_2 and M_3 and stored temporarily in W/Z registers. (Examine the contents of the address bus and the data bus in Figure 8.10.) In the next two cycles, the contents of the program counter are stored on the stack. This is the address where the microprocessor will continue the execution of the program after the completion of the subroutine. Figure 8.11 shows the contents of the program counter, the stack pointer register, and the stack during the execution of the CALL instruction.

RET EXECUTION

At the end of the subroutine, when the instruction RET is executed, the program execution sequence is transferred to the memory location 2043H. (The address 2043H was stored in the top two locations of the stack (23FEH and 23FFH) during the CALL instruction. Figure 8.12 shows the sequence of events that occurs as the instruction RET is executed.

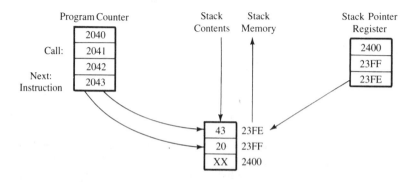

FIGURE 8.11

Contents of the Program Counter, the Stack Pointer, and the Stack During the Execution of CALL Instruction

Instruction: RET

Memory Address	Code (H)
207F	C9

Contents of Stack Memory	
23FE	43
23FF	20

Machine Cycles	Stack Pointer (23FE)	Address Bus (AB)	Program Counter	Data Bus (DB)	Internal Registers (W)(Z)
M₁ Opcode Fetch	23FE	207F	2080	C9 Opcode	
M₂ Memory Read	23FF	23FE		43 (Stack) → 43	43
M₃ Memory Read	2400	23FF		20 (Stack−1) → 20	20
M₁ Opcode Fetch of Next Instruction		2043 (W)(Z) ◀	2044		2043 (W)(Z)

FIGURE 8.12
Data Transfer During the Execution of the RET Instruction

M_1 is a normal Opcode Fetch cycle. However, during M_2 the contents of the stack pointer register are placed on the address bus, rather than those of the program counter. Data byte 43H from the top of the stack is fetched and stored in the Z register, and the stack pointer register is upgraded to the next location, 23FFH. During M_2, the next byte — 20H — is copied from the stack and stored in register W, and the stack pointer register is again upgraded to the next location, 2400H.

The program sequence is transferred to location 2043H by placing the contents of the W/Z registers on the address bus at the beginning of the next instruction cycle.

8.21 Illustrative Program: Traffic Signal Controller

PROBLEM STATEMENT

Write a program to provide the given on/off time to three traffic lights (Green, Yellow, and Red) and two pedestrian signs (WALK and DON'T WALK). The signal lights and signs are turned on/off by the data bits of an output port as shown below:

Lights	Data Bits	On Time
1. Green	D_0	15 seconds
2. Yellow	D_2	5 seconds
3. Red	D_4	20 seconds
4. WALK	D_6	15 seconds
5. DON'T WALK	D_7	25 seconds

The traffic and pedestrian flow are in the same direction; the pedestrian should cross the road when the Green light is on.

PROBLEM ANALYSIS

The problem is primarily concerned with providing various time delays for a complete sequence of 40 seconds. The on/off times for the traffic signals and pedestrian signs are as follows:

Time Sequence in Seconds	DON'T WALK D_7	WALK D_6	D_5	Red D_4	D_3	Yellow D_2	D_1	Green D_0		Hex Code
0										
(15) ↓	0	1	0	0	0	0	0	1	=	41H
15										
(5) ↓	1	0	0	0	0	1	0	0	=	84H
20										
(20) ↓	1	0	0	1	0	0	0	0	=	90H
40										

The Green light and the WALK sign can be turned on by sending data byte 41H to the output port. The 15-second delay can be provided by using a 1-second subroutine and a counter with a count of 15_{10}. Similarly, the next two bytes, 84H and 90H, will turn on/off the appropriate lights/signs as shown in the flowchart (Figure 8.13). The necessary time delays are provided by changing the values of the count in the counter.

PROGRAM

Memory Address	Code	Mnemonics		Comments
XX00	31		LXI SP, XX99	;Initialize stack pointer at location XX99H
01	99			
02	XX			;High-order address (page) of user memory
03	3E	START:	MVI A, 41H	;Load accumulator with the bit pattern for
04	41			Green light and WALK sign
05	D3		OUT PORT#	;Turn on Green light and WALK sign
06	PORT#			
07	06		MVI B, 0FH	;Use B as a counter to count 15 seconds. B is
08	0F			decremented in the subroutine
09	CD		CALL DELAY	;Call delay subroutine located at XX50H
0A	50			
0B	XX			;High-order address (page) of user memory
0C	3E		MVI A, 84H	;Load accumulator with the bit pattern for
0D	84			Yellow light and DON'T WALK

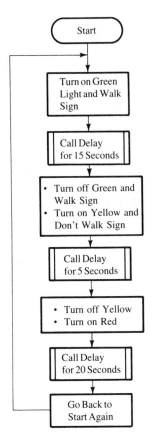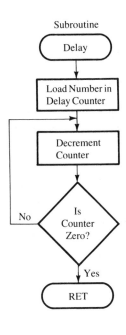

FIGURE 8.13
Flowchart for Traffic Signal Controller

0E	D3	OUT PORT#	;Turn on Yellow light and DON'T WALK and
0F	PORT#		turn off Green light and WALK
10	06	MVI B, 05	;Set up 5-second delay counter
11	05		
12	CD	CALL DELAY	
13	50		
14	XX		;High-order address of user memory
15	3E	MVI A, 90H	;Load accumulator with the bit pattern for Red
16	90		light and DON'T WALK
17	D3	OUT PORT#	;Turn on Red light, keep DON'T WALK on,
18	PORT#		and turn off Yellow light
19	06	MVI B, 14H	;Set up the counter for 20-second delay
1A	14		

1B	CD		CALL DELAY	
1C	50			
1D	XX			
1E	C3		JMP START	;Go back to location START to repeat the
1F	03			sequence
20	XX			

DELAY: This is a 1-second delay subroutine and provides delay according to the parameter specified in register B

;*Input:* Number of seconds is specified in register B

;*Output:* None

;*Registers Modified:* Register B

XX50	D5	DELAY:	PUSH D	;Save contents of DE and accumulator
51	F5		PUSH PSW	
52	11	SECOND:	LXI D, Count	;Load register pair DE with data byte for
53	LO			1-second delay
54	HI			
55	1B	Loop:	DCX D	;Decrement register pair DE
56	7A		MOV A, D	
57	B3		ORA E	;OR (D) and (E) to set Zero flag
58	C2		JNZ LOOP	;Jump to Loop if delay count is not equal to 0
59	55			
5A	XX			
5B	05		DCR B	;End of 1 second delay; decrement the counter
5C	C2		JNZ SECOND	;Is this the end of time needed? If not, go
5D	52			back to repeat 1-second delay
5E	XX			;High-order memory address of user memory
5F	F1		POP PSW	;Retrieve contents of saved registers
60	D1		POP D	
61	C9		RET	;Return to main program

PROGRAM DESCRIPTION

The stack pointer register is initialized at XX99H so that return addresses can be stored on the stack whenever a CALL instruction is used. As shown in the flowchart this program loads the appropriate bit pattern in the accumulator, sends it to the output port, and calls the delay routine. Register B is loaded in the main program and used in the subroutine to provide appropriate timing.

The DELAY subroutine is similar to the delays discussed in Chapter 7 except it requires the instruction RET at the end of the routine.

This example illustrates the type of subroutine that is called many times from various locations in the main program, as illustrated in Figure 8.14.

In this program, the subroutine is called from the locations XX09, 0A, and 0BH. The return address, XX0C, is stored on the stack, and the stack pointer is decremented by two to location XX97H. At the end of the subroutine, the contents of the top two locations

FIGURE 8.14
Multiple-Calling for
a Subroutine

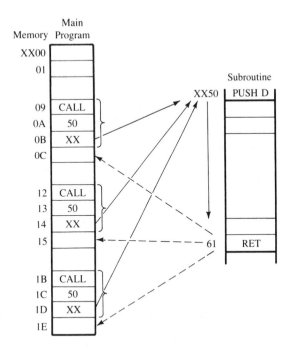

of the stack (XX0C) are retrieved, the stack pointer register is incremented by two to the original location (XX99H), and the main program is resumed. This sequence is repeated two more times in the main program, as shown in Figure 8.14.

8.22   Subroutine Documentation and Parameter Passing

In a large program, subroutines are scattered all over the memory map, and are called from many locations. Various information is passed between a calling program and a subroutine, a procedure called **parameter passing**. Therefore, it is important to document a subroutine clearly and carefully. The documentation should include at least

1. Functions of the subroutine
2. Input/Output parameters
3. Registers used or modified
4. List of other subroutines called by this subroutine

The delay subroutine in the traffic-signal controller program shows one example of subroutine documentation.

FUNCTIONS OF THE SUBROUTINE

It is important to state clearly and precisely what the subroutine does. A user should understand the function without going through the instructions.

INPUT/OUTPUT PARAMETERS

In the delay subroutine illustrated in Section 8.21, the information concerning the number of seconds is passed from the main program to the subroutine by loading an appropriate count in register B. In this example, a register is used to pass the parameter. The parameters passed to a subroutine are listed as **inputs**, and parameters returned to calling programs are listed as **outputs**.

When many parameters must be passed, R/W memory locations are used to store the parameters, and HL registers are used to point to parameter locations. Similarly, the stack is also used to store and pass parameters.

REGISTERS USED OR MODIFIED

Registers used in a subroutine also may be used by the calling program. Therefore, it is necessary to save the register contents of the calling program on the stack at the beginning of the subroutine and to retrieve the contents before returning from the subroutine.

In the delay subroutine, the contents of registers DE, the accumulator, and the flag register are pushed on the stack because these registers are used in the subroutine. The contents are restored at the end of the routine using the LIFO method. However, the contents of registers that pass parameters should not be saved on the stack because this could cause irrelevant information to be retrieved and passed on to the calling program.

LIST OF SUBROUTINES CALLED

If a subroutine is calling other subroutines, the user should be provided with a list. The user can check what parameters need to be passed to various subroutines and what registers are modified in the process.

8.3   CONDITIONAL CALL AND RETURN INSTRUCTIONS

In addition to the unconditional CALL and RET instructions, the 8085/8080A instruction set includes eight conditional Call instructions and eight conditional Return instructions. The conditions are tested by checking the respective flags. In case of a conditional Call instruction, the program is transferred to the subroutine if the condition is met; otherwise, the main program is continued. In case of a conditional Return instruction, the sequence returns to the main program if the condition is met; otherwise the sequence in the subroutine is continued. If the Call instruction in the main program is conditional, the Return instruction in the subroutine can be conditional or unconditional. The conditional Call and Return instructions are listed for reference.

CONDITIONAL CALL

CC	Call subroutine if Carry flag is set (CY = 1)
CNC	Call subroutine if Carry flag is reset (CY = 0)
CZ	Call subroutine if Zero flag is set (Z = 1)
CNZ	Call subroutine if Zero flag is reset (Z = 0)

CM	Call subroutine if Sign flag is set (S = 1, negative number)
CP	Call subroutine if Sign flag is reset (S = 0, positive number)
CPE	Call subroutine if Parity flag is set (P = 1, even parity)
CPO	Call subroutine if Parity flag is reset (P = 0, odd parity)

CONDITIONAL RETURN

RC	Return if Carry flag is set (CY = 1)
RNC	Return if Carry flag is reset (CY = 0)
RZ	Return if Zero flag is set (Z = 1)
RNZ	Return if Zero flag is reset (Z = 0)
RM	Return if Sign flag is set (S = 1, negative number)
RP	Return if Sign flag is reset (S = 0, positive number)
RPE	Return if Parity flag is set (P = 1, even parity)
RPO	Return if Parity flag is reset (P = 0, odd parity)

ADVANCED SUBROUTINE CONCEPTS 8.4

In the last section, one type of subroutine (multiple-calling of a subroutine by a main program) was illustrated. However, other types of subroutine techniques, such as nesting, and multiple ending, are briefly illustrated below.

NESTING

The programming technique of a subroutine calling another subroutine is called **nesting**. This process is limited only by the number of available stack locations. When a subroutine calls another subroutine, all return addresses are stored on the stack. Nesting is illustrated in Figure 8.15.

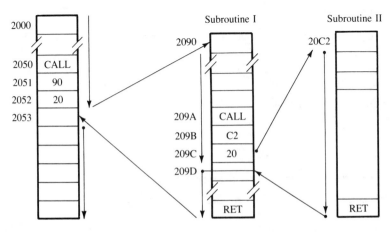

FIGURE 8.15
Nesting of Subroutines

FIGURE 8.16
Multiple Ending Subroutine

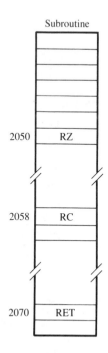

The main program in Figure 8.15 calls the subroutine from location 2050H. The address of the next instruction, 2053H, is placed on the stack, and the program is transferred to the subroutine at 2090H. Subroutine I calls Subroutine II from location 209AH. The address 209DH is placed on the stack, and the program is transferred to Subroutine II. The sequence of execution returns to the main program, as shown in Figure 8.15.

MULTIPLE ENDING SUBROUTINES

Figure 8.16 illustrates three possible endings to one CALL instruction. The subroutine has two conditional returns (RZ—Return on Zero, and RC—Return on Carry) and one unconditional return (RET). If the Zero flag (Z) is set, the subroutine returns from location 2050H. If the Carry flag (CY) is set, it returns from location 2058H. If neither the Z nor the CY flag is set, it returns from location 2070H. This technique is illustrated in Chapter 9, Section 9.42.

SUMMARY

To implement a subroutine, the following steps are necessary:

1. The stack pointer register must be initialized, preferably at the highest memory location of the R/W memory.

2. The CALL (or conditional Call) instruction should be used in the main program accompanied by the RET (or conditional Return) instruction in the subroutine.

The instructions CALL and RET are similar to the instructions PUSH and POP. The similarities and differences are as follows:

CALL and RET	**PUSH and POP**
1. When CALL is executed, the micro-processor automatically stores the 16-bit address of the instruction next to CALL on the stack.	**1.** The programmer uses the instruction PUSH to save the contents of a register pair on the stack.
2. When CALL is executed, the stack pointer register is decremented by two.	**2.** When PUSH is executed, the stack pointer register is decremented by two.
3. The instruction RET transfers the contents of the top two locations of the stack to the program counter.	**3.** The instruction POP transfers the contents of the top two locations of the stack to the specified register pair.
4. When the instruction RET is executed, the stack pointer is incremented by two.	**4.** When the instruction POP is executed, the stack pointer is incremented by two.
5. In addition to the unconditional CALL and RET instructions, there are eight conditional CALL and RETURN instructions.	**5.** There are no conditional PUSH and POP instructions.

ASSIGNMENTS

1. Check the appropriate answer in the following statements.
- **a.** A stack is
  - (1) an 8-bit register in the microprocessor.
  - (2) a 16-bit register in the microprocessor.
  - (3) a set of memory locations in R/WM reserved for storing information temporarily during the execution of a program.
  - (4) a 16-bit memory address stored in the program counter.
- **b.** A stack pointer is
  - (1) a 16-bit register in the microprocessor that indicates the beginning of the stack memory.
  - (2) a register that decodes and executes 16-bit arithmetic expressions.
  - (3) the first memory location where a subroutine address is stored.
  - (4) a register in which flag bits are stored.
- **c.** When a subroutine is called, the address of the instruction following the CALL instruction is stored in/on the

      (1) stack pointer.

      (2) accumulator.

      (3) program counter.

      (4) stack.

d. When the RET instruction at the end of a subroutine is executed

      (1) the information where the stack is initialized is transferred to the stack pointer.

      (2) the memory address of the RET instruction is transferred to the program counter.

      (3) two data bytes stored in the top two locations of the stack are transferred to the program counter.

      (4) two data bytes stored in the top two locations of the stack are transferred to the stack pointer.

e. Whenever the POP H instruction is executed

      (1) data bytes in the HL pair are stored on the stack.

      (2) two data bytes at the top of the stack are transferred to the HL register pair.

      (3) two data bytes at the top of the stack are transferred to the program counter.

      (4) two data bytes from the HL register that were previously stored on the stack are transferred back to the HL register.

2. Read the following program and answer the questions given below:

Line No.	Mnemonics
1	LXI SP, 0400H
2	LXI B, 2055H
3	LXI H, 22FFH
4	LXI D, 2090H
5	PUSH H
6	PUSH B
7	MOV A, L
↓	↓
20	POP H

    a. What is stored in the stack pointer register after the execution of line 1?

    b. What is the memory location of the stack where the first data byte will be stored?

    c. What is stored in memory location 03FEH when line 5 (PUSH H) is executed?

    d. After the execution of line 6 (PUSH B), what is the address in the stack pointer register, and what is stored in stack memory location 03FDH?

    e. Specify the contents of register pair HL after the execution of line 20 (POP H).

3. The following program has a delay subroutine located at location 2060H. Read the program and answer the questions given at the end of the program.

Memory Locations	Mnemonics	
2000	LXI SP, 20CDH	;Main Program
2003	LXI H, 0008H	
2006	MVI B, 0FH	
2008	CALL 2060H	
200B	OUT 01H	
↓	DCR B	
	↓	
	CONTD.	
2060	PUSH H	:Delay Subroutine
2061	PUSH B	
	MVI B, 05H	
	LXI H, COUNT	
	↓	
↓	POP B	
	POP H	
	RET	

a. When the execution of the CALL instruction located at 2008H–200AH is completed, list the contents stored at 20CCH and 20CBH, the contents of the program counter, and the contents of the stack pointer register.

b. List the stack locations and their contents after the execution of the instructions PUSH H and PUSH B in the subroutine.

c. List the contents of the stack pointer register after the execution of the instruction PUSH B located at 2061H.

d. List the contents of the stack pointer register after the execution of the instruction RET in the subroutine.

4. Write a program to add the two Hex numbers 7A and 46 and to store the sum at memory location XX98H and the flag status at location XX97H.

5. In assignment 4, display the sum and the flag status at two different output ports.

6. Write a program to meet the following specifications:

a. Initialize the stack pointer register at XX99H.

b. Clear the memory locations starting from XX90H to XX9FH.

c. Load register pairs B, D, and H with data 0237H, 1242H, and 4087H, respectively.

d. Push the contents of the register pairs B, D, and H on the stack.

   e. Execute the program and verify the memory locations from XX90H to
      XX9FH.
7. Write a program to clear the initial flags and to load data byte FFH into the accumulator and increment the byte by using the instruction INR. Mask all the flags
   except the CY flag and display the CY flag at PORT0 (or store the results on the
   stack). Modify the program to load byte FFH in the accumulator again, add 01H,
   and display the CY flag at PORT1 (or store the results on the stack). Explain
   your answer.
8. Write a 20 ms time delay subroutine using register pair BC. Clear the Z flag without affecting any other flags in the flag register and return to the main program.
9. Write a program to control a railway crossing signal that has two alternately flashing red lights, with a 1-second on time for each light.
10. Write a program to simulate a flashing yellow light with 750 ms on time.
    Use bit D_7 to control the light. (*Hint:* To simulate flashing, the light must be
    turned off.)
11. In the DELAY subroutine of the Illustrative Program for a traffic signal controller
    (Section 8.21), add the following instructions as suggested: PUSH B at the begin-
    ning of the subroutine (memory location XX50H) and POP B at the end of the
    subroutine (just before RET). Make any necessary changes in the memory
    addresses of the other instructions in the subroutine. Explain your output results if
    the program is executed.
12. In Assignment 11, specify the output if the instruction POP B is deleted.

Code Conversion, BCD Arithmetic, and 16-Bit Data Operations

In microcomputer applications, various number systems and codes are used to input data or to display results. The ASCII (American Standard Code For Information Interchange) keyboard is a commonly used input device for disk-based microcomputer systems. Similarly, alphanumeric characters (letters and numbers) are displayed on a CRT (cathode ray tube) terminal using the ASCII code. However, inside the microprocessor data processing is usually performed in binary. In some instances, arithmetic operations are performed in BCD numbers. Therefore, data must be converted from one code to another code. The programming techniques used for code conversion fall into four general categories:

1. Conversion based on the position of a digit in a number (BCD to binary and vice versa).
2. Conversion based on hardware consideration (binary to seven-segment code using table look-up procedure).
3. Conversion based on sequential order of digits (binary to ASCII and vice versa).
4. Decimal adjustment in BCD arithmetic operations. (This is an adjustment rather than a code conversion.)

This chapter discusses these techniques with various examples written as subroutines. The subroutines are written to demonstrate industrial practices in writing software, and can be verified on single-board microcomputers. In addition, instructions related to 16-bit data operations are introduced and illustrated.

OBJECTIVES

Write programs and subroutines to

☐ Convert a packed BCD number (0–99) into its binary equivalent.

☐ Convert a binary digit (0 to F) into its ASCII Hex code and vice versa.

☐ Select an appropriate seven-segment code for a given binary number using the table look-up technique.

☐ Convert a binary digit (O to F) into its ASCII Hex code and vice versa.

☐ Decimal adjust 8-bit BCD addition and subtraction.

☐ Perform such arithmetic operations as multiplication and subtraction using 16-bit data related instructions.

☐ Demonstrate uses of instructions such as DAD, PCHL, XTHL, and XCHG.

9.1   BCD TO BINARY CONVERSION

In most microprocessor-based products, data are entered and displayed in decimal numbers. For example, in an instrumentation laboratory, readings such as voltage and current are maintained in decimal numbers, and data are entered through a decimal keyboard. The system-monitor program of the instrument converts each key into an equivalent 4-bit binary number, and stores two BCD numbers in an 8-bit register or a memory location. These numbers are called **packed BCD**. Even if data are entered in decimal digits, it is inefficient to process data in BCD numbers because, in each 4-bit combination, digits A through F go unused. Therefore, BCD numbers are generally converted into binary numbers for data processing.

The conversion of a BCD number into its binary equivalent employs the principle of *positional weighting* in a given number.

For example: $72_{10} = 7 \times 10 + 2$

The digit 7 represents 70, based on its second position from the right. Therefore, converting 72_{BCD} into its binary equivalent requires multiplying the second digit by 10, and adding the first digit.

Converting a 2-digit BCD number into its binary equivalent requires the following steps:

1. Separate an 8-bit packed BCD number into two 4-bit unpacked BCD digits: BCD_1 and BCD_2.

2. Convert each digit into its binary value according to its position.

3. Add both binary numbers to obtain the binary equivalent of the BCD number.

Example
9.1

Convert $(72)_{BCD}$ into its binary equivalent.

Solution

$$72_{10} = 0111 \quad 0010_{BCD}$$

Step 1: $0111 \quad 0010 \rightarrow 0000 \quad 0010$ Unpacked BCD_1
$\rightarrow 0000 \quad 0111$ Unpacked BCD_2

Step 2: Multiply BCD_2 by 10 (7 × 10)

Step 3: Add BCD_1 to the answer in Step 2.

The multiplication of BCD_2 by 10 can be performed by various methods. One method is multiplication with repeated addition: add 10 seven times. This technique is illustrated in the next program.

9.11 Illustrative Program: 2-Digit BCD to Binary Conversion

PROBLEM STATEMENT

A BCD number between 0 and 99 is stored in a R/W memory location called the **Input Buffer**. Write a main program and a conversion subroutine (BCDBIN) to convert the BCD number into its equivalent binary number. Store the result in a memory location defined as the **Output Buffer**.

PROGRAM

START:	LXI SP, STACK	;Initialize stack pointer	
	LXI H, INBUF	;Point HL index to the Input Buffer memory location where BCD ;number is stored	
	LXI B, OUTBUF	;Point BC index to the Output Buffer memory where binary ;number will be stored	
	MOV A, M	;Get BCD number	
	CALL BCDBIN	;Call BCD to binary conversion routine	
	STAX B	;Store binary number in the Output Buffer	
	HLT	;End of program	

BCDBIN: ;Function: This subroutine converts a BCD number into its binary equivalent
;Input: A 2-digit packed BCD number in the accumulator
;Output: A binary number in the accumulator
;No other register contents are destroyed

		;Save BC registers	Example:	Assume BCD number is 72:
PUSH B				
PUSH D		;Save DE registers	A	$0111 \quad 0010 \rightarrow 72_{10}$
MOV B,A		;Save BCD number	B	$0111 \quad 0010 \rightarrow 72_{10}$
ANI 0FH		;Mask most significant four bits	A	$0000 \quad 0010 \rightarrow 02_{10}$
MOV C,A		;Save unpacked BCD_1 in C	C	$0000 \quad 0010 \rightarrow 02_{10}$
MOV A,B		;Get BCD again	A	$0111 \quad 0010 \rightarrow 72_{10}$
ANI F0H		;Mask least significant four bits	A	$0111 \quad 0000 \rightarrow 70_{10}$
RRC		;Convert most significant four		
RRC		;bits into upacked BCD_2		
RRC				
RRC			A	$0000 \quad 0111 \rightarrow 07_{10}$
MOV D,A		;Save BCD_2 in D	D	$0000 \quad 0111 \rightarrow 07_{10}$
XRA A		;Clear accumulator		
MVI E,0AH		;Set E as multiplier of 10	E	$0000 \quad 1010 \rightarrow 0AH$

SUM: ADD E   ;Add 10 until (D) = 0   Add E as many times as (D)
         DCR D   ;Reduce BCD₂ by one
         JNZ SUM   ;Is multiplication complete?   After adding E seven times A
                        ;If not, go back and add again.   contains: 0100 0110
         ADD C   ;Add BCD₁   C   +0000 0010
         POP D   ;Retrieve previous contents   A   0100 1000 → 48H
         POP B
         RET

PROGRAM DESCRIPTION

1. In writing assembly language programs, the use of labels is a common practice. Rather than writing a specific memory location or a port number, a programmer uses such labels as INBUF (Input Buffer) and OUTBUF (Output Buffer). Using labels gives flexibility and ease of documentation.
2. The main program initializes the stack pointer and two memory indexes. It brings the BCD number into the accumulator and passes that parameter to the subroutine.
3. After returning from the subroutine, the main program stores the binary equivalent in the Output Buffer memory.
4. The subroutine saves the contents of the BC and DE registers because these registers are used in the subroutine. Even if this particular main program does not use the DE registers, the subroutine may be called by some other program in which the DE registers are being used. Therefore, it is a good practice to save the registers that are used in the subroutine, unless parameters are passed to the subroutine. The accumulator contents are not saved because that information is passed on to the subroutine.
5. The conversion from BCD to binary is illustrated in the subroutine with the example of 72_{BCD} converted to binary.

The illustrated multiplication routine is easy to understand; however, it is rather long and inefficient. Another method is to multiply BCD_2 by shifting, as illustrated in Assignments 3 and 4 at the end of this chapter.

PROGRAM EXECUTION

To execute the program on a single-board computer, complete the following steps:

1. Assign memory addresses to the instructions in the main program and in the subroutine. Both can be assigned consecutive memory addresses.
2. Define STACK: the stack location with a 16-bit address in the R/W memory (such as 2099H).
3. Define INBUF (Input Buffer) and OUTBUF (Output Buffer): two memory locations in the R/W memory (e.g., 2050H and 2060H).
4. Enter a BCD byte in the Input Buffer (e.g., 2050H).
5. Enter and execute the program.
6. Check the contents of the Output Buffer memory location (2060H) and verify your answer.

See Assignments 1–4 at the end of this chapter.

BINARY TO BCD CONVERSION   **9.2**

In most microprocessor-based products, numbers are displayed in decimal. However, if data processing inside the microprocessor is performed in binary, it is necessary to convert the binary results into their equivalent BCD numbers just before they are displayed. Results are quite often stored in R/W memory locations called the **Output Buffer**.

The conversion of binary to BCD is performed by dividing the number by the powers of ten; the division is performed by the subtraction method.

For example, assume the binary number is

$$1 \quad 1 \quad 1 \quad 1 \quad 1 \quad 1 \quad 1 \quad 1_2 \quad (\text{FFH}) \quad = \quad 255_{10}$$

To represent this number in BCD requires twelve bits or three BCD digits, labelled here as BCD_3 (MSB), BCD_2, and BCD_1 (LSB),

$$= \quad 0 \quad 0 \quad 1 \quad 0 \quad \quad 0 \quad 1 \quad 0 \quad 1 \quad \quad 0 \quad 1 \quad 0 \quad 1$$
$$\qquad BCD_3 \qquad\qquad BCD_2 \qquad\qquad BCD_1$$

The conversion can be performed as follows:

Step 1:	If the number is less than 100, go to Step 2; otherwise, divide by 100 or subtract 100 repeatedly until the remainder is less than 100. The quotient is the most significant BCD digit BCD_3.	**Example** 255 -100 -100	$=$ $=$	155 55 BCD_3	**Quotient** 1 1 $= \quad 2$
Step 2:	If the number is less than 10, go to Step 3; otherwise divide by 10 repeatedly until the remainder is less than 10. The quotient is BCD_2.	55 -10 -10 -10 -10 -10	$=$ $=$ $=$ $=$ $=$	45 35 25 15 05 BCD_2	1 1 1 1 1 $= \quad 5$
Step 3:	The remainder from step 2 is BCD_1.			BCD_1	$= \quad 5$

These steps can be converted into a program as illustrated next.

9.21 Illustrative Program: Binary to Unpacked BCD Conversion

PROBLEM STATEMENT

A binary number is stored in memory location BINBYT. Convert the number into BCD, and store each BCD as two unpacked BCD digits in the Output Buffer. To perform this task, write a main program and two subroutines: one to supply the powers of ten, and the other to perform the conversion.

PROGRAM

This program converts an 8-bit binary number into a BCD number; thus it requires twelve bits to represent three BCD digits. The result is stored as three unpacked BCD digits in three Output-Buffer memory locations.

```
START:    LXI SP,STACK      ;Initialize stack pointer
          LXI H, BINBYT     ;Point HL index where binary number is stored
          MOV A,M           ;Transfer byte
          CALL PWRTEN       ;Call subroutine to load powers of 10
          HLT
```

PWRTEN: ;This subroutine loads the powers of 10 in register B and calls the binary to BCD conversion
          ;routine
          ;Input: Binary number in the accumulator
          ;Output: Powers of ten and stores BCD_1 in the first Output-Buffer memory
          ;Calls BINBCD routine and modifies register B

```
          LXI H,OUTBUF      ;Point HL index to Output-Buffer memory
          MVI B,64H         ;Load 100 in register B
          CALL BINBCD       ;Call conversion
          MVI B,0AH         ;Load 10 in register B
          CALL BINBCD
          MOV M,A           ;Store BCD₁
          RET
```

BINBCD: ;This subroutine converts a binary number into BCD and stores BCD_2 and BCD_3 in the
          ;Output Buffer.
          ;Input: Binary number in accumulator and powers of 10 in B
          ;Output: BCD_2 and BCD_3 in Output Buffer
          ;Modifies accumulator contents

```
          MVI M,FFH         ;Load buffer with (0 − 1)
NXTBUF:   INR M             ;Clear buffer and increment for each subtraction
          SUB B             ;Subtract power of 10 from binary number
          JNC NXTBUF        ;Is number > power of 10? If yes, add 1 to buffer memory
          ADD B             ;If no, add power of 10 to get back remainder
          INX H             ;Go to next buffer location
          RET
```

PROGRAM DESCRIPTION

This program illustrates the concepts of the **nested subroutine** and the **multiple-call subroutine**. The main program calls the PWRTEN subroutine; in turn, the PWRTEN calls the BINBCD subroutine twice.

1. The main program transfers the byte to be converted to the accumulator and calls the PWRTEN subroutine.
2. The subroutine PWRTEN supplies the powers of ten by loading register B and the address of the first Output-Buffer memory location, and calls conversion routine BINBCD.
3. In the BINBCD conversion routine, the Output-Buffer memory is used as a register. It is incremented for each subtraction loop. This step also can be achieved by using a register in the microprocessor. The BINBCD subroutine is called twice, once after loading register B with 64H (100_{10}), and again after loading register B with 0AH (10_{10}).
4. During the first call of BINBCD, the subroutine clears the Output Buffer, stores BCD_3, and points the HL registers to the next Output-Buffer location. The instruction ADD B is necessary to restore the remainder because one extra subtraction is performed to check the borrow.
5. During the second call of BINBCD, the subroutine again clears the output buffer, stores BCD_2, and points to the next buffer location. BCD_3 is already in the accumulator after the ADD instruction, which is stored in the third Output-Buffer memory by the instruction MOV M,A in the PWRTEN subroutine.

This is an efficient subroutine; it combines the functions of storing the answer and finding a quotient. However, two subroutines are required, and the second subroutine is called twice for a conversion.

See Assignments 5–8 at the end of this chapter.

BCD TO SEVEN-SEGMENT LED CODE CONVERSION

9.3

When a BCD number is to be displayed by a seven-segment LED, it is necessary to convert the BCD number to its seven-segment code. The code is determined by hardware considerations such as common cathode or common anode LED; the code has no direct relationship to binary numbers. Therefore, to display a BCD digit at a seven-segment LED, the **table look-up technique** is used.

In the table look-up technique, the codes of the digits to be displayed are stored sequentially in memory. The conversion program locates the code of a digit based on its magnitude, and transfers the code to the MPU to send out to a display port. The table look-up technique is illustrated in the next program.

9.31 Illustrative Program: BCD to Common Cathode LED Code Conversion

PROBLEM STATEMENT

A set of three packed BCD numbers (six digits) representing time and temperature are stored in memory locations starting at XX50H. The seven-segment codes of the digits 0 to 9 for a common cathode LED are stored in memory locations starting at XX70H, and the Output-Buffer memory is reserved at XX90H.

Write a main program and two subroutines, called UNPAK and LEDCOD, to unpack the BCD numbers and select an appropriate seven-segment code for each digit. The codes should be stored in the Output-Buffer memory.

PROGRAM

```
LXI SP,STACK        ;Initialize stack pointer
LXI H, XX50H        ;Point HL index where BCD digits are stored
MVI D,03H           ;Number of digits to be converted is placed in D
CALL UNPAK          ;Call subroutine to unpack BCD numbers
HLT                 ;End of conversion
```

UNPAK: ;This subroutine unpacks the BCD number into two single digits.
            ;Input: Starting memory address of the packed BCD numbers in HL registers
            :   : Number of BCDs to be converted in register D
            ;Output: Unpacked BCD into accumulator and output
                       Buffer address in BC
            ;Calls subroutine LEDCOD

```
           LXI B,BUFFER        ;Point BC index to the buffer memory
NXTBCD:    MOV A,M             ;Get packed BCD number
           ANI F0H             ;Masked BCD₁
           RRC                 ;Rotate four times to place BCD₂ as unpacked single digit BCD
           RRC
           RRC
           RRC
           CALL LEDCOD         ;Find seven-segment code
           INX B               ;Point to next buffer location
           MOV A,M             ;Get BCD number again
           ANI 0FH             ;Separate BCD₁
           CALL LEDCOD
           INX B
           INX H               ;Point to next BCD
           DCR D               ;One conversion complete, reduce BCD count
           JNZ NXTBCD          ;If all BCDs are not yet converted, go back to convert next BCD
           RET
```

LEDCOD: ;This subroutine converts an upacked BCD into its seven-segment LED code
           ;Input :An unpacked BCD in accumulator
                  :Memory address of the buffer in BC register
           ;Output: Stores seven-segment code in the output buffer

```
           PUSH H              ;Save HL contents of the caller
```

```
        LXI H,CODE       ;Point index to beginning of seven-segment code
        ADD L            ;Add BCD digit to starting address of the code
        MOV L,A          ;Point HL to appropriate code
        MOV A,M          ;Get seven-segment code
        STAX B           ;Store code in buffer
        POP H
        RET


CODE:   3F               ;Digit 0:  Common cathode codes
        06               ;Digit 1
        5B               ;Digit 2
        4F               ;Digit 3
        66               ;Digit 4
        6D               ;Digit 5
        7D               ;Digit 6
        07               ;Digit 7
        7F               ;Digit 8
        6F               ;Digit 9
        00               ;Invalid Digit
```

PROGRAM DESCRIPTION/OUTPUT

1. The main program initializes the stack pointer, the index for BCD digits, and the counter for the number of digits; and calls the UNPAK subroutine.
2. The UNPAK subroutine transfers a BCD number into the accumulator, and unpacks it into two BCD digits by using the instructions ANI and RRC. This subroutine also supplies the address of the buffer memory to the next subroutine, LEDCOD. The subroutine is repeated until counter D becomes zero.
3. The LEDCOD subroutine saves the memory address of the BCD number and points the HL register to the beginning address of the code.
4. The instruction ADD L adds the BCD digit in the accumulator to the starting address of the code. After storing the sum in register L, the HL register points to the seven-segment code of that BCD digit.
5. The code is transferred to the accumulator and stored in the buffer.

This illustrative program uses the technique of the nested subroutine (one subroutine calling another). Parameters are passed from one subroutine to another; therefore, you should be careful in using Push instructions to store register contents on the stack. In addition, the LEDCOD subroutine does not account for a situation if by adding the register L a carry is generated. (See Assignment 12.)

See Assignments 9–12 at the end of this chapter.

9.4 BINARY TO ASCII AND ASCII TO BINARY CODE CONVERSION

The American Standard Code for Information Interchange (known as ASCII) is used commonly in data communication. It is a seven-bit code, and its 128 (2^7) combinations are assigned different alphanumeric characters (see Appendix E). For example, the hexadecimal numbers 30H to 39H represent 0 to 9 ASCII decimal numbers, and 41H to 5AH represent capital letters A through Z; in this code, bit D_7 is zero. In serial data communication, bit D_7 can be used for parity checking (see Chapter 16, Serial I/O and Data Communication).

The ASCII keyboard is a standard input device for entering programs in a microcomputer. When an ASCII character is entered, the microprocessor receives the binary equivalent of the ASCII Hex number. For example, when the ASCII key for digit 9 is pressed, the microprocessor receives the binary equivalent of 39H, which must be converted to the binary 1001 for arithmetic operations. Similarly, to display digit 9 at the terminal, the microprocessor must send out the ASCII Hex code (39H). These conversions are done through software, as in the following illustrative program.

9.41 Illustrative Program: Binary to ASCII Hex Code Conversion

PROBLEM STATEMENT

An 8-bit binary number (e.g., 9FH) is stored in memory location XX50H.

1. Write a program to
   a. Transfer the byte to the accumulator.
   b. Separate the two nibbles (as 09 and 0F).
   c. Call the subroutine to convert each nibble into ASCII Hex code.
   d. Store the codes in memory locations XX60H and XX61H.
2. Write a subroutine to convert a binary digit (0 to F) into ASCII Hex code.

MAIN PROGRAM

```
LXI SP,STACK      ;Initialize stack pointer
LXI H,XX50H       ;Point index where binary number is stored
LXI D,XX60H       ;Point index where ASCII code is to be stored
MOV A,M           ;Transfer byte
MOV B,A           ;Save byte
RRC               ;Shift high-order nibble to the position of low-order nibble
RRC
RRC
RRC
```

```
        CALL ASCII          ;Call conversion routine
        STAX D              ;Store first ASCII Hex in XX60H
        INX D               ;Point to next memory location, get ready to store next byte
        MOV A,B             ;Get number again for second digit
        CALL ASCII
        STAX D
        HLT
```

ASCII: ;This subroutine converts a binary digit between 0 and F to ASCII Hex code
          ;Input: Single binary number 0 to F in the accumulator
          ;Output: ASCII Hex code in the accumulator

```
        ANI 0FH             ;Mask high-order nibble
        CPI 0AH             ;Is digit less than 10₁₀?
        JC CODE             ;If digit is less than 10₁₀, go to CODE to add 30H
        ADI 07H             ;Add 7H to obtain code for digits from A to F
CODE:   ADI 30H             ;Add base number 30H
        RET
```

PROGRAM DESCRIPTION

1. The main program transfers the binary data byte from the memory location to the accumulator.
2. It shifts the high-order nibble into the low-order nibble, calls the conversion subroutine, and stores the converted value in the memory.
3. It retrieves the byte again and repeats the conversion process for the low-order nibble.

In this program, the masking instruction ANI is used once in the subroutine rather than twice in the main program as illustrated in the program for BCD to Common Cathode LED Code Conversion (Section 9.31).

9.42 Illustrative Program: ASCII Hex to Binary Conversion

PROBLEM STATEMENT

Write a subroutine to convert an ASCII Hex number into its binary equivalent. A calling program places the ASCII number in the accumulator, and the subroutine should pass the conversion back to the accumulator.

SUBROUTINE

ASCBIN: ;This subroutine converts an ASCII Hex number into its binary
           ;equivalent

```
;Input:  ASCII Hex number in the accumulator
;Output: Binary equivalent in the accumulator

SUI 30H        ;Subtract 0 bias from the number
CPI 0AH        ;Check whether number is between 0 and 9
RC             ;If yes, return to main program
SUI 07H        ;If not, subtract 7 to find number between A and F
RET
```

PROGRAM DESCRIPTION

This subroutine subtracts the ASCII weighting digits from the number. This process is exactly opposite to that of the Illustrative Program that converted binary into ASCII Hex (Section 9.41). However, this program uses two return instructions, an illustration of the multiple-ending subroutine.

See Assignments 13 and 14 at the end of this chapter.

9.5   BCD ADDITION

In some applications, input/output data are presented in decimal numbers, and the speed of data processing is unimportant. In such applications, it may be convenient to perform arithmetic operations directly in BCD numbers. However, the addition of two BCD numbers may not represent an appropriate BCD value. For example, the addition of 34_{BCD} and 26_{BCD} results in 5AH, as shown below:

$$
\begin{array}{rclll}
34_{10} & = & 0011 & 0100_{BCD} \\
+26_{10} & = & 0010 & 0110_{BCD} \\
\hline
60_{10} & = & 0101 & 1010 \rightarrow 5AH
\end{array}
$$

The microprocessor cannot recognize BCD numbers; it adds any two numbers in binary. In BCD addition, any number larger than 9 (from A to F) is invalid and needs to be adjusted by adding 6 in binary. For example, after 9, the next BCD number is 10; however, in Hex it is A. The Hex number A can be adjusted as a BCD number by adding 6 in binary. The BCD adjustment in an 8-bit binary register can be shown as follows:

$$
\begin{array}{rclcccccccc}
A & = & 0 & 0 & 0 & 0 & & 1 & 0 & 1 & 0 \\
+6 & = & 0 & 0 & 0 & 0 & & 0 & 1 & 1 & 0 \\
\hline
& & 0 & 0 & 0 & 1 & & 0 & 0 & 0 & 0 \rightarrow 10_{BCD}
\end{array}
$$

Any BCD sum can be adjusted to proper BCD value by adding 6 when the sum exceeds 9. In case of packed BCD, both BCD_1 and BCD_2 need to be adjusted; if a carry is generated by adding 6 to BCD_1, the carry should be added to BCD_2, as shown in the following example.

Add two packed BCD numbers: 77 and 48									Example 9.2

Addition

Solution

$$
\begin{array}{rcllll llll}
77 & = & 0 & 1 & 1 & 1 & 0 & 1 & 1 & 1 \\
+48 & = & 0 & 1 & 0 & 0 & 1 & 0 & 0 & 0 \\
\hline
125 & = & 1 & 0 & 1 & 1 & 1 & 1 & 1 & 1
\end{array}
$$

The value of the least significant four bits is larger than 9. Add 6.

$$
\begin{array}{llll}
 & +0 & 1 & 1 & 0 \\
\hline
\text{CY}\,\boxed{1} & 0 & 1 & 0 & 1
\end{array}
$$

The value of the most significant four bits is larger than 9. Add 6 and the carry from the previous adjustment.

$$
\begin{array}{llll llll}
 & +0 & 1 & 1 & 0 \\
\hline
\text{CY}\,\boxed{1}\;\; 0 & 0 & 1 & 0 & 0 & 1 & 0 & 1
\end{array}
$$

In this example, the carry is generated after the adjustment of the least significant four bits for the BCD digit, and is again added to the adjustment of the most significant four bits.

A special instruction called DAA (Decimal Adjust Accumulator) performs the function of adjusting a BCD sum in the 8085/8080A instruction set. This instruction uses the Auxiliary Carry flip-flop (AC) to sense that the value of the least four bits is larger than 9 and adjusts the bits to the BCD value. Similarly, it uses the Carry flag (CY) to adjust the most significant four bits. However, the AC flag is used internally by the microprocessor; this flag is not available to the programmer through any Jump instruction.

INSTRUCTION

DAA: Decimal Adjust Accumulator
        This is a 1-byte instruction.
        It adjusts an 8-bit number in the accumulator to form two BCD numbers
        by using the process described above.
        It uses the AC and the CY flags to perform the adjustment.
        All flags are affected.

It must be emphasized that instruction DAA:

☐ Adjusts a BCD sum.
☐ Does not convert a binary number into BCD numbers.
☐ Works only with addition when BCD numbers are used; does not work with subtraction (except with the 8080A made by NEC, Nippon Electric Company; this is an enhancement added by NEC).

9.51 Illustrative Program: Addition of Unsigned BCD Numbers

PROBLEM STATEMENT

A set of ten packed BCD numbers is stored in the memory location starting at XX50H.

1. Write a program with a subroutine to add these numbers in BCD. If a carry is generated, save it in register B, and adjust it for BCD. The final sum will be less than 9999_{BCD}.
2. Write a second subroutine to unpack the BCD sum stored in registers A and B, and store them in the output-buffer memory starting at XX60H. The most significant digit (BCD_4) should be stored at XX60H, and the least significant digit (BCD_1) at XX63H.

PROGRAM

START:	LXI SP, STACK	;Initialize stack pointer
	LXI H, XX50H	;Point index to XX50H
	MVI C, COUNT	;Load register C with the count of BCD numbers to be added
	XRA A	;Clear accumulator
	MOV B,A	;Clear register B to save carry
NXTBCD:	CALL BCDADD	;Call subroutine to add BCD numbers
	INX H	;Point to next memory location
	DCR C	;One addition of BCD number is complete, decrement the counter
	JNZ NXTBCD	;If all numbers are added go to next step, otherwise go back
	LXI H,XX63H	;Point index to store BCD_1 first
	CALL UNPAK	;Unpack the BCD stored in the accumulator
	MOV A,B	;Get ready to store high-order BCD–BCD_3 and BCD_4
	CALL UNPAK	;Unpack and store BCD_3 and BCD_4 at XX61H and XX60
	HLT	

BCDADD: ;This subroutine adds the BCD number from the memory to the accumulator and decimal
;adjusts it. If the sum is larger than eight bits, it saves the carry and decimal adjusts the
;carry sum
;Input: The memory address in HL register where the BCD number is stored
;Output: Decimal adjusted BCD number in the accumulator and the carry in register B

	ADD M	;Add packed BCD byte and adjust it for BCD sum
	DAA	
	RNC	;If no carry, go back to next BCD
	MOV D,A	;If carry is generated, save the sum from the accumulator
	MOV A,B	;Transfer CY sum from register B and add 01
	ADI 01H	
	DAA	;Decimal adjust BCD from B
	MOV B,A	;Save adjusted BCD in B
	MOV A,D	;Place BCD_1 and BCD_2 in the accumulator
	RET	

UNPAK: ;This subroutine unpacks the BCD in the accumulator and the carry register, and stores
;them in the output buffer
;Input: BCD number in the accumulator, and the buffer address in HL registers
;Output: Unpacked BCD in the output buffer

	MOV D,A	;Save BCD number

ANI 0FH	;Mask high-order BCD
MOV M,A	;Store low-order BCD
DCX H	;Point to next memory location
MOV A,D	;Get BCD again
ANI F0H	;Mask low-order BCD
RRC	;Convert the most significant four bits into unpacked BCD
RRC	
RRC	
RRC	
MOV M,A	;Store high-order BCD
DCX H	;Point to the next memory location
RET	

PROGRAM DESCRIPTION

1. The expected maximum sum is 9999, which requires two registers. The main program clears the accumulator to save BCD_1 and BCD_2, clears register B to save BCD_3 and BCD_4, and calls the subroutine to add the numbers. The BCD bytes are added until the counter C becomes zero.

2. The BCDADD subroutine is an illustration of the multiple ending subroutine. It adds a byte, decimal adjusts the accumulator and, if there is no carry, returns the program execution to the main program. If there is a carry, it adds 01 to the carry register B by transferring the contents to the accumulator and decimal adjusting the contents. The final sum is stored in registers A and B.

3. The main program calls the UNPAK subroutine, which takes the BCD number from the accumulator (e.g., 57_{BCD}), unpacks it into two separate BCDs (e.g., 05_{BCD} and 07_{BCD}), and stores them in the output buffer. When a subroutine stores a BCD number in memory, it decrements the index because BCD_1 is stored first.

See Assignments 15–16 at the end of this chapter.

BCD SUBTRACTION 9.6

When subtracting two BCD numbers, the instruction DAA cannot be used to decimal adjust the result of two packed BCD numbers; the instruction applies only to addition. Therefore, it is necessary to devise a procedure to subtract two BCD numbers. Two BCD numbers can be subtracted by using the procedure of 100's complement (also known as 10's complement), similar to 2's complement. The 100's complement of a subtrahend can be added to a minuend as illustrated:

For example, $82 - 48 \ (=34)$ can be performed as follows:

| 100's complement of subtrahend | 52 | $(100 - 48 = 52)$ |
| Add minuend | + 82 | |

1/34

The sum is 34 if the carry is ignored. This is similar to subtraction by 2's complement. However, in an 8-bit microprocessor, it is not a simple process to find 100's complement of a subtrahend (100_{BCD} requires twelve bits). Therefore, in writing a program, 100's complement is obtained by finding 99's complement and adding 01.

9.61   Illustrative Program: Subtraction of Two Packed BCD Numbers

PROBLEM STATEMENT

Write a subroutine to subtract one packed BCD number from another BCD number. The minuend is placed in register B, and the subtrahend is placed in register C by the calling program. Return the answer into the accumulator.

SUBROUTINE

```
SUBBCD:      ;This subroutine subtracts two BCD numbers and adjusts the result to
             ;BCD values by using the 100's complement method
             ;Input: A minuend in register B and a subtrahend in register C
             ;Output: The result is placed in the accumulator
             MVI A,99H
             SUB C          ;Find 99's complement of subtrahend
             INR A          ;Find 100's complement of subtrahend
             ADD B          ;Add minuend to 100's complement of subtrahend
             DAA            ;Adjust for BCD
             RET
```

See Assignments 17 and 18 at the end of this chapter.

9.7   INTRODUCTION TO ADVANCED INSTRUCTIONS AND APPLICATIONS

The instructions discussed in the last several chapters deal primarily with 8-bit data (except LXI). However, in some instances data larger than eight bits must be manipulated, especially in arithmetic manipulations and stack operations. Even if the 8085/8080A is an 8-bit microprocessor, its architecture allows specific combinations of two 8-bit registers to form 16-bit registers. Several instructions in the instruction set are available to manipulate 16-bit data. These instructions will be introduced in this section.

9.71   16-Bit Data Transfer (Copy) and Data Exchange Group

LHLD: Load HL registers direct
             This is a 3-byte instruction
             The second and third bytes specify a memory location (the second byte
             is a line number and the third byte is a page number)

Transfers the contents of the specified memory location to L register
Transfers the contents of the next memory location to H register

SHLD: Store HL registers direct

This is a 3-byte instruction

The second and third bytes specify a memory location (the second byte is a line number and the third byte is a page number)

Stores the contents of L register in the specified memory location

Stores the contents of H register in the next memory location

XCHG: Exchange the contents of HL and DE

This is a 1-byte instruction

The contents of H register are exchanged with the contents of D register, and the contents of L register are exchanged with the contents of E register

---

Memory locations 2050H and 2051H contain 3FH and 42H, respectively, and register pair DE contains 856FH. Write instructions to exchange the contents of DE with the contents of the memory locations.

Example 9.3

Memory

Before Instructions: D | 85   6F | E | 3F | 2050
    | 42 | 2051

Instructions

Machine Code	Mnemonics							
2A	LHLD 2050H						3F	2050
50							42	2051
20		H	42	3F	L			
EB	XCHG	D	42	3F	E		3F	2050
		H	85	6F	L		42	2051
22	SHLD						6F	2050
50							85	2051
20		H	85	6F	L			

9.72 Arithmetic Group

Operation: Addition with Carry

    ADC R   These instructions add the contents of the operand, the

    ADC M   carry, and the accumulator. All flags are affected

    ACI 8-Bit

| Example 9.4 | Registers BC contain 2793H, and registers DE contain 3182H. Write instructions to add these two 16-bit numbers, and place the sum in memory locations 2050H and 2051H. |

Before instructions: B | 27 | 93 | C
                       D | 31 | 82 | E

Instructions

MOV A,C	A	93		F	93H
ADD E	A	15	CY = 1	F	+ 82H
MOV L,A	H		15	L	1/15H
MOV A,B					27H
ADC D					+31H
MOV H,A	H	59	15	L	59H
SHLD 2050H

Operation: Subtraction with Carry
    SBB R   These instructions subtract the contents of the operand and
    SBB M   the borrow from the contents of the accumulator
    SBI 8-Bit

| Example 9.5 | Registers BC contain 8538H and registers DE contain 62A5H. Write instructions to subtract the contents of DE from the contents of BC, and place the result in BC. |

Instructions

MOV A,C   (B) 85 | 38 (C)
SUB E   —
MOV C,A   (D) 62 | A5 (E)
MOV A,B   −1 | 1/93
SBB D   (B) 22 | 93 (C)
MOV B,A

Operation: Double Register ADD
    DAD Rp   Add register pair to register HL
             This is a 1-byte instruction
    DAD B   Adds the contents of the operand (register pair or stack pointer)
    DAD D   to the contents of HL registers
    DAD H   The result is placed in HL registers
    DAD SP   The Carry flag is altered to reflect the result of the 16-bit addi-
             tion. No other flags are affected
             The instruction set includes four instructions

Write instructions to display the contents of the stack pointer register at output ports.

Example 9.6

Instructions

```
LXI H, 0000H    ;Clear HL
DAD SP          ;Place the stack pointer contents in HL
MOV A, H        ;Place high-order address of the stack pointer in the accumulator
OUT PORT1
MOV A, L        ;Place low-order address of the stack pointer in the accumulator
OUT PORT2
```

The instruction DAD SP adds the contents of the stack pointer register to the HL register pair, which is already cleared. This is the only instruction in the 8085/8080A that enables the programmer to examine the contents of the stack pointer register.

9.73 Instructions Related to the Stack Pointer and the Program Counter

XTHL : Exchange Top of the Stack with H and L

The contents of L are exchanged with the contents of the memory location shown by the stack pointer, and the contents of H are exchanged with the contents of memory location of the stack pointer + 1.

Write a subroutine to set the Zero flag and check whether the instruction JZ (Jump on Zero) functions properly, without modifying any register contents other than flags.

Example 9.7

Subroutine

```
CHECK:     PUSH H
           MVI L, FFH      ;Set all bits in L to logic 1
           PUSH PSW        ;Save flags on the top of the stack
           XTHL            ;Set all bits in the top stack location
           POP PSW         ;Set Zero flag
           JZ NOEROR
           JMP ERROR
NOEROR:    POP H
           RET
```

The instruction PUSH PSW places the flags in the top location of the stack, and the instruction XTHL changes all the bits in that location to logic 1. The instruction POP PSW sets all the flags. If the instruction JZ is functioning properly, the routine returns to the calling program; otherwise, it goes to the ERROR routine (not shown). This example shows that the flags can be examined, and they can be set or reset to check malfunctions in the instructions.

SPHL: Copy H and L Registers into the Stack Pointer Register
The contents of H specify the high-order byte and the contents of L specify the low-order byte
The contents of HL registers are not affected

This instruction can be used to load a new address in the stack pointer register. (For an example, see SPHL in the instruction set, Appendix F.)

PCHL: Copy H and L Registers into the Program Counter
The contents of H specify the high-order byte and the contents of L specify the low-order byte

---

Example 9.8

Assume that the HL registers hold address 2075H. Transfer the program to location 2075H.

Solution

The program can be transferred to location 2075H by using Jump instructions. However, PCHL is a 1-byte instruction that can perform the same function as the Jump instruction. (For an illustration, see the instruction PCHL in the instruction set, Appendix F.)

This instruction is commonly used in monitor programs to transfer the program control from the monitor program to the user's program (see illustration in Chapter 17, Section 17.3).

9.74 Miscellaneous Instructions

CMC: Complement the Carry Flag (CY)
If the Carry flag is 1, it is reset; and if it is 0, it is set
STC: Set the Carry Flag

These instructions are used in bit manipulation, usually in conjunction with rotate instructions. (See the instruction set in Appendix F for examples.)

9.8 MULTIPLICATION

Multiplication can be performed by repeated addition; this technique is used in BCD-to-binary conversion. It is, however, an inefficient technique for a large multiplier. A more efficient technique can be devised by following the model of manual multiplication of decimal numbers. For example

$$
\begin{array}{r}
108 \\
\times \ \ 15 \\
\end{array}
$$

Step 1: (108×5) $=$ 540
Step 2: Shift left and add (108×1) $=$ $+108$
                                                      1620

In this example, the multiplier multiplies each digit of the multiplicand, starting from the farthest right, and adds the product by shifting to the left. The same process can be applied in binary multiplication.

9.81   Illustrative Program: Multiplication of Two 8-Bit Unsigned Numbers

PROBLEM STATEMENT

A multiplicand is stored in memory location XX50H and a multiplier is stored in location XX51H. Write a main program to

1. Transfer the two numbers from memory locations to the HL registers.
2. Store the product in the Output Buffer at XX90H.

Write a subroutine to

1. Multiply two unsigned numbers placed in registers H and L.
2. Return the result into the HL pair.

```
            MAIN PROGRAM
            LXI SP, STACK
            LHLD XX50H       ;Place contents of XX50 in L register and contents of XX51 in
                             ;H register
            XCHG             ;Place multiplier in D and multiplicand in E
            CALL MLTPLY      ;Multiply the two numbers
            SHLD XX90H       ;Store the product in locations XX90 and 91H
            HLT
```

Subroutine

```
;MLTPLY: This subroutine multiplies two 8-bit unsigned numbers
;Input: Multiplicand in register E and multiplier in register D
;Output: Results in HL register

MLTPLY:   MOV A,D        ;Transfer multiplier to accumulator
          MVI D,00H      ;Clear D to use in DAD instruction
          LXI H,0000H    ;Clear HL
          MVI B,08H      ;Set up register B to count eight rotations
NXTBIT:   RAR            ;Check if multiplier bit is 1
          JNC NOADD      ;If not, skip adding multiplicand.
          DAD D          ;If multiplier is 1, add multiplicand to HL and place partial result in HL
NOADD:    XCHG           ;Place multiplicand in HL.
          DAD H          ;And shift left
          XCHG           ;Retrieve shifted multiplicand
          DCR B          ;One operation is complete, decrement counter
          JNZ NXTBIT     ;Go back to next bit
          RET
```

PROGRAM DESCRIPTION

1. The objective of the main program is to demonstrate use of the instructions LHLD, SHLD, and XCHG. The main program transfers the two bytes (multiplier and multiplicand) from memory locations to the HL registers by using the instruction LHLD, places them in the DE register by the instruction XCHG, and places the result in the Output Buffer by the instruction SHLD.
2. The multiplier routine follows the format — add and shift to the left — illustrated at the beginning of Section 9.8. The routine places the multiplier in the accumulator and rotates it eight times until the counter (B) becomes zero. The reason for clearing D is to use the instruction DAD to add register pairs.
3. After each rotation, when a multiplier bit is 1, the instruction DAD D performs the addition, and DAD H shifts bits to the left. When a bit is 0, the subroutine skips the instruction DAD D and just shifts the bits.

9.9   SUBTRACTION WITH CARRY

The instruction set includes several instructions specifying arithmetic operations with carry (for example, add with carry or subtract with carry, Section 9.72). Descriptions of these instructions convey an impression that these instructions can be used to add (or subtract) 8-bit numbers when the addition generates carries. In fact, in these instructions when a carry is generated, it is added to bit D_0 of the accumulator in the next operation. Therefore, these instructions are used primarily in 16-bit addition and subtraction, as shown in the next program.

9.91   Illustrative Program: 16-Bit Subtraction

PROBLEM STATEMENT

A set of five 16-bit readings of the current consumption of industrial control units is monitored by meters and stored at memory locations starting at XX50H. The low-order byte is stored first (e.g., at XX50H), followed by the high-order byte (e.g., at XX51H). The corresponding maximum limits for each control unit are stored starting at XX90H. Subtract each reading from its specified limit, and store the difference in place of the readings. If any reading exceeds the maximum limit, call the indicator routine and continue checking.

MAIN PROGRAM

```
            LXI D,2050H        ;Point index to readings
            LXI H,2090H        ;Point index to maximum limits
            MVI B,05H          ;Set up B as a counter
    NEXT:   CALL SBTRAC
            INX D              ;Point to next location
            INX H
```

```
        DCR B
        JNZ NEXT
        HLT
```

Subroutine

```
;SBTRAC: This subroutine subtracts two 16-bit numbers
;Input: The contents of registers DE point to reading locations
;       The contents of registers HL point to maximum limits
;Output: The results are placed in reading locations, thus destroying the initial readings
;The comment section illustrates one example, assuming the following data:
```

Memory Contents

The first current reading	=	6790H	2050	= 90H	LSB
			2051	= 67H	MSB
Maximum limit	=	7000H	2090	= 00H	LSB
			2091	= 70H	MSB

```
                         ;Illustrative Example
SBTRAC:   MOV A,M        ;(A)   =   00H     LSB of maximum limit
          XCHG           ;(HL)  =   2050H
          SUB M          ;(A)   =   0000    0000
                          (M)   =   0111    0000    (2's complement of 90H)
                                ─────────────────
                                1   0111    0000    Borrow flag is set to
                                                    indicate the result is in
                                                    2's complement.

          MOV M,A        ;Store at 2050H
          XCHG           ;(HL)  =   2090H
          INX H          ;(HL)  =   2091H
          INX D          ;(DE)  =   2051H
          MOV A,M        ;(A)   =   70H     MSB of the maximum limit
          XCHG           ;(HL)  =   2051H
          SBB M          ;(A)   =   0111    0000    (70H)
                          (M)   =   1001    1001    2's complement of 67H
                          (CY)  =              1    Borrow flag
          CC INDIKET     ;Call Indicate subroutine if reading is higher than the
                          maximum limit

          MOV M,A
          RET
```

PROGRAM DESCRIPTION

This is a 16-bit subtraction routine that subtracts one byte at a time. The low-order bytes are subtracted by using the instruction SUB M. If a borrow is generated, it is accounted for by using the instruction SBB M (Subtract with Carry) for high-order bytes. In the illustrative example, the first subtraction (00H − 90H) generates a borrow that is subtracted from high-order bytes. The instruction XCHG changes the index pointer alternately between the set of readings and the maximum limits.

SUMMARY

The following code conversion and 16-bit arithmetic techniques were illustrated in this chapter:

☐ BCD to binary (Section 9.1)
☐ Binary to BCD (Section 9.2)
☐ BCD to seven-segment LED code (Section 9.3)
☐ Binary to ASCII code and ASCII to binary (Section 9.4)
☐ BCD addition and subtraction (Sections 9.5 and 9.6)
☐ Multiplication of two 8-bit unsigned numbers and 16-bit subtraction with carry (Section 9.7)

Review of Instructions

The instructions introduced and illustrated in this section are summarized below.

16-Bit Data Transfer (Copy) and Data Exchange Instructions

☐ LHLD 16-Bit   Load HL registers direct
☐ SHLD 16-Bit   Store HL registers direct
☐ XCHG   Exchange the contents of HL with DE
☐ XTHL   Exchange the top of the stack with HL
☐ SPHL   Copy HL registers into the stack pointer
☐ PCHL   Copy HL registers into the program counter

Arithmetic Instructions Used in 16-Bit Operations

Addition: The following instructions add the contents of the operand, the carry, and the accumulator.

ADC R	Add register contents with carry
ADC M	Add memory contents with carry
ACI 8-bit	Add immediate 8-bit data with carry

Subtraction: The following instructions subtract the contents of the operand and the borrow from the contents of the accumulator.

SBB R	Subtract register contents with borrow
SBB M	Subtract memory contents with borrow
SBI 8-bit	Subtract immediate 8-bit data with borrow

LOOKING AHEAD

This chapter included various types of code conversion techniques and illustrated applications of more advanced instructions. The illustrative programs were written as independent modules, similar to the circuit boards of an electronic system. Now, what is needed is to link these modules to perform a specific task.

However, single-board microcomputer systems are unsuitable for writing and coding programs with more than 50 instructions. Coding becomes cumbersome, modifications become tedious, and trouble-shooting becomes next to impossible. To write a large program, therefore, it is necessary to have access to an assembler and a disk-based system, which will be discussed in the next chapter.

ASSIGNMENTS

Section 9.1: BCD-to-Binary Conversion

1. Rewrite the BCDBIN subroutine to include storing results in the Output Buffer. Eliminate unnecessary PUSH and POP instructions.
2. Modify the program (Section 9.11) to convert a set of numbers of 2-digit BCD numbers into their binary equivalents and store them in the Output Buffer. The number of BCD digits in the set is specified by the main program in register D and passed on as a parameter to the subroutine.
3. Rewrite the multiplication section using the RLC (Rotate Left) instruction. *Hints:* Rotating left once is equivalent to multiplying by two. To multiply a digit by ten, rotate left three times and add the result of the first rotation (times 10 = times 8 + times 2).
4. In Assignment 3, multiplication is performed by rotating the high-order digit to the left. However, in the BCDBIN subroutine, just before the multiplication section, the high-order digit BCD_2 is shifted right to place it in the low-order position. Rewrite the subroutine to combine the two operations. *Hint:* Rotating BCD_2 right once from the high-order position is equivalent to multiplying it by eight.

Section 9.2: Binary-to-BCD Conversion

5. Assume the STACK is defined as 20B8H in the illustrative program to convert binary to unpacked BCD (Section 9.21). Specify the stack addresses and their (symbolic) contents when the BINBCD subroutine is called the second time.
6. Rewrite the main program to supply the powers of ten in registers B and C, and to store converted BCD numbers in the Output Buffer. Modify the BINBCD subroutine to accomodate the changes in the main program, and eliminate the PWRTEN subroutine.
7. Rewrite the program to convert a given number of binary data bytes into their BCD equivalents, and store them as unpacked BCDs in the Output Buffer. The number of data bytes is specified in register D in the main program. The converted numbers should be stored in groups of three consecutive memory locations.

If the number is not large enough to occupy all three locations, zeros should be loaded in those locations.

8. A set of ten BCD readings is stored in the Input Buffer. Convert the numbers into binary and add the numbers. Store the sum in the Output Buffer; the sum can be larger than FFH.

Section 9.3: BCD-to-Seven-Segment LED Code Conversion

9. List the common cathode and the common anode seven-segment LED look-up table to include hexadecimal digits from 0 to F. (See Figure 11.11 for the diagram.)

10. A set of data is stored as unpacked (single digit) BCD numbers in memory from XX50H to XX5FH. Write a program to look up the common cathode LED code for each reading and store the code from XX55H to XX64H (initial data can be eliminated).

11. Design a counter to count continuously from 00H to FFH with 500 ms delay between each count. Display the count at PORT1 and PORT2 (one digit per port) with a common anode seven-segment LED code.

12. Modify the LEDCOD subroutine to account for a carry when the instruction ADD L is executed. For example, if the starting address of the CODE table is 02F9, the codes of digits larger than six will be stored on page 03H. The subroutine given in illustrative program to convert BCD to LED code (Section 9.31) does not account for such a situation. *Hint:* Check for the carry (CY) after the addition, and increment H whenever a carry is generated.

Section 9.4: Binary to ASCII Code Conversion

13. A set of ASCII Hex digits is stored in the Input-Buffer memory. Write a program to convert these numbers into binary. Add these numbers in binary, and store the result in the Output-Buffer memory.

14. Extend the program in Assignment 13 to convert the result from binary to ASCII Hex code.

Section 9.5: BCD Addition

15. Write a counter program to count continuously from 0 to 99 in BCD with a delay of 750 ms between each count. Display the count at an output port.

16. Modify the illustrative program for the addition of unsigned numbers (Section 9.51) to convert the unpacked BCD digits located at XX60 to XX63 into ASCII characters, and store them in the Output Buffer.

Section 9.6: BCD Subtraction

17. Design a down-counter to count from 99 to 0 in BCD with 500 ms delay between each count. Display the count at an output port. *Hint:* Check for the low-order digit; when it reaches zero, adjust the next digit to nine.

18. Write a program to subtract a 2-digit BCD number from another 2-digit BCD number; the numbers are stored in two consecutive memory locations. Rather than using the hundred's complement method, subtract one BCD digit at a time, and decimal adjust each digit after subtraction. (The instruction DAA cannot be used in subtraction.) Display the result at an output port. Verify that if the subtrahend is larger than the minuend, the result will be negative and will be displayed as 100's complement.

Section 9.7: Advanced Instructions and Applications

19. A set of 16-bit readings is stored in memory locations starting at 2050H. Each reading occupies two memory locations: the low-order byte is stored first, followed by the high-order byte. The number of readings stored is specified by the contents of register B. Write a program to add all the readings and store the sum in the Output-Buffer memory. (The maximum limit of a sum is 24 bits.)

20. In Assignment 19, save the contents of the stack pointer from the main program, point the stack pointer to location 2050H, and transfer the readings to registers by using the POP instruction. Add the readings as in Assignment 19; however, retrieve the original contents of the stack pointer after the addition is completed.

21. Assume that the monitor program stores a memory address in the DE registers. When a Hex key is pressed to enter a new memory address, the keyboard subroutine places the 4-bit code of the key pressed in the accumulator. Write a subroutine to shift out the most significant four bits of the old address, and to insert the new code from the accumulator as the least significant four bits in register E.

Hint: Place the memory address in the HL registers, and use the instruction DAD H four times; this will shift all bits to the left by four positions, and will clear the least significant four bits.

22. A pair of 32-bit readings is stored in groups of four consecutive memory locations; the memory location with the lowest memory address in each group contains the least significant byte. Write a program to add these readings; if a carry is generated, call an error routine.

Software Development Systems and Assemblers

A **software development system** is a computer that enables the user to develop programs (**software**) with the assistance of other programs. The development process includes writing, modifying, testing, and debugging of the user programs. Programs such as Editor, Assembler, Loader, and Debugger enable the user to write programs in mnemonics, translate mnemonics into binary code, and debug the binary code. All the activities of the computer—hardware and software—are directed by another program, called the **operating system** of the computer.

This chapter describes a microprocessor-based software development system, its hardware, and related programs. It also describes a widely used operating system, CP/M and its assembler, and illustrates the use of the assembler to write assembly language programs.

OBJECTIVES

- ☐ Describe the components of a software development system.
- ☐ List various types of floppy disks, and explain how information is stored on the disk.
- ☐ Define the operating system of a microcomputer, and explain its function.
- ☐ Explain the functions of these programs: Editor, Assembler, Loader, and Debugger.
- ☐ List the advantages of the assembler over manual assembly.
- ☐ List the assembler directives, and explain their functions.
- ☐ Write assembly language programs with appropriate directives.

10.1 MICROPROCESSOR-BASED SOFTWARE DEVELOPMENT SYSTEMS

A **software development system** is simply a computer that enables the user to write, modify, debug, and test programs. In a microprocessor-based development system, a microcomputer is used to develop software for a particular microprocessor. Generally, the microcomputer has a large R/W memory (64K), disk storage, and a video terminal with ASCII keyboard. The system includes programs that enable the user to develop software in either assembly language or high-level languages. This text will focus on developing programs in the **8085/8080A assembly language**.

Conceptually, this type of microcomputer is similar to a single-board microcomputer except that it has features that can assist in developing large programs. Programs are accessed and stored under a file name (title), and they are written by using other programs such as text editors and assemblers. The system (I/Os, files, programs, etc.) is managed by a program called the **operating system**. The hardware and software features of a typical software development system are described in the next sections.

10.11 System Hardware and Storage Memory

Figure 10.1 shows a typical software development system; it includes an ASCII keyboard, a CRT terminal, an MPU board with 64K R/W memory and disk controllers, and two disk

FIGURE 10.1
A Typical Software Development System
SOURCE: Photograph courtesy of TeleVideo Systems, Inc.

drives. The disk controller is an interfacing circuit through which the MPU can access a disk and provide Read/Write control signals. The disk drives have Read/Write elements that read and write data on the disk. Two types of disks are in common use: 5¼-inch and 8-inch diameter, they are known as mini-floppy and floppy disk, respectively. A 5¼-inch single-density disk can store about 90K bytes of data, while an 8-inch disk is capable of storing 240K bytes of data. The storage capacity can be doubled by using double-density disks, and quadrupled by using both sides of the disks. The TeleVideo 802 system (Figure 10.1) is designed for two 5¼-inch, double-density, double-sided disks; each disk has a storage capacity of 340K bytes of memory. Another development in floppy disks is the availability of even smaller-sized disks for portable microcomputers. At present, the size is not yet standardized, but sizes are around 3-inch. A typical disk is described below.

FLOPPY DISK

A **floppy disk** (Figure 10.2) is made of a thin magnetic material (iron oxide) that can store logic 0s and 1s in the form of magnetic directions. The surface of the disk is divided into a number of concentric tracks, with each track divided into sectors, as shown in Figure 10.2. The large hole in the center of the disk is locked by the disk drive when it spins the disk. The small hole shown in the figure is known as the *indexing hole*. The disk drive uses this hole as a reference to count the sectors. The oblong cutout, called the *head*

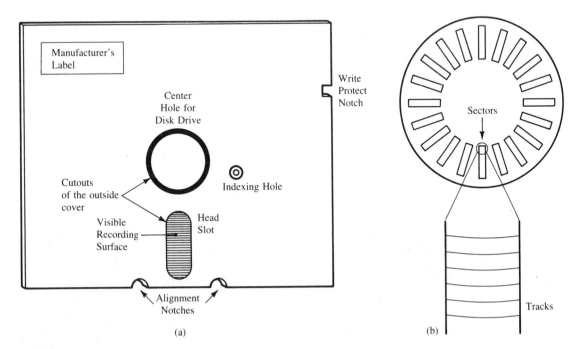

FIGURE 10.2
A Typical 5¼-Inch Floppy Disk (a) and Its Sectors and Tracks (b)

slot, is the reading/recording segment; this is the only segment of the surface that comes in contact with the disk drive. At the edge of the disk, near the head slot, is a notch called the Write Protect notch. In the 5¼-inch disk, if the disk notch is covered, data cannot be written on the disk; the disk is "Write Protected." An 8-inch disk, on the other hand, is "Write Protected" if the notch is left open rather than covered.

Floppy disks are further classified as either soft-sectored or hard-sectored. Figure 10.2 shows a soft-sectored disk; it has one hole as a reference to the first sector, and the other sectors are formatted by using software. In a hard-sectored disk, each sector is identified with a separate hole.

Each sector and track is assigned binary addresses. The MPU can access information on the disk with the sector and the track addresses; however, the access is semi-random. Going from one track to another, access is random. Once the track is found, the system waits for the index hole and then locates the sector serially by counting the sectors. Once data bytes are located, they are transferred to the system's R/W memory serially over a single line (see the discussion of serial I/O in Chapter 16). That means a byte is first converted into a stream of eight bits, sent over a single line to the system, and then converted back into a parallel byte and stored in R/W memory. These data transfer functions between a floppy disk and the system are performed by the **disk controller** and controlled by the **operating system**, also known as the Disk Operating System (DOS) described in Section 10.12.

HARD DISK

Another memory storage form used with computers is called a **hard disk** or **Winchester disk**. The hard disk is similar to the floppy disk except that the magnetic material is coated on a rigid aluminum base and enclosed in a sealed container. While it is highly precise and reliable, the hard disk requires sophisticated controller circuitry; thus, it is expensive. However, its storage capacity is large. Hard disks are available in these sizes: 3½-inch, 5¼-inch, 8-inch, and 14-inch. Storage capacity ranges from several megabytes to several gigabytes.

10.12   Operating Systems and CP/M

The **operating system** of a computer is a group of programs that manages or oversees all the operations of the computer. The computer transfers information constantly among peripherals such as a floppy disk, printer, keyboard, and video monitor. It also stores user programs under file names on a disk. (A **file** is defined as related records stored as a single entity.) The operating system is responsible primarily for managing the files on the disk and the communication between the computer and its peripherals.

Each computer has its own operating system. CP/M (Control Program/Monitor) is by far the most widely used operating system for microcomputers designed around the 8085/8080A and the Z-80 microprocessors. The CP/M design is, for the most part, independent of the machine, so that microcomputer manufacturers can adapt it to their own designs with minimum changes. Other popular microcomputers, such as the TRS-80 (Radio Shack), Cromemco, or North Star, have their own operating systems. To illustrate the operation of a software development system, CP/M is briefly described in reference to a system with 64K R/W memory.

CP/M

The operating system is divided into three components: BIOS (Basic Input/Output System), BDOS (Basic Disk Operating System), and CCP (Console Command Processor).

BIOS The BIOS program consists of input/output routines; it manages data transfer between the microprocessor and various peripherals. This section of CP/M is accessible to the user. Each manufacturer modifies I/O port addresses in this section according to the hardware design in a particluar system.

BDOS The BDOS program directs the activities of the disk controller and manages the file allocation on the disk and is not accessible to the user. The BDOS program allocates memory spaces under a file name.

CCP The CCP program reads and interprets the CP/M commands from the keyboard. These commands include operations such as listing the programs on the disk, copying, erasing, and renaming a file. CCP also transfers the program control from CP/M to user or other programs.

When CP/M is loaded into a system's R/W memory, it occupies approximately 6K of memory at the highest available locations, as shown in Figure 10.3. In addition, the first 256 locations (from 0000 to 00FFH) are reserved for system parameters. The rest of the R/W memory (approximately 58K) is available for the user. Once the operating system is

FIGURE 10.3
CP/M Memory Map with
64K R/W Memory

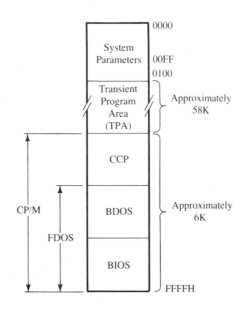

loaded into R/W memory, the user can write, assemble, test, and debug programs by using **utility programs** (described in the next section).

10.13 Tools for Developing Assembly Language Programs

The CP/M operating system includes programs called **utility programs**. These programs can be classified in two categories: file management utilities, and program development utilities. The file management utilities are programs that enable the user to perform functions such as copying, printing, erasing, and renaming files. The program development utilities enable the user to write, assemble, and test assembly language programs; they include programs such as Editor, Assembler, Loader, and Debugger.

EDITOR

The Editor is a program that allows the user to enter, modify, and store a group of instructions or text under a file name. To write text, the user must call the Editor under CP/M control. As soon as the Editor program is transferred from the disk to the system memory, the program control is transferred from CP/M to the Editor program. The Editor has its own commands, and the user can enter and modify text by using those commands. Some Editor programs, such as "Word Star," are very easy to use. At the completion of writing a program, the exit command of the Editor will save the program on the disk under the file name, and will transfer the program control to CP/M. This file is known as a *source file* or a *source program*. If the source file is intended to be a program in the 8085/8080A assembly language, the user should follow the syntax of the assembly language and the rules of the assembler program that is described next. The Editor program is not concerned with whether one is writing a letter or an assembly language program.

ASSEMBLER

The Assembler (ASM) is a program that translates mnemonics into the Intel Hex code of the 8085/8080A microprocessor and generates a file called the *Hex file*. This function is similar to manual assembly, whereby the user looks up the code for each mnemonic in the listing. In addition to translating mnemonics, the Assembler performs various functions, such as error checking and memory allocations. The Assembler is described in more detail in Section 10.2.

LOADER

The Loader (LOAD) is a program that takes the Hex file generated by the assembler and generates a file in binary code called the COM file or the object code. The COM file is the only executable file: i.e., the only file that can be executed by the microcomputer. To execute the program, the COM file is called under CP/M control and executed.

DEBUGGER

The Debugger, also known as DDT (Dynamic Debugging Tool), is a program that allows the user to test and debug the object file. The user can employ this program to perform the following functions:

☐ Make changes in the object code.

☐ Examine and modify the contents of memory.

☐ Set breakpoints, execute a segment of the program, and display register contents after the execution.

☐ Trace the execution of the specified segment of the program, and display the register and memory contents after the execution of each instruction.

☐ Disassemble a section of the program: i.e., convert the object code into the source code or mnemonics.

In the CP/M assembler, translating mnemonics into binary code is a two-step process: first, the source file is converted into the Hex file by the ASM program; then, the Hex file is converted into the binary object file by the LOAD program. This is called **program assembly**, and the two programs in combination (ASM and LOAD) can be viewed as the **CP/M assembler**. In addition, the assembler also generates the print (PRN) file and the backup (BAK) file. The PRN file is generated for documentation, and the BAK file is generated when the user calls the ASM file for reediting; the BAK file is the copy of the previous file before the user begins to reedit. The BAK file is generated as a precautionary measure, in the event the user wishes to go back to the previous file. At the completion of the assembly process, the CP/M user will have the following five files:

☐ ASM File: This is the source file written by the user.

☐ HEX File: This is generated by the assembler program and contains the program code in hexadecimal notations.

☐ PRN File: This is the print file generated by the assembler program for documentation purposes. It contains memory locations, Hex code, mnemonics, and comments.

☐ COM File: This is the executable file generated by the loader program, and it contains binary code.

☐ BAK File: When the ASM file is called for reediting, the previous file is saved as the BAK file.

ASSEMBLERS 10.2

The assembler, as previously described, is a program that translates assembly language mnemonics or source code into binary executable code. This translation requires that the source program be written strictly according to the specified syntax of the assembler. The assembly language source program includes three types of statements:

1. The program statements in 8085/8080A mnemonics that are to be translated into binary code.

2. Comments that are reproduced as part of the program documentation.

3. Directives to the assembler that specify items such as starting memory locations, label definitions, and required memory spaces for data.

The first two types of statements have been used throughout Part II of this book; the format of these statements as they appear in an assembly language source program is identical to the format used here. The third type — directive statements — and their functions will be described in the next sections.

10.21 Assembly Language Format

A typical assembly language programming statement is divided into four parts called **fields**: *label, operation code* (opcode), *operand,* and *comments*. These fields are separated by *delimiters* for the CP/M assembler, as shown in Table 10.1.

TABLE 10.1
Delimiters Used in Assembler Statements

Delimiter	Placement
1. Colon	After label (optional)
2. Space	Between an opcode and an operand
3. Comma	Between two operands
4. Semicolon	Before the beginning of a comment

The assembler statements have a free-field format, which means that any number of blanks can be left between the fields. As mentioned before, comments are optional but are generally included for good documentation. Similarly, a label for an instruction is also optional, but its use greatly facilitates specifying jump locations. As an example, a typical assembly language statement is written as follows:

Label	Opcode	Operand	Comments
START:	LXI	SP, 20FFH	;Initialize stack pointer

Delimiters include the colon following START, the space following LXI, the comma following SP, and the semicolon preceding the comment.

10.22 Assembler Directives

The **assembler directives** are the instructions to the assembler concerning the program being assembled; they also are called *pseudo instructions* or *pseudo opcodes*. These instructions are neither translated into machine code nor assigned any memory locations in the object file. Some of the important assembler directives for the CP/M assembler are listed and described here.

Assembler Directives	Example	Description
1. ORG (Origin)	ORG 0100H	The next block of instructions should be stored in memory locations starting at 0100H.

2. END	END	End of assembly. The HLT instruction suggests the end of a program, but that does not necessarily mean it is the end of the assembly.
3. EQU (Equate)	PORT1 EQU 02H	The value of the term PORT1 is equal to 02H. Generally, this means the PORT1 has the port address 02H.
	INBUF EQU 2099H	The value of the term INBUF is 2099H. This may be the memory location used as Input Buffer.
	STACK EQU INBUF +1	The equate can be expressed by using the label of another equate. This example defines the stack as next location of INBUF.
4. DB (Define Byte)	DATA: DB A2H, 9FH	Initializes an area byte by byte. Assembled bytes of data are stored in successive memory locations until all values are stored. This is a convenient way of writing a data string. The label is optional.
5. DW (Define Word)	DW 2050H	Initializes an area two bytes at a time.
6. DS (Define Storage)	OUTBUF: DS 4	Reserves a specified number of memory locations. In this example, four memory locations are reserved for OUTBUF.

10.23   Advantages of the Assembler

The **assembler** is a tool for developing programs with the assistance of the computer. Assemblers are absolutely essential for writing industry-standard software; manual assembly is too difficult for programs with more than 50 instructions. The assembler performs many functions in addition to translating mnemonics, and it has several advantages over manual assembly. The salient features of the assembler are as follows:

1. The assembler translates mnemonics into binary code with speed and accuracy, thus eliminating human errors in looking up the codes.
2. The assembler assigns appropriate values to the symbols used in a program. This facilitates specifying jump locations.
3. It is easy to insert or delete instructions in a program; the assembler can reassemble the entire program quickly with new memory locations and modified addresses for jump locations. This avoids rewriting the program manually.
4. The assembler checks syntax errors, such as wrong labels and expressions, and provides error messages. However, it cannot check logic errors in a program.

5. The assembler can reserve memory locations for data or results.

6. The assembler can provide files for documentation.

7. A program such as DDT can be used in conjunction with the assembler to test and debug an assembly language program.

10.3 WRITING PROGRAMS USING AN ASSEMBLER

This section deals primarily with writing programs using the CP/M assembler. The following examples are taken from previous chapters, in which they were already assembled using manual assembly. An assembler source program is identical to a program the user writes with paper and pencil, except that the assembler source program includes assembler directives.

10.31 Illustrative Program: Unconditional Jump to Set up a Loop

The following program is taken from Chapter 5 (Section 5.42). Its source program is rewritten here for the assembler.

SOURCE PROGRAM

;This program monitors the switch positions of the input port and turns on/off devices
;connected to the output port.

```
PORT0      EQU 00H          ;Input port address.
PORT1      EQU 01H          ;Output port address.
           ORG 2000H        ;Start assembling the program from location 2000H.
START:     IN PORT0         ;Read input switches.
           OUT PORT1        ;Turn on devices.
           JMP START        ;Go back and read switches again.
           END
```

This program illustrates the following assembler directives:

☐ ORG The object code will be stored starting at the location 2000H.

☐ EQU The program defines two equates, PORT0 and PORT1. In this program it would have been easier to write port addresses directly with the instructions. The equates are essential in development projects in which hardware and software design are done concurrently. In such a situation, equates are convenient. Equates are also useful in long programs because it is easy to change or define port addresses by defining equates.

☐ Label The program illustrates one label: START.

☐ END The end of assembly.

TWO-PASS ASSEMBLER

To assemble the program, the assembler scans through the program twice; this is known as a **two-pass assembler**. In the first pass, the first memory location is determined from the ORG statement, and the counter known as the location counter is initialized. Then the assembler scans each instruction and records locations in the address column of the first byte of each instruction; the location counter keeps track of the bytes in the program. The assembler also generates a symbol table during the first pass. When it comes across a label, it records the label and its location. In the second pass, each instruction is examined, and mnemonics and labels are replaced by their machine codes in Hex notation as shown below.

Pass 1

Address Hex	Machine Code Hex	Label Opcode	Operand	Symbol Table
2000		START: IN	PORT0	PORT0 00H
2002		OUT	PORT1	PORT1 01H
2004		JMP	START	START 2000H

Pass 2

2000	DB00
2002	D301
2004	C30020

ASSEMBLED PRINT FILE

The file lists the memory addresses of the first byte of each instruction.

;This program monitors the switch positions of the input port and turn on/off devices connected to the output port

---

0000 =	PORT0	EQU 00H	;Input port address
0001 =	PORT1	EQU 01H	;Output port address
2000		ORG 2000H	;Start assembling program from location ;2000H
2000 DB00	START:	IN PORT0	;Read input switches
2002 D301		OUT PORT1	;Turn on devices
2004 C30020		JMP START	;Go back and read switches again
2007		END	

10.32   Illustrative Program: Addition with Carry

The following program is from Chapter 6 (Section 6.32). The program adds six bytes of data stored in memory locations starting at 2050H and stores the sum in the Output Buffer memory in two consecutive memory locations.

Data (H):   A$_2$, FA, DF, E5, 98, and 8B.

SOURCE PROGRAM

```
;Addition with Carry
INBUF       EQU 2050H                 ;Input Buffer location
COUNTR      EQU 06H                   ;Number of bytes to add
            ORG 2000H
            XRA A                     ;Clear accumulator
            MOV B,A                   ;Set up B for carry
            MVI C,COUNTR              ;Set up C to count bytes
            LXI H,INBUF               ;Point to data address
NXTBYT:     ADD M
            JNC NXTMEM
            INR B                     ;If there is carry, add 1
NXTMEM:     INX H                     ;Point to next data byte
            DCR C                     ;One is added, decrement counter
            JNZ NXTBYT                ;Get next byte if all bytes not yet added
            LXI H,OUTBUF              ;Point index to output buffer
            MOV M,A                   ;Store low-order byte of the sum
            INX H
            MOV M,B                   ;Store high-order byte of the sum
            HLT
OUTBUF:     DS 2                      ;Reserve two memory locations
            ORG 2050H                 ;Assemble next instructions starting at 2050H
DATA:       DB 0A2H,0FAH,0DFH,0E5H,98H
            DB 8BH
            END
```

This program illustrates two more assembler directives—DB (Define Byte) and DS (Define Storage)—and the use of the ORG statement to store data starting at location 2050H. A data byte or an address that begins with Hex digits (A through F) should be preceded by 0; otherwise, the assembler cannot interpret it as a Hex number (see the data string above). The assembled program is shown below.

PRINT FILE

```
            ;Addition with Carry
2050 =      INBUF     EQU 2050H       ;Input Buffer location
0006 =      COUNTR    EQU 06H         ;Number of bytes to add
2000                  ORG 2000H
2000 AF               XRA A           ;Clear accumulator
2001 47               MOV B,A         ;Set up B for carry
2002 0E06             MVI C,COUNTR    ;Set up C to count bytes
2004 215020           LXI H,INBUF     ;Point to data address
2007 86      NXTBYT   ADD M
```

Address	Code	Label	Instruction	Comment
2008	D20C20		JNC NXTMEM	
200B	04		INR B	;If there is carry, add 1
200C	23	NXTMEM:	INX H	;Point to next data byte
200D	0D		DCR C	;Decrement counter
200E	C20720		JNZ NXTBYT	;Get next byte if all bytes
				;not yet added
2011	211820		LXI H,OUTBUF	;Point index to Output
2014	77		MOV M,A	;Store low-order byte
2015	23		INX H	
2016	70		MOV M,B	;Store high-order byte
2017	76		HLT	
2018		OUTBUF:	DS 2	;Reserve two memory
				;locations
2050			ORG 2050H	;Assemble next instructions
				;starting at 2050H
2050	A2FADFE598	DATA:	DB 0A2H,0FAH,0DFH,0E5H,98H	
2055	8B		DB 8BH	
2056			END	

The print file shows the memory addresses of the first byte of each instruction; this is a typical printout of an assembly language program. The file also shows that two memory locations (2018H and 2019H) are reserved for OUTBUF, and six locations are used to store data starting from 2050H.

ERROR MESSAGES

In addition to translating the mnemonics into object code, the assembler also gives error messages. The two types of error messages are terminal error messages and source program error messages. In the first case, the assembler is not able to complete the assembly. In the second case, the assembler is able to complete the assembly, but it lists the errors.

SUMMARY

A software development system and an assembler are essential tools for writing large assembly language programs. These tools facilitate the writing, assembling, testing, and debugging of assembly language programs.

A disk-based microcomputer, its operating system, and assembler programs can serve as a development system. All the operations of the computer are managed and directed by the operating system of the computer. The Assembler and other utility programs assist the user in developing software. The Editor allows the user to enter text, the Assembler translates mnemonics into machine code and provides error messages. The Debugger (DDT) assists in debugging the program.

The program assembled using the Assembler is in many ways similar to that of the hand assembly program except that the program written for the Assembler includes assembler directives concerning how to assemble the program. The Assembler has many advantages over manual assembly; without the Assembler, it would be extremely difficult to develop industry-standard software.

ASSIGNMENTS

1. Check the appropriate answer in the following statements:
    a. The process of accessing information on a floppy disk is
        (1) random.
        (2) serial.
        (3) semi-random.
    b. The operating system of a computer is defined as
        (1) hardware that operates the floppy disk.
        (2) a program that manages files on the disk.
        (3) a group of programs that manages and directs hardware and software in the system.
    c. The Editor is
        (1) an assembly language program that reads and writes information on the disk.
        (2) a high-level language program that allows the user to write programs.
        (3) a program that allows the user to write, modify, and store text in the computer system.
    d. The Assembler is
        (1) a compiler that translates statements from high-level language into assembly language.
        (2) a program that translates mnemonics into binary code.
        (3) an operating system that manages all the programs in the system.
    e. A file is
        (1) a group of related records stored as a single entity.
        (2) a program that transfers information between the system and the floppy disk.
        (3) a program that stores data.
    f. In the CP/M operating system, the LOAD program
        (1) loads object file in the system.
        (2) executes other programs.
        (3) generates binary file from Hex file.
    g. A hard-sectored disk is
        (1) a floppy disk in which each sector is identified with a hole.
        (2) a hard disk that stores information on an aluminum-based magnetic surface.
        (3) a double-density, double-sided floppy disk.

h. A disk controller is

(1) a program that manages the files on the disk.

(2) a circuit that interfaces the disk with the microcomputer system.

(3) a mechanism that controls the spinning of the disk.

2. Write a print file for the following program with the starting location 0100H, and list the errors in the source file. Assume that the subroutine BCDBIN is written separately.

```
        ORG 0100
        LXI SP, STACK      ;Initialize stack pointer
        LXI H, INBUF       ;Input buffer
        LXI B, OUTBUF      ;Output buffer
        MVI D, 0AH         ;Initialize counter
NEXT:   MOV A, M           ;Get byte
        CALL BCDBIN        ;Call BCD to binary routine
        STAX B             ;Store result
        DCR D
        JNZ NEXT
INBUF:  DW
OUTBUF: DW
        HLT
```

3. Rewrite the illustrative program in Section 9.31 for a BCD to common-cathode LED code conversion to assemble it with the assembler.

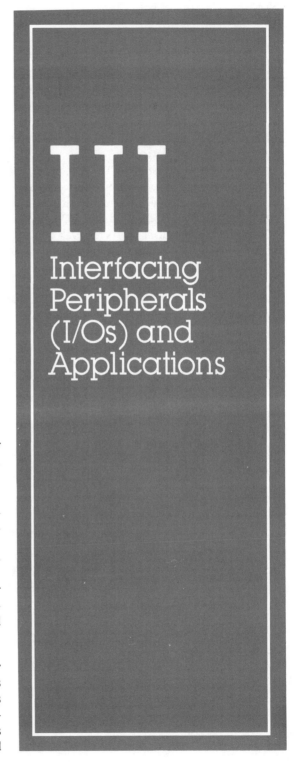

III
Interfacing Peripherals (I/Os) and Applications

Part III of this book is concerned with the interfacing of peripherals (I/Os) and design processes of microcomputer-based systems. The primary objectives of Part III are

1. To examine the concepts and processes of data transfer between the microprocessor and peripherals.
2. To apply the concepts for interfacing peripherals with the microprocessor.
3. To synthesize the concepts of microprocessor architecture, software, and interfacing by designing a simple microprocessor-based system, and by discussing the process of troubleshooting.

The primary function of the **microprocessor (MPU)** is to accept data from input devices such as keyboards and A/D converters, read instructions from memory, process data according to the instructions, and send the results to output devices such as LEDs, printers, and video monitors. These input and output devices are called either **peripherals** or **I/Os**; memory can be viewed as a special type of I/O. Designing logic circuits (hardware) and writing instructions (software) to enable the microprocessor to communicate with these peripherals is called **interfacing**, and the logic circuits are called **I/O ports** or **interfacing devices**.

The microprocessor (MPU) communicates with the peripherals in either of two formats: **asynchronous** or **synchronous**. Similarly, it transfers data in either of two modes: **parallel I/O** or **serial I/O**. The 8085/8080A identifies peripherals either as **memory-mapped I/O** or **peripheral I/O** based on their interfacing logic circuits. Data transfer between the microprocessor and its peripherals can take place under various conditions, as shown in the chart. The modes, the techniques, the instructions, and the conditions of data transfer are briefly described in the following paragraphs and summarized in the chart.

FORMATS OF DATA TRANSFER: SYNCHRONOUS AND ASYNCHRONOUS

Synchronous means at the same time; the transmitter and receiver are synchronized with the same clock.

Asynchronous means at irregular intervals. The synchronous format is used in high-speed data transmission and the asynchronous format is used for low-speed data transmission. Data transfer between the microprocessor and the peripherals is primarily asynchronous.

MODES OF DATA TRANSFER: PARALLEL AND SERIAL

The microprocessor receives (or transmits) binary data in either of two modes: parallel or serial. In the parallel mode, the entire word (4-bit, 8-bit, or 16-bit) is transferred at one time. In the 8085/8080A, an 8-bit word is transferred simultaneously over the eight data lines. The peripherals commonly used for parallel data transfer are keyboards, seven-segment LEDs, data converters, and memory.

In the serial mode, data are transferred one bit at a time over a single line between the microprocessor and a peripheral. For data transmission from the microprocessor to a peripheral, a word is converted into a stream of eight bits; this is called parallel-to-serial conversion. For reception, a stream of eight bits is converted into a parallel word; this

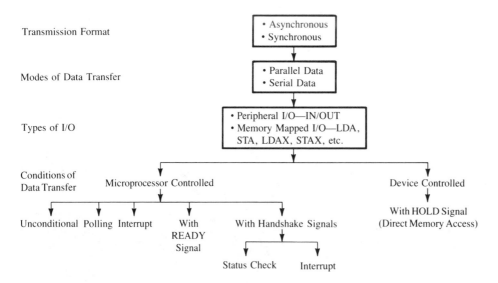

Process of Data Transfer Between the 8085/8080A Microprocessor and Peripherals

is called serial-to-parallel conversion. The serial I/O mode is commonly used with peripherals such as teletypes (TTY), CRT terminals, printers, and cassette tapes.

TYPES OF I/O: PERIPHERAL AND MEMORY-MAPPED

In peripheral I/O, a peripheral is identified with an 8-bit address. The 8085/8080A has two instructions—IN and OUT—to implement data transfer between the microprocessor and peripherals. These are 2-byte instructions; the second byte specifies the address or the port number of a peripheral. The instruction IN transfers (copies) data from an input device to the accumulator, and the instruction OUT transfers data from the accumulator to an output device.

In memory-mapped I/O, a peripheral is connected as if it were a memory location, and it is identified with a 16-bit address. Data transfer is implemented by using memory-related instructions such as STA; LDA; MOV M, R; and MOV R, M.

CONDITIONS OF DATA TRANSFER

The process of data transfer between the microprocessor and the peripherals is controlled either by the microprocessor or by the peripherals, as shown in the chart. Data transfer is generally implemented under the microprocessor control when the peripheral response is slow relative to that of the microprocessor.

MICROPROCESSOR-CONTROLLED DATA TRANSFER

Most peripherals respond slowly in comparison with the speed of the microprocessor. Therefore, it is necessary to set up conditions for data transfer so that data will not be lost during the transfer. Microprocessor-controlled data transfer can take place under five different conditions: unconditional, polling (also known as status check), interrupt, with READY signal, and with handshake signals. These conditions are described briefly.

Unconditional Data Transfer　In this form of data transfer, the microprocessor assumes that a peripheral is always available. For example, to display data at an LED port, the microprocessor simply enables the port, transfers data, and goes on to execute the next instruction.

Data Transfer with Polling (Status Check)　In this form of data transfer, the microprocessor is kept in a loop to check whether data are available; this is called polling. For example, to read data from an input keyboard in a single-board microcomputer, the microprocessor can keep polling the port until a key is pressed.

Data Transfer with Interrupt　In this condition, when a peripheral is ready to transfer data, it sends an interrupt signal to the microprocessor. The microprocessor stops the execution of the program, accepts the data from the peripheral, and then returns to the program. In the interrupt technique, the processor is free to perform other tasks rather than held in a polling loop.

Data Transfer with READY Signal　When peripheral response time is slower than the execution time of the microprocessor, the READY signal can be used to add T-states, thus extending the execution time. This process provides sufficient time for the peripheral to complete the data transfer. The technique is commonly used in a system with slow memory chips.

Data Transfer with Handshake Signals　In this data transfer, signals are exchanged between the microprocessor and a peripheral prior to actual data transfer; these signals are called handshake signals. The function of handshake signals is to ensure the readiness of the peripheral and to synchronize the timing of the data transfer. For example, when an A/D converter is used as an input device, the microprocessor needs to wait because of the slow conversion time of the converter. At the end of the conversion, the A/D converter sends the Data Ready

(DR), also known as End of Conversion, signal to the microprocessor. Upon receiving the DR signal, the microprocessor reads the data and acknowledges by sending a signal to the converter that the data have been read. During the conversion period, the microprocessor keeps checking the DR signal; this technique is called the status check with handshake signals. This status check method is functionally similar to the polling method and achieves the same results.

Rather than using the handshake signals for the status check, the signals can be used to implement data transfer with interrupt. In the above example of the A/D converter, the DR signal can be used to interrupt the microprocessor.

Handshake signals prevent the microprocessor from reading the same data more than once, from a slow device, and from writing new data before the device has accepted the previous data.

PERIPHERAL-CONTROLLED DATA TRANSFER

The last category of data transfer shown in the chart is device-controlled I/O. This type of data transfer is employed when the peripheral is much faster than the microprocessor. For example, in the case of Direct Memory Access (DMA), the DMA controller sends a HOLD signal to the microprocessor, the microprocessor releases its data bus and the address bus to the DMA controller, and data are transferred at high speed without the intervention of the microprocessor.

CHAPTER TOPICS

Chapter 11 addresses the basic concepts of parallel I/O. It includes examples of interfacing simple devices such as keyboards and seven-sgement LEDs. Memory interfacing is illustrated also as a special type of I/O. In addition, the chapter deals with topics such as key debounce, multiplexing, display scanning, bus contention, and an application of the READY signal.

Chapter 12 deals primarily with interrupts. It includes the 8080A interrupt and the 8085 interrupts, with examples.

Chapter 13 is concerned with the interfacing of data converters. After reviewing the basic concepts underlying data converters, the chapter presents examples of interfacing data converters.

Chapter 14 deals with programmable interface devices used in the SDK-85 system. These devices can be set up to perform I/O tasks by writing instructions in their control registers, thus the title programmable devices. While most I/O tasks discussed in Chapters 11–13 are performed with software, Chapter 14 focuses, instead, on hardware. The chapter includes several illustrations of interfacing using programmable devices from the Intel family, such as the 8155/8156 (Memory with I/O and Timer), the 8755/8355 (EPROM/ROM with I/O), and the 8279 (Programmable Keyboard Display Interface).

Chapter 15 is an extension of the topics examined in Chapter 14. It includes general-purpose programmable interface devices, such as the 8255A (Programmable Peripheral Interface), the 8253 (Timer), the 8259A (Interrupt Controller), and the 8257 (DMA Controller).

Chapter 16 deals with serial I/O. It includes the software approach to serial data transfer, using I/O ports as well as the SID and SOD signals of the 8085. This chapter also illustrates the hardware approach to serial I/O, using the 8251A (Programmable Communication Interface).

Chapter 17 is concerned with the process of designing a microprocessor-based product. The primary objective of this chapter is to synthesize the concepts, using both hardware and software, discussed in all the previous chapters. It includes two projects: (1) the design of a single-board microcomputer, and (2) bidirectional data transfer between two microcomputers. It also includes in-circuit emulation as a troubleshooting technique.

Chapter 18 reviews other microprocessors and suggests the trends in microprocessor technology.

It describes some other 8-bit microprocessors, such as the Zilog Z80, National Semiconductor NSC800, Motorola 6800 and 6809, and MOS Technology 6502. It also discusses various Intel single-chip microcomputers, and 16-bit and 32-bit microprocessors.

PREREQUISITES

☐ Basic concepts of microprocessor architecture, memory, and I/Os (see Part I).
☐ Familiarity with the 8085/8080A instruction set and programming techniques (see Part II).

Parallel Input/Output and Interfacing Applications

11

In the parallel I/O data mode, the 8085/8080A accepts eight bits of data on its data bus from peripherals such as switches, Hex keyboards, and A/D converters. Similarly, it sends out eight bits of data on its data bus to output devices such as LEDs, seven-segment LEDs, and D/A converters. Each I/O device is assigned a binary address, called a *device address* or *port number,* through an appropriate interfacing logic circuit. When the microprocessor executes a data transfer instruction for an I/O device, it sends the appropriate address on the address bus, sends the control signal, enables the device, and transfers data. When these I/O tasks are accomplished by means of input/output (IN/OUT) instructions, the process is called peripheral I/O. When I/O tasks are accomplished by means of memory-related data transfer instructions (LDA, STA, etc.), the process is called memory-mapped I/O.

This chapter deals with techniques of interfacing the 8085/8080A microprocessor with various I/O devices for parallel data transfer. Specifically, the chapter deals with how the microprocessor selects an I/O device, what hardware chips are necessary, what software instructions are used, and how data are transferred. It illustrates techniques such as multiplexing, key debounce, and key matrix scan with examples and circuit diagrams. In addition, it includes memory interfacing with and without Wait states and a discussion about the bus contention.

OBJECTIVES

☐ Recognize the device address (port number) assigned to an I/O device by analyzing the associated logic circuits.

☐ Interface an I/O device to a microcomputer for a specified device address by using logic gates and

MSI chips such as decoders, latches, and buffers.
□ Analyze a multiplexed output display port, and write a program to display data using the multiplexing technique.
□ Explain the key debounce, and write a program to read data from a keyboard by using software key debounce.
□ Analyze the interfacing circuit of a matrix keyboard, and write a keyboard subroutine to read data from a matrix keyboard.

□ Design memory-mapped I/O ports for a given address, and write instructions to read and write from these ports.
□ Interface memory for a given memory map.
□ Explain the term *bus contention* and illustrate a way to avoid the bus contention by using appropriate logic circuits.
□ Define the term *memory-access time,* and explain how the READY signal is used to interface slow memories.

11.1   BASIC INTERFACING CONCEPTS

The approach to designing an interfacing circuit for an I/O device is determined primarily by the instructions to be used for data transfer. An I/O device can be interfaced with the 8085/8080A microprocessor either as a peripheral I/O or as a memory-mapped I/O. In the peripheral I/O, the instructions IN/OUT are used for data transfer, and the device is identified by an 8-bit address. In the memory-mapped I/O, memory-related instructions are used for data transfer, and the device is identified by a 16-bit address. However, the basic concepts in interfacing I/O devices are similar in both methods. Peripheral I/O is described in the following section, and memory-mapped I/O is described in Section 11.4.

11.11   Peripheral I/O Instructions

The 8085/8080A microprocessor has two instructions for data transfer between the processor and the I/O device, as discussed in Chapter 5. The instruction IN (Code DB) inputs data from an input device (such as a keyboard) into the accumulator, and the instruction OUT (Code D3) sends the contents of the accumulator to an output device such as an LED display. These are 2-byte instructions with the second byte specifying the address or the port number of an I/O device. For example, the OUT instruction is typically written as follows:

Memory Address	Machine Code	Mnemonics	Comments
2050	D3	OUT, 01H	;Output accumulator contents to the port with device address 01H.
2051	01		

If the output port with the address 01H is designed as an LED display, the instruction OUT will display the contents of the accumulator at the port. The second byte of this OUT instruction can be any of the 256 combinations of eight bits, from 00H to FFH. Therefore, the 8085/8080A can communicate with 256 different output ports with device addresses ranging from 00H to FFH. Similarly, the instruction IN can be used to accept data from

256 different input ports. Now the question remains: How does one assign a device address or a port number to an I/O device from among 256 combinations? The decision is arbitrary and somewhat dependent on available logic chips. In order to understand a device address, it is necessary to examine how the microprocessor executes IN/OUT instructions.

11.12 I/O Execution

The execution of I/O instructions can best be illustrated using the example of the OUT instruction given in the previous section (11.11). The 8085/8080A executes the OUT instruction in three machine cycles, and it takes ten T-states (clock periods) to complete the execution. However, there are some differences bewteen the 8085 and the 8080A machine cycles which will be discussed later.

OUT INSTRUCTION (8085)

In the first machine cycle, M_1 (Opcode Fetch, Figure 11.1), the 8085 places the high-order memory address 20H on $A_{15}-A_8$ and the low-order address 50H on AD_7-AD_0. At the same time, ALE goes high and $IO/\overline{M}$ goes low. The ALE signal indicates the availability of the address on AD_7-AD_0, and it can be used to demultiplex the bus. The $IO/\overline{M}$, being low, indicates that it is a memory-related operation. At T_2, the microprocessor sends the $\overline{RD}$ control signal which is combined with $IO/\overline{M}$ (externally, see Chapter 3) to generate the $\overline{MEMR}$ signal, and the processor fetches the instruction code D3 using the data bus. When the 8085 decodes the machine code D3, it finds out that the instruction is a 2-byte instruction and that it must read the second byte.

In the second machine cycle, M_2 (Memory Read), the 8085 places the next address, 2051H, on the address bus and gets the device address 01H via the data bus.

In the third machine cycle, M_3 (I/O Write), the 8085 places the device address 01H on the low-order (AD_7-AD_0) as well as the high-order ($A_{15}-A_8$) address bus. The $IO/\overline{M}$ signal goes high to indicate that it is an I/O operation. At T_2, the accumulator contents are placed on the data bus (AD_7-AD_0), followed by the control signal $\overline{WR}$. By ANDing the $IO/\overline{M}$ and $\overline{WR}$ signals, the $\overline{IOW}$ signal can be generated to enable an output device.

Figure 11.1 shows the execution timing of the OUT instruction. The information necessary for interfacing an output device is available during T_2 and T_3 of the M_3 cycle. The data byte to be displayed is on the data bus, the 8-bit device address is available on the low-order as well as high-order address bus, and availability of the data byte is indicated by the $\overline{WR}$ control signal. The availability of the device address on both segments of the address bus is redundant information; in peripheral I/O, only one segment of the address bus (low or high) is sufficient for interfacing. The data byte remains on the data bus only for two T-states, then the processor goes on to execute the next instruction. Therefore, the data byte must be latched now, before it is lost, using the device address and the control signal (Section 11.13).

IN INSTRUCTION

When the microprocessor executes the instruction IN to accept data from an input port, events similar to the execution of the OUT instruction take place. During machine cycle

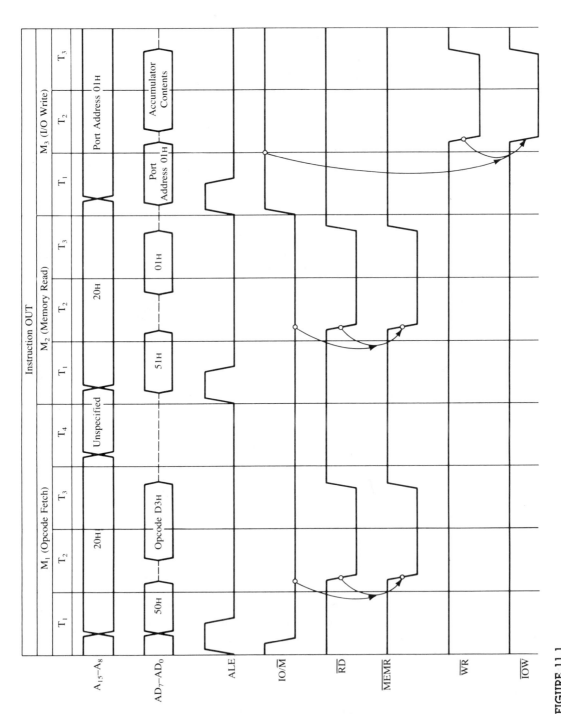

FIGURE 11.1
8085 Timing for Execution of OUT Instruction

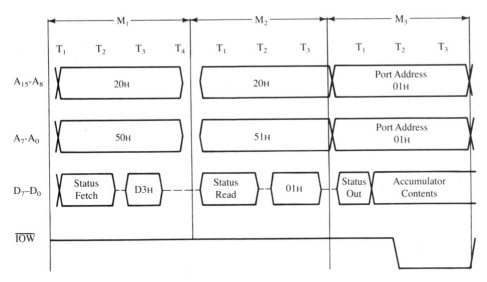

FIGURE 11.2
8080A Timing for Execution of OUT Instruction

M_3, the address of the input port is placed on the address bus, the control signal $\overline{IOR}$ is sent to enable the port, and data are transferred from the input device (such as a keyboard) to the accumulator via the data bus.

8080A MACHINE CYCLE

Figure 11.2 shows the 8080A instruction cycle for the OUT instruction. Functionally, the 8085 and the 8080A machine cycles are similar even though the contents of the data bus during the T_1 state are different. In the 8080A, the status information is placed on the data bus; on the other hand, in the 8085 the low-order address is placed on the bus AD_7–AD_0. However, the critical information required for I/O interfacing occurs during T_2 and T_3 of machine cycle M_3, which is similar in both microprocessors.

11.13 Device Selection and Data Transfer

In general, peripherals are connected in parallel on the data and address buses. To select an appropriate peripheral, the device address on the address bus and the control signal during the M_3 cycle can be used as follows:

1. Decode the address bus to generate a unique pulse corresponding to the device address on the bus; this is called the **device address pulse**.
2. Combine (AND) the device address pulse with the control signal to generate a device-select pulse that is generated only when both signals are asserted.
3. Use the device select pulse to activate the interfacing device (I/O port).

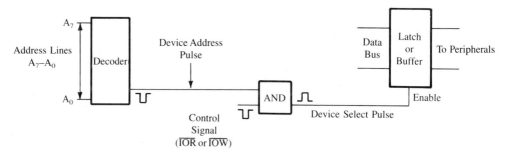

FIGURE 11.3
Block Diagram of I/O Interface

The block diagram (Figure 11.3) illustrates these steps for interfacing an I/O device. In Figure 11.3, address lines A_7–A_0 are connected to a decoder, which will generate a unique pulse corresponding to each address on the address lines. This pulse is combined with the control signal to generate a device select pulse, which is used to enable an output latch or an input buffer.

Figure 11.4 shows a practical decoding circuit for the output device with address 01H. Address lines A_7 to A_0 are connected to the 8-input NAND gate that functions as a decoder. Line A_0 is connected directly, and lines A_7 to A_1 connected through the inverters. When the address bus carries address 01H, gate G_1 generates a low pulse; otherwise, the output remains high. Gate G_2 combines the output of G_1 and the control signal $\overline{IOW}$ to generate a device select pulse when both input signals are low. Meanwhile (as was shown in the timing diagram—Figure 11.1, machine cycle M_3), the contents of the accumulator are placed on the data bus and are available on the data bus for a few microseconds and, therefore, must be latched for display. The device select pulse clocks the data into the latch for display by the LEDs.

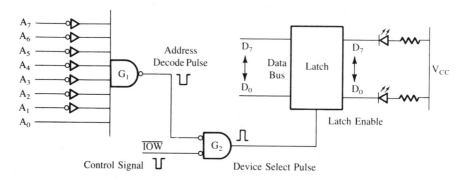

FIGURE 11.4
Decode Logic for LED Output Port

NOTE: To use this circuit with the 8085, the bus AD_7–AD_0 must be demultiplexed.

DIFFERENCES BETWEEN 8085 AND 8080A INTERFACING

If the 8085 low-order bus is demultiplexed, the interfacing steps described above are identical for both microprocessors. If bus AD_7–AD_0 is not demultiplexed, the address of the I/O device is not available on the bus when the control signal goes low. However, the device address is available on the high-order address bus, A_{15}–A_8, throughout machine cycle M_3; therefore, address lines A_{15}–A_8 should be used for decoding instead of A_7–A_0, as in Figure 11.4.

In all subsequent discussions, it will be assumed that in an 8085 system, the demultiplexed address bus is available for I/O interfacing except when special purpose programmable I/O devices are being used. The examples in the following sections are applicable to both microprocessors.

11.14 Absolute vs. Linear-Select Decoding

In Figure 11.4, all eight address lines are decoded to generate one unique output pulse; the device will be selected only with the address, 01H. This is called **absolute decoding** and is a good design practice. However, to minimize the cost, the output port can be selected by using one address line, as shown in Figure 11.5; this is called **linear-select decoding**. As a result, the device has multiple addresses.

In Figure 11.5, address line A_0 and control signal $\overline{IOW}$ are combined to generate the **device select** pulse. This port will be addressed whenever $A_0 = 0$. Lines A_1 through A_7 are unused and can assume "don't care" states. In this circuit, the output port will be selected by addresses such as $00, 02 \ldots FEH$. Such multiple addresses will not create serious problems in small systems, provided the designer is aware of them.

11.15 Input Interfacing

Figure 11.6 shows an example of interfacing an 8-key input port. The basic concepts behind this circuit are similar to the interfacing concepts explained earlier.

The address lines are decoded by using an 8-input NAND gate. When address lines A_7–A_0 are high (FFH), the output of the NAND gate goes low and is combined with control signal $\overline{IOR}$ in gate G_2. When the MPU executes the instruction (IN FFH), gate G_2 generates the device-select pulse that is used to enable the tri-state buffer. Data from the keys are put on the data bus D_7–D_0 and loaded into the accumulator. The circuit for the input port in Figure 11.6 differs from the output port in Figure 11.4 as follows:

FIGURE 11.5
Linear-Select Decoding:
Device with Multiple Addresses

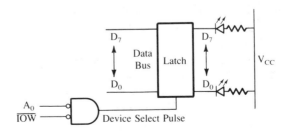

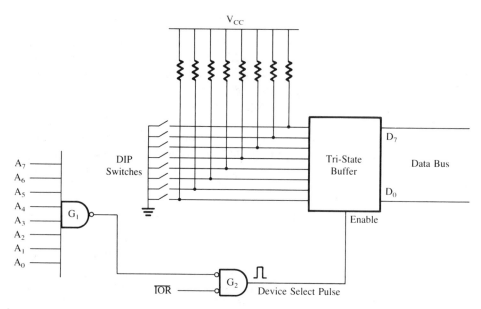

FIGURE 11.6
Decode Logic for a Dip-Switch Input Port

1. Control signal $\overline{\text{IOR}}$ is used in place of $\overline{\text{IOW}}$.
2. The tri-state buffer is used as an interfacing port in place of the latch.
3. In Figure 11.6, data flow from the keys to the accumulator; on the other hand, in Figure 11.4, data flow from the accumulator to the LEDs.

11.16   Interfacing I/Os Using Decoders

Various techniques and circuits can be used to interface an I/O device to the microprocessor. However, all of these techniques should follow the three basic steps suggested in Section 11.13. Figures 11.4 and 11.6 illustrate an approach to device selection using an 8-input NAND gate. Figure 11.5 illustrates a technique using minimum hardware; this technique has the disadvantage of having multiple addresses for the same device. Figure 11.7 illustrates another scheme of I/O interfacing.

In this circuit, a 4-to-16 decoder and a 4-input NAND gate are used to decode the address bus. The output of the NAND gate is used to enable (active low) the 4-to-16 decoder. The output of the decoder (line 5) goes low when the enable line = 0 and the address lines have the following values: $A_3 = 0$, $A_2 = 1$, $A_1 = 0$ and $A_0 = 1$ (0101 = 5H). The output of the NAND gate goes low when A_7, A_6, A_5, and A_4 are all 1s. When address lines A_7–A_0 carry the address F5H, then decoder line 5 generates a device address pulse that is combined with control signal $\overline{\text{IOW}}$ to generate a device select pulse. If decoder line 5 is ANDed with the control signal $\overline{\text{IOR}}$, it will generate a pulse to enable the input port with the address F5H. In a system, an input port and an output port can

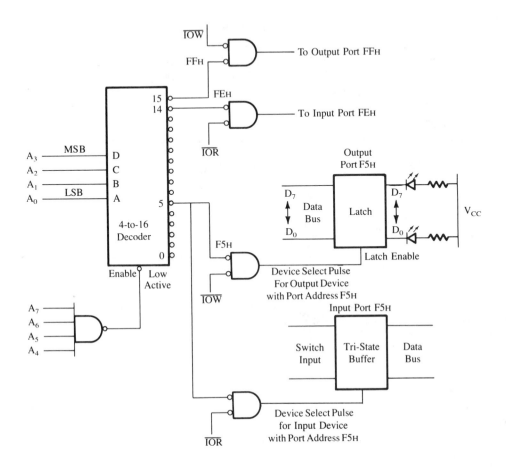

FIGURE 11.7
Decode Logic for I/O Devices Using 4-to-16 Decoder

have the same I/O port address, as shown in Figure 11.7; the ports are differentiated by control signals.

The circuit in Figure 11.7 can be used to enable sixteen different input or output ports with addresses from F0H to FFH. An additional input port with address FEH and an output port with address FFH are shown as examples.

11.17   Review of Important Concepts

In peripheral I/O, the basic concepts and the steps in designing an interfacing circuit can be summarized as follows:

1. When an I/O instruction is executed, the 8085/8080A microprocessor places the device address (port number) on the low-order as well as the high-order address bus.

2. Either the high-order bus (A_{15}–A_8) or the low-order bus (A_7–A_0) can be decoded to generate the pulse corresponding to the device address on the bus.

3. The device address pulse is ANDed with the appropriate control signal ($\overline{IOR}$ or $\overline{IOW}$) and, when both signals are asserted, the I/O port is selected.

4. As interfacing devices, a latch is used for an output port and a tri-state buffer is used for an input port.

5. The address bus can be decoded by using either the absolute- or the linear-select decoding technique. A decoder or discrete gates can be used for absolute decoding and an address line can be used directly for linear-select decoding. The linear-select decoding technique reduces the component cost, but the I/O device ends up with multiple addresses.

11.2 INTERFACING OUTPUT DISPLAYS

This section concerns the analysis and design of practical circuits for data display. The section includes three different types of circuits. The first illustrates the simple display of binary data with LEDs; the second illustrates an application of seven-segment LEDs with the table look-up procedure; and the third illustrates the principle of multiplexing.

11.21 Illustration: LED Display for Binary Data

PROBLEM STATEMENT

1. Analyze the interfacing circuit in Figure 11.8(a), identify the address of the output port, and explain the circuit operation.

2. Explain similarities between (a) and (b) in Figure 11.8.

3. Write instructions to display binary data at the port.

CIRCUIT ANALYSIS

Address bus A_7–A_0 is decoded by using an 8-input NAND gate. The output of the NAND gate goes low only when the address lines carry the address FFH. The output of the NAND gate is combined with the microprocessor control signal $\overline{IOW}$ in a NOR gate (connected as negative AND). The output of NOR gate 74LS2 goes high to generate a device-select pulse when both inputs are low (or both signals are asserted). Meanwhile, the contents of the accumulator have been put on the data bus. The device-select pulse is used as a clock pulse to activate the D-type latch, and the data are latched and displayed.

In this circuit, the LED cathodes are connected to the $\overline{Q}$ output of the latch. The anodes are connected to +5 V through resistors to limit the current flow through the diodes. When the data line (for example D_0) has 1, the output $\overline{Q}$ is 0 and the corresponding LED is turned on. If the LED anode were connected to Q, its cathode would be connected to the ground. In this configuration, the D flip-flop would not be able to supply the necessary current to the LED.

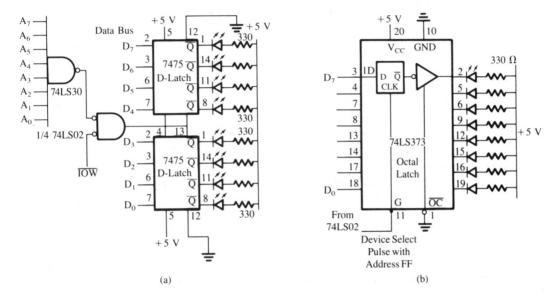

FIGURE 11.8
Interfacing LED Output Port Using the 7475 D-Type Latch (a) and Using the
74LS373 Octal D-Type Latch (b)

Figure 11.8(b) uses the 74LS373 octal latch as an interfacing device, and both circuits (a) and (b) are functionally similar. The 74LS373 includes D-latches (flip-flops) followed by tri-state buffers (see Figure 2.23 for details). This device has two control signals: Enable (G) to clock data in the flip-flops and Output Control ($\overline{OC}$) to enable the buffers. In this circuit, the 74LS373 is used as a latch; therefore, the tri-state buffers are enabled by grounding the $\overline{OC}$ signal.

PROGRAM

Address (LO)	Machine Code	Mnemonics	Comments
00	3E	MVI A, DATA	;Load accumulator with data
01	DATA*		
02	D3	OUT FFH	;Output accumulator contents to port FFH
03	FF		
04	76	HLT	;End of program

PROGRAM DESCRIPTION

Instruction MVI A loads the accumulator with the data you enter, and instruction OUT FFH identifies the LED port as the output device and displays the data.

*Enter data you wish to display.

11.22   Illustration: Seven-Segment LED Display as an Output Device

PROBLEM STATEMENT

1. Design a seven-segment LED output port with the device address C8H. (Available chips: 8212 I/O, 74LS138 3-to-8 decoder, 2-input NAND gate, a NOR gate, common anode seven-segment LED.

2. Explain the operation of each chip and of the overall circuit.

3. Write a program to count continuously from 0 to F with a 100 ms delay between each count.

4. Display the count at the port using the table look-up technique, assuming the seven-segment code is stored in memory.

HARDWARE DESCRIPTION

The design problem specifies two MSI (Medium Scale Integration) chips—the decoder (74SL138), and an I/O device (the 8212)—and a common anode seven-segment LED. Functional descriptions of these devices are given below.

Decoder   Figure 11.9 shows the 74LS138 3-to-8 decoder used for decoding the address lines. The chip has three chip enable pins (one active high and two active low), three input lines, and eight output lines. When the chip is enabled, one output signal goes low corresponding to the address on the input lines; when it is not enabled, all output lines remain high. The chip is described in Chapter 2, Section 2.53.

The 8212 I/O Device   The 8212 is a 24-pin I/O device with eight D-type latches, each followed by a tri-state buffer, illustrated in Figure 11.10(a). It has eight input lines (DI_1–DI_8) and eight output lines (DO_1–DO_8).* The 8212 can be used as an input or an output device, and the function (input or output) is determined by pin MD (Mode). However, the 8212 cannot be used simultaneously for input and output in the same circuit, its mode pin is hardwired. It has two device select signals:[†] $\overline{DS_1}$ (active low) and DS_2 (active high). In addition, it has three pins: $\overline{CLR}$ (Clear), STB (Strobe), and $\overline{INT}$ (Interrupt).

At first, the 8212 appears to be a complex device; however, functionally, it is an extension of the latch (the 74LS373 or the 8282) described in Chapter 2, Section 2.55. In its simplest format, the 8212 is a latch with a tri-state buffer and additional control logic. The control logic consists of four signals: $\overline{DS_1}$, DS_2, MD, and STB; this configuration allows the chip to be used as either an input device or an output device. When MD is high the 8212 functions as a latch, and when MD is low it functions as a tri-state buffer. Its output logic is shown in simplified form in Figure 11.10(b) and explained in the next paragraph. Its input logic is described in Section 11.31.

---

*In most other MSI chips, the input/output lines are numbered from 0 to 7 to correspond with the data bus. The 8212 is an earlier chip, however, and this numbering convention was not followed.

[†]The terms Chip Enable, Chip Select, and Device Select are synonymous.

Output Logic In the output mode, Figure 11.10(b), pins MD, STB, and $\overline{\text{CLR}}$ are high. When MD is high, the output of gate G_2 — Figure 11.10(b) — is high, which enables the tri-state buffer. The D flip-flop functions as a latch. Similarly, the output of gate G_4 is low, which makes the STB signal nonfunctional. When the device is selected ($\overline{\text{DS}}_1 = 0$ and $\text{DS}_2 = 1$), the output signals of gates G_1, G_3, and G_5 go high, and the clock signal of the flip-flop goes high. The data on pins DI flow to the output of the flip-flops and are latched when the clock pulse goes low.

SEVEN-SEGMENT LED

A seven-segment LED consists of seven light emitting diode segments and one segment for the decimal point. These LEDs are arranged as shown in Figure 11.11(a). To display a number, the necessary segments are lit by sending an appropriate signal for current flow through diodes. For example, to display an 8, all segments must be lit. To display 1,

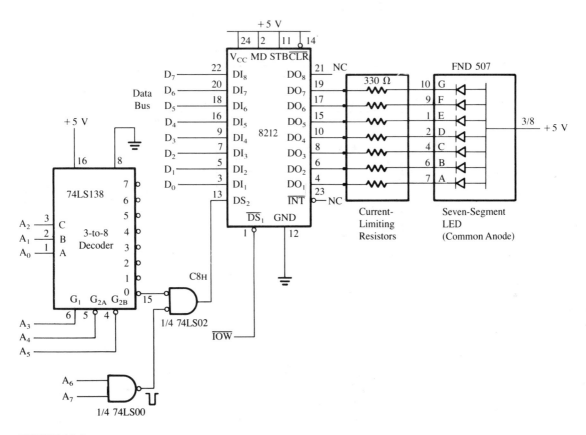

FIGURE 11.9
Seven-Segment LED Output Port Using 3-to-8 Decoder and 8212 as an Interfacing Device

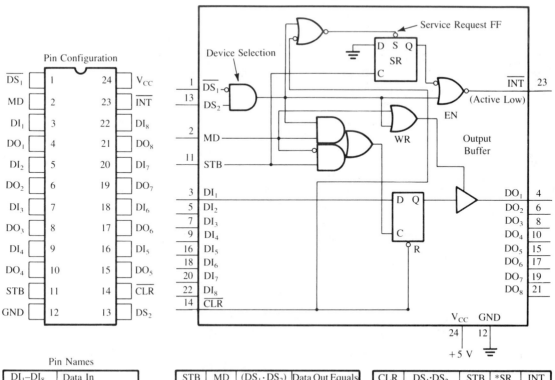

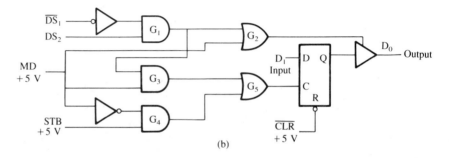

FIGURE 11.10

8212 Logic Diagram and Pin Configuration (a) and 8212 Output Logic Control (b)

SOURCE: (a): Intel Corporation, *Family User's Manual* (Santa Clara, Calif.: 1979), p. 6-80.

FIGURE 11.11
Seven-Segment LED: LED
Segments (a); Common Anode
LED (b); Common Cathode
LED (c)

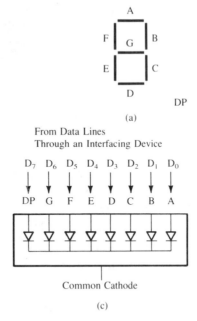

(a)

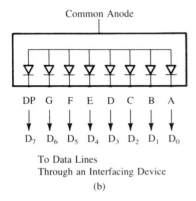

Common Anode

DP G F E D C B A

D₇ D₆ D₅ D₄ D₃ D₂ D₁ D₀

To Data Lines
Through an Interfacing Device

(b)

From Data Lines
Through an Interfacing Device

D₇ D₆ D₅ D₄ D₃ D₂ D₁ D₀

DP G F E D C B A

Common Cathode

(c)

segments B and C must be lit. Seven-segment LEDs are available in two types: common cathode and common anode. They can be represented schematically as in Figure 11.11(b) and (c). Current flow in these diodes should be limited to 20 mA.

The seven segments, A through G, are usually connected to data lines D_0 through D_6, respectively. If the decimal-point segment is being used, data line D_7 is connected to DP, otherwise it is left open. The binary code required to display a digit is determined by the type of the seven-segment LED (common cathode or common anode), the connections of the data lines, and the logic required to light the segment. For example, to display digit 7 at the LED in Figure 11.9, the requirements are as follows:

1. It is a common anode seven-segment LED, and logic 0 is required to turn on a segment.
2. To display digit 7, segments A, B, and C should be turned on.
3. The binary code should be:

Data Lines	D_7	D_6	D_5	D_4	D_3	D_2	D_1	D_0		
Bits	X	1	1	1	1	0	0	0	=	78H
Segments	NC	G	F	E	D	C	B	A		

The code for each digit can be determined by examining the connections of the data lines to the segments and the logic requirements.

Circuit Analysis Figure 11.9 shows the decoding circuit and seven-segment LED with 8212 connected as an output port. The device address of this port can be identified by examining the signals that activate the device select signal DS_2 (high) and the $\overline{DS_1}$ (low).

DS_2 is connected to the NOR gate 74LS02 (shown as negative AND), and $\overline{DS}_1$ is connected to the control signal $\overline{IOW}$. The NOR gate has two inputs: one from the 3-to-8 decoder 74LS138 and the other from the NAND gate. Output line 0 from the decoder goes low when address lines A_5–A_0 have the following signals:

A_5 A_4	A_3	A_2 A_1 A_0
0 0	1	0 0 0
Active Low	Active High	Logic Levels for Line 0
Decoder Enable Lines		Input Lines

The other input to the NOR gate from the NAND gate goes low when lines A_7 and A_6 are 1. Therefore, output port 8212 is enabled by the control signal $\overline{IOW}$ and device address C8H, as shown below:

A_7 A_6	A_5 A_4 A_3	A_2 A_1 A_0
1 1	0 0 1	0 0 0 = C8H
Input to the NAND Gate	Decoder Enable Lines	Input to the Decoder

When the microprocessor executes instruction D3 C8 (OUT C8H), the steps in sending the data to the output device are as follows:

1. In the third machine cycle (M_3), the device address C8H is placed on the address bus A_7 through A_0.
2. The address is decoded by the decoding logic (decoder, NAND, and NOR gates); and the device select line DS_2 of port 8212 is enabled.
3. The other device select line ($\overline{DS}_1$) of the 8212 is enabled by the control signal $\overline{IOW}$ and the output port is selected for data transfer.
4. Meantime, the contents of the accumulator (data to be displayed) are already placed on the data bus.
5. Because the mode signal MD is high, the 8212 functions as an output device. The MD at logic 1 enables the tri-state buffers.
6. When the 8212 is selected, the data on the data bus flow to output lines DO_1–DO_8.
7. Data are latched and displayed by the seven-segment LED.

Current Requirements   The circuit in Figure 11.9 uses a common anode seven-segment LED. Each segment requires 10 to 15 mA of current ($I_{D\;max} = 19$ mA) for appropriate illumination. The tri-state buffers of the 8212 can sink 15 mA when the output is low and can supply approximately 1 mA when the output is high. In this circuit, the common anode LED segments are turned on by zeros on the output of the 8212. If common cathode seven-segment LEDs were used in this circuit, the output of the 8212 would have to be high to drive the segments. The current supplied would be about 1 mA, which might not be sufficient to make the segments visible.

Minimizing the Hardware   Figure 11.9 uses more chips than are actually required in the laboratory experiments in order (1) to illustrate different ways of interfacing I/O devices, and (2) to use the technique of absolute decoding (i.e., the output device in Figure 11.9 cannot be selected by any address other than C8H). The hardware can be minimized by connecting one address line directly to the DS_2 line and control signal $\overline{IOW}$ to $\overline{DS_1}$. (To perform a laboratory experiment with the program given below, but with minimum hardware, see Experimental Assignment 2 at the end of this chapter.)

PROGRAM

The following program, which simply displays each of the sixteen hexadecimal digits sequentially, assumes that you are familiar with the table look-up procedure used in Chapter 9 and the delay calculations explained in Chapter 7. The seven-segment codes for the common anode LEDs are stored sequentially in memory locations starting at location CODE. The program includes a subroutine labelled DELAY that provides a 100 ms time delay.

	Mnemonics		**Comments**
	LXI	SP, STACK	;Initialize stack pointer
START:	LXI	H,CODE	;Load starting address of seven-segment code table
	MVI	B,10H	;Set up a counter to count 16_{10} digits
NEXT:	MOV	A,M	;Find seven-segment code
	OUT	C8H	;Display digit at the port
	CALL	DELAY	;Wait 100 ms
	INX	H	;Point to next code
	DCR	B	;Decrement the counter
	JNZ	NEXT	;If the display count $\neq$ F, go to the next count
	JMP	START	;If the display count $=$ F, repeat the sequence
DELAY:	LXI	D,COUNT	;Load DE pair with delay count
LOOP:	DCX	D	
	MOV	A,D	
	ORA	E	;Check for zero flag
	JNZ	LOOP	;Repeat until count in DE is zero
	RET		
			;Common anode seven-segment code for hexadecimal numbers
CODE:	40		;0
	79		;1
	24		;2
	30		;3
	19		;4
	12		;5

02	;6
78	;7
00	;8
18	;9
08	;A
03	;b
46	;C
21	;d
06	;E
0E	;F

PROGRAM DESCRIPTION

The HL register pair is loaded with the memory address of CODE, in which the first seven-segment code is stored. The count is initialized by placing 10H in register B. A code character is moved to the accumulator from the memory location "pointed to" by the HL register pair, beginning with location CODE. The code character is sent to port C8H for display at the seven-segment LED. Each digit is latched for display during the 100 ms delay provided by the DELAY subroutine. Upon returning from the subroutine, register pair HL is incremented by 1, and register B is decremented by 1. If register B is not 0, the program jumps to location NEXT to display the next digit. If register B is 0, the program jumps to location START and the sequence repeats.

11.23 Multiplexing

In the previous problem, one output port with seven data lines (eight data lines if decimal point is used) was required to display one Hex digit. To display several digits with this technique, additional hardware is required in proportion to the number of digits to be displayed — which can be costly. The number of hardware chips needed for multiple-digit display can be minimized by using the technique called **multiplexing**, whereby the data lines and output ports are time shared by various seven-segment LEDs.

The basic circuit for multiplexed display is illustrated in Figure 11.12. The circuit has two output ports: one port (P_A) to drive LED segments, and a second port (P_B) to turn on the corresponding cathodes. The output data lines of port P_A are connected to seven segments of each LED, and the output lines of port P_B are connected to the cathodes of each LED. The code of the first digit to be displayed at LED-1 is sent on the data lines by outputing to port P_A. The corresponding seven segment LED is turned on by sending a bit to the cathode through port P_B. Next, LED-2 is turned on and LED-1 is turned off. Each seven-segment LED is turned on and off sequentially. The cycle is repeated fast enough that the display appears stable.

In a common cathode seven-segment LED, all segments are driven by the output lines, which should supply at least 10 mA to 15 mA of current to each segment. The cathode should sink seven or eight times that current. MSI output devices (such as the 8212) are limited in current capacity; therefore, additional transistors or ICs, called **segment** and **digit drivers**, are required, as shown in Figure 11.12 and illustrated in the next problem.

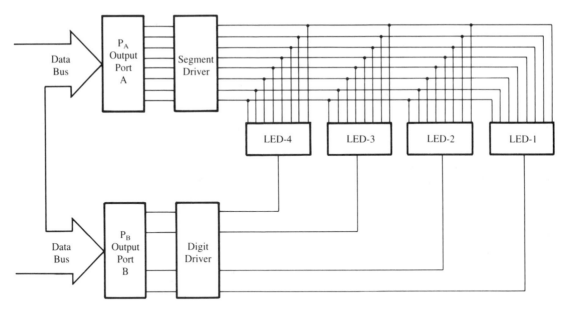

FIGURE 11.12
Block Diagram of Multiplexed Output Display

11.24 Illustration: Seven-Segment Display with Multiplexing

PROBLEM STATEMENT

1. Design a four seven-segment LED display using the technique of multiplexing.
2. Write a program to display the sign 8085.

HARDWARE DESCRIPTION

Figure 11.13 shows the complete schematic which includes 8-input NAND gates to decode the address bus and two 8212s as interfacing devices. In addition, SN 75491 is used as the seven-segment driver, and SN 75492 is used as the digit driver. The explanation of these chips is as follows.

SN 75491 — Segment Driver The SN 75491 is a quad device that has four darlington pair transistors in a package. It can source or sink 50 mA current (approx. 12.5 mA/pair). Figure 11.14 shows both the device and a simplified diagram. Pin A, the base of the transistor, is connected to one of the data lines of the output port and emitter E is connected to one of the LED segments. Two chips of SN 75491 are required for eight data lines (D_0–D_7).

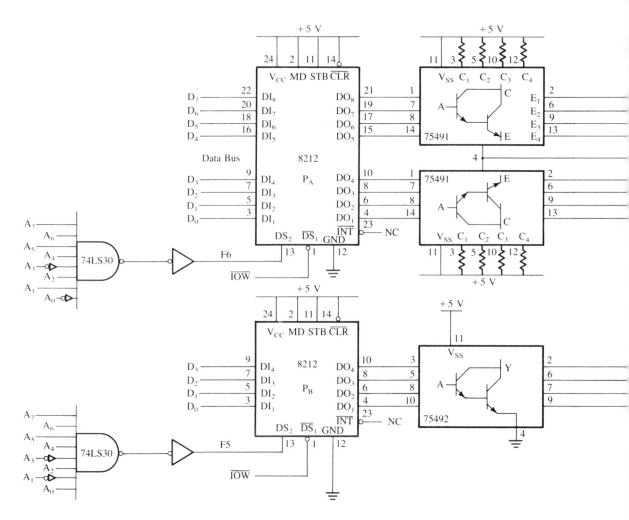

FIGURE 11.13
Multiplexed Output Display

SN 75492 — Digit Driver   The SN 75492 (Figure 11.15) has six darlington pairs in a package and can sink 250 mA of total current. The base of the transistor, pin A, is connected to one of the data lines of a second output port, see Figure 11.15(b). The collector, pin Y, is connected to the common cathode of a seven-segment LED. One chip can drive six seven-segment LEDs.

Circuit Analysis   The circuit (Figure 11.13) has two 8212s as output ports, identified as port P_A and port P_B. Port P_A is assigned the device address F6H by decoding the address

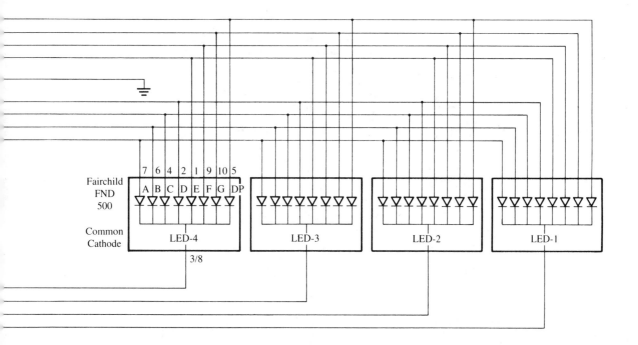

bus with an 8-input NAND gate and Hex inverters. An inverter is necessary to enable DS_2, which requires a high signal. Control signal $\overline{IOW}$ is connected directly to $\overline{DS_1}$, and the output data lines of port P_A are connected to the segment drivers of the SN 75491. Similarly, port P_B is assigned the device address F5H, and its output lines are connected to the digit drivers of the SN 75492. To display a digit, the seven-segment code for the digit is sent to port P_A, and the corresponding cathode is turned on by sending a one to port P_B. Each seven-segment LED is thus turned on and off in sequence, and the loop is repeated continuously.

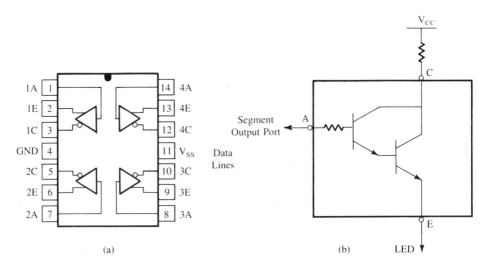

Figure 11.14

SN 75491 (a) and a Simplified Diagram of SN 75491 (b)

SOURCE: Courtesy of Texas Instruments Incorporated.

PROGRAM

START:	MVI	B,01H	;Initialize digit code
	MVI	C,04H	;Initialize counter for four LEDs
	LXI	H,CODES	;Load HL with CODE memory location — HL is used as a CODE pointer
NEXT:	MOV	A,M	;Transfer seven-segment code to the accumulator
	OUT	F6H	;Send code to port P_A
	MOV	A,B	;Load accumulator with digit code
	OUT	F5H	;Turn on LED
	INX	H	;Increment CODE pointer
	RLC		;Rotate left to change digit code for next LED
	MOV	B,A	;Save digit code
	DCR	C	;Decrement LED counter
	JNZ	NEXT	;Is the fourth LED on? If not, go back to turn on next LED
	JMP	START	;Start sequence again
CODES:			;Seven-segment codes for:
	6D		;digit 5
	7F		;digit 8
	3F		;digit 0
	7F		;digit 8

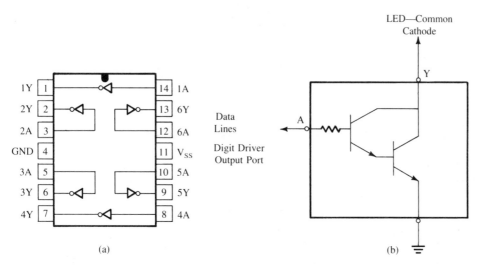

FIGURE 11.15
SN 75492 (a) and a Simplified Diagram of SN 75492 (b)
SOURCE: Courtesy of Texas Instruments Incorporated.

PROGRAM DESCRIPTION

This program assumes that the seven-segment codes for the four Hex digits to be displayed are stored in memory locations CODES through CODES +3. It begins by initializing register B to 01H. This register will always contain the digit code to the next LED to be displayed, thus:

00000001 will turn on LED-1
00000010 will turn on LED-2
00000100 will turn on LED-3
00001000 will turn on LED-4

Register C is then initialized to 04H to serve as a counter, and the HL register pair is initialized to "point to" location CODES.

First, the code pointed to by the HL is transferred to the accumulator and sent to port P_A to drive the segments. The LED digit code stored in register B is then sent to port P_B, where it will turn off the LED presently being displayed and turn on the next LED to be displayed.

Register pair HL is incremented to point to the next seven-segment code, the LED digit code in the accumulator is shifted one place to the left and saved in register B, and the count in register C is decreased by one. If the count in register C goes to zero, indicating that all four LED codes have been displayed, the program re-initializes all registers and begins the display sequence again, from location CODES. If the count in register C is not 0, the next code in the sequence is displayed in the next LED to the left.

This program permits the display of any four Hex digits desired, simply by changing codes in the memory locations.

11.3   INTERFACING INPUT KEYBOARDS

This section deals with interfacing keyboards to input data to the microprocessor using either on/off keys or push-button keys. In the case of on/off keys, the data are very easily read by identifying the device. However, in the case of a push-button key, the metal contact bounces a few times, closing and opening the contacts before providing a steady reading. Such bouncing can be mistaken as several readings. Therefore, the microprocessor must wait until the key settles to a steady state; this is known as **key debounce**. In addition, the push-button keys are arranged in two ways on a keyboard. In one arrangement, each key is connected independently between ground and power supply. In the second case, keys are arranged in a matrix format. This section will illustrate three different ways of entering data in the microprocessor: reading data from a DIP (on/off) switch, reading data from push-button keys and matrix keys by using the software technique.

11.31   Illustration: Data Input from a DIP Switch

PROBLEM STATEMENT

Read the data from the input port in Figure 11.16, and continue reading the input port until a key closure is found. When data are available on the switch, read the input port and display the data at an available output port. Identify the device address of the input port, and explain the circuit operation.

CIRCUIT ANALYSIS

The decoding circuit in Figure 11.16 is similar to the circuit in Figure 11.8; address lines A_7–A_0 are decoded by using an 8-input NAND gate. The output of the NAND gate goes low when the address lines carry address FFH, which is combined with control signal $\overline{IOR}$ in the NOR gate instead of with the $\overline{IOW}$ signal as in Figure 11.8. Even though both decoding circuits are the same, the control signal, $\overline{IOR}$ or $\overline{IOW}$, determines whether the microprocessor reads data as input from a device or sends data as output to a device.

8212 AS INPUT DEVICE

In Figure 11.16, the 8212 is connected as an input device; mode MD is low, input lines DI_1–DI_8 are connected to the DIP switch, and output lines DO_1–DO_8 are connected to the microprocessor data bus. The 8212 functions as an input device when the mode signal is low. Figure 11.17 shows the simplified logic of the 8212 in the input mode. When the mode pin is low, all tri-state buffers are disabled until the device is selected. However, when the STB is high, the output of G_4 and G_5 go high, and external data can be loaded

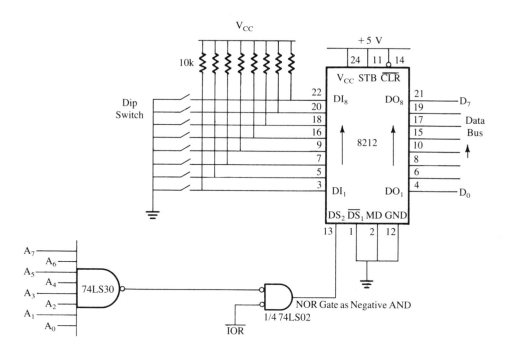

FIGURE 11.16
Interfacing DIP Switch as Input Port

into the flip-flops even if the 8212 is not selected. When the microprocessor executes the IN instruction and selects the 8212, the tri-state buffers are enabled and the data flow from Q to the data bus.

In Figure 11.16, the STB signal is connected high to accept the data from the switches. The input data are entered through the DIP switch; one side of the switches is connected to the pull-up resistors. When no switch is closed (that is, the absence of data), this is indicated by all 1s (FFH). When the 8212 is enabled by the output pulse (active high) of the NOR gate, which is connected to pin DS_2, the data on the DIP switch go to the accumulator via the data bus.

PROGRAM

	Mnemonics		Comments
START:	IN	FFH	;Read data from input port FFH
	CPI	FFH	;Check for switch closed
	JZ	START	;If not, go back and check again
	CMA		;Complement input to indicate the key pressed
	OUT	PORT	;Display data
	HLT		;End of program

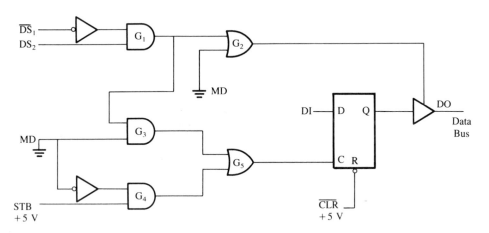

FIGURE 11.17
Simplified Logic Diagram of the 8212 in the Input Mode

PROGRAM DESCRIPTION

The program reads the input port and checks whether there is any data by comparing the reading with FFH. If no switch is closed, the instruction JZ (Jump On Zero) keeps the program in the first loop. Once it finds that a key is pressed, the program falls through the loop, and complements the data to indicate 1s for the key pressed.

11.32   Key Debounce

When a mechanical push-button key is pressed or released, the metal contacts of the key momentarily bounce before giving a steady-state reading, as shown in Figure 11.18. Therefore, it is necessary that the bouncing of the key should not be read as an input. The key bounce can be eliminated from input data by the **key-debounce technique**, using either hardware or software.

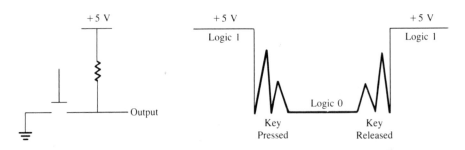

FIGURE 11.18
Key Bounce

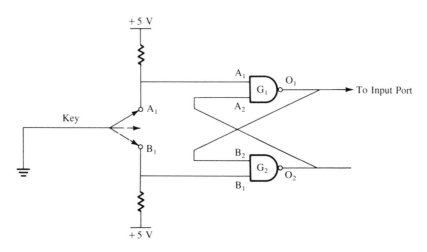

FIGURE 11.19
Key Debounce Circuit Using Two NAND Gates

KEY DEBOUNCE USING HARDWARE

Figure 11.19 shows a key debounce circuit. In this circuit, the outputs of the NAND gates do not change even if the key is released from position A_1. The outputs change when the key makes a contact with position B_1.

When the key is connected to A_1, A_1 goes low. If one of the inputs to gate G_1 is low, the output O_1 becomes 1 which makes B_2 high. Because line B_1 is already high, the output of O_2 goes low, which makes A_2 low. When the key connection is released from A_1, it goes high, but because A_2 is low the output doesn't change. When the key makes contact with B_1, the outputs change. This means when the key goes from one contact ($+5$ V) to another contact (ground), the output does not change during the transition period, thus eliminating multiple readings.

KEY DEBOUNCE USING SOFTWARE

In the software technique, when a key closure is found, the microprocessor waits for at least 10 ms before it accepts the key as an input. The flowchart in Figure 11.21 illustrates the software technique.

The flowchart (Figure 11.21) begins by reading the input port and checks whether the previous key has been released. This will eliminate the problem that would otherwise occur if someone were to press a key and hold it for a long time. Once the key is released, it is debounced by waiting 10 ms. (The waiting period can be anywhere from 10 to 50 ms.) The program reads the keyboard and checks for a key closure. If a key closure is found, it is debounced again by waiting 10 ms, and the binary code corresponding to the key pressed is found either by the table look-up procedure or by setting up a counter.

11.33 Illustration: Reading Push-Button Keys with Debounce

PROBLEM STATEMENT

Write a keyboard program to read the input port 07H, debounce the key closure, and display the equivalent binary code for the key at one of the available output ports on your system. For example, when the K_0 key is pressed, the binary code 0000 should be displayed, and when the K_7 key is pressed, the binary code 0111 should be displayed.

CIRCUIT ANALYSIS

The circuit in Figure 11.20 is similar to Figure 11.16 except that the DIP switches are replaced by push-button keys and the 8212 is replaced by the 74LS244 octal buffer (Figure 2.13). The 74LS244 is a simpler device than the 8212; it is a tri-state octal buffer with two active low enable signals ($1\overline{G}$ and $2\overline{G}$). Each enable signal controls a group of four buffers in the package.

The address bus is decoded by using the 8-input NAND gate and Hex inverters. When the address on the address bus is 07H, the NAND gate generates the device address

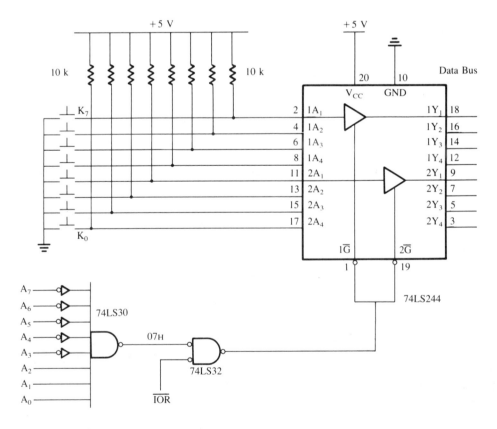

FIGURE 11.20
Push-Button Keyboard as an Input Port

pulse, which is combined with control signal $\overline{\text{IOR}}$ in 74LS32. The output of the 74LS32 (active low) enables the buffers and data from the keys are placed on the data bus. When no key is pressed, the output of the buffer is FFH because the keys are connected to the power supply through the pull-up resistors. When one of the keys is closed, the corresponding data bit goes low and the others remain high. For example, when key 7 is closed, the output of the buffer is 7FH (0111 1111); however, the binary code of the key (0111) must be generated using software techniques.

PROGRAM

The program alongside the flowchart shown in Figure 11.21 finds the key code by using register B as a code indicator, rather than the table look-up procedure.

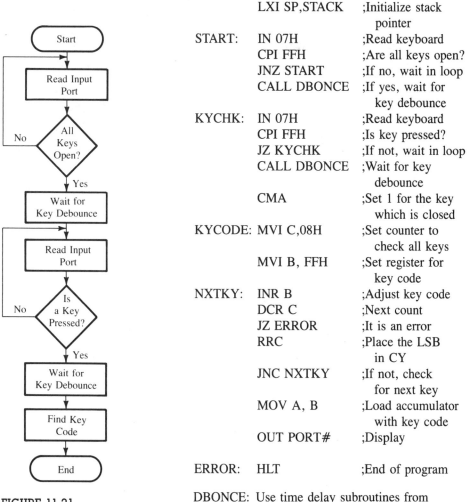

	LXI SP,STACK	;Initialize stack pointer
START:	IN 07H	;Read keyboard
	CPI FFH	;Are all keys open?
	JNZ START	;If no, wait in loop
	CALL DBONCE	;If yes, wait for key debounce
KYCHK:	IN 07H	;Read keyboard
	CPI FFH	;Is key pressed?
	JZ KYCHK	;If not, wait in loop
	CALL DBONCE	;Wait for key debounce
	CMA	;Set 1 for the key which is closed
KYCODE:	MVI C,08H	;Set counter to check all keys
	MVI B, FFH	;Set register for key code
NXTKY:	INR B	;Adjust key code
	DCR C	;Next count
	JZ ERROR	;It is an error
	RRC	;Place the LSB in CY
	JNC NXTKY	;If not, check for next key
	MOV A, B	;Load accumulator with key code
	OUT PORT#	;Display
ERROR:	HLT	;End of program
DBONCE:	Use time delay subroutines from Chapter 7	

FIGURE 11.21
Flowchart of Key Input
with Debounce

PROGRAM DESCRIPTION

The program reads input port 07H and compares it with FFH to check whether all keys are open. If all keys are open, instruction CPI sets the Zero flag, and the program waits for key debounce. After waiting 10 ms, it checks the input port for a key closure. Once a key closure is found, it waits again for the key debounce. The next instruction (CMA) complements the contents of the accumulator, which sets one for the key closed. Register B is used to store a key code, and register C is used to keep an account whether all keys are checked. The Carry flag is checked for a key closure by rotating the accumulator contents to the right. If there is no closure, the accumulator contents are rotated until a key closure is found. For every rotation, the binary code is adjusted by incrementing register B. The binary code for the key pressed is displayed by moving the key code from register B to the accumulator. After eight rotations, if a key closure has not been found, register C becomes zero and the program ends, indicating an error.

11.34   Matrix Keyboard as Input Device

In the previous problem, the number of lines necessary increases in proportion to the number of keys connected. For a large number of keys, such a technique is cumbersome. To reduce the number of connections, keys arranged in a matrix form (Figure 11.22) are used. Figure 11.22 shows sixteen keys arranged in four rows and four columns. When a key is pressed, it shorts one row and one column; otherwise, the row and the column do not have any connection. This keyboard requires eight lines to make all the connections instead of the sixteen lines required if the keys are connected, as in Figure 11.21.

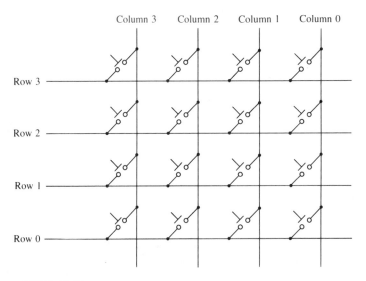

FIGURE 11.22
Matrix Keyboard

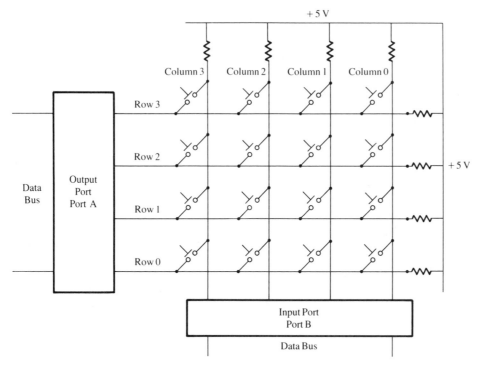

FIGURE 11.23
Matrix Keyboard Connections

The interfacing of a matrix keyboard is shown in Figure 11.23. It has two ports: an output port and an input port. Rows are connected to the output port, and columns are connected to the input port.

The software technique called **matrix scan** is used to read the data from the keyboard. In a matrix scan, rows are grounded by outputting 0s to all the rows through port A and a key closure is checked by reading the data on columns through input port B.

11.35 Illustration: Matrix Keyboard Subroutine

PROBLEM STATEMENT

Write a keyboard subroutine with a key debounce to read the data from the matrix keyboard shown in Figure 11.24 and display the equivalent binary key code.

CIRCUIT ANALYSIS

Figure 11.24 shows the connections of a matrix keyboard. The columns and rows are connected only when a key is pressed; otherwise, they remain high (+5 V). Port P_A is an output port with the device address F5H (see Figure 11.8 for further explanation of the

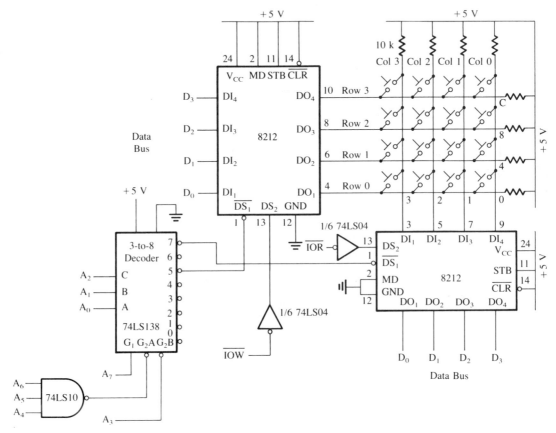

FIGURE 11.24
Interfacing Matrix Keyboard

device address). The data bus of the 8085/8080A is connected to the input lines of the 8212, and the four rows of the keyboard are connected to output lines DO_1–DO_4 of the 8212. The four columns of the keyboard are connected to the input port P_B with the device address F7H. When no key is pressed, all columns remain high. During the scan, one row at a time will be brought low. If a key in that row is pressed, then the corresponding column will also go low.

PROBLEM ANALYSIS

This problem is similar to the previous problem, except that additional steps are necessary because of the matrix key arrangement. The problem is divided into four steps, as shown in the flowchart in Figure 11.25.

Step 1: Check whether all keys are open. In this step, the program grounds all the rows by sending zeros to the output port. It reads the input port to check the key release, and debounces the key release by waiting for 10 ms.

Step 2: Check a key closure. In this step, the program checks for a key closure by reading the input port. If all keys are open, the input reading on data lines D_3–D_0 should be 1111; if one of the keys is closed, the reading will be less than 1111. (Data lines D_7–D_4 are not connected; therefore, the data on these lines should be masked.)

Step 3: Identify the key. This is a somewhat complex procedure. Once a key closure is found, the key should be identified by grounding one row at a time and checking each column for zero. Figure 11.25 shows that two loops are set up, the outer loop grounds one row at a time, and the inner loop checks each column for zero.

Step 4: Find the binary key code for the key. The binary key code is identified through the counter procedure. For each row, the inner loop is repeated four times to check four columns and, for every column check, the counter is incremented. For four rows, the inner loop is repeated sixteen times, and the counter is incremented from 0 to F, thus maintaining the binary code in the counter. Once the key is identified, the code is transferred from the counter to the accumulator.

KEYBOARD SUBROUTINE

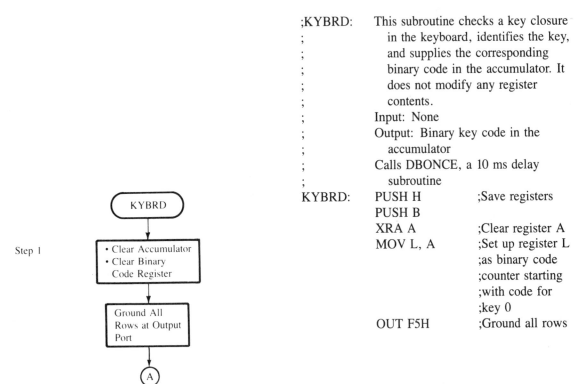

```
;KYBRD:    This subroutine checks a key closure
;          in the keyboard, identifies the key,
;          and supplies the corresponding
;          binary code in the accumulator. It
;          does not modify any register
;          contents.
;          Input: None
;          Output: Binary key code in the
;                  accumulator
;          Calls DBONCE, a 10 ms delay
;                  subroutine
KYBRD:    PUSH H          ;Save registers
          PUSH B
          XRA A           ;Clear register A
          MOV L, A        ;Set up register L
                          ;as binary code
                          ;counter starting
                          ;with code for
                          ;key 0
          OUT F5H         ;Ground all rows
```

Step 1

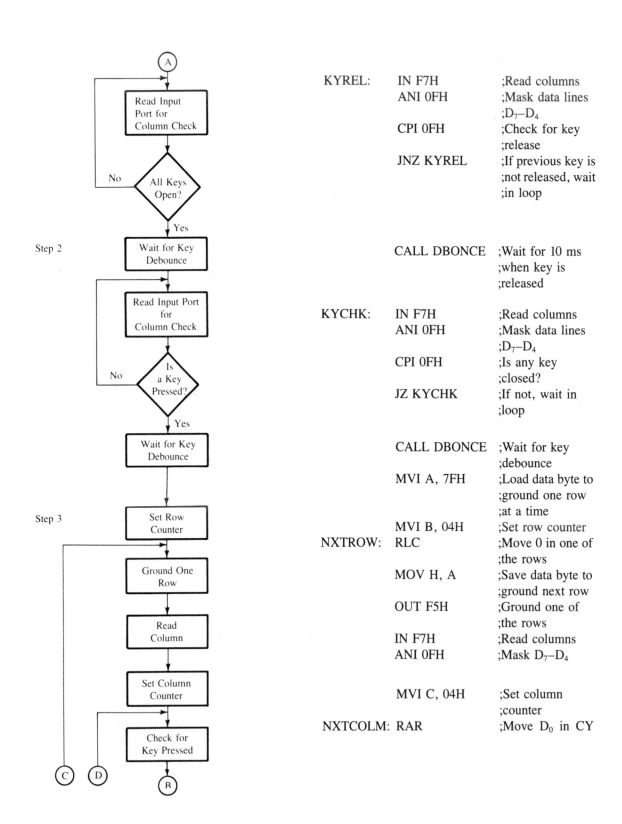

KYREL:	IN F7H	;Read columns	
	ANI 0FH	;Mask data lines	
		;D_7-D_4	
	CPI 0FH	;Check for key	
		;release	
	JNZ KYREL	;If previous key is	
		;not released, wait	
		;in loop	

CALL DBONCE ;Wait for 10 ms
;when key is
;released

KYCHK:	IN F7H	;Read columns
	ANI 0FH	;Mask data lines
		;D_7-D_4
	CPI 0FH	;Is any key
		;closed?
	JZ KYCHK	;If not, wait in
		;loop

CALL DBONCE ;Wait for key
;debounce

MVI A, 7FH ;Load data byte to
;ground one row
;at a time

MVI B, 04H ;Set row counter

NXTROW: RLC   ;Move 0 in one of
;the rows

MOV H, A ;Save data byte to
;ground next row

OUT F5H ;Ground one of
;the rows

IN F7H ;Read columns
ANI 0FH ;Mask D_7-D_4

MVI C, 04H ;Set column
;counter

NXTCOLM: RAR ;Move D_0 in CY

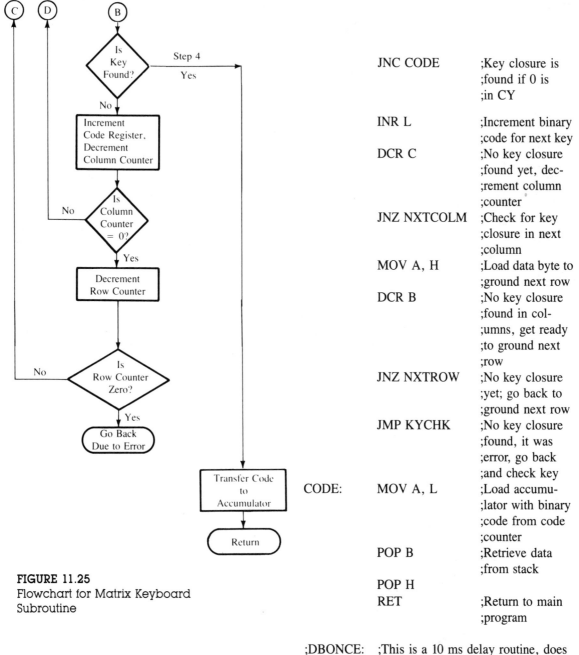

FIGURE 11.25
Flowchart for Matrix Keyboard Subroutine

	JNC CODE	;Key closure is ;found if 0 is ;in CY
	INR L	;Increment binary ;code for next key
	DCR C	;No key closure ;found yet, dec- ;rement column ;counter
	JNZ NXTCOLM	;Check for key ;closure in next ;column
	MOV A, H	;Load data byte to ;ground next row
	DCR B	;No key closure ;found in col- ;umns, get ready ;to ground next ;row
	JNZ NXTROW	;No key closure ;yet; go back to ;ground next row
	JMP KYCHK	;No key closure ;found, it was ;error, go back ;and check key
CODE:	MOV A, L	;Load accumu- ;lator with binary ;code from code ;counter
	POP B	;Retrieve data ;from stack
	POP H	
	RET	;Return to main ;program

```
;DBONCE:   ;This is a 10 ms delay routine, does
;              not destroy any register contents
;          ;Input: None
;          ;Output: None
```

```
DBOUNCE:  PUSH H          ;Save register
                          ;contents
          PUSH PSW
          LXI H,COUNT     ;Load HL pair
                          ;with delay count
LOOP:     DCX H
          MOV A, H
          ORA L           ;Set Zero flag if
                          ;(HL) = 0
          JNZ LOOP        ;If count ≠ 0,
                          ;repeat loop
          POP PSW         ;Restore register
                          ;contents
          POP H
          RET
```

PROGRAM DESCRIPTION

In the beginning of the subroutine, the contents of register pairs HL and BC are saved on the stack and registers A and L are cleared. Register L is set up to store the binary code for the keys 0 to F. The binary code for the 0-key is placed in register L by clearing the register. The OUT instruction grounds all the rows, and the IN instruction reads the columns. Because data lines D_4–D_7 are not connected and may have any random data, the ANI instruction masks the lines D_4–D_7.

The next instruction, CPI 0FH, checks whether all keys are open or whether the previous key pressed has been released. If all the keys are open, D_0–D_3 will be high and the Compare instruction will set the Zero flag; otherwise, the program stays in the loop KYREL until all keys are open. The subroutine DBONCE provides a 10-ms delay and eliminates the key bounce while a key is being released.

Once all keys are open, the program reads the columns from the input port to check a key closure. If any of the keys is closed, the column reading will have one zero, and the program will fall through the KYCHK loop. The DBONCE subroutine will debounce the key closure. At this point in the program, a key closure is found, but the key is not identified. For example, if any one of the keys (0, 4, 8, or C) along the 0 column is pressed, the microprocessor will read the binary data as 1110. For each column, data will be as follows:*

---

*Binary data represents data lines D_0, D_1, D_2, and D_3, in that order.

Keys	Column 0	Keys	Column 1	Keys	Column 2	Keys	Column 3
0 =	1110	1 =	1101	2 =	1011	3 =	0111
4 =	1110	5 =	1101	6 =	1011	7 =	0111
8 =	1110	9 =	1101	A =	1011	B =	0111
C =	1110	D =	1101	E =	1011	F =	0111

To identify the key pressed, one row is grounded at a time and each column is checked for a key closure. This is done by setting up two counters — register B for the row counter and register C for the column counter. The instruction MVI B, 04H sets up the row counter to ground four rows, one at a time. The instruction MVI A, 7FH loads the accumulator with the binary digits 0111 1111 and the next instruction, RLC (Rotate Left), moves the 0 bit from the D_7 position to D_0. When the OUT instruction sends the contents of the accumulator to port F5H, it grounds the 0 row and the IN instruction reads the columns. Register C is set up as a column counter to check four columns. The instruction RAR (Rotate Accumulator Right through Carry) moves bit D_0 into the carry. If D_0 is 0, no carry flag is set, and the key pressed must be the 0 key. The program jumps to location CODE where the contents of register L are moved into the accumulator as a key code; register L is cleared for a key code in the beginning of the program.

If the RAR instruction sets the Carry flag that means bit $D_0 = 1$ and the key 0 is open. Next, the code counter (L) is incremented by one for the next key code. The column counter is decremented by one, and the program jumps to NXTCOLM to check the next column. This loop is repeated four times and in the process, the code counter is incremented four times. The zero in register C suggests that no key is closed in row 0 and in columns 0 to 3. The program falls through the loop, and the instruction MOV A,H loads the digit code into the accumulator. The row counter is decremented, and the program returns to ground the next row (Row 1) by rotating the digit code. The column counter is set again, and each column is checked for a key closure. The row counter (B) and the column counter (C) loop the program until a key closure is found. Every time the program repeats the loop, register L is incremented.

To understand how a binary key code is obtained corresponding to each key from 0 to F, it is necessary to examine the binary digits generated by the hardware listed in the table. There is no direct relationship between the hardware digit pattern and the number of the key. For example, the 0 key generates the pattern 1110; however, it requires the code 0000 to identify it as the 0 key. In this program, register L is used to generate the binary code corresponding to the number of a key. As each key is checked sequentially, register L is incremented from 0 to F.

MEMORY-MAPPED I/O   11.4

The memory-mapped I/O technique uses the memory-related data transfer instructions (LDA; STA; MOV M, A; etc.) and memory-control signals ($\overline{\text{MEMR}}$ and $\overline{\text{MEMW}}$) to transfer data between the accumulator (or registers) and an I/O device. The microprocessor views an I/O device as if it were one of the memory locations. The memory-mapped I/O technique is similar in many ways to the peripheral I/O technique. To understand the similarities, it is necessary to review how a data byte is transferred from the 8085/8080A microprocessor to a memory location or vice versa. For example, the following instruction will transfer the contents of the accumulator to the memory location 8000H.

Memory Address	Machine Code	Mnemonics	Comments
2050	32	STA 8000H	;Store contents of accumulator in memory location 8000H
2051	00		
2052	80		

The instruction STA is a 3-byte instruction; the second and third bytes specify the memory location. In the above example, if an output device instead of a memory location is connected with the address 8000H, the accumulator contents will be transferred to the output device. This is called the **memory-mapped I/O technique**.

On the other hand, the instruction LDA (Load Accumulator Direct) transfers the data from a memory location to the accumulator. The instruction LDA is a 3-byte instruction; the second and third bytes specify the memory location. In the memory-mapped I/O technique, an input device (keyboard) is connected instead of a memory. The input device will have the 16-bit address specified by the LDA instruction. When the microprocessor executes the LDA instruction, the accumulator receives data from the input device rather than from a memory location. To use memory-related instructions for data transfer, the control signals Memory Read ($\overline{\text{MEMR}}$) and Memory Write ($\overline{\text{MEMW}}$) should be connected to I/O devices instead of $\overline{\text{IOR}}$ and $\overline{\text{IOW}}$ signals, and the 16-bit address bus (A_{15}–A_0) should be decoded. The hardware details will be described later in Sections 11.41 and 11.42.

ADDITIONAL MEMORY-RELATED DATA TRANSFER INSTRUCTIONS

In addition to the instructions STA and LDA, the following memory-related data transfer instructions also can be used for memory-mapped I/O.

☐ MOV M, R: Copy data from register to memory location. The memory location is specified by the contents of the HL pair.

☐ MOV R, M: Copy data from memory location to register. The memory location is specified by the contents of the HL pair.

☐ LDAX B (or D): Copy data in the accumulator from the memory location specified by the contents of the BC (or DE) pair.

☐ STAX B (or D): Copy data from the accumulator to the memory location specified by the contents of the BC (or DE) pair.

(These instructions were discussed and illustrated in Chapter 6.)

The example we discussed earlier in this section is illustrated below using the instruction MOV M,A.

Memory Address	Machine Code	Mnemonics	Comments
2050	21	LXI H,8000H	;Load HL pair with address 8000H
51	00		
52	80		
53	77	MOV M,A	;Transfer contents of accumulator to memory location 8000H

These instructions can be used to output data to the device with address 8000H. To design a 16-bit device address, it is necessary to examine how the microprocessor executes the memory-related data transfer instruction.

EXECUTION OF MEMORY-RELATED DATA TRANSFER INSTRUCTIONS

The execution of memory-related data transfer instructions is similar to the execution of IN or OUT instructions, except that the memory-related instructions have 16-bit addresses. The microprocessor requires four machine cycles (thirteen T-states) to execute the instruction STA (Figure 11.26). The machine cycle M_4 for the STA instruction is similar to the machine cycle M_3 for the OUT instruction.

For example, to execute the instruction STA 8000H in the fourth machine cycle (M_4), the microprocessor places memory address 8000H on the entire address bus (A_{15}–A_0). The accumulator contents are sent on the data bus, followed by the control signal Memory Write $\overline{MEMW}$ (active low).

On the other hand, in executing the OUT instruction (Figures 11.1 and 11.2), the 8-bit device address is repeated on the low-order address bus (A_0–A_7) as well as on the high-order bus, and the $\overline{IOW}$ control signal is used. To identify an output device, either the low-order or the high-order bus can be decoded. In the case of the STA instruction, the entire bus must be decoded.

Device selection and data transfer in memory-mapped I/O require three steps that are similar to those required in peripheral I/O:

1. Decode the address bus to generate the device address pulse.
2. AND the control signal with the device address pulse to generate the device select pulse.
3. Use the device select pulse to enable the I/O port.

11.41 Illustration: LED Display for Binary Data

The interfacing of the LED display illustrated in this section (Figure 11.27) is similar to Figure 11.8, except that the memory-mapped I/O technique is used here. Additional hardware is used to decode the high-order address bus, and control signal $\overline{MEMW}$ is used instead of control signal $\overline{IOW}$.

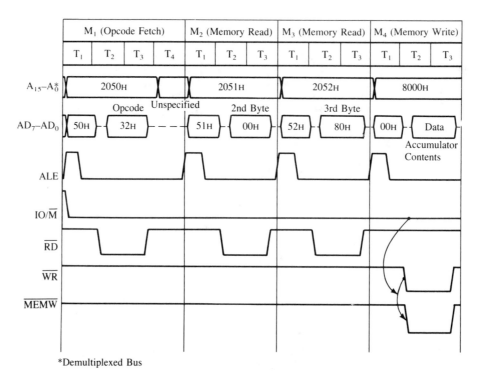

FIGURE 11.26
Timing for Execution of the Instruction: STA 8000H

CIRCUIT ANALYSIS

Figure 11.27 shows that the high-order address bus, $A_{15}-A_8$, is decoded using an additional 8-input NAND gate. The outputs of the two NAND gates and control signal $\overline{\text{MEMW}}$ are ANDed using the 3-input NOR gate 74LS27. When the microprocessor places the address FFFFH on the address bus and sends control signal $\overline{\text{MEMW}}$, the output of the 74LS27 goes high and enables the D latches (7475).

PROGRAM

Address (LO)	Machine Code	Mnemonics	Comments
00	3E	MVI A,DATA	;Load accumulator with data
01	DATA		
02	32	STA FFFFH	;Output accumulator contents to device with address FFFFH
03	FF		
04	FF		
05	76	HLT	;End of program

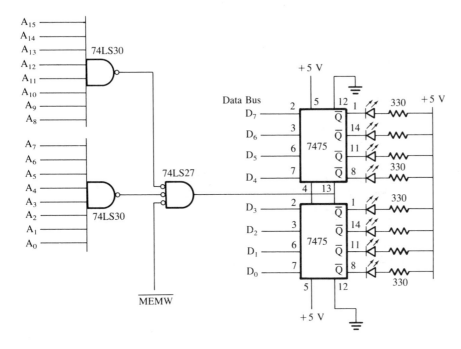

FIGURE 11.27
Memory-Mapped I/O: LED Display

PROGRAM DESCRIPTION

The program is similar to the program in Section 11.21. This program uses the instruction STA with the 16-bit address instead of the instruction OUT with the 8-bit address. The instruction STA FFFFH identifies the device and displays the contents of the accumulator.

11.42 Illustration: Seven-Segment LED Display as an Output Device with Memory-Mapped I/O

The design of the seven-segment LED display (Figure 11.28) is similar to that used in the problem in Section 11.22 (Figure 11.9), except that this design uses the memory-mapped I/O technique. The address lines are decoded using 8-input and 4-input NAND gates (74LS30 and 74LS20), and a 3-to-8 decoder (74LS138). The control signal $\overline{\text{MEMW}}$ is connected through an inverter to one of the device select signals (DS$_2$) of the 8212; the other device select signal ($\overline{\text{DS}_1}$) is enabled by the output of the decoder.

CIRCUIT ANALYSIS

To enable the 3-to-8 decoder, address lines A_{15}–A_3 should be high. Address line A_{15} is connected directly to the active high enable of the decoder. When lines A_{14}–A_3 are high, the outputs of the NAND gates go low and enable the decoder. If the input to the decoder (A_2, A_1, and A_0) is 0 0 0, the 0 line of the decoder goes low and enables $\overline{\text{DS}_1}$, and the

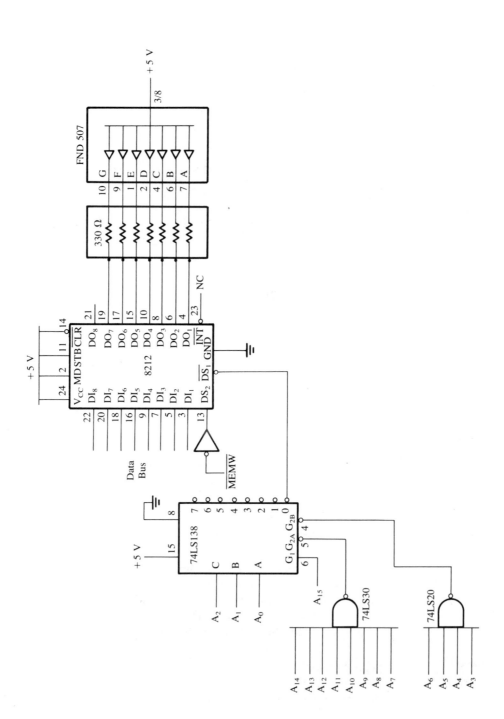

FIGURE 11.28
Memory-Mapped I/O: Seven-Segment LED Display

control signal $\overline{\text{MEMW}}$ enables DS_2. Therefore, the device address of the LEDs in Figure 11.28 should be as follows:

$$A_{15} \longleftarrow \qquad\qquad\qquad\qquad \longrightarrow A_4 \quad A_3 \quad A_2 \quad A_1 \quad A_0$$
$$1 \quad 1 \quad 1 \quad 1 \quad\quad 1 \quad 1 \quad 1 \quad 1 \quad\quad 1 \quad 1 \quad 1 \quad 1 \quad\quad 1 \quad 0 \quad 0 \quad 0 \quad = \quad \text{FFF8H}$$

PROGRAM

The instructions will be identical to the instructions in Section 11.22, except that the instruction STA FFF8H should be used instead of the instruction OUT F8H.

11.43 Review of Important Concepts

Memory-mapped I/O is in many ways similar to peripheral I/O, except that in memory-mapped I/O, the device has a 16-bit address, and memory-related control signals are required to identify the device. Memory-mapped I/O and peripheral I/O techniques are compared in Table 11.1.

TABLE 11.1

Comparison of Memory-Mapped I/O and Peripheral I/O

Characteristics	Memory-Mapped I/O	Peripheral I/O
1. Device address	16-bit	8-bit
2. Control signals for Input/Output	$\overline{\text{MEMR}}/\overline{\text{MEMW}}$	$\overline{\text{IOR}}/\overline{\text{IOW}}$
3. Instructions available	Memory-related instructions such as STA; LDA; LDAX; STAX; MOV M, R; ADD M; SUB M; ANA M; etc.	IN and OUT
4. Data transfer	Between any register and I/O	Only between I/O and the accumulator
5. Maximum number of I/Os possible	The memory map (64K) is shared between I/Os and system memory	The I/O map is independent of the memory map; 256 input devices and 256 output devices can be connected
6. Execution speed	13 T-states (STA, LDA) 7 T-states (MOV M, R)	10 T-states
7. Hardware requirements	More hardware is needed to decode 16-bit address	Less hardware is needed to decode 8-bit address
8. Other features	Arithmetic or logical operations can be directly performed with I/O data	Not available

An examination of Table 11.1 shows that the selection of the I/O technique will be determined primarily by the type of application; the advantages seem to balance the disadvantages. In systems in which 64K memory is a requirement, peripheral I/O becomes essential; on the other hand, in control applications in which the number of I/Os exceed the limit (256) and direct data manipulation is preferred, memory-mapped I/O may have an advantage.

11.5 INTERFACING MEMORY

The topic of **interfacing memory** had been discussed briefly, in Chapters 2 and 3, in the context of the memory map of a given system. Two types of memory — R/WM and ROM (or EPROM) — and their communication process with the microprocessor were illustrated. To read from a memory chip, the 8085/8080A places the 16-bit address of a memory location on the address bus, sends the Memory Read ($\overline{\text{MEMR}}$) signal, and fetches the word via the 8-bit data bus. To write a word in a memory location, the microprocessor places the 16-bit address on the address bus and an 8-bit word on the data bus, and sends the control signal $\overline{\text{MEMW}}$. The process of reading from and writing in memory is similar to reading data from an input port (such as a keyboard) and writing data to an output port, respectively. Memory, therefore, can be viewed as another I/O device. However, it is a special type of I/O that requires additional considerations before interfacing with the microprocessor. Some of these considerations for R/W memory are as follows:

1. Memory requires a 16-bit address. Some address lines from the 16-bit address are used to select the chip, and others are used to address a specific memory location.
2. Memory has internal buffers (input and output) that should be enabled to read from or write in a location. Not enabling memory buffers at the appropriate times may result in bus contention, whereby two or more devices attempt to use the data bus simultaneously (see Section 11.52).
3. Memory has its own response time to Read or Write commands from the microprocessor, which should be considered carefully in interfacing memory. If the memory response time is much slower than the execution speed of the microprocessor, Wait states may be needed in interfacing memory (see Section 11.53).

These considerations are equally valid for ROM or EPROM, except that data cannot be written in these memories. Two examples of memory interfacing are illustrated in the following sections.

11.51 Illustration: Interfacing 2114 Memory Chip

PROBLEM STATEMENT

Interface 1024 (1K) bytes of R/W memory to an 8085 system, with the memory map from 3000H to 33FFH. Use 2114 (1024 × 4) memory chips (Figure 11.29) and the 74LS138 (3-to-8 decoder).

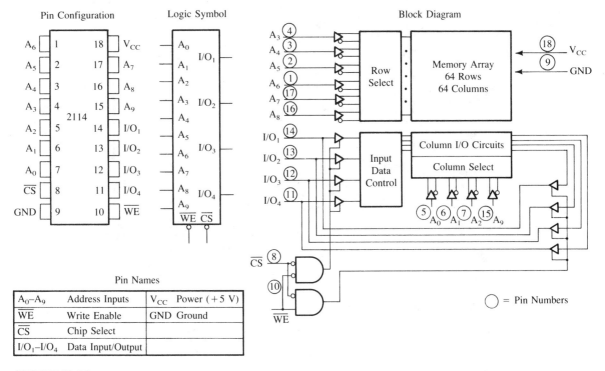

FIGURE 11.29
Memory Chip-2114: Logic and Block Diagram
SOURCE: Intel Corporation, *Family User's Manual* (Santa Clara, Calif.: 1979), p. 6-173.

PROBLEM ANALYSIS

The memory chip 2114 is a static R/W memory, organized in 1024×4 format, which means it has 1024 registers (locations) with four I/O lines (Figure 11.29). Two chips must be connected in parallel to form an 8-bit memory word. The memory chip has two control signals — $\overline{CS}$ (Chip Select) and $\overline{WE}$ (Write Enable) — both active low. The block diagram shows that when both control signals are low, the input buffers are enabled, and a data byte can be written in the selected location. When $\overline{WE}$ is high, a data byte can be read just by selecting the chip; the $\overline{CS}$ signal enables the output buffers.

As shown in Figure 11.30, the chip requires ten address lines, A_9–A_0, to address 1024 locations, and the remaining six lines of the address bus can be used for the chip select ($\overline{CS}$). The logic levels on these six lines determine the memory map of the chip. To design the memory map from 3000H to 33FFH, the logic levels on the address lines A_{15} to A_{10} should be as follows:

A_{15}	A_{14}	A_{13}	A_{12}	A_{11}	A_{10}	A_9	A_8 ←	→ A_0		
0	0	1	1	0	0	0	0 ←	→ 0	=	3000H
						1	1 ←	→ 1	=	33FFH

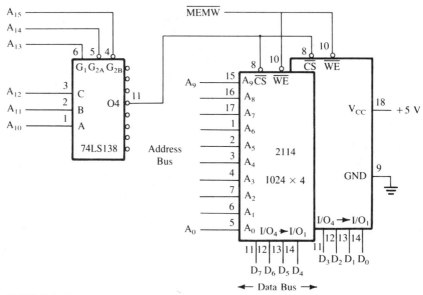

FIGURE 11.30
Interfacing Memory: The 2114

The six high-order address lines can be decoded easily using the 74LS138 3-to-8 decoder, as shown in Figure 11.30. Address lines A_{12}, A_{11}, and A_{10} are used as input to the decoder, and the other three lines are used to enable the decoder. When the input to the decoder is 100, output line 4 goes active and selects the memory chip.

However, in this memory design, the $\overline{CS}$ signal enables the memory output buffers; data can be read simply by selecting the memory chip. Memory may place a data byte on the data bus before the low-order address on AD_7–AD_0 gets off the bus; which may cause bus contention, as described in the next section.

11.52   Bus Contention

Bus contention is defined as a condition in which two or more output buffers are enabled; that is, more than one device attempts to use the data bus. The bus contention usually arises in a transition period when one device is being deselected while another is being selected. In the 8085, bus contention can occur if memory places a data byte on bus AD_7–AD_0 before the low-order address goes off the bus. This may be a potential problem in the schematic shown in Figure 11.30. The bus timings are shown in Figure 11.31.

The $\overline{CS}$ signal is generated within 30 ns after the trailing edge of ALE; this delay is caused in the decoding network. The output from memory can become active in as much as 20 ns (t_{CX}: Chip Selection to Output Active = 20 ns, as shown in Table 11.2). This means the output buffers of memory will go active within 50 ns after the trailing edge of ALE. However, the 8085 specifies that the address hold time is at least 100 ns, which will cause 50 ns of bus contention. The reason for the bus contention is that the memory output

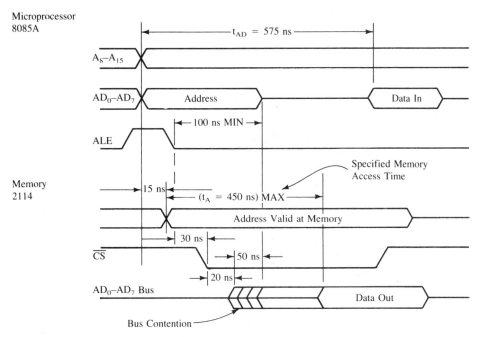

FIGURE 11.31

Timing Waveforms: Reading Data from 2114 Memory

SOURCE: MOSTEK, *Memory Data Book and Designer's Guide* (Carroliton, Texas: 1980), p.

buffer is enabled by the $\overline{\text{CS}}$ signal which is generated as soon as the address is placed on the address bus. The contention problem can be resolved in two ways: by delaying the $\overline{\text{CS}}$ signal by approximately 50 ns, or by using a memory chip with an additional control to enable the memory output buffers.

Figure 11.32 shows a circuit to delay the $\overline{\text{CS}}$ signal. The $\overline{\text{CS}}$ signal is delayed until the $\overline{\text{MEMR}}$ or $\overline{\text{MEMW}}$ signal can enable the decoder; this will avoid bus contention.

FIGURE 11.32

Circuit to Avoid Bus Contention

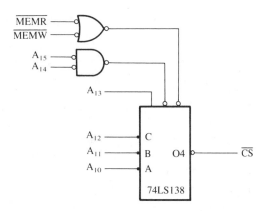

TABLE 11.2
2114 Memory: Read and Write Timings

| Symbol | Parameter | 2114, 2114L | | Unit |
		Min.	Max.	
	Read Cycle*			
t_{RC}	Read cycle time	450		ns
t_A	Access time		450	ns
t_{CO}	Chip selection to output valid		120	ns
t_{CX}	Chip selection to output active	20		ns
t_{OTD}	Output 3-state from deselection		100	ns
t_{OHA}	Output hold from address change	50		ns
	Write Cycle†			
t_{WC}	Write cycle time	450		ns
t_W	Write time	200		ns
t_{WR}	Write release time	0		ns
t_{OTW}	Output 3-state from write		100	ns
t_{DW}	Data to write time overlap	200		ns
t_{DH}	Data hold from write time	0		ns

NOTES:
*A Read occurs during the overlap of a low $\overline{CS}$ and a high $\overline{WE}$.
†A Write occurs during the overlap of a low $\overline{CS}$ and a low $\overline{WE}$.

SOURCE: Intel Corporation, *Family User's Manual* (Santa Clara, Calif.: 1979).

Figure 11.33 shows Intel 2142 (1024 × 4) memory chip and its Read timing diagram. This chip has a control signal, called OD (Output Disable), which is used to control the output buffers. This signal is usually connected to $\overline{MEMR}$. The timing waveforms show that a data byte is placed on the data bus after the OD signal goes low, which is controlled by $\overline{MEMR}$. This allows sufficient time for the low-order address to go off bus AD_7–AD_0, thus avoiding bus contention. During the Write operation, OD is high and the output buffers remain disabled. The chip also has an additional Chip Select (CS_2) signal, which provides more flexibility in some memory designs; ordinarily it is tied high.

11.53   Memory Access Time and Wait States

The **memory response** is defined in terms of the **memory access time** t_A; this is the time delay between the memory address on the address bus and the data byte from memory on the data bus (see t_A in Figure 11.31). The notation for access time varies from one memory chip to another and from one manufacturer to another. Some of the terms used are t_{ACC}, t_{AA} and t_A. Figure 11.31 also shows the parameter t_{AD} (575 ns); this is the time interval between the valid address on the address bus and valid data on the data bus. Memory must place data before the t_{AD} interval is completed; at t_{AD} the 8085 begins to read data. Figure 11.34 shows typical timings of these parameters for a system with 320 ns clock period. If the memory access time is too long compared to the t_{AD} of the microprocessor, data may be lost. In such a case, clock periods are added, by using the READY signal, until memory has enough time to place data on the data bus. This is illustrated in the next

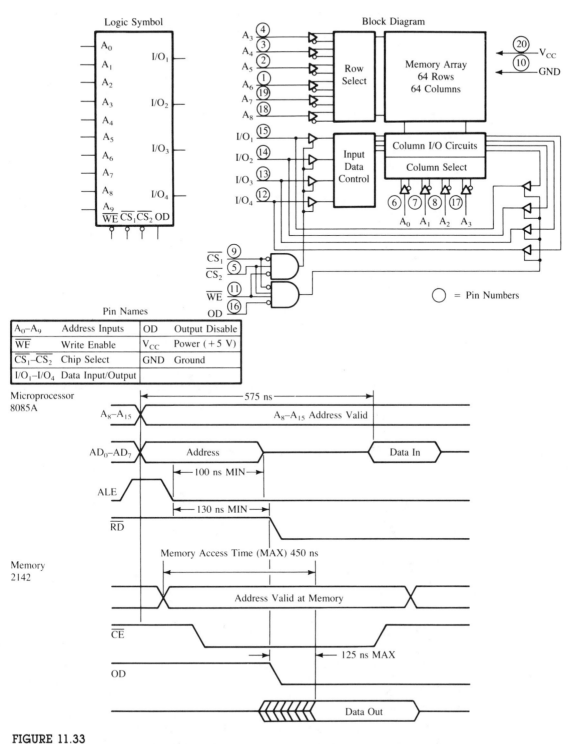

FIGURE 11.33

2142 Memory Chip and Its Read Timing Without Bus Contention

SOURCE: Memory chip: Intel Corporation, *Family User's Manual* (Santa Clara, Calif.: 1979), p. 6-145. Timing: Adapted from MOSTEK, *Memory Data Book and Designer's Guide* (Carroliton, Texas: 1980).

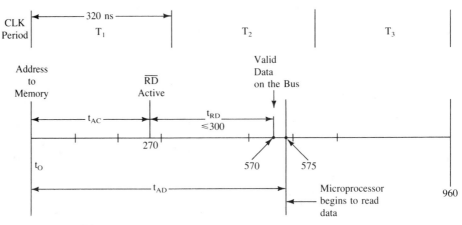

t_{AC} = Address to $\overline{RD}$
t_{RD} = $\overline{RD}$ to Valid Data
t_{AD} = Address to Valid Data In

FIGURE 11.34
Typical Timings for an 8085 System with 320 ns Clock Period

section. The other option in interfacing slow memory is to reduce the clock frequency. This will reduce the speed of the whole system; however, in some systems, it may not affect their overall performance.

11.54   Illustration: Interfacing Memory Using Wait States

PROBLEM STATEMENT

1. Explain the 2716 EPROM memory chip and the interfacing circuit shown in Figure 11.35.
2. Explain the function of the READY signal and how Wait states are generated.

1. THE 2716 EPROM

Figure 11.35 shows the logic diagram of the 2716. It is a 2048 × 8 memory chip with two control signals: $\overline{CE}$ (Chip Enable) and $\overline{OE}$ (Output Enable). It requires eleven address lines (A_{10}–A_0), and the $\overline{RD}$ signal to enable the output buffers. This chip can be programmed in college laboratories using an EPROM programmer. The V_{PP} pin should be connected to +25 V during the programming mode; otherwise, it is connected to +5 V. A program can be erased by exposing the chip to ultraviolet light, and the chip can be reprogrammed.

2. INTERFACING CIRCUIT

Figure 11.35 shows that the eleven address lines (A_{10}–A_0) of the address bus are connected to the address lines of the chip to identify 2048 registers. This circuit uses IO/$\overline{M}$ and $\overline{RD}$ as shown, instead of generating $\overline{MEMR}$ separately. The figure shows that IO/$\overline{M}$ and A_{15}

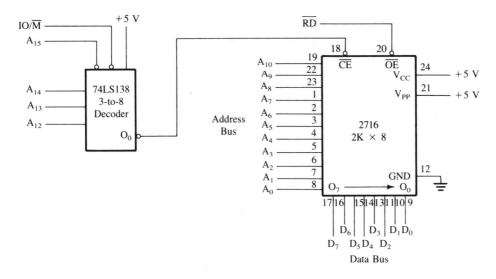

FIGURE 11.35
Interfacing EPROM: The 2716

are connected to active low enable lines of the decoder, and the active high enable line is tied to +5 V. Address lines A_{14}, A_{13}, and A_{12} are used as the input to the decoder, and line A_{11} is not being used. The 0 output line of the decoder is used to select the chip, and control signal $\overline{RD}$ is directly connected to the $\overline{OE}$ (Output Enable) of the memory chip. The decoder is enabled only for memory-related operations because IO/$\overline{M}$ is one of the enabling signals of the decoder. Assuming address line A_{11} is at logic 0, the memory map will be as follows:

A_{15}	A_{14}	A_{13}	A_{12}	A_{11}	A_{10}←			→A_0		
0	0	0	0	0	0	0	0	0	=	0000H
0	0	0	0	0	1	1	1	1	=	07FFH

The timing diagram of the Memory Read cycle is shown in Figure 11.36. The access time is 450 ns; this is the time the memory takes to place a data byte on the data bus after receiving an address. The 8085 microprocessor with clock of 320 ns will begin reading data 575 ns after the address is valid. This leaves 125 ns (575 − 450 = 125 ns) for delays in the decoding circuits. This calculation can be stated in simplified form as follows:

t_{AD} for 8085 = t_{ACC} (Memory) + Decoding Delays + Bus Driver Delays

t_{AD} (8085A): A_0–A_{15} Valid to Valid Data In = 575 ns
t_{ACC} (2716): Address to Output Delay or Access Time = 450 ns
Decoder/Driver Delays < 100 ns

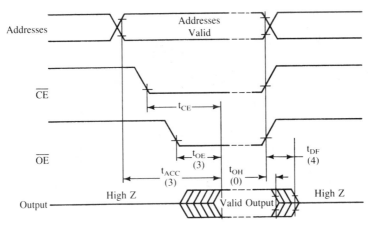

FIGURE 11.36
Timing Waveforms: Memory Read Cycle
SOURCE: Intel Corporation, *Family User's Manual* (Santa Clara, Calif.: 1979), p. 6-80.

In this particular circuit, 450 ns access time is adequate. However, this memory will be too slow for a 5 MHz version (8085A-2) of the microprocessor chip, which has $t_{AD} = 350$ ns. In such a case, the READY signal can be used to extend t_{AD}, as shown in Figure 11.37.

3. READY SIGNAL AND WAIT STATES

The 8085/8080A microprocessor has a READY signal that can be used to generate Wait states.

READY   This is an input signal to the 8085/8080A microprocessor. When it is low, the MPU waits and adds clock cycles, called Wait states, until READY goes high, and then the MPU completes the Read or Write cycle.

In Figure 11.37, the ALE is connected to the clock input of the D flip-flop (F/F_1). When the ALE goes high, the output of F/F_1 goes high. At the next clock, the output (Q)

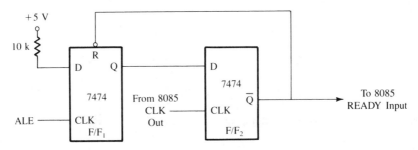

FIGURE 11.37
Circuit to Add One Wait State

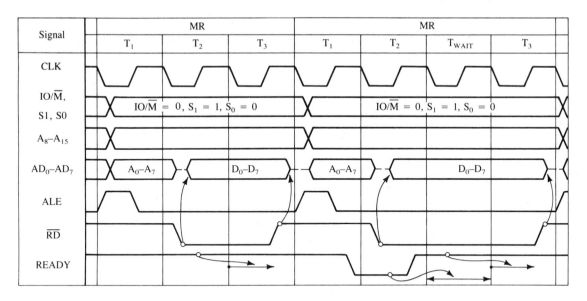

FIGURE 11.38

Memory Read Machine Cycles (With and Without WAIT States)

SOURCE: Intel Corporation, *Family User's Manual* (Santa Clara, Calif.: 1979), p. 2-11.

of F/F$_2$ goes low, which pulls the READY signal low and resets F/F$_1$. This makes Q high in the next clock period. Thus, the output (Q) is low only for one clock period, adding one wait state (clock = 200 ns) to every machine cycle, as shown in Figure 11.38. This technique allows enough time for memory to place data on the data bus.

Figure 11.38 shows two Memory Read machine cycles. The first machine cycle represents the Memory Read operation without the Wait state, while the second includes one Wait state. During T$_2$ of the machine cycle, the microprocessor checks the READY line; if it is low, the microprocessor inserts one Wait state. Again it checks the READY line during the Wait state. If the line is high, the microprocessor goes to T$_3$, and if it is low, it inserts the next Wait state. Figure 11.38 shows how one Wait state extends the Read signal, thus extending t$_{AD}$ by one clock period.

SUMMARY

This chapter began with a discussion of the basic concepts in interfacing I/O devices. These concepts deal with the execution of I/O instructions, device selection, and the process of data transfer in peripheral I/O.

Based on these concepts, six illustrations were presented. The illustrations included examples such as multiplexed seven-segment display and matrix keyboard. Similarly, the concepts in memory-mapped I/O were illustrated with examples.

In addition, topics related to memory interfacing were examined. The illustrations included topics such as the bus contention and applications of the READY signal in interfacing memory.

ASSIGNMENTS

1. Specify the 8085/8080A peripheral I/O instructions and explain why the peripheral I/O technique is limited to 256 input and 256 output peripherals.
2. Is it possible to interface an input device and an output device with the same device address? If yes, what is the major difference in their device select logic?
3. What is the reason to latch data in interfacing LED as an output device?
4. Explain the need for buffers in interfacing an input keyboard.
5. In the peripheral I/O method, explain why data cannot be transferred directly from a register to an output port without using the accumulator (*Hint:* See the execution of the OUT instruction).
6. Identify the device address in Figure 11.4 if high-order address lines A_8–A_{15} are connected to the 8-input NAND gate instead of low-order address lines A_0–A_7.
7. Explain the reason for decoding the high-order address lines in interfacing an I/O device with the 8085.
8. Explain the reason for multiple addresses to an I/O device.
9. What is multiplexing?
10. What is the advantage of a matrix keyboard?
11. Specify the control signal necessary to interface a keyboard using the memory-mapped I/O technique.
12. List two advantages of the memory-mapped I/O technique.
13. In the memory-mapped I/O, can data be transferred directly from a register to an I/O port without using the accumulator?
14. Explain how a memory can be viewed as an I/O device.
15. Explain why a memory interfacing circuit does not need external latches and buffers.
16. Check the appropriate answer in the following statements.
    a. In peripheral I/O, the high-order bus can be used for decoding because
        (1) the I/O device has a 16-bit address.
        (2) the device address is duplicated on the high-order bus.
        (3) the low-order bus is multiplexed.
    b. In the memory-mapped I/O, the device is assigned a 16-bit address because
        (1) the data byte is transferred using sixteen address lines.
        (2) the address bus has sixteen lines.
        (3) the memory data-transfer instructions require a 16-bit address.
    c. The software key debounce can be accomplished by
        (1) holding a key for more than 10 ms.
        (2) using a pair of NAND gates.

(3) using an appropriate delay loop.

d. In the 8212, when the mode pin is high
   (1) the tri-state buffer is enabled and the device functions as a latch.
   (2) the device select pin (DS_2) goes high.
   (3) the device functions as an input device.

e. In the 8212, when the mode pin is low
   (1) the tri-state buffer is enabled by the device select signals ($\overline{DS_1}$ and DS_2).
   (2) the device select signal ($\overline{DS_1}$) goes low.
   (3) the device functions as a latch.

f. To design 2K (2048) bytes of memory with 1024×1 size memory chips would require
   (1) eight chips.
   (2) sixteen chips.
   (3) two chips.

g. In interfacing the 2114 static memory, the $\overline{MEMR}$ signal is not required because
   (1) the Chip Select logic enables the output buffers.
   (2) the $\overline{MEMW}$ enables the input buffers.
   (3) the $\overline{MEMW}$ enables the output buffers.

h. To interface a slow memory, Wait states are added by
   (1) extending the time of the Chip Select logic.
   (2) causing the READY signal to go low.
   (3) causing the READY signal to go high.

17. Identify the device address of the output port in Figure 11.39. (Assume that the don't care lines are at logic 0.)

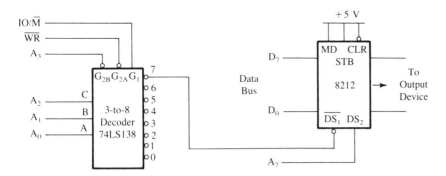

FIGURE 11.39

18. Write a program to display the sign 8085 moving from right to left, for the circuit shown in Figure 11.13 (Section 11.24, Multiplexing).

19. Identify the memory map of the circuit shown in Figure 11.40.

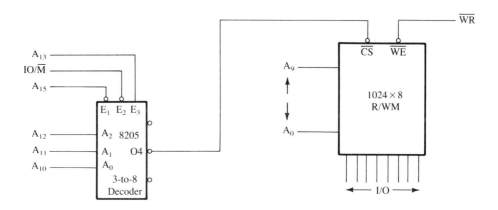

FIGURE 11.40
Memory Interfacing Schematic

20. Figure 11.41 shows the DIP switch as an input port, the LED display as an output port, and the 8205 as a decoder. However, the device select signals $\overline{DS_1}$ (active low) of the 8212s are yet to be connected to the outputs of the decoder.

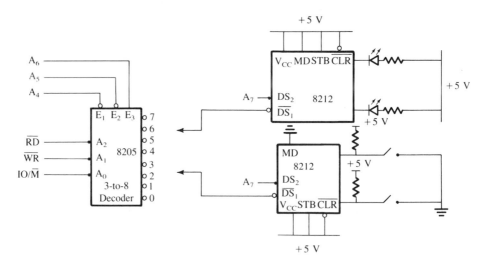

FIGURE 11.41

    a. Identify the output lines of the decoder that can be connected to the $\overline{DS_1}$ of the 8212s.

    b. Identify the device addresses of the ports. (Assume that the don't care lines are at logic 0.)

21. Redraw the schematic in Figure 11.9 using the latch 74LS373 in place of the 8212. (See Chapter 2, Figure 2.23 for the 74LS373 logic symbol.)

22. Redraw the schematic in Figure 11.16 using the octal buffer 74LS244 (see Chapter 2, Figure 2.13 for logic symbol) in place of the 8212.

23. In Figure 11.24, one 8212 is connected as the output port and the other is connected as the input port. Replace both 8212s with Intel's 8282 latches and redraw the schematic. (See Chapter 2, Figure 2.23 for the 8282 logic symbol.)

INTERFACING EXPERIMENTS

Interfacing I/O devices with a microcomputer is a very important aspect of microprocessor applications. The basic principles of I/O interfacing were presented in this chapter, and interfacing applications were illustrated with schematics and programs. The illustrations described in this chapter are suitable for laboratory verification, and I/O interfacing can be performed with any single-board microcomputer based on the 8085/8080A or the Z80. Single-board microcomputers are available from various manufacturers; widely used systems include the Intel SDK-85, the E & L Instruments MMD1, the NEC TK-80A, and the SD Systems Starter Kit.

To perform I/O interfacing with the microcomputer, the following signal lines should be available:

☐ **Address Bus:** Preferably the entire bus $A_{15}-A_0$ or at least the low-order bus A_7-A_0
☐ **Data Bus:** D_7-D_0
☐ **Control Signals:** $\overline{IOR}$, $\overline{IOW}$, $\overline{MEMR}$, and $\overline{MEMW}$
☐ **Other Signals (Optional):** INTR, $\overline{INTA}$, READY, RST 5.5, RST 6.5, or RST 7.5
☐ **Power:** +5 V and Ground

In most single-board microcomputers, the necessary signals are made available to the user.

Modifications in Illustrations

This chapter includes ten illustrations of various interfacing applications, and most of them use the technique of absolute decoding. Even though absolute decoding is a highly recommended practice, it increases the number of ICs to be connected and the time required to perform these experiments. Furthermore, the ICs used in the illustrations may not be available in your laboratory. Therefore, the examples suggested as experimental assignments are better suited for performing I/O interfacing experiments than the illustrations. In these assignments, hardware is simplified, but the programs illustrated in this chapter can be used. In addition, the suggested experimental assignments can be used as problem solving exercises.

Experimental Assignments

1. The schematic shown in Figure 11.42 is similar to the schematic shown in Figure 11.8 except it does not have the 8-input NAND gate.

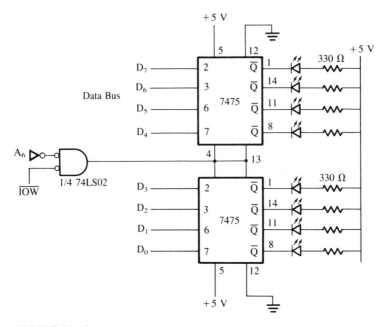

FIGURE 11.42
Interfacing LED Output Port

*Connect A_{14} in place of A_6 if the bus is multiplexed.

    a. Identify the device address (port number) of the output port, assuming the don't care address lines are at logic 1.
    b. What is the device address if all the don't care lines are at logic 0?
    c. What is the port address if address line A_{15} is connected in place of A_7?
    d. Write a program to turn on one LED at a time in a sequence starting at D_7. The LED turn-on pattern should appear as a rotating light from left to right; each LED should remain on for 500 ms.

2. Refer to Figure 11.9.
    a. Connect the circuit in Figure 11.9 (Section 11.22: Seven-Segment LED Display as an Output Device) with the following modification. Eliminate the decoding logic of port address C8H and connect address line A_7 (or A_{15}) directly to device select signal DS_2 of the 8212.
    b. Identify the output device address assuming all don't care address lines = 1.
    c. What is the device address if all don't care address lines = 0?
    d. Write a program to count down continuously from 9 to 0.

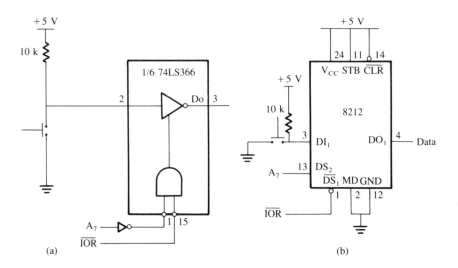

FIGURE 11.43

e. Display the count at the output port using the table look-up technique, assuming the seven-segment code is stored in memory location.

f. Redraw the schematic in Figure 11.9 using the 74LS373 octal latch in place of the 8212.

g. Explain the difficulties in using a common cathode seven-segment LED in relation to the LED current requirement.

3. a. Connect the circuit shown in Figure 11.43 (a) or (b).

b. Identify the device address of the input port, assuming the don't care address lines = 0.

c. Write a program to count the number of times the key is pressed and display the count for each key closure. The program should include 20 ms key debounce and terminate after the tenth count.

d. Modify the program in step c to flash FFH at an output port after the tenth count.

e. Observe effects on a key count, both by reducing the time delay for the key debounce to 5 ms and by eliminating the key debounce.

4. a. Connect the circuit shown in Figure 11.24 (Illustration: Matrix Keyboard Subroutine, Section 11.35) with the following modifications:

☐ Eliminate the decoding circuit.
☐ Connect address line A_7 to DS_2 and control signal $\overline{IOW}$ to $\overline{DS1}$ of port P_A.
☐ Connect address line A_6 to DS_2 and control signal $\overline{IOR}$ to $\overline{DS1}$ of port P_B.

b. Identify the device addresses of the input port and the output port, assuming the don't care address lines = 0.

c. Write a program to check if the key F is pressed. When a key closure is detected for the key F, debounce the key and call the emergency subroutine to flash FF at an output port.

Interrupts

The interrupt I/O is a process of data transfer whereby an external device or a peripheral can inform the processor that it is ready for communication and it requests attention. The process is initiated by an external device and is asynchronous, meaning that it can be initiated at any time without reference to the system clock. However, the response to an interrupt request is directed or controlled by the microprocessor.

The interrupt requests are classified in two categories: maskable interrupt and nonmaskable interrupt. A maskable interrupt request can be ignored or delayed by the microprocessor if it is performing some critical task; however, the microprocessor has to respond to a nonmaskable request immediately. The maskable interrupt is somewhat like a telephone that can be kept off the hook when one is not interested in receiving any calls. The nonmaskable interrupt is like a smoke detector that requires immediate attention when it is set off.

The interrupt process allows the microprocessor to respond to these external requests for attention or service on a demand basis and leaves the microprocessor free to perform other tasks. On the other hand, in the polled or the status check I/O, the microprocessor remains in a loop, doing nothing, until the device is ready for data transfer. For example, in the keyboard routine (Chapter 11),

the processor stays in the loop until a key is pressed and cannot perform any other tasks.

This chapter first describes the interrupt process, which is functionally similar in both the 8085 and the 8080A microprocessors. It includes discussion of how multiple interrupts are implemented with one interrupt line and how priorities are determined. The 8085 has four additional interrupt signals that are described later in the chapter. Two examples of the interrupt I/O are illustrated: a clock timer with the 60 Hz power line as the interrupting source, and a software breakpoint routine. The chapter also includes a brief explanation of the interrupt controller, the 8259, and the I/O process called Direct Memory Access (DMA).

OBJECTIVES

☐ Explain an interrupt process and the difference between a nonmaskable and a maskable interrupt.

☐ Explain the instructions EI, DI, and RST, and their functions in the 8080A (8085) interrupt process.

☐ List the eight steps to initiate and implement the 8080A (8085) interrupt.

☐ Design and implement an interrupt with a given RST instruction.

☐ Explain how to connect multiple interrupts with the INT/INTR interrupt lines and how to determine their priorities using logic circuits.

☐ List the 8085 interrupts and their vectored memory locations.

☐ Explain the instructions SIM and RIM, and illustrate how to use them for the 8085 interrupts.

☐ Explain how to use a RST instruction to implement a software breakpoint.

☐ Explain features of the programmable interrupt controller, the 8259A, and the Direct Memory Access (DMA) data transfer.

12.1 THE 8080A INTERRUPT

The 8080A interrupt process is controlled by the Interrupt Enable flip-flop, which is internal to the processor and can be set or reset by using software instructions. If the flip-flop is enabled and the input to the interrupt signal INT (pin 14) goes high, the microprocessor is interrupted. This is a maskable interrupt and can be disabled. The 8080A has only one interrupt signal; it does not have a nonmaskable interrupt. The 8085 has an interrupt signal called INTR (pin 10), functionally identical with the 8080A interrupt. However, the 8085 has additional interrupt signals as well. To avoid confusion, we will refer to the interrupt process that is common to both the processors as the 8080A interrupt. The best way to describe the 8080A interrupt process is to compare it to a telephone with a blinking light instead of a ring.

Assume that you are reading an interesting novel at your desk where there is a telephone. In order for you to receive and respond to a telephone call, the following steps should occur:

1. The telephone system should be enabled, meaning that the receiver should be on the hook.
2. You should glance at the light at certain intervals to check whether someone is calling.
3. If you see a blinking light, you should pick up the receiver, say hello, and wait for a response. Once you pick up the phone, the line is busy, and no more calls can be received until you replace the receiver.
4. Assuming that the caller is your roommate, the request may be: It is going to rain today. Will you please shut all the windows in my room?
5. You insert a bookmark on the page you are reading.
6. You replace the receiver on the hook.
7. You shut your roommate's windows.
8. You go back to your book, find your mark, and start reading again.

Steps 6 and 7 may be interchanged, depending on the urgency of the request. If the request is critical and you do not want to be interrupted while attending to the request, you are likely to attend to the request first, then put the receiver back on the hook. The 8080A interrupt process can be described in terms of those eight steps.

Step 1: The interrupt process should be enabled by writing the instruction EI in the main program. This is similar to keeping the phone receiver on the hook. The instruction EI sets the Interrupt Enable flip-flop. The instruction DI resets the flip-flop and disables the interrupt process.

Instruction EI (Enable Interrupt)

☐ This is a 1-byte instruction.
☐ The instruction sets the Interrupt Enable flip-flop and enables the interrupt process.
☐ System reset or an interrupt disables the interrupt process.

Instruction DI (Disable Interrupt)

☐ This is a 1-byte instruction.
☐ The instruction resets the Interrupt Enable flip-flop and disables the interrupt.
☐ It should be included in a program segment where an interrupt from an outside source cannot be tolerated.

Step 2: When the microprocessor is executing a program, it checks the INT line (INTR in the 8085) during the execution of each instruction.

Step 3: If the line INT is high and the interrupt is enabled, the microprocessor completes the current instruction, disables the Interrupt Enable flip-flop and sends a signal called $\overline{\text{INTA}}$ — Interrupt Acknowledge (active low). The processor cannot accept any interrupt requests until the interrupt flip-flop is enabled again.

Step 4: The signal $\overline{\text{INTA}}$ is used to insert an instruction, preferably, a restart (RST) instruction, through *additional hardware*. The RST instruction is a 1-byte call instruction (explained below) that transfers the program control to a specific memory location on page 00H and restarts the execution at that memory location after executing Step 5.

Step 5: If the microprocessor receives an RST instruction, it saves the memory address of the next instruction on the stack. This is similar to inserting a bookmark. The program is transferred to the CALL location.

Step 6: Assuming that the task to be performed is written as a subroutine at the specified location, the processor performs the task. This subroutine is known as a service routine.

Step 7: The service routine should include the instruction EI to enable the interrupt again. This is similar to putting the receiver back on the hook.

Step 8: At the end of the subroutine, the RET instruction retrieves the memory address where the program was interrupted and continues the execution. This is similar to finding the page where you were interrupted by the phone call and continuing to read.

We will elaborate further on the restart instructions and additional hardware mentioned in Step 4.

RST (RESTART) INSTRUCTIONS

The 8085/8080A instruction set includes eight RST (Restart) instructions. These are 1-byte Call instructions and transfer the program execution to a specific location on page 00H, as listed in Table 12.1.

TABLE 12.1
Restart Instructions

Mnemonics	Binary Code								Hex Code	Call Location in Hex
	D_7	D_6	D_5	D_4	D_3	D_2	D_1	D_0		
RST 0	1	1	0	0	0	1	1	1	C7	0000
RST 1	1	1	0	0	1	1	1	1	CF	0008
RST 2	1	1	0	1	0	1	1	1	D7	0010
RST 3	1	1	0	1	1	1	1	1	DF	0018
RST 4	1	1	1	0	0	1	1	1	E7	0020
RST 5	1	1	1	0	1	1	1	1	EF	0028
RST 6	1	1	1	1	0	1	1	1	F7	0030
RST 7	1	1	1	1	1	1	1	1	FF	0038

To implement Step 4 in the interrupt process, insert one of these instructions in the microprocessor by using external hardware and the signal $\overline{INTA}$ (Interrupt Acknowledge), as shown in Figure 12.1.

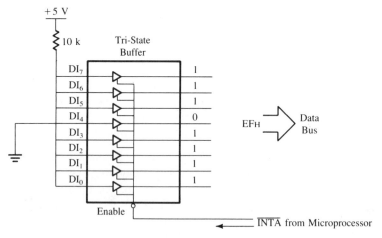

FIGURE 12.1
A Circuit to Implement the Instruction RST 5

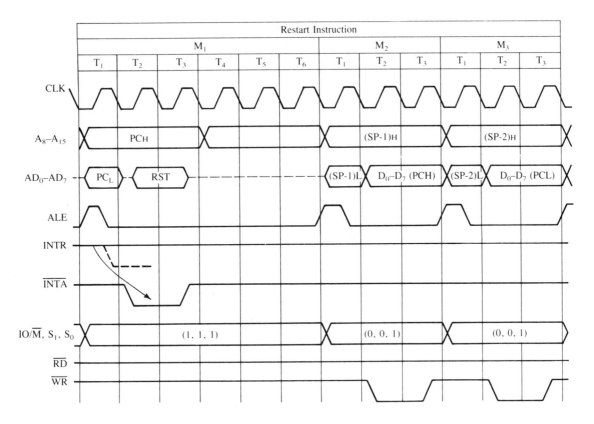

FIGURE 12.2

8085 Timing of the Interrupt Acknowledge Machine Cycle and Execution
of an RST Instruction

SOURCE: Intel Corporation, *MCS 80/85 Student Study Guide* (Santa Clara, Calif.: Author, 1979), p. 2-90.

In Figure 12.1, the instruction RST 5 is built using resistors and a tri-state buffer. Figure 12.2 shows the timing of the 8085 Interrupt Acknowledge machine cycle. In response to the INTR (Interrupt Request) high signal, the 8085 sends the $\overline{\text{INTA}}$ (Interrupt Acknowledge) low signal, which is used to enable the buffer, and the RST instruction is placed on the data bus during M_1. During M_1, the program counter holds the memory address of the next instruction, which should be stored on the stack so that the program can continue after the service routine. During M_2, the address of the stack pointer minus one (SP − 1) location is placed on the address bus, and the high-order address of the program counter is stored on the stack. During M_3, the low-order address of the program counter is stored in the next location (SP − 2) of the stack.

The machine cycle M_1 of the interrupt acknowledge is identical with the Opcode Fetch cycle, with two exceptions. The $\overline{\text{INTA}}$ signal is sent out instead of the $\overline{\text{RD}}$ signal, and the status lines (IO/$\overline{\text{M}}$, S_0 and S_1) are 1 1 1 instead of 0 1 1 (see Figure 12.2). During M_1, the RST 5 is decoded, a 1-byte Call instruction to location 0028H. The machine cycles M_2 and M_3 are Memory Write cycles that store the contents of the program counter on the stack, and then a new instruction cycle begins.

In this next instruction cycle, the program is transferred to location 0028H. However, there are only eight memory locations available for RST 5 if RST 6 is being used in the system; RST 6 begins at 0030H. If the service routine requires more than eight locations, the routine is written somewhere else in R/W memory, and the Jump instruction is written at 0028H to specify the address of the service routine. All these steps are illustrated in the following example.

12.11   Illustration: An Implementation of the 8080A Interrupt

PROBLEM STATEMENT

1. Write a main program to count continuously in binary with a one-second delay between each count.

2. Write a service routine at XX70H to flash FFH five times when the program is interrupted, with some appropriate delay between each flash.

MAIN PROGRAM

Memory Address	Label	Mnemonics	Comments
XX00		LXI SP, XX99H	;Initialize stack pointer
03		EI	;Enable interrupt process
04		MVI A, 00H	;Initialize counter
06	NXTCNT:	OUT PORT1	;Display count
08		MVI C, 01H	;Parameter for 1-second delay
0A		CALL DELAY	;Wait one second
0D		INR A	;Next count
0E		JMP NXTCNT	;Continue

Delay Routine   Use delay subroutine illustrated in Chapter 8, Section 8.21.

Service Routine

Memory Address	Label	Mnemonics	Comments
XX70	SERV:	PUSH B	;Save contents
71		PUSH PSW	
72		MVI B, 0AH	;Load register B for five flashes and five blanks
74		MVI A, 00H	;Load 00 to blank display
76	FLASH:	OUT PORT1	

78	MVI C, 01H	;Parameter for 1-second delay
7A	CALL DELAY	
7D	CMA	;Complement display count
7E	DCR B	;Reduce count
7F	JNZ FLASH	
82	POP PSW	
83	POP B	
84	EI	;Enable interrupt process
85	RET	;Service is complete; go back to main program

DESCRIPTION OF THE INTERRUPT PROCESS

1. The main program initializes the stack pointer at 99H and enables the interrupts. The program will count continuously from 00H to FFH with a delay of one second between each count.
2. To interrupt the processor, push the switch. The INT line goes high.
3. Assuming the switch is pushed when the processor is executing the instruction OUT at memory location XX06H, the following sequence of events occurs:
   a. The microprocessor completes the execution of the instruction OUT.
   b. It senses that the line INT is high, and that the interrupt is enabled.
   c. The microprocessor disables the interrupt, stops execution, and sends out a control signal $\overline{INTA}$ (Interrupt Acknowledge).

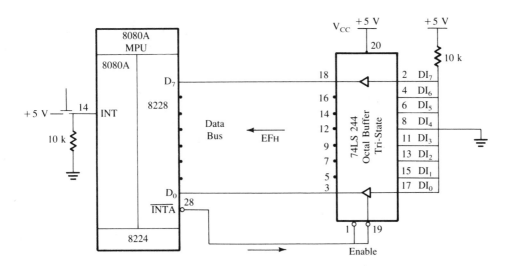

FIGURE 12.3
Schematic to Implement the 8080A Interrupt
NOTE: The 8085 can be substituted for the 8080A with appropriate changes in pin connections.

d. The $\overline{\text{INTA}}$ (active low) enables the tri-state buffer, and the instruction EFH is placed on the data bus.

e. The microprocessor saves the address XX08H of the next instruction (MVI C, 01H) on the stack at locations 98H and 97H, and the program is transferred to memory location 0028H. The locations 0028-29-2AH should have the following Jump instruction to transfer the program to the service routine.

JMP   XX70H

(However, you do not have access to write at 0028H in the monitor program. See the next section.)

4. The program jumps to the service routine at XX70H.

5. The service routine saves the registers which are being used in the subroutine and loads the count ten in register B to output five flashes and also five blanks.

6. The service routine enables the interrupt before returning to the main program.

7. When the service routine executes the RET instruction, the microprocessor retrieves the memory address XX08H from the top of the stack and continues the binary counting.

TESTING INTERRUPT ON A SINGLE-BOARD COMPUTER SYSTEM

Step 3e in the above description assumes that you are designing the system and have access to locations in EPROM or ROM on page 00H. In reality, you have no direct access to restart locations if the system has already been designed. Then how do you transfer the program control from a restart location to the service routine?

In single-board microcomputers, some restart locations are usually reserved for users, and the system designer provides a Jump instruction at a restart location to jump somewhere in R/W memory. For example, in Intel's SDK-85 system, R/W memory begins at page 20H, and you may find the following instruction in the monitor program at memory location 0028H:

0028   JMP 20C2H

If instruction RST 5 is inserted as shown in Figure 12.3, it transfers the program to location 0028H, and the monitor transfers the program from 0028H to location 20C2H. To implement the interrupt shown in Figure 12.3, you need to store the Jump instruction as shown below:

20C2 C3 JMP SERV
20C3 70
20C4 20

This instruction will transfer the program to the service routine located at 2070H.

ISSUES IN IMPLEMENTING INTERRUPTS

In the above illustration, some questions remain unanswered:

1. *Is there a minimum pulse width required for the INTR (INT) signal?*

The microprocessor checks INTR, one cycle before the end of an instruction cycle. In the 8085, the Call instructions require 18 T-states; therefore, the INTR pulse should be high at least for 17.5 T-states. In a system with 3 MHz clock frequency (such as the SDK-85 system), the input pulse to INTR should be at least 5.8 μs long.

2. *How long can the INTR pulse stay high?*

The INTR pulse can remain high until the interrupt flip-flop is set by the EI instruction in the service routine. If it remains high after the execution of the EI instruction, the processor will be interrupted again, as if it were a new interrupt. In Figure 12.3 (Section 12.11), the manual push button will keep the INTR high for more than 20 ms; however, the service routine has a delay of 1 second, and the EI instruction is executed at the end of the service routine.

3. *Can the microprocessor be interrupted again before the completion of the first interrupt service routine?*

The answer to this question is determined by the programmer. After the first interrupt, the interrupt process is automatically disabled. In the Illustrative Program in Section 12.11, the service routine enables the interrupt at the end of the service routine; in this case, the microprocessor cannot be interrupted before the completion of this routine. If instruction EI is written at the beginning of the routine, the microprocessor can be interrupted again during the service routine. (See Experimental Assignment 1 at the end of this chapter.)

12.12   Multiple Interrupts and Priorities

The 8080A microprocessor has one INT pin for the interrupt and eight Restart instructions. This raises two questions.

1. How to connect more than one interrupting device?
2. What happens if two or more interrupting devices request service simultaneously?

The schematic in Figure 12.4 implements multiple interrupting devices using an 8-to-3 priority encoder that determines the priorities among interrupting devices. If you examine the instruction code for eight RST instructions, you will notice that bits D_5, D_4, and D_3 change in a binary sequence and that the others are always at logic 1 (see Table 12.1).

The encoder provides appropriate combinations on its output lines A_0, A_1, and A_2, which are connected to data lines D_3, D_4, and D_5 through a tri-state buffer. The eight inputs to the encoder are connected to eight different interrupting devices.

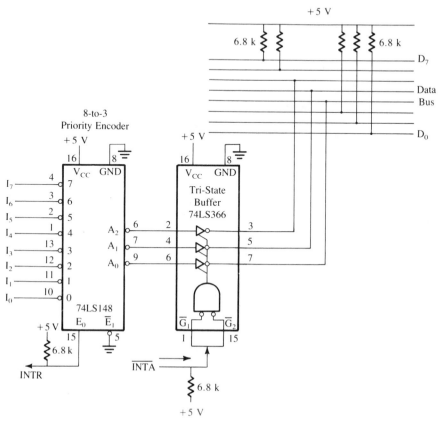

FIGURE 12.4
Multiple Interrupts Using a Priority Encoder

When an interrupting device requests service, one of the input lines goes low, which makes line E_0 high and interrupts the microprocessor. When the interrupt is acknowledged and the signal $\overline{INTA}$ enables the tri-state buffer, the code corresponding to the input is placed on lines D_5, D_4, and D_3. For example, if the interrupting device on line I_5 goes low, the output of the encoder will be: 010. This code is inverted by the buffer 74LS366 and combined with other high data lines. Thus, the instruction 1110   1111 (EFH) is placed on the data bus. This is instruction RST 5. Similarly, any one of the RST instructions can be generated and placed on the data bus. If there are simultaneous requests, the priorities are determined by the encoder; it responds to the higher-level input, ignoring the lower-level input. One of the drawbacks of this scheme is that the interrupting device connected to the input I_7 always has the highest priority. The interrupt scheme shown in Figure 12.4 also can be implemented by using a special device called a Priority Interrupt

Controller—8214. This device includes a status register and a priority comparator in addition to an 8-to-3 priority encoder. Today, however, this device is being replaced by a more versatile one called a Programmable Interrupt Controller—8259, (described briefly later in this chapter).

THE 8085 INTERRUPTS 12.2

The 8085 has five interrupt inputs (Figure 12.5). One is called INTR, which is identical with the INT input in the 8080A. The other four are automatically vectored (transferred) to specific locations on memory page 00H without any external hardware. They do not require the $\overline{\text{INTA}}$ signal or an input port; the necessary hardware is already implemented inside the 8085. These interrupts and their call locations are as follows:

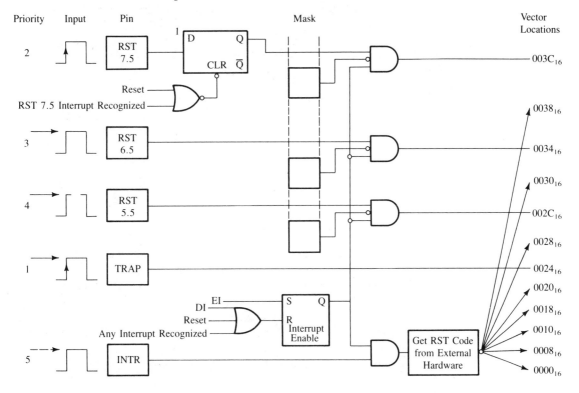

FIGURE 12.5
The 8085 Interrupts and Vector Locations

SOURCE: Intel Corporation, *MCS 80/85 Student Study Guide* (Santa Clara, Calif.: Author, 1979).

Interrupts		Call Locations
1. TRAP	$\longrightarrow$	0024H
2. RST 7.5	$\longrightarrow$	003CH
3. RST 6.5	$\longrightarrow$	0034H
4. RST 5.5	$\longrightarrow$	002CH

The TRAP has the highest priority, followed by RST 7.5, 6.5, 5.5, and INTR, in that order.

12.21   TRAP

TRAP, a nonmaskable interrupt known as NMI, is analogous to the smoke detector described earlier: It has the highest priority; it need not be enabled; and it cannot be disabled. It is level- and edge-sensitive, meaning that the input should go high and stay high to be acknowledged. It cannot be acknowledged again until it makes a transition from high to low to high.

Figure 12.5 shows that when this interrupt is triggered, the program control is transferred to location 0024H without any external hardware or the interrupt enable instruction EI. TRAP is generally used for such critical events as power failure and emergency shut-off.

12.22   RST 7.5, 6.5, and 5.5

These maskable interrupts (shown in Figure 12.6) are enabled under program control with two instructions: EI (Enable Interrupt) described earlier, and SIM (Set Interrupt Mask) described below:

Instruction   SIM: Set Interrupt Mask

☐ This is a 1-byte instruction.
☐ This instruction reads the contents of the accumulator and enables or disables the interrupts according to the contents of the accumulator.
☐ Bits D_7 and D_6 of the accumulator are used for serial I/O and do not affect the interrupts. $D_6 = 1$ enables the serial I/O.
☐ Bit D_3 is a control bit and should $= 1$, in order for bits D_0, D_1, and D_2 to be effective. Logic 0 in D_0, D_1, and D_2 will enable the corresponding interrupts, and logic 1 will disable the interrupts.
☐ Bit D_4 is additional control for the RST 7.5. If $D_4 = 1$, the RST 7.5 flip-flop is reset. This is used to override RST 7.5 without servicing it.

The mnemonic SIM is confusing. The wording — Set Interrupt Mask — implies that the instruction masks the interrupts. However, the instruction must be executed in order to use the interrupts. The process required to enable these interrupts can be likened to a switchboard controlling three telephone extensions in a company. Let us assume these phone extensions are assigned to the president (RST 7.5), the vice-president (RST 6.5)

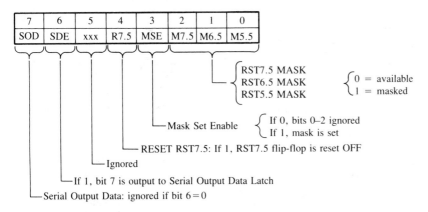

FIGURE 12.6
Interpretation of the Accumulator Bit Pattern

SOURCE: Intel Corporation, *Assembly Language Programming Manual* (Santa Clara, Calif.: Author, 1979), p. 3-59.

and the manager (RST 5.5), in that priority, and are monitored by their receptionist according to the instructions given. The protocols of placing a telephone call to one of the executives and of interrupting the microprocessor using RST 7.5, 6.5, and 5.5 can be compared as follows:

Placing a telephone call	Interrupting the 8085 (Figure 12.6)
1. The switchboard is functional and all telephone lines are open.	1. The interrupt process is enabled. The instruction EI sets the Interrupt Enable flip-flop, and one of the inputs to the AND gates is set to logic 1 (Figure 12.5). These AND gates activate the program transfer to various vectored locations.
2. All executives leave instructions on the receptionist's desk as to whether they wish to receive any phone calls.	2. An appropriate bit pattern is loaded into the accumulator.
3. The receptionist reads the instructions.	3. If bit $D_3 = 1$, the respective interrupts are enabled according to bits D_2–D_0.
4. The receptionist is on duty, and sends calls through for whomever is available.	4. RST 7.5, 6.5, and 5.5 are being monitored.
5. The receptionist is busy typing. Phone calls can be received directly according to previous instructions.	5. If bit $D_3 = 0$, bits D_2–D_0 have no effect on previous conditions.
6. No calls for the president now. Call back later.	6. Bit $D_4 = 1$, this resets RST 7.5.

This analogy can be extended to the interrupt INTR, which is viewed as one telephone line shared by eight engineers with a switchboard operator (external hardware) who rings the appropriate extension.

The entire interrupt process (except TRAP) is disabled by resetting the Interrupt Enable flip-flop (Figure 12.5). The flip-flop can be reset in one of the three ways: by instruction DI, system Reset, or by recognition of an interrupt request. Figure 12.5 shows that these three signals are ORed and the output of the OR gate is used to reset the flip-flop.

TRIGGERING LEVELS

These interrupts are sensitive to different types of triggering as listed below:

- ☐ **RST 7.5** This is positive-edge sensitive and can be triggered with a short pulse. The request is stored internally by the D flip-flop (Figure 12.5) until the microprocessor responds to the request or until it is cleared by Reset or by bit D_4 in SIM instruction.
- ☐ **RST 6.5** and **RST 5.5** These interrupts are level sensitive, meaning that the triggering level should be on until the microprocessor completes the execution of the current instruction. If the microprocessor is unable to respond to these requests immediately, they should be stored or held by external hardware.

Example 12.1

Enable all the interrupts in an 8085 system.

Instructions

EI	;Enable interrupts
MVI A, 08H	;Load bit pattern to enable RST 7.5, 6.5 and 5.5
SIM	;Enable RST 7.5, 6.5, and 5.5

Bit $D_3 = 1$ in the accumulator makes the instruction SIM functional, and bits D_2, D_1, and $D_0 = 0$ enable the interrupts 7.5, 6.5 and 5.5.

Example 12.2

Reset the 7.5 interrupt from Example 12.1.

Instructions

MVI A, 18H	;Set $D_4 = 1$
SIM	;Reset 7.5 interrupt flip-flop

PENDING INTERRUPTS

Because there are several interrupt lines, when one interrupt request is being served, other interrupt requests may occur and remain pending. The 8085 has an additional instruction called RIM (Read Interrupt Mask) to sense these pending interrupts.

The RIM instruction loads the accumulator with the following information:

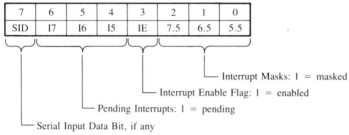

7	6	5	4	3	2	1	0
SID	I7	I6	I5	IE	7.5	6.5	5.5

Interrupt Masks: 1 = masked
Interrupt Enable Flag: 1 = enabled
Pending Interrupts: 1 = pending
Serial Input Data Bit, if any

FIGURE 12.7
Interpretation of the Accumulator Bit Pattern for the RIM Instruction

SOURCE: Intel Corporation, *Assembly Language Programming Manual* (Santa Clara, Calif.: Author, 1979), p. 3-49.

Instruction RIM: Read Interrupt Mask

☐ This is a 1-byte instruction.
☐ This instruction loads the accumulator with eight bits indicating the current status of the interrupt masks, the interrupt enable, pending interrupts, and serial input data. See Figure 12.7.

Assuming the microprocessor is completing an RST 7.5 interrupt request, check to see if RST 6.5 is pending. If it is pending, enable RST 6.5 without affecting any other interrupts; otherwise, return to the main program.

Example
12.3

Instructions

```
        RIM         ;Read interrupt mask.
        MOV B,A     ;Save mask information.
        ANI 20H     ;Check whether RST 6.5 is pending.
        JNZ NEXT
        EI
        RET         ;RST 6.5 is not pending, return to main program.
NEXT:   MOV A,B     ;Get bit pattern; RST 6.5 is pending.
        ANI 0DH     ;Enables RST 6.5 by setting D₁ = 0.
        ORI 08H     ;Enable SIM by setting D₃ = 1.
        SIM
        JMP SERV    ;Jump to service routine for RST 6.5.
```

The instruction RIM checks for a pending interrupt. Instruction ANI 20H masks all the bits except D_5 to check pending RST 6.5. If $D_5 = 0$, the program control is transferred to the main program. $D_5 = 1$ indicates that RST 6.5 is pending. Instruction ANI 0DH sets $D_1 = 0$ (RST 6.5 bit for SIM), instruction ORI sets $D_3 = 1$ (this is necessary for SIM to be effective), and instruction SIM enables RST 6.5 without affecting any other interrupts. The JMP instruction transfers the program to the service routine (SERV) written for RST 6.5.

12.23   Illustration: Interrupt-Driven Clock

PROBLEM STATEMENT

Design a 1-minute timer using a 60 Hz power line as an interrupting source. The output ports should display minutes and seconds in BCD. At the end of the minute, the output ports should continue displaying one minute and zero seconds.

HARDWARE DESCRIPTION

This 1-minute timer is designed with a 60 Hz AC line. The circuit (Figure 12.8) uses a step-down transformer, the 74121 monostable multivibrator, and interrupt pin RST 6.5. After the interrupt, program control is transferred to memory location 0034H in the monitor program.

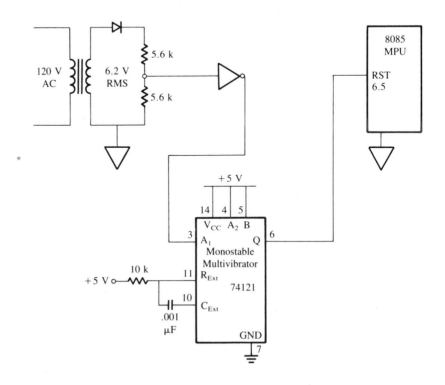

FIGURE 12.8
Schematic of Interrupt-Driven Timer Clock

The AC line with 60 Hz frequency has a period of 16.6 ms, that means it can provide a pulse every sixtieth of a second with 8.3 ms pulse width which is too long for the interrupt. The interrupt flip-flop is enabled again within 6 μs in the timer service routine; therefore, the pulse should be turned off before the EI instruction in the service routine is executed. The 74121 monostable multivibrator is used to provide appropriate pulse width. Another option is to use the 7474 positive-edge triggered flip-flop. The output of the transformer is connected to the clock of the 7474 with D input tied high. Output Q is connected to INTR to interrupt the processor, and the output pulse can be turned off by using INTA. If RST 6.5 is used for the interrupt, an additional output port is necessary to clear the flip-flop (see Assignment 4 at the end of this chapter).

MONITOR PROGRAM

0034	JMP RWM	;This is RST 6.5; go to location in user memory to give Restart access to the user

MAIN PROGRAM

	LXI SP, STACK	Initialize stack pointer
	MVI A, 1DH	;Load bit pattern to enable RST 6.5 and disable others
	SIM	;Enable RST 6.5
	LXI B, 0000H	;Set up register B for minutes and register C for seconds
	MVI D, 3C	;Set up register D to count 60_{10} interrupts
	EI	;Enable interrupts
DSPLAY:	MOV A, B	
	OUT PORT1	;Display minutes at PORT1
	MOV A, C	
	OUT PORT2	;Display seconds at PORT2
	JMP DSPLAY	
RWM:	JMP TIMER	;This is RST 6.5 vector location 0034H; go to TIMER routine to upgrade the clock

INTERRUPT SERVICE ROUTINE

;Section I		
TIMER:	DCR D	;One interrupt occurred; reduce count by 1
	EI	;Enable interrupts
	RNZ	;Has 1 second elapsed? If not, go back to main program
;Section II	DI	;No other interrupts allowed
	MVI D, 3CH	;1 second is complete; load register D again to count 60 interrupts
	MOV A, C	
	ADD 01H	;Increment "Second" register

```
            DAA                 ;Decimal adjust "Seconds"
            MOV C, A            ;Save "BCD" seconds
            CPI 60H
            EI
            RNZ                 ;Is time = 60 seconds? If not, go back to main
                                   program
;Section III DI                 ;Disable interrupts
            MVI C, 00H          ;60 seconds complete, clear "Second" register
            INR B               ;Increment "Minutes"
            RET                 ;1 minute elapsed
```

PROGRAM DESCRIPTION

The main program clears registers B and C to store minutes and seconds, respectively; enables the interrupts; sets up register D to count 60 interrupts; and displays the starting time in minutes (00) and seconds (00). Instruction SIM enables RST 6.5 by reading 1DH from the accumulator.

When the first pulse interrupts the processor, program control is transferred to memory location 0034H, as mentioned earlier. (Check location 0034H in your monitor program; you may find a Jump instruction to transfer the control to a memory location in R/W memory. Write a Jump instruction at that location to locate the service routine labelled TIMER.)

In the service routine (Section I), register D is decremented every second, the interrupt is enabled, and the program is returned to the main routine. This is repeated 60 times. After the sixtieth interrupt, counter D goes to zero and the program enters Section II. In this section, counter D is reloaded, the "second" register is incremented and adjusted for BCD, and the program is returned to the main routine. In this section, instruction DI is used as a precaution to avoid any interrupts from other sources. For the next 60 interrupts, the program remains in Section I. When Section II is repeated 60 times, the program goes to Section III where the "minute" register is incremented and the "second" register is cleared. To avoid further interrupts, the interrupt is disabled and the program is returned to the main routine where one minute and zero seconds are displayed continuously.

In this particular program, the service routine does not save any register contents by using PUSH instructions before starting the service routine. However, in most service routines, register contents must be saved because the interrupt is asynchronous and can occur at any time.

12.3 RESTART AS SOFTWARE INSTRUCTIONS

External hardware is necessary to insert an RST instruction when an interrupt is requested to INTR (INT in the 8080A). However, the fact that RST is a software instruction is quite often overlooked or misunderstood. RST instructions are commonly used to set up software breakpoints as a debugging technique. A breakpoint is a Restart (RST) instruction in a program where the execution of the program stops temporarily and program control is transferred to the RST location. The program should be transferred from the RST location to the breakpoint service routine to allow the user to examine register or memory contents when specified keys are pressed. After the breakpoint routine, the program should return to executing the main program at the breakpoint. The breakpoint procedure allows the user to test programs in segments. For example, if RST 6 is written in a program, the program execution is transferred to location 0030H; it is equivalent to a 1-byte call instruction. This can be used to write a software breakpoint routine as illustrated next.

12.31 Illustrative Program: Implementation of Breakpoint Technique

PROBLEM STATEMENT

Implement a breakpoint facility at RST 5 for user. When the user writes RST 5 in the program, the program should

1. Be interrupted at the instruction RST 5.
2. Display the accumulator content and the flags when Hex key A (1010_2) is pressed.
3. Exit the breakpoint routine and continue execution when the *Zero* key (0000_2) is pressed.

Assume that when a keyboard routine (KBRD) is called, it returns the binary key code of the key pressed in the accumulator.

PROBLEM ANALYSIS

The breakpoint routine should display the accumulator contents and the flags when a user writes the RST instruction in a program. The technique used to display register contents after executing a segment of the user's program is as follows:

1. Store the register contents on the stack.
2. Assign (arbitrarily) a key from the keyboard for the accumulator display. (In this problem Hex key A from the keyboard is assigned to display the accumulator contents.)
3. Wait for the key to be pressed, and retrieve the contents from the stack by manipulating the stack pointer when the key is pressed.
4. Assign a key to return to the user's program. (In this problem, it is the *Zero* key.)

This approach assumes that a keyboard subroutine can be called from your monitor program, and that the codes associated with each key are known.

BREAKPOINT SUBROUTINE

```
;BRKPNT: This is a breakpoint subroutine; it can be implemented with the
;        instruction RST 5. It displays the accumulator and the flags when the
;        A key is pressed, and returns to the calling program when the Zero key
;        is pressed
```

```
;Input: None
;Output: None
;Does not modify any register contents
;Calls: KBRD subroutine. The KBRD is a keyboard subroutine that checks a key
;        pressed. The routine identifies the key and places its binary code in the
;        accumulator
BRKPNT:    PUSH PSW        ;Save registers
           PUSH B
           PUSH D
           PUSH H
KYCHK:     CALL KBRD        ;Check for a key
           CPI 0AH          ;Is it key A?
           JNZ RETKY        ;If not, check Zero key
           LXI H, 0007H     ;Load stack pointer displacement count; see program
                               description
           DAD SP           ;Place memory address in HL, where (A) is stored
           MOV A,M
           OUT PORT1        ;Display accumulator contents
           DCX H            ;Point HL to the location of the flags
           MOV A,M
           OUT PORT2        ;Display flags
           JMP KYCHK        ;Go back and check next key
RETKY:     CPI 00H          ;Is it Zero key?
           JNZ KYCHK        ;If not, go and check key program
           POP H            ;Retrieve registers
           POP D            ;
           POP B
           POP PSW
           RET
```

PROGRAM DESCRIPTION

The breakpoint routine saves all the registers on the stack, and the address in the stack pointer is decremented accordingly. (In this particular problem, registers BC and DE need not be saved. These registers are saved here for the assignments given at the end of the chapter.) The accumulator contents are stored in the seventh memory location from the top of the stack, and the flags in the sixth memory location.

When key A is pressed, the HL register adds seven to the stack pointer contents and places that address in HL register (DAD SP), without modifying the contents of the stack pointer. This is an important point, if the stack pointer is varied, appropriate contents may not be retrieved with POP and RET instructions.

The subroutine displays the accumulator and the flags at the two output ports and returns to the main program.

ADDITIONAL I/O CONCEPTS AND PROCESSES 12.4

The 8080A interrupt I/O, described earlier, is limited because of its single interrupt pin and hardware requirements to determine interrupt priorities. To circumvent these limitations, a programmable interrupt controller such as the 8259A is used to implement and extend the capability of the 8080A interrupt. Another I/O process, Direct Memory Access (DMA), is commonly used for high-speed data transfer. This I/O process is implemented also by using a programmable device such as DMA controller 8257. A programmable device is generally a multi-function chip, and the microprocessor can specify and/or modify its functions by writing appropriate bits in the control register of the device. The concepts of programmable devices are discussed in Chapter 14. The intent here is to maintain the continuity in the discussion of the interrupt I/O and to introduce the concept of Direct Memory Access (DMA). The interrupt controller and the DMA process will be described briefly in the next sections — see Chapter 15 for further details.

12.41 Programmable Interrupt Controller: the 8259A

The 8259A is a programmable interrupt-managing device, specifically designed for use with the interrupt signals (INTR/INT) of the 8085/8080A microprocessors. The primary features of the 8259A are as follows:

1. It manages eight interrupt requests.
2. It can vector an interrupt request anywhere in the memory map through program control without additional hardware for restart instructions. However, all eight requests are spaced at the interval of either four locations or eight locations.
3. It can resolve eight levels of interrupt priorities in a variety of modes.
4. With additional 8259A devices, the priority scheme can be expanded to 64 levels.

One of the major limitations of the 8085/8080A interrupt scheme is that all requests are vectored to memory locations on page 00H, which is reserved for ROM or EPROM, and access to these locations is difficult after a system has been designed. In addition, the process of determining priorities is limited, and extra hardware is required to insert Restart instructions. The 8259A overcomes these limitations and provides many more flexible options. The 8259A is an upgraded version of, and fully compatible with, its predecessor, the 8259. The 8259A can be employed with such 16-bit Intel microprocessors as the 8086/8088 as well.

The 8259A block diagram (Figure 12.9) includes control logic, registers for interrupt requests, priority resolver, cascade logic, and data bus. The registers manage interrupt requests, while the priority resolver determines their priority. The cascade logic is used to connect additional 8259A devices.

Block Diagram

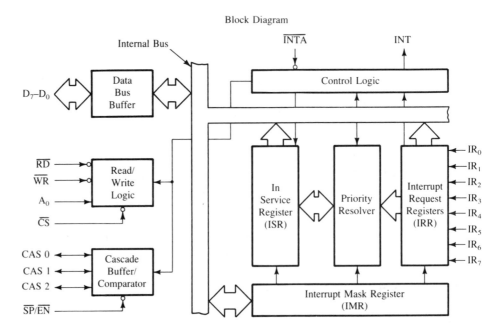

FIGURE 12.9

The 8259A Block Diagram

SOURCE: Intel Corporation, *MCS — 80/85 Family User's Manual* (Santa Clara, Calif.: Author, 1979), p. 6-132.

8259A INTERRUPT OPERATION

Implementing interrupts in the simplest format without cascading requires two specific instructions. The instructions are written by the MPU in the device registers (explained in Chapter 15). The first instruction specifies features such as mode, and/or memory space between two consecutive interrupt levels. The second instruction specifies high-order memory address. After these instructions have been written, the following sequence of events should occur:

1. One or more interrupt request lines go high requesting the service.
2. The 8259A resolves the priorities and sends an INT signal to the MPU.
3. The MPU acknowledges the interrupt by sending $\overline{INTA}$.
4. After the $\overline{INTA}$ has been received, the opcode for the CALL instruction (CDH) is placed on the data bus.
5. Because of the CALL instruction, the MPU sends two more $\overline{INTA}$ signals.
6. At the first $\overline{INTA}$, the 8259A places the low-order 8-bit address on the data bus and, at the second $\overline{INTA}$, it places high-order 8-bit address of the interrupt vector. This completes the 3-byte CALL instruction.
7. The program sequence of the MPU is transferred to the memory location specified by the CALL instruction.

The 8259A includes additional features such as reading the status and changing the interrupt mode during a program execution.

12.42 Direct Memory Access (DMA)

The direct memory access (DMA) is a process of communication or data transfer controlled by an external peripheral. In situations in which the microprocessor-controlled data transfer is too slow, the DMA is generally used; e.g., data transfer between a floppy disk and R/W memory of the system.

The 8085/8080A microprocessor has two pins available for this type of I/O communication: HOLD (Hold) and HLDA (Hold Acknowledge). Conceptually, this is an important I/O technique; it introduces two new signals available on the 8085/8080A — HOLD and HLDA.

☐ HOLD — Hold. This is an active high input signal to the 8085/8080A from another master requesting the use of the address and data buses. After receiving the HOLD request, the MPU relinquishes the buses in the following machine cycle. All buses are tri-stated and a Hold Acknowledge (HLDA) signal is sent out. The MPU regains the control of buses after HOLD goes low.

☐ HLDA — Hold Acknowledge. This is an active high output signal indicating that the MPU is relinquishing the control of the buses.

Typically, an external peripheral such as a DMA controller sends a request — a high signal — to the HOLD pin (Figure 12.10). The processor completes the execution of the current machine cycle; floats (high impedance state) the address, the data, and the control lines; and sends the Hold Acknowledge (HLDA) signal. The DMA controller takes control of the buses and transfers data directly between source and destination, thus bypassing the

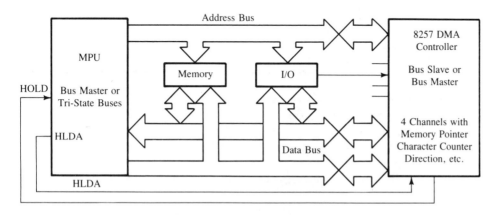

FIGURE 12.10
DMA Data Transfer

SOURCE: Intel Corporation, *MCS 80/85 Student Study Guide* (Santa Clara, Calif.: Author, 1979), p. 2-21.

microprocessor. At the end of data transfer, the controller terminates the request by sending a low signal to the HOLD pin, and the microprocessor regains control of the buses. Typically, DMA controllers are programmable LSI chips. One such chip, the Intel 8257, is described in Chapter 15.

SUMMARY

□ The interrupt is an asynchronous process of communication with the micro-processor, initiated by an external peripheral.

□ The 8080A has a maskable interrupt that can be enabled or disabled using the instructions EI and DI, respectively.

□ The 8080A has eight RST instructions that are equivalent to 1-byte Calls to specific locations on memory page 00H.

□ In the interrupt process, the RST instructions (0 to 7) are implemented using external hardware and the $\overline{\text{INTA}}$ signal.

□ The 8085 has five interrupt inputs, one nonmaskable and four maskable. These four interrupts are implemented without any external hardware. The fifth interrupt is identical to the 8080A interrupt.

□ The instruction SIM is necessary to implement the interrupts 7.5, 6.5, and 5.5.

□ The instruction RIM can be used to check whether any interrupt requests are pending.

□ The RST instructions are software commands and can be used in a program to jump to their vectored locations on memory page 00H.

□ A programmable interrupt controller such as the 8259A is used commonly to implement and extend the capability of the 8080A interrupt.

□ The Direct Memory Access (DMA) is a process of high speed data transfer under the control of external devices such as a DMA controller.

ASSIGNMENTS

1. Check whether the following statements are true or false.
   a. If the 8080A microprocessor is interrupted while executing a 3-byte instruction (assuming the interrupt is enabled), the processor will acknowledge the interrupt request immediately, even before the completion of the instruction.   (T/F)
   b. When an 8085 system is Reset, all the interrupts including the TRAP are disabled.   (T/F)
   c. When the 8085/8080A microprocessor acknowledges an interrupt, it disables the interrupt system (except TRAP).   (T/F)
   d. Instruction EI (Enable Interrupt) is necessary to implement the TRAP interrupt, but external hardware and the SIM instruction are unnecessary.   (T/F)

FIGURE 12.11
Schematic for an Interrupt

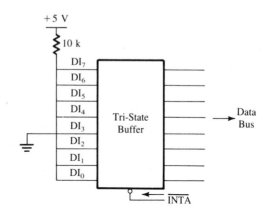

e. If instruction RST 4 is written in a program, the program will jump to
   location 0020H without any external hardware.   (T/F)

f. If a DMA request is sent to the microprocessor with a high signal to the
   HOLD pin, the microprocessor acknowledges the request after completing
   the present machine cycle.   (T/F)

g. Instruction RIM is used to disable the interrupts 7.5, 6.5, and 5.5.   (T/F)

h. The execution of instructions MVI A, 10H, and SIM will enable all three
   interrupts (7.5, 6.5, and 5.5).   (T/F)

2. a. Identify the RST instruction in Figure 12.11.

   b. Specify the restart memory location when the microprocessor is interrupted.

   c. If the instruction in the monitor program at 0030 is JMP 20BFH and the service
      routine is written at 2075H, what instruction is necessary (at 20BFH) to locate
      the service routine?

3. The main program is stored beginning at 0100H. The main program (at 0120H) has
   called the subroutine at 0150H, and when the microprocessor is executing the instruction at location 0151 (LXI), it is interrupted. Read the program, then answer
   the questions that follow:

	Memory Address	Mnemonics
START:	0100	LXI SP, 0400H
	0103	EI
	↓	↓
	0120	CALL 0150H
SUB:	0150	PUSH B
	0151	LXI B, 10FFH

0154   MOV C,A

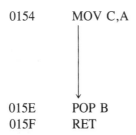

015E   POP B
015F   RET

    a. Specify the contents of stack location 03FFH.
    b. Specify the stack locations where the contents of registers B and C are stored.
    c. When the program is interrupted, what is the memory address stored on
       the stack?

4. Redraw the schematic in Figure 12.8 with the following changes, and modify the
service routine accordingly.
    a. Replace monostable multivibrator 74121 by positive-edge trigger flip-flop 7474.
    b. Design an output port, and use bit D_7 to clear the flip-flop.
    c. Modify Section I of the timer routine to clear the flip-flop at an appropriate
       place.

5. Answer the following questions in reference to Figure 12.4.
    a. What is the instruction placed on the data bus when input line I_6 of the encoder
       goes low, thus requesting the interrupt service?
    b. If three input lines (I_2, I_4, and I_5) go low simultaneously, explain how the
       priority is determined among the three requests, and specify the instruction that
       is placed on the data bus.

6. A program is stored in memory from 2000H to 205F. To check the first segment of
the program up to location 2025H, a breakpoint routine call is inserted at location
2026H. (Refer to the Illustrative Program in Section 12.31 for the breakpoint subroutine.) If the stack pointer is initialized at 2099H, answer the following
questions:
    a. Specify the contents of memory locations 2098H and 2097H.
    b. Specify the memory locations where the accumulator contents and the flags are
       stored when the microprocessor executes instruction PUSH PSW in the break-
       point routine.
    c. Specify the memory locations where HL register contents are stored after exe-
       cuting the instruction PUSH H.
    d. Specify the contents of the stack pointer when the breakpoint routine returns
       from the KBRD routine.
    e. What address is placed in the program counter when instruction RET is
       executed?

7. Modify the breakpoint routine in Section 12.31 to display the memory location
where the breakpoint is inserted in a program (for example, location 2026H in
Assignment 6.a).

8. Modify the breakpoint routine to display the contents of the BC, DE, and HL registers when the user pushes the Hex keys *1*, *2*, and *3*. (The respective Hex codes are 01, 02, and 0.3.)

EXPERIMENTAL ASSIGNMENTS

1. a. Build the circuit shown in Figure 12.3. Enter and execute the program given in the illustration.

  b. Verify the interrupt process by pushing the *Interrupt* key.

  c. Replace the instruction EI at location XX03 by the NOP instruction. Push the *Interrupt* key and verify whether an interrupt request can be accepted by the microprocessor.

  d. Interrupt the processor; when the processor is in the middle of the service routine, push the *Interrupt* key again. Explain why the processor does not accept any interrupts during the service routine.

  e. In the routine SERV, write instruction EI at the beginning of the service routine. Push the interrupt key, and explain your observation. (You may notice interesting results because the manual key keeps INTR high too long.)

2. a. Build the circuit shown in Figure 12.8 and implement the interrupt-driven clock.

  b. Rewrite the program to simulate a 5-minute egg timer.

  c. Modify the program in Experimental Assignment 2.a to flash FF with some appropriate delay to indicate the completion of the 5-minute period.

Interfacing Data Converters

The microprocessor is a logic device; it processes digital signals that are binary and discontinuous. On the other hand, the real-world physical quantities such as temperature and pressure are continuous. These are represented by equivalent electrical quantities called analog signals. Even though an analog signal may represent a real physical parameter with accuracy, it is difficult to process or store the analog signal for later use without introducing considerable error. Therefore, in microprocessor-based industrial products, it is necessary to translate an analog signal into a digital signal. The electronic circuit that translates an analog signal into a digital signal is called an analog-to-digital, or A/D converter (ADC). Similarly, a digital signal needs to be translated into an analog signal to represent a physical quantity (e.g., to regulate a machine). This translator is called a digital-to-analog, or D/A converter (DAC). Both A/D and D/A are also known as data converters and are now available as integrated circuits.

This chapter focuses on interfacing data converters with the 8085/8080A microprocessor. First, D/A converters are discussed, including the basic concepts in the conversion process and their interfacing applications. A/D converters are discussed later because some A/D conversion techniques include D/A converters in the conversion process. The

chapter includes illustrations of successive approximation and dual-slope integrating converters.

OBJECTIVES

- ☐ Explain the functions of data converters.
- ☐ Explain the basic circuit of a D/A converter and define the terms: *resolution* and *settling time*.
- ☐ Calculate the analog output of a D/A converter for a given digital input signal.

☐ Design a circuit to interface an 8-bit D/A converter with the 8085/8080A microprocessor, and verify the analog output for a digital signal.
☐ Interface a 10- or 12-bit D/A converter with an 8-bit microprocessor.
☐ Explain the basic concepts underlying the successive approximation A/D converter and the integrator type A/D converter.

☐ Write a program for a software-controlled A/D converter.
☐ Interface an 8-bit A/D converter with the 8085/8080A, using status check, Wait states, and interrupt.

13.1 DIGITAL-TO-ANALOG (D/A) CONVERTERS

Digital-to-Analog converters can be broadly classified in three categories: **current output**, **voltage output**, and **multiplying type**. The current output DAC, as the name suggests, provides current as the output signal. The voltage output DAC internally converts the current signal into the voltage signal. The voltage output DAC is slower than the current output DAC because of the delay in converting the current signal into the voltage signal. However, in many applications, it is necessary to convert current into voltage by using an external operational amplifier. The multiplying DAC is similar to the other two types except its output represents the product of the input signal and the reference source (Figure 13.3 will explain the reference source), and the product is linear over a broad range. Conceptually, there is not much difference between these three types; any DAC can be viewed as a multiplying DAC.

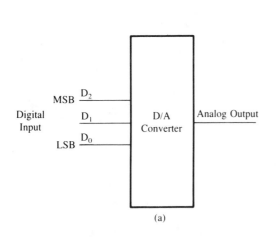

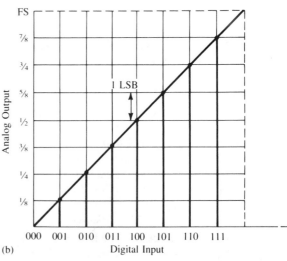

FIGURE 13.1
A 3-Bit D/A Converter: Block Diagram (a) and Digital Input vs. Analog Output (b)

D/A converters are available as **integrated circuits**. Some are specially designed to be compatible with the microprocessor. Typical applications include digital voltmeters, peak detectors, panel meters, programmable gain and attenuation, and stepping motor drive.

13.11 Basic Concepts

Figure 13.1(a) shows a block diagram of a 3-bit D/A converter; it has three digital input lines (D_2, D_1, and D_0) and one output line for the analog signal. The three input lines can assume eight ($2^3 = 8$) input combinations from 000 to 111, D_2 being the most significant bit (MSB) and D_0 being the least significant bit (LSB). If the input ranges from 0 to 1 V, it can be divided into eight equal parts ($\frac{1}{8}$ V); each successive input is $\frac{1}{8}$ V higher than the previous combination, as shown in Figure 13.1(b).

The following points can be summarized from the graph:

1. The 3-bit D/A converter has eight possible combinations. If a converter has n input lines, it can have 2^n input combinations.
2. If the full-scale analog voltage is 1 V, the smallest unit or the LSB (001_2) is equivalent to $\frac{1}{2^n}$ of 1 V. This is defined as resolution. In this example, the LSB = $\frac{1}{8}$ V.
3. The MSB represents half of the full-scale value. In this example, the MSB (100_2) = $\frac{1}{2}$ V.
4. For the maximum input signal (111_2), the output signal is equal to the value of the full-scale input signal minus the value of the 1 LSB input signal. In this example, the maximum input signal (111_2) represents $\frac{7}{8}$ V.

Calculate the values of the LSB, MSB, and full-scale output for an 8-bit DAC for the 0 to 10 V range.

Example
13.1

Solution

1. LSB = $\frac{1}{2^8}$ = $\frac{1}{256}$
   For 10 V, LSB = 10 V/256 = 39 mV
2. MSB = $\frac{1}{2}$ full scale = 5 V
3. Full-Scale Output = (Full-Scale Value − 1 LSB)
   $$= 10 \text{ V} - .039 \text{ V}$$
   $$= 9.961 \text{ V}$$

13.12 D/A Converter Circuits

Input signals representing appropriate binary values can be simulated by an operational amplifier with a summing network as shown in Figure 13.2.

The input resistors R_1, R_2, and R_3 are selected in binary weighted proportion; each has double the value of the previous resistor. If all three inputs are 1 V, the total current

FIGURE 13.2
Summing Amplifier with Binary
Weighted Input Resistors

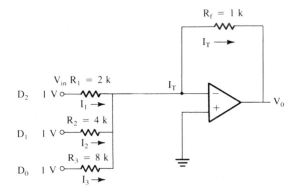

I_T is as follows:

$$I_T = I_1 + I_2 + I_3$$
$$= \frac{V_{in}}{R_1} + \frac{V_{in}}{R_2} + \frac{V_{in}}{R_3}$$
$$= \frac{V_{in}}{1\ k}\left(\frac{1}{2} + \frac{1}{4} + \frac{1}{8}\right)$$
$$= 0.875\ mA$$

The voltage output V_0:

$$V_0 = -R_f I_T$$
$$= -(1\ k)(0.875\ mA)$$
$$= -0.875\ V$$
$$= \tfrac{7}{8}\ V$$

This example shows that for the input $= 111_2$, the output is equal to either $\frac{7}{8}$ mA or $\frac{7}{8}$ V representing the D/A conversion process.

The following points can be inferred from the above example:

1. A D/A converter circuit requires three elements: resistor network with appropriate weighting, switches, and a reference source.
2. The output can be a current signal or converted into a voltage signal using an operational amplifier.
3. The time required for conversion, called settling time, is dependent on the response time of the switches and the output amplifier (for a voltage output DAC).

R/2R LADDER NETWORK

One major drawback of designing a DAC as shown in Figure 13.2 is the requirement for various precision resistors. The R/2R ladder network shown in Figure 13.3 uses only two resistor values. The resistors are connected in such a way that for any number of inputs, the total current I_T is in binary proportion. The R/2R ladder network (or a similar

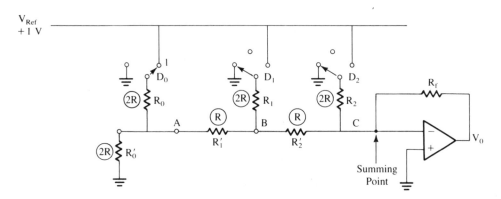

$$= \text{Values of resistors}$$

FIGURE 13.3
R/2R Ladder Network

network called an inverted ladder) is used commonly in designing integrated D/A converters. The interfacing of 8-bit and 10-bit integrated D/A converters is illustrated in the next two sections.

13.15 Illustration: Interfacing an 8-bit D/A Converter with the 8085/8080A

PROBLEM STATEMENT

1. Design an output port with the address FFH to interface the 1408 D/A converter that is calibrated for a 0 to 10 V range (Figure 13.4(a)).
2. Write a program to generate a continuous ramp waveform.
3. Explain the operation of the 1408 in Figure 13.4(b) which is calibrated for a bipolar range ±5 V. Calculate the output V_O if the input is 10000000_2.

HARDWARE DESCRIPTION

The circuit shown in Figure 13.4(a) includes an 8-input NAND gate and a NOR gate (negative AND) as the address decoding logic, the 74LS373 as a latch, and an industry-standard 1408 D/A converter. The OUT instruction with port address FFH enables the latch.

The 1408 is an 8-bit D/A converter compatible with TTL and CMOS logic, with the settling time around 300 ns. It has eight input data lines A_1 (MSB) through A_8 (LSB); the convention of labelling MSB to LSB is opposite to that of what is normally used for the data bus in the microprocessor. It requires 2 mA reference current for full-scale input and two power supplies $V_{CC} = +5$ V and $V_{EE} = -15$ V (V_{EE} can range from -5 V to -15 V).

The total reference current source is determined by the resistor R_{14} and the voltage V_{Ref}. The resistor R_{15} is generally equal to R_{14} to match the input impedance of the

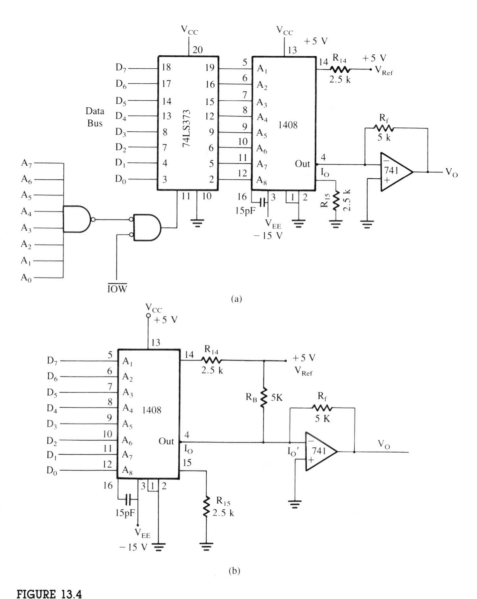

FIGURE 13.4
Interfacing the 1408 D/A Converter: Voltage Output in Unipolar Range (a) and in Bipolar Range (b)

reference source. The output current I_O is calculated as follows:

$$I_O = \frac{V_{Ref}}{R_{14}}\left(\frac{A_1}{2} + \frac{A_2}{4} + \frac{A_3}{8} + \frac{A_4}{16} + \frac{A_5}{32} + \frac{A_6}{64} + \frac{A_7}{128} + \frac{A_8}{256}\right)$$

Inputs A_1 through $A_8 = 0$ or 1.

This formula is an extension of the 3-bit formula for the current I_T to the 8-bit current I_O. For full scale input (D_7 through $D_0 = 1$)

$$I_O = \frac{5\ V}{2.5\ k}\left(\frac{1}{2} + \frac{1}{4} + \frac{1}{8} + \frac{1}{16} + \frac{1}{32} + \frac{1}{64} + \frac{1}{128} + \frac{1}{256}\right)$$
$$= 2\ mA\ (255/256)$$
$$= 1.992\ mA$$

The output is 1 LSB less than the full-scale reference source of 2 mA. The output voltage V_O for the full-scale input is

$$V_O = 2\ mA\ (255/256) \times 5\ k$$
$$= 9.961\ V$$

PROGRAM

To generate a continuous waveform, the instructions are as follows:

```
           MVI A, 00H        ;Load accumulator with the first input
D/A:       OUT FFH           ;Output to DAC
           MVI B, COUNT      ;Set up register B for delay
DELAY:     DCR B
           JNZ DELAY
           INR A             ;Next input
           JMP D/A           ;Go back to output
```

Program Description   This program outputs 00 to FF continuously to the D/A converter. The analog output of the DAC starts at 0 and increases up to 10 V (approximately) as a ramp. When the accumulator contents go to 0, the next cycle begins; and thus, the ramp signal is generated continuously. The ramp output of the DAC can be observed on an oscilloscope with an external sync.

The delay in the program is necessary for two reasons:

1. The time needed for a microprocessor to execute an output loop is likely to be less than the settling time of the DAC.
2. The slope of the ramp can be varied by changing the delay.

OPERATING THE D/A CONVERTER IN A BIPOLAR RANGE

The 1408 in Figure 13.4(b) is calibrated for the bipolar range from -5 V to $+5$ V by adding the resistor R_B (5.0 k) between the reference voltage V_{Ref} and the output pin 4. The resistor R_B supplies 1 mA (V_{Ref}/R_B) current to the output in the opposite direction of the current generated by the input signal. Therefore, the output current for the bipolar operation I_O' is

$$I_O' = I_O - \frac{V_{Ref}}{R_B}$$

$$= \frac{V_{Ref}}{R_{14}}\left(\frac{A_1}{2} + \frac{A_2}{4} + \frac{A_3}{8} + \frac{A_4}{16} + \frac{A_5}{32} + \frac{A_6}{64} + \frac{A_7}{128} + \frac{A_8}{256}\right) - \frac{V_{Ref}}{R_B}$$

When the input signal is equal to zero, the output V_O is

$$V_O = I_O'R_f$$

$$= \left(I_O - \frac{V_{Ref}}{R_B}\right)R_f$$

$$= \left(0 - \frac{5\ V}{5\ k}\right)(5\ k)\ (I_O = 0\ \text{for input} = 0)$$

$$= -5\ V$$

Output V_O when the input = 10000000

$$V_O = \left(I_O - \frac{V_{Ref}}{R_B}\right)R_f$$

$$= \left(\frac{V_{Ref}}{R_{14}} \times \frac{A_1}{2} - \frac{V_{Ref}}{R_B}\right)R_f;\qquad (A_2 - A_8 = 0)$$

$$= \left(\frac{5\ V}{2.5\ k} \times \frac{1}{2} - \frac{5\ V}{5\ k}\right)5\ k$$

$$= (1\ mA - 1\ mA)5\ k = 0\ V$$

13.14   Microprocessor-Compatible D/A Converters

In response to the growing need for interfacing data converters with the microprocessor, specially designed microprocessor-compatible D/A converters are now available. These D/A converters generally include a latch on the chip (see Figure 13.5), thus eliminating the need for an external latch as in Figure 13.4.

Figure 13.5 shows the block diagram of the Analog Devices AD558, which includes a latch and an output op amp internal to the chip. It can be operated with one power supply voltage between $+4.5$ V to $+16.5$ V. To interface the AD558 with the microprocessor, two signals are required: Chip Select ($\overline{CS}$) and Chip Enable ($\overline{CE}$).

Figure 13.5 shows one example of interfacing the AD558 with the 8085/8080A. The address line A_7 through an inverter is used for the Chip Select, which assigns the port address 80H (assuming all other address lines are at logic 0) to the DAC port. The control signal $\overline{IOW}$ is used for the Chip Enable. The program shown in Section 13.13 can be used to generate ramp waveforms.

Figure 13.5(b) shows the timing of latching data in relation to the control signals, while Figure 13.5(c) shows the truth table of the control logic. When both signals $\overline{CS}$ and $\overline{CE}$ are at logic 0, the latch is transparent, meaning the input is transferred to the DAC section. When either $\overline{CS}$ or $\overline{CE}$ goes to logic 1, the input is latched in the register and held until both control signals go to logic 0.

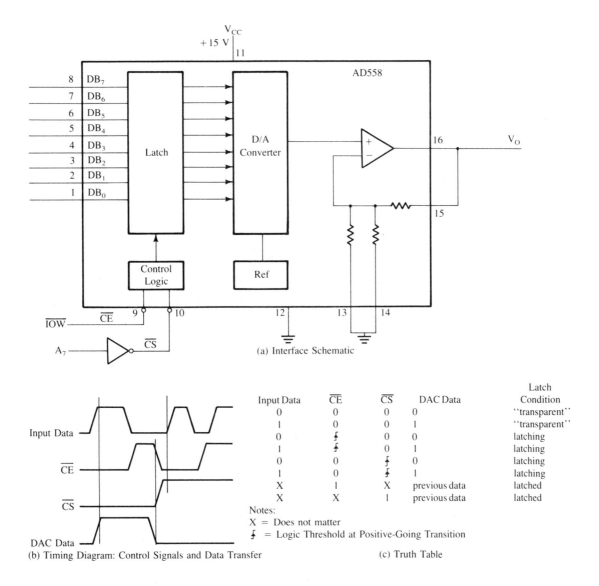

FIGURE 13.5

Interfacing the AD558 (Microprocessor-Compatible D/A Converter) with the 8085/8080A

SOURCE: B and C: Analog Devices, Inc., *Data Acquisition Components and Subsystems* (Norwood, Mass.: Author, 1980), p. 9-18.

13.15 Interfacing a 10-Bit D/A Converter

In many D/A converter applications, 10- or 12-bit resolution is required. However, the 8-bit microprocessor has only eight data lines. Therefore, to transfer ten bits, the data bus

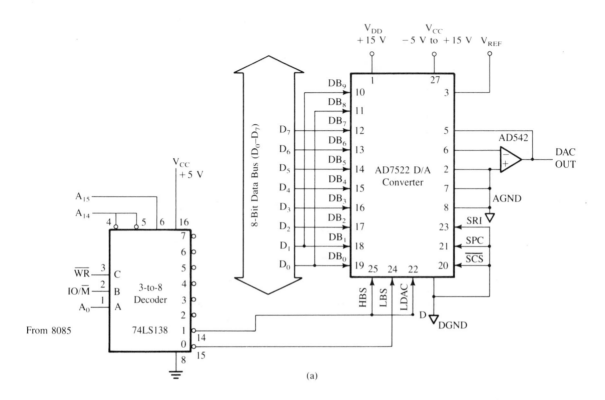

(a)

FIGURE 13.6

Interfacing 10-Bit DAC (AD7522) with the 8085/8080A (a) and a Timing Diagram for Loading the Input Data (b)

SOURCE: Analog Devices, Inc., *Data Acquisition Components and Subsystems* (Norwood, Mass.: Author, 1980), p. 9-73.

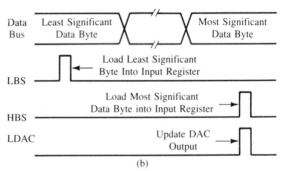

(b)

is time shared by using two output ports: one for the first eight bits and the second for the remaining two bits. A disadvantage of this method is that the DAC output assumes an intermediate value between the two output operations. This difficulty can be circumvented by using a double buffered DAC such as Analog Devices AD7522, as shown in Figure 13.6(a).

The AD7522 is a CMOS 10-bit D/A converter with an input buffer and a holding register. The ten bits are loaded into the input register in two steps using two output ports. The low-order eight bits are loaded with the control line LBS, and the remaining two bits are loaded with the control line HBS. Then all ten bits are switched into a holding register for the conversion by enabling the line LDAC. The last operation (enabling the line LDAC) can be combined with the loading of the second byte as shown in Figure 13.6(a); otherwise, this operation will require three output ports.

HARDWARE DESCRIPTION

Figure 13.6(a) shows a schematic of interfacing the AD7522 with the 8085. It is a memory-mapped I/O with multiple addresses. The attempt here is to minimize the chip count.

The three input signals to the decoder are address line A_0 and two control signals IO/$\overline{M}$ and $\overline{WR}$. To enable the line LBS, the input to the decoder should be 000; this results in the port address 8000H. ($A_{15} = 1$, $A_{14} = 0$, and the lines A_{13} to A_1 are assumed at logic 0.) When a data byte is sent to the port address 8000H in a memory-mapped I/O, the $\overline{WR}$ and IO/$\overline{M}$ signals go low along with A_0, and the line LBS is enabled. Similarly, the address 8001H enables the lines HBS and LDAC. Figure 13.6(b) shows the timing diagram for loading input data into the converters.

The following instructions illustrate how to load the maximum input of ten bits (all 1s) into the D/A converter.

```
LXI B, 03FFH    ;Load ten bits at logic 1 in BC register
LXI H, 8000H    ;Load HL with port address for low-order 8-bits
MOV M, C        ;Load eight bits (D₇–D₀) in the DAC
INX H           ;Point to port address 8001H
MOV M, B        ;Load two bits (D₉ and D₈) and switch all ten bits into holding register
                    for conversion
HLT
```

ANALOG-TO-DIGITAL (A/D) CONVERTERS 13.2

The A/D conversion is a quantizing process whereby an analog signal is represented by equivalent binary states; this is opposite to the D/A conversion process. Analog-to-Digital converters can be classified into two general groups based on the conversion technique. One technique involves comparing a given analog signal with the internally generated equivalent signal. This group includes successive approximation, counter, and flash-type converters. The second technique involves changing an analog signal into time or frequency and comparing these new parameters against known values. This group includes integrator converters and voltage-to-frequency converters. The trade-off between the two techniques is based on accuracy vs. speed. The successive approximation and the flash type are faster but generally less accurate than the integrator and the voltage-to-frequency type converters. Furthermore, the flash type is expensive and difficult to design for high accuracy.

The most commonly used A/D converters — the successive approximation and the integrator — are discussed in this section with several interfacing examples. The successive approximation A/D converters are used in applications such as data loggers and instrumentation, where conversion speed is important. On the other hand, integrating type converters are used in applications such as digital meters, panel meters, and monitoring systems, where the conversion accuracy is critical.

13.21   Basic Concepts

Figure 13.7(a) shows a block diagram of a 3-bit A/D converter. It has one input line for an analog signal and three output lines for digital signals. Figure 13.7(b) shows the graph of the analog input voltage (0 to 1 V) and the corresponding digital output signal. It shows eight (2^3) discrete output states from 000_2 to 111_2, each step being $\frac{1}{8}$ V apart. This is defined as the resolution of the converter. The LSB, the MSB, and the full-scale output are calculated the same way as in D/A converters.

FIGURE 13.7

A 3-Bit A/D Converter: Block Diagram (a) and Analog Input vs. Digital Output (b)

SOURCE: Analog Devices, Inc., *Integrated Circuit Converters, Data Acquisition Systems, and Analog Signal Conditioning Components* (Norwood, Mass.: Author, 1979), p. I-18.

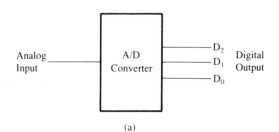

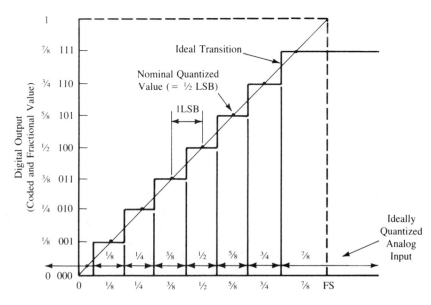

In A/D conversion, another critical parameter is **conversion time**. This is defined as the total time required to convert an analog signal into its digital output, and is determined by the conversion technique used and by the propagation delay in various circuits.

13.22 Successive Approximation A/D Converter

Figure 13.8(a) shows the block diagram of a successive approximation A/D converter. It includes three major elements: the D/A converter, the successive approximation register (SAR), and the comparator. The conversion technique involves comparing the output of the D/A converter V_O with the analog input signal V_{in}. The digital input to the DAC is generated using the successive approximation method (explained below). When the DAC output matches the analog signal, the input to the DAC is the equivalent digital signal.

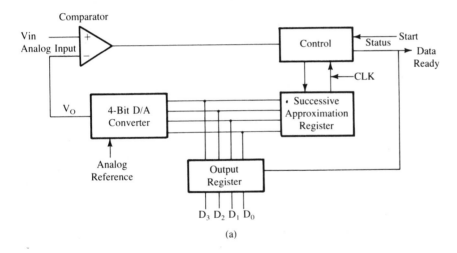

(a)

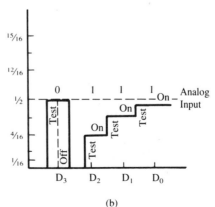

FIGURE 13.8
Successive Approximation
A/D Converter: Block Diagram
(a) and Conversion Process for
a 4-Bit Converter (b)

(b)

The successive approximation method of generating input to the DAC is similar to weighing an unknown material (e.g., less than 1 gram) on a chemical balance with a set of such fractional weights as ½ gm, ¼ gm, ⅛ gm, etc. The weighing procedure begins with the heaviest weight (½ gm), and subsequent weights (in decreasing order) are added until the balance is tipped. The weight that tips the balance is removed, and the process is continued until the smallest weight is used. In case of a 4-bit A/D converter, bit D_3 is turned on first and the output of the DAC is compared with an analog signal. If the comparator changes the state, indicating that the output generated by D_3 is larger than the analog signal, bit D_3 is turned off in the SAR and bit D_2 is turned on. The process continues until the input reaches bit D_0. Figure 13.8(b) illustrates a 4-bit conversion process. When bit D_3 is turned on, the output exceeds the analog signal and, therefore, bit D_3 is turned off. When the next three successive bits are turned on, the output becomes approximately equal to the analog signal.

The successive approximation conversion process can be accomplished through either the software or hardware approach. In the software approach, an A/D converter is designed using a D/A converter, and the microprocessor plays the role of the counter and the SAR. For the hardware approach, a complete ADC, including a tri-state buffer, is now available as an integrated circuit on a chip. The interfacing of both types of A/D converters is illustrated in the next section.

13.23   Illustration: Software-Controlled A/D Converter

PROBLEM STATEMENT
1. Explain the interfacing circuit and A/D conversion process in Figure 13.9.
2. Write a program to perform the successive approximation A/D conversion using a D/A converter.

INTERFACING CIRCUIT

The D/A converter section of the interfacing circuit in Figure 13.9 is the same as that shown in Figure 13.5; it includes the address decoding logic with the output port address 80H and the D/A converter. The analog signal is connected to pin *15* and compared internally in the comparator with the output of the DAC. The output of the comparator is fed to the base of the transistor, and the collector of the transistor is connected to the data bus (line D_7) through tri-state buffer 74LS365. The enable logic of the buffer is controlled by signals $\overline{\text{IOR}}$ and address line A_6. The microprocessor can monitor data line D_7 by reading the 74LS365 as the input port with the port address 40H (assuming the don't care lines are at logic 0).

When the analog signal is higher than the DAC output, the comparator output (pin *16*) is low, the transistor is turned off, the collector is high, and the MPU reads logic 1 at data line D_7. When the analog signal is less than the DAC output, the comparator output is high and data line D_7 is low.

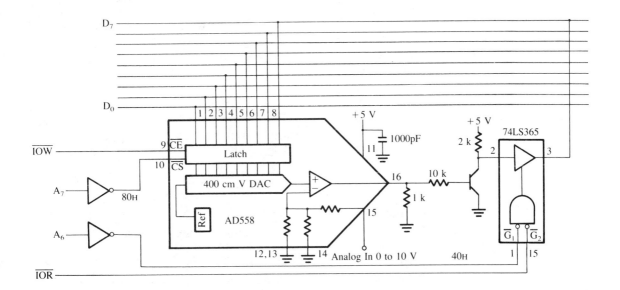

FIGURE 13.9

Software-Controlled Successive Approximation A/D Converter

SOURCE: Douglas Grant, *Interfacing the AD558 Dacport to Microprocessors,* Application Note (Norwood, Mass.: Analog Devices, 1980).

PROGRAM

```
              LXI SP, STACK      ;Initialize stack pointer
              LXI B, 8000H       ;Set up register B to add successive digits and set
                                    up register C to store successive approximation
                                    values
              MOV D, 08H         ;Set up register D as counter to count eight rotations
                                    of the bit in register B
              MOV A, B           ;Set D₇ = 1
NEXTRY:       ADD C              ;Add previous value
              MOV C, A           ;Save bits in C
              OUT 80H            ;Start conversion
              CALL DELAY         ;Wait during settling time, approximate
                                    delay = 200 µs
              IN 40H             ;Read comparator output
              RAL                ;Check bit D₇
              JC NXTBIT          ;If bit D₇ = 1, analog signal is larger than DAC
                                    output. Turn on next bit
              MOV A, B           ;If bit D₇ = 0, analog signal is less than DAC
                                    output. Turn off previous bit
```

```
              CMA
              ANA C
              MOV C, A          ;Save after turning off previous bit
NXTBIT:       MOV A, B
              RRC               ;Turn on next bit
              MOV B, A
              DCR D
              JNZ NEXTRY        ;Have not yet turned all eight bits; go back
              MOV A, C          ;Display digital value
              OUT PORT1
              HLT
```

Program Description   Initially, the instruction LXI B clears register C to save successive approximation values, and sets bit D_7 in register B to logic 1, which is shifted to the right eight times. Register D is set up to count eight rotations. The instruction ADD C adds a bit from register B to the previous answer saved in register C. The OUT instruction starts the conversion, and after the settling delay the microprocessor reads bit D_7, which indicates the output of the comparator. If bit $D_7 = 1$, the transistor is off, and the analog signal is larger than the DAC output. The program jumps to location NXTBIT, where the bit in register B is shifted right to the next position and the counter is decremented. If the bit in register B is not yet rotated through eight positions, the program goes back to add the new bit to register C. After adding a bit if the transistor is turned on, the microprocessor reads logic 0 at line D_7, and the bit is turned off by complementing and adding to the previous value in register C.

Output   The digital output for a given analog signal is stored in register C, which is displayed at PORT1.

13.24   Interfacing 8-Bit A/D Converters

As an integrated circuit, the A/D converter includes all three elements — SAR, DAC, and comparator — on a chip (Figure 13.10). In addition, it has a tri-state output buffer. Typically, it has two control lines, START (or CONVERT) and DATA READY (or BUSY); they are TTL compatible and can be active low or high depending upon the design.

A pulse to the *START* pin begins the conversion process, and disables the tri-state output buffer. At the end of the conversion period, DATA READY becomes active and the digital output is made available at the output buffer. To interface an A/D converter with the microprocessor, the microprocessor should

1. Send a pulse to the *START* pin. This can be derived from a control signal such as Write ($\overline{WR}$).
2. Wait until the end of the conversion. The end of the conversion period can be verified either by status checking (polling) or through the READY signal or the interrupt.

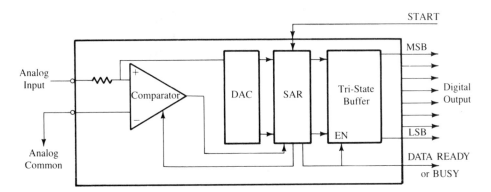

FIGURE 13.10
Block Diagram of a Typical Successive-Approximation A/D Converter as an
Integrated Circuit

3. Read the digital signal at an input port. Three examples of interfacing an A/D converter
using status check, READY signal, and the interrupt are shown below. An example of
using handshake signals is given in Chapter 14.

INTERFACING AN 8-BIT A/D CONVERTER
USING STATUS CHECK

Figure 13.11(a) is a schematic showing interfacing of the Analog Devices AD570 A/D
converter. This is a typical 8-bit successive approximation A/D converter and requires
+5 V and −15 V power supplies. The analog input can range from 0 to +10 V or ±5 V.
Its B/$\overline{\text{C}}$ (Blank and $\overline{\text{Convert}}$) input signal is similar to the START pulse shown in
Figure 13.10, and pin $\overline{\text{DR}}$ represents the DATA READY signal. The output can be
available in two modes: one in which data are present at the output at all times except
during the conversion, or with the data available at the output after the conversion when
the converter is selected for Read operation. In Figure 13.11, B/$\overline{\text{C}}$ and $\overline{\text{DR}}$ lines are
generally low and data are available at the output except during the conversion.

Figure 13.11(b) shows the timing diagram of the conversion process. As the B/$\overline{\text{C}}$
signal goes high, the output is disabled (high impedance) and the $\overline{\text{DR}}$ goes high. The
falling edge of the B/$\overline{\text{C}}$ signal initiates the conversion cycle. When the conversion is
completed (typically 25 μs), the $\overline{\text{DR}}$ goes low and, within 500 ns, the new data are
available on the data lines. If the B/$\overline{\text{C}}$ line is caused to go high during the conversion, the
conversion is abandoned, as shown in Figure 13.11(b).

The interfacing circuit in Figure 13.11(a) shows two input ports: one with the
address 82H to read digital data, the other with the address 81H to read the status of the
$\overline{\text{DR}}$ signal. Port 80H is used just to start the conversion by writing in the port. Two crossed
coupled NAND gates are used to ensure a sufficiently long B/$\overline{\text{C}}$ pulse to initiate the
conversion process. When the microprocessor writes to port 80H, the output of the gate

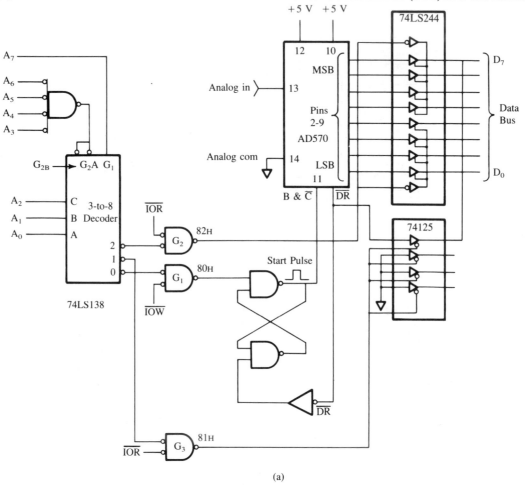

(a)

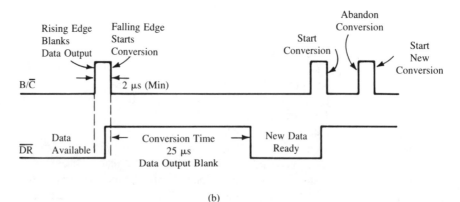

(b)

FIGURE 13.11
Interfacing the AD570 Using the Status Check (a) and a Timing Diagram for the A/D Conversion Process (b)

SOURCE: Adapted from Analog Devices, Inc., *Integrated Circuit Converters, Data Acquisition Systems, and Analog Signal Conditioning Components* (Norwood, Mass.: Author, 1979), p. 10-18.

G_1 goes low and $B/\overline{C}$ goes high. Subsequently, the $\overline{DR}$ goes high, which resets the $B/\overline{C}$ low through the NAND gates. When the microprocessor reads port 81H, the buffer 74125 is enabled and data line D_7 is checked for the status of the $\overline{DR}$ signal. The necessary instructions to initiate the conversion and to read output are shown below.

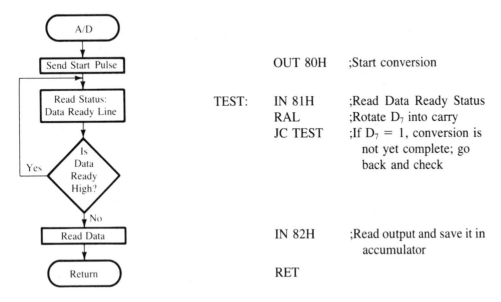

	OUT 80H	;Start conversion
TEST:	IN 81H	;Read Data Ready Status
	RAL	;Rotate D_7 into carry
	JC TEST	;If $D_7 = 1$, conversion is not yet complete; go back and check
	IN 82H	;Read output and save it in accumulator
	RET	

FIGURE 13.12
Flowchart of A/D Conversion Process

INTERFACING MICROPROCESSOR-COMPATIBLE A/D CONVERTER USING WAIT STATES

To reduce the number of chips needed to interface data converters with the microprocessor, manufacturers have begun to include latches, buffers, and control logic on the same chip with a data converter. In the previous example, two tri-state buffers were required as input ports to interface the AD570—one to check status and another to accept data. These two chips can be eliminated by using a microprocessor-compatible A/D converter such as the AD7574 (illustrated in Figure 13.13).

The AD7574 is an 8-bit successive approximation ADC with 15 μs conversion time. It is designed to be operated as a memory-mapped input device with two control signals: a Chip Select ($\overline{CS}$) for a decoded device address, and a Read/Write ($\overline{RD}$) signal.

Figure 13.13 shows an example of interfacing the AD7574 with the 8085. In this schematic, both control signals $\overline{CS}$ and $\overline{RD}$ are tied together and driven by the memory-mapped decoded address 8000H. However, the primary concern in interfacing a slow device such as an A/D converter is that the microprocessor's execution speed is much faster than the conversion speed of the converter. In the previous example, an additional input port is built for the status check, and the microprocessor is kept in a loop reading

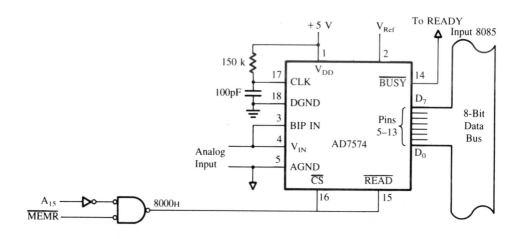

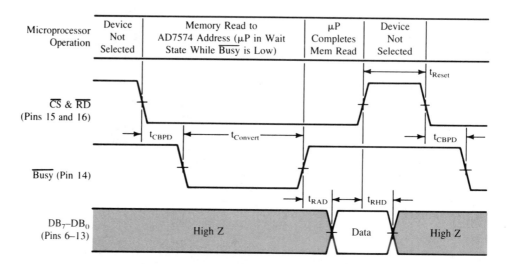

AD7574 Slow Memory Mode Timing Diagram
($\overline{CS}$ and $\overline{RD}$ Tied Together)

AD7574 Inputs	AD7574 Outputs		AD7574 Operation
$\overline{CS}$ & $\overline{RD}$	$\overline{BUSY}$	DB_7-DB_0	
H	H	High Z	Not Selected
⌐	H→L	High Z	Start Conversion
L	L	High Z	Conversion in Progress, μP in Wait State
L	⌐	High Z→Data	Conversion Complete, μP Reads Data
⌐	H	Data→High Z	Converter Reset and Deselected
H	H	High Z	Not Selected

FIGURE 13.13

Interfacing the AD7574 Using the Ready Signal

SOURCE: Timing diagram and truth table are from Analog Devices, Inc., *Integrated Circuit Converters, Data Acquisition Systems, and Analog Signal Conditioning Components* (Norwood, Mass.: Author, 1979), p. 10-85.

the input port until the end of the conversion. In this example, the microprocessor is made to wait until the end of the conversion by connecting the $\overline{\text{BUSY}}$ signal (similar to DATA READY) to the microprocessor READY input.

Conversion is initiated by executing a Memory Read to the ADC port 8000H. As the conversion begins, the $\overline{\text{BUSY}}$ signal goes low, pulling the READY input low, and the microprocessor enters a *Wait* state until the conversion is complete. At the end of the conversion, $\overline{\text{BUSY}}$ goes high, which pulls READY high, and the microprocessor completes the Read operation.

INTERFACING AN A/D CONVERTER USING INTERRUPT

In the previous two examples, the synchronization between the high speed microprocessor and the slow responding A/D converters is accomplished either by using the status check or using the READY line. In both instances, the microprocessor has to wait until the end of the conversion time. However, this wait can be avoided by using the interrupt technique illustrated in Figure 13.14.

Figure 13.14(a) shows the interfacing of the National Semiconductor ADC 0801 with the 8085 MPU, using the interrupt. Address line A_{15} with an inverter is used for Chip Select ($\overline{\text{CS}}$), and the control signals $\overline{\text{MEMR}}$ and $\overline{\text{MEMW}}$ are connected to $\overline{\text{RD}}$ and $\overline{\text{WR}}$ signals, respectively. The ADC 0801 includes control logic that is specially designed to implement interfacing with the interrupt.

The conversion is initiated when the $\overline{\text{CS}}$ and $\overline{\text{WR}}$ signals go low (Figure 13.14(b)). At the end of the conversion, the $\overline{\text{INTR}}$ signal goes low, and is used to interrupt the MPU through an inverter. When the service routine reads the data byte, the $\overline{\text{RD}}$ signal causes the $\overline{\text{INTR}}$ to go high as shown in the timing diagram, Figure 13.14(b). This chip includes the control logic to set $\overline{\text{INTR}}$ at the end of a conversion and to reset it when data are read. This also can be done by using discrete components external to the converter. However, by including this logic on the converter chip, extra components necessary for interfacing are eliminated.

To implement data transfer using the interrupt as shown in Figure 13.14(a), the main program should enable the microprocessor interrupts (EI) and initiate a conversion by writing to port 8000H. At the end of the conversion, the microprocessor is interrupted by using RST 6.5, which transfers the program control to location 0034H. The service routine should read the data (LDA 8000H), enable the 8085 interrupts for the next reading, initiate the next cycle of the conversion, and return to the main program.

13.25 Integrating A/D Converters

Integrating A/D converters use an indirect conversion method. An analog signal is converted into a proportional time period, which is then measured using a digital counter. Several variations of this technique are used. The most commonly known — the dual-slope conversion method — is described below.

DUAL-SLOPE A/D CONVERTERS

Figure 13.15(a) is a block diagram of a typical dual-slope converter. It includes an integrator, comparator, counter, control logic, and a reference voltage. The conversion process follows three steps.

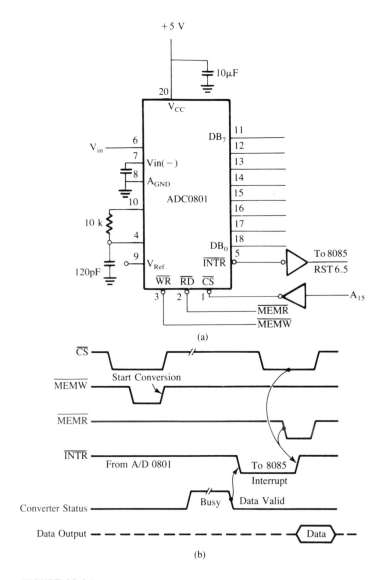

FIGURE 13.14

The ADC 0801 Using the Interrupt: Interface (a) and Timing Diagram for Reading
Data from A/D Converter (b)

SOURCE: B: National Semiconductor, *Data Conversion/Acquisition Data Book* (Santa Clara, Calif.: Author, 1980), p. 5-25.

1. The switch S_1 connects the analog voltage V_{in} for a fixed count, shown in Figure 13.15(b) as period T_1. During this period, the capacitor is charged with the current I_c resulting in a linear ramp at the integrator output.

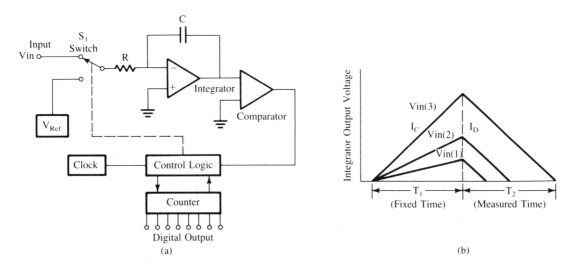

FIGURE 13.15
Dual-Slope A/D Converter: Block Diagram (a) and Conversion Process (b)

2. After the period T_1, the control logic switches the integrator input to the reference voltage V_{Ref} of the opposite polarity of the voltage Vin, and the counter is reset.
3. The counter starts counting again from zero as the capacitor begins to discharge with the current I_D for the period T_2. This results in a ramp with the opposite slope, and the counter is stopped when the ramp crosses the zero level. The counter reading is the equivalent digital signal for the analog input voltage Vin.

In Figure 13.15(b), the total charge in the capacitor while charging and discharging must be equal. Therefore

$$I_c T_1 = I_D T_2$$
$$VinT_1 = V_{Ref}T_2 \text{ (I_c and I_D are proportional to Vin and V_{Ref} respectively)}$$
$$T_2 = \frac{Vin}{V_{Ref}} \times T_1$$

Since T_1 and V_{Ref} are constant, the counter output for period T_2 is proportional to the analog input voltage V_{in}. The output voltage of the integrator reaches the final value proportional to the magnitude of the input voltage (Figure 13.15(b)). However, the slope during the capacitor discharge is constant; thus, the higher voltage takes a longer period.

The characteristics of the integrating A/D converter can be summarized as follows:

1. The conversion accuracy is high.
2. The conversion speed is slow.
3. The noise-rejection level is high.

Interfacing an integrator-type converter with the microprocessor involves considerations similar to those involved in interfacing a successive approximation converter (discussed in Section 13.24); therefore, they are not discussed again.

SUMMARY

☐ D/A converters transform a digital signal into an equivalent analog signal, and A/D converters transform an analog signal into an equivalent digital signal.

☐ Resolution of a converter determines the degree of accuracy in conversion. And it is equal to $\frac{1}{2^n}$ (n is the number of bits).

☐ Settling Time (for DAC) and Conversion Time (for ADC) are important parameters in selecting data converters; they suggest the speed of data conversion.

☐ D/A converters are classified into three categories according to their output function: current, voltage, and multiplying.

☐ The successive approximation A/D converter is a high speed converter and uses a D/A converter to compare an analog signal with an internally generated signal.

☐ A successive approximation A/D converter is available as an integrated circuit on a chip or can be designed by using software and a D/A converter.

☐ The integrating type A/D converter is a high accuracy converter. It is based on the principle of converting an analog signal into a time period and measuring the time period with a digital counter.

☐ A/D converters can serve as input devices and D/A converters can serve as output devices to microprocessor-based systems.

☐ A/D converters can be interfaced with the microprocessor by using techniques such as status check, READY signal, and interrupt.

☐ When 12-bit (or 16-bit) converters are interfaced with an 8-bit microprocessor, data are transferred in two (or three) stages using multiple ports.

ASSIGNMENTS

1. Calculate the output current for the 1408, Figure 13.4(a), if the input is 82H and the converter is calibrated for a 0 to 2 mA current range.
2. What is the voltage output in Assignment 1?
3. Figure 13.4(b) shows a circuit that is calibrated for -5 V to $+5$ V. Calculate the output voltage if the input is 45H.
4. What changes are necessary in the ramp program, Figure 13.4(a), to limit the peak voltage to 7.5 V?
5. Modify the program (Figure 13.4(a)) to generate a square wave with the amplitude of 5 V and a 1 kHz frequency.
6. Calculate the resolution of a 12-bit D/A converter.
7. A 12-bit D/A converter is calibrated over the range 0 to 10 V. Calculate the outputs if the input is 01H and 82H.

8. Calculate the analog voltages corresponding to the LSB and the MSB for a 12-bit A/D converter calibrated for a 0 to 5 V range.

9. In Figure 13.11, assume that the data line D_0 is connected to the line ($\overline{DR}$), instead of D_7, to check the status, and make the necessary changes in the instructions.

10. Change the circuit in Figure 13.11 from the peripheral I/O to the memory-mapped I/O, and assign the port addresses as 8000H to 8002H. Assume that the unused address lines are at logic 0. Rewrite the instructions.

11. Modify the circuit in Figure 13.11 to interface a 12-bit A/D converter.

12. In reference to Figure 13.13, write a subroutine to initiate conversion, read an output signal, and store data in the memory location specified by the main program.

EXPERIMENTAL ASSIGNMENTS

1. **a.** Connect the circuit as shown in Figure 13.4(a) and calibrate the D/A converter for 0 to 10 V.
   b. Write a DELAY routine for a 100 μs delay, and enter the program.
   c. Measure the frequency and the slope of the ramp on an oscilloscope.
   d. Change the DELAY routine to 500 μs. Measure the frequency and the slope of the ramp.
   e. Modify the program to limit the maximum peak voltage of the ramp to 5 V.
   f. Modify the program to generate a triangular waveform.
   g. Modify the program as suggested below:
      (1) Store some random data at locations XX50H to XX5FH.
      (2) Change instructions to call out the data in sequence. Display on an oscilloscope.
      (3) Continue displaying the data to observe a stable pattern.
      (4) Eliminate the DELAY routine and observe the output.

2. **a.** Connect the circuit as shown in Figure 13.9, and calibrate the D/A converter for 0 to 10 V.
   b. Write a DELAY routine for a 200 μs delay, and enter the program. Verify digital outputs for five different analog voltages.
   c. Modify the program to eliminate the counter (MOV D, 08H) and perform the same function by using the instruction RRC. (*Hint:* Check for the Carry flag after the instruction RRC. If the Carry flag is set, that means in the previous iteration D_0 was 1).
   d. Eliminate the instructions CALL DELAY and observe the output for four different input readings in the ascending and the descending order. Explain your results.
   e. Design a software controlled counter A/D converter using the circuit in Figure 13.9 (*Hint:* This is similar to a ramp generation in the D/A converter. Start from the count zero input to the DAC and continue incrementing the count until the output of the DAC exceeds the analog input.)

SDK-85
Programmable
Interface Devices

A programmable interface device is designed to perform various input/output functions. Such a device can be set up to perform specific functions by writing an instruction (or instructions) in its internal register, called the control register. Furthermore, functions can be changed anytime during execution of the program by writing a new instruction in the control register. These devices are flexible, and multifunctional. They are widely used in microprocessor-based products.

In the last three chapters, simple integrated circuits, such as latches and buffers, were used to interface I/O devices. Among the I/O devices used so far, the 8212 is more flexible than others. The 8212 is a combination of latches and tri-state buffers that can be used either as an input or an output device, depending upon the selected mode signal. However, the mode pin must be hardwired. In a programmable device, on the other hand, functions are determined through software instructions. A programmable interface device can be viewed as multiple 8212s, but also performing many other functions such as time delays, counting, and interrupts. In fact, it consists of many devices on a single chip, interconnected through a common bus. This is a hardware approach through software control to performing the I/O functions discussed in the last three chapters. This approach, a trade-off between hardware and software, should reduce programming.

This chapter describes several programmable devices used in the Intel SDK-85 system: the 8155/8156 I/Os and timer, the 8355/8755 I/Os, and the 8279 Keyboard/Display Interface. These devices can be grouped into two categories: devices specifically designed to be compatible with the 8085 multiplexed bus, and general purpose devices. The first two devices — the 8155 and the 8755 — are specifically designed to be compatible with the 8085, while the 8279 is a general purpose device. The Intel family of support devices includes several other general purpose devices that will be discussed in the next chapter.

This chapter first describes the basic concepts underlying these programmable devices. Based on these concepts, three devices — the 8155, the 8755, and the 8279 — are discussed in the context of the SDK-85 single-board microcomputer. This discussion will enable the user to perform laboratory experiments using the SDK-85 or to build additional display ports on the system. The 8155 and the 8755 are multi-purpose chips. Their memory sections have been discussed already in Chapter 3; only the programmable I/Os and the timer are discussed in this chapter.

OBJECTIVES

☐ List the elements and characteristics of a typical programmable device.
☐ Explain the functions of handshake signals.
☐ Explain the block diagram of the 8155/56 I/O section and timer.
☐ Design an interfacing circuit for the 8155 I/O ports and the timer, and write initialization instructions.
☐ Set up the 8155 I/O ports in the handshake mode and write initialization instructions.
☐ Set up the 8155 timer to generate a pulse after a given time delay or a continuous waveform.
☐ Explain the block diagram of the 8355/8755 I/O section.
☐ Design an interfacing circuit for the 8355/8755 I/O ports, and write initialization instructions.
☐ Explain the block diagram of the 8279 Keyboard/Display Interface and its operation.
☐ Write instructions to initialize the 8279 in a given mode.

14.1   BASICS IN PROGRAMMABLE I/OS

The I/O functions of a programmable device are determined through software instructions. The MPU writes an appropriate instruction (or instructions) in the device to define its I/O functions.

In order to understand the principles underlying a programmable device, it is helpful to review the functions performed by the interfacing I/O devices, as discussed in the previous chapters.

1. A latch is used as an output port to hold and display data.
2. A tri-state buffer is used as an input port to read data from devices such as a keyboard or data converters.
3. A tri-state buffer is used as a 1-bit input port to check the status and determine whether the device is ready to input data.
4. An interrupt signal can be generated by an interfacing device (such as the 8212).

Therefore, a programmable device should include at least these functions in its hardware. In addition, it should have control logic, chip select logic, and a register (or registers) in which to write an instruction for defining its hardware functions. As background for understanding such a device, the next section will examine the functions of the 8212 and suggest a conceptual approach to making it programmable.

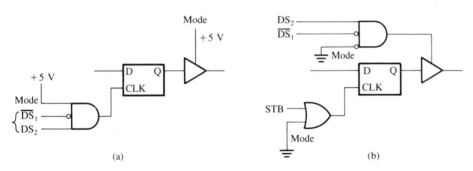

FIGURE 14.1
Simplified Logic of the 8212: The Output Mode (a) and the Input Mode (b)

14.11 Making the 8212 Programmable

The **8212** in its simplest format is a **D-latch with a tri-state buffer**. It can function either in the output mode (Figure 14.1(a)), or in the input mode (Figure 14.1(b)). These figures represent logical functions, not actual inside hardware. The input/output functions of the 8212 are determined by the mode signal. When it is high, the 8212 is an output device; and when it is low, it is an input device. Rather than having a hardwired mode signal, the 8212 can be made programmable by adding a register called the **control register** (Figure 14.2). The MPU could write $D_0 = 0$ or 1 into the control register of this hypothetical 8212, and thus make the mode of the 8212 programmable.

Now the question is: How would the MPU communicate with the control register? The same way it would with any other peripheral, through a port address. Figure 14.2 shows that the address line A_0 would enable the 8212 when it goes low, and would enable the control register when it goes high. This hypothetical chip would be selected through the NAND gate when the address lines A_7 through A_1 are all high. Therefore, the MPU could access the control register through the port address FFH; and the 8212 through FEH.

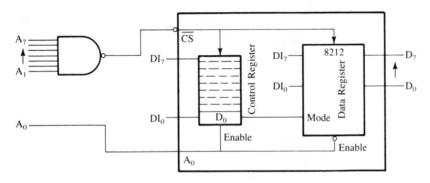

FIGURE 14.2
A Hypothetical 8212 with a Control Register

To set up the 8212 as an output port and display data stored at a memory location (e.g., 2050H) the following instructions are necessary.

INSTRUCTIONS

MVI A, 01H	;Set $D_0 = 1$, D_1 through D_7 are don't care lines
OUT FFH	;Write in the control register
LXI H, 2050H	;Point index to 2050H
MOV A, M	;Get data
OUT FEH	;Display at the output port

14.12   The 8212 with Status Check

The 8212 shown in Figure 14.2 can perform only limited I/O functions. In the discussion of interfacing A/D converters in Chapter 13, Figure 13.11 showed that an additional input port is needed to check the status of the $\overline{DR}$ (Data Ready) line. The programmable 8212 can be expanded to include one more input register called the status register, as shown in Figure 14.3. The hypothetical chip shown in Figure 14.3 has three control lines: $\overline{CS}$, A_1, and A_0. The status register can be accessed when $A_1 = 0$ and $A_0 = 1$. The decode logic that selects the chip ($\overline{CS}$) is similar to that of Figure 14.2, but has one fewer address line. Therefore, the port addresses of the registers and the 8212 are as follows:

Control Register = FFH (A_1 and $A_0 = 1$)
Status Register = FDH ($A_1 = 0$ and $A_0 = 1$)
8212 = FEH ($A_1 = 1$, $A_0 = 0$)

Example 14.1

Set up the hypothetical 8212 in Figure 14.3 as an input port to read the data from an A/D converter if the $\overline{DR}$ signal is low. (Assume that the $\overline{DR}$ signal is connected to D_0.)

INSTRUCTIONS

	MVI A, 00H	;Set D_0 of the control register to logic 0
	OUT FFH	;Write in the control register to set 8212 as an input
READ:	IN FDH	;Read the status port
	ANI 01H	;Mask D_1 through D_7
	JNZ READ	;If D_0 of the status port is high, wait in the loop until it goes low
	IN FEH	;Now D_0 is low; read the input port
	↓	
	Continue	

14.13   Programmable Devices with Handshake Signals

The MPU and peripherals operate at different speeds; therefore, signals are exchanged prior to data transfer between the fast-responding MPU and slow-responding peripherals such as printers and data converters. These signals are called **handshake signals**. The

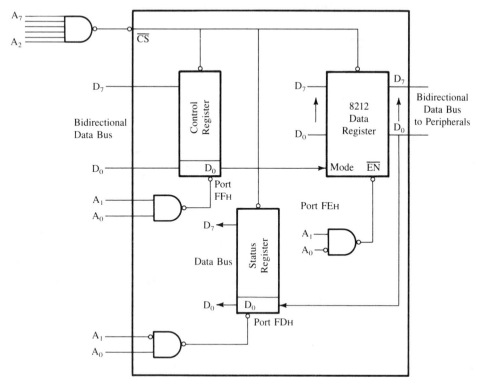

FIGURE 14.3
A Hypothetical 8212 with a Status Register

exchange of handshake signals prevents the MPU from writing over the previous data before a peripheral has had a chance to accept it, or from reading the same data before a peripheral has had time to send the next data byte. These signals are generally provided by programmable devices. Figure 14.4(a) shows a programmable device in the input mode with two handshake signals (STB and IBF) and one interrupt signal (INTR). Now the MPU has two ways of finding out whether a peripheral is ready: either by checking the status of a handshake signal, or through the interrupt technique as explained below.

DATA INPUT WITH HANDSHAKE

The steps in data input from a peripheral such as a keyboard are as follows:

1. A peripheral strobes or places a data byte in the input port and informs the interfacing device by sending handshake signal STB (Strobe).
2. The device informs the peripheral that its input port is full — do not send the next byte until this one has been read. This message is conveyed to the peripheral by sending handshake signal IBF (Input Buffer Full).

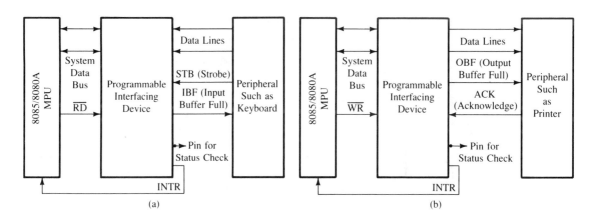

FIGURE 14.4
Interfacing Device with Handshake Signals for Data Input (a) and Data Output (b)

3. The MPU keeps checking the status until a byte is available. Or the interfacing device informs the MPU, by sending an interrupt, that it has a byte to be read.
4. The MPU reads the byte by sending control signal $\overline{RD}$.

DATA OUTPUT WITH HANDSHAKE

Figure 14.4(b) shows the programmable device in the output mode using the same two handshake signals, except that they are labelled differently. The steps in data output to a peripheral such as a printer are as follows:

1. The MPU writes a byte into the output port of the programmable device by sending control signal $\overline{WR}$.
2. The device informs the peripheral, by sending handshake signal OBF (Output Buffer Full), that a byte is on the way.
3. The peripheral acknowledges the byte by sending back the ACK (Acknowledge) signal to the device.
4. The device interrupts the MPU in order to ask for the next byte, or the MPU finds out that the byte has been acknowledged through the status check.

Examination of Figure 14.4 shows the following similarities among the handshake signals:

1. Handshake signals ACK and STB are input signals to the device and perform similar functions, although they are called by different names.
2. Handshake signals OBF and IBF are output signals from the device and perform similar functions (Buffer Full).

The active levels and labels of these signals are arbitrary and vary considerably from device to device. For example, in the 8155 (R/W Memory with I/O) both input signals are called STB (Strobe); in the 8255 (Programmable Peripheral Interface) one input signal is called STB (Strobe) and the other is called ACK (Acknowledge).

14.14 Review of Important Concepts

The above examples suggest that a programmable I/O device is likely to have the following elements:

1. A control register in which the MPU can write an instruction.
2. A status register that can be read by the MPU.
3. I/O devices or registers.
4. Control logic.
5. Chip Select logic.
6. Bidirectional data bus.
7. Handshake signals and Interrupt logic.

A programmable I/O device is programmed by writing a specific word, called the **control word**, according to the internal logic; its status can be verified by reading the status register. This I/O device can be expanded to include elements such as multiple I/O ports, counters, and parallel to serial registers. The programmable devices used in the Intel SDK-85 system — the 8155/8156, the 8355 (or 8755), and the 8279 — are described in detail in the next sections.

THE 8155/8156 and 8355/8755 MULTIPURPOSE PROGRAMMABLE DEVICES | 14.2

The 8155 and the 8355 are two multipurpose programmable devices specifically designed to be compatible with the 8085 microprocessor. The ALE, IO/$\overline{M}$, $\overline{RD}$, and $\overline{WR}$ signals from the 8085 can be connected directly to these devices; this eliminates the need for external demultiplexing of the low-order bus AD_7–AD_0 and generation of the control signals such as $\overline{MEMR}$, $\overline{MEMW}$, $\overline{IOR}$, and $\overline{IOW}$.

The 8155 includes 256 bytes of R/W memory, three I/O ports, and a timer. The 8156 is identical with the 8155, except that the 8156 requires Chip Enable (CE) active high. The 8355 includes 2K of ROM and two I/O ports. The 8755 is similar to the 8355, except that the 8755 is EPROM. The programmable I/O sections of these devices are illustrated in the following sections.

14.21 THE 8155/8156 PROGRAMMABLE I/O PORTS AND TIMER

The 8155/8156 is a device with two sections: the first is 256 bytes of R/W memory, and the second is a programmable I/O. Functionally, these two sections can be viewed as two independent chips. The I/O section includes two 8-bit parallel I/O ports (A and B), one 6-bit port (C), and a timer (Figure 14.5). All the ports can be configured simply as

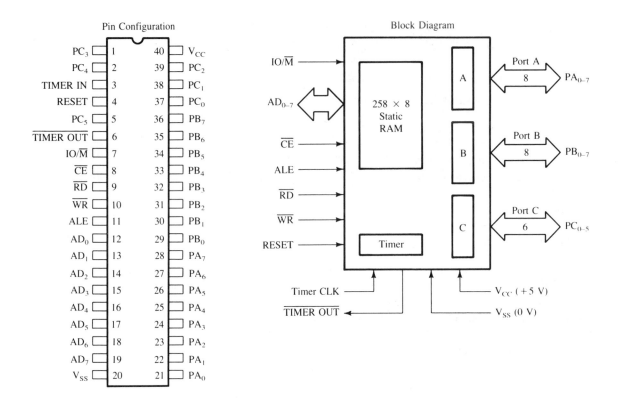

FIGURE 14.5
8155 Pin Configuration and Block Diagram
SOURCE: Intel Corporation, *MCS — 80/85 Family User's Manual* (Santa Clara, Calif.: Author, 1979), p. 6-17.

input/output ports — similar to the 8212. Ports A and B also can be programmed in the handshake mode, each port using three signals as handshake signals from port C. The timer is a 14-bit down-counter and has four modes. Pins *PA*, *PB*, and *PC*, shown in Figure 14.5, correspond to ports A, B, and C.

CONTROL LOGIC

The control logic of the 8155 is specifically designed to eliminate the need for externally demultiplexing lines AD_7–AD_0 and generating separate control signals for memory and I/O. Figure 14.5 shows five control signals; all except the Chip Enable ($\overline{CE}$) are input signals directly generated by the 8085.

☐ $\overline{CE}$ — Chip Enable: This is a master Chip Select signal connected to the decoded high-order bus.
☐ IO/$\overline{M}$ — When this signal is low, the memory section is selected, and when it is high, the I/O section (including timer) is selected.

☐ ALE—Address Latch Enable: This signal latches the low-order address AD_7–AD_0, $\overline{CE}$, and $IO/\overline{M}$ into the chip.

☐ $\overline{RD}$ and $\overline{WR}$—These are control signals to read from and write into the chip registers and memory.

☐ RESET—This is connected to RESET OUT of the 8085 and this resets the chip and initializes I/O ports as input.

THE 8155 I/O PORTS

The I/O section of the 8155 includes a control register, three I/O ports, and two registers for the timer (Figure 14.6). The expanded block diagram of the I/O section (Figure 14.6) represents a typical programmable I/O as discussed in Section 14.12. In that section, two address lines plus the Chip Select logic were used to determine port addresses. The 8155 I/O section requires three address lines — AD_2 to AD_0 and the Chip Enable logic to specify one of the seven registers. In addition, two control signals, $\overline{RD}$ and $\overline{WR}$, are necessary to read from and write into these I/O registers.

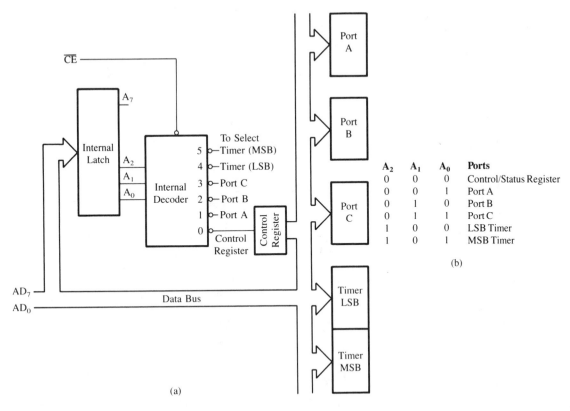

A_2	A_1	A_0	Ports
0	0	0	Control/Status Register
0	0	1	Port A
0	1	0	Port B
0	1	1	Port C
1	0	0	LSB Timer
1	0	1	MSB Timer

(b)

(a)

FIGURE 14.6
Expanded Block Diagram of the 8155 (a) and Its I/O Address: Selection (b)

To communicate with peripherals through the 8155 the following steps are necessary:

1. Determine the addresses (port numbers of the registers and I/Os) based on the Chip Enable logic and address lines AD_0, AD_1, and AD_2.
2. Write a control word in the control register to specify I/O functions of the ports and the timer characteristics.
3. Write I/O instructions to port addresses to communicate with peripherals.
4. Read the status register, if necessary, to verify the status of the I/O ports and the timer. In simple applications, this step is not necessary.

CHIP ENABLE LOGIC AND PORT ADDRESSES

Address lines AD_2 to AD_0, also shown as A_2 to A_0 after internal demultiplexing, select one of the registers, as shown in Figure 14.6(b). Address lines A_3 to A_7 are don't care lines; however, the logic levels on the corresponding high-order lines, A_{11} to A_{15}, will be duplicated on lines A_3 to A_7, as explained in the next example.

Example 14.2

Determine the addresses of the control/status register, I/O ports, and timer registers in Figure 14.7.

Solution   To select the chip, the output line O_4 of the 8205 (3-to-8) decoder (Figure 14.7) should go low. Therefore, the logic levels of A_{15} to A_{11} should be as follows:

$$
\begin{array}{cc|ccc}
A_{15} & A_{14} & A_{13} & A_{12} & A_{11} \\
0 & 0 & 1 & 0 & 0 \\
\end{array}
$$

↑	↑
Enable lines of the 8205	Input logic to activate the output line 4 of the 8205

By combining five high-order address lines with three low-order address lines (A_2–A_0), the port numbers in Figure 14.8 will range from 20H to 25H, as shown below.

A_{15}	A_{14}	A_{13}	A_{12}	A_{11}	AD_2	AD_1	AD_0	Addresses	Ports
0	0	1	0	0	0	0	0	= 20H	Control or status register
					0	0	1	= 21H	Port A
		(2H)			0	1	0	= 22H	Port B
					0	1	1	= 23H	Port C
		⇓			1	0	0	= 24H	Timer (LSB)
A_7	A_6	A_5	A_4	A_3	1	0	1	= 25H	Timer (MSB)

This raises a question: How is it possible to combine five high-order address lines with three low-order address lines to generate a port address? To find an answer to this question, examine the execution of either the IN or the OUT instruction. When these

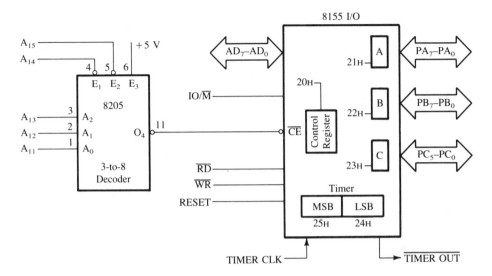

FIGURE 14.7
Interfacing 8155 I/O Ports (Schematic from the SDK-85 System)

instructions are executed, the high-order and low-order address buses carry the same information. In this case, the logic levels required on lines A_{15} to A_{11} for the Chip Enable are also duplicated on the address lines from A_7 through A_3, as shown above.

CONTROL WORD

The I/O ports and the timer can be configured by writing a control word in the control register. The control register bits are defined as shown in Figure 14.8.

In this control word, outputs are defined with logic 1 and inputs with logic 0. The first two LSBs, D_0 and D_1, determine I/O functions of ports A and B; and the MSBs, D_7 and D_6, determine timer functions. Bits D_2 and D_3 determine the functions of port C; and their combination specifies one of the four alternatives, from simple I/O to interrupt I/O, as shown in Figure 14.8(b). Bits D_4 and D_5 are used only in the interrupt mode to enable or disable internal flip-flops of the 8155. These bits do not have any effect on the Interrupt Enable flip-flop (INTE) of the MPU.

The next section shows an application of the 8155 to design two output ports for the SDK-85 system. An application of the 8155 in the handshake mode is illustrated later.

14.22 Illustration: Interfacing Seven-Segment LED Output Ports Using the 8155

PROBLEM STATEMENT

1. Design two seven-segment LED displays using ports A and B of the 8155.
2. Write initialization instructions and display data bytes at each port.

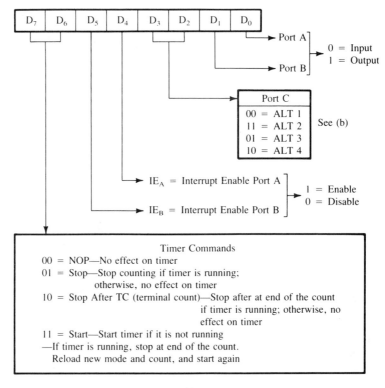

(a)

Table: ALT 1–ALT 4: Port C Bit Assignments, Defined by Bits D_3 and D_2 in the Control Register

ALT	D_3	D_2	PC_5	PC_4	PC_3	PC_2	PC_1	PC_0
ALT 1	0	0	I	I	I	I	I	I
ALT 2	1	1	O	O	O	O	O	O
ALT 3	0	1	O	O	O	$\overline{STB}_A$	BF_A	$INTR_A$
ALT 4	1	0	$\overline{STB}_B$	BF_B	$INTR_B$	$\overline{STB}_A$	BF_A	$INTR_A$

I = Input, STB = Strobe, INTR = Interrupt Request
O = Output, BF = Buffer Full, Subscript A = Port A
                                                B = Port B

(b)

FIGURE 14.8
Control Word Definition in the 8155 (a) and Table of Port C Bit Assignments (b)

HARDWARE DESCRIPTION

Figure 14.9 shows two seven-segment output ports: port A with the Hewlett Packard HP 5082/7340, and port B with the Fairchild FND 507, and 9370. The HP 5082 includes an internal decoder/driver, while the FND 507 is driven by a separate decoder/driver 9370.

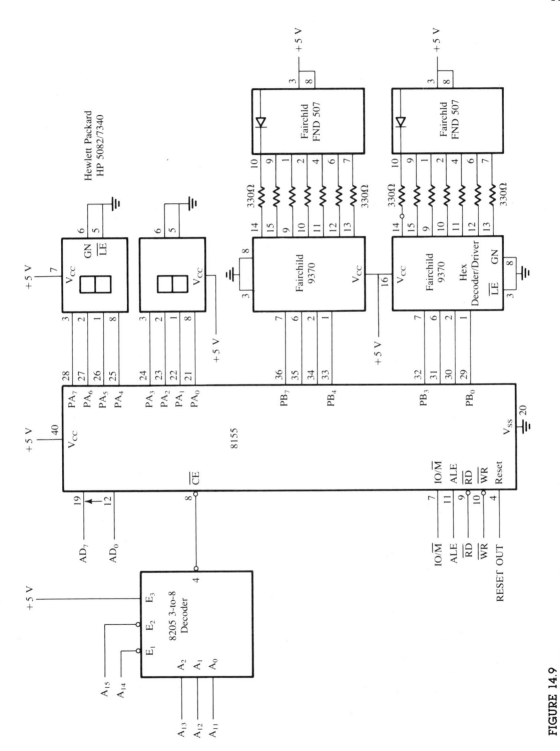

FIGURE 14.9
Interfacing 8155 I/O Ports with Seven-Segment LEDs

Both are functionally similar; however, a seven-segment display with an internal built-in decoder/driver is more expensive.

The decode logic is the same as that used in the previous discussion; therefore, the port addresses are as follows:

$$\begin{array}{ll}\text{Control Register} & = 20\text{H} \\ \text{Port A} & = 21\text{H} \\ \text{Port B} & = 22\text{H}\end{array}$$

CONTROL WORD

To configure ports A and B as outputs, the control word is as follows:

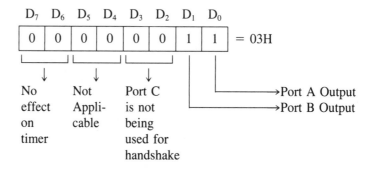

PROGRAM

```
MVI A, 03H        ;Initialize ports A and B as output ports.
OUT 20H
MVI A, BYTE1
OUT 21H           ;Display BYTE1 at port A.
MVI A, BYTE2
OUT 22H           ;Display BYTE2 at port B.
HLT
```

PROGRAM DESCRIPTION

The instruction MVI A, 03H initializes ports A and B as simple output ports, and the following instructions display data BYTE1 and data BYTE2 at ports A and B, respectively.

14.23   The 8155 Timer

The timer section of the 8155 has two 8-bit registers; fourteen bits are used for counter, two bits for the timer mode, and it requires a clock as an input. This 14-bit down-counter provides output in four different modes, as described below.

Figure 14.10(a) shows two registers for a 14-bit count, one for LSB (low significant byte) and one for MSB (most significant byte). The most significant bits M_2 and M_1 are

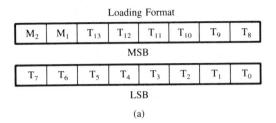

Loading Format

M_2	M_1	T_{13}	T_{12}	T_{11}	T_{10}	T_9	T_8

MSB

T_7	T_6	T_5	T_4	T_3	T_2	T_1	T_0

LSB

(a)

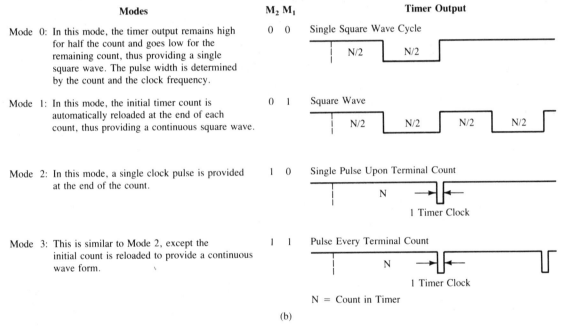

Modes M_2 M_1 **Timer Output**

Mode 0: In this mode, the timer output remains high   0   0   Single Square Wave Cycle
for half the count and goes low for the
remaining count, thus providing a single
square wave. The pulse width is determined
by the count and the clock frequency.

Mode 1: In this mode, the initial timer count is   0   1   Square Wave
automatically reloaded at the end of each
count, thus providing a continuous square wave.

Mode 2: In this mode, a single clock pulse is provided   1   0   Single Pulse Upon Terminal Count
at the end of the count.

Mode 3: This is similar to Mode 2, except the   1   1   Pulse Every Terminal Count
initial count is reloaded to provide a continuous
wave form.

N = Count in Timer

(b)

FIGURE 14.10
Timer Loading Format (a) and Modes (b)

used to specify the timer mode. To operate the timer, a 14-bit count and mode bits are
loaded in the registers. An appropriate control word starts the counter, which decrements
the count at each clock pulse. The timer outputs vary according to the mode specified
(Figure 14.10(b)).

The timer can be stopped either in the midst of counting, or at the end of a count
(applicable to Modes 1 and 3). In addition, the actual count at a given moment can be
obtained by reading the status register. These details will be described later.

14.24   Illustration: Designing a Square Wave Generator Using the 8155 Timer

PROBLEM STATEMENT

Design a square wave generator with a pulse width of 100 μs by using the 8155 timer. Set up the timer in Mode 1 if the clock frequency is 3 MHz. Use the same decode logic and the port addresses as in Example 14.2 (Figure 14.7).

PROBLEM ANALYSIS

Timer Count   The pulse width required is 100 μs; therefore, the count should be calculated for the period of 200 μs. The timer output stays high for only half the count.

$$\text{Clock Period} = 1/f = 1/3 \times 10^6 = 330 \text{ ns}$$

$$\text{Timer Count} = \frac{\text{Pulse Period}}{\text{Clock Period}} = \frac{200 \times 10^{-6}}{330 \times 10^{-9}} = 606$$

$$\text{Count} = 025\text{EH}$$

Assuming the same decode logic for the 8155 Chip Enable line as in Example 14.2, the port addresses for the timer registers are

$$\text{Timer LSB} = 24\text{H}$$
$$\text{Timer MSB} = 25\text{H}$$

The least significant byte, 5EH (of the count 025EH), should be loaded in the timer register with address 24H.

The most significant byte is determined as follows:

$$
\begin{array}{cc@{\qquad}cccccc}
M_2 & M_1 & T_{13} & T_{12} & T_{11} & T_{10} & T_9 & T_8 \\
0 & 1 & 0 & 0 & 0 & 0 & 1 & 0 \\
\end{array}
= 42\text{H}
$$

Timer Mode 1   MSB

Therefore, 42H should be loaded in the timer register with the address 25H.

Control Word   Assuming the same configuration for ports A and B as before, only bits D_7 and D_6 should be set to 1 to start the counter (see control word definition in Figure 14.8).

Therefore, Control Word: 1100 0011 = C3H

Initialization Instructions

```
MVI A, 5EH      ;LSB of the count
OUT 24H         ;Load the LSB timer register
```

```
MVI A, 42H      ;MSB of the count
OUT 25H         ;Load the MSB timer register
MVI A, C3H
OUT 20H         ;Start the timer
HLT
```

14.25   The 8155 I/O Ports in Handshake Mode

In the handshake mode, data transfer occurs between the MPU and peripherals using control signals called handshake signals. Two I/O ports of the 8155, A and B, can be configured in the handshake mode; each uses three signals from port C as control signals (Figure 14.11). Another alternative (ALT 3 in the Table in Figure 14.8) available in the 8155 is to configure port A in the handshake mode with three control signals from port C; configure port B as simple I/O; and configure the remaining three bits of port C as outputs. The details of configuring ports A and B in the handshake mode by using the pins of port C are given below.

CONTROL SIGNALS IN HANDSHAKE MODE

When both ports A and B are configured in the handshake mode, port A uses the lower three signals of port C (PC_0, PC_1, and PC_2), and port B uses the upper three signals (PC_3, PC_4, and PC_5), as shown in Figure 14.11. The functions of these signals are as follows:

□ $\overline{STB}$ **(Strobe Input):** This is an input handshake signal from a peripheral to the 8155. The low on this signal informs the 8155 that data are strobed into the input port.

□ **BF (Buffer Full):** This is an active high signal, indicating the presence of a data byte in the port.

□ **INTR (Interrupt Request):** This signal is generated by the rising edge of the $\overline{STB}$ signal if the interrupt flip-flop (INTE) is enabled. This signal can be used to interrupt the MPU.

□ **INTE (Interrupt Enable):** This is an internal flip-flop used to enable or disable the interrupt capability of the 8155. The interrupts for port A and port B are controlled by bits D_4 and D_5, respectively, in the control register.

FIGURE 14.11
8155 with Handshake Mode

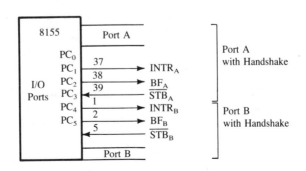

These control signals can be used to implement either interrupt I/O or status check I/O.

INPUT

Figure 14.12(a) shows the sequence of events and timing in data input to the 8155; they can be described as follows:

1. An external peripheral places data in the input port and informs the 8155 by causing the $\overline{STB}$ signal to go low.

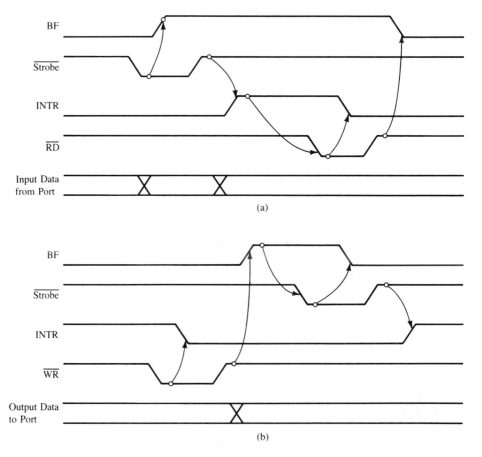

(a)

(b)

FIGURE 14.12

Timing Waveforms of the 8155 I/O Ports with Handshake: Input Mode (a) and Output Mode (b)

SOURCE: Intel Corporation, *MCS—80/85 Family User's Manual* (Santa Clara, Calif.: Author, 1979), p. 6-30.

2. The falling edge of the $\overline{\text{STB}}$ sets signal BF (Buffer Full) high, informing the peripheral to wait.
3. When the $\overline{\text{STB}}$ goes high, the rising edge of the $\overline{\text{STB}}$ can generate signal INTR if the internal interrupt flip-flop INTE is set. The interrupt flip-flops are set or reset by the control word.
4. The last step is to transfer data from the 8155 input port to the MPU. This can be done either by interrupting the MPU with the INTR signal or by checking the status of signal BF. The MPU can check the status by reading the status register (described later). When the MPU reads data, the INTR and BF signals are reset. When the BF signal goes low, it informs the peripheral that the port is empty, and the device is ready for the next byte.

OUTPUT

The sequence of events and timing in data output from the 8155 port to a peripheral are as follows (see Figure 14.12(b)):

1. When the output port is empty, the MPU writes a byte in the port.
2. The falling edge of the $\overline{\text{WR}}$ signal resets the INTR signal and the rising edge sets the BF (Buffer Full) signal high, which is used to inform the peripheral that a byte is available in the port.
3. After receiving the data byte, the peripheral acknowledges by sending the $\overline{\text{STB}}$ signal (active low).
4. The $\overline{\text{STB}}$ signal resets the BF signal low and generates the interrupt request by setting INTR high. Now the MPU can be informed by the interrupt signal to send the next byte, or the MPU can sense that the port is empty through status check.

STATUS WORD

The MPU can read the status register to check the status of the ports or the timer. The control register and the status register have the same port address; they are differentiated only by the $\overline{\text{RD}}$ and $\overline{\text{WR}}$ signals. The status register bits are defined in Figure 14.13.

14.26 Illustration: Interfacing I/O Ports in Handshake Mode Using the 8155

PROBLEM STATEMENT

Design an interfacing circuit using the 8155 to read and display data from an A/D converter to meet the following requirements:

1. Set up port A in the handshake mode to read data from an A/D converter.
2. Set up port B as an output port to display data at seven-segment LEDs.
3. Use line PC_3 from port C to initiate a conversion.

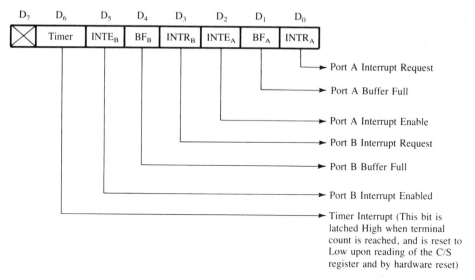

FIGURE 14.13
Status Word Definition

SOURCE: Intel Corporation, *MCS—80/85 Family User's Manual* (Santa Clara, Calif.: Author, 1979), p. 6-20.

4. Use the same decode logic as in Example 14.2 (Figure 14.7) to assign I/O port addresses.

5. Use the 8155 timer to record the conversion time.

PROBLEM ANALYSIS

Figure 14.14 shows an interfacing circuit that uses the 8155 I/O ports as follows:

1. Port A is configured as an input port in the handshake mode for reading data from the A/D converter.

2. Port B is configured as a simple output port for seven-segment LEDs.

3. The upper half of port C is a simple output port, and bit PC_3 is being used to start conversion.

4. The lower half of port C provides handshake signals for port A. Bit PC_2 is being used as a strobe ($\overline{STB}$) to inform the 8155 that the conversion is complete and that the output of the converter has been placed in port A.

INPUT WITH STATUS CHECK

The circuit shows that the INTR signal (bit PC_0) is not being used. This suggests that port A is configured for status check and not for interrupt I/O. Therefore, the control word (see Figure 14.8) required to set up the ports as specified above and the masking byte to check the Data Ready ($\overline{DR}$) line are as follows:

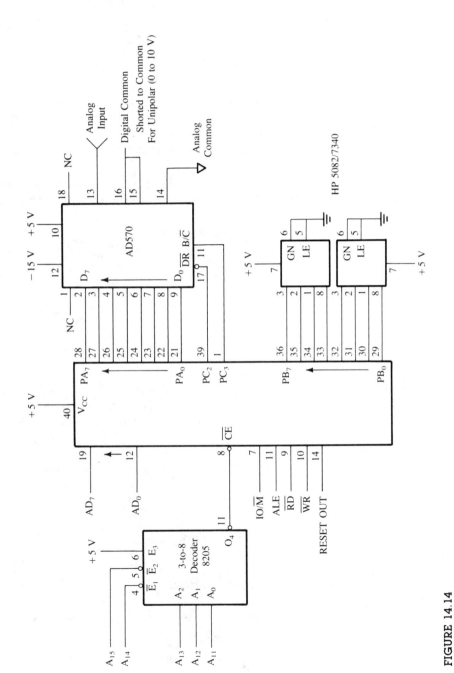

FIGURE 14.14

Interfacing the A/D Converter AD570 in the Handshake Mode

Control Word

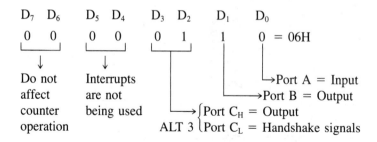

D_7 D_6 D_5 D_4 D_3 D_2 D_1 D_0

0   0   0   0   0   1   1   0 = 06H

Do not   Interrupts   →Port A = Input
affect   are not   →Port B = Output
counter   being used   →⎰Port C_H = Output
operation   ALT 3 ⎱Port C_L = Handshake signals

Status Word   The MPU needs to check bit D_1 of the status register to verify the end of conversion and the availability of data in port A. The status word will have the following information (see Figure 14.13):

D_7	D_6	D_5	D_4	D_3	D_2	D_1	D_0
X	X	X	X	X	X	BF_A	X
	Timer	$INTE_B$	BF_B	$INTR_B$	$INTE_A$		$INTR_A$

When the status word is masked with byte 02H, the availability of a data byte in port A can be verified.

8155 TIMER

The timer can be used to calculate the conversion time. When a conversion begins, the timer should be started with a known count, and at the end of conversion the timer should be stopped. The difference between the two counts multiplied by the clock period of the timer should provide a fairly accurate reading of the conversion time.

To start the timer, set bits D_7 and D_6 of the control register to 1 without affecting the other bits of the register. Therefore, to start the timer, the control word should be:

$$= 1 \ 1 \quad 0 \ 0 \ 0 \ 1 \ 1 \ 0 \quad = C6H$$

Start   I/O Assignments
Timer

To stop the timer, the control word should be:

$$0 \ 1 \quad 0 \ 0 \ 0 \ 1 \ 1 \ 0 \quad = 46H$$

Stop   I/O Assignments
Timer

PORT ADDRESSES

The decode logic is the same as in Example 14.2; therefore, the I/O port addresses range from 20H (control register) to 25H (Timer — MSB).

PROGRAM

	MVI A, 06H	;Control word for I/O ports
	OUT 20H	;Set up ports as specified
	MVI A, 00H	;Load 0000H in the timer registers
	OUT 24H	
	OUT 25H	
	MVI A, 08H	;Byte to set $PC_3 = 1$
	OUT 23H	;Send START pulse
	MVI A, C6H	;Control word to start timer
	OUT 20H	;Start timer
	MVI A, 00H	;Byte to set $PC_3 = 0$
	OUT 23H	;Start conversion
STATUS:	IN 20H	;Read status register
	ANI 02H	;Check status of $\overline{DR}$
	JZ STATUS	;If $BF_A = 0$, wait in the loop until a data byte is available
	MVI A, 46H	;Byte to stop counter
	OUT 20H	;Stop counter
	IN 21H	;Read A/D converter output
	OUT 22H	;Display data at port B
	IN 24H	;Read LSB of timer count
	MOV L, A	;Save timer count in register L
	IN 25H	;Read MSB of timer count
	ANI 3FH	;Delete D_7 and D_6 from the MSB; they represent timer mode
	MOV H, A	;Save MSB timer count in H
	LHLD RWM	;Store timer count from HL register in R/W memory locations
	HLT	

PROGRAM DESCRIPTION

The comments are self explanatory; however, some explanation is needed for the timer count, start conversion (convert) pulse, and status check.

The program loads 0000H in the timer register, and after the first decrement, the count becomes 3FFFH. This is a 14-bit counter, with bits D_{15} and D_{14} reserved to specify the mode. However, in this particular problem, the counter mode is irrelevant. This program assumes that the A/D conversion time is less than the time period given by the maximum count. The difference between the initial count and the final count will provide the necessary value to calculate the conversion time. The program does not perform this subtraction; it just stores the final count in two consecutive memory locations labelled as RWM.

The second item needing explanation is the start conversion (convert) pulse. This is an active high pulse provided by turning on and off bit PC_3 in port C.

Finally, instruction IN 20H reads the status register, and instructions ANI 02 and JZ check whether the buffer in port A (BF_A) is full. The program stays in the loop until the BF_A goes high, indicating the availability of data.

INTERRUPT I/O

This example illustrates all the important I/O operations of the 8155 except the interrupt I/O in the handshake mode. To implement the interrupt I/O in the above example, the $INTR_A$—the output bit PC_0—should be connected to a vectored interrupt such as RST 6.5 and the control word should be changed accordingly (see assignment 15 at the end of this chapter).

14.27 Interfacing the 8355/8755 Programmable I/O Ports

The 8355/8755 is a 2K-byte (2048 × 8) memory with two I/O ports; each I/O line of the ports can be programmed either as input or output. The 8355 is ROM and the 8755 is EPROM; the interfacing of the memory sections of these devices was discussed in Chapter 3. Figure 14.15 shows: (a) the block diagram of the 8755, and (b) the internal control registers called Data Direction Registers (DDR). Each bit in the DDR registers controls the corresponding bit in the I/O ports. The port addresses of the DDR registers and I/O ports are determined by the Chip Enable ($\overline{CE}$) logic and address lines AD_0 and AD_1. The table, Figure 14.15(c), shows the logic levels required for address lines AD_0 and AD_1 to select a port. These logic levels are combined with $\overline{CE}$ logic to determine the port addresses, as explained below.

Figure 14.16 is a schematic from the SDK-85 system. The interfacing logic shows the 3-to-8 decoder; its output line 0 is connected to the $\overline{CE}$ signal of the 8755. (The schematic in Appendix C2 shows how to connect LED displays to 8755 I/O ports.)

To select the 8755, the logic on the address lines should be as follows:

A_{15}/AD_7	A_{14}/AD_6	A_{13}/AD_5	A_{12}/AD_4	A_{11}/AD_3	AD_2	AD_1	AD_0		Selected Register
0	0	0	0	0	X	0	0	= 00	A
						0	1	= 01	B
						1	0	= 02	DDR A
						1	1	= 03	DDR B

The logic levels on the high-order address lines (A_{15}–A_{11}) are duplicated on the low-order address lines (AD_7–AD_3).

Each bit of port A and port B can be programmed by writing control words in their respective DDR registers; logic 0 in a DDR register specifies input mode for the corresponding bit in the I/O port. For example, byte F0H in the DDR_A specifies that lines PA_0 to PA_3 are inputs and lines PA_4 to PA_7 are outputs.

FIGURE 14.15

8755 Block Diagram (a), Data
Direction Register (b), and I/O
Selection Table (c)

SOURCE: A: Intel Corporation, *MCS—80/85
Family User's Manual* (Santa Clara, Calif.:
Author, 1979), p. 6-45.

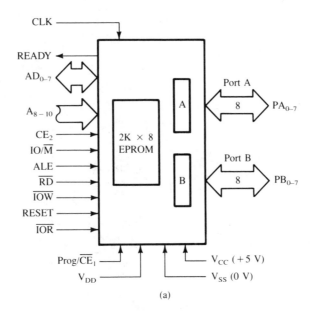

(a)

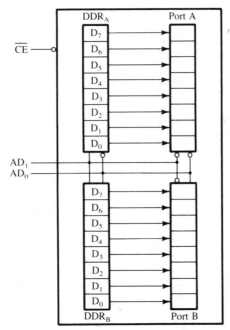

(b)

Table: I/O Selection	AD₁	AD₀	Port
	0	0	A
	0	1	B
	1	0	DDR$_A$
	1	1	DDR$_B$

(c)

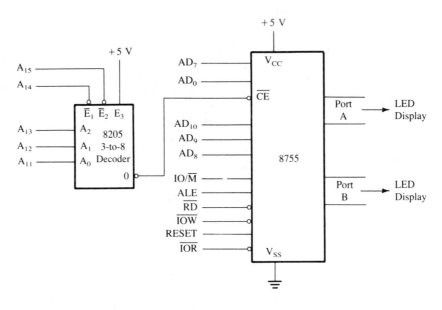

FIGURE 14.16
Interfacing the 8755 I/O Ports

Example
14.3

Write initialization instructions to configure port A and port B as output ports, and display 32H at port A.

Instructions

MVI A, FFH   ;Control word to set up all bits as output bits
OUT 02H   ;Initialize port A as output
OUT 03H   ;Initialize port B as output
MVI A, 32H
OUT 00H   ;Display 32H at port A
HLT

14.3 THE 8279 PROGRAMMABLE KEYBOARD/DISPLAY INTERFACE

The 8279 is a hardware approach to interfacing a matrix keyboard and a multiplexed display. Chapter 11 illustrated the software approach to interfacing a matrix keyboard and a multiplexed display of seven-segment LEDs. The disadvantage of the software approach is that the microprocessor is occupied for a considerable amount of time in checking the keyboard and refreshing the display. The 8279 relieves the processor from these two tasks. The disadvantage of using the 8279 is the cost. The trade-offs between the hardware approach and the software approach are the production cost vs. the processor time and the software development cost.

The 8279 (Figure 14.17) is a 40-pin device with two major segments: keyboard and display. The keyboard segment can be connected to a 64-contact key matrix. Keyboard entries are debounced and stored in the internal FIFO (First-In–First-Out) memory, while an interrupt signal is generated with each entry. The display segment can provide a sixteen-character scanned display interface with such devices as LEDs. This segment has 16×8 R/W memory (RAM), which can be used to read/write information for display purposes. The display can be set up either in right-entry or left-entry format.

14.31   Block Diagram of the 8279

The block diagram (Figure 14.18) shows four major sections of the 8279: keyboard, scan, display, and MPU interface. The functions of these sections are described below.

KEYBOARD SECTION

This section has eight lines (RL_0–RL_7) that can be connected to eight columns of a keyboard, plus two additional lines: Shift and CNTL/STB (Control/Strobe). The status of the *SHIFT* key and the *Control* key can be stored along with a key closure. The keys are automatically debounced, and the keyboard can operate in two modes: two-key lockout or N-key rollover. In the two-key lockout mode, if two keys are pressed almost simultaneously, only the first key is recognized. In the N-key rollover mode, simultaneous keys are recognized and their codes are stored in the internal buffer; it can also be set up so that no key is recognized until only one key remains pressed.

The keyboard section also includes 8×8 FIFO (First-In–First-Out) RAM. The FIFO RAM consists of eight registers that can store eight keyboard entries; each is then read in the order of entries. The status logic keeps track of the number of entries and provides an IRQ (Interrupt Request) signal when the FIFO is not empty.

SCAN SECTION

The scan section has a scan counter and four scan lines (SL_0–SL_3). These four scan lines can be decoded using a 4-to-16 decoder to generate sixteen lines for scanning. These lines can be connected to the rows of a matrix keyboard and the digit drivers of a multiplexed display.

DISPLAY SECTION

The display section has eight output lines divided into two groups, A_0–A_3 and B_0–B_3. These lines can be used, either as a group of eight lines or as two groups of four, in conjunction with the scan lines for a multiplexed display. The display can be blanked by using the $\overline{BD}$ line. This section includes 16×8 display RAM. The MPU can read from or write into any of these registers.

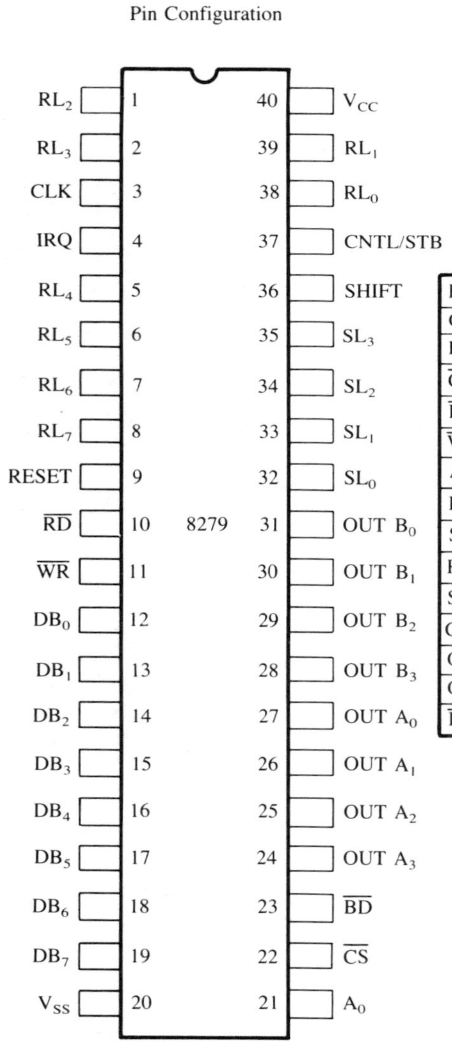

Logic Symbol

V_{CC}

Key Data: RL_{0-7} (8), SHIFT, CNTL/STB

Scan: SL_{0-3} (4)

Display Data: OUT A_{0-3} (4), OUT B_{0-3} (4), $\overline{BD}$

IRQ, Data Bus (8), $\overline{RD}$, $\overline{WR}$, $\overline{CS}$, A_0, Reset, CLK

CPU Interface

V_{SS}

Pin Names

	I/O	
DB_{0-7}	I/O	Data Bus (Bidirectional)
CLK	I	Clock Input
RESET	I	Reset Input
$\overline{CS}$	I	Chip Select
$\overline{RD}$	I	Read Input
$\overline{WR}$	I	Write Input
A_0	I	Buffer Address
IRO	O	Interrupt Request Output
SL_{0-3}	O	Scan Lines
RL_{0-7}	I	Return Lines
SHIFT	I	Shift Input
CNTL/STB	I	Control Strobe Input
OUT A_{0-3}	O	Display (A) Outputs
OUT B_{0-3}	O	Display (B) Outputs
$\overline{BD}$	O	Blank Display Output

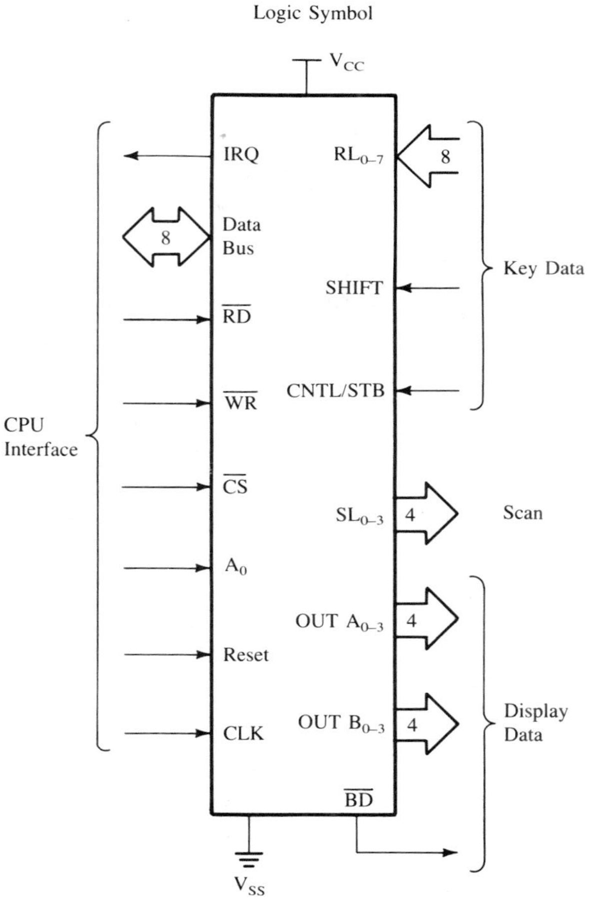

Pin Configuration

		8279		
RL_2	1		40	V_{CC}
RL_3	2		39	RL_1
CLK	3		38	RL_0
IRQ	4		37	CNTL/STB
RL_4	5		36	SHIFT
RL_5	6		35	SL_3
RL_6	7		34	SL_2
RL_7	8		33	SL_1
RESET	9		32	SL_0
$\overline{RD}$	10		31	OUT B_0
$\overline{WR}$	11		30	OUT B_1
DB_0	12		29	OUT B_2
DB_1	13		28	OUT B_3
DB_2	14		27	OUT A_0
DB_3	15		26	OUT A_1
DB_4	16		25	OUT A_2
DB_5	17		24	OUT A_3
DB_6	18		23	$\overline{BD}$
DB_7	19		22	$\overline{CS}$
V_{SS}	20		21	A_0

FIGURE 14.17
The 8279 Logic Pinout

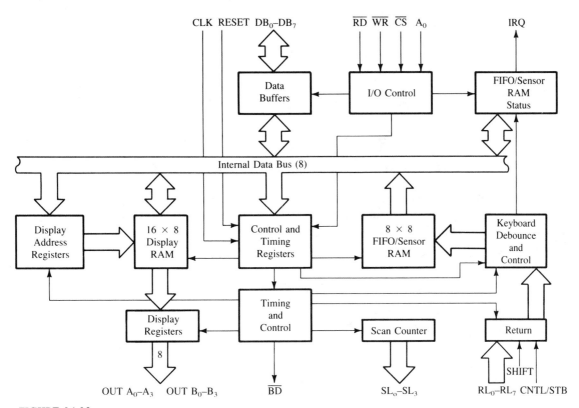

FIGURE 14.18
The 8279 Logic Block Diagram

SOURCE: Intel Corporation, *Peripheral Design Handbook* (Santa Clara, Calif.: Author, 1981), p. 1-397.

MPU INTERFACE SECTION

This section includes eight bidirectional data lines (DB_0–DB_7), one Interrupt Request line (IRQ), and six lines for interfacing, including the buffer address line (A_0).

When A_0 is high, signals are interpreted as control words or status; when A_0 is low, signals are interpreted as data. The IRQ line goes high whenever data entries are stored in the FIFO. This signal is used to interrupt the MPU to indicate the availability of data.

14.32 Programming the 8279

The 8279 is a complex device that can accept eight different commands to perform various functions.* The discussion here is specific to the circuit in the SDK-85 system.

The initialization commands can specify

---

*It is beyond the scope of this book to illustrate all the functions the 8279 can perform.

1. left or right entry and key rollover.
2. clock frequency prescaler.
3. starting address and incrementing mode of the FIFO RAM.
4. RAM address to read and write data and incrementing mode.
5. blanking format.

In order to illustrate important command words, the next section will illustrate the keyboard/display circuit from the SDK-85 system.

14.33   Illustration: SDK-85 Keyboard Schematic

Figure 14.19 shows the keyboard/display circuit from the SDK-85 system.

1. Explain the functions of various components in the circuit.
2. Explain the decoding logic, and identify the port addresses of the 8279 registers.
3. Explain the initialization instructions given later.

CIRCUIT DESCRIPTION

Figure 14.19 shows the following components:

☐ The 8279 Programmable Keyboard/Display Interface.
☐ A matrix keyboard with 22 keys.
☐ Six seven-segment LEDs: DS_1–DS_6. (Only one is shown; other five are identical.)
☐ The 74LS156 decoder with open collector outputs.
☐ Transistors as current drivers.
☐ The 8205 decoder for the decoding logic.

Lines RL_0–RL_7 (Return Lines) of the 8279 are connected to the columns of the matrix keyboard, and the output lines (A_0–A_3 and B_0–B_3) are connected to drive the LED segments through the transistors. The three scan lines are connected to the decoder, the 74LS156, to generate eight decoded signals. In this circuit, six output lines of the decoder are connected as digit drivers to turn on six seven-segment LEDs; two output lines are unused. In addition, the first three output lines are also used to scan the rows of the keyboard. The 8279 has four scan lines that can be decoded to generate sixteen output lines to drive sixteen displays. The data lines of the 8279 are connected to the data bus of the 8085, and the IRQ (Interrupt Request) is connected to the RST 5.5 of the system.

Four signals — $\overline{RD}$, $\overline{WR}$, CLK, and RESET OUT — are connected directly from the 8085. The system has a 3.072 MHz clock; and when the 8279 is reset, the clock prescaler is set to 31. This divides the clock frequency by 31 to provide the scan frequency of approximately 100 kHz. The RESET signal also sets the 8279 in the mode of sixteen-character display with two-key lockout keyboard.

After the initialization of the 8279, the respective codes are sent to the display RAM to display any characters. The 8279 takes over the task of displaying the characters by outputting the codes and digit strobes. To read the keyboard, the 8279 scans the columns; if a key closure is detected, it debounces the key. If a key closure is valid, it loads the key code into the FIFO, and the IRQ line goes high to interrupt the system.

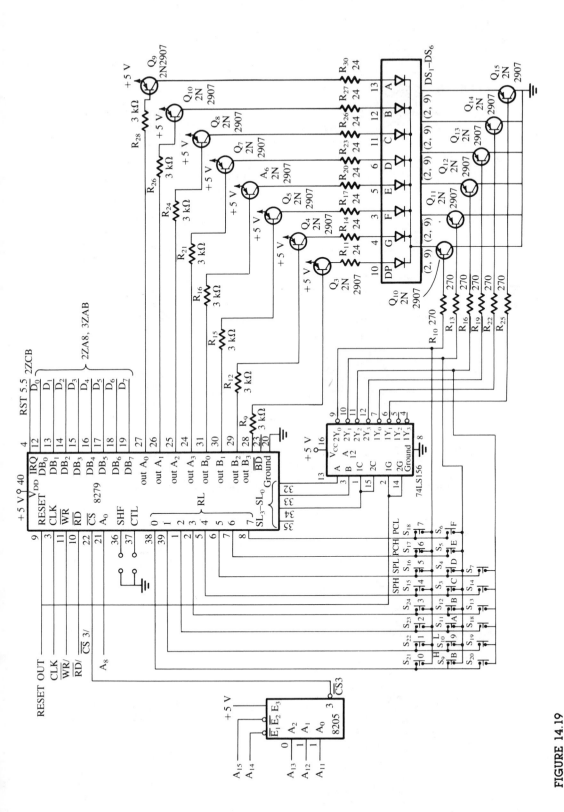

FIGURE 14.19

SDK-85 Keyboard/Display Circuit

SOURCE: Intel Corporation, *SDK-85 User's Manual* (Santa Clara, Calif.: Author, 1978), Appendix B.

DECODING LOGIC AND PORT ADDRESSES

The port addresses of the 8279 registers are determined by two signals: $\overline{CS}$ and A_0. The $\overline{CS}$ signal of the 8279 is connected to the $\overline{CS}$-3 output of the 8205 decoder, and A_0 is directly connected to the address line A_8 of the 8085. For commands and status, A_0 should be high. For data transfer, A_0 should be low. By examining the decoder input lines and assuming logic 0 for the don't care address lines, one can determine that the port addresses are as follows:

A_{15}	A_{14}	A_{13}	A_{12}	A_{11}	A_{10}	A_9	A_8	A_7	A_6	A_5	A_4	A_3	A_2	A_1	A_0	
0	0	0	1	1	0	0	I/O	0	0	0	0	0	0	0	0	= 1900H/1800H

↓ Decoder Enable ↓ Decoder Input ↓ Don't Care ↓ A_0 of 8279 ↓ Don't Care

Command/Status Port: 1900H

Data Port: 1800H

INITIALIZATION INSTRUCTIONS

In the SDK-85 system, the 8279 is initialized for the keyboard/display mode: Two-Key Lockout; Left Entry; and 8-bit, 8-Character Display. The RESET signal sets the clock prescaler to 31; thus, the scan frequency is approximately 100 kHz. When the 8279 detects a key closure, the IRQ signal interrupts the 8085, using RST 5.5. The interrupt service routine sends the command word to read from the keyboard (Command Port 1900H), reads the character data from the keyboard (Data Port 1800H), and stores it in the input buffer of the system's R/W memory. The following instructions illustrate the initialization and the interrupt-service routine.

Initialization

Keyboard/Display Mode

MVI A, 00H	;Control word to set mode: Left	0 0 0 D D K K K
	;entry, 8-character, 2-key lockout	
	;encoded scan keyboard	
STA 1900H	;Initialize 8279	

Interrupt Routine to Read Keyboard

PUSH H		
PUSH PSW		**Read FIFO RAM: Control Word**
LXI H, 1900H	;Keyboard control	0 1 0 A1 X A A A
	;register address	

MVI M, 40H	;Control word to read
	;from keyboard
DCR H	;Data Port Address
	;1800H
MOV A,M	;Read data

Data Format

D_7	D_6	D_5 D_4 D_3	D_2 D_1 D_0
CNTL	SHFT	ROW	COL

ANI 3FH	;Mask D_7 and D_6.
	;CNTL, *Shift* keys are
	;not being used
STA IBUFF	;Store in R/W memory
POP PSW	
POP H	
RET	

To display characters, the routine determines whether it is displaying a 4-digit memory address or a 2-digit data value. Then it sends the control word to read the display RAM.

For example, to display a 4-digit memory address, the control word instructions are as follows:

MVI A, 90H	;Control word to write
	;starting at first RAM
	;location
STA 1900H	
MVI A,CODE	;Load seven-segment code
STA 1800H	;Output the code

Write Display RAM Control Word

1 0 0 A_1 A A A A

To display a 2-digit data value, the control instructions are as follows:

MVI A,94H	;Control word to display data
STA 1900H	

In this example, the control word 94H points to the fifth memory location in the display RAM; the first four locations are reserved for memory addresses.

SUMMARY

This chapter was concerned with the basic concepts (such as control register, control logic, chip select logic, and handshake signals) underlying a programmable device. The characteristics of a programmable device were discussed using the 8212 as a hypothetical example, and the important concepts related to a programmable device were

reviewed in Section 14.14. Based on these concepts, three programmable devices —
the 8155/8156 (R/W memory with I/O), the 8355/8755 (ROM/EPROM with I/O), and
the 8279 (keyboard/display interface) — were discussed with examples from Intel's
single-board microcomputer system, the SDK-85.

The 8155 is a multipurpose device and includes memory, timer, and I/O ports.
Interfacing applications of the I/O ports in various modes (including handshake) and
the timer were illustrated with examples. Similarly, interfacing the 8355/8755 I/O ports
was illustrated, and the 8279 (keyboard/display interface) was discussed, using the
circuit from the SDK-85 system.

ASSIGNMENTS

1. List the internal components generally found in a programmable device.
2. In a programmable device, how does the MPU differentiate between the control
   register and the status register if both registers have the same port address?
3. Explain the functions of handshake signals.
4. Explain the difference between setting the 8155 I/O ports in ALT 1 and ALT 3.
5. Specify the handshake signals for port B of the 8155 if port B is connected as an
   input port in the interrupt mode. Explain the function of each handshake signal.
6. Port B of the 8155 is set up in the handshake mode, and the reading of the status
   word is 20H. Is the port set up for status check or interrupt I/O?
7. Explain how the bits in the DDR register specify the I/O functions of ports A and
   B in the 8355/8755.
8. List the major components of the 8279 keyboard/display interface, and explain
   their functions.
9. In Figure 14.7, specify all the port addresses if the output line 7 of the decoder is
   connected to $\overline{CE}$.
10. In Figure 14.7, assume that the decoder is eliminated and address line A_{15} is con-
    nected to $\overline{CE}$ through an inverter. Specify the addresses of ports A, B, and C as-
    suming all don't care lines are at logic 0.
11. Can any port be accessed with port address FDH in Assignment 10?
12. Write the instructions to set up the 8155 timer in Mode 3 with count 3FF8H.
13. In Assignment 12, specify the output if the clock frequency is 3 MHz and the
    count is 3080H.
14. Calculate the count for the 8155 timer to obtain the square wave of the 500 μs
    period if the clock frequency is 1 MHz.
15. Modify the circuit in Figure 14.14 to connect the A/D converter with interrupt
    I/O. Use RST 6.5 for the interrupt.
16. In Assignment 15, write the instructions in the main program to enable the
    RST 6.5 interrupt. Write a service routine to read a data byte, store it in memory
    location XX70H, and start the next conversion. (Ignore all the specifications re-
    lated to the timer in the illustration.)

EXPERIMENTAL ASSIGNMENTS

1. a. Connect the seven-segment displays to the 8755 I/O ports shown in Figure 14.16. (See Appendix B2 for the schematic.)
  b. Initialize all bits of ports A and B as output and display a data byte at each port.
  c. Change the command word to initialize bits PA_7–PA_0 of port A as output and bits PB_7–PB_0 of port B as input. Output a data byte to both the ports and observe the results.
  d. Change the command word to initialize bits PA_7–PA_0 as output, bits PB_7–PB_4 as input, and bits PB_3–PB_0 as output. Output a data byte to both the ports and observe the results.
2. a. Connect the A/D converter AD570 as an input (Figure 14.14).
  b. Set up port A as an input port in ALT 3 with interrupt I/O. Use RST 6.5 for the interrupt.
  c. Write a main program to

  ☐ initialize port A as an input and port C for handshake signals.
  ☐ start conversion.
  ☐ display data at an output port.
  ☐ set up a continuous loop for displaying data.

  d. Write a service routine to

  ☐ read a data byte.
  ☐ start conversion for the next reading.

  e. Record data for various analog signals.
3. a. Set up the 8155 timer as shown in Section 14.24.
  b. Enter and execute the given program.
  c. Measure the square wave output on an oscilloscope.
  d. Calculate the frequency and the pulse width of the square wave if bits T_{13}–T_0 all = 0.
  e. Load the count from step (d), start the counter, and measure the frequency and the pulse width of the output.

General Purpose Programmable Peripheral Devices

This chapter is an extension of Chapter 14, except that the programmable devices discussed in this chapter are designed for general purpose use. This chapter describes several programmable devices from the Intel family of support devices: the 8255A Peripheral Interface, the 8253 Interval Timer, the 8259A Interrupt Controller, and the 8257 DMA controller.

The 8255A and the 8253, two widely used general purpose programmable devices, can be compatible with any microprocessor. The 8255A includes three programmable ports, one of which can be used for bidirectional data transfer. This is an important additional feature in comparison with the 8155 I/O ports. The 8253 timer is similar to the 8155 timer, except that it has three 16-bit independent timers with various modes.

The next two devices—the 8259A Interrupt Controller and the 8257 DMA controller—were introduced briefly in Chapter 12. These devices illustrate the implementation of interrupts and of Direct Memory Access by using programmable devices. If you are not familiar with the concepts underlying programmable devices and handshake signals, you are strongly advised to read Section 14.1 before reading this chapter.

OBJECTIVES

☐ List the elements of the 8255A Programmable Peripheral Interface (PPI) and explain its various operating modes.

☐ Set up the 8255A I/O ports in the simple I/O and bit set/reset (BSR) mode.

☐ Design an interfacing circuit to set up the 8255A in the handshake mode (Mode 1) and write in-

structions to transfer data under status check I/O
and interrupt I/O.

☐ List operating modes of the 8253 timer and write
instructions to set up the timer in the various
modes.

☐ Explain the functions of the 8259A interrupt controller and its operation in the fully nested mode.

☐ Explain the process of the Direct Memory Access
(DMA) and the functions of various elements of
the 8257.

15.1 THE 8255A PROGRAMMABLE PERIPHERAL INTERFACE

The 8255A is a widely used, programmable, parallel I/O device. It can be programmed
to transfer data under various conditions, from simple I/O to interrupt I/O. It is flexible,
versatile, and economical (when multiple I/O ports are required), but somewhat
complex. It is an important general purpose I/O device that can be used with almost any
microprocessor.

The 8255A has 24 I/O pins that can be grouped primarily in two 8-bit parallel
ports: A and B, with the remaining eight bits as port C. The eight bits of port C can be
used as individual bits or be grouped in two 4-bit ports: C_{UPPER} (C_U) and C_{LOWER} (C_L) as
in Figure 15.1(a). This device is like three 8212s with many more additional features. The
functions of these ports are defined by writing a control word in the control register.

Figure 15.1(b) shows all the functions of the 8255A, classified according to two
modes: the Bit Set/Reset (BSR) mode and the I/O mode. The BSR mode is used to set

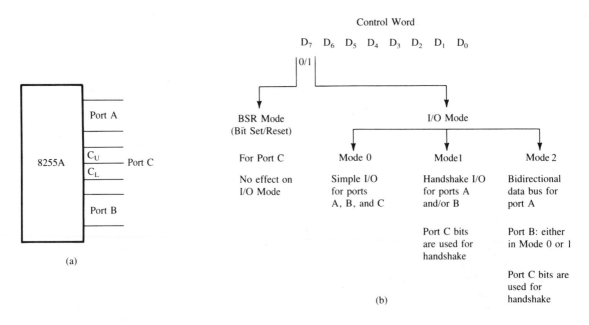

FIGURE 15.1
8255A I/O Ports (a) and Their Modes (b)

or reset the bits in port C. The I/O mode is further divided into three modes: Mode 0, Mode 1, and Mode 2. In Mode 0, all ports function as simple I/O ports. Mode 1 is a handshake mode whereby ports A and/or B use bits from port C as handshake signals. In the handshake mode, two types of I/O data transfer can be implemented: status check and interrupt. In Mode 2, port A can be set up for bidirectional data transfer using handshake signals from port C, and port B can be set up either in Mode 0 or Mode 1.

15.11 Block Diagram of the 8255A

The block diagram in Figure 15.2(a) shows two 8-bit ports (A and B), two 4-bit ports (C_U and C_L), the data bus buffer, and control logic. Figure 15.2(b) shows a simplified but expanded version of the internal structure, including a control register. This block diagram includes all the elements of a programmable device; port C performs functions similar to that of the status register in addition to providing handshake signals.

CONTROL LOGIC

The control section has six lines. Their functions and connections are as follows:

- $\overline{\text{RD}}$ **(Read):** This control signal enables the Read operation. When the signal is low, the MPU reads data from a selected I/O port of the 8255A.
- $\overline{\text{WR}}$ **(Write):** This control signal enables the Write operation. When the signal goes low, the MPU writes into a selected I/O port or the control register.
- **RESET (Reset):** This is an active high signal; it clears the control register and sets all ports in the input mode.
- $\overline{\text{CS}}$, **A_0, and A_1:** These are device select signals. $\overline{\text{CS}}$ is connected to a decoded address, and A_0 and A_1 are generally connected to MPU address lines A_0 and A_1, respectively.

The $\overline{\text{CS}}$ signal is the master Chip Select, and A_0 and A_1 specify one of the I/O ports or the control register as given below:

$\overline{\text{CS}}$	A_1	A_0	Selected
0	0	0	Port A
0	0	1	Port B
0	1	0	Port C
0	1	1	Control Register
1	X	X	8255A is not selected.

As an example, the port addresses in Figure 15.3(a) are determined by the $\overline{\text{CS}}$, A_0, and A_1 lines. The $\overline{\text{CS}}$ line goes low when $A_7 = 1$ and A_6 through A_2 are at logic 0. When these signals are combined with A_0 and A_1, the port addresses range from 80H to 83H, as shown in Figure 15.3(b).

CONTROL WORD

Figure 15.2(b) shows a register called the **control register**. The contents of this register, called the **control word**, specify an I/O function for each port. This register can be

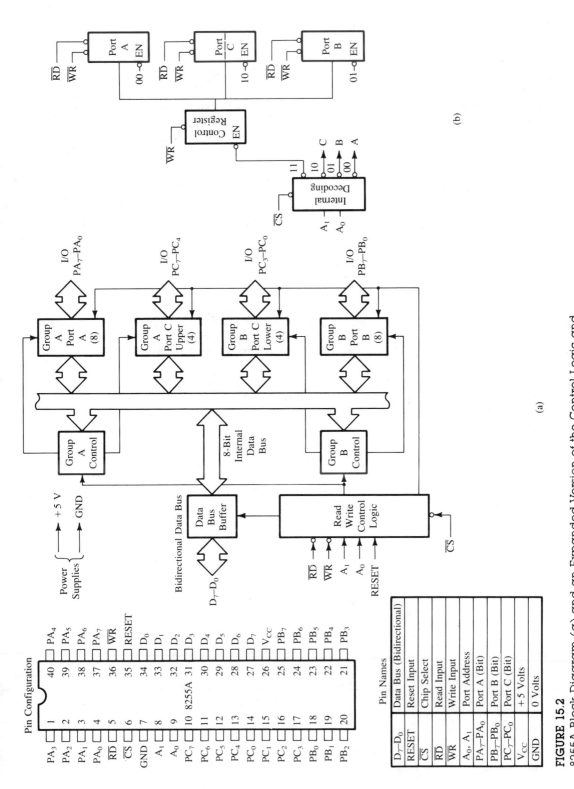

FIGURE 15.2

8255A Block Diagram (a) and an Expanded Version of the Control Logic and I/O Ports (b)

SOURCE: A: Intel Corporation, *MCS—80/85 Family User's Manual* (Santa Clara, Calif.: Author, 1979), p. 6-162.

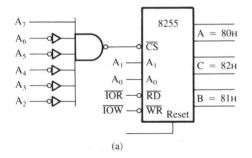

$\overline{CS}$			Hex Address	Port
A_7 A_6 A_5 A_4 A_3 A_2	A_1 A_0			
1 0 0 0 0 0	0 0		= 80H	A
	0 1		= 81H	B
	1 0		= 82H	C
	1 1		= 83H	Control Register

(a)　　　　　　　　　　　　　　　　　　(b)

FIGURE 15.3
8255A Chip Select Logic (a) and I/O Port Addresses (b)

accessed to write a control word when A_0 and A_1 are at logic 1, as mentioned previously. The register is not accessible for a Read operation.

Bit D_7 of the control register specifies either the I/O function or the Bit Set/Reset function, as classified in Figure 15.1(b). If bit $D_7 = 1$, bits D_6–D_0 determine I/O functions in various modes, as shown in Figure 15.4. If bit $D_7 = 0$, port C operates in the Bit Set/Reset (BSR) mode. The BSR control word does not affect the functions of ports A and B (the BSR mode will be described later).

To communicate with peripherals through the 8255A, three steps are necessary:

1. Determine the addresses of ports A, B, and C and of the control register according to the Chip Select logic and address lines A_0 and A_1.
2. Write a control word in the control register.
3. Write I/O instructions to communicate with peripherals through ports A, B, and C.

Examples of the various modes are given in the next section.

15.12 Mode 0: Simple Input or Output

In this mode, ports A and B can be viewed as equivalent to two 8212s and port C as equivalent to two 4-bit 8212s. Each port (or half-port, in case of C) can be programmed to function as simply an input port or an output port. The input/output features in Mode 0 are as follows:

1. Outputs are latched.
2. Inputs are not latched.
3. Ports do not have handshake or interrupt capability.

---

1. Identify the port addresses in Figure 15.5.
2. Identify the Mode 0 control word to configure port A and port C_U as output ports and port B and port C_L as input ports.

Example
15.1

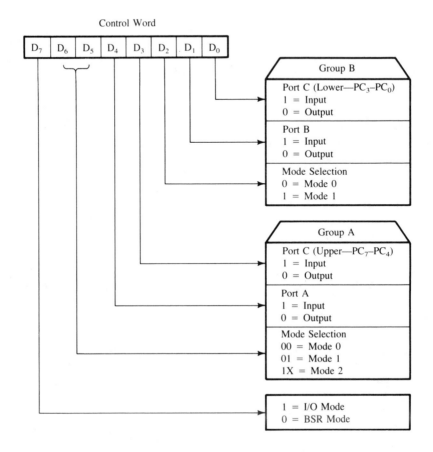

FIGURE 15.4
8255A Control Word Format for I/O Mode

SOURCE: Adapted from Intel Corporation, *Peripheral Design Handbook* (Santa Clara, Calif.: Author, 1981), p. 1-336.

3. Write a program to read the DIP switches and display the reading from port B at port A and from port C_L at port C_U.

Solution

1. Port Addresses This is a memory-mapped I/O; when the address line A_{15} is high, the Chip Select line is enabled. Assuming all don't care lines are at logic 0, the port addresses are as follows:

$$
\begin{aligned}
\text{Port A} &= 8000\text{H} \ (A_1 = 0, A_0 = 0) \\
\text{Port B} &= 8001\text{H} \ (A_1 = 0, A_0 = 1) \\
\text{Port C} &= 8002\text{H} \ (A_1 = 1, A_0 = 0) \\
\text{Control Register} &= 8003\text{H} \ (A_1 = 1, A_0 = 1)
\end{aligned}
$$

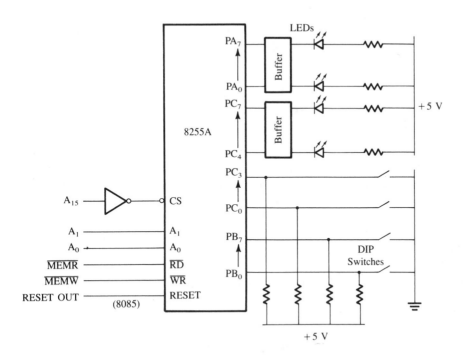

FIGURE 15.5
Interfacing 8255A I/O Ports in Mode 0

2. Control Word

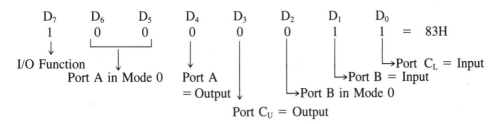

3. Program

MVI	A, 83H	;Load accumulator with the control word
STA	8003H	;Write the control word in the control register and initialize all the ports
LDA	8001H	;Read switches at port B
STA	8000H	;Display the reading at port A
LDA	8002H	;Read switches at port C

```
ANI     0FH     ;Mask the upper four bits of port C; these bits are not input data
RLC             ;Rotate and place data in the upper half of the accumulator
RLC
RLC
RLC
STA     8002H   ;Display data at Port C_U
HLT
```

Program Description The circuit is designed for memory-mapped I/O; therefore, the instructions are written as if all the 8255A ports are memory locations.

The ports are initialized by placing the control word 83H in the control register. The instructions STA and LDA are equivalent to the instructions OUT and IN, respectively.

In this example, the low four bits of port C are configured as input and the high four bits are configured as output; even though port C has one address for both halves C_U and C_L (8002H), Read and Write operations are differentiated by the control signals $\overline{MEMR}$ and $\overline{MEMW}$. When the MPU reads port C (e.g., LDA 8002H), it receives eight bits in the accumulator. However, the high-order bits (D_7–D_4) must be ignored because the input data bits are in PC_3–PC_0. To display these bits at the upper half of port C, bits (PC_3–PC_0) must be shifted to PC_7–PC_4.

15.13 BSR (Bit Set/Reset) Mode

The BSR mode is concerned only with the eight bits of port C, which can be set or reset by writing an appropriate control word in the control register. A control word with bit $D_7 = 0$ is recognized as a BSR control word, and it does not alter any previously transmitted control word with bit $D_7 = 1$; thus the I/O operations of ports A and B are not affected by a BSR control word. In the BSR mode, individual bits of port C can be used for applications such as an on/off switch.

BSR CONTROL WORD

This control word, when written in the control register, sets or resets one bit at a time, as specified in Figure 15.6.

Example 15.2	Write a BSR control word subroutine to set bits PC_7 and PC_3 and reset them after 10 ms. Use the schematic in Figure 15.3 and assume that a delay subroutine is available.	

Solution

BSR CONTROL WORDS

		D_7	D_6	D_5	D_4	D_3	D_2	D_1	D_0		
To set bit PC_7	=	0	0	0	0	1	1	1	1	=	0FH
To reset bit PC_7	=	0	0	0	0	1	1	1	0	=	0EH
To set bit PC_3	=	0	0	0	0	0	1	1	1	=	07H
To reset bit PC_3	=	0	0	0	0	0	1	1	0	=	06H

FIGURE 15.6
8255A Control Word Format
in the BSR Mode

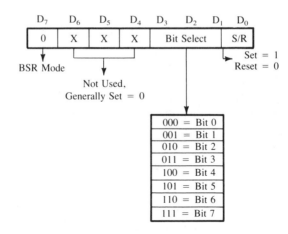

PORT ADDRESS

Control register address = 83H (refer to Figure 15.3(b)).

SUBROUTINE

```
BSR:    MVI  A, 0FH      ;Load byte in accumulator to set PC₇
        OUT  83H         ;Set PC₇ = 1
        MVI  A, 07H      ;Load byte in accumulator to set PC₃
        OUT  83H         ;Set PC₃ = 1
        CALL DELAY       ;This is a 10-ms delay
        MVI  A, 06H      ;Load accumulator with the byte to reset PC₃
        OUT  83H         ;Reset PC₃
        MVI  A, 0EH      ;Load accumulator with the byte to reset PC₇
        OUT  83H         ;Reset PC₇
        RET
```

From an analysis of the above routine, the following points can be noted:

1. To set/reset bits in port C, a control word is written in the control register and not in port C.
2. A BSR control word affects only one bit in port C.
3. The BSR control word does not affect the I/O mode.

15.14 Illustration: Interfacing A/D Converter Using the 8255A in Mode 0 and BSR Mode

PROBLEM STATEMENT

Design an interfacing circuit to read data from an A/D converter, using the 8255A in the memory-mapped I/O.

1. Set up port A to read data.

2. Set up bit PC_0 to start conversion and bit PC_7 to read the ready status of the converter.

PROBLEM ANALYSIS

The Chip Select logic in Figure 15.7 is the same as in Figure 15.5; therefore, the assigned port addresses range from 8000H for port A to 8003H for the control register. The control signals $\overline{MEMR}$ and $\overline{MEMW}$ specify the memory-mapped I/O.

MODE 0: CONTROL WORD

The configuration of the ports is specified as follows:

☐ Port A: As an input port.
☐ Port C_L: As an output port because bit PC_0 is used to start conversion.
☐ Port C_U: As an input port to read the status at PC_7.
☐ Port B: Not used.

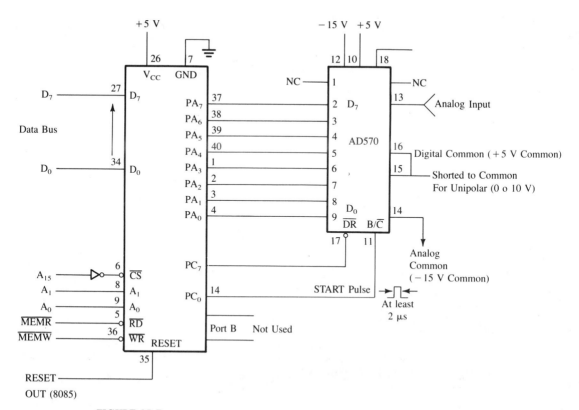

FIGURE 15.7

Schematic: Interfacing the A/D Converter AD570 Using the 8255A in Mode 0 and BSR Mode

Therefore, the control word necessary to meet the requirements is as follows:

D_7	D_6	D_5	D_4	D_3	D_2	D_1	D_0		
1	0	0	1	1	0	0	0	=	98H

I/O function — Mode 0 for port A — Port A input — Port C_U input — Port B is not used — Port C_L output

BSR CONTROL WORD FOR START PULSE

Bit PC_0 is used as a START pulse. To set and reset PC_0, the BSR control word is as follows (refer to Figure 15.6):

D_7	D_6	D_5	D_4	D_3	D_2	D_1	D_0		
0	0	0	0	0	0	0	1/0	=	01H to set

BSR mode — Don't care — Bit 0 — 1 = set / 0 = reset   = 00H to reset

SUBROUTINE

```
A/D:    LXI   H, 8003H    ;Point the index to control register
        MVI   A, 98H      ;Load the mode control word
        MOV M, A          ;Write in the control register to set up A and C_U
                              as inputs
        MVI   A, 01H      ;Load BSR control word to set PC_0
        MOV M, A          ;Turn on the START pulse
        CALL DELAY        ;Wait
        MVI   A, 00H      ;Load BSR control word to reset PC_0
        MOV M, A          ;Start conversion
READ:   MOV A, M          ;Read port C
        RAL               ;Place PC_7 in the carry
        JC    READ        ;Wait in the loop until the end of conversion
        LDA   8000H       ;Read A/D converter
        RET
```

PROGRAM DESCRIPTION

Instruction MOV M, A initializes the 8255A ports by placing the control word in the control register. To provide a START pulse to the converter, bit PC_0 is set to 1; it is turned off after the appropriate delay. The end of conversion is checked by verifying the status of line PC_7. When PC_7 goes low, instruction LDA 8000H reads and places data in the accumulator.

15.15   Mode 1: Input or Output with Handshake

In Mode 1, handshake signals are exchanged between the MPU and peripherals prior to data transfer. The features of this mode include

1. Two ports (A and B) function as 8-bit I/O ports. They can be configured either as input or output ports.
2. Each port uses three lines from port C as handshake signals. The remaining two lines of port C can be used for simple I/O functions.
3. Input and output data are latched.
4. Interrupt logic is supported.

In the 8255A, the specific lines from port C used for handshake signals vary according to the I/O function of a port. Therefore, input and output functions in Mode 1 are discussed separately.

MODE 1: INPUT CONTROL SIGNALS

Figure 15.8(a) shows the associated control signals used for handshaking when ports A and B are configured as input ports. Port A uses the upper three signals: PC_3, PC_4, and

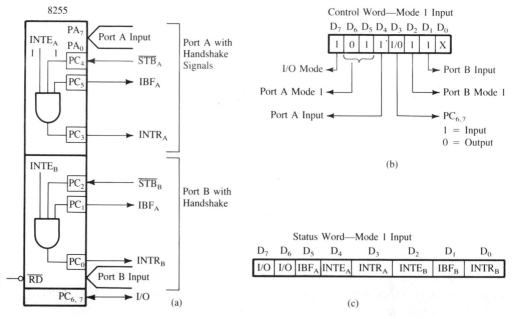

FIGURE 15.8
8255A Mode 1: Input Configuration

SOURCE: Adapted from Intel Corporation, *Peripheral Design Handbook* (Santa Clara, Calif.: Author, 1981), pp. 1-341 and 1-346.

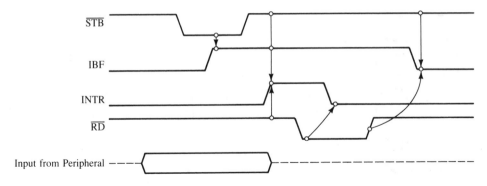

FIGURE 15.9
8255A Mode 0: Timing Waveforms for Strobed Input (with Handshake)
SOURCE: Adapted from Intel Corporation, *Peripheral Design Handbook* (Santa Clara, Calif.: Author, 1981), p. 1-341.

PC_5. Port B uses the lower three signals: PC_2, PC_1, and PC_0. The functions of these signals are as follows:

- $\overline{STB}$ **(Strobe Input):** This signal (active low) is generated by a peripheral device to indicate that it has transmitted a byte of data. The 8255A, in response to $\overline{STB}$, generates IBF and INTR, as shown in Figure 15.9.
- **IBF (Input Buffer Full):** This signal is an acknowledgment by the 8255A to indicate that the input latch has received the data byte. This is reset when the MPU reads the data (Figure 15.9).
- **INTR (Interrupt Request):** This is an output signal that may be used to interrupt the MPU. This signal is generated if $\overline{STB}$, IBF, and INTE (Internal flip-flop) are all at logic 1. This is reset by the falling edge of the $\overline{RD}$ signal (Figure 15.9).
- **INTE (Interrupt Enable):** This is an internal flip-flop used to enable or disable the generation of the INTR signal. The two flip-flops $INTE_A$ and $INTE_B$ are set/reset using the BSR mode. The $INTE_A$ is enabled or disabled through PC_4, and $INTE_B$ is enabled or disabled through PC_2.

CONTROL AND STATUS WORDS

Figure 15.8(b) uses control words derived from Figure 15.4 to set up port A and port B as input ports in Mode 1. Similarly, Figure 15.8(c) also shows the status word, which will be placed in the accumulator if port C is read.

PROGRAMMING THE 8255A IN MODE 1

The 8255A can be programmed to function using either status check I/O or interrupt I/O. Figure 15.10(a) shows a flowchart for the status check I/O. In this flowchart, the MPU continues to check data status through the IBF line until it goes high. This is a simplified flowchart and does not show how to handle data transfer if two ports are being used. The technique is similar to that of Mode 0 combined with the BSR mode. The disadvantage of the status check I/O with handshake is that the MPU is tied up in the loop.

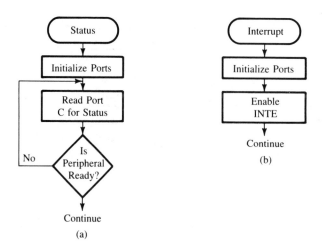

FIGURE 15.10
Flowcharts: Status Check I/O (a) and Interrupt I/O (b)

The flowchart in Figure 15.10(b) shows the steps required for the interrupt I/O, assuming that vectored interrupts are available. The confusing step in the interrupt I/O is to set INTE either for port A or port B. Figure 15.8(a) shows that the $\overline{STB}$ signal is connected to pin PC_4 and the $INTE_A$ is also controlled by the pin PC_4. (In port B, pin PC_2 is used for the same purposes.) However, the $INTE_A$ is set or reset in the BSR mode and the BSR control word has no effect when ports A and B are set in Mode 1.

In case the INTR line is used to implement the interrupt, it may be necessary to read the status of $INTR_A$ and $INTR_B$ to identify the port requesting an interrupt service and to determine the priority through software, if necessary.

MODE 1: OUTPUT CONTROL SIGNALS

Figure 15.11 shows the control signals when ports A and B are configured as output ports. These signals are defined as follows:

- ☐ **$\overline{OBF}$ (Output Buffer Full):** This is an output signal that goes low when the MPU writes data into the output latch of the 8255A. This signal indicates to an output peripheral that new data are ready to be read (Figure 15.12). It goes high again after the 8255A receives an $\overline{ACK}$ from the peripheral.
- ☐ **$\overline{ACK}$ (Acknowledge):** This is an input signal from a peripheral that must output a low when the peripheral receives the data from the 8255A ports (Figure 15.12).
- ☐ **INTR (Interrupt Request):** This is an output signal, and it is set by the rising edge of the $\overline{ACK}$ signal. This signal can be used to interrupt the MPU to request the next data byte for output. The INTR is set when $\overline{OBF}$, $\overline{ACK}$ and INTE are all one (Figure 15.12) and reset by the falling edge of $\overline{WR}$.

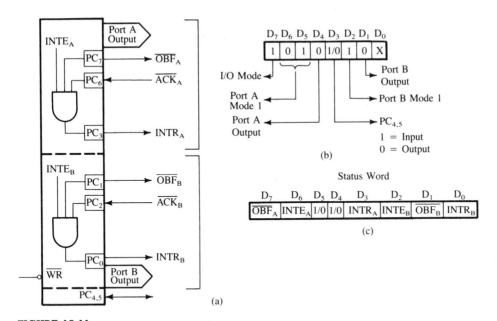

FIGURE 15.11
8255A Model: Output Configuration
SOURCE: Adapted from Intel Corporation, *Peripheral Design Handbook* (Santa Clara, Calif.: Author, 1981), p. 1-342.

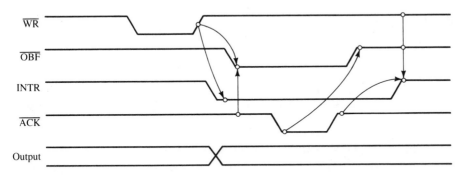

FIGURE 15.12
8255 Mode 1: Timing Waveforms for Strobed (with Handshake) Output
SOURCE: Adapted from Intel Corporation, *Peripheral Design Handbook* (Santa Clara, Calif.: Author, 1981), p. 1-342.

☐ **INTE (Interrupt Enable):** This is an internal flip-flop to a port and needs to be set to generate the INTR signal. The two flip-flops $INTE_A$ and $INTE_B$ are controlled by bits PC_6 and PC_2, respectively, through the BSR mode.

☐ **PC_{4-5}:** These two lines can be set up either as input or output.

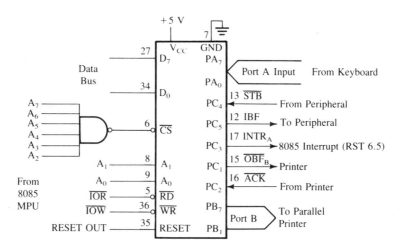

FIGURE 15.13
Interfacing the 8255A in Mode 1 (Strobed Input/Output)

CONTROL AND STATUS WORDS

Figure 15.11(b) shows the control word used to set up ports A and B as output ports in Mode 1. Similarly, Figure 15.11(c) also shows the status word, which will be placed in the accumulator if port C is read.

15.16   Illustration: An Application of the 8255A in the Handshake Mode (Mode 1)

PROBLEM STATEMENT

Figure 15.13 shows an interfacing circuit using the 8255A in Mode 1. Port A is designed as the input port for a keyboard with interrupt I/O, and port B is designed as the output port for a printer with status check I/O.

1. Find port addresses by analyzing the decode logic.
2. Determine the control word to set up port A as input and port B as output in Mode 1.
3. Determine the BSR word to enable $INTE_A$ (port A).
4. Determine the masking byte to verify the $\overline{OBF}_B$ line in the status check I/O (port B).
5. Write initialization instructions and a printer subroutine to output characters that are stored in memory.

1. Port Addresses   The 8255A is connected as peripheral I/O. When the address lines A_7–A_2 are all 1, the output of the NAND gate goes low and selects the 8255A. The individual ports are selected as follows:

$$
\begin{aligned}
\text{Port A} &= \text{FCH } (A_1 = 0, A_0 = 0) \\
\text{Port B} &= \text{FDH } (A_1 = 0, A_0 = 1)
\end{aligned}
$$

Port C   =   FEH $(A_1 = 1, A_0 = 0)$
Control Register   =   FFH $(A_1 = 1, A_0 = 1)$

2. Control Word to Set Up Port A as Input and Port B as Output in Mode 1

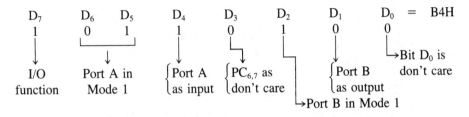

D_7	D_6	D_5	D_4	D_3	D_2	D_1	D_0	= B4H
1	0	1	1	0	1	0	0	

I/O function → ; Port A in Mode 1 ← ; Port A as input ; $PC_{6,7}$ as don't care ; Port B in Mode 1 ; Port B as output ; Bit D_0 is don't care

In the above control word, all bits are self explanatory, and bits D_3 and D_0 are in a don't care logic state. To generate interrupt signal $INTR_A$, flip-flop $INTE_A$ should be set to 1, which can be accomplished by using the BSR Mode to set PC_4.

  The output to the printer (port B) is status-controlled. Therefore, the status of line $\overline{OBF_B}$ can be checked by reading bit D_1 of port C_L.

3. BSR Word to Set $INTE_A$
To set the Interrupt Enable flip-flop of port A ($INTE_A$), bit PC_4 should be 1.

D_7	D_6	D_5	D_4	D_3	D_2	D_1	D_0	= 09H
0	0	0	0	1	0	0	1	

BSR mode → ; Don't care ; Bit PC_4 ; Bit set

4. Status Word to Check $\overline{OBF_B}$

D_7	D_6	D_5	D_4	D_3	D_2	$\overline{D_1}$	D_0
X	X	X	X	X	X	$\overline{OBF_B}$	X

Masking byte: 02H

5. Initialization Program

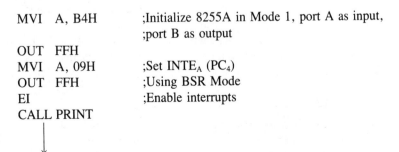

```
MVI   A, B4H        ;Initialize 8255A in Mode 1, port A as input,
                    ;port B as output
OUT   FFH
MVI   A, 09H        ;Set INTE_A (PC_4)
OUT   FFH           ;Using BSR Mode
EI                  ;Enable interrupts
CALL PRINT
```

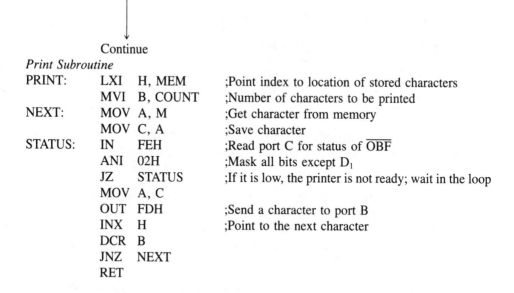

Continue

Print Subroutine

```
PRINT:     LXI   H, MEM        ;Point index to location of stored characters
           MVI   B, COUNT      ;Number of characters to be printed
NEXT:      MOV   A, M          ;Get character from memory
           MOV   C, A          ;Save character
STATUS:    IN    FEH           ;Read port C for status of OBF
           ANI   02H           ;Mask all bits except D₁
           JZ    STATUS        ;If it is low, the printer is not ready; wait in the loop
           MOV   A, C
           OUT   FDH           ;Send a character to port B
           INX   H             ;Point to the next character
           DCR   B
           JNZ   NEXT
           RET
```

KEYBOARD SERVICE ROUTINE

This is given as Assignment 7 at the end of the chapter.

PROGRAM DESCRIPTION

This I/O design using the 8255A in Mode 1 allows two operations: outputting to the printer and data entry through the keyboard. The printer interfacing is designed with the status check and the keyboard interfacing with the interrupt.

In the PRINT subroutine, the character is placed in the accumulator, and the status is read by the instruction IN FEH. Initially, port B is empty, bit PC_1 ($\overline{OBF_B}$) is high, and the instruction OUT FDH sends the first character to port B. The rising edge of the $\overline{WR}$ signal sets signal $\overline{OBF}$ low, indicating the presence of a data byte in port B, which is sent out to the printer (Figure 15.12). After receiving a character, the printer sends back an acknowledge signal ($\overline{ACK}$), which in turn sets $\overline{OBF_B}$ high indicating that port B is ready for the next character, and the PRINT subroutine continues.

If a key is pressed during the PRINT, a data byte is transmitted to port A and the $\overline{STB_A}$ goes low, which sets IBF_A high. The initialization routine should set the $INTE_A$ flip-flop. When the $\overline{STB_A}$ goes high, all the conditions (i.e., $IBF_A = 1$, $INTE_A = 1$) to generate $INTR_A$ are met. This signal, which is connected to the RST 6.5, interrupts the MPU, and the program control is transferred to the service routine. This service routine would read the contents of port A, enable the interrupts, and return to the PRINT routine.

15.17 Mode 2: Bidirectional Data Transfer

This mode is used primarily in applications such as data transfer between two computers or floppy disk controller interface. In this mode, port A can be configured as the bidirectional port and port B either in Mode 0 or Mode 1. Port A uses five signals from

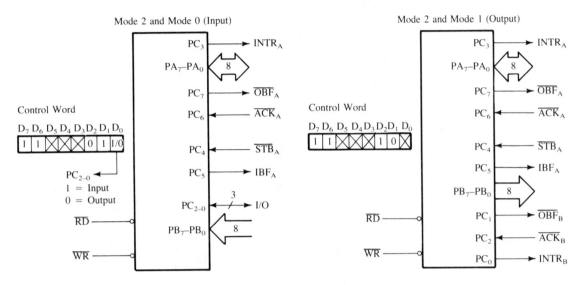

FIGURE 15.14
8255A Mode 2: Bidirectional Input/Output

SOURCE: Intel Corporation, *Peripheral Design Handbook* (Santa Clara, Calif.: Author, 1981), p. 1-345.

port C, as controls signals for data transfer. The remaining three signals from port C can be used either as simple I/O or as handshake for port B. Figure 15.14 shows two configurations of Mode 2. This mode is discussed in detail in Chapter 17.

THE 8253 PROGRAMMABLE INTERVAL TIMER 15.2

The 8253 programmable interval timer/counter is functionally similar to the software-designed counters and timers described in Chapter 7. It generates accurate time delays and can be used for applications such as a real-time clock, an event counter, a digital one-shot, a square wave generator, and a complex waveform generator.

The 8253 includes three identical 16-bit counters that can operate independently in any one of the six modes (to be described later). It is packaged in a 24-pin DIP and requires a single +5 V power supply. To operate a counter, a 16-bit count is loaded in its register and, on command, it begins to decrement the count until it reaches 0. At the end of the count, it generates a pulse that can be used to interrupt the MPU. The counter can count either in binary or BCD. In addition, a count can be read by the MPU while the counter is decrementing.

15.21 Block Diagram of the 8253

Figure 15.15 is the block diagram of the 8253; it includes three counters (0, 1, and 2), a data bus buffer, Read/Write control logic, and a control register. Each counter has two input signals—Clock (CLK) and GATE—and one output signal—OUT.

Pin Configuration

Block Diagram

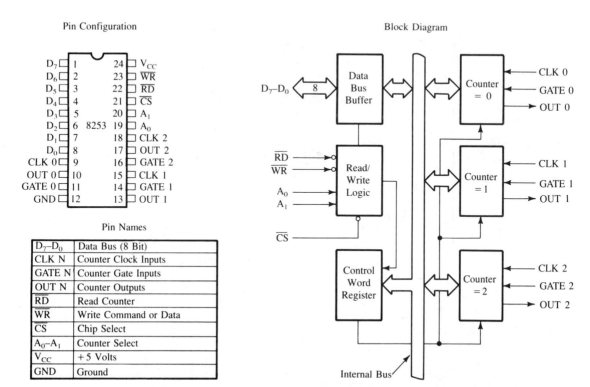

Pin Names

D₇–D₀	Data Bus (8 Bit)
CLK N	Counter Clock Inputs
GATE N	Counter Gate Inputs
OUT N	Counter Outputs
$\overline{RD}$	Read Counter
$\overline{WR}$	Write Command or Data
$\overline{CS}$	Chip Select
A₀–A₁	Counter Select
V_CC	+5 Volts
GND	Ground

FIGURE 15.15
8253 Block Diagram

SOURCE: Intel Corporation, *MCS—Family User's Manual* (Santa Clara, Calif.: Author, 1979), p. 6-161.

DATA BUS BUFFER

This tri-state, 8-bit, bidirectional buffer is connected to the data bus of the MPU.

CONTROL LOGIC

The control section has five signals: $\overline{RD}$ (Read), $\overline{WR}$ (Write), $\overline{CS}$ (Chip Select), and the address lines A₀ and A₁. In the peripheral I/O mode, the $\overline{RD}$ and $\overline{WR}$ signals are connected to $\overline{IOR}$ and $\overline{IOW}$, respectively. In memory-mapped I/O, these are connected to $\overline{MEMR}$ (Memory Read) and $\overline{MEMW}$ (Memory Write). Address lines A₀ and A₁ of the MPU are usually connected to lines A₀ and A₁ of the 8253, and $\overline{CS}$ is tied to a decoded address.

The control word register and counters are selected according to the signals on lines A₀ and A₁, as shown below:

A₁	A₀	Selection
0	0	Counter 0

0	1	Counter 1
1	0	Counter 2
1	1	Control Register

CONTROL WORD REGISTER

This register is accessed when lines A_0 and A_1 are at logic 1. It is used to write a command word which specifies the counter to be used, its mode, and either a Read or a Write operation. However, the control word register is not available for a Read operation. The control word format is shown in Figure 15.16.

MODE

The 8253 can operate in six different modes, as shown in Figure 15.17. The gate of a counter is used either to disable or enable counting, as shown in Figure 15.18.

15.22 Programming the 8253

The 8253 can be programmed to provide various types of output (Figure 15.17) through Write operations, or to check a count while counting through Read operations. The details of these operations are given below.

WRITE OPERATIONS

To initialize a counter, the following steps are necessary.

1. Write a control word into the control register.
2. Load the low-order byte of a count in the counter register.
3. Load the high-order byte of a count in the counter register.

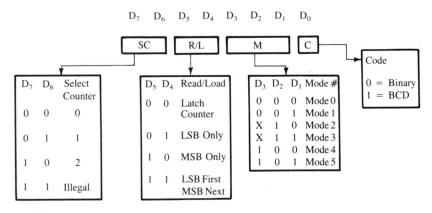

FIGURE 15.16
8253 Control Word Format

SOURCE: Adapted from Intel Corporation, *MCS 80/85 Student Study Guide* (Santa Clara, Calif.: Author, 1978), p. 1-310.

Mode 0: Interupt on Terminal Count

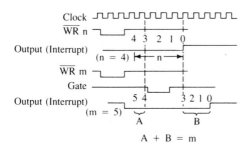

Mode 1: Programmable One-Shot

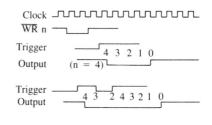

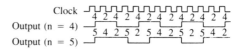

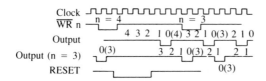

$A + B = m$

Mode 2: Rate Generator Clock

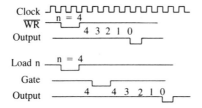

Mode 3: Square Wave Generator

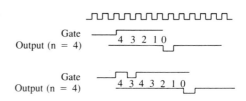

Mode 4: Software Triggered Strobe

Mode 5: Hardware Triggered Strobe

FIGURE 15.17
Six Modes of the 8253

SOURCE: Intel Corporation, *Peripheral Design Handbook* (Santa Clara, Calif.: Author, 1981), p. 1-312.

With a clock (maximum 2 MHz) and an appropriate gate signal to one of the counters, the above steps should start the counter and provide appropriate output according to the control word.

READ OPERATIONS

In some applications, especially in event counters, it is necessary to read the value of the count in progress. This can be done by either of two methods. One method involves reading a count after inhibiting (stopping) the counter to be read. The second method involves reading a count while the count is in progress (known as reading on the fly).

In the first method, counting is stopped (or inhibited) by controlling the gate input or the clock input of the selected counter, and two I/O read operations are performed by

Modes / Signal Status	Low or Going Low	Rising	High
0	Disables counting	—	Enables counting
1	—	(1) Initiates counting (2) Resets output after next clock	—
2	(1) Disables counting (2) Sets output immediately high	(1) Reloads counter (2) Initiates counting	Enables counting
3	(1) Disables counting (2) Sets output immediately high	Initiates counting	Enables counting
4	Disables counting	—	Enables counting
5	—	Initiates counting	—

FIGURE 15.18
Gate Settings of a Counter

SOURCE: Intel Corporation, *Peripheral Design Handbook* (Santa Clara, Calif.: Author, 1981), p. 1-311.

the MPU. The first I/O operation reads the low-order byte, and the second I/O operation reads the high-order byte.

In the second method, an appropriate control word is written into the control register to latch a count in the output latch, and two I/O Read operations are performed by the MPU. These Read/Write operations are illustrated below.

15.23   Illustration: The 8253 as a Counter

PROBLEM STATEMENT

1. Identify the port addresses of the control register and counter 2 in Figure 15.19.
2. Calculate the clock frequency of counter 2, and calculate the time delay if the counter is loaded with the count of $50,000_{10}$.
3. Write a subroutine to initialize counter 2 in Mode 0 with a count of $50,000_{10}$. The subroutine should also include reading counts on the fly; when the count reaches zero, it should return to the main program.
4. Write a main program to display seconds by calling the subroutine as many times as necessary.

1. Port Addresses   The Chip Select is enabled when $A_7 = 1$ (see Figure 15.19), and the control register is selected when A_1 and $A_0 = 1$. Similarly, counter 2 is selected when $A_1 = 1$ and $A_0 = 0$. Assuming that the unused address lines A_6 to A_2 are at logic 0, the port addresses will be as follows:

$$\text{Control Register} = 83H$$
$$\text{Counter 2} = 82H$$

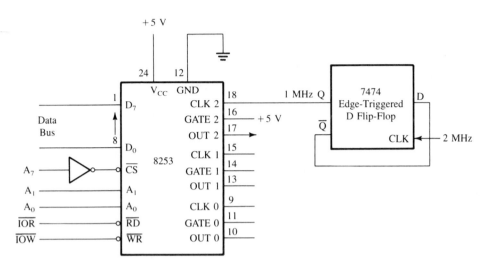

FIGURE 15.19
Schematic: Interfacing the 8253

2. Clock Frequency and Time Delay The system clock frequency is 2 MHz, which is divided by two with a D flip-flop. The output of the flip-flop changes on the rising edge; therefore, the output frequency that is fed to CLK2 is 1 MHz.

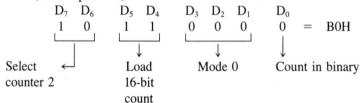

Time Delay $= 50,000 \times 1 \ \mu s = 50$ ms

FIGURE 15.20
Clock Frequency Waveform

3. Subroutine Counter To initialize the 8253 for counter 2 in Mode 0, the following control word is necessary (see Figure 15.16):

Control Word (Load Operation)

D_7	D_6	D_5	D_4	D_3	D_2	D_1	D_0		
1	0	1	1	0	0	0	0	=	B0H

Select counter 2 ←   Load 16-bit count   Mode 0   Count in binary

Control Word for Latching: Bits D_5 and D_4 should be 0 = 80H

Subroutine

COUNTER:	MVI A, B0H	;Load control word in the accumulator to initialize counter 2
	OUT 83H	;Write in the control register
	MVI A, LOBYTE	;Load accumulator with the low-order byte of the count 50000
	OUT 82H	;Load counter 2 with the low-order byte
	MVI A, HIBYTE	;Load accumulator with the high-order byte of the count 50000
	OUT 82H	;Load counter 2 with the high-order byte
READ:	MVI A, 80H	;Load control word in accumulator to latch a count
	OUT 83H	;Write the control word in the control register
	IN 82H	;Read low-order byte
	MOV D, A	;Store low-order byte in register D
	IN 82H	;Read high-order byte
	ORA D	;Logical OR low- and high-order bytes to set Zero flag
	JNZ READ	;If the counter is $\neq 0$, go back and read the next count
	RET	

Subroutine Description The subroutine has two segments. In the first segment, counter 2 is initialized by writing a control word in the control register and a 16-bit count specified as LOBYTE and HIBYTE in the counter register. The hexadecimal value equivalent to 50000_{10} must be calculated.

In the second segment (beginning at READ), a control word is written into the control register to sample a count, and the 16-bit count is read by performing two input operations. The reading of the counter is repeated until the counter reaches 0; the Zero flag is checked by ORing the low- and high-order bytes.

4. Main Program The subroutine COUNTER provides 50 ms delay; if this routine is called twenty times, the total delay will be one second.

Program

	LXI SP, STACK	;Initialize stack pointer
	MVI B, 00H	;Clear register B to save number of seconds
SECOND:	MVI C, 14H	;Set up register C to count 20_{10}
WAIT:	CALL COUNTER	;Wait for 50 ms
	DCR C	
	JNZ WAIT	;Is this one second; if not, go back and wait 50 ms
	MVI A, B	

```
         ADI   01              ;Add one second
         DAA
         OUT   PORT1
         MOV   B, A            ;Save seconds
         JMP   SECOND          ;Go back and start counting the next second
```

Program Description The main program initializes the 8253 twenty times by loading register C with the count of 14H(20) and setting up the WAIT loop. At the end of the loop, it increments the seconds in register B, decimal adjusts the byte, and displays seconds. The sequence is repeated until register B reaches 99_{BCD}. After the 99th second, register B is cleared and the clock sequence is repeated.

This program is just to demonstrate the Read and Write operations of the 8253; this clock design does not take into account the errors caused by the delay in executing the program instructions. A better way of designing a real-time clock is to interrupt the MPU at the end of a count (see Assignment 14 at the end of this chapter).

15.3 THE 8259A PROGRAMMABLE INTERRUPT CONTROLLER

The 8259A is a programmable interrupt controller designed to work with Intel microprocessors 8080A, 8085, 8086, and 8088. The 8259A interrupt controller can

1. Manage eight interrupts according to the instructions written into its control registers. This is equivalent to providing eight interrupt pins on the processor in place of one INTR/INT pin.
2. Vector an interrupt request anywhere in the memory map. However, all eight interrupts are spaced at the interval of either four or eight locations. This eliminates the major drawback of the 8085/8080A interrupts, in which all interrupts are vectored to memory locations on page 00H.
3. Resolve eight levels of interrupt priorities in a variety of modes, such as fully nested mode, automatic rotation mode, and specific rotation mode (to be explained later).
4. Mask each interrupt request individually.
5. Read the status of pending interrupts, in-service interrupts, and masked interrupts.
6. Be set up to accept either the level-triggered or the edge-triggered interrupt request.
7. Be expanded to 64 priority levels by cascading additional 8259s.
8. Be set up to work with either the 8085/8080A microprocessor mode or the 8086/8088 microprocessor mode.

The 8259A is upward compatible with its predecessor, the 8259. The main difference between the two is that the 8259A can be used with Intel's 8086/88 16-bit microprocessors. It also includes additional features such as the level-triggered mode, buffered mode, and automatic-end-of-interrupt mode. To simplify the explanation of the 8259A, illustrative examples will not include the cascade mode or the 8086/88 mode, and will be limited to modes commonly used with the 8085/8080A. (For additional details, see Appendix D.)

15.31   Block Diagram of the 8259A

Figure 15.21 shows the internal block diagram of the 8259A. It includes eight blocks: control logic, Read/Write logic, data bus buffer, three registers (IRR, ISR, and IMR), priority resolver, and cascade buffer. This diagram shows all the elements of a programmable device, plus additional blocks. These blocks are similar to the blocks in a programmable device. The functions of some of these blocks need explanation, which is given below.

READ/WRITE LOGIC

This is a typical Read/Write control logic. When the address line A_0 is at logic 0, the controller is selected to write a command or read a status. The Chip Select logic and A_0 determine the port address of the controller.

CONTROL LOGIC

This block has two pins: INT (Interrupt) as an output, and $\overline{INTA}$ (Interrupt Acknowledge) as an input. The INT is connected to the interrupt pin of the MPU. Whenever a valid interrupt is asserted, this signal goes high. The $\overline{INTA}$ is the Interrupt Acknowledge signal from the MPU.

INTERRUPT REGISTERS AND PRIORITY RESOLVER

The Interrupt Request Register (IRR) has eight input lines (IR_0–IR_7) for interrupts. When these lines go high, the requests are stored in the register. The In-Service Register (ISR) stores all the levels that are currently being serviced, and the Interrupt Mask Register (IMR) stores the masking bits of the interrupt lines to be masked. The Priority Resolver (PR) examines these three registers, and determines whether INT should be sent to the MPU.

CASCADE BUFFER/COMPARATOR

This block is used to expand the number of interrupt levels by cascading two or more 8259As. In order to simplify the discussion, this block will not be mentioned again.

15.32   Interrupt Operation

To implement interrupts, the Interrupt Enable flip-flop in the microprocessor should be enabled by writing the EI instruction, and the 8259A should be initialized by writing control words in the control register. The 8259A requires two types of control words: Initialization Command Words (ICWs) and Operational Command Words (OCWs). The ICWs are used to set up the proper conditions and specify RST vector addresses. The OCWs are used to perform functions such as masking interrupts, setting up status-read operations, etc. After the 8259A is initialized, the following sequence of events occurs when one or more interrupt request lines go high:

Block Diagram

Pin Configuration

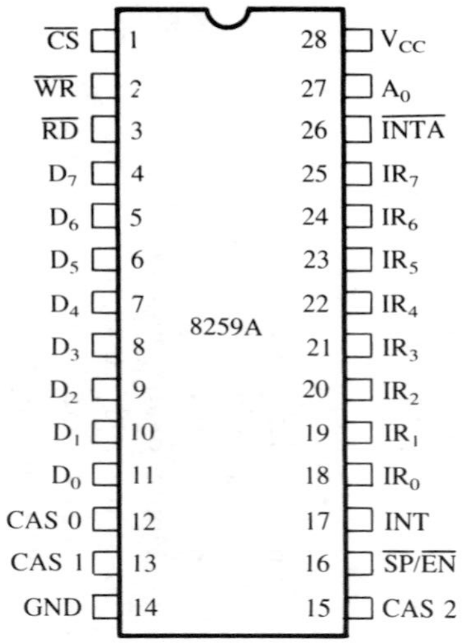

IR_0 IR_1 IR_2 IR_3 IR_4 IR_5 IR_6 IR_7

Interrupt Request Register (IRR)

Control Logic

INT

$\overline{INTA}$

Priority Resolver

Interrupt Mask Register (IMR)

In-service Register (ISR)

Internal Bus

Data Bus Buffer

D_7–D_0

Read/ Write Logic

$\overline{RD}$
$\overline{WR}$
A_0
$\overline{CS}$

Cascade Buffer/ Comparator

CAS 0
CAS 1
CAS 2
$\overline{SP}/\overline{EN}$

8259A

1	$\overline{CS}$		28	V_{CC}
2	$\overline{WR}$		27	A_0
3	$\overline{RD}$		26	$\overline{INTA}$
4	D_7		25	IR_7
5	D_6		24	IR_6
6	D_5		23	IR_5
7	D_4		22	IR_4
8	D_3		21	IR_3
9	D_2		20	IR_2
10	D_1		19	IR_1
11	D_0		18	IR_0
12	CAS 0		17	INT
13	CAS 1		16	$\overline{SP}/\overline{EN}$
14	GND		15	CAS 2

Pin Names

D_7–D_0	Data Bus (Bidirectional)
$\overline{RD}$	Read Input
$\overline{WR}$	Write Input
A_0	Command Select Address
$\overline{CS}$	Chip Select
CAS_2–CAS_0	Cascade Lines
$\overline{SP}/\overline{EN}$	Slave Program/Enable Buffer
INT	Interrupt Output
$\overline{INTA}$	Interrupt Acknowledge Input
IR_0–IR_7	Interrupt Request Inputs

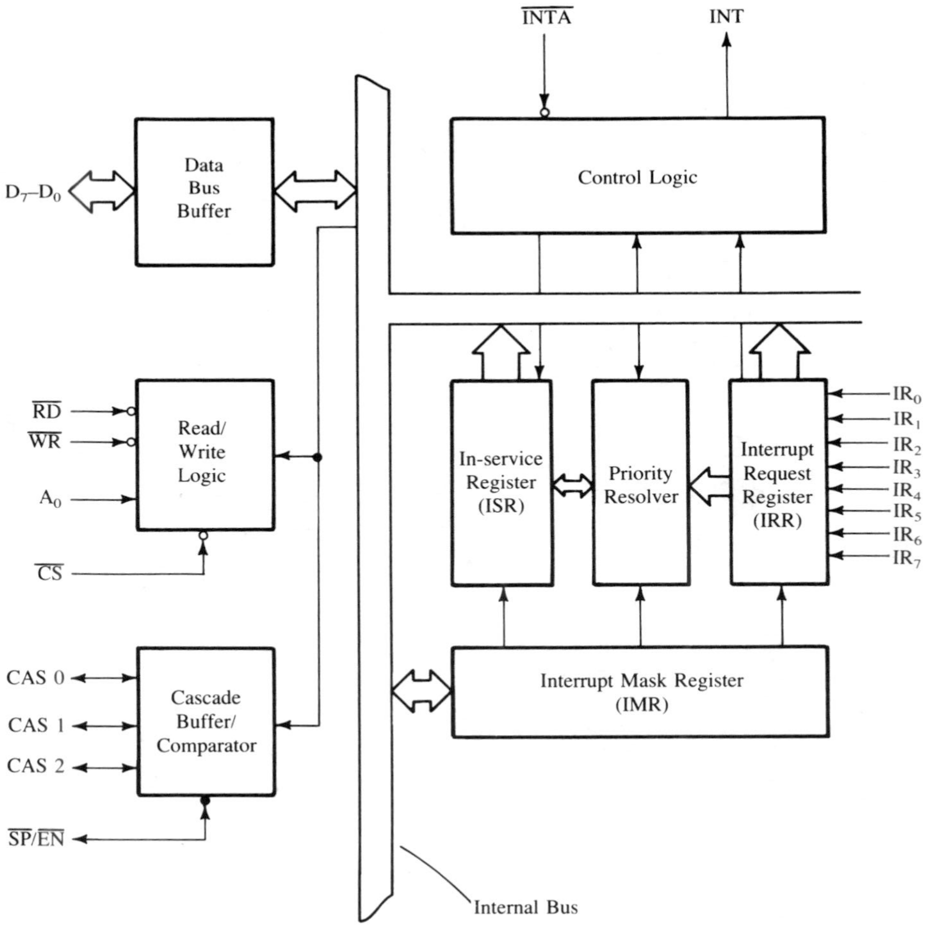

FIGURE 15.21

The 8259A Block Diagram

SOURCE: Intel Corporation, *MCS—80/85 Family User's Manual* (Santa Clara, Calif.: Author, 1979), p. 6-132.

1. The IRR stores the requests.
2. The priority resolver checks three registers: the IRR for interrupt requests, the IMR for masking bits, and the ISR for the interrupt request being served. It resolves the priority and sets the INT high when appropriate.
3. The MPU acknowledges the interrupt by sending $\overline{\text{INTA}}$.
4. After the $\overline{\text{INTA}}$ is received, the appropriate priority bit in the ISR is set to indicate which interrupt level is being served, and the corresponding bit in the IRR is reset to indicate that the request is accepted. Then, the opcode for the CALL instruction is placed on the data bus.
5. When the MPU decodes the CALL instruction, it places two more $\overline{\text{INTA}}$ signals on the data bus.
6. When the 8259A receives the second $\overline{\text{INTA}}$, it places the low-order byte of the CALL address on the data bus. At the third $\overline{\text{INTA}}$, it places the high-order byte on the data bus. The CALL address is the vector memory location for the interrupt; this address is placed in the control register during the initialization.
7. During the third $\overline{\text{INTA}}$ pulse, the ISR bit is reset either automatically (Automatic-End-of-Interrupt—AEOI) or by a command word that must be issued at the end of the service routine (End-of-Interrupt—EOI). This option is determined by the initialization command word (ICW).
8. The program sequence is transferred to the memory location specified by the CALL instruction.

15.33 Priority Modes and Other Features

Many types of priority modes are available under software control in the 8259A, and they can be changed dynamically during the program by writing appropriate command words. Commonly used priority modes are discussed below. (See Appendix D for additional details.)

1. Fully Nested Mode   This is a general purpose mode in which all IRs (Interrupt Requests) are arranged from highest to lowest, with IR_0 as the highest and IR_7 as the lowest.

   In addition, any IR can be assigned the highest priority in this mode; the priority sequence will then begin at that IR. In the example below, IR_4 has the highest priority, and IR_3 has the lowest priority:

IR_0	IR_1	IR_2	IR_3	IR_4	IR_5	IR_6	IR_7
4	5	6	7	0	1	2	3
			↑	↑			
			Lowest	Highest			
			priority	priority			

2. Automatic Rotation Mode   In this mode, a device, after being serviced, receives the lowest priority. Assuming that the IR_2 has just been serviced, it will receive the seventh priority, as shown below:

IR_0	IR_1	IR_2	IR_3	IR_4	IR_5	IR_6	IR_7
5	6	7	0	1	2	3	4

3. Specific Rotation Mode   This mode is similar to the automatic rotation mode, except that the user can select any IR for the lowest priority, thus fixing all other priorities.

END OF INTERRUPT

After the completion of an interrupt service, the corresponding ISR bit needs to be reset to update the information in the ISR. This is called the End-of-Interrupt (EOI) command. It can be issued in three formats:

1. Nonspecific EOI Command   When this command is sent to the 8259A, it resets the highest priority ISR bit.

2. Specific EOI Command   This command specifies which ISR bit to reset.

3. Automatic EOI   In this mode, no command is necessary. During the third $\overline{\text{INTA}}$, the ISR bit is reset. The major drawback with this mode is that the ISR does not have information on which IR is being serviced. Thus, any IR can interrupt the service routine, irrespective of its priority, if the Interrupt Enable flip-flop is set.

ADDITIONAL FEATURES OF THE 8259A

The 8259A is a complex device with various modes of operation. These modes are listed below for reference; the user should refer to the 8085 User's Manual for details.

☐ Interrupt Triggering: The 8259A can accept an interrupt request with either the edge-triggered mode or the level-triggered mode. The mode is determined by the initialization instructions.
☐ Interrupt Status: The status of the three interrupt registers (IRR, ISR, and IMR) can be read, and this status information can be used to make the interrupt process versatile.
☐ Poll Method: The 8259A can be set up to function in a polled environment. The MPU polls the 8259A rather than each peripheral.

15.34 Programming the 8259A

As mentioned before, the 8259A requires two types of command words: Initialization Command Words (ICWs) and Operational Command Words (OCWs). The 8259A can be initialized with four ICWs; the first two are essential, and the other two are optional based on the modes being used. These words must be issued in a given sequence. Once initialized, the 8259A can be set up to operate in various modes by using three different OCWs; however, they no longer need be issued in a specific sequence.

Figure 15.22 shows the bit specification of the first two ICWs. The ICW1 (Figure 15.22(a)) specifies

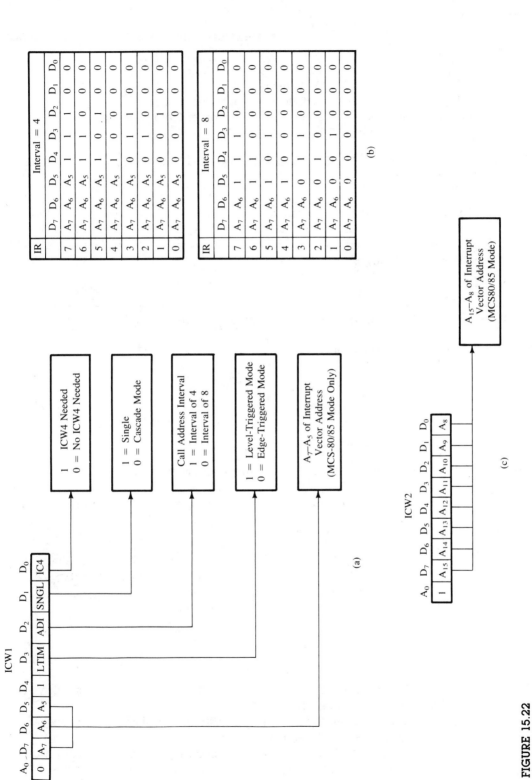

FIGURE 15.22

Initialization Command Words for the 8259A

SOURCE: Intel Corporation, *MCS—80/85 Family User's Manual* (Santa Clara, Calif.: Author, 1979), pp. 6-136 and 6-139.

1. single or multiple 8259As in the system.
2. 4- or 8-bit interval between the interrupt vector locations.
3. the address bits A_7–A_5 of the CALL instruction, and the rest are supplied by the 8259A, as shown in Figure 15.22(b).

The ICW_2 (Figure 15.22(c)) specifies the high-order byte of the CALL instruction.

EXAMPLES

Figure 15.23 shows the schematic of an interrupt-driven system using the 8259A. Four sources are connected to the IR lines of the 8259A: Emergency Signal, Keyboard, A/D Converter, and Printer. Of these, the Emergency Signal has the highest priority and the Printer has the lowest priority.

Example 15.3

Explain the following initialization instructions in reference to Figure 15.23.

Initialization Instructions

```
DI
MVI A, 76H      ;ICW₁
OUT 80H         ;Initialize 8259A
MVI 20H         ;ICW₂
OUT 81H         ;Initialize 8259A
```

Solution

1. The DI instruction disables the interrupts so that the initialization process will not be interrupted.
2. The command word 76H specifies the following parameters, (see Figure 15.22(a)):

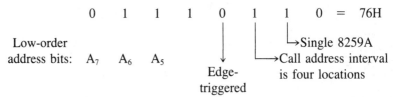

$$0 \quad 1 \quad 1 \quad 1 \quad 0 \quad 1 \quad 1 \quad 0 \quad = \quad 76H$$

Low-order address bits: A_7 A_6 A_5

Edge-triggered

→Single 8259A
→Call address interval is four locations

Low-Order Byte of the IR_0 Call Address (see Figure 15.22(b)):

A_7	A_6	A_5	A_4	A_3	A_2	A_1	A_0	
0	1	1	0	0	0	0	0	= 60H

The address bits A_4–A_0 are supplied by the 8259A. The subsequent addresses are four locations apart (e.g., IR_1 = 64H).

3. The port address of the 8259A for ICW_1 is 80H; A_0 should be at logic 0, and the other bits are determined by the decoder.
4. Command word ICW_2 is 20H, which specifies the high-order byte of the Call address.
5. The port address of ICW_2 is 81H; A_0 should be at logic 1.

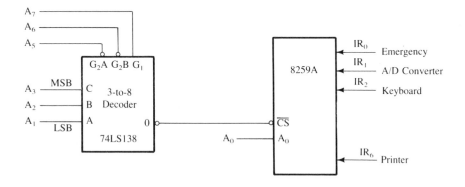

FIGURE 15.23
Schematic of an Interrupt System Using the 8259A

Explain the interrupt process in the fully nested mode relative to Figure 15.24. Assume that the 8259A is initialized with the same instructions as in the previous example.

Example
15.4

Figure 15.24 shows that the interrupts are enabled by the main program, and the 8259A is initialized. After the initialization, the 8259A is set in the fully nested mode by default, unless a different Operational Command Word (OCW) is issued. During the main program, the printer has made a request. Because the interrupts are enabled, the program is transferred first to the vectored location 2078H for IR_6, and then to the service routine. The ISR_6 bit is also set to indicate that IR_6 is being serviced.

Solution

During the IR_6 service routine, the keyboard makes a request (IR_2). Even though IR_2 has a higher priority than the IR_6, the request is not acknowledged until the IR_6 service routine enables the interrupts through the EI instruction. When IR_2 is acknowledged, bit ISR_2 is set, and the program is vectored to the location 2068H and then to the service routine.

At the end of the IR_2 service routine, the instruction EOI (End-of-Interrupt) informs the 8259A that the service has been completed, and the highest ISR bit (ISR_2) has been reset. The program returns to the IR_6 service routine, completes the service, sends the EOI, and then returns to the main program. The EOI in this routine resets the ISR_6 bit.

The format for the nonspecific EOI command is as follows (also refer to Appendix F2).

A_0	D_7	D_6	D_5	D_4	D_3	D_2	D_1	D_0		
0	0	0	1	0	0	0	0	0	=	20H with port address 80H

The nonspecific EOI command can be used in the fully nested mode because it always resets the bit of the highest priority; however, in other priority modes, it may reset the wrong bit. It is always safe to use a specific EOI command; the format is as follows:

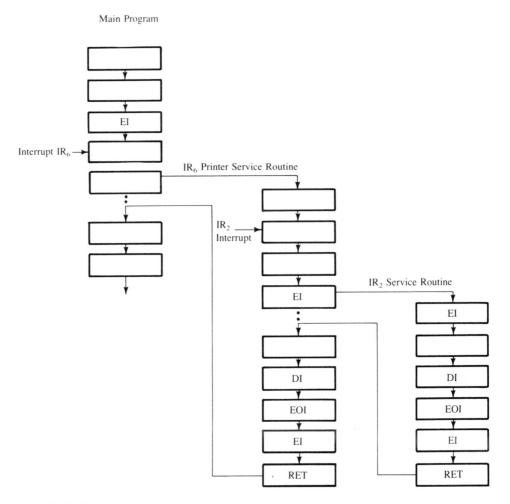

FIGURE 15.24
Interrupt Process: Fully Nested Mode

SOURCE: John Beaston, *Using the Programmable Interrupt Controller,* Intel Application Note AP-31 (Santa Clara, Calif.: Intel Corporation, May 1978), p. 10.

DIRECT MEMORY ACCESS (DMA) AND THE 8257 DMA CONTROLLER 15.4

Direct Memory Access is an I/O technique commonly used for high speed data transfer; for example, data transfer between system memory and a floppy disk. In status check I/O and interrupt I/O, data transfer is relatively slow because each instruction needs to be fetched and executed. In DMA, the MPU releases the control of the buses to a device called a DMA controller. The controller manages data transfer between memory and a peripheral under its control, thus bypassing the MPU. Conceptually, this is an important I/O technique; it introduces two new signals available on the 8085/8080A — HOLD and HLDA (Hold Acknowledge).

☐ HOLD — This is an active high input signal to the 8085/8080A from another master requesting the use of the address and data buses. After receiving the Hold request, the MPU relinquishes the buses in the following machine cycle. All buses are tri-stated and the Hold Acknowledge (HLDA) signal is sent out. The MPU regains the control of the buses after HOLD goes low.

☐ HLDA (Hold Acknowledge) — This is an active high output signal indicating that the MPU is relinquishing control of the buses.

A DMA controller uses these signals as if it were a peripheral to requesting the MPU for the control of the buses. The MPU communicates with the controller by using the Chip Select line, buses, and control signals. However, once the controller has gained control, it plays the role of a processor for data transfer. To perform this function the DMA controller should have

1. a data bus,
2. an address bus,
3. Read/Write control signals, and
4. control signals to disable its role as a peripheral and to enable its role as a processor. This process is called switching from the slave mode to the master mode.

For all practical purposes, the DMA controller is a microprocessor with a limited instruction set. As an illustration, a programmable DMA controller, the Intel 8257, is described below.

15.41 THE 8257 DMA CONTROLLER

The 8257 is a programmable, 4-channel, direct memory access controller. This means that four peripherals can request data transfer, and the request priorities are determined internally. Figure 15.25 shows the three blocks of the 8257, similar to any programmable device: data bus buffer, Read/Write logic and four channels. In addition, the 8257 has control logic of its own to manage data transfer. Each channel can transfer 16,384 (16K) bytes. The MPU provides a 15-bit starting address, a 14-bit count for the number of bytes, and the direction for data transfer. The important features of each block are described below in a simplified version.

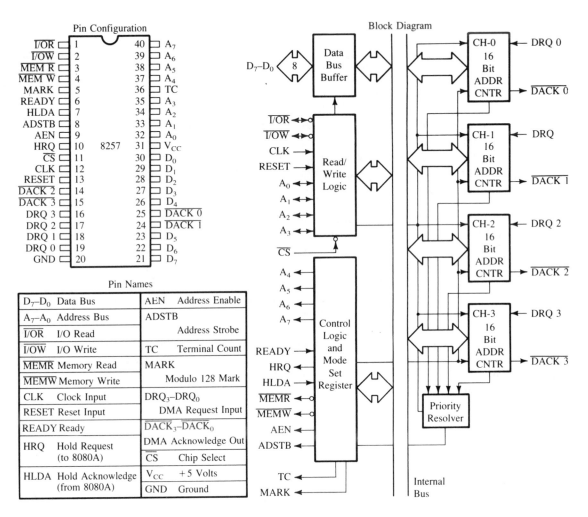

Pin Configuration

I/OR	1	40	A$_7$
I/OW	2	39	A$_6$
MEM R	3	38	A$_5$
MEM W	4	37	A$_4$
MARK	5	36	TC
READY	6	35	A$_3$
HLDA	7	34	A$_2$
ADSTB	8	33	A$_1$
AEN	9	32	A$_0$
HRQ	10	31	V$_{CC}$
CS	11	30	D$_0$
CLK	12	29	D$_1$
RESET	13	28	D$_2$
DACK 2	14	27	D$_3$
DACK 3	15	26	D$_4$
DRQ 3	16	25	DACK 0
DRQ 2	17	24	DACK 1
DRQ 1	18	23	D$_5$
DRQ 0	19	22	D$_6$
GND	20	21	D$_7$

(8257)

Pin Names

D$_7$–D$_0$	Data Bus	AEN	Address Enable
A$_7$–A$_0$	Address Bus	ADSTB	Address Strobe
I/OR	I/O Read		
I/OW	I/O Write	TC	Terminal Count
MEMR	Memory Read	MARK	Modulo 128 Mark
MEMW	Memory Write		
CLK	Clock Input	DRQ$_3$–DRQ$_0$	DMA Request Input
RESET	Reset Input		
READY	Ready	DACK$_3$–DACK$_0$	DMA Acknowledge Out
HRQ	Hold Request (to 8080A)		
		CS	Chip Select
HLDA	Hold Acknowledge (from 8080A)	V$_{CC}$	+5 Volts
		GND	Ground

FIGURE 15.25
Block Diagram of the 8257 DMA Controller
SOURCE: Intel Corporation, *MCS—80/85 Family User's Manual* (Santa Clara, Calif.: Author, 1981), p. 6-132.

DMA CHANNELS

The 8257 has four identical channels, each with two signals: DRQ (DMA Request) and DACK (DMA Acknowledge). Each channel has two 16-bit registers, one for the memory address where data transfer should begin, and the second for a 14-bit count. Bits D$_{15}$ and D$_{14}$ of the count register specify the DMA function—Write, Read, or Verify—as shown in Figure 15.26(a).

Figure 15.26 also shows two additional 8-bit registers: the control register, called the Mode Set Register (Figure 15-26b), and the Status Register (Figure 15.26c). The

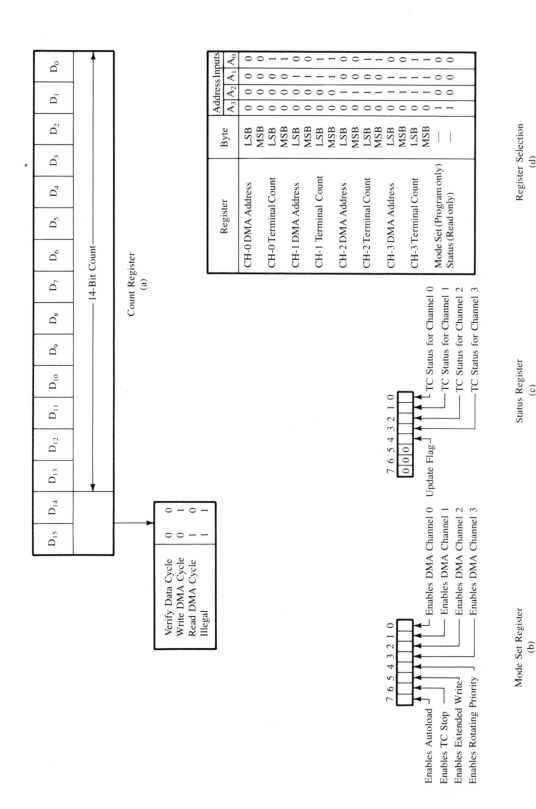

FIGURE 15.26
Registers in a DMA Channel

control word in the Mode Set Register enables or disables channels and determines other functions. The port addresses of each register are determined by four address lines (Figure 15.26d) and Chip Select logic. For example,

A_3	A_2	A_1	A_0	
0	0	0	0	selects Channel 0 DMA address
0	0	0	1	selects Channel 0 terminal count address
1	0	0	0	selects mode/status

The Mode Set register is defined as follows:

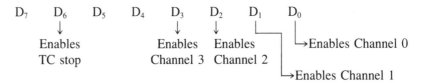

Bits D_4, D_5, and D_7 are assumed to be zero (and are not described here, in order to maintain clarity).

NEED FOR 8212 AND SIGNAL ADSTB

The 8257 has eight address lines, but requires sixteen address lines to address a memory location. The additional eight lines are generated by using the signal ADSTB to strobe a high-order memory address into the 8212 from the data bus.

SIGNAL AEN (ADDRESS ENABLE)

The AEN output signal is used to disable (float) the system data bus and control bus. This signal is necessary to switch the 8257 from the slave mode to the master mode.

Example 15.5

1. Explain the DMA interfacing circuit shown in Figure 15.27.
2. Write an initialization program to transfer 256 bytes of data from a peripheral (floppy disk) to memory, starting at 2050H. After the transfer, the DMA operation should be terminated.

Solution

The functions of the various components in the circuit are as follows:

1. The 8212 (in the upper half of Figure 15.27) is used to demultiplex the 8085 bus in order to generate the low-order address bus (A_7–A_0). This 8212 is a part of the MPU circuit, and is not related to the DMA operation (except that $\overline{DS}_1$ is controlled by AEN).
2. The 74LS257 is a multiplexer used to generate control signals. Again, this is also the part of the MPU circuit, and is not related to the DMA operation (except that $\overline{OE}$ is controlled by AEN).
3. The port addresses of the registers in the 8257 are as follows. These port assignments assume the $\overline{CS}$ signal of the 8257 is connected to address line A_7 through an inverter and A_6–A_4 are at logic 0.

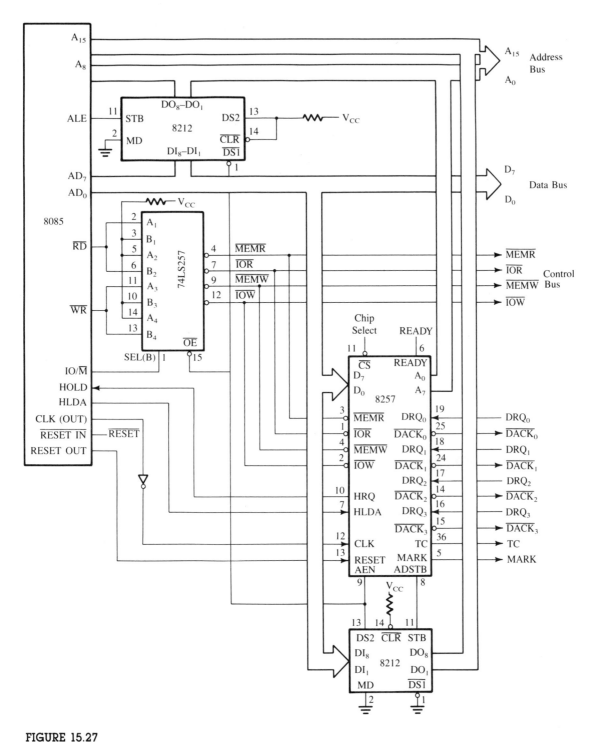

FIGURE 15.27
Schematic of Interfacing 8257 DMA Controller

SOURCE: Intel Corporation, *MCS — 80/85 Family User's Guide* (Santa Clara, Calif.: Author, 1981), p. 6-125.

	A_7	A_6	A_5	A_4	A_3	A_2	A_1	A_0		
Mode Register:	1	0	0	0	1	0	0	0	=	88H
Ch 0/DMA Register	1	0	0	0	0	0	0	0	=	80H
Ch 0/Count Register	1	0	0	0	0	0	0	1	=	81H

4. The 8212 connected to the DMA controller accepts data during the DMA operation. The high-order address (20H) of the memory location 2050H is sent to A_{15}–A_8 as an output of the 8212.

INITIALIZATION

The following steps should be followed to initialize the 8257 and transfer 256 bytes of data. (See Figure 15.26 for the definitions of control words.)

Instructions

1. Send mode word to mode register

D_7	D_6	D_5	D_4	D_3	D_2	D_1	D_0			
0	1	0	0	0	0	0	1	=	41H	MVI A, 41H

     ↓   ↓   OUT 88H

   Enables   Enables

   TC stop   Channel 0

2. Send low-order byte count FF to count register   MVI A, FFH

                                                       OUT 81H

3. Send high-order byte count including direction for write mode: MVI A, 40H

   $D_{15} = 0$, $D_{14} = 1$ (D_{13}–$D_8 = 0$)   OUT 81H

4. Send-low order byte (50H) of the memory location 2050H to the   MVI A, 50H

   DMA register of channel 0   OUT 80H

5. Send high-order byte (20H) to the DMA register channel 0   MVI A, 20H

                                                         OUT 80H

DMA EXECUTION

The process of data transfer from the peripheral to the system memory under the DMA controller can be classified under two modes: the slave mode and the master mode.

Slave Mode In the slave mode, the DMA controller is treated as a peripheral, using the following steps:

1. The MPU selects the DMA controller through Chip Select.
2. The MPU writes the command mode and terminal count in channel registers by accessing the register through A_0–A_3 and through the control signals $\overline{IOR}$ and $\overline{IOW}$.

In this mode, the signals shown in the Read/Write logic block are used; the address lines A_7 to A_4 and the control signals $\overline{MEMR}$, $\overline{MEMW}$ from the control logic block are in tri-state. The other signals are not being used.

Master Mode After the initialization, the 8257 in master mode keeps checking for a DMA request, and the steps in data transfer can be listed as follows:

1. When the peripheral is ready for data transfer, it sends a high signal to DRQ.
2. When the DRQ has been received and the channel enabled, the control logic sets HRQ (Hold Request) high. (HRQ is connected to the HOLD signal of the 8085.)
3. In the next cycle, the MPU relinquishes the buses and sends the HLDA (Hold Acknowledge) signal to the 8257.
4. After receiving the HLDA signal, the control logic generates $\overline{\text{DACK}}$ (DMA Acknowledge) and sends the acknowledgment to the peripheral.
5. Meanwhile, the 8257 enables the signal AEN (Address Enable). AEN disables the MPU demultiplexed address bus A_7–A_0 ($\overline{\text{DS}}_1$ of the upper 8212 goes high and the control signal $\overline{\text{OE}}$ of 74LS157 is set high). The entire bus, A_7–A_0, of the 8257 becomes output.
6. The low-order byte of the memory location is placed on the A_7–A_0 of the 8257.
7. When the AEN signal is high, the ADSTB (Address Strobe) signal goes high and places the high-order byte of the memory location, generated by the lower 8212, on address bus A_{15}–A_8. Data transfer continues until the count reaches zero.

DESIGN TRENDS IN PROGRAMMABLE DEVICES 15.5

As microprocessor technology advances, more and more functions are being designed in programmable devices. The following chips are examples:

☐ 8271 — Programmable Floppy Disk Controller
☐ 8275 — Programmable CRT Controller
☐ 8295 — Dot Matrix Printer Controller

Designing a wide variety of I/O functions on one chip is a recent trend. A 40-pin package seems to be the upper limit; a very few LSI chips are designed in a 48- or 64-pin package. Intel recently announced a chip called MUART, which is briefly described below to indicate trends in technology.

THE 8256 MUART

This chip is known as a Multifunction Universal Asynchronous Receiver-Transmitter (MUART) and is housed in a 40-pin package. It performs most of the functions that are performed individually by the chips described in this chapter and the next chapter. It is a programmable device and includes

1. a programmable UART for serial I/O (described in Chapter 16)
2. two 8-bit I/O ports; port 1 can be programmed for handshake I/O
3. an 8-level priority interrupt controller

4. five 8-bit programmable timer/counters — four of which can be cascaded to function as 16-bit counters

5. a programmable baud generator

6. a programmable system clock

If pins are available, manufacturers are likely to design more and more I/O functions in the same package. In order to combine various I/Os in one package, quite a few compromises have been made in the 8256. The address and data lines — input from the MPU to the chip — are multiplexed. This is not a general purpose chip; it is designed to function with the Intel microprocessors, such as the 8085/86/88, that can use ALE (Address Latch Enable) to demultiplex the bus internally.

SUMMARY

In this chapter, four programmable devices were described: the 8255A (PPI), the 8253 (timer), the 8259A (interrupt controller), and the 8257 (DMA controller). These are general purpose devices, and each is designed to serve different purposes in the I/O communication process. The common element among them is that the functions of these devices can be programmed by writing instructions in their control registers. Applications of these devices were demonstrated with illustrations and examples, and design trends in programmable devices were suggested using the 8256 MUART as an example.

ASSIGNMENTS

1. List the oeprating modes of the 8255A Programmable Peripheral Interface.
2. Specify the handshake signals and their functions if port A of the 8255A is set up as an output port in Mode 1.
3. Specify the bit of a control word for the 8255, which differentiates between the I/O mode and the BSR mode.
4. Specify the two control words that are necessary to set bit PC_6 (assume that the other ports are not being used).
5. Port A of the 8255A is set up in Mode 1, and the status word is read as 18H. Is there an error in the status word?
6. List the necessary conditions to generate INTR when port A of the 8255A is set up as an output port in Mode 1.
7. Write initialization instructions and a service routine to read the keyboard (Figure 15.13) and store the reading in the input buffer memory INBUF. Assume keys are debounced and decoded.
8. Specify the conditions to start the timer 8253.

9. List the major components of the 8259A interrupt controller and explain their functions.
10. Explain why each channel in the 8257 DMA controller is restricted to 16K bytes of data transfer.
11. Write initialization instructions for the 8255A to set up:

   ☐ Port A as an output port in Mode 0.
   ☐ Port B as an output port in Mode 1 for interrupt I/O.
   ☐ Port C_U as an output port in Mode 0.

12. In Figure 15.5, connect the system address lines A_9 and A_8 to A_1 and A_0 lines of the 8255A, respectively. Specify the port addresses.
13. Set up the 8253 as a square wave generator with a 1 ms period, if the input frequency to the 8253 is 1 MHz.
14. Design a five-minute clock (timer) using the 8253 and the interrupt technique. Display minutes and seconds.
15. Write initialization instructions for the 8259A Interrupt Controller to meet the following specifications:

   ☐ Interrupt vector address: 2090H
   ☐ Call address interval of eight bits.
   ☐ Nested mode.

EXPERIMENTAL ASSIGNMENTS

1. **a.** Connect the circuit as shown in Figure 15.7.
   b. Write initialization instructions, and store binary readings in memory buffer for five different analog signals.
   c. Modify the circuit to record the data, using the interrupt RST 6.5.
   d. Modify the initialization instructions.
   e. Write the service routine to record the data.
   f. Store data in memory for five different analog signals.
2. **a.** Set up the 8253 timer as shown in Figure 15.19.
   b. Write instructions to obtain a square wave with the period of 500 μs.
   c. Enter the instructions and execute the program.
   d. Measure the square wave output on an oscilloscope.
   e. Calculate the pulse width if the count is 8000H.
   f. Load the count in step e, start the counter, and measure the pulse width of the output.

Serial I/O and Data Communication

The 8085/8080A microprocessor is a parallel device; it transfers eight bits of data simultaneously over eight data lines. This is the **parallel I/O mode** discussed in previous chapters. However, in many situations, the parallel I/O mode is either impractical or impossible. For example, parallel data communication over a long distance can become very expensive. Similarly, devices such as a CRT terminal or a cassette tape are not designed for parallel I/O. In these situations, the serial I/O mode is used, whereby one bit at a time is transferred over a single line.

In serial transmission (from the MPU to a peripheral), an 8-bit parallel word should be converted into a stream of eight serial bits; this is known as **parallel-to-serial conversion**. In serial reception, the MPU receives a stream of eight bits, and they should be converted into an 8-bit parallel word; this is known as **serial-to-parallel conversion**. For example, when the letter *A* or the digit *7* is pressed on a terminal keyboard, the MPU receives equivalent alphanumeric (letters and numbers) binary code in eight serial bits. This process raises several questions about the serial I/O mode.

☐ In serial I/O, how does the MPU identify a peripheral and what are the conditions of data transfer: unconditional, using the status check, or using the interrupt?

☐ What are the codes for alphanumeric data?
☐ What are the requirements of transmission: synchronization, speed, error check, etc.?
☐ What are the standards for interfacing various types of equipment?
☐ What are the trade-offs between software and hardware approaches in implementing serial I/O?

These questions concern basic concepts in serial data communication and are discussed in this chapter. The illustrations include both software and hardware controlled serial I/O, as well as uses of the SOD (Serial Output Data) and SID (Serial Input Data) pins — specially designed signals for serial I/O in the 8085.

OBJECTIVES

☐ Explain how data transfer occurs in the serial I/O mode and how it differs from the parallel I/O mode.

☐ Explain the terms: *synchronous* and *asynchronous transmission, simplex, half* and *full duplex transmission; ASCII code; baud (rate);* and *parity check.*

☐ Explain how data bits are transmitted (or received) in the asynchronous format, and calculate the delay required between two successive bits for a given baud.

☐ Explain the two standards of transmission: current loop and RS-232C.

☐ Design an interfacing circuit and write programs to set up software controlled data communication between a microcomputer and a teletype (or a CRT terminal).

☐ Write instructions to transmit and receive data using the serial I/O lines (SID and SOD) in an 8085 system.

☐ Explain the block diagram and the functions of each block of the Intel 8251 USART (Programmable Communication Interface).

☐ Design an interfacing circuit using the 8251, and write initialization instructions to set up data communication between a microcomputer and a serial peripheral.

16.1 BASIC CONCEPTS IN SERIAL I/O

The basic concepts concerning the serial I/O mode can be classified into the categories as shown; they will be discussed in the following sections.

1. I/O requirements
2. Alphanumeric codes
3. Transmission format
4. Serial transmission standards
5. Software vs. programmable hardware approaches

16.11 I/O Requirements

The 8085/8080A MPU identifies a serial I/O peripheral in the same manner that it identifies any other peripheral — through a decoded port address and the control signals $\overline{IOR}$ and $\overline{IOW}$. The control signal $\overline{IOR}$ is used to receive data, and $\overline{IOW}$ is used to transmit data, as shown in Figure 16.1.

FIGURE 16.1
Block Diagram: Serial I/O and Control Signals

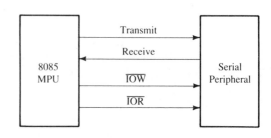

Similarly, the memory-mapped I/O technique can be employed using the memory-related control signals $\overline{\text{MEMR}}$ and $\overline{\text{MEMW}}$. The primary differences between parallel I/O and serial I/O are the number of data lines and the number of bits transferred by the I/O instructions. The 8085/8080A MPU can transfer bits serially under various conditions depending upon the type of peripheral and its interfacing logic. Serial I/O data transfer can be unconditional, with the status check, or with the interrupt.

16.12 Alphanumeric Codes

A computer is a binary machine; in order to communicate with the computer in alphabetic letters and decimal numbers, translation codes are necessary. The commonly used code is known as ASCII, the American Standard Code for Information Interchange. It is a 7-bit code with 128 (2^7) combinations, and each combination from 00H to 7FH is assigned to a letter, a decimal number, a symbol, or a machine command (see Appendix G). For example, hexadecimals 30H to 39H represent numerals 0 to 9; 41H to 5AH represent capital letters A through Z; 21H to 2FH represent various symbols; and the initial codes 00H to 1FH represent machine commands such as Carriage Return (CR) or Line Feed (LF). Devices that use ASCII characters include ASCII terminals, teletype machines (TTY), and printers. When the key 9 is pressed on an ASCII terminal, the computer receives 39H in binary, and the system programs (as shown in Chapter 9) translate ASCII characters into appropriate binary or BCD numbers.

Another code, called EBCDIC (Extended Binary Coded Decimal Interchange Code), is widely used in IBM computers. This is an 8-bit code representing 256 combinations; however, several combinations are not being used.

16.13 Transmission Format

A transmission format is concerned with issues such as synchronization, direction of data flow, speed, errors, and medium of transmission (telephone lines for example). These topics are described briefly below.

SYNCHRONOUS VS. ASYNCHRONOUS TRANSMISSION

Serial communication occurs either in synchronous or asynchronous format. In the synchronous format, a receiver and a transmitter are synchronized; a block of characters is transmitted along with the synchronization information, as in Figure 16.2(a). This format is generally used for high speed transmission (more than 20 k bits/second).

The asynchronous format is character-oriented. Each character carries the information of the START and the STOP bits, shown in Figure 16.2(b). When no data are being transmitted, a receiver stays high at logic 1, called MARK; logic 0 is called SPACE. Transmission begins with one START bit (low), followed by a character and one or two STOP bits (high). This is also known as **framing**. Figure 16.2(b) shows the transmission of eleven bits for an ASCII character in the asynchronous format: one START bit, eight character bits, and two STOP bits. The format shown in Figure 16.2(b) is similar to Morse code, but the dots and dashes are replaced by logic 0s and 1s. The asynchronous format is generally used in low speed transmission (less than 20 k bits/second).

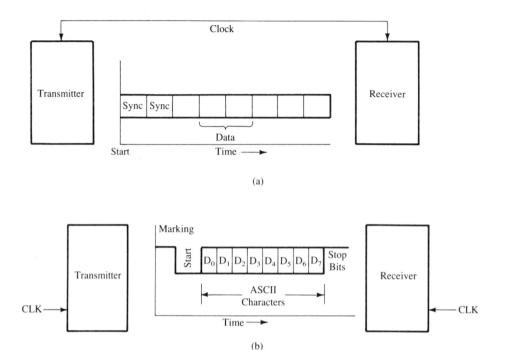

FIGURE 16.2
Transmission Format: Synchronous (a) and Asynchronous (b)

SIMPLEX AND DUPLEX TRANSMISSION

Serial communication also can be classified according to the direction and simultaneity of data flow.

In **simplex transmission**, data are transmitted in only one direction. A typical example is the transmission from a microcomputer to a printer.

In **duplex transmission**, data flow in both directions. However, if the transmission goes one way at a time, it is called **half duplex**; if it goes both ways simultaneously, it is called **full duplex**. Generally, transmission between two computers or between a computer and a terminal is full duplex.

PARITY CHECK

During transmission, data bits may change (e.g., because of noise) and a wrong character may be received by a receiver. The MSB bit in the ASCII code can be used to check an error; this process is called **parity check**.

To check the parity, the transmitter simply counts whether the number of 1s in a character is odd or even, and transmits that information to the receiver as the MSB bit. The receiver checks the MSB bit and the number of 1s in the received character. If there is an error, the receiver sends back an error message to the transmitter.

The parity check can be either odd or even, depending upon the system. In an odd parity system, when a character has an even number of 1s, bit D_7 is set to 1 and an odd number of 1s is transmitted. For example, the code for the character G is 47H (01000111) with four 1s. When the character G is transmitted in an odd parity system, the transmitter will set bit D_7 to 1, making the code C7H (11000111). On the other hand, the character I (49H = 01001001) has three 1s; when the character I is transmitted, bit D_7 is set to 0, keeping the code 49H. The parity check cannot detect multiple errors in any given character.

The 8085/8080A microprocessor sets a parity flag when the number of 1s in the accumulator is even. This flag can be used for the parity check in an 8085/8080A system.

BAUD

The rate at which the bits are transmitted — bits/second — is called a **baud** in serial I/O; however, technically, it is defined as the number of signal changes/second. Each piece of equipment has its own baud requirement. For example, a teletype (TTY) generally runs on a 110 baud. However, in most terminals and printers, the baud is adjustable, typically, in the range of 50 to 9600 baud.

MODEM

A **modem** (Modulator/Demodulator) is a circuit that translates digital data into audio tone frequencies for transmission over telephone lines and converts audio frequencies into digital data for reception. The modulation technique generally used is called **frequency shift keying** (FSK); it converts logic 1 (MARK) and logic 0 (SPACE) into audio tones around 1200 and 2200 Hz frequencies.

Computers can exchange information over telephone lines by using two modems — one on each side (Figure 16.3). A calling computer (or a terminal) contacts a receiving computer through a telephone number, and a communication link is established after control signals have been exchanged between computers and modems.

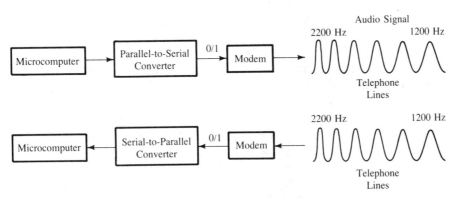

FIGURE 16.3
Communication Between Two Computers Using Modems

A typical process of communication is shown in Figure 16.3. A parallel word is converted into serial bits; in turn, they generate two audio frequencies according to logic 0 or 1, and these audio frequencies are transmitted over telephone lines. At the receiving end, audio frequencies are converted back into 0s and 1s, and serial bits are converted into a parallel word that can be read by the receiving computer.

16.14 Standards

In serial I/O, data can be transmitted either as current or as voltage. Typically, 20 mA (or 60 mA) current loops are used in teletype equipment. When a teletype is marking or at logic 1, current flows; when it is at logic 0 (or SPACE), current is interrupted. The advantage of the current loop method is that signals are relatively noise free and suitable for transmission over a distance.

When data are transmitted as voltage, the commonly used standard is known as **RS-232C**. It is defined in reference to Data Terminal Equipment (DTE) and Data Communication Equipment (DCE)—terminal and modem—as shown in Figure 16.4(a); however, its voltage levels are not compatible with TTL logic levels.

To appreciate the difficulties and confusion in this standard, one has to examine its historical background. The RS-232 standard was developed during the initial days of computer timesharing, long before the existence of TTL logic, and its primary focus was on compatibility between a terminal and a modem. However, the same standard is now being used for communications between computers and peripherals, and the roles of a data terminal and a modem have become ambiguous. Should a printer be considered a terminal or a modem? Actually, it can be either. Therefore, the lines used for transmission and reception will differ, depending on how the manufacturer defines the role of its peripheral.

RS-232C

Figure 16.4(b) shows the RS-232C 25-pin connector and its signals. The signals are divided into four groups: **data signals**, **control signals**, **timing signals**, and **grounds**. For data lines, the voltage level from $+3$ V to $+15$ V is defined as logic 0, and from -3 V to -15 V as logic 1 (normally, voltage levels are ±12 V). This is negative true logic. Because of incompatibility with TTL logic, voltage translators called **line drivers** and **line receivers** are required to interface TTL logic with the RS-232 signals. These are described in Section 16.42.

The minimum interface requires three lines: pins 2, 3, and 7, as shown in Figure 16.4(a). These lines are defined in relation to the DTE; the terminal transmits on pin 2 and receives on pin 3. On the other hand, the DCE transmits on pin 3 and receives on pin 2 (see the Illustration in Section 16.42). Typically, data transmission with a handshake requires eight lines. Specific functions of handshake lines differ in different peripherals and, therefore, should be referred to in the manufacturers' manuals.

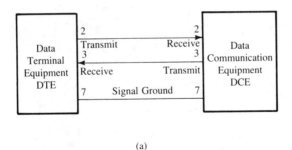

(a)

Signals	Pins	Signals
	1	Protective Ground
Secondary Transmitted Data	14	
	2	Transmitted Data (T × D) ⟶ DCE
Transmission Signal Element Timing (DCE Source)	15	
	3	Received Data (R × D) ⟶ DTE
Secondary Received Data	16	
	4	Request to Send (RTS) ⟶ DCE
Receiver Signal Element Timing (DCE Source)	17	
	5	Clear to Send (CTS) ⟶ DTE
Unassigned	18	
	6	Data Set Ready (DSR) ⟶ DTE
Secondary Request to Send	19	
	7	Signal Ground
DCE ⟵ Data Terminal Ready (DTR)	20	
	8	Received Line Signal Detector
Signal Quality Detector	21	
	9	(Reserved for Data Set Testing)
Ring Indicator	22	
	10	(Reserved for Data Set Testing)
Data Signal Rate Selector (DTE/DCE Source)	23	
	11	Unassigned
Transmit Signal Element Timing (DTE Source)	24	
	12	Sec. Rec'd. Line Sig. Detector
Unassigned	25	
	13	Sec. Clear to Send

FIGURE 16.4

Minimum Configuration of Control Signals Between DTE and DCE (a), and RS-232C Signal Definitions and Pin Assignments (b)

SOURCE: B: Courtesy of the Electronic Industries Association and available from them at 2001 Eye Street, NW, Washington, D.C. 20006, (202) 457-4900.

16.15 Software vs. Programmable Hardware Approaches

Conceptually, the software and the hardware approaches to serial data transfer are similar. Data transmission from a microcomputer to a serial peripheral involves converting a parallel word into a stream of serial bits and sending out one bit at a time with appropriate time delay using one data line of an output port. In data reception, this process is reversed.

In the software approach, the delay is set up by using a counter and a loop, as in Chapter 7, and the entire word is rotated through the data bit connected to the serial peripheral. In the hardware approach, these functions are performed by a programmable chip that contains a counter and parallel-to-serial and serial-to-parallel registers.

The software approach is suitable for slow speed asynchronous data communication in which timing requirements are not critical. The approach is simple and inexpensive. The hardware approach is suitable for both asynchronous and synchronous formats. Because hardware chips are programmable, the approach is flexible to accommodate changing requirements.

16.16   Review of Important Concepts

The basic concepts concerning serial I/O discussed in the previous sections are summarized in Table 16.1. In the following sections, these concepts will be illustrated through both the software and the hardware approaches for asynchronous serial I/O, which is widely used in microcomputers. Synchronous transmission will not be discussed here.

TABLE 16.1
Summary of Synchronous and Asynchronous Serial Transmission

| Format | Serial Transmission | |
	Synchronous	Asynchronous
Data format:	Groups of characters	One character at a time
Speed:	High (20 k bits/second) or higher	20 k bits/second or lower
Framing information:	Sync characters are sent with each group	START and STOP bits with every character
Implementation:	Hardware	Hardware or software
Data direction:	Simplex, half and full duplex	Simplex, half and full duplex

16.2   SOFTWARE-CONTROLLED ASYNCHRONOUS SERIAL I/O

In the **asynchronous serial I/O format**, each character includes framing information (START and STOP bits). Figure 16.5 shows a stream of eleven bits for the ASCII character K; including one START bit and two STOP bits. The character bits are transmitted beginning with the LSB — bit D_0. The bit time — the delay between two successive bits — is determined by the transmission rate (baud).

Typically, a teletype (TTY) sends (or receives) ten ASCII characters per second. If each character has 11 bits, the TTY transmits 110 bits/second:

$$\text{TTY transmission rate} \quad = \quad 110 \text{ bits/second}$$
$$\text{Time for each bit} \quad = \quad 1 \text{ second}/110 = 9.1 \text{ ms}$$

FIGURE 16.5
TTY Serial Bit Format

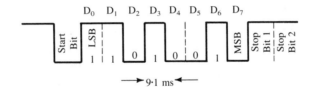

Therefore, to transmit a character to a teletype, the MPU should add framing information and send out one bit at a time at the interval of 9.1 ms. Software necessary for data transmission is given in Section 16.21.

Data reception in the serial mode involves the reverse process — receiving one bit at a time and forming an 8-bit parallel word. When a key is pressed on a TTY, it sends out the character bits and framing information at the interval of 9.1 ms in the same format, beginning with the START bit and the LSB(D_0) and terminating with D_7 and the STOP bits, as shown in Figure 16.5. Software necessary for data reception is given in Section 16.22.

16.21 Illustration: Data Transmission to Teletype (TTY)

PROBLEM STATEMENT

1. Explain the interfacing circuit shown in Figure 16.6.
2. Write a program to transmit a message in ASCII characters from an 8085/8080A single-board computer to a teletype with a 20 mA current loop and 110 baud. The ASCII characters required for the message are stored without a parity check in memory locations starting at XX70H; and the end of the message is indicated by the carriage return.
3. At the end of the message, the teletype should return to the beginning of the second line and wait.

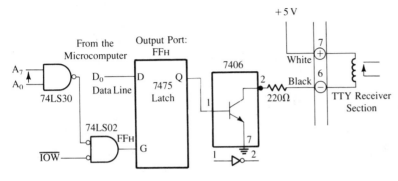

FIGURE 16.6
TTY Interfacing Circuit for Data Transmission

HARDWARE DESCRIPTION

A teletype is an asynchronous machine that can receive or transmit ASCII characters. The receiver section consists of a printer that converts a digital bit pattern into an ASCII character and prints it on a paper. The transmitter section consists of a keyboard that generates an ASCII bit pattern when a key is pressed.

When no character is being received, the printer stays high in MARK position, and 20 mA current continues to flow until a START bit is received. The START bit is low, and it interrupts the current flow. The printer waits for the next 8-bit pattern, decodes the pattern, prints a character, and prepares to receive the next character during the two STOP bits.

Similarly, when no character is being transmitted, the output of the keyboard section stays high, and the receiver (in this case, the microcomputer) waits until the logic level goes from high to low. When a key is pressed, the keyboard section generates eleven bits; each bit is represented by a pulse width of 9.1 ms.

In interfacing the teletype, the MPU views the device as two different peripherals (a printer and a keyboard) thus requiring two ports. The printer section is interfaced through an output port and the keyboard section is interfaced through an input port. .

CIRCUIT ANALYSIS

Figure 16.6 shows the 7475 D-latch as the output port with device address FFH. The address bus is decoded using an 8-input NAND gate, and combined with the control signal $\overline{\text{IOW}}$ to clock the latch. When the instruction OUT FFH is executed, the clock goes high, and bit D_0 is transferred to output Q. The bit is latched as the clock goes low. If Q is high, 20 mA current flows in the TTY circuit.

PROBLEM ANALYSIS

To transmit a character to a TTY with a 110 baud, eleven bits must be transmitted with an interval of 9.1 ms. This transmission requires a counter and a time delay subroutine of 9.1 ms. The counter can be set up to count all eleven bits or just eight character bits with separate START and STOP bits. In addition, the program should include a table look-up procedure to transfer the message from the memory to the microprocessor, and a Compare instruction to check the last ASCII character for the Carriage Return. The following program transfers the message by using two subroutines.

MAIN PROGRAM

```
            LXI   SP, XX90H    ;Initialize stack pointer
            LXI   H, XX70H     ;Set up HL as memory index pointer
            MVI   A, 01H
            OUT   FFH          ;Set output of Q to 1 to keep TTY in MARK
                                 position
TRNSMT:     MOV   A, M         ;Transfer character from memory to accumulator
            CPI   0DH          ;Is this Carriage Return?
            MOV   B, A         ;Save character
            JZ    LAST         ;End of message if this is Carriage Return
```

```
                CALL OUTTTY      ;Call routine that transmits a character serially
                INX   H          ;Point to next character
                JMP   TRNSMT     ;Go back to transmit next character
LAST:           CALL OUTTTY      ;Transmit Carriage Return
                MVI   B, 0AH     ;Load B with Line Feed
                CALL OUTTTY      ;Transmit Line Feed
                HLT
;OUTTTY: This subroutine converts parallel eight bits into a stream of serial bits and
;          transmits them to a teletype with 110 baud. The contents of registers A
;          and C are modified.
;        INPUT: ASCII character in register B
;        OUTPUT: No output to any other program even though it sends out
;             serial bits
;        CALLS: BITTIME subroutine for 9.1 ms delay
```

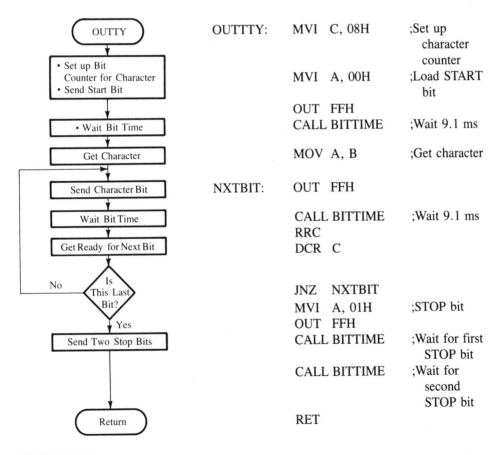

```
OUTTTY:   MVI  C, 08H      ;Set up
                             character
                             counter
          MVI  A, 00H      ;Load START
                             bit
          OUT  FFH
          CALL BITTIME     ;Wait 9.1 ms

          MOV  A, B        ;Get character

NXTBIT:   OUT  FFH

          CALL BITTIME     ;Wait 9.1 ms
          RRC
          DCR  C

          JNZ  NXTBIT
          MVI  A, 01H      ;STOP bit
          OUT  FFH
          CALL BITTIME     ;Wait for first
                             STOP bit
          CALL BITTIME     ;Wait for
                             second
                             STOP bit
          RET
```

FIGURE 16.7
Flowchart of Data Transmission to TTY

PROGRAM DESCRIPTION

The main program is similar to the program illustrated in Section 6.52, Figure 6.18. It transfers a character from memory to the microprocessor, checks whether it is the Carriage Return, and if it is other than the Carriage Return, the program calls the subroutine OUTTTY. This subroutine sends out eleven bits at the interval of 9.1 ms as shown in the flowchart (Figure 16.7). However, two instructions in the main program need additional explanation.

The first one is MVI A, 01H. This instruction is included as a precaution, in case the output of the flip-flop is not in the MARK position when the power is turned on. The second instruction is labelled as LAST. This instruction calls the subroutine again and transmits the Carriage Return. The reason is that the Compare instruction sets the Zero flag when the character of the Carriage Return is compared, and the program jumps to location LAST before transmitting the character.

The subroutine OUTTTY is not an efficient routine; however, it is easy to understand. More efficient routines are suggested in the assignment section at the end of this chapter. The subroutine BITTIME is left as an exercise.

16.22   Illustration: Data Reception from TTY

PROBLEM STATEMENT

1. Write a subroutine to receive a character from a TTY with 110 baud and save the character in the accumulator.
2. Explain the interfacing circuit (Figure 16.8).

CIRCUIT ANALYSIS

Figure 16.8 shows that a tri-state buffer is used as the input port with the device address 00H, and data line D_7 is used to receive data from the TTY.

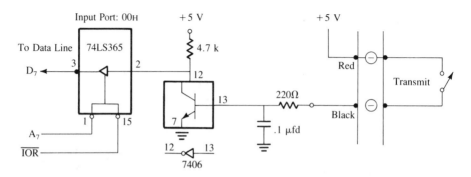

FIGURE 16.8
TTY Interfacing Circuit for Data Reception

PROBLEM ANALYSIS

The initial requirements for receiving data from the TTY are similar to those for checking the key closure of a Hex keyboard. The MPU needs to check whether the START bit is received. Similarly, it is necessary to read a data bit in the middle of the pulse, rather than at the beginning, to avoid errors in transition. This can be accomplished by waiting half the delay period (4.05 ms) following the arrival of the START bit and then reading the next eight bits at the interval of the full delay period (9.1 ms). Reading a bit in the middle of the pulse allows slight variations in receiver and transmitter frequencies.

The TTY transmits a character starting with the LSB; however, in this circuit the serial bit is received over data line D_7. Therefore, a parallel word can be formed by shifting bits to the right whenever a bit is read, and eventually the LSB will reach its proper position.

SUBROUTINE

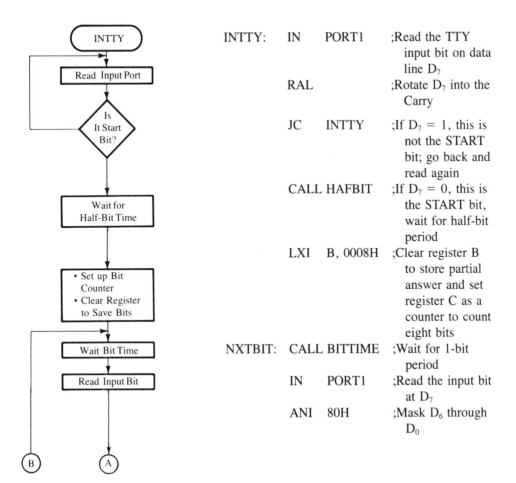

INTTY:	IN	PORT1	;Read the TTY input bit on data line D_7
	RAL		;Rotate D_7 into the Carry
	JC	INTTY	;If $D_7 = 1$, this is not the START bit; go back and read again
	CALL HAFBIT		;If $D_7 = 0$, this is the START bit, wait for half-bit period
	LXI	B, 0008H	;Clear register B to store partial answer and set register C as a counter to count eight bits
NXTBIT:	CALL BITTIME		;Wait for 1-bit period
	IN	PORT1	;Read the input bit at D_7
	ANI	80H	;Mask D_6 through D_0

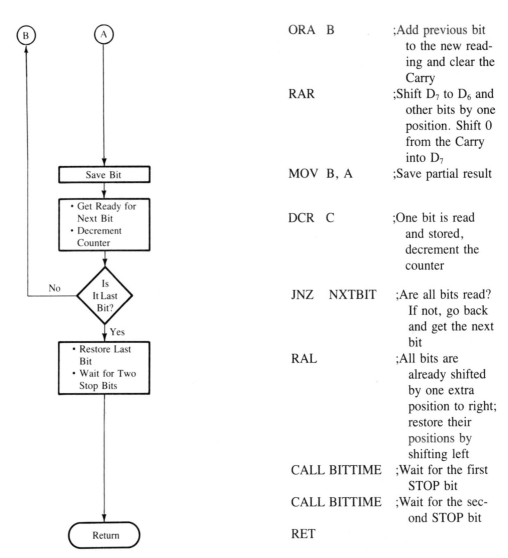

ORA B	;Add previous bit to the new reading and clear the Carry
RAR	;Shift D_7 to D_6 and other bits by one position. Shift 0 from the Carry into D_7
MOV B, A	;Save partial result
DCR C	;One bit is read and stored, decrement the counter
JNZ NXTBIT	;Are all bits read? If not, go back and get the next bit
RAL	;All bits are already shifted by one extra position to right; restore their positions by shifting left
CALL BITTIME	;Wait for the first STOP bit
CALL BITTIME	;Wait for the second STOP bit
RET	

FIGURE 16.9
Flowchart of Data Reception from TTY

PROGRAM DESCRIPTION

Initially, the subroutine stays in the loop until bit D_7 goes from high (MARK) to low, indicating the START bit. After waiting for half the bit period, all subsequent readings are sampled approximately in the middle of a bit.

The instruction LXI B clears register B to save the partial results and sets up register C as a counter to count eight input bits. However, the instructions after

CALL BITTIME are critical to the conversion of a serial bit pattern to a parallel word as explained below.

Instruction IN reads each bit of the character being received starting from bit D_0 and places the bit in D_7 of the accumulator. Instruction ANI 80H clears bits D_6 through D_0, with only one bit, (D_7), preserved. Instruction ORA B clears the Carry and always adds bit D_7 to the previous results. Therefore, after instruction RAR, bit D_7 is always 0 and the input reading is placed in the position of bit D_6 of the accumulator. After the eighth reading, bit D_0 of character is placed into the Carry. Therefore, it is necessary to shift left once to restore the bit pattern. The next two STOP bits are not saved; the subroutine just waits for two bit periods.

THE 8085 — SERIAL I/O LINES: SOD AND SID 16.3

The 8085 microprocessor has two pins specially designed for software-controlled serial I/O. One is called SOD (Serial Output Data), and the other is called SID (Serial Input Data). Data transfer is controlled through two instructions: SIM and RIM. Instructions SIM and RIM are used for entirely different processes: interrupt and serial I/O. These instructions have already been discussed in the context of the 8085 interrupt process (Chapter 12); now the focus is on their uses in serial I/O.

SERIAL OUTPUT DATA (SOD)

The instruction SIM is necessary to output data serially from the SOD line. It can be interpreted for serial output as in Figure 16.10.

Instructions

```
MVI A, 80H    ;Set D₇ in the accumulator = 1
RAR           ;Set D₆ = 1 and bring Carry into D₇
SIM           ;Output D₇
```

In this set of instructions, the serial output line is enabled by rotating 1 into bit position D_6; the instruction SIM outputs the Carry bit through bit position D_7.

SERIAL INPUT DATA (SID)

Instruction RIM is used to input serial data through the SID line. Instruction RIM can be interpreted for serial I/O as in Figure 16.11.

FIGURE 16.10
Interpretation of Accumulator
Contents by the SIM Instruction

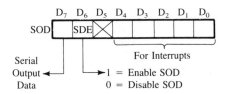

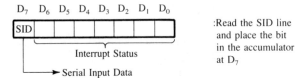

D$_7$ D$_6$ D$_5$ D$_4$ D$_3$ D$_2$ D$_1$ D$_0$

| SID | | | | | | | |

Interrupt Status

Serial Input Data

:Read the SID line
and place the bit
in the accumulator
at D$_7$

FIGURE 16.11
Interpretation of Accumulator Contents After the RIM Instruction

In the context of serial I/O, instruction RIM is similar to instruction IN, except RIM reads only one bit and places it in the accumulator at D$_7$.

The SID and SOD lines in the 8085 eliminate the need for an input port and an output port in the software-controlled serial I/O. Essentially, the SID is a 1-bit input port and SOD is a 1-bit output port. Similarly, instruction RIM is equivalent to a 1-bit IN instruction and instruction SIM is equivalent to a conditional 1-bit OUT instruction. The software necessary to implement serial I/O using SID and SOD lines is conceptually similar to that illustrated in Section 16.2. The two subroutines, OUTTTY and INTTY, described in Section 16.2, are illustrated below using SOD and SID lines.

16.31 Illustration: Data Transmission to TTY Using SOD Line

PROBLEM STATEMENT

Rewrite the subroutine OUTTY (Section 16.21) using the 8085 SOD line. The input to the subroutine is an ASCII character in register B.

SUBROUTINE*

The following subroutine SODTTY (Serial Output Data to TTY) is similar to the routine OUTTTY, except that it sets the counter for eleven bits and repeats the loop eleven times. The STOP bits are sent out using the instruction STC (Set Carry).

```
            ;Input: An ASCII character without parity check in register B
            ;Output: None

SODTTY:     MVI   C, 0BH        ;Set up counter C to count eleven bits
            XRA   A             ;Reset Carry to 0
NXTBIT:     MVI   A, 80H        ;Set D7 = 1 in the accumulator
            RAR                 ;Bring Carry in D7 and set D6 = 1
            SIM                 ;Output D7
            CALL BITTIME        ;Wait for 9.1 ms
            STC                 ;Set Carry = 1
```

_____

*This subroutine is adapted from John Wharton, *Using the 8085 Serial Lines,* Application Note AP 29 (Santa Clara, Calif.: Intel Corporation, 1977).

```
MOV  A, B        ;Place ASCII character in the accumulator
RAR              ;Place ASCII D₀ in the Carry, shift 1 in D₇, and
                     continue shifting for each loop
MOV  B, A        ;Save
DCR  C           ;One bit transmitted, decrement counter
JNZ  NXTBIT      ;If all bits are not transmitted, go back
RET
```

Subroutine Description This is an efficient subroutine based on the same serial I/O concepts discussed earlier. However, it uses some programming tricks to output data. To understand these tricks, it is necessary to examine the role of the following instructions, illustrated with an example of the ASCII letter G (47H = 0100 0111):

1. MVI A, 10000000 (80H)
   RAR

   When D_7 is rotated into D_6, the SOD line is enabled for each loop and the contents of the Carry are placed in D_7.
2. STC
   MOV A, B
   RAR

   Instruction STC places 1 into the Carry, and instruction MOV A, B places ASCII character in the accumulator. Instruction RAR brings 1 from the Carry into D_7 and places ASCII bit into the Carry.
3. In the second iteration, the first RAR (described in step 1) places ASCII bit from the Carry into D_7, and 1 from 80H into D_6. Instruction SIM outputs ASCII bit from bit D_7.
4. The logic 1's, set by instruction STC and saved in register B, are shifted right by one position in every iteration. In the ninth iteration when ASCII D_7 is sent out, register B will have all 1's from D_0 to D_7. In the last two iterations, logic 1's are sent out as STOP bits.
5. The contents of the accumulator after execution of these instructions are as follows (assume ASCII letter G is being transmitted):

*Input from Main
Program:*   (B) = 47H   0   1   0   0   0   1   1   1   (B)
Subroutine
SODTTY:

		CY	D_7	D_6	D_5	D_4	D_3	D_2	D_1	D_0	
XRA		0	0	0	0	0	0	0	0	0	(A)
MVI A, 80H		0	1	0	0	0	0	0	0	0	(A)
RAR	$D_0 \to 0$	0	0	1	0	0	0	0	0	0	(A)
SIM			0 ———— →SOD								
				OUTPUT							
STC		1									
		↓									
MOV A,B		1	0	1	0	0	0	1	1	1	(A)
RAR		1	1	0	1	0	0	0	1	1	(A)

16.32   Illustration: Data Reception from TTY Using SID Line

PROBLEM STATEMENT

Rewrite the subroutine INTTY (Section 16.22) using the 8085 SID line.

SUBROUTINE*

The following subroutine, SIDTTY (Serial Input Data from TTY), is conceptually similar to routine INTTY. However, this subroutine uses the RIM instruction to input serial data.

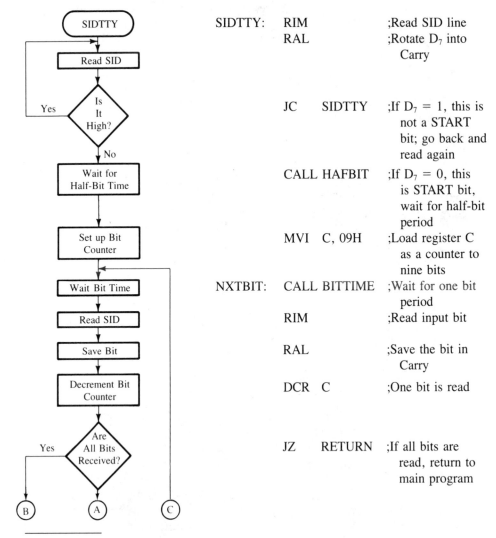

SIDTTY:	RIM		;Read SID line
	RAL		;Rotate D_7 into Carry
	JC	SIDTTY	;If $D_7 = 1$, this is not a START bit; go back and read again
	CALL	HAFBIT	;If $D_7 = 0$, this is START bit, wait for half-bit period
	MVI	C, 09H	;Load register C as a counter to nine bits
NXTBIT:	CALL	BITTIME	;Wait for one bit period
	RIM		;Read input bit
	RAL		;Save the bit in Carry
	DCR	C	;One bit is read
	JZ	RETURN	;If all bits are read, return to main program

---

*This subroutine is adapted from John Wharton, *Using the 8085 Serial Lines,* Application Note AP 29 (Santa Clara, Calif.: Intel Corporation, 1977).

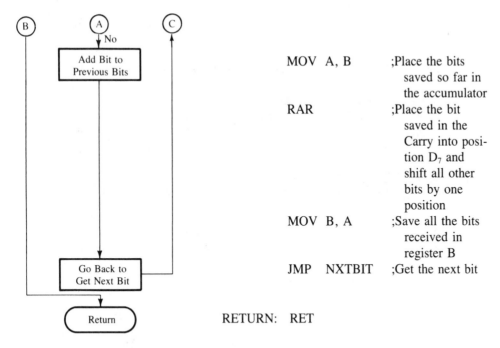

MOV A, B   ;Place the bits
             saved so far in
             the accumulator

RAR   ;Place the bit
             saved in the
             Carry into posi-
             tion D_7 and
             shift all other
             bits by one
             position

MOV B, A   ;Save all the bits
             received in
             register B

JMP NXTBIT ;Get the next bit

RETURN: RET

FIGURE 16.12
Flowchart of Data Transmission from TTY Using SID Line

SUBROUTINE DESCRIPTION

The flowchart of this subroutine is slightly different from the flowchart of the routine INTTY. The difference is in the procedure of saving a bit and forming a parallel word.

After the first bit (D_0) is read, it is saved in the Carry with instruction RAL. The bit is stored and shifted right by using the instruction RAR. This procedure is repeated eight times. In the ninth iteration, the subroutine returns to the main program, ignoring the last two STOP bits.

HARDWARE-CONTROLLED SERIAL I/O USING PROGRAMMABLE CHIPS

16.4

The hardware approach to serial I/O incorporates the same basic principles and requirements necessary for the software approach. The functions performed separately under software control must be combined in one chip. These functions and requirements for the software approach are summarized below.

1. An input port and an output port are required for interfacing.
2. In data transmission, the MPU converts a parallel word into a stream of serial bits.
3. In data reception, the MPU converts serial bits into a parallel word.

4. Data transfer is synchronized between the MPU and slow responding peripherals through time delays.

An integrated circuit called **USART** (Universal Synchronous/Asynchronous Receiver/Transmitter) incorporates all the features described above on the chip, as well as many more sophisticated features used for serial data communication. It is a programmable device; i.e., its functions and specifications for serial I/O can be determined by writing instructions in its internal registers. The Intel 8251A USART is a device widely used in serial I/O; the device and its applications are described in the next section.

16.41   The 8251A Programmable Communication Interface

The 8251A is a programmable chip designed for synchronous and asynchronous serial data communication, packaged in a 28-pin DIP. The 8251A is the enhanced version of its predecessor, the 8251, and it is compatible with the 8251. Figure 16.13 shows the block diagram of the 8251A. It includes five sections: Read/Write Control Logic, Transmitter, Receiver, Data Bus Buffer, and Modem Control.

The control logic interfaces the chip with the MPU, determines the functions of the chip according to the control word in its register (to be explained below), and monitors the data flow. The transmitter section converts a parallel word received from the MPU into serial bits and transmits them over the TxD line to a peripheral. The receiver section receives serial bits from a peripheral, converts them into a parallel word, and transfers the word to the MPU. The modem control is used to establish data communication through modems over telephone lines. The 8251A is a complex device, capable of performing various functions. For the sake of clarity, this chapter focuses only on the asynchronous mode of serial I/O, and excludes any discussion of the synchronous mode and the modem control. The asynchronous mode is often used for data communication between the MPU and serial peripherals such as terminals and floppy disks.

Figure 16.14 shows an expanded version of the 8251A block diagram. The block diagram shows all the elements of a programmable chip; it includes the interfacing signals, the control register, and the status register. The functions of various blocks are described below.

READ/WRITE CONTROL LOGIC AND REGISTERS

This section includes R/W control logic, six input signals, control logic, and three buffer registers: data register, control register, and status register. The input signals to the control logic are as follows.

Input Signals

☐ $\overline{\text{CS}}$ — **Chip Select:** When this signal goes low, the 8251A is selected by the MPU for communication. This is usually connected to a decoded address bus.
☐ **C/$\overline{\text{D}}$ — Control/Data:** When this signal is high, the control register or the status register is addressed; when it is low, the data buffer is addressed. The control register and the status register are differentiated by $\overline{\text{WR}}$ and $\overline{\text{RD}}$ signals, respectively.

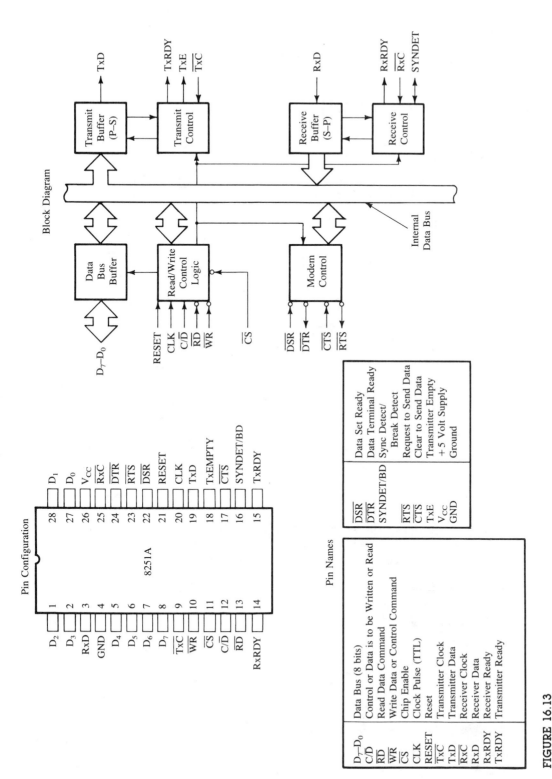

FIGURE 16.13

The 8251A: Block Diagram, Pin Configuration, and Description

SOURCE: Intel Corporation, *MCS—80/85 Family User's Manual* (Santa Clara, Calif.: Author, 1979), p. 6-160.

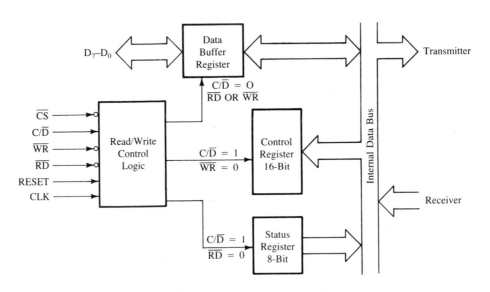

FIGURE 16.14
The 8251A: Expanded Block Diagram of Control Logic and Registers

☐ $\overline{WR}$ — **Write:** When this signal goes low, the MPU either writes in the control register or sends output to the data buffer. This is connected to $\overline{IOW}$ or $\overline{MEMW}$.

☐ $\overline{RD}$ — **Read:** When this signal goes low, the MPU either reads a status from the status register or accepts (inputs) data from the data buffer. This is connected to either $\overline{IOR}$ or $\overline{MEMR}$.

☐ **RESET** — **Reset:** A high on this input resets the 8251A and forces it into the idle mode.

☐ **CLK** — **Clock:** This is the clock input, usually connected to the system clock. This clock does not control either the transmission or the reception rate. The clock is necessary for communication with the microprocessor.

Control Register   This 16-bit register for a control word consists of two independent bytes: the first byte is called the **mode instruction** (word) and the second byte is called **command instruction** (word). This register can be accessed as an output port when the C/$\overline{D}$ pin is high.

Status Register   This input register checks the ready status of a peripheral. This register is addressed as an input port when the C/$\overline{D}$ pin is high; it has the same port address as the control register.

Data Buffer   This bidirectional register can be addressed as an input port and an output port when the C/$\overline{D}$ pin is low. Table 16.2 summarizes all the interfacing and control signals.

TABLE 16.2
Summary of Control Signals for the 8251A

$\overline{CS}$	C/$\overline{D}$	$\overline{RD}$	$\overline{WR}$	Function
0	1	1	0	MPU writes instructions in the control register
0	1	0	1	MPU reads status from the status register
0	0	1	0	MPU outputs data to the Data Buffer
0	0	0	1	MPU accepts data from the Data Buffer
1	X	X	X	USART is not selected

TRANSMITTER SECTION

The transmitter accepts parallel data from the MPU and converts them into serial data. It has two registers: a buffer register to hold eight bits and an output register to convert eight bits into a stream of serial bits (Figure 16.15). The MPU writes a byte in the buffer register; whenever the output register is empty, the contents of the buffer register are transferred to the output register. This section transmits data on the TxD pin with the appropriate framing bits (START and STOP). Three output signals and one input signal are associated with the transmitter section.

☐ **TxD—Transmit Data:** Serial bits are transmitted on this line.
☐ **TxC—Transmitter Clock:** This input signal controls the rate at which bits are transmitted by the USART. The clock frequency can be 1, 16, or 64 times the baud.

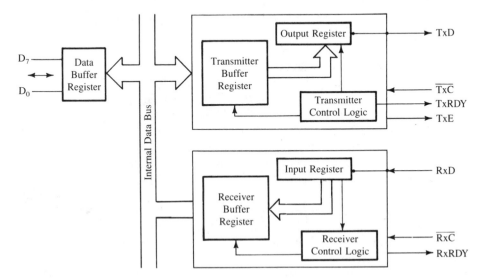

FIGURE 16.15
The 8251A: Expanded Block Diagram of Transmitter and Receiver Sections

☐ **TxRDY — Transmitter Ready:** This is an output signal. When it is high, it indicates that the buffer register is empty and the USART is ready to accept a byte. It can be used either to interrupt the MPU or to indicate the status. This signal is reset when a data byte is loaded into the buffer.

☐ **TxE — Transmitter Empty:** This is an output signal. Logic 1 on this line indicates that the output register is empty. This signal is reset when a byte is transferred from the buffer to the output register.

RECEIVER SECTION

The receiver accepts serial data on the RxD line from a peripheral and converts them into parallel data. The section has two registers: the receiver input register and the buffer register (Figure 16.15).

When the RxD line goes low, the control logic assumes it is a START bit, waits for half a bit time, and samples the line again. If the line is still low, the input register accepts the following bits, forms a character, and loads it into the buffer register. Subsequently, the parallel byte is transferred to the MPU when requested. In the asynchronous mode, two input signals and one output signal are necessary, as described below.

☐ **RxD — Receive Data:** Bits are received serially on this line and converted into a parallel byte in the receiver input register.

☐ **$\overline{RxC}$ — Receiver Clock:** This is a clock signal that controls the rate at which bits are received by the USART. In the asynchronous mode, the clock can be set to 1, 16, or 64 times the baud.

☐ **RxRDY — Receiver Ready:** This is an output signal. It goes high when the USART has a character in the buffer register and is ready to transfer it to the MPU. This line can be used either to indicate the status or to interrupt the MPU.

INITIALIZING THE 8251A

To implement serial communication, the MPU must inform the 8251A of all details such as mode, baud, stop bits, parity, etc. Therefore, prior to data transfer, a set of control words must be loaded into the 16-bit control register of the 8251A. In addition, the MPU must check the readiness of a peripheral by reading the status register. The control words are divided into two formats: mode words and command words. The mode word specifies the general characteristics of operation (such as baud, parity, number of stop bits), the command word enables data transmission and/or reception, and the status word provides the information concerning register status and transmission errors. Figure 16.16 shows the definitions of these words.

To initialize the 8251A in the asynchronous mode, a certain sequence of control words must be followed. After a Reset operation (system Reset or through instruction), a mode word must be written in the control register followed by a command word. Any control word written into the control register immediately after a mode word will be interpreted as a command word, that means a command word can be changed anytime during the operation. However, the 8251A should be reset prior to writing a new mode word, and it can be reset by using the Internal Reset bit (D_6) in the command word.

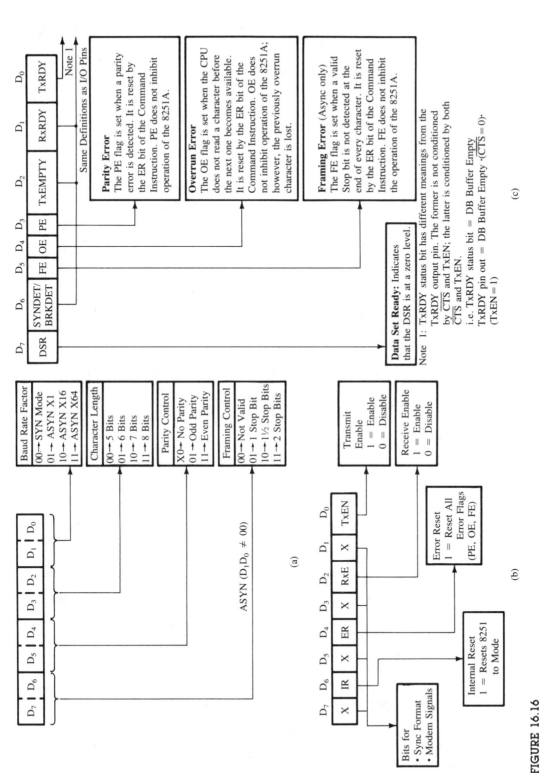

FIGURE 16.16

Mode Word Format (a), Command Word Format (b), and Status Word Format (c)

SOURCE: A and C: Intel Corporation, *Peripheral Design Handbook* (Santa Clara, Calif.: Author, 1981), pp. 2-249 and 1-174.

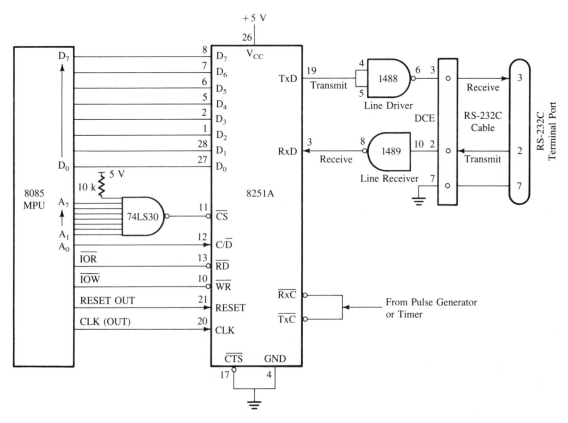

FIGURE 16.17
Schematic of Interfacing a RS-232 Terminal with an 8085 System Using the 8251A

16.42   Illustration: Interfacing a RS-232 Terminal Using the 8251A

PROBLEM STATEMENT

1. Identify the port addresses of the control register, the status register, and the data register in Figure 16.17.

2. Explain the RS-232 signals and the operations of the line driver (MC 1488) and the line receiver (MC 1489) shown in Figure 16.17.

3. Specify the initialization instructions and the status word to transmit characters with the following parameters if the transmitter clock frequency (TxC) is 153.6 kHz.

☐ Asynchronous mode with 9600 baud
☐ Character length = seven bits and two stop bits
☐ No parity check

4. Write instructions to initialize the 8251A, to read the status word, and set up a loop until the transmitter (TxRDY) is ready.

1. PORT ADDRESSES

a. The Chip Select line of the 8251 is enabled when the address lines A_7 through A_1 are at logic 1. To select the control register or the status register, the C/$\overline{D}$ line should be high, which means that address line A_0 should be 1. Therefore, the port address of the control register and the status register = FFH.

   The control register is an output port and the status register is an input port; they are identified by $\overline{WR}$ and $\overline{RD}$ signals, even if their port addresses are the same.

b. The data register is selected when the C/$\overline{D}$ line goes low; thus, A_0 should be low. The port address of the data register = FEH. The register is bidirectional, and the same address is used to receive or transmit data. The input and output functions are identified by $\overline{RD}$ and $\overline{WR}$ signals.

2. RS-232C SIGNALS, LINE DRIVERS AND LINE RECEIVERS

Figure 16.17 shows that three RS-232 signals — TxD, RxD, and Ground — are being used for serial communication between the CRT terminal and the 8085 system. The terminal transmits data on pin 2 and receives on pin 3; on the other hand, the 8085 system receives on pin 2 and transmits on pin 3 using the 8251A. Therefore, the terminal is connected as the DTE and the system plays the role of the DCE; the 8251A is part of the 8085 system.

   Data transmitted over the TxD line (pin 19 of the 8251A), are at the TTL logic level. These bits are converted to RS-232 voltage levels and negative logic by line driver MC 1488. The line driver converts logic 1 to -10 V and logic 0 to $+10$ V (approximately). The output voltage levels of the line driver are decided primarily by its power supply voltages.

   Data received by the 8251A over the RxD line (pin 3) should be at the TTL logic level. Therefore, the RS-232 signals at pin 2 of the connector are converted to the positive TTL logic level by line receiver MC 1489.

3. INITIALIZATION

The control words necessary for the given specifications are as follows:

Mode Word Refer to Figure 16.16(a)

D_7	D_6	D_5	D_4	D_3	D_2	D_1	D_0	
1	1	0	0	1	0	1	0	= CAH

Two STOP Bits	No Parity	7-Bit Character	Baud
			= $\overline{TxC}/16$
			= 153.6 k/16
			= 9600

In a mode word, bits D_1 and D_0 can specify a baud factor that divides the clock frequency (TxC) to provide three different transmission rates. In this illustration, TxC is sixteen times the specified baud.

Command Word Refer to Figure 16.16(b)

D_7	D_6	D_5	D_4	D_3	D_2	D_1	D_0	
X	0	X	1	X	X	X	1	= 11H

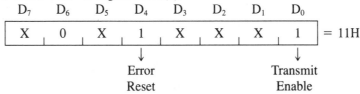

Error   Transmit
Reset   Enable

In this command word, bit D_0 enables the transmitter, bit D_4 ignores any errors, and bit D_6 prevents reset of the 8251A; all other bits are don't care. In this illustration, bit D_4 also can assume don't care logic level.

Status Word Refer to Figure 16.16(c)

D_7	D_6	D_5	D_4	D_3	D_2	D_1	D_0	
X	X	X	X	X	X	X	1	= 01H

Transmitter
Ready

The MPU should check bit D_0 before transferring a character to the 8251A; it indicates the status of the pin TxRDY. When a byte is transferred from the transmitter buffer to the output register (see Figure 16.15 for the block diagram), bit D_0 is set to 1, and it is reset when the MPU loads the next byte in the buffer. Bit D_2 (TxEMPTY) indicates the status of the output register; this bit usually is not used except in applications such as half duplex mode.

4. INITIALIZATION INSTRUCTIONS

```
SETUP:     MVI A, CAH      ;Load the mode word
           OUT FFH         ;Write mode word in control register
           MVI A, 11H      ;Load the command word to enable transmitter
           OUT FFH         ;Enable the transmitter
STATUS:    IN   FFH        ;Read status register
           ANI 01H         ;Mask all bits except D0
           JZ   STATUS     ;If D0 = 0, the transmitter buffer is full; go back
                             and wait
```

Figure 16.18 shows the contents of various registers after the initialization. Mode word CAH and command word 11H are loaded in the control register by the OUT FFH instructions. The MPU checks the transmitter status by reading the status register and examining bit D_0 (Transmitter Ready).

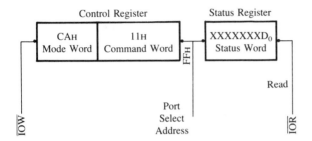

FIGURE 16.18
Control Register Contents After Initialization

When a character is transferred from the buffer register to the output (parallel-to-serial) register, bit D_0 is set to 1, indicating to the MPU that the transmitter is ready to accept the next character.

16.43 Illustration: Data Transmission to a CRT Terminal Using the 8251A in the Status Check Mode

PROBLEM STATEMENT

Write a program including the initialization of the USART—the 8251A—to transmit a message from an 8085/8080A single-board microcomputer to a CRT terminal (Figure 16.17). The requirements are as follows:

1. A message is stored as ASCII characters (without parity) in memory locations starting at XX70H.
2. The message specifies the number of characters to be transmitted as the first byte (excluding the first byte) and concludes with the characters for the Carriage Return and the Line Feed.
3. The initialization instructions are the same as in the previous illustration (Figure 16.17).
4. The program should check status before it transmits a character.

PROGRAM

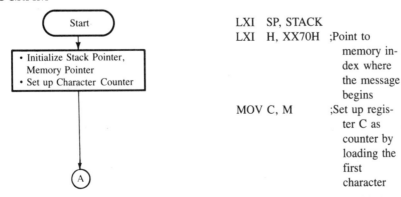

```
LXI  SP, STACK
LXI  H, XX70H   ;Point to
                 memory in-
                 dex where
                 the message
                 begins
MOV  C, M        ;Set up regis-
                 ter C as
                 counter by
                 loading the
                 first
                 character
```

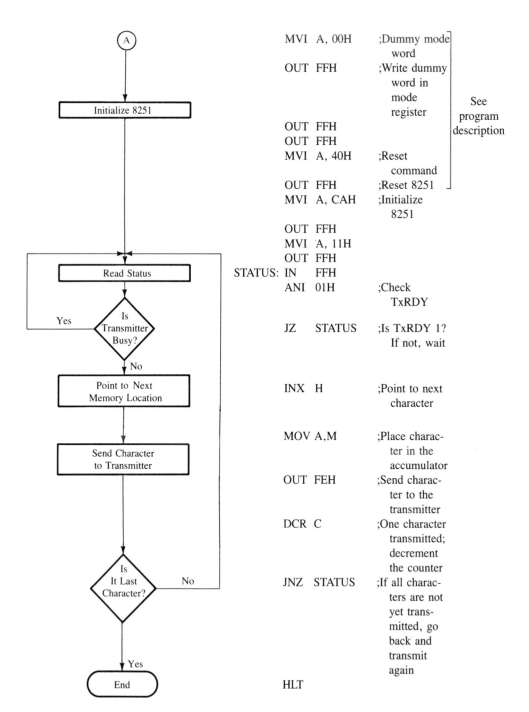

FIGURE 16.19
Flowchart for Transmitting Message from
Single-Board Microcomputer Using the 8251A

```
;Message — HELLO
XX70    08      ;Number of characters to follow
   71   48      ;Letter H
   72   45      ;Letter E
   73   4C      ;Letter L
   74   4C      ;Letter L
   75   4F      ;Letter O
   76   21      ;Exclamation
   77   0D      ;Carriage Return
   78   0A      ;Line Feed
```

PROGRAM DESCRIPTION

According to the problem statement, the first character of the message specifies the number of characters to be transmitted. Therefore, the instruction MOV C,M loads the first character (in this case 08H) in register C and sets that register as the counter.

Before the initialization of the 8251A, the dummy mode word and the reset command are sent to the control register. Initially, the control register may have any random command; therefore, it is a good practice to reset the 8251. However, it expects the first instruction as a mode word followed by a command word. Therefore, the reset command is sent after sending three dummy mode words which are recommended to avoid problems when it is turned on.

16.44   Illustration: Data Reception from a Keyboard Using the 8251A in the Interrupt Mode

PROBLEM STATEMENT

Design an interfacing circuit using the 8251A to receive serial data from an ASCII keyboard. When a key is pressed, the 8085 MPU should be interrupted (Figure 16.20).

PROBLEM ANALYSIS

Figure 16.20(a) shows a schematic of the 8251A connected as memory-mapped I/O to receive serial data from a keyboard. When a key is pressed, the receiver section receives serial data, forms a character, and transfers a parallel byte to the buffer register. At this point, the output line RxRDY goes high and interrupts the MPU. The service routine as shown in the flowchart in Figure 16.20(b) transfers the character from the receiver buffer section to the MPU and returns to the main program.

SUMMARY

1. In serial I/O communication, a word is transmitted one bit at a time over a single line by converting a parallel word into a stream of serial bits. On the other hand, a word is received by converting a stream of bits into a parallel word.

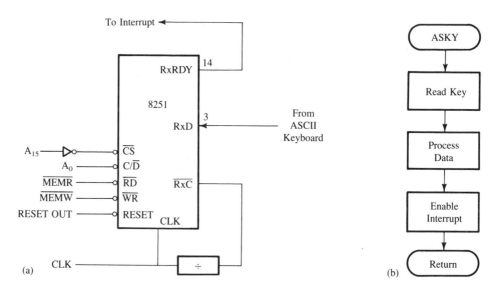

FIGURE 16.20
Interfacing Keyboard Using the 8251A (a) and the Flowchart of Keyboard Interrupt Service Routine (b)

2. Serial data communication can be either synchronous or asynchronous. The synchronous mode is used for high speed and the asynchronous mode is used for low speed data communication.

3. The MPU identifies a serial peripheral through a decoded address and an appropriate control signal. Data transfer occurs under various conditions — unconditional, status check, and interrupt — depending upon logic design.

4. In software-controlled serial transmission, the MPU converts a parallel word into serial bits by using time delays and transmits bits over one data line of an output port.

5. In software-controlled serial reception, the MPU converts a serial word into a parallel word by using time delays and receives bits over one data line.

6. In the 8085, two specially designed 1-bit ports are provided for serial I/O: SOD and SID. Data transfer is controlled through two instructions: SIM and RIM.

7. The 8251 is a programmable serial I/O chip known as USART, which can perform all the functions of serial I/O.

DEFINITION OF TERMS

☐ ASCII (American Standard Code for Information). A 7-bit alphanumeric code commonly used in computers.

☐ EBCDIC (Extended Binary Coded Decimal Interchange Code). An 8-bit alphanumeric code used primarily in IBM computers.

☐ Asynchronous Serial Data Transmission. In this format, the transmitter is not synchronized with the receiver by the same master clock. A transmitted character includes information about the starting and ending of the character.

☐ Synchronous Serial Data Transmission. In this format, the transmitter is synchronized with the receiver on the same frequency.

☐ Simplex Transmission. One-way data communication.

☐ Duplex Transmission. Two-way data communication. Full duplex is simultaneous in both directions and half duplex is one direction at a time.

☐ Baud (Rate). The number of signal changes per second. In serial I/O, it is equal to bits per second, the rate of data transmission.

☐ Current Loop. The transmission of serial data bits as current signals.

☐ RS-232C. A data communications standard that defines voltage signals in reference to data terminal equipment and data communication equipment.

☐ SID (Serial Input Data Line). A specially designed 1-bit input port in the 8085 to receive serial data.

☐ SOD (Serial Output Data). A specially designed 1-bit output port in the 8085 to transmit serial data.

☐ USART (Universal Synchronous/Asynchronous Receiver/Transmitter). A programmable chip designed for synchronous/asynchronous serial data communication.

ASSIGNMENTS

1. Check whether the following statements are true or false.
   a. Serial data communication cannot be implemented using the memory-mapped I/O technique. (T/F)
   b. ASCII is an 8-bit binary code that represents 256 different characters. (T/F)
   c. In the synchronous serial I/O format, all eight bits are sent simultaneously. (T/F)
   d. In the half duplex transmission mode, data flow is bidirectional between the MPU and a serial peripheral, but not simultaneously. (T/F)
   e. In serial transmission from the MPU to a peripheral, bit D_0 is transmitted first after the START bit. (T/F)
   f. In serial reception from a peripheral to the MPU, bit D_7 of a character is received first after the START bit. (T/F)
   g. In a system with the odd parity check, the letter A is transmitted with the code C1H. (T/F)
   h. In a system with the even parity check, the letter M is transmitted with the code 4CH. (T/F)
   i. The delay between the successive bits for 9600 baud rate is approximately 0.1 ms. (T/F)
   j. RS-232C is a 25-pin serial I/O voltage standard compatible with TTL logic. (T/F)

k. To enable the 8085 serial output data line (SOD), bits D_7 and D_6 of the accumulator should be at logic 1. (T/F)

l. The instruction RIM is equivalent to the instruction IN with one input data line (D_7). (T/F)

m. The 8085 SID and SOD lines receive and transmit characters starting from bit D_7 after the START bit. (T/F)

2. Write delay loops for BITTIME and half BITTIME for 1200 baud if the system frequency is 3 MHz.

3. Write a program to transmit letters A–Z from the MPU to the TTY in Figure 16.6.

4. Write a subroutine to receive an ASCII character from the terminal to the 8085 system (Figure 16.17) and store the ASCII code in the input buffer INBUF at location 2070H.

5. Write a program to receive ASCII characters from the terminal to the 8085 system (Figure 16.17) and to transmit the same characters back to the terminal to display on the CRT.

6. In Figure 16.20, specify the port addresses of the control register and the data register.

7. Specify the control word and the command word for data communication having the following specifications (Figure 16.20):

   a. asynchronous mode

   b. 1200 baud ($\overline{TxC} = \overline{RxC}$ = 76.8 kHz)

   c. 8-bit character

   d. even parity

   e. one STOP bit

8. In Figure 16.20, instruction LDA FFFFH loads 05H in the accumulator of the MPU. Explain the meaning of the accumulator contents.

9. Write instructions to check the parity error (Figure 16.20). If an error occurs, write a command word to disable the receiver, reset the error, and call the ERROR routine.

10. Write an interrupt service routine for the RST 6.5 interrupt in Figure 16.20 to receive a character from the keyboard and store the character in memory location INBUF.

EXPERIMENTAL ASSIGNMENTS

1. **a.** Connect the circuit as shown in Figure 16.6 to transmit data from a single-board microcomputer to a teletype or modify the circuit in Figure 16.6 to use the SOD line of the SDK-85 system.

   b. Write the subroutine BITTIME for a 9.1 ms delay.

    c. Write a program to transmit the message: "Welcome Home." Store the ASCII characters for the message in memory and use the table look-up technique to transmit the message.

2. a. Connect the circuit as shown in Figure 16.8 to receive data from TTY or modify the circuit in Figure 16.8 to use the SID line of the SDK-85 system.

    b. Write the subroutine HAFBIT for a 4.05 ms delay.

    c. Write a program to receive two numbers in ASCII, convert the numbers in decimal digits, and store them in memory.

3. a. Connect the circuit shown in Figure 16.17 to receive and transmit ASCII characters.

    b. Connect the clock with 4.8 kHz frequency to $\overline{\text{RxC}}$ and $\overline{\text{TxC}}$ pins of the 8251A. (Use a pulse generator or set up the 8155 timer for 4.8 kHz.)

    c. Write initialization instructions to set up the 8251A for the asynchronous mode, 300 baud, and 7-bit character with no parity.

    d. Write a program to receive a character from the terminal and echo the character back to the terminal for display. Use the status check technique.

Microprocessor Applications

Microcomputer systems based on the 8085/8080A microprocessor were introduced at the beginning of the book, an overview of the instruction set was given in Chapter 4, and Chapters 5 through 9 were devoted to programming techniques. Various types of I/O data transfer and interfacing concepts were later discussed in detail in Chapters 11 through 16. This chapter is concerned with integrating or synthesizing all the concepts of the microprocessor architecture, software, and interfacing discussed previously, by designing a microprocessor system.

Designing a single-board microcomputer is the best possible choice, since it can incorporate all the important concepts related to the microprocessor. Furthermore, it allows expansion to include various types of interfacing. An interfacing circuit to set up bidirectional communication using the 8255A is demonstrated as an example of further expansion.

OBJECTIVES

☐ Design a single-board microcomputer based on the 8085 MPU and general purpose peripherals.
☐ Write the necessary software to enable a user to execute programs on the system.

☐ List the primary features of the in-circuit emulator and explain its applications in troubleshooting microprocessor based systems.
☐ Design an interfacing circuit, and write the necessary software to set up communication between two microcomputers, using the 8255A in the bidirectional mode.

17.1 DESIGNING A MICROCOMPUTER SYSTEM

PROJECT STATEMENT

Design a single-board microcomputer to meet the following specifications:

- ☐ Input: Hex keyboard with a minimum of 20 keys
- ☐ Output: Six seven-segment LEDs to display memory address and data
       One LED port to display binary data
- ☐ Memory: 2K of EPROM — 2716 (2048 × 8)
       1K of R/W Static Memory — 2114 (1024 × 4)
- ☐ Microprocessor: 8085A
- ☐ System Frequency: 1 MHz
- ☐ Peripheral Devices: 8255A PPI, bus drivers, 3-to-8 decoders, and Hex decoder/drivers
       for display

The system should allow a user to enter and execute programs, and the buses should have enough driving capacity to interface with additional peripherals. As machine codes are entered, the memory address and data should be displayed by seven-segment LEDs. The last two keys pressed should also be displayed at the binary port. Seven-segment LEDs and the binary port also should be available as output ports to display the results when programs are executed.

17.11 Project Analysis

In analyzing the specifications of a microprocessor-based product it is essential to consider both hardware and software, simultaneously. Both are interrelated, and each will have an impact on the other. The functions of the single-board microcomputer according to the specifications given above can be classified into three categories:

1. Check the keyboard for data or functions.
2. Display memory address, data, and results.
3. Execute programs.

KEYBOARD

The keyboard in this design is an input port with keys arranged in the matrix format. (Interfacing a matrix keyboard was discussed in Chapter 11.) The keyboard program should wait in a loop for a key to be pressed. When a key is pressed, the program should provide a binary equivalent of the key.

The keys are divided into two groups: one group is for Hex digits from 0 to F and the second is concerned with various functions. The number of keys used to recognize a memory address and the technique used to display it have a major impact on software design. Basically, there are two approaches to recognizing and displaying Hex keys. One approach is to begin with Hex keys, identify them as memory or data, and then specify a function. The MMD1 Microdesigner system designed by E & L Instruments uses this approach with two separate keys for identifying high-order and low-order memory addresses. In the second approach, a function is specified first and then data are accepted. The Intel SDK-85 system uses the second approach.

In this project's design, the first approach will be used to simplify the software and program execution.

DISPLAY

The display consists of four seven-segment LEDs for memory address, two seven-segment LEDs for data, and one LED port for displaying binary data. These are also to be used as display for results after executing a program. Therefore, these displays can be designed as output ports. Furthermore, this is not a scanned display, so the monitor program can simply output binary data to the ports and wait for the next key to be pressed. In the seven-segment LED ports, binary data will be converted into seven-segment code using decoder drivers.

EXECUTE

This is the simplest function of the three and can be performed with one instruction: PCHL. The user provides the memory address where the program is stored and presses the *Execute* key. Assuming the memory address is stored in HL registers, instruction PCHL simply loads the program counter with the specified memory address, and the program control is transferred from the monitor program to the user's program.

The above functions are divided into two categories, hardware design and software design, which are discussed in detail in the following sections.

17.12 Hardware Design

This single-board microcomputer is designed around the 8085A microprocessor; however, all other peripheral components are general purpose devices. Devices that are specially designed to work with the 8085 microprocessor (such as the 8155 R/W memory with I/O or the 8755 EPROM with I/O) are excluded from the design to keep the process as general as possible.

The hardware section is divided into five subsystems as follows (Figure 17.1):

1. 8085-based MPU and its bus architecture
2. Memory (R/W Memory and EPROM)
3. Input/Output (keyboard and displays)
4. Frequency and power requirements
5. Externally triggered signals (Reset, Interrupts, etc.)

The block diagram of the system (Figure 17.1) shows that the first three subsystems are interconnected through the bus architecture and the last two are connected directly to the MPU. These subsystems are described below.

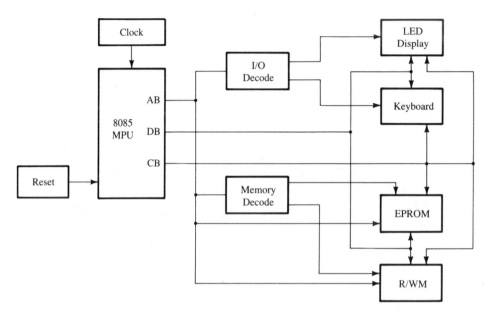

FIGURE 17.1
Block Diagram of a Single-Board Microcomputer

THE 8085 MPU AND ITS BUS ARCHITECTURE

This single-board microcomputer is expected to be used for general purpose interfacing; therefore, the buses need more driving capacity than that of the 8085 microprocessor. Similarly, peripherals specially designed to be compatible with the 8085 are not used in this design problem; therefore, the low-order address bus must be demultiplexed, and I/O and memory-related control signals must be generated.

Address Bus Figure 17.2 shows the 74LS244, an octal bus driver used with the high-order address bus to increase its driving capacity. Typically, the 8085 buses can source 400 μA (I_{OH} = −400 μA) and sink 2 mA (I_{OL} = 2 mA) of current; they can drive one TTL logic load. The 74LS244 driver is capable of sourcing 15 mA and sinking 24 mA of current.

The low-order address bus is demultiplexed by using the ALE signal (Address Latch Enable) and the 8212 as a latch. At the beginning of each machine cycle, ALE goes high during T_1 (see Chapter 3, Figure 3.3), and this signal is connected to the DS_2 line to enable the 8212. As ALE goes low, the address on bus AD_7–AD_0 is latched, and the eight output lines of the 8212 serve as the low-order address bus (A_7–A_0). The address on the output of the 8212 remains latched until the next ALE signal. In addition to demultiplexing the address bus, the 8212 can serve as a bus driver; it can source 1 mA and sink 15 mA of current.

Data Bus Figure 17.2 shows the 74LS245 as an 8-bit bidirectional bus driver to increase the driving capacity of the data bus. The 74LS245 can sink 24 mA and source 15 mA of

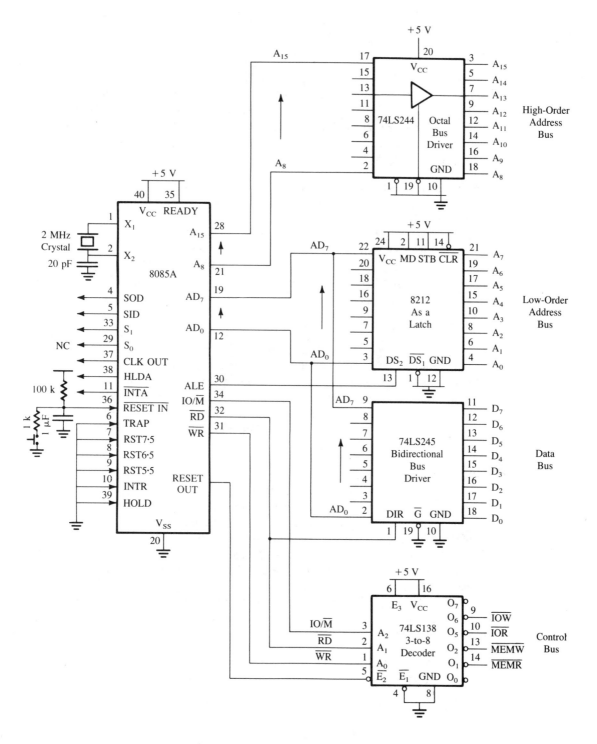

FIGURE 17.2
Schematic of the 8085 MPU with Demultiplex Address Bus and Control Signals

current. The 74LS245 has eight bidirectional data lines; the direction of the data flow is determined by the direction control line (DIR). Figure 17.2 shows that the bus driver is enabled by grounding the enable signal ($\overline{G}$). The direction of the data flow is determined by connecting the $\overline{RD}$ signal from the MPU to the DIR signal. When the MPU is writing to peripherals, the $\overline{RD}$ is high and data flow from the MPU to peripherals. When it is reading from peripherals, the $\overline{RD}$ is low and data flow towards the MPU.

Control Bus   The 8085 generates three signals: IO/$\overline{M}$ (I/O or memory), $\overline{RD}$ (Read), and $\overline{WR}$ (Write). The IO/$\overline{M}$ signal differentiates between I/O and memory functions. When IO/$\overline{M}$ is high, it is an I/O-related function; when IO/$\overline{M}$ is low, it is a memory-related function. Therefore, by combining IO/$\overline{M}$ with $\overline{RD}$ and $\overline{WR}$ signals, appropriate control signals can be generated.

Figure 17.2 shows that three signals — IO/$\overline{M}$, $\overline{RD}$, and $\overline{WR}$ — are used as inputs to the 74LS138 3-to-8 decoder to generate four control signals — $\overline{IOR}$, $\overline{IOW}$, $\overline{MEMR}$, and $\overline{MEMW}$. These signals can be used for interfacing with any peripherals.

MEMORY DESIGN

This single-board microcomputer includes two types of memory: 2K of EPROM and 1K of R/W memory. The monitor program of the system is stored in the EPROM. The monitor program should begin at memory address 0000H because the program counter is cleared to that address whenever the system is reset. Therefore, the memory map of EPROM with 2K bytes of memory should be placed in the range from 0000H to 07FFH as shown in Figure 17.3. However, there are no such restrictions for the memory map of R/W memory; it can be mapped anywhere from 0800H to FFFFH in this system.

EPROM Memory   Figure 17.3 shows the design of EPROM using the 2716 (2048 × 8) and the 74LS138 (3-to-8 decoder). The eleven address lines (A_{10}–A_0) of the MPU from the bus drivers are connected directly to pins A_{10} to A_0 of the 2716 to decode 2048 memory locations. The rest of the address lines (A_{15}–A_{11}) are decoded by the 74LS138. Output line O_0 of the decoder is used for the Chip Enable ($\overline{CE}$) line of the memory chip. To enable the memory chip, address lines A_{15} to A_{11} should be at logic 0, because A_{15} and A_{14} are used to enable line $\overline{E_1}$ (active low) of the decoder, and lines A_{13}, A_{12}, and A_{11} are inputs to the decoder. Line $\overline{E_2}$ is enabled either by $\overline{MEMR}$ or $\overline{MEMW}$; this is an anti-bus-contention circuit (see Chapter 11, section 11.51). By combining address lines A_{10} to A_0 with the decoding lines, the memory map of EPROM will range from 0000H to 07FFH, as shown below.

A_{15}	A_{14}	A_{13}	A_{12}	A_{11}	A_{10}		A_0	**Address**			
0	0	0	0	0	0	————	0	0	0	0	0
0	0	0	0	0	1	————	1	0	7	F	F

Decoder enable active low   Decoder input   Lines to decode 2048 memory registers

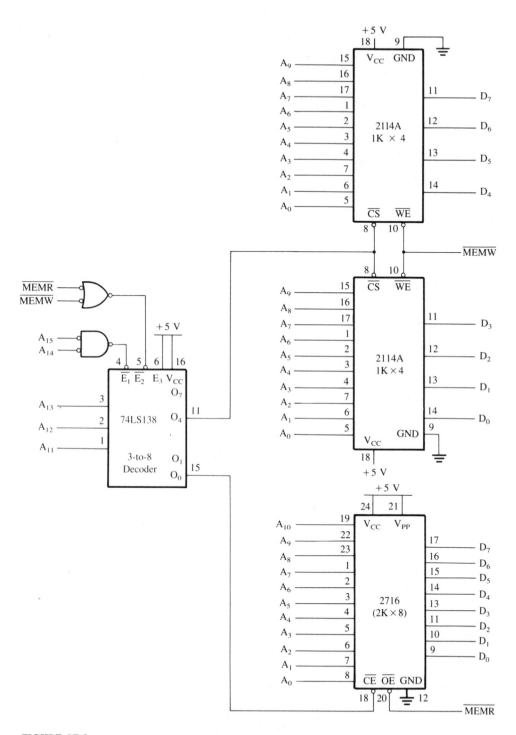

FIGURE 17.3
Schematic of Memory Design

R/W Memory   The system R/W memory (1K bytes) is designed with 2114 memory chips, which are organized 1024 × 4 bits. Figure 17.3 shows two 2114s in parallel to make up 1024 bytes of memory. The ten address lines, A_9 to A_0, from the MPU are connected to the ten address pins, A_9 to A_0, of the memory chips to decode the 1024 memory locations. The Chip Select ($\overline{CS}$) logic is generated from the same decoder as for EPROM. When output line O_4 of the decoder goes low, these memory chips are enabled; thus, the memory map of this R/W memory ranges from 2000H to 23FFH, as shown below.

A_{15}	A_{14}	A_{13}	A_{12}	A_{11}	A_{10}	A_9	——————	A_0	**Address**
0	0	1	0	0	X	0	——————	0	2000H
0	0	1	0	0	X	1	——————	1	23FFH

However, this memory will occupy four more pages of memory space because address line A_{10} is in the don't care state (see assignment 2 at the end of this chapter).

INPUT/OUTPUT (I/Os)

The system includes a matrix keyboard as an input, and six seven-segment LEDs and eight simple LEDs as outputs. The matrix keyboard requires two ports, one input port and one output port. Similarly, since this is not a scanned display, the six seven-segment LEDs require three output ports and the other eight LEDs need an additional port (Figure 17.4).

Keyboard   The matrix keyboard has twenty keys arranged in 4 × 5 format and inter-faced with the MPU through the 8255A programmable peripheral (Figure 17.4). Port A of the 8255A is an output port for the rows and port B is an input port for the columns. Port C is not being used. The 8255A is enabled by using output line O_0 of the 3-to-8 decoder and two address lines, A_1 and A_0. The port addresses of the 8255A are as follows:

A_7	A_6	A_5	A_4	A_3	A_2	A_1	A_0			
1	0	0	0	0	0	0	0	=	80H	Port A
						0	1	=	81	Port B
						1	0	=	82	Port C
						1	1	=	83	Control Register

Decoder enable lines	Decoder inputs

LED Displays   The six seven-segment LEDs are interfaced with the MPU using the 8255A and the 9370 Hex decoder drivers. The 9370 has four data lines as binary input. This input is decoded internally, and the corresponding seven-segment code is placed on the output lines. To display memory address and data requires 24 lines (all three ports) of the 8255A and 6 decoders. Figure 17.4 shows only two LEDs connected to port A; the other four LEDs are connected to ports B and C (not shown in figure). The decode logic of the 8255A is similar to that of the keyboard; the output line of the 3-to-8 decoder determines the decode logic of the 8255A. The addresses of the 8255A ports are as follows:

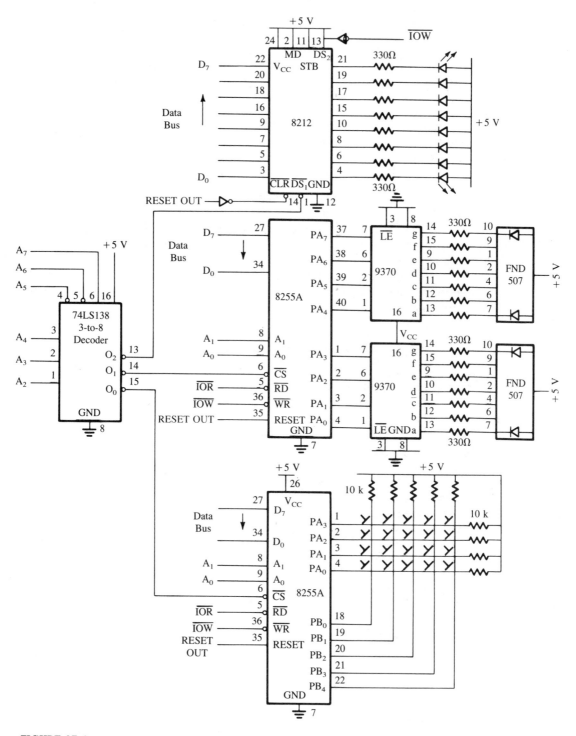

FIGURE 17.4

Schematic of Keyboard and Display

∗ NOTE: The connections to ports PB and PC are identical to port PA (therefore, they are not shown here).

A_7	A_6	A_5	A_4	A_3	A_2	A_1	A_0			
1	0	0	0	0	1	0	0	=	84H	Port A
						0	1	=	85H	Port B
						1	0	=	86H	Port C
						1	1	=	87H	Control Register

Decoder enable lines

Decoder inputs

Similarly, the 8212 LED port is enabled by output line O_2 of the decoder. However, in this port address lines A_1 and A_0 are in the don't care state. Assuming these lines are at logic 0, the LED port address is 88H. It is important to note the following point about this output port. The 8212 is capable of sinking the necessary current for the LEDs (approximately 10 to 15 mA); however, the 8212 cannot source sufficient current if the LEDs are connected by grounding their cathodes. Furthermore, these LEDs cannot be driven by the output of the 8255A without an additional driver because the 8255A can sink current around 3 mA.

FREQUENCY AND POWER REQUIREMENTS

The 8085A can operate with a maximum clock frequency of 3 MHz. To obtain 3 MHz operating frequency, the clock logic should be driven by double the desired frequency (6 MHz). The 8085 has two clock inputs: X_1 and X_2 at pins 1 and 2. These inputs can be driven with a crystal, an LC tuned circuit, or an RC network.

Figure 17.5(a) shows a 2 MHz crystal with 20 pF capacitor to drive the clock inputs. This input frequency is divided in half internally, and the system will run on 1 MHz clock frequency. The capacitor is required to assure oscillator start-up at the correct frequency. Figure 17.5(b) shows an alternative method of providing a clock input using an RC network.

The 8085 and other components used in this system require one power supply with +5 V. The current requirement of the power supply is determined primarily by the display

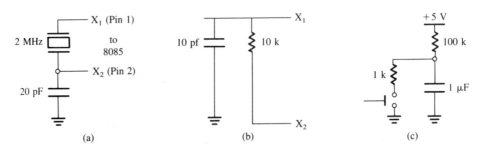

(a)   (b)   (c)

FIGURE 17.5
Clock and Reset Circuits: Clock Circuit with Crystal (a), RC Clock Circuit (b), and Reset Circuit (c)

load and the peripherals of the system; the MPU and memory components of the system require less than 400 mA.

EXTERNAL TRIGGER SIGNALS

As discussed in Chapter 2, the 8085 has provision for four external input signals: Reset, Interrupt, Ready, and Hold. Of these signals, the RESET is used in this system, and the others are disabled.

Reset The $\overline{\text{RESET IN}}$ is an active low signal used to reset the system. When this pin goes low, the program counter is set to 0, the Interrupt Enable and HLDA flip-flops are reset, and all buses are placed in tri-state. The reset circuit shown in Figure 17.5(c) is an RC network with a sufficiently long time constant. When the *Reset* key is pushed, the $\overline{\text{RESET IN}}$ goes low and slowly rises to +5 V, providing sufficient time for the MPU to reset the system.

Interrupts The 8085 has five interrupt signals, all of them active high. In this system, interrupts are not used; therefore, they need to be grounded as shown in the circuit. Otherwise, the floating interrupt pins can cause the system to malfunction. To allow the use of interrupt signals for further expansion of the system, the pins can be grounded using switches.

HOLD This is an active high signal used in the DMA. This signal is also grounded in this system.

READY When this signal is high, it indicates that the memory or peripheral is ready to send or receive data. When READY goes low, the MPU enters the Wait state until READY goes high, then the MPU completes the Read or Write cycle. This signal is used primarily to synchronize slow peripherals with the MPU. To prevent the MPU from entering the Wait state, this pin is tied high.

A complete single-board microcomputer can be built from Figures 17.2, 17.3, and 17.4. The next step is to write a monitor program that can perform the functions specified in the design problem.

17.13 Software Design

In microprocessor-based systems, software design is a more demanding task than hardware design. Industrial experience suggests that 70 percent of the total design effort is devoted to writing and troubleshooting software. Software is not designed in isolation from nor after the completion of hardware design—these are concurrent processes.

The most puzzling aspect of software design is where to begin and how to synthesize all the functions in a single program. The place to begin is with a list of the functions to be performed. In the project analysis section, three functions are listed: check keyboard, display, and execute. Next check the hardware requirements. Examination of the hardware design reveals the following clues:

1. The program should begin at location 0000H.
2. Initial memory locations should be reserved for interrupt restarts.
3. Programmable peripherals need initialization instructions.
4. As the system is turned on, the first user memory location and its contents should be displayed.
5. Two keys are available to identify the high-order and low-order memory address.

By combining the functions to be performed and the clues obtained from hardware design, the task can be divided into the following steps:

1. Initialize programmable peripherals.
2. Display memory address and data.
3. Check for a key and obtain its binary code.
4. Determine whether it is a Hex key or a function key.
5. If it is a Hex key, determine whether it is a data byte or memory address.
6. If it is a function key, identify and perform its function.

The first two steps are simple. The initialization is determined by peripheral devices and their decode logic (discussed in the previous section). The display involves loading the accumulator with the appropriate data bytes and sending them out to three output ports.

The third step, checking a key of a matrix keyboard, is more challenging. However, this task has already been completed in Chapter 11. The keyboard subroutine given in Chapter 11 (Section 11.33, Figure 11.25) can be used here with a few minor modifications. Assuming 20 keys are available on the keyboard, a sequential binary code from 00H to 13H can be assigned to account for all the keys. The first sixteen keys will be assigned to Hex data, and the remaining keys can be assigned to other functions.

The fourth step involves differentiating between a Hex key and a function key. After obtaining a key code in step 3, this is a simple task: if the binary code of a key pressed is larger than 00001111 (0FH), it is a function key. This can be determined by using the compare (CPI) instruction.

In step 5, whether a key is part of a memory address will be determined by two special keys reserved for high-order and low-order memory addresses.

The last step determines the function: either storing a data byte or executing a program. Storing data involves transferring a data byte to a specified memory location. Executing a program involves loading the program counter with the starting memory address of the program, using the instruction PCHL.

Now, the question is: Where does the program end? In reality, this program never stops until a user executes a program. The primary function of this program is to monitor the keyboard. Therefore, after checking and storing data, the program should go back to step 3 to check the next key. However, if the *Execute* key is pressed, the program exits from the keycheck loop and the control is transferred to the user program. The thinking process discussed in the above steps is represented in the flowcharts shown in Figures 17.6 and 17.7. The flowcharts show the sequence of steps and loops the program will follow to perform the functions specified in the project statement. Now, the next steps are to code

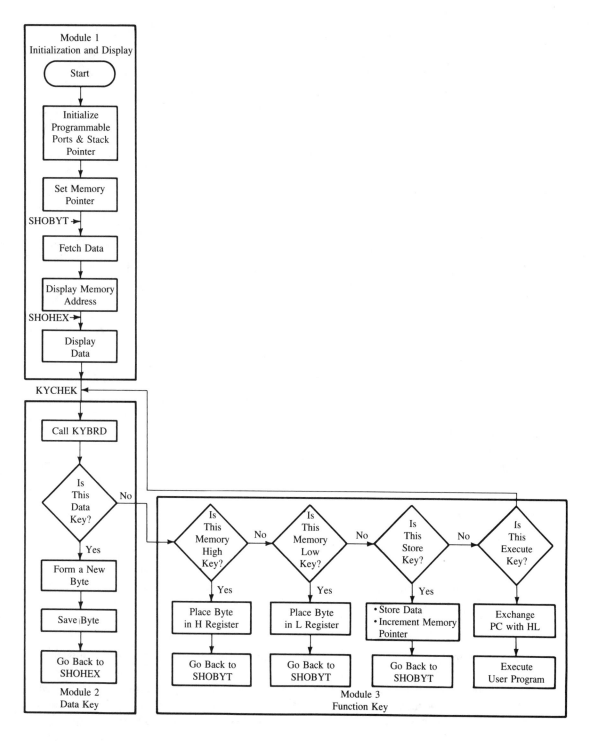

FIGURE 17.6
Flowchart of System Monitor Program

FIGURE 17.7
Flowchart of Module 4:
Keyboard Subroutine

Module 4
Keyboard Subroutine

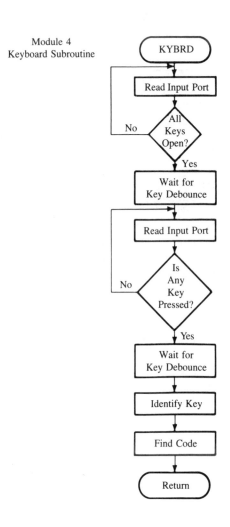

this program in 8085/8080A assembly language, and to test it on prototype hardware, using an in-circuit emulator (to be discussed later).

PROGRAM CODING

Assuming that program coding is to be performed by a team, the task must be broken down into small, manageable, and independent modules. It is not always possible to break logic flow into independent subroutine modules. However, the symbols or labels to be used by various members of the team, called **global symbols**, must be agreed upon by the team.

As shown in the flowchart, the coding task is divided into four modules.

☐ Module 1: Initialization and Display
☐ Module 2: Data (Hex) Key

☐ Module 3: Function Key
☐ Module 4: Keyboard Subroutine

Of the four, Modules 1 and 4 are logically independent. Modules 2 and 3 are logically interrelated, but are divided here arbitrarily for convenience. The symbols that might be used by different team members happen to fall in Module 1. Modules 2 and 3 require two entry points to return to some locations in Module 1. These are defined as global symbols:

1. SHOBYT: Transfer of data byte from memory to register B
2. SHOHEX: Data display

In addition to these global symbols, the output ports, function keys, starting memory address, and stack pointer must be either labelled or defined.

MODULE 1: INITIALIZATION AND DISPLAY

This module transfers the program execution from the reset location (0000H) to the starting location (0040H), leaving memory spaces for interrupt restarts. In this system, the memory space from 0000H to 0040H need not be left for RST locations because interrupts are not being used. However, these memory locations are left empty in case RST locations are needed to include interrupts. The module initializes the programmable ports and the stack location and displays the first user memory location (2000H) and its contents.

```
;Module 1: Initialization and Display
;Labels for this module are defined as follows:
STACK       EQU 2400H          ;This is one location beyond the last memory
                               ;address in R/W memory; the stack begins
                               ;at 23FFH
KEYWRD      EQU 8BH            ;Control word to initialize keyboard 8255:
                               ;Port A output, Port B input in Mode 0, Port C
                               ;is assumed input
PPIKEY      EQU 83H            ;Control register address of keyboard 8255
LEDWRD      EQU 80H            ;Control word to initialize display 8255: All
                               ;ports A, B, C are outputs
PPILED      EQU 87H            ;Control register address of display 8255
R/WM        EQU 2000H          ;Starting address of the user memory
OUTHI       EQU 86H            ;Port C of the Display 8255 is assigned for
                               ;high-order memory address
OUTLO       EQU 85H            ;Port B of the Display 8255 is assigned for
                               ;low-order memory address
OUTHEX      EQU 84H            ;Port A of the Display 8255 is assigned for
                               ;data
HIKY        EQU 10H            ;Key code for high-order memory address
LOKY        EQU 11H            ;Key code for low-order memory address
STORKY      EQU 12H            ;Key code for Store key
```

```
EXCTKY      EQU  13H              ;Key code for Execute key

            ORG  0000H
            JMP  START            ;Transfer program from 0000H to 0040H
            ORG  0040H
START:      LXI  SP,STACK         ;Initialize the stack
            MVI  A,KEYWRD         ;Load accumulator with control word for
                                  ;keyboard 8255 (PPI)
            OUT  PPIKEY           ;Initialize 8255 for keyboard
            MVI  A, LEDWRD        ;Load accumulator with control word for
                                  ;seven-segment LED 8255
            OUT  PPILED           ;Initialize 8255 for seven-segment LEDs
            LXI  H,R/WM           ;Point HL to first user memory location
SHOBYT:     MOV  B,M              ;Transfer byte from memory to B
                                  ;This is a global symbol, reentry point for
                                  ;Store key
            MOV  A,H              ;Transfer high-order memory address
            OUT  OUTHI            ;Display high-order memory address
            MOV  A,L
            OUT  OUTLO            ;Display low-order memory address
SHOHEX:     MOV  A,B              ;Get Hex data byte for display
            OUT  OUTHEX           ;Display Hex data
;Continue to Module 2 at location KYCHEK
```

MODULE 2: DATA (HEX) KEY

The module calls the keyboard subroutine and checks whether it is a data key. If it is a data key, the module forms a byte in register B. The user is expected to press two Hex data keys to enter a byte. However, the user might press more than two data keys in sequence, either to correct initial mistakes or just to see what happens when more keys are pressed. This module accounts for such modifications by rejecting the initial keys and preserving the code of the last two keys.

The module uses register B to form a byte. When the first key code is received from the keyboard subroutine, the four high-order bits from the previous data in register B are shifted out, the four low-order bits are shifted into the high-order position, and the newly arrived four bits are placed in the low-order position as shown below.

| Example 17.1 | Assume that register B contains 47H either as random data or as the previously stored byte. A programmer intends to enter 3E (MVI A) and pushes two keys, 3 and E, in that order. The program module will accept these keys as follows: |

Previous byte in B: (B) = 0 1 0 0   0 1 1 1 → 47H

After the first key: (B) = 0 1 1 1   0 0 1 1 → 73H
                                           New Key

After the second key: (B) = 0 0 1 1   1 1 1 0 → 3EH
                                        Next New Key

If more than two keys are pressed, only the codes of the last two keys will be held in the register, and this data byte will be stored if the user pushes the STORE key (to be explained in the mext module).

```
;Module 2:  Data (Hex) Key
KYCHEK:     CALL KYBRD      ;Check for a key
            CPI   HIKY       ;Check for a data key; is code less than
                            ;function key?
            JNC   MEMHI      ;If it is not a data key, jump to check whether it is
                            ;high-order memory address key
            MOV C,A          ;Save data key temporarily in register C
            MOV A,B          ;Get previous data byte
            RLC              ;Shift low-order nibble into MSB position
            RLC
            RLC
            RLC
            ANI   FOH        ;Eliminate low-order bits to make room for a new
                            ;key code
            ORA   C          ;Place new key code in accumulator
            MOV B,A          ;Save Hex byte
            JMP   SHOHEX     ;Go back and display new byte
```

MODULE 3: FUNCTION KEY

This module is concerned with checking various function keys and performing the designated function of each key. If it is a *Memory Address* key (MEM$_{HI}$ or MEM$_{LO}$), the program stores the previous Hex byte from Module 2 in the HL registers, returns to location SHOBYT, and displays the memory address and data at that location.

If it is the *Store* key, the program stores the Hex byte in the memory location specified by the contents of the HL registers, increments (HL), and returns to location SHOBYT.

If it is the *Execute* key, the program simply loads the contents of HL registers in the program counter and the program control is transferred to the user's program.

```
;Module 3:  Function Key
MEMHI:      CPI   HIKY       ;Is this MEM_HI key?
            JNZ   MEMLO      ;If not, jump to check MEM_LO key
            MOV H,B          ;If it is MEM_HI key, store it in register H
            JMP   SHOBYT     ;Go back to display new address and data
MEMLO:      CPI   LOKY       ;Is this MEM_LO key?
            JNZ   STORE      ;If not, jump to check Store key
            MOV L,B          ;If it is MEM_LO key, store it in register L
            JMP   SHOBYT     ;Go back to display new address and data
STORE:      CPI   STORKY     ;Is this Store key?
            JNZ   EXECUTE    ;If not, jump to check Execute key
            MOV M,B          ;Store data byte in memory
            INX   H          ;Point to next memory location
```

	JMP	SHOBYT	;Go back to display new address and data
EXECUTE:	CPI	EXCTKY	;Is this *Execute* key?
	JNZ	KYCHEK	;If it is not *Execute* key this is an error, go ;back to check next key
	PCHL		;Place memory address in program counter and ;execute user program

MODULE 4: KEYBOARD SUBROUTINE

This is the keyboard routine (Figure 17.7) that was explained in Chapter 11 (Section 11.33, Figure 11.25). The modifications required are: Change the 4×4 key matrix to a 4×5 matrix, which involves modifying the number for columns; include additional codes for function keys; and define equates for the input and the output ports of the keyboard.

17.14 Prototype Building and Testing

Microprocessor-based products hardly ever are completely built and tested as complete systems during the initial stages of design. A completely built system is difficult to troubleshoot. Traditional approaches, such as signal injection and isolating trouble spots, are ineffective for troubleshooting bus-oriented systems. Therefore, a system is built and tested in stages. Each subsystem—such as keyboard, display, and memory—should be built and tested separately as an independent module.

Now, the question is: How can a module be tested without building a system? An answer can be found in such everyday incidents as testing a light bulb or trying to start a car with a dead battery. The light bulb can be tested by plugging it into a working socket and the car can be started with a jumper cable. There are two principles involved in these examples: (1) borrowing resources from a working system and (2) substitution. These principles can be used in testing each separate subsystem of a microprocessor-based product. A working system is needed that can create an environment similar to the complete prototype system, and that is generous enough to share its resources with hardware modules to be built. Such a working system, called an **in-circuit emulator**, is described briefly in Section 17.21.

Assuming that such an in-circuit emulator is available, each subsystem of the single-board microcomputer can be built and tested simultaneously. Similarly, as software modules are written, they can be tested first on a software development system (discussed in Chapter 10). Finally, hardware and software can be integrated and tested by using an in-circuit emulator.

17.2 DEVELOPMENT AND TROUBLESHOOTING TOOLS

In bus-oriented systems, there is constant flow of data, which continuously changes the logic states. This flow of data is controlled by software instructions. Therefore, to examine what is happening inside the system, special instruments, capable of capturing data in relation to instructions, are required. Three such instruments are discussed briefly in the next section: In-circuit Emulator, Logic State Analyzer, and Signature Analyzer.

17.21 In-Circuit Emulator

The in-circuit emulation technique has become an essential part of the design process for microprocessor-based products. In-circuit emulation is the execution of a prototype software program in prototype hardware under the control of a software development system. To perform an in-circuit emulation, the microprocessor is removed from the prototype design board, and a 40-pin cable from an in-circuit emulator is plugged into the socket previously occupied by the microprocessor. The in-circuit emulator performs all the functions of the replaced microprocessor; in addition, it allows the prototype hardware to share all its resources, such as software, memory, and I/Os. It provides a window for looking into the dynamic, real-time operation of the prototype hardware. At present, a wide variety of in-circuit emulators are available, ranging from universal emulators with complete software development systems to stand-alone microprocessor units. Figure 17.8(a) shows an universal in-circuit emulator (9508) manufactured by Gould Inc.; it is designed to emulate various microprocessors with plug-in boards. Figure 17.8(b) shows a stand-alone in-circuit emulator (EM — 188) designed by Advanced Micro Systems.

EMULATION PROCESS

To test subsystems (such as I/O and memory) using an in-circuit emulator, the minimum prototype hardware required is a 40-pin microprocessor socket, without the microprocessor, and a power supply. All other resources can be borrowed from the in-circuit emulator. As more and more prototype hardware is built, fewer and fewer resources from the in-circuit emulator will be required. In the final stage, total software and hardware are integrated for testing. A hardware prototype can be viewed as a fetus growing in stages in the womb of an in-circuit emulator; until the fetus is fully developed and functioning independently, the in-circuit emulator provides the necessary environment and resources.

FEATURES OF IN-CIRCUIT EMULATOR

An in-circuit emulator is a software/hardware troubleshooting instrument. It can be a stand-alone unit or part of a software development system. A small program can be entered directly into the emulator, or a program can be transferred into the emulator from a host computer system through an RS-232 serial link. Once a program is loaded, a user can interact with the emulator through its keyboard or a terminal. The emulator has its own software commands to perform various debugging functions. The main capabilities of an in-circuit emulator can be listed as follows:

☐ **Downloading:** Facilities to transfer programs between a software development system or a host computer and the in-circuit emulator.
☐ **Resource Sharing:** The in-circuit emulator allows the system being tested to share its memory and I/O ports. The memory and I/O ports of the in-circuit emulator can be assigned any addresses, which will avoid conflict with memory and I/Os of the prototype; this is called memory and I/O mapping.

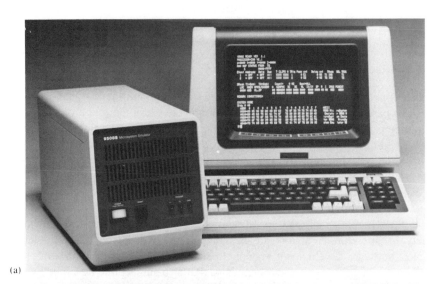

(a)

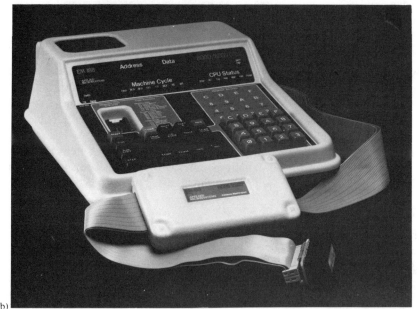

(b)

FIGURE 17.8
In-Circuit Emulators: Universal In-Circuit Emulator—9508 (a) and Stand-Alone
In-Circuit Emulator—EM 188 (b)

SOURCE: A: Photograph courtesy of Gould Inc., Design & Test Systems Division, Santa Clara, Calif. B: Photograph courtesy of Applied Micro Systems.

☐ **Debugging Tools:** Breakpoints
Mnemonic Display
Real-Time Trace
In-Line Assembly
Disassembly
Register Display/Modifications

DEBUGGING TOOLS

The debugging tools listed above are used in troubleshooting programs. Single-stepping and setting breakpoints have already been discussed in Chapter 5. The others are briefly discussed below.

Real-Time Trace   The in-circuit emulator has R/W memory used as a buffer to store the last several (such as 128) bus operations and these can be displayed on the screen. The display is like a snapshot of all the bus operations in real time. A typical display is shown in Figure 17.9. The user can specify several requirements, such as a memory address and certain data conditions for recognizing an event, in order to trigger and display a trace. Similarly, a trace can be observed between two breakpoints or at a specified delay after a certain event. The real-time trace is a valuable tool in debugging microprocessor-based products.

In-Line Assembly   This allows the user to change data or instructions while the software is in the in-circuit emulator.

Disassembly   After instructions are changed in the in-circuit emulator, this facility can write mnemonics in software.

Register Display   This displays the register contents after the execution of instructions.

17.22   Logic State Analyzer

The logic state analyzer, also known as the logic analyzer, is a multitrace digital oscilloscope especially designed to use with microprocessor-related products. In a multitrace scope, the timing relationships of several signals can be observed with respect to some triggering event or events. For example, a four-trace scope can show the timing relationships of four signals. In a microprocessor-related product, the user is interested in observing digital signals on the address bus, the data bus, the control bus and, possibly, an external instrument relative to a specified triggering event or events. Furthermore, data display should be in a conveniently readable format, such as Hex or binary. The logic analyzer performs these functions.

A typical logic analyzer designed primarily to work with the microprocessor has a 40-pin probe plus an auxiliary probe to gather external information. It includes Read-Only

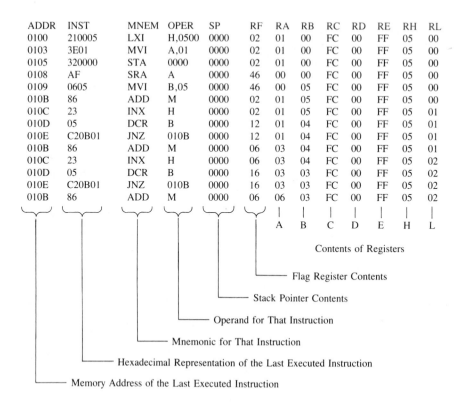

ADDR	INST	MNEM	OPER	SP	RF	RA	RB	RC	RD	RE	RH	RL
0100	210005	LXI	H,0500	0000	02	01	00	FC	00	FF	05	00
0103	3E01	MVI	A,01	0000	02	01	00	FC	00	FF	05	00
0105	320000	STA	0000	0000	02	01	00	FC	00	FF	05	00
0108	AF	SRA	A	0000	46	00	00	FC	00	FF	05	00
0109	0605	MVI	B,05	0000	46	00	05	FC	00	FF	05	00
010B	86	ADD	M	0000	02	01	05	FC	00	FF	05	00
010C	23	INX	H	0000	02	01	05	FC	00	FF	05	01
010D	05	DCR	B	0000	12	01	04	FC	00	FF	05	01
010E	C20B01	JNZ	010B	0000	12	01	04	FC	00	FF	05	01
010B	86	ADD	M	0000	06	03	04	FC	00	FF	05	01
010C	23	INX	H	0000	06	03	04	FC	00	FF	05	02
010D	05	DCR	B	0000	16	03	03	FC	00	FF	05	02
010E	C20B01	JNZ	010B	0000	16	03	03	FC	00	FF	05	02
010B	86	ADD	M	0000	06	06	03	FC	00	FF	05	02

                                                                  A   B   C   D   E   H   L

Contents of Registers

Flag Register Contents

Stack Pointer Contents

Operand for That Instruction

Mnemonic for That Instruction

Hexadecimal Representation of the Last Executed Instruction

Memory Address of the Last Executed Instruction

A 14-bus-cycle printout of an 8080A microcomputer prototype program segment annotated with data-column identifiers.

FIGURE 17.9

Display of a Real-Time Trace Using an In-Circuit Emulator

SOURCE: Tod Archer, *Simplifying Microprocessor-Based Product Design* (Beaverton, Ore.: Tektronix, 1979), p. 6-10.

Memory (ROM) to store instructions related to the analyzer, R/W buffer memory to store data from a product under test, a microprocessor to monitor data gathering, and a keyboard to specify operations and enter data in Hex or octal format. The analyzer can be triggered to gather information at a specified event related to the microprocessor in the product under test or in relation to an external word. The analyzer in a trace mode takes a snapshot of real-time information at a specific trigger, stores it in its buffer memory and displays it on its CRT.

The in-circuit emulator is a valuable tool during the initial stages of product development and, in later stages, the logic analyzer can perform some of the trouble-shooting functions.

17.23   Signature Analyzer

The signature analyzer is an instrument used in troubleshooting microprocessor products either in the field or during production. This instrument converts the complex serial data stream present at the intersections of logic circuits, called nodes, into a 4-digit pattern, called a signature. Conceptually, a signature is similar to a voltage level specified on the schematic of an analog product. To troubleshoot an analog product, voltages are measured at various locations until the measured reading does not match the specified reading, thus isolating the trouble. The signature analyzer is used in the same manner.

DATA TRANSFER BETWEEN TWO MICROCOMPUTERS IN DISTRIBUTED PROCESSING   17.3

As the VLSI technology is improving, the cost of hardware is decreasing. It is becoming economical to design dedicated microcomputers to perform or monitor specific tasks where the speed of data processing is less important. These dedicated microcomputers are usually controlled by a high speed computer, an approach called **distributed data processing**. The high speed computer is known as a **master** and the dedicated computer is called a **slave**. Parallel I/O with handshake is used to transfer data between a master and a slave, and the data transfer is bidirectional. The bidirectional communication between two microcomputers can be accomplished using the 8255A PPI in Mode 2, as illustrated in the next project.

PROJECT STATEMENT

Design an interfacing circuit to set up bidirectional data communication in the master-slave format between two 8085A microcomputers. Use the 8255 PPI as the interfacing device with the master and a tri-state buffer with the slave microcomputer. Write necessary software to transfer a block of data from the master to the slave.

17.31   Project Analysis

Figure 17.10 shows a block diagram to set up the bidirectional communication between the master and slave MPUs. The block diagram shows two bidirectional data buses — master and slave — interconnected through the 8255A, which serves as an interfacing device of the master MPU. Port A of the 8255A is used for bidirectional data transfer, and four signals from port C are used for handshaking. The communication process is similar to Mode 1 of the 8255A. When the master MPU writes a data byte in the 8255A, the $\overline{\text{OBF}}$ signal goes low to inform the slave that a byte is available, and the slave acknowledges when it reads the byte. Similarly, two other handshake signals are used when the slave transfers a data byte to the master.

   The master requires I/O ports to read and write data and to check the status of handshake signals. Similarly, the slave MPU requires I/O ports to perform Read and Write operations. Therefore, it is necessary to analyze carefully these I/O functions between the

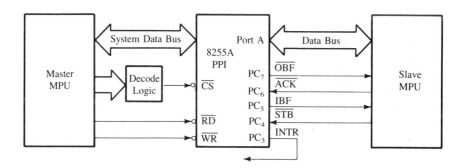

FIGURE 17.10
Block Diagram of Bidirectional Communication Between Two Computers Using the 8255A

MPUs. Data transfer can be accomplished either by status check or interrupt. The speed of handling data is of more importance to the master MPU than to the slave MPU. Therefore, the master MPU is generally set up in the interrupt mode and the slave MPU in the status check mode. However, for this example, both MPUs are set up under the status check mode; the interrupt mode is left as an assignment. The data transfer operations between the two MPUs under the status check I/O can be listed as follows.

DATA TRANSFER FROM MASTER MPU TO SLAVE MPU

1. The master MPU reads the status of $\overline{OBF}$ to verify whether the previous byte has been read by the slave MPU. This is an input function for the master MPU.
2. The master writes data into port A and the 8255A informs the slave by causing the signal $\overline{OBF}$ to go low. This is an output function for the master MPU.
3. The slave checks the $\overline{OBF}$ signal from the master for data availability. This is an input function for the slave MPU.
4. The slave MPU reads data from port A and acknowledges the reading at the same time by making the signal $\overline{ACK}$ low. This is an input function for the slave MPU.

DATA TRANSFER FROM SLAVE TO MASTER MPU

5. The slave MPU checks the handshake signal IBF (Input Buffer Full) to find out whether port A is available (empty) to transfer a data byte. This is an input function for the slave MPU.
6. The slave MPU places a data byte on the data bus and informs the 8255A by enabling the $\overline{STB}$ (Strobe) signal. This is an output function for the slave MPU.
7. The 8255A causes the IBF (Input Buffer Full) to go high, and the master MPU reads the signal to find out whether a data byte is available. This is an input function for the master MPU.
8. Finally, the master reads the data byte. This is an input function for the master MPU.

This analysis leads to certain hardware requirements that are discussed in the next section.

17.32   Hardware Description

In the first four steps described in the previous section, the master MPU performs one input and one output operation, and the slave MPU performs two input operations. They use two handshake signals: $\overline{OBF}$ (Output Buffer Full) and $\overline{ACK}$ (Acknowledge). Steps 5 through 8 are mirror images of the first four steps. The slave MPU performs one input and one output operation, and the master MPU performs two input operations. They use two additional handshake signals: IBF (Input Buffer Full) and $\overline{STB}$ (Strobe). These steps suggest that the master MPU and the slave MPU require three input ports and one output port each. However, if port A is a bidirectional port and port C is a status port, they will meet all the Read/Write requirements of the master MPU. Additional ports need to be designed for the slave MPU.

Figure 17.11 shows the complete schematic of the necessary ports and their decoding logic. The address bus of the master MPU is decoded by using an 8-input NAND gate and the 8255A is selected when all lines are high, thus assigning the following port addresses:

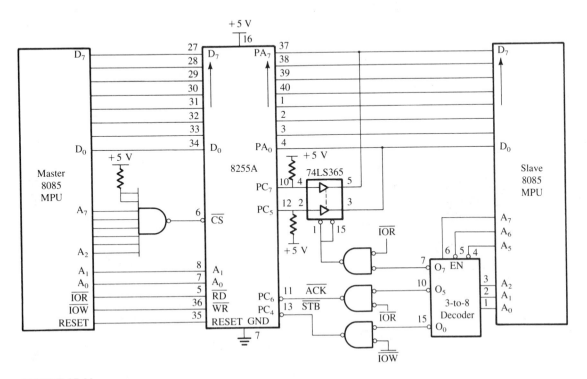

FIGURE 17.11

Schematic: Bidirectional Communication Between the Master and Slave MPUs

SOURCE: Adapted from Peter Rony, "Interfacing Fundamentals: Bidirectional I/Os Using Two Semaphores." Reprinted with permission from the April 1981 issue of *Computer Design*, copyright 1981 Computer Design Publishing Company.

$$\begin{aligned}\text{Control Register} &= \text{FFH} \quad (A_1 \text{ and } A_0 = 1)\\ \text{Port A} &= \text{FCH} \quad (A_1 \text{ and } A_0 = 0)\\ \text{Port C} &= \text{FEH} \quad (A_1 = 1, A_0 = 0)\end{aligned}$$

Port A is configured in Mode 2 using the four signals from port C as shown in the schematic. The INTR signals are unnecessary and, therefore, are not shown. The master MPU checks the $\overline{\text{ACK}}$ and the $\overline{\text{STB}}$ signals by reading the status bits of $\overline{\text{OBF}}$ and IBF in port C.

The other two handshake signals — $\overline{\text{OBF}}$ and IBF — are tied, respectively, to bits D_7 and D_0 of the slave data bus through a tri-state buffer so that they can be read by the slave MPU. The decode logic for three input ports and one output port is generated by using the 74LS138 (3-to-8) decoder. Assuming the don't care address lines (A_4 and A_3) are at logic 0, the eight output lines of the decoder can be enabled with the addresses from 80H to 87H. Two output lines of the decoder are combined with the $\overline{\text{IOR}}$ control signal to generate two input device select pulses (85H and 87H). Input device select pulse 87H is used to read status on the data lines D_7 and D_0. The decoder line with address 80H is combined with the $\overline{\text{IOW}}$ signal to generate the $\overline{\text{STB}}$ signal.

CONTROL WORD — MODE 2

To set up the 8255A in the bidirectional mode (Mode 2), the bits of the control word are defined as follows:

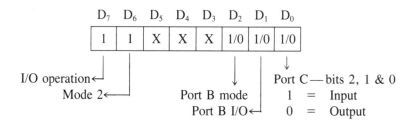

Examination of the control word definition shows that bits D_2 to D_0 are irrelevant in this example because port B and the remaining bits of port C are not being used. Therefore, the required control word is COH.

STATUS WORD — MODE 2

The status of the I/O operation in Mode 2 can be verified by reading the contents of port C. The status word format is as follows:

D_7	D_6	D_5	D_4	D_3	D_2	D_1	D_0
$\overline{\text{OBF}}_A$	INTE_1	IBF_A	INTE_2	INTR_A	X	X	X

for port B

The status of the signal $\overline{\text{OBF}}$ can be checked by rotating bit D_7 into the Carry, and the status of the signal IBF can be checked by ANDing the status word with data byte 20H.

READ AND WRITE OPERATIONS OF THE SLAVE MPU

A data byte can be read by the slave MPU from port A simply by sending an active-low device select pulse to the $\overline{ACK}$ signal; there is no need to build an input port. Similarly, a data byte can be written by the slave MPU into port A by causing the $\overline{STB}$ signal to go low.

17.33 Program

MASTER PROGRAM

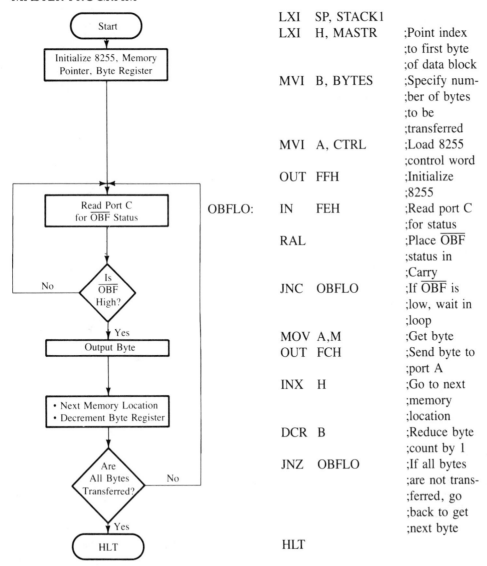

	LXI	SP, STACK1	
	LXI	H, MASTR	;Point index ;to first byte ;of data block
	MVI	B, BYTES	;Specify num- ;ber of bytes ;to be ;transferred
	MVI	A, CTRL	;Load 8255 ;control word
	OUT	FFH	;Initialize ;8255
OBFLO:	IN	FEH	;Read port C ;for status
	RAL		;Place $\overline{OBF}$;status in ;Carry
	JNC	OBFLO	;If $\overline{OBF}$ is ;low, wait in ;loop
	MOV	A,M	;Get byte
	OUT	FCH	;Send byte to ;port A
	INX	H	;Go to next ;memory ;location
	DCR	B	;Reduce byte ;count by 1
	JNZ	OBFLO	;If all bytes ;are not trans- ;ferred, go ;back to get ;next byte
	HLT		

FIGURE 17.12
Flowchart of Master Program

SLAVE PROGRAM

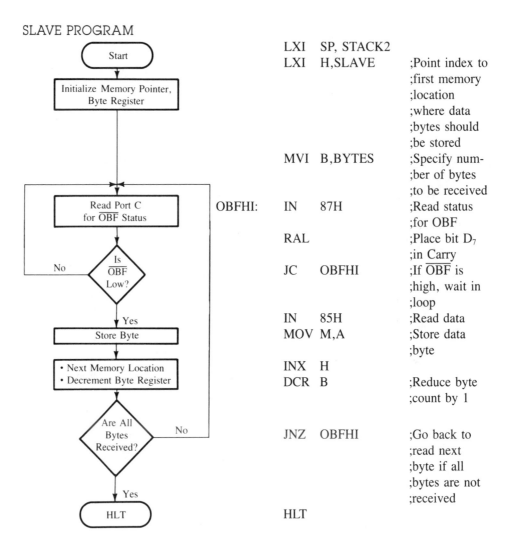

	LXI	SP, STACK2	
	LXI	H,SLAVE	;Point index to ;first memory ;location ;where data ;bytes should ;be stored
	MVI	B,BYTES	;Specify num- ;ber of bytes ;to be received
OBFHI:	IN	87H	;Read status ;for OBF
	RAL		;Place bit D_7 ;in Carry
	JC	OBFHI	;If $\overline{OBF}$ is ;high, wait in ;loop
	IN	85H	;Read data
	MOV	M,A	;Store data ;byte
	INX	H	
	DCR	B	;Reduce byte ;count by 1
	JNZ	OBFHI	;Go back to ;read next ;byte if all ;bytes are not ;received
	HLT		

FIGURE 17.13
Flowchart of Slave Program

PROGRAM COMMENTS

1. The flowcharts in Figure 17.12 and Figure 17.13 show that both programs check for the status line $\overline{OBF}$. The master program waits until the $\overline{OBF}$ goes high, then writes a byte in port A. On the other hand, the slave program waits until the $\overline{OBF}$ goes low, then reads data.

2. When the master MPU writes a data byte, it is latched by port A, and the data byte is placed on the slave data bus when the $\overline{ACK}$ goes low. The timing diagram in

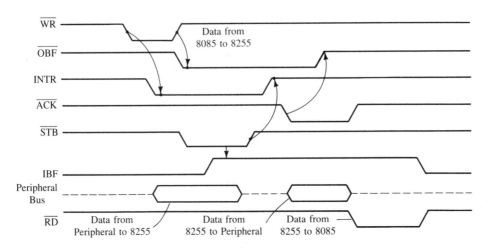

FIGURE 17.14

Timing Diagram Mode 2

SOURCE: Adapted from Intel Corporation, *Peripheral Design Handbook* (Santa Clara, Calif.: Author, 1981), p. 5-133.

Figure 17.14 shows that when the slave MPU reads data, the $\overline{\text{ACK}}$ signal goes low, and the falling edge of the $\overline{\text{ACK}}$ signal sets the $\overline{\text{OBF}}$ signal high for the master MPU to write the next byte.

3. The programs given above can transfer a block of data from the master MPU to the slave MPU but not vice versa. To transfer a block of data from the slave MPU to the master MPU, additional instructions are necessary (see Assignment 7 at the end of this chapter). These instructions should monitor the IBF signal in both programs and Read/Write operations should be interchanged. The master MPU should wait until IBF goes high to read a data byte, and the slave MPU should wait until IBF goes low to write a byte.

4. The timing diagram in Figure 17.14 shows an INTR signal to implement data transfer using the interrupt. However, the signal is irrelevant in this project; it is given in Figure 17.14 for Assignment 8 at the end of this chapter.

SUMMARY

In this chapter, two design projects were illustrated: a single-board microcomputer, and bidirectional data communication between two microcomputers. In addition, debugging tools such as the in-circuit emulator and the logic analyzer, and the signature analyzer were introduced.

The first project brought together all the concepts of the microprocessor architecture, software, and interfacing discussed in previous chapters. The necessary steps for designing hardware and software were demonstrated. The complete schematic and the monitor program were included in the illustration.

The second project—bidirectional communication between two microcomputers—used the 8255A in Mode 2 to set up the communication protocol. It illustrated the uses of handshake signals to transfer data between the master MPU and the slave MPU, and the program demonstrated the status check technique for the bidirectional data transfer.

ASSIGNMENTS

Section 17.1

1. Design the LED output port using two 7474 D-latches in place of the 8212 shown in Figure 17.4.
2. Explain why 1K of R/W memory in Figure 17.3 occupies more than 1K of memory space. Redesign this memory using a separate 3-to-8 decoder for absolute addressing.
3. The seven-segment display (Figure 17.4) uses a decoder driver 9370. Replace the decoder driver with the table look-up software technique.
4. Modify the schematic in Figure 17.4 to replace the seven-segment display with a scanned display.
5. Modify the software to include the table look-up technique in Assignment 3 and Assignment 4.
6. Modify the monitor program (Section 17.13) to include a software breakpoint routine using the RST 5.

Section 17.3

7. Write necessary software to transfer 100 bytes of data from the slave MPU to the master MPU using the status check I/O (see Figure 17.11).
8. Connect the INTR signal to RST 6.5 (8085 system) to interrupt the master MPU when data transfer is required. Modify the master program to implement data transfer under the interrupt I/O mode.
   Hints:

   ☐ The main program should enable INTE1 and INTE2, using the BSR mode.
   ☐ The interrupt service routine should verify whether it is a Read or a Write request.

Trends in Microprocessor Technology and Bus Standards

The microprocessor has had an impact on industries as diversified as machine tools, chemical processes, medical instrumentation, and sophisticated guidance control. Some applications require simple timing and bit set/reset functions, while others require high speed data processing capability. Therefore, a number of different microprocessor families are being designed to meet these diversified requirements. Microprocessors range from single-chip micro-controllers (microcomputers) to general purpose 32-bit microprocessors. In the present state of microprocessor technology, 4-bit microprocessors are rarely used and generally not available, except for the Texas Instruments TMS-1000 series. At the other extreme, 32-bit microprocessors are commercially available and have begun to invade the territories of traditional mainframe computers. This chapter will examine recent trends in this fast-changing technology and their implications for industry.

The microprocessor topics in this book have been discussed in the context of the widely used 8085/8080A microprocessor. However, various other 8-bit microprocessors are available, with varying degrees of capability. Four such microprocessors (and their families) will be discussed briefly in this chapter. In addition to general purpose 8-bit microprocessors, microprocessor technology has evolved

in two directions. At one extreme is the complete microcomputer on a single chip geared towards dedicated applications. At the other direction are the 16-bit and 32-bit general purpose microprocessors similar to mini- and mainframe computers. This chapter includes brief descriptions of single-chip microcomputers, and of 16-bit and 32-bit microprocessors.

In addition to examining recent trends in

microprocessor technology, this chapter discusses various bus standards used in microprocessor-based products.

OBJECTIVES

☐ List important characteristics of the contemporary 8-bit microprocessors such as the Z80, the NSC800, the MC6800 and 6809, and the MCS6502.

☐ List the elements of a single-chip microcomputer (microcontroller), and compare the characteristics of representative microcontrollers from the Intel family.

☐ Describe important features of 16-bit microprocessors and explain the concepts of memory segmentation, parallel processing, queueing, and coprocessing.

☐ Compare the features of the Intel iAPX8086/8088 and the Motorola MC68000 16-bit microprocessors.

☐ Explain the design features of 32-bit microprocessors, and describe the characteristics of the Intel iAPX 432 and the Bell Labs Bellmac 32-A.

☐ Explain the necessity for bus standards and list important features of the S-100 (IEEE-696) bus, the STD bus, the Multibus (IEEE-796), and the GPIB (IEEE-488).

18.1 CONTEMPORARY 8-BIT MICROPROCESSORS

The Intel 8008, which was later superseded by the Intel 8080A, was the first 8-bit microprocessor. Just about the same time, Motorola brought out the MC6800 as an improvement over the first 8008, but with substantially different architecture. Within a few years, Zilog designed the Z80 and Intel came up with the 8085 as an improvement over the 8080A. Both are upward machine-language compatible with the 8080A. Recently, National Semiconductor introduced an 8-bit microprocessor — the NSC800 — combining the features of the 8085 and the Z80. Other popular microprocessors are those of the MOS Technology MCS6500 series, which was designed as an improvement over the Motorola 6800; however, they are neither hardware nor software compatible. In recent years, Motorola came up with the MC6809, a vastly improved version of the MC6800. The 8085/8080A has been discussed throughout this text; these other contemporary 8-bit microprocessors will be discussed in the next few sections.

18.11 The Z80

The Z80 microprocessor is manufactured by Zilog, using N-channel MOS technology. It is upward software compatible with the 8080A. Its instruction set has 158 basic instructions, which includes the 8080A instruction set. However, the Zilog mnemonics are different from the Intel mnemonics, even though the machine codes are identical for the 8080A set. Furthermore, the Z80 instruction set does not include two serial I/O instructions (RIM and SIM) of the 8085. Figure 18.1 shows the Z80 signals and its internal registers. The Z80 is not pin compatible with the 8080A or the 8085.

The Z80 microprocessor requires one +5 V power supply and can operate with 2.5 MHz single-phase clock frequency. The faster versions of the Z80 — the Z80A and the Z80B — can operate with 4 MHz and 6 MHz clock frequency, respectively. The Z80 chip has sixteen address lines to address 64K memory and eight data lines. No lines are

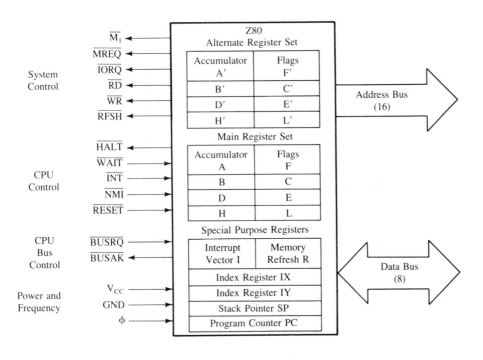

FIGURE 18.1

Z80 Microprocessor: Signals and Internal Registers

SOURCE: Adapted from MOSTEK, *Z80 Microcomputer Data Book* (Carroliton, Texas: Author, 1981), pp. III-8 and III-11.

multiplexed. Zilog recently announced a new microprocessor, the Z800. This 8-bit micro-processor is upward software compatible with the Z80, but it can address 500K bytes of memory and can operate with 25 MHz clock frequency. The expanded instruction set includes instructions such as "multiply and divide." It has addressing modes suited for multiuser, multiprocessing systems.

The Z80 has two interrupt lines: one is compatible with the 8080A interrupt line, and the second is a nonmaskable interrupt (NMI). An additional significant feature of the Z80 is its on-board logic ($\overline{\text{RFSH}}$) to refresh dynamic memories. This allows the user to use dynamic memories in a system without having to build an additional refresh circuit. Dynamic memory chips, in general, are much less expensive than static memory chips.

The internal architecture of the Z80 (Figure 18.1) includes all the 8080A regis-ters: A, B, C, D, E, H, L, the flag register, the program counter, and the stack pointer. In addition, it has the entire set of 8-bit alternate registers, shown as A' through L'. However, access to the alternate set of registers is only through an instruction called exchange (EXX). This instruction exchanges the contents of the alternate registers. In essence, the alternate set of registers is used as temporary storage. Figure 18.1 shows two 16-bit index registers (IX and IY), one 8-bit Interrupt Vector Register (IV), and one 7-bit Memory Refresh Register (R). The two index registers in the Z80 allow various types of memory addressing modes — a significant improvement over the 8085/8080A, in which memory addressing is restricted primarily to the HL register.

The instruction set of the Z80 is the most powerful set among the 8-bit microprocessors. It includes instructions to transfer data from one block of memory to another (LDIR = Load, Increment, and Repeat) and to search the entire memory for an 8-bit character (CPIR = Compare, Increment, and Repeat). Some of its Jump instructions perform more than one function, such as Decrement B and Jump if Nonzero (DJNZ). The group of instructions called "Bit Manipulation," can test, set, or reset a bit in any register or a memory location. In addition, the Z80 has an extensive set of I/O instructions that include block input/output instructions and various modes of interrupts.

The Z80 microprocessor is supported by peripheral devices such as the parallel I/O (PIO), the clock timer circuit (CTC), the Direct Memory Access Controller (DMA), and the serial I/O (SIO and DART).

18.12   The NSC800

The NSC800 is an 8-bit microprocessor manufactured by National Semiconductor (Figure 18.2). It is a low-power device that combines features of the 8085 and the Z80; its power consumption is 5 percent of that of the NMOS devices. It is ideally suited for low-power or battery-operated applications.

The NSC800 has a bus structure similar to that of the 8085: a multiplexed bus with the status signals S_0, S_1, and IO/$\overline{M}$. It has a very powerful interrupt scheme that combines the 8085 and the Z80 interrupts. It includes refresh logic for dynamic memory, and on-board clock circuitry for the system clock. Unlike the 8085, however, it does not support serial I/O.

The instruction set and mnemonics are identical with those of the Z80. The instruction set does not include the RIM and SIM instructions as in the 8085. Its architecture includes all the Z80 registers.

National Semiconductor has special purpose devices compatible with its multiplexed bus and status signals, such as the NSC810 RAM-I/O-Timer and the NSC830 ROM-I/O. These devices are similar to Intel devices such as the 8155 and the 8755.

In summary, the NSC800 is a high-performance, low-power microprocessor that combines the software capability of the Z80 with the bus structure of the 8085. In addition, it combines features such as interrupts, clock circuitry, and refresh logic on the same chip.

18.13   The MC6800

The MC6800 microprocessor is manufactured by Motorola using N-channel MOS technology. It was developed at about the same time as the Intel 8080A. Both microprocessors were developed as improvements over Intel's first 8-bit microprocessor, the 8008. However, the MC6800 has a different architecture than its competitor, the Intel 8080A.

The MC6800 has sixteen address lines and eight data lines. It requires one +5 V power supply — a significant improvement over the 8080A — and runs on a 1 MHz standard clock signal with two phases: ϕ_1 and ϕ_2. However, the chip does not include a clock logic. It has two interrupt lines: a regular interrupt and a nonmaskable interrupt.

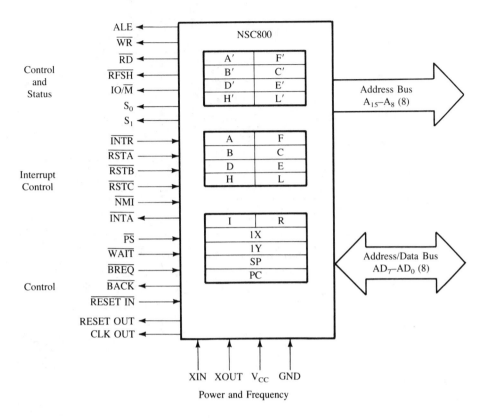

FIGURE 18.2
NSC800 Microprocessor and Internal Registers
SOURCE: Courtesy of National Semiconductor, Inc.

Figure 18.3 shows the internal architecture of the MC6800. It has two 8-bit accumulators and one index register. The other three registers — the program counter, the stack pointer, and the status register — are similar to the registers in the 8080A.

The MC6800 instruction set includes 72 basic instructions and makes extensive use of memory referencing. The set does not include typical direct I/O instructions (IN/OUT); it has only memory-mapped I/O. It has simple timing and control signals; the clock period is the same as the machine cycle. In general, the MC6800 is a much simpler microprocessor than the 8080A.

THE MC6809

The 6809 is the latest improved version of the 6800 family of processors. It is faster, and has more registers and instructions than the 6800. However, its machine code is not compatible with that of the 6800. This difficulty is circumvented by the use of the cross-assembler, which produces 6809 machine code from 6800 mnemonics. Figure 18.4

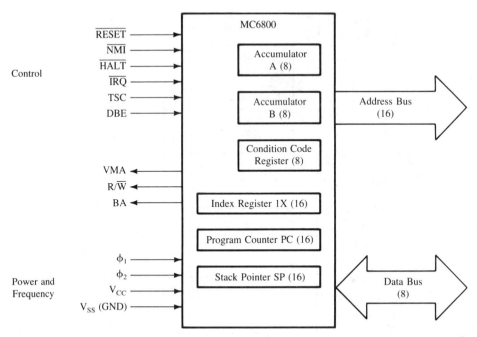

FIGURE 18.3
Motorola MC6800 Microprocessor with Internal Registers
SOURCE: Courtesy of Motorola, Inc.

shows the internal architecture of the 6809. In comparison with the 6800, the 6809 has an additional Index Register, User Stack Pointer and 8-bit Direct Page Register. It has clock logic on the chip and one additional interrupt line, called Fast Interrupt Request (FIRQ).

The instruction set is more powerful than that of the 6800 and includes many new instructions. The Direct Page Register allows direct addressing anywhere in memory. Three new addressing modes have been added. The stack pointers have indexing capability, and some instructions can use two accumulators as a 16-bit accumulator. With an improved instruction set and additional indexing capability, the 6809 has eliminated most of the limitations of the 6800 and become more suitable for handling high level languages.

18.14   The MCS6500

The MCS6500 series consists of nine microprocessors sharing the same instruction set and addressing modes. They differ in packaging and system interface; two of them are housed in a 40-pin package and the others in a 28-pin package. The series was designed as an improvement over the Motorola MC6800. However it is neither hardware nor software compatible with the MC6800.

Figure 18.5 shows the architecture of the 6502, the member of the 6500 series that is most comparable to the MC6800. The 6502 has sixteen address lines, eight data lines,

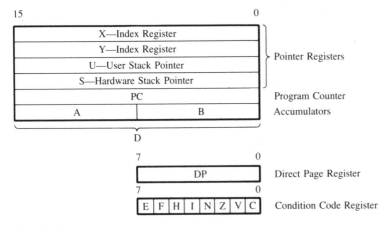

FIGURE 18.4
Motorola MC6809: Internal Registers

SOURCE Motorola, *MC6809-MC6809E Programming Manual* (Austin, Texas: Author, 1981), p. 1-3.

and two interrupt lines. Like the MC6800, the 6502 requires one +5 V power supply and runs on a 1 MHz standard clock with two phases: ϕ_1 and ϕ_2, the same as that of the MC6800. The important features of the 6502 are its on-chip clock logic and its simplicity. It has fewer control signals than any other microprocessor described here.

The 6502 has one accumulator as opposed to the two accumulators in the 6800. It has two 8-bit index registers and one 8-bit stack pointer. The high-order address for the stack pointer is 01H, supplied by the microprocessor, and the stack is restricted to 256 bytes on page 01. The instruction set is similar to that of the 6800. Two important features of the instruction set are indirect addressing anywhere in the memory map, and the ability to operate in the BCD mode.

18.15 Review of 8-Bit Microprocessors

The architectures of the Z80 and the 8085 are register-oriented. The Z80 has a larger and more powerful instruction set than the 8085, and it is software compatible with the 8085, except for serial I/O instructions. As the first designer and manufacturer of the microprocessor, Intel has a substantial sales lead over Z80. However, the Z80 has become the basis of many disk-based microcomputers. The NSC800 is a recent entry in the field. It is best suited for low-powered applications, and it has combined the features of the Z80 and the 8085. However, it is more expensive than the Z80 or 8085. In contrast to the register-oriented Z80, NSC800, and 8085, the 6800, the 6809, and the 6502 are memory-reference oriented. They include fewer registers in their architecture than the 8085. The best feature of the 6502 is its simplicity, while the 6809 may be viewed as perhaps one of the most powerful 8-bit processors. However, all of these microprocessors are so powerful that they are hardly ever used to their full capacity in control applications. In

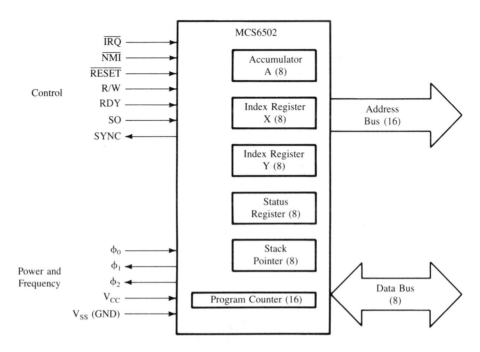

FIGURE 18.5
MOS Technology: The MCS6502 Microprocessor with Internal Registers

many instances, therefore, they are selected for product design on such grounds as familiarity, product support, and compatibility with existing systems.

18.2 SINGLE-CHIP MICROCOMPUTERS

Single-chip microcomputers, also known as microcontrollers, are used primarily to perform dedicated functions. They are used as independent controllers in machines or as slaves in distributed processing as described in Chapter 17. Generally, they include all the essential elements of a computer on a single chip: MPU, R/W memory, ROM, and I/O lines. Typical examples of the single-chip microcomputers are the Intel 8048 family and 8051 family, the Motorola 6801, the MOS Technology 370, the Fairchild F8 (2-chip), the Texas Instruments TMS1000 series, and Zilog Z8.

Most of these microcomputers have an 8-bit word size (except the TMS1000, with only 4-bits), at least 64 bytes of R/W memory, and 1K bytes of ROM. The range of I/O lines varies considerably, from 16 to 32 lines. However, most of these devices cannot be easily programmed in college laboratories unless they include EPROM on the chip, such as the Intel 8048 and 8051. A variety of single-chip microcomputers is available on the market to meet diversified industry needs. To illustrate the trend, four different single-chip microcomputers from the Intel family are described below.

FIGURE 18.6
Block Diagram: The 8048

SOURCE: Adapted from Intel Corporation, *Intel Microcontroller Handbook* (Santa Clara, Calif.: Author, 1984), p. 16-7.

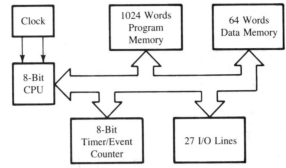

18.21 Intel 8048 Family

The members of the 8048 family are Intel's earliest single-chip 8-bit devices; and they are used primarily in low-cost, high-volume control applications. The family includes five devices that differ in the memory size and operating frequencies (2 MHz and 4 MHz).

Figure 18.6 shows the block diagram of the 8048. It includes 27 I/O lines, 1K ROM or EPROM, 64 bytes of R/W memory, and one 8-bit counter/timer. It has an 8-bit accumulator, and 64 bytes of "scratchpad" memory that can be used as general purpose registers. It has a 12-bit counter and can address 4K of memory: 1K internal and 3K external. The 12-bit address bus is multiplexed with I/O ports: the low-order bus is multiplexed with DB_0 to DB_7, and the four high-order lines are multiplexed with pins P_{20} to P_{23}. The chip includes the address latch enable (ALE), which makes it compatible with the specially designed device, such as the 8155.

The instruction set is versatile and especially suited for control applications. It includes bit manipulation, BCD operations, conditional branching, and table look-up. It also includes a simple scheme for an external interrupt and a single-step trouble-shooting mode.

Another trend in designing single-chip microcomputers is to include an A/D converter and/or a serial I/O port on the same chip. For example, the 8022 microcomputer includes the features of the 8048 plus a two-channel, 8-bit A/D converter.

18.22 Intel 8051 Single-Chip Family

The Intel 8051 is the latest single-chip microcomputer family. At the high end of the single-chip device spectrum in terms of its capability and versatility, it is designed for use in sophisticated real-time instrumentation and industrial control. It can operate with a 12 MHz clock and has a very powerful instruction set.

Figure 18.7 shows a block diagram of the chip. It includes the following features:

☐ 4K bytes of ROM or EPROM
☐ 128 bytes of data memory plus 21 special-function registers (SFR—not included in figure)
☐ four programmable I/O ports (32 I/O lines)
☐ two 16-bit timer/event counters

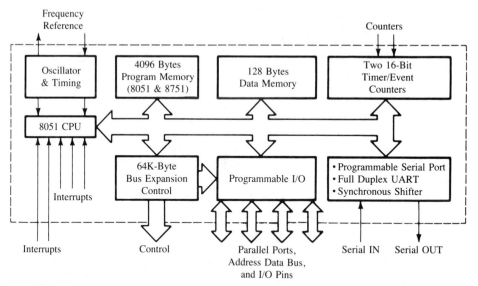

FIGURE 18.7
Block Diagram: The 8051

SOURCE: Adapted from Bob Koehler, "Microcontroller Doubles as Boolean Processors," *Electronic Design* vol. 28, no. 11; copyright Hayden Publishing Company, Inc., 1980.

☐ a serial I/O port with a UART
☐ five interrupt lines: two for external signals and three for internal operations

The 8051 is known as a "bit and byte processor." The instruction set includes binary and BCD arithmetic operations, bit set/reset functions, and all logical functions. However, its real power comes from its ability to handle Boolean functions. On any addressable bit, the processor can perform functions such as Set, Clear, Complement, Jump If Set or Not Set, and Jump If Set Then Clear. It can also perform logical functions with two bits and place the result in the Carry flag.

The 8051 can use its 32 I/O lines as 32 individual bits or as four 8-bit parallel ports. It can service five interrupts: two external, two from the counters, and one from the serial I/O port. The chip includes two 16-bit counters that can operate in three different modes, and a serial I/O port that can operate in the full duplex mode.

18.23 Universal Peripheral Interface (UPI): The 8041 Family

These chips are designed primarily to function as slave MPUs in distributed processing. The UPI is a single-chip microcomputer that is in many ways similar to the 8048. However, it includes a data bus, an input/output register, and a status register. These registers perform functions similar to handshaking and synchronizing data transfer between the UPI and the master. When a master writes a data byte in the register, an interrupt is generated to inform the 8041, and the device reads the data byte with a special instruction. On the other hand, to transfer a data byte from the slave to the master, the 8041 checks the status register for the handshaking signal before it writes a data byte.

18.24 Analog Signal Processor: The 2920

The 2920 is a single-chip microcomputer specially designed to process analog signals. Most microprocessors are not able to process high speed analog signals because of their slow response. The 2920 is designed with special architecture and a suitable instruction set for handling high speed signal processing. In addition to the MPU and memory, the chip includes all necessary devices such as A/D and D/A converters, multiplexer to handle four different inputs, sample and hold circuit, and demultiplexer.

The 2920 is widely used for acquiring and processing analog signals. Typical applications include areas such as telecommunication, signal processing, guidance and control, speech processing, and industrial automation.

18.25 Review of Intel Single-Chip Microcomputers

Examination of the various examples discussed above shows that the single-chip microcomputer plays a vital role in control applications and is an important segment of microprocessor technology. These devices are designed for special purpose applications, and the circuitry on the chip varies according to its objectives. Applications range from bit set/reset functions to processing high speed analog signals.

16-BIT MICROPROCESSORS 18.3

The 16-bit microprocessor families are designed primarily to compete with minicomputers and are oriented towards high-level languages. Their applications sometimes overlap those of the 8-bit microprocessor and may compete with those of mainframe computers. They have powerful instruction sets and are capable of addressing megabytes of memory. Typical examples of widely used 16-bit microprocessors include Intel iAPX 8086/8088, Zilog Z8001/8002, Digital Equipment LSI-11, Texas Instruments TMS9900, Motorola 68000, and National Semiconductor NS16000.

Apart from design concepts and instruction sets, one of the critical factors that decides the capability of the microprocessor is the number of pins available. One trend is to stay within the 40-pin package size and take advantage of the existing production and testing facilities. The 40-pin package either limits the size of the memory that can be addressed or necessitates multiplexing of several functions. Intel, Zilog (Z8002), and Digital Equipment have stayed with the 40-pin package. Another trend is to go beyond the 40-pin limit to a 48-pin size or to a 64-pin size. National Semiconductor (NS16000) and Zilog (Z8001) have chosen the 48-pin package. Motorola and Texas Instruments have selected the 64-pin package. The primary objectives of these 16-bit microprocessors can be summarized as follows:

1. Increase memory addressing capacity
2. Increase execution speed
3. Provide a powerful instruction set
4. Facilitate programming in high-level languages

These objectives can be met by using various design concepts. To illustrate differences in design philosophies, the next two sections will describe briefly two 16-bit microprocessors: the Intel iAPX 8086/8088 and Motorola MC68000.

18.31   Intel iAPX 8086/8088

The Intel iAPX 8086/8088 is a 16-bit microprocessor housed in a 40-pin package and capable of addressing one megabyte of memory. Various versions of this chip can operate with clock frequencies from 4 MHz to 8 MHz. Figure 18.8 shows internal registers; the shaded portions of the figure are identical with the 8085/8080A registers. This microprocessor includes fourteen 16-bit registers, of which the top four registers (AX, BX, CX, and DX) are used as general purpose accumulators. These four can also be used as 8-bit registers. The next four 16-bit registers are used primarily as memory pointers and index registers; they hold part of a 20-bit memory address (see Memory Segmentation below). They can also be used as general purpose registers. The next four 16-bit registers are used to specify a segment of the 1-megabyte memory. The last two registers are similar to the program counter and flag register in the 8085/8080A, but have four additional flags.

The 8088 is functionally similar to the 8086, except that it has an 8-bit data bus. Its internal architecture and instruction set are identical with those of the 8086. The only difference is that a 16-bit data word must be transferred in two segments in the 8088. The 8088 can be viewed as an 8-bit microprocessor with the execution power of a 16-bit microprocessor. The next few paragraphs describe the features of the 8086 architecture that meet the objectives described above.

MEMORY SEGMENTATION

To increase the memory addressing capacity, the concept of memory segmentation is employed in this device. This concept involves combining the addresses from two 16-bit registers to form a 20-bit effective address. A segment register provides a base address, and another register supplies an offset address. For example, to fetch an instruction from the 256th location on page 0, the address can be formed as follows:

1. Define the memory segment by loading 0000H in the Code Segment Register.
2. The Instruction Pointer should hold 00FFH as the offset.
3. The processor shifts the address in the Code Segment Register by four bits to the left and adds the content of the Instruction Pointer to form the 20-bit address:

$$
\begin{array}{lcccc}
\text{Code Segment:} & 0 & 0 & 0 & 0 \\
\text{Instruction Pointer:} & & 0 & 0 & F & F \\
\text{Effective Address:} & 0 & 0 & 0 & F & F
\end{array}
$$

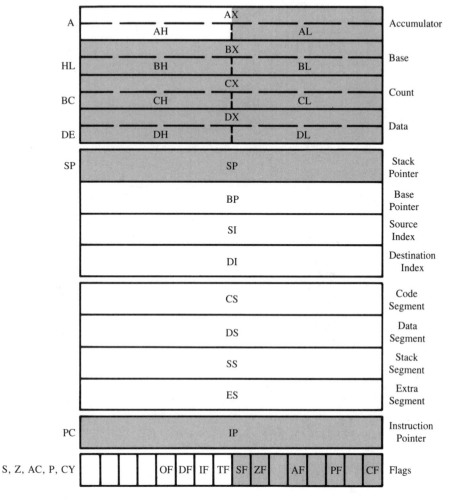

FIGURE 18.8
The 8086 Programming Registers (The Shaded Portions Show Areas Equivalent to the 8085)

SOURCE: Intel Corporation, *iAPX 86, 88 User's Manual* (Santa Clara, Calif.: Author, 1981), p. 2-9.

The new address can be obtained by redefining the address in the Code Segment Register and by using an appropriate count from the Instruction Pointer. By having four segment registers, the 1-megabyte memory space can be conveniently divided into different sections such as program, data, strings, and variables.

PARALLEL PROCESSING

The 8086 includes two processors called Execution Unit and Bus Interface Unit, shown in Figure 18.9. The concept of dividing work between two processors and processing it

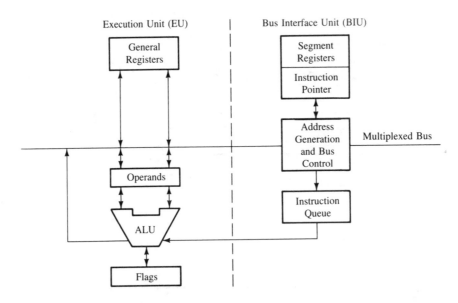

FIGURE 18.9
Execution and Bus Interface Units (EU and BIU) of the 8086
SOURCE: Intel Corporation, *iAPX 86, 88 User's Manual* (Santa Clara, Calif.: Author, 1981), p. 2-5.

simultaneously speeds up the execution. The execution process in the 8086 is similar to that of the 8085/8080A: fetch, decode, and execute. However, in the 8-bit processor, the buses are idle during the execution cycle. This idle time is avoided in the 8086, by assigning execution to the Execution Unit and fetching to the Bus Interface Unit. During the execution, the Bus Interface Unit fetches instructions and places them on a queue, as shown in Figure 18.9.

COPROCESSING

In addition to the 8086, Intel has designed a series of special function devices such as the 8089 (I/O Processor) and the 8087 (Numeric Processor). These processors are compatible with the 8086 in the master-slave relationship. They are designed with additional instructions and can be assigned dedicated functions to increase the overall execution speed of large systems.

INSTRUCTION SET

The 8086 has a large instruction set, consisting of 135 basic instructions, which can operate on individual bits, bytes, 16-bit words, and 32-bit double words. The set includes instructions such as multiply, divide, and bit and string manipulation.

MODULAR PROGRAMMING

In addition to the powerful instruction set, the chip design is oriented towards modular programming, which is highly desirable for high-level languages. The memory-segmentation concept facilitates programming of independent modules that can communicate with each other as well as share common data.

18.32 Motorola MC68000

This 16-bit microprocessor has a 32-bit internal architecture housed in a 64-pin package. It is capable of addressing sixteen megabytes of memory, and the clock frequency ranges from 4 MHz to 10 MHz for different versions of the chip.

Figure 18.10 shows the internal architecture of the device. It includes seventeen 32-bit, general purpose registers, a 32-bit program counter, and a 16-bit status register. The general purpose registers are divided into three groups: eight data registers, seven address registers, and two stack pointers. The contents of the data registers can be accessed as bytes, 16-bit words, or 32-bit words, and the contents of the address registers can be accessed as 16-bit or 32-bit addresses. The 68000 can operate in two different modes: the user mode and the supervisor mode. The supervisor mode is designed primarily for operating systems; in this mode, some privileged system control instructions can be used. Some of its other features can be described as follows.

NONSEGMENTED MEMORY

To increase the memory addressing capacity, Motorola increased the number of pins in its package. The chip is designed with 23 separate lines to address eight megawords (sixteen

FIGURE 18.10
Programming Registers
of the 68000

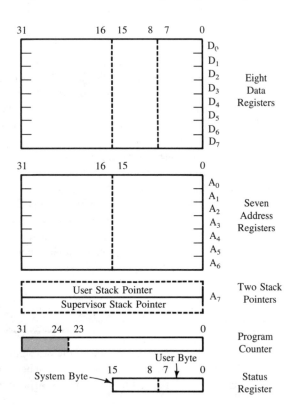

megabytes). Similarly, its program counter is 32 bits long; however, only the low-order 24 bits are necessary to address the entire memory map.

INSTRUCTION SET

The 68000 has one of the most powerful yet simple instruction sets. It includes 56 basic instructions and can operate on five different types of data: bit, byte, BCD, 16-bit word, and 32-bit word. It has only memory-mapped I/O but includes fourteen memory-addressing modes. To cite one example of its powerful set, its MOV instruction can transfer data from any source to any destination. It includes instructions such as Multiply and Divide and special instructions to deal with numbers longer than 32 bits. Its orientation towards high-level languages comes primarily from its instruction set.

ASYNCHRONOUS AND SYNCHRONOUS CONTROL LINES

The 68000 has a special way of handling slow and fast peripherals. It has two sets of control signals, called asynchronous and synchronous signals. Communication with asynchronous peripherals is handled through the control lines called Upper Data Strobe (UDS), Lower Data Strobe (LDS), and Data Acknowledge (DACK). The DACK signal is similar to a handshake line; the bus cycle is not terminated until the signal, DACK, is received. The 6800 family offers some synchronous peripherals, and communication with these peripherals is handled through the control signals called Valid Peripheral Address (VPA), Valid Memory Address (VMA), and Enable (E).

18.33   Review of 16-Bit Microprocessors

The 8086 and the 68000 are designed with two distinct philosophies. The 8086 uses only 40 pins and multiplexes most of the functions. It has employed several new architectural concepts such as memory segmentation, parallel processing, queueing, and coprocessing. On the other hand, the 68000 has adopted a 64-pin package and simplified its architecture. Both are oriented towards high-level languages and will perform some functions of mini- and mainframe computers.

The 16-bit microprocessors are too powerful to perform the functions of general purpose 8-bit microprocessors; therefore, they are less likely to replace 8-bit processors. Competition with the general purpose 8-bit microprocessors will come from another direction, the single-chip microcomputers. However, the single-chip microcomputers do not adapt well as vehicles for learning basic concepts, and the 16-bit microprocessors are too complex and cumbersome for instructional purposes. It appears, therefore, that the 8-bit microprocessors will dominate the instructional arena for a considerable period.

18.4   32-BIT MICROPROCESSORS

Several manufacturers have announced the development of 32-bit microprocessors. Some are available for commercial uses and some are being used within their own organizations. These microprocessors are known either as **supermicros** or **micro-mainframes**. As the names suggest, they are designed to compete with the traditional mini- and mainframe computers. Examples of the 32-bit microprocessors include devices such as the iAPX 432 (Intel), the Bellmac-32A (Bell Labs), the MC68020 (Motorola), and the NS 32032 (National Semiconductor). Motorola and National have two chips — the MC68000 and the NS 16032 — that have a 32-bit internal architecture and a 16-bit external data bus; they can be classified either as 16-bit or 32-bit microprocessors.

Some of the features of 32-bit microprocessors are as follows. These processors

- □ can address large memory space.
- □ are faster and more precise in arithmetic calculations than 16-bit microprocessors.
- □ require a package with more than 40 pins.
- □ are oriented towards high-level languages.
- □ have object-oriented architecture (explained later).
- □ perform many functions through hardware that were traditionally performed through software.

These microprocessors are not all based on the same design philosophy, some are single-chip and others are multiple-chip. To illustrate differences between design philosophies, two microprocessors, the Intel iAPX 432 and the Bellmac-32A will be discussed. Some of the general characteristics of these two microprocessors are shown in Table 18.1.

18.41   Intel iAPX 432

The iAPX 432 is a 3-chip unit: 43201, 02, and 03. The 43201 fetches and decodes instructions, the 43202 executes instructions, and the 43203 performs I/O interfacing. These chips are tied together by a processor-memory interconnect bus (Figure 18.11). Like

TABLE 18.1

Comparison of Two 32-Bit Microprocessors: Intel iAPX 432 and Bellmac-32A

	BELLMAC-32A[16,24]	INTEL iAPX 432[18]
Year of Commercial Introduction	1982*	1981
Technology	2.5-μm DOMINO CMOS	HMOS
No. of Transistors	146,000	219,000 ON 3 Chips
Size of Chip	160,000 mil^2	100,000 mil^2 Each
Power Dissipation	0.7 Watt at 8 MHz	2.5 Watts/Chip
Pin Count	63 Active 84 Total	64 Per Chip
Basic Clock Frequency	10 MHz	8 MHz
Direct Address Range (Bytes)	2^{32}	2^{24} Real; 2^{40} Virtual
No. of General Purpose Registers	16 User-Visible	No Registers Visible To User
No. of Basic Instructions	169	221
No. of Addressing Modes	18	5

NOTE: *Currently for internal use only.
SOURCE: Amar Gupta and Hoo-min D. Toong, "An Architectural Comparison of 32-Bit Microprocessors," *IEEE Micro* 3, no. 1 (February 1983): (© 1983 IEEE).

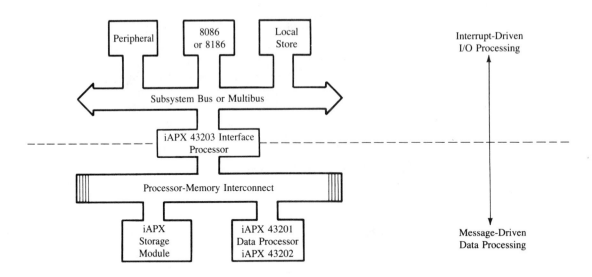

FIGURE 18.11

The Intel iAPX 432: 3-Chip 32-Bit Microprocessor

SOURCE: Amar Gupta and Hoo-min D. Toong, "An Architectural Comparison of 32-Bit Microprocessors," *IEEE Micro* 3, no. 1 (February 1983): 14 (© 1983 IEEE).

the 8086, the iAPX 432 uses the segmented memory scheme with each segment 2^{16} bytes long. It has 2^{24} segments; thus, it is capable of addressing 2^{40} bytes of virtual memory.

The instruction lengths range from 6 bits to 344 bits. The iAPX 432 can manipulate 8-bit characters, 16/32-bit integers, 32/64/80-bit floating point variables, bit strings, arrays, and records. The device is designed to support high-level languages, and is particularly suited for a language such as Ada. The instruction set is object oriented, the object is defined as data structures organized in a given manner. Single instructions can manipulate entire data structures. There are no registers available to users; functions traditionally performed by registers are executed through microinstructions. This is also known as microcoding, in which a group of instructions are written in the internal memory of the processor and executed in response to user instruction.

18.42   Bellmac-32A

The Bellmac-32A is a single-chip device housed in an 84-pin package. The device is intended for internal use, for products within the Bell organization. It is capable of addressing 2^{32} bytes of memory. The architecture of the device has two distinct functional units: the Fetch Unit and the Execution Unit (Figure 18.12). It has sixteen registers, each 32 bits wide. One register is used as a program counter and three registers are used to support the functions of operating systems. Figure 18.12 shows that the instructions fetched from memory are placed in the instruction queue, the arithmetic address unit performs all address calculations, and the ALU performs the execution.

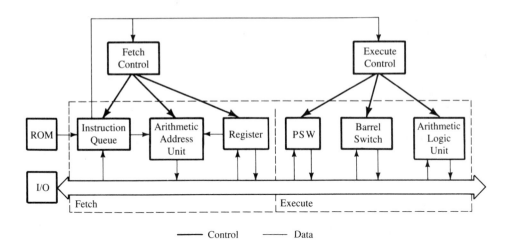

FIGURE 18.12

The Bellmac-32A Internal Architecture

SOURCE: Amar Gupta and Hoo-min D. Toong, "An Architectural Comparison of 32-Bit Microprocessors," *IEEE Micro* 3, no. 1 (February 1983): 13 (© 1983 IEEE).

The instruction set includes 169 instructions and can manipulate bytes, half words, words, and bit fields. The instruction set is designed to support high-level languages and is particularly suited for the C language. Single instructions can transfer blocks of data from memory to memory. However, it does not support either floating point or decimal arithmetic; it is suited for real-time applications.

18.43 Review of 32-Bit Microprocessors

The 32-bit microprocessors are oriented towards high-level languages. They can address a large memory space, execute instructions at high speed, and perform arithmetic operations with high precision. These microprocessors suggest a trend toward replacing software functions with hardware. They are designed to perform the functions normally found in mainframe computers.

A question quite often raised is: Will there be 48-bit or 64-bit microprocessors in the near future? It is difficult to answer such a question; however, we can speculate on the basis of present trends. The 32-bit mainframe computers have been in use for more than a decade (such as IBM 370, for commercial purposes). Similarly, 64-bit computers are being used for specialized scientific work. Harris Corporation recently announced a 48-bit minicomputer. However, the CPUs of these computers are less likely to be single-chip microprocessors, as suggested by the 3-chip iAPX 432 device and the 84-pin requirement for the Bellmac-32A. Therefore, it appears that single-chip microprocessors, with words larger than 32 bits, are technically feasible but — practically speaking — improbable.

18.5 BUS INTERFACE STANDARDS

The microcomputer is a bus-oriented system whereby subsystems or peripherals are interconnected through the bus architecture. The design approach should be such that systems are modular, expandable, and multipurpose. For example, a microcomputer with 32K memory should be expandable to 64K memory without any design changes as the user's needs change. The user should be able to select a peripheral from any manufacturer and plug it into the system. Similarly, the user should be able to print out programs as well as collect data from various instruments. To design microcomputers with such features, a common understanding of equipment specifications among manufacturers is needed; this is known as **defining standards**. In the field of electronics, these standards are generally defined by professional organizations such as IEEE (Institute for Electrical and Electronics Engineers); EIA (Electronic Industries Association), or the standards are forced upon the industry either by a dominant manufacturer or by common practice. The need for expandability and modularity gave rise to various bus standards, as listed in Table 18.2. The bus S-100, the Standard Bus, the Multibus, and the GPIB are described here, others were described in Chapter 16.

TABLE 18.2
Bus Standards

Buses	I/O Mode	Applications/Description
1. S-100 (IEEE-696)	Parallel	To interconnect various components within the microcomputer. It has 100 signals.
2. STD Bus	Parallel	This is a bus competing with S-100. It has 56 signals.
3. Multibus (IEEE-796)	Parallel	Interface between modules with the master/slave type communication. It has 86 signals.
4. GPIB (IEEE-488)	Parallel	Interface between the microcomputer and measurement equipment such as a voltmeter. It has 24 signals.
5. RS-232 C	Serial	Interface between the microcomputer and serial peripherals such as a terminal and a printer (see Chapter 16).
6. RS-422 and RS-423	Serial	High speed serial communication for distances longer than 20 meters.
7. Current Loop	Serial	Interface with current operated peripherals such as Teletype (see Chapter 16).

18.51 S-100 (IEEE 696) and Standard Bus

The primary force behind the development of these buses is their expandability. This type of bus allows the user to plug in additional peripherals (including memory) without any design changes and also facilitates troubleshooting. The bus design is based on the concept of the "mother board," a printed circuit board with parallel foil strips. Several edge connectors, connected to the foil strips, are included in a system, and some edge connectors are left empty for the user.

BUS INTERFACE

The bus signals are divided into four groups, as shown in Figure 18.13: power, data, address, and control. The S-100 bus has 100 signals, and the STD bus has 56 signals.

The S-100 bus was originally developed by MITS and IMASAI in 1975, even before the existence of a 16-bit microprocessor. The bus quickly became popular with hobbyists and it became the de-facto industry standard. Initially, several lines were undefined, causing contradictory uses by manufacturers. Eventually, IEEE adopted the S-100, with some modifications, as the IEEE-696 standard. This bus has 24 address lines, 16 data lines, 11 interrupts, and provision for multiprocessing.

The STD bus was recently (1981) developed by Pro-Log Corporation and MOSTEK, as a simple bus structure for 8-bit microprocessors. It is a 56-pin bus with 8 data lines, 16 address lines, 22 control lines, and 10 power lines. It is a better-defined bus, an improvement over the original S-100 bus. However, the S-100 is so widely used that the STD bus may have difficulty demonstrating its superiority to industry.

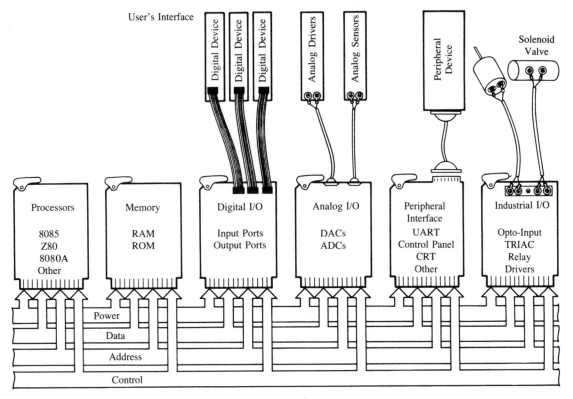

FIGURE 18.13
Bus Interface

SOURCE: Courtesy of Pro-Log Corporation, Monterey, Calif.

18.52   Multibus (IEEE 796)

The multibus is an 86-line (optional 60-line) bus developed by Intel Corporation to connect independent modules (or microcomputers) of various microprocessors to share resources. Each board can operate independently using its own memory and I/Os for dedicated functions. They can access a system's resources such as a hard disk or printer through the multibus.

The bus includes twenty address lines, sixteen bidirectional data lines, numerous control lines, and multiple power and ground lines; the bus control can be managed by IC devices such as the Intel 8218 or 8288. A multibus system can have many masters; therefore, control logic is required for arbitration and data flow when multiple requests are made to access the bus. Simultaneous requests to access the bus are handled through either serial or parallel techniques by control signals.

18.53   GPIB Interface Bus (IEEE 488)

This bus was developed to facilitate interfacing of programmable instruments (such as printers, digital voltmeters, and digital tape recorders) with computers. Initially, the bus was developed by Hewlett-Packard; later, it was accepted as the IEEE 488 Interface Standard. The bus standard is also known as the General Purpose Interface Bus (GPIB) or the Hewlett-Packard Interface Bus (HP-IB).

Some of the features of this bus are the following:

1. Data transfer among the interconnected devices is digital.
2. Fifteen devices may be connected to one continuous bus.
3. Total transmission path is limited to twenty meters or two meters per device.
4. Data rate on any signal line is limited to 1M-byte/sec.

BUS SIGNALS

The bus has 24 signals: eight bidirectional data lines, five general bus management lines, three handshake lines, and eight grounds. Figure 18.14 shows four types of devices that can be connected to the bus. These devices are classified as follows:

1. *Listener* is a device capable of receiving data when addressed; fourteen devices can listen at a time. Examples include printers and display devices.
2. *Talker* is a device capable of transmitting data when addressed; only one device can be active at a time. Examples include tape readers and voltmeters.
3. *Listener/Talker* is a device that can receive as well as transmit data over the interface. A programmable digital voltmeter (DVM) is a listener/talker device.
4. *Controller* is a device that controls signals and specifies which device can talk and which device can listen. A microcomputer with an appropriate I/O card can serve as a controller.

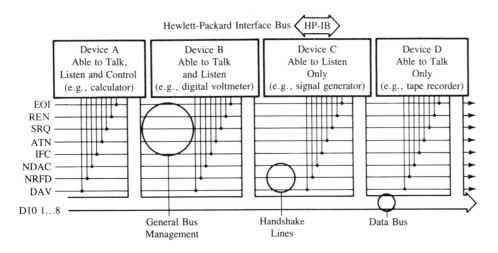

Hewlett-Packard Interface Bus

FIGURE 18.14
GPIB (IEEE 488) Bus Interface

SOURCE: Hewlett-Packard Company, *Tutorial Description of the Hewlett-Packard Interface Bus* (Palo Alto, Calif.: Author, 1980), p. 8, reproduced with permission.

SUMMARY

In this chapter, various microprocessors — from 8-bit to 32-bit — and single-chip microcontrollers from the Intel family were discussed, compared, and contrasted in terms of their characteristics and applications. Future trends in microprocessor technology were suggested.

Eight-bit microprocessors contemporary to the 8085/8080A were discussed in Section 18.1. These processors were classified primarily into two groups: register-oriented and memory-referenced. The Z80 and the NSC800 appear to have combined the best features of both the groups.

Single-chip microcomputers (also known as microcontrollers) and their applications were discussed in Section 18.2. These microcontrollers are specially designed to be geared towards certain applications, and their characteristics differ according to their areas of application.

Microprocessors with 16- and 32-bit words were discussed in Sections 18.3 and 18.4, respectively. They are designed to facilitate uses of high-level languages, and are expected to compete with mini- and mainframe computers. New architectural concepts such as memory segmentation, parallel processing, and queueing were employed in designing some of these processors, and some are designed with a package larger than 40 pins.

In addition, various bus standards were discussed.

References

Advanced Micro Devices Inc. *The 8080A/9080A Microprocessor Handbook*. Sunnyvale, Calif.: Author, 1979.

Analog Devices Inc. *Data Acquisition Components and Subsystems*. Norwood, Mass.: 1980.

Analog Devices Inc. *Integrated Circuit Converters Data Acquisition Systems and Analog Signal Conditioning Components*, Norwood, Mass.: Author, 1979.

Archer, Tod. *Simplifying Microprocessor-Based Product Design*. Beaverton, Ore.: Tektronix, 1979.

Burton, D. P., and A. L. Dexter. *Microprocessor Systems Handbook*. Norwood, Mass.: Analog Devices, 1979.

Coffron, James. *Practical Hardware Details for 8080, 8085, Z80, and 6800 Microprocessor Systems*. Englewood Cliffs, N. J.: Prentice-Hall Inc., 1981.

DeJong, M. L., et al. "Microcomputer Interfacing: Characteristics of the 8253 Programmable Interval Timer." *Computer Design* 17, no. 2 (February 1978): 136–140.

Floyd, Thomas. *Digital Logic Fundamentals*. 2nd ed. Columbus, Ohio: Charles E. Merrill Publishing Co., 1980.

E & L Instruments Inc. *Micro Designer (MMD1) User's Manual*. Derby, Conn.: Author, 1976.

Electronic Industries Association. *Interface Between Data Terminal Equipment and Data Communication Equipment Employing Serial Binary Data Interchange: RS-232-C Standard*. Washington, D. C.: Author, 1969. Reaffirmed in June 1981.

Gaonkar, Ramesh. "Data Conversion." In *Integrated Circuits Applications Handbook*, edited by Arthur Seidman. New York: John Wiley & Sons, 1983.

Goldsbrough, Paul. *Microcomputer Interfacing with the 8255 PPI Chip*. Indianapolis, Ind.: Howard W. Sams, 1979.

Grant, Douglas. *Interfacing the AD558 Dacport to Microprocessors*, Application Note. Norwood, Mass.: Analog Devices, 1980.

Hewlett Packard Company, *Tutorial Description of the Hewlett-Packard Interface Bus*. Palo Alto, Calif.: Author, 1980.

Hogan, Thom. *CP/M User's Guide*, Berkeley, Calif.: Osborne/McGraw-Hill, 1981.

Intel Corporation. *Microcontroller Handbook*. Santa Clara, Calif.: Author, 1984.

Intel Corporation. *Microprocessor and Peripheral Handbook*. Santa Clara, Calif.: Author, 1983.

Intel Corporation. *Peripheral Design Handbook*. Santa Clara, Calif.: Author, 1981.

Intel Corporation. *iAPX 86,88 User's Manual*. Santa Clara, Calif.: Author, 1981.

Intel Corporation. *MCS—80/85 Family User's Manual*. Santa Clara, Calif.: Author, 1979.

Intel Corporation. *8080/8085 Assembly Language Programming Manual*. Santa Clara, Calif.: Author, 1979.

Intel Corporation. *SDK-85 User's Manual*. Santa Clara, Calif.: Author, 1978.

Intel Corp. *8080 Microcomputer Systems User's Manu-*

al. Santa Clara, Calif.: Author, 1975.

Intersil Inc. *Data Book 1981,* Cupertino, Calif.: Author, 1981.

Larsen, D. G., et al. "Microcomputer Interfacing: A Demonstration Program for the 8253 Timer." *Computer Design* 17, no. 3 (March 1978): 134–136.

Larsen, David, Jonathan Titus, and Christopher Titus. *8080/8085 Software Design Book 2,* Indianapolis, Ind.: Howard W. Sams, 1979.

Larsen, David, Jonathan Titus, and Christopher Titus. *8080/8085 Software Design Book 1.* Indianapolis, Ind.: Howard W. Sams, 1977.

Leibson, Steve. "The Input/Output Primer, Part 5: Character Codes." *Byte* (June 1982): 242–258.

Leibson, Steve. "The Input/Output Primer, Part 4: The BCD and Serial Interfaces." *Byte* (May 1982): 202–220.

Leventhal, Lance. *Introduction to Microprocessors: Software, Hardware, Programming.* Englewood Cliffs, N. J.: Prentice Hall Inc., 1978.

MOSTEK. *Memory Data Book and Designer's Guide,* Carroliton, Texas: Author, 1980.

National Semiconductor Inc. *Linear Data Handbook,* Santa Clara, Calif.: Author, 1982.

Osborne, Adam, and Gerry Kane. *4- & 8-bit Microprocessor Handbook,* Berkeley, Calif.: Osborne/McGraw-Hill, 1981.

Pasahow, Edward. *Microprocessors and Microcomputers.* New York: McGraw-Hill Book Co., 1981.

Pro-Log Corporation, *Series 7000 STD Bus Technical Manual and Product Catalog.* Monterey, Calif.: Author, 1981.

Rony, Peter. "Interfacing Fundamentals: A Comparison of Block Diagrams for I/O Techniques." *Computer Design* (February 1982): 175–177.

Rony, Peter. "Interfacing Fundamentals: 2-Wire Handshake Using Two Microcomputers." *Computer Design* (June 1981): 156–160.

Rony, Peter. "Interfacing Fundamentals: Bidirectional I/O Using Two Semaphores." *Computer Design* (April 1981): 184–188.

Rony, Peter. "Interfacing Fundamentals: Conditional I/O Using Two Microcomputers." *Computer Design* (August 1980): 136–138.

Rony, Peter. "Interfacing Fundamentals: Conditional I/O Using a Semaphore." *Computer Design* (April 1980): 166–167.

Rony, Peter. *Interfacing & Scientific Data Communications Experiments.* Indianapolis, Ind.: Howard W. Sams, 1979.

Sloan, M. E. *Introduction to Minicomputers and Microcomputers.* Reading, Mass.: Addison-Wesley Publishing Co., 1980.

Texas Instruments Inc. *The TTL Data Book for Design Engineers.* 2nd ed. Dallas, Texas: Author, 1976.

Titus, Christopher, et al. *16-Bit Microprocessors.* Indianapolis, Ind.: Howard W. Sams, 1981.

Titus, Jonathan, et al. *Microcomputer-Analog Converter Software and Hardware Interfacing.* Indianapolis, Ind.: Howard W. Sams, 1978.

Tocci, Ronald, and Lester Laskowski. *Microprocessors and Microcomputers: Hardware and Software.* Englewood Cliffs, N. J.: Prentice-Hall Inc., 1979.

Toomey, Paul. *The AD7574 Analog to Microprocessor Interface,* Application Note. Norwood, Mass.: Analog Devices, 1982.

Zaks, Rodney. *Microprocessor from Chips to Systems,* Berkeley, Calif.: Sybex Inc., 1977.

Number Systems

Computers communicate and operate in binary digits 0 and 1; on the other hand, human beings generally use the decimal system with ten digits, from 0–9. Other number systems are also used, such as octal with eight digits, from 0–7, and hexadecimal (Hex) system with digits from 0–15. In the hexadecimal system, digits 10 through 15 are designated as A through F, respectively, to avoid confusion with the decimal numbers, 10 to 15.

A positional scheme is usually used to represent a number in any of the number systems. This means that each digit will have its value according to its position in a number. The number of digits in a position is also referred to as the base. For example, the binary system has base 2, the decimal system has base 10, and the hexadecimal system has base 16.

NUMBER CONVERSION A.1

A number in any base system can be represented in a generalized format as follows:

$$N = A_n B^n + A_{n-1} B^{n-1} + ------ + A_1 B^1 + A_0 B^0$$

$$N = \text{number}, B = \text{base}, A = \text{any digit in that base}$$

For example, number 154 can be represented in various number systems as follows:

Decimal: 154   = $1 \times 10^2 + 5 \times 10^1 + 4 \times 10^0$ =   154

Octal: 232   = $2 \times 8^2 + 3 \times 8^1 + 2 \times 8^0$
                       =   128   +   24   +   2   =   154

Hexadecimal: 9A   = $9 \times 16^1 + A \times 16^0$
                       =   144   +   10   =   154

Binary: 10011010   = $1 \times 2^7 + 0 \times 2^6 + 0 \times 2^5 + 1 \times 2^4 + 1 \times 2^3 + 0 \times 2^2 + 1 \times 2^1 + 0 \times 2^0$
                       =   128   +   0   +   0   +   16   +   8   +   0   +   2   +   0   =   154

The above example also shows how to convert a given number in any system into its decimal equivalent.

CONVERSION TABLE: DECIMAL, BINARY, OCTAL,
  AND HEXADECIMAL

Decimal	Hex	Binary	Octal
0	0	0000	00
1	1	0001	01
2	2	0010	02
3	3	0011	03
4	4	0100	04
5	5	0101	05
6	6	0110	06
7	7	0111	07
8	8	1000	10
9	9	1001	11
10	A	1010	12
11	B	1011	13
12	C	1100	14
13	D	1101	15
14	E	1110	16
15	F	1111	17

HOW TO CONVERT A NUMBER FROM BINARY INTO
  HEXADECIMAL AND OCTAL

Example

Convert the binary number 1   0   0   1   1   0   1   0 into its Hex and octal equivalents.

Hexadecimal

Step 1: Starting from the right (LSB) arrange the binary digits in groups of four.
          1   0   0   1   1   0   1   0

Step 2: Convert each group into its equivalent Hex number.
          9   A

Octal

Step 1: Starting from the right (LSB) arrange the binary digits in groups of three.

1 0   0 1 1   0 1 0

Step 2: Convert each group into its equivalent octal number.

2   3   2

2'S COMPLEMENT AND ARITHMETIC OPERATIONS   A.2

The 8085/8080A microprocessor performs the subtraction of two binary numbers using the 2's complement method. In digital logic circuits, it is easier to design a circuit to add numbers than to design a circuit to subtract numbers. The 2's complement of a binary number is equivalent to its negative number; thus by adding the complement of the subtrahend (the number to be subtracted) to the minuend, a subtraction can be performed. The method of 2's complement is explained below with the examples from the decimal number system.

DECIMAL SUBTRACTION

Subtract the following two decimal numbers using the borrow method and the 10's complement method: $(52 - 23)$

Example
A.1

$$\text{Minuend: } 52 = 5 \times 10 + 2$$
$$\text{Subtrahend: } 23 = 2 \times 10 + 3$$

Borrow
Method

Step 1: To subtract 3 from 2, 10 must be borrowed from the second place of the minuend.

$$52 = 4 \times 10 + 12$$

Step 2: The subtraction of the digits in the first place and the second place is as follows.

$$
\begin{array}{rcl}
52 & = & 4 \times 10 + 12 \\
-23 & = & 2 \times 10 + \ \ 3 \\
\hline
 & & 2 \times 10 + \ \ 9 = 29
\end{array}
$$

Step 1: Find 9's complement of the subtrahend (23), meaning subtract each digit of the subtrahend from 9.

10's
Complement
Method

9's complement of 23:
$$
\begin{array}{r}
9 \ \ 9 \\
-2 \ \ 3 \\
\hline
7 \ \ 6
\end{array}
$$

Step 2: Add 1 to the 9's complement to find the 10's complement of the subtrahend.

$$10\text{'s complement of } 23: \quad \begin{array}{r} 76 \\ +\ 1 \\ \hline 77 \end{array}$$

The reason to find the 9's complement is to demonstrate a similar procedure to find the 2's complement of a binary number. However, in reality, the 10's complement of 23 is equivalent to subtracting 23 from 100.

Step 3: Add 10's complement of the subtrahend (77) to the minuend (52) to subtract 23 from 52.

$$\begin{array}{rr} 10\text{'s complement of } 23: & 77 \\ \text{Minuend:} & +\ 52 \\ \hline & 1\ \ 29 \end{array} = 29 \quad \text{(By dropping the most significant digit)}$$

The elimination of the most significant bit is equivalent to subtracting 100 from the sum. This is necessary to compensate for the 100 that was added to find the 10's complement of 23.

Example A.2

Perform the subtraction of the following two numbers using the borrow method and the 10's complement method: $23 - 52$.

Borrow Method

$$\begin{array}{rr} \text{Minuend:} & 2\ 3 \\ \text{Subtrahend:} & 5\ 2 \end{array}$$

Step 1: The subtraction of the digits in the first place results in: $3 - 2 = 1$.

Step 2: To subtract the digits in the second place, a borrow is required from the third place. Assuming the borrow is available from the third place, the digit 5 can be subtracted from 2 as follows:

$$\begin{array}{r} 1\ \ 2 \\ -\ \ \ 5 \\ \hline \bar{1}\ \ 7 \end{array} \quad \text{(the nonexistent borrow is shown with the bar)}$$

$$\text{Result:} \quad \begin{array}{r} 23 \\ -\ 52 \\ \hline \bar{1}\ \ 71 \end{array}$$

The same result is obtained with the 10's complement method, as shown below.

10's Complement Method

Step 1: Find the 9's complement of the subtrahend (52).

$$9\text{'s complement of } 52: \quad \begin{array}{r} 9\ \ 9 \\ -5\ \ 2 \\ \hline 4\ \ 7 \end{array}$$

Step 2: Add 1 to the 9's complement to find 10's complement: $47 + 1 = 48$

Step 3: Add the 10's complement of the subtrahend to the minuend.

10's complement of 52:   48

Minuend: 23

71 (this is negative 29, expressed in 10's complement)

By examining these two examples, the following conclusions can be drawn and these conclusions can be used for any number system.

1. The complement of a number is its equivalent negative number.
2. A number can be subtracted by using its complement.
3. The sum of a number and its complement results in 0 if the most significant digit of the sum is ignored.
4. When the subtrahend is larger than the minuend, the result of the 10's complement method is negative, and it is expressed in terms of 10's complement. The same result can be obtained by borrowing a digit from the most significant position.

PROCEDURE TO FIND 2'S COMPLEMENT OF A BINARY NUMBER

Step 1: Find 1's complement. This amounts to replacing 0 by 1 and 1 by 0.

Step 2: To find 2's complement, add 1 to the 1's complement. This is similar to the procedure of 10's complement.

Find the 2's complement of the binary number:

Example A.3

$$0\ \ 0\ \ 0\ \ 1\quad 1\ \ 1\ \ 0\ \ 0\quad (1CH\ or\ 28_{10})$$

Step 1: Find 1's complement, meaning replace 0 with 1 and 1 with 0.

1's complement	=	1 1 1 0	0 0 1 1

Step 2: Add 1   +   1

2's complement = 1 1 1 0   0 1 0 0

By examining the result of the example, the following rule can be stated to find the 2's complement of a binary number, instead of the above procedure of the 1's complement.

Rule 1: Start at the LSB of a given number, and check all the bits to the left. Keep all the bits as they are up to and including the least significant 1.

Rule 2: After the first 1, replace all 0's with 1's and 1's with 0's.

These rules can be applied to the given binary number (1CH) as illustrated below:

```
Binary Number:   0   0   0   1     1   1   0   0 ◄─────┐
                 └──────────┘     └──────┘           │
                       ↓               ↓        Start Here
              Replace 0 with 1    Keep as they are
                and 1 with 0
2's complement:   1   1   1   0   0     1   0   0
```

The 2's complement of the number can be verified by adding the complement to the original number as follows, and the sum should be 0:

```
Binary Number:   0   0   0   1     1   1   0   0
2's Complement:  1   1   1   0     0   1   0   0
              1     0   0   0   0     0   0   0   0  (ignore the MSB)
```

BINARY SUBTRACTION USING 2'S COMPLEMENT

The binary subtraction can be performed by using 2's complement method, and if the result is negative, it is expressed in terms of 2's complement.

Example A.4

Subtract 32H (0011 0010) from 45H (0100 0101).

```
        Subtrahend:  32H  =  0  0  1  1    0  0  1  0
2's complement of 32H   =  1  1  0  0    1  1  1  0
                              +
          Minuend:  45H  =  0  1  0  0    0  1  0  1
                   CY      1         1    1
                        ─────────────────────────
                        0  0  0  1    0  0  1  1   =   13H
```

Example A.5

Subtract 45H (0100 0100) from 32H (0011 0010).

```
        Subtrahend:  45H  =  0  1  0  0    0  1  0  1
2's complement of 45H   =  1  0  1  1    1  0  1  1
                              +
          Minuend:  32H  =  0  0  1  1    0  0  1  0
                   CY   =     1  1         1
                        ─────────────────────────
                        1  1  1  0    1  1  0  1   =   EDH
```

The result is negative and it is expressed in 2's complement. This can be verified by taking the 2's complement of the result; the 2's complement of the result should be 13H as in Example 4.

```
        Result EDH    =  1  1  1  0    1  1  0  1
Two's complement of EDH  =  0  0  0  1    0  0  1  1   =   13H
```

SIGNED NUMBERS

To perform the arithmetic operations with signed numbers (positive and negative), the sign must be indicated as well as the magnitude of the number. In 8-bit microprocessors, bit D_7 is used to indicate the sign of a number; 0 in D_7 indicates a positive number and 1 indicates a negative number. Bit D_7 can be used to indicate the sign of a number because:

1. The 8085/8080A performs the subtraction of two numbers using 2's complement and, if the result is negative, it saves (shows) the result in the form of 2's complement.
2. 2's complement of all the 7-bit numbers have 1 in D_7.

When a programmer uses bit D_7 to indicate the sign of a number, the magnitude of the number can be represented by seven bits (D_6–D_0). For example, number 74H is represented with sign as follows:

$$
\begin{array}{ccccccccc}
 & & D_7 & D_6 & D_5 & D_4 & D_3 & D_2 & D_1 & D_0 \\
+74H & = & 0 & 1 & 1 & 1 & 0 & 1 & 0 & 0 \\
-74H & = & 1 & 0 & 0 & 0 & 1 & 1 & 0 & 0 \quad \text{(2's complement of 74H)}
\end{array}
$$

sign   magnitude

However, the microprocessor cannot differentiate between a positive number and a negative number. For example, in the above illustration, $-74H$ can be interpreted as the unsigned positive number 8CH or the bit pattern. It is the responsibility of the programmer to provide the necessary interpretation.

SUBTRACTION PROCESS IN THE 8085/8080A MICROPROCESSOR

The 8085/8080A performs the following operations when it subtracts (SUB or SUI) two binary numbers:

Step 1: Finds one's complement of the subtrahend.

Step 2: Finds two's complement of the subtrahend by adding 1 to the result of Step 1.

Step 3: Adds the two's complement of the subtrahend to the minuend.

Step 4: Complements the CY flag.

These steps are internal to the microprocessor and invisible to the user; only the result is available to the user.

Show the internal steps performed by the microprocessor to subtract the following unsigned numbers:
a. FAH − 62H
b. 62H − FAH

Example A.6

a. Minuend: FAH $=$ 1 1 1 1   1 0 1 0
     Subtrahend: 62H $=$ 0 1 1 0   0 0 1 0

Step 1: 1's complement of 62H $=$ 1 0 0 1   1 1 0 1
Step 2: Add 1 $+$ 1

            2's complement of 62H $=$ 1 0 0 1   1 1 1 0
Step 3: Add minuend (FAH) $+1$ 1 1 1   1 0 1 0
                                     ─────────────────────────
                                      1 1 0 0 1   1 0 0 0
Step 4: Complement CY   0 1 0 0 1   1 0 0 0
            Result: 0 1 0 0 1   1 0 0 0 $=$ 98H
            Flags: CY $=$ 0, S $=$ 1, Z $=$ 0, P $=$ 0.

b. Minuend: 62H $=$ 0 1 1 0   0 0 1 0
    Subtrahend: FAH $=$ 1 1 1 1   1 0 1 0

Step 1: 1's complement of FAH $=$ 0 0 0 0   0 1 0 1
Step 2: Add 1 $+$ 1

            2's complement of FAH $=$ 0 0 0 0   0 1 1 0
Step 3: Add minuend (62H) $+0$ 1 1 0   0 0 1 0
                                     ─────────────────────────
                                      0 0 1 1 0   1 0 0 0
Step 4: Complement CY   1 0 1 1 0   1 0 0 0
            Result: 1 0 1 1 0   1 0 0 0 $=$ 68H (CY $=$ 1)
            Flags: CY $=$ 1, S $=$ 0, Z $=$ 0, P $=$ 0

This result is negative and expressed in 2's complement of the magnitude.

Results   a. FAH $-$ 62H $=$ 98H (positive), CY $=$ 0, S $=$ 1
           b. 62H $-$ FAH $=$ 68H (negative), CY $=$ 1, S $=$ 0

These results and associated flags appear to be confusing. In Example A.6a, the result is positive but the sign flag indicates that it is negative. On the other hand, in Example A.6b, the result is negative but the sign flag indicates that it is positive. This confusion can be explained as follows:

1. This subtraction is concerned with the unsigned numbers; therefore, the sign flag is irrelevant. In signed arithmetic, the number FAH is invalid because it is an 8-bit number.
2. The programmer can check whether the result indicates the true magnitude by checking the CY flag. If CY is reset, the result is positive, and if CY is set, the result is expressed in 2's complement.

Example   In Example A.6a, assume that the numbers are signed numbers, and interpret the result.
A.7   *Minuend:* FAH
            This is a negative number because $D_7 = 1$; therefore, this must be represented in 2's complement. The magnitude of the number can be found by taking the 2's complement of FAH:

$$\begin{aligned} \text{FAH} &= 1\ 1\ 1\ 1\quad 1\ 0\ 1\ 0 \\ \text{2's complement of FAH} &= 0\ 0\ 0\ 0\quad 0\ 1\ 1\ 0 \\ &= 06\text{H (magnitude)} \end{aligned}$$

Subtrahend: 62H (This is a positive number because $D_7 = 0$.)
   The problem given in 6a can be represented as follows:

$$\begin{aligned} \text{FAH} - 62\text{H} &= (-06\text{H}) - (+62\text{H}) \\ &= -68\text{H} \end{aligned}$$

The final result is -68H, which will be in the form of its 2's complement:

$$\begin{aligned} -68\text{H} &= -(0\ 1\ 1\ 0\quad 1\ 0\ 0\ 0) \\ \text{2's complement of 68H} &= 1\ 0\ 0\ 1\quad 1\ 0\ 0\ 0 \\ &= 98\text{H} \end{aligned}$$

The final answer is the same as before; however, it will be interpreted as a negative number with the magnitude of 68H. When signed numbers are used in arithmetic operations, the sign flag will indicate the proper sign of the result.

Add the following two positive numbers and interpret the sign flag: $+41$H, $+54$H

$$\begin{array}{lllllllll} 41\text{H} = & 0 & 1 & 0 & 0 & 0 & 0 & 0 & 1 \\ + & & & & & & & & \\ \underline{54\text{H}} = & \underline{0} & \underline{1} & \underline{0} & \underline{1} & \underline{0} & \underline{1} & \underline{0} & \underline{0} \\ 95\text{H} = & 1 & 0 & 0 & 1 & 0 & 1 & 0 & 1 \end{array}$$

$\text{S} = 1,\ \text{CY} = 0,\ \text{Z} = 0$

This is an addition of two positive numbers; therefore, the sign flag indicates that the sum is larger than seven bits. This is also known as overflow. If this would have been the sum of two unsigned numbers, the sign flag has no significance.

How to Use the Intel SDK-85 System

B.11   System Description

The SDK-85 is a single-board microcomputer from Intel, designed with the 8085 micro-processor, primarily for training purposes. This system is widely used in college laboratories. Figure B.1 shows the functional block diagram of the system. It includes: the 8085

SOURCE: Appendix B is adapted from class notes by James Delaney, Onondaga Community College.

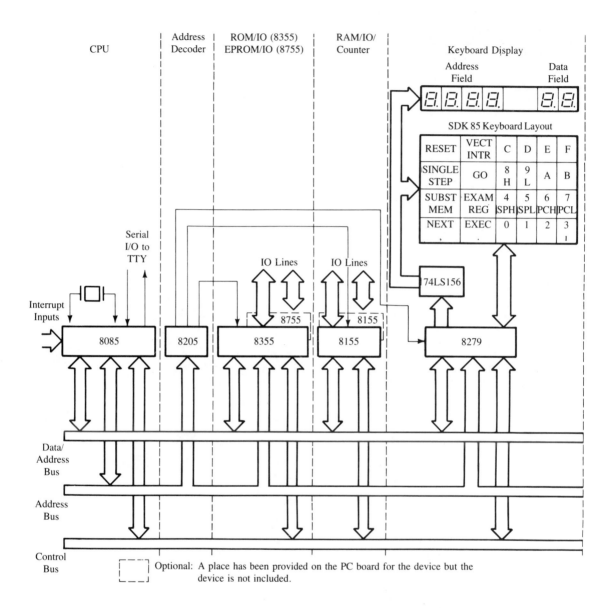

FIGURE B.1
SDK-85 Functional Block Diagram and Keyboard

SOURCE: Intel Corporation, *SDK—85 User's Manual* (Santa Clara, Calif.: Author, 1978), p. 5-2.

microprocessor, the 8755 (or 8355) as EPROM, the 8155 (R/W Memory with I/O), Hex keyboard, and six seven-segment LEDs for display. The keyboard and the display are interfaced with the 8085 through the keyboard/display controller the 8279.

The keyboard enables the user to enter and store the 8085 Hex machine code representing the 8085 assembly language programs in R/W memory. A program can be executed using the function keys on the keyboard, and the result can be displayed by the seven-segment LEDs. The LEDs are also used to display memory addresses and their contents while entering, modifying, or examining the programs.

THE 8755 EPROM (OR THE 8355 ROM)

This is a 2K memory with the memory map from 0000H to 07FFH. The system monitor program is stored permanently in this memory; the program can be examined but cannot be modified. This program continuously monitors the keyboard and displays the Hex keys at the LEDs. The primary function of the system monitor is to enable the user to enter, modify, and execute a program.

The 8755 also includes two I/O ports that can be used to interface with additional I/O devices.

THE 8155

This chip has 256 bytes of R/W memory, two I/O ports, and one timer. The memory map of the 8155 ranges from 2000H to 20FFH; however, the memory locations from 20C2H to 20FFH are reserved for the use of the monitor or some other functions. In this memory, the user can enter a program and execute it using the keyboard.

The I/O ports can be used to interface additional devices, and the timer can be used to provide pulses or time delays.

THE 8279

This is a programmable device used to handle keyboard and display. It displays memory addresses and data from its internal memory at the LEDs using the scanned technique. When a key is pressed, the 8085 is interrupted, and a new key is stored in the internal memory of the 8279 and displayed.

THE 8205 AND THE 74LS156

The 8205 is a 3-to-8 decoder used to decode the address lines and provide Chip Select signals to the memory chips: the 8155 and the 8355 and to the 8279. Similarly, the 74LS156 is also used as a decoder for the column lines of the keyboard/display chip, and the output lines of the decoder are used to scan the columns of the keyboard and control the cathodes of the seven-segment LEDs.

B.12   Keyboard

The keyboard has 24 keys; 16 keys for Hex digits, from 0–F, and the other eight keys for various functions, as shown below:

1. RESET: Reset the system.
2. SUBST MEM: Locate memory location to examine or modify its contents.

3. NEXT: Store the displayed data byte in memory and go to the next memory location and display its contents.

4. GO: Locate memory location to start execution.

5. EXEC: Start execution

6. VECT INTR: Jump to 20CEH

7. SINGLE STEP: Execute the program, one instruction at a time.

8. EXAM REG: Display the contents of registers.

B.13 Memory Map

The memory map of the system is shown in Table B.1. The user memory ranges from 2000H to 20FFH; however, the locations starting at 20C2H to 20FFH are reserved for user interrupts and the monitor stack. Table B.2 shows the list of memory locations and their contents.

B.14 Available Subroutines

The monitor program includes several subroutines, which the user can access by calling their respective addresses. Some of the subroutines are listed below:

TABLE B.1
SDK-85 Memory Map

Memory	
0000 07FF	Monitor ROM (2K)
0800 0FFF	Expansion ROM (2K)
1000 17FF	Open
1800 1FFF	1800 — Keyboard/Display Controller — Data Loc 1900 — Keyboard/Display Controller
2000 20FF	User R/W Memory (256 Bytes)
2100 27FF	User R/W Memory (Foldback)
2800 28FF	Expansion Space for User R/WM
2900 2FFF	Expansion Foldback
3000 7FFF	Open
8000 FFFF	Memory Space Where Expansion Buffers Are Enabled

TABLE B.2
Monitor Reserved RAM Locations

20C2	RST 5	The monitor program transfers these Restart instructions to these locations. Users may write Jump instructions to locate service routines.
20C5	RST 6	
20C8	RST 6.5 (Hardwired User Interrupt)	
20CB	RST 7	
20CE	VECT INTR	
20D1 — 20FF:	Reserved for Monitor Stack and Register Information	

☐ *UPDAD (0363H):* This subroutine displays the contents of the DE register in the address field; the contents of all the registers are affected.

☐ *UPDDT (036EH):* This subroutine displays the contents of the accumulator in the data field; the contents of all the registers are affected.

☐ *DELAY (05F1H):* This is a delay subroutine; the delay is determined by the contents of the DE register. Registers A, D, E, and the flags are affected.

USING THE SDK-85   B.2

The SDK-85 can be used to:

☐ Enter programs in its R/W memory (2000H–20C1H).
☐ Examine and modify the contents of memory.
☐ Execute programs.
☐ Debug programs using Single Step, Breakpoint, Register Examine, and Interrupt facilities.

After the execution of a program, results can be displayed at the system's seven-segment LEDs by calling appropriate display routines from the monitor program. Additional seven-segment LEDs can also be connected to programmable I/O ports (8155 or 8355), if necessary.

B.21 How to Enter a Program

To enter the program illustrated in Chapter 4 (Section 4.3) starting at location 2000H:

	Displays	
Press	**Address Field**	**Data Field**
RESET	−8 0	8 5
SUBST MEM		

	Displays	
Press	**Address Field**	**Data Field**

Press	Address Field	Data Field	
2 0 0 0	2 0 0 0		
NEXT	2 0 0 0	* *.	
3 E	2 0 0 0	3 E.	MVI A, 32H
NEXT	2 0 0 1	* *.	
3 2	2 0 0 1	3 2.	
NEXT	2 0 0 2	* *.	
0 6	2 0 0 2	0 6.	MVI B, 48H
NEXT	2 0 0 3	* *.	
4 8	2 0 0 3	4 8.	
NEXT	2 0 0 4	* *.	
8 0	2 0 0 4	8 0.	ADD B
NEXT	2 0 0 5	* *.	
4 F	2 0 0 5	4 F.	MOV C, A
NEXT	2 0 0 6	* *.	
7 6†	2 0 0 6	7 6.	HLT

To terminate the program entry, use RESET or EXEC.
To modify the contents of a memory location press:

1. SUBST / MEM , Memory Address, and NEXT : Memory address and its contents will be displayed.

2. New data byte, and NEXT : New data byte will be stored, and the next memory location and its contents will be displayed.

B.22   To Execute the Program

Press

RESET
GO 2 0 0 0   Starting Location
EXEC   E   Execution Complete

RESULTS

This program does not send any result to an output port. Therefore, to verify the result that is stored in register C and in the accumulator, EXAM / REG key† should be used as described in Section B.27.

---

†The HLT instruction should be replaced by the RST1 (Code CF) to use exam register key.

B.23   Why RESET Can Be Hazardous to Your Program

In the 8085, the RESETIN is asynchronous; therefore, the RESET key in the SDK-85 system may modify the register contents or even clear the memory location indicated by the program counter at the time of RESET.

   If the program ends with the HLT instruction, the memory location immediately following that instruction may be cleared by the RESET. Similarly, RESET may modify the contents of internal register. Therefore, if you need to examine the register contents, terminate the program with the instruction RST 1 (Machine Code CF) instead of HLT. The RST 1 instruction returns the program control to the monitor program.

   If a program with delays, such as a counter, is being executed and, if RESET is used, the program may not run properly at the next attempt. When the RESET is pressed, it may clear the contents of the memory location indicated by the program counter. In a program with a delay loop, the most likely place for modification to occur is the Jump instruction.

   For example, if you are running the Illustrative Program for a zero-to-nine counter (Section 7.3) and you press RESET, you will most likely clear the memory location XX0B (C2: JNZ instruction). Before you run the program again, check the machine code of your program.

B.24   How to Display Results at the SDK-85 LED Port

The SDK-85 display is managed by the programmable controller the 8279 using the scanned technique. The port cannot be accessed by simply writing the OUT instruction. However, a data byte can be displayed by calling the subroutine UPDDT (Update Data). This subroutine displays the contents of the accumulator. But this subroutine cannot be used, without modification, for a changing display in a counter because the subroutine modifies the contents of all the registers. Two examples are illustrated below.

To display the output in the above illustration B.21 (from Section 4.3), add the following instructions:

Example
B.1

Memory	Code	Mnemonics	
2006	CD	CALL UPDDT	;Subroutine UPDDT displays (A)
2007	6E		;Subroutine location 036EH
2008	03		
2009	76	HLT	

To display the count in the Illustrative Program for a zero-to-nine counter (Section 7.3), add the following instructions starting at location 2003 and make changes in the memory addresses of the subsequent instructions.

Example
B.2

2003	F5	DSPLAY: PUSH PSW	;Save register contents
2004	C5	PUSH B	

2005	D5	PUSH D	
2006	E5	PUSH H	
2007	CD	CALL UPDDT	;Call subroutine to display count
2008	6E		
2009	03		
200A	E1	POP H	;Restore register contents
200B	D1	POP D	
200C	C1	POP B	
200D	F1	POP PSW	
200E	Continue	LXI H	
	LOOP:	DCX H	

The OUT instruction in the program is replaced by the CALL to the subroutine UPDDT. However, before the CALL instruction, all register contents are saved on the stack and the contents are restored before continuing with the program.

B.25   Building Additional Displays on the Board

The SDK-85 has two devices with programmable I/Os: the 8155 and the 8355. Additional seven-segment LEDs can be connected to these ports. Figure B.2 shows the schematic to connect four seven-segment LEDs (Dialco 745-0007). These LEDs include a binary to seven-segment decoding circuit; therefore, only four connections per LED must be made. These output ports have port addresses as 00H and 01H, as shown in the schematic. However, these ports must be initialized before they can function as output ports. The initialization instructions are given below.

Example B.3	Modify the program given above in Item 1 (from Section 4.3) to display the output at the port 00H.		
	2000	3E	MVI A, FFH	;Initialization words for port 00 and 01

2000	3E	MVI A, FFH	;Initialization words for port 00 and 01
2001	FF		
2002	D3	OUT 02H	;Set up port 00 as output
2003	02		
2004	D3	OUT 03H	;Set up port 01 as output
2005	03		
2006	3E	MVI A, 32H	;This is the beginning of the program
2007	32		
2008	06	MVI B, 48H	
2009	48		
200A	80	ADD B	
200B	4F	MOV C,A	;Save result in register C

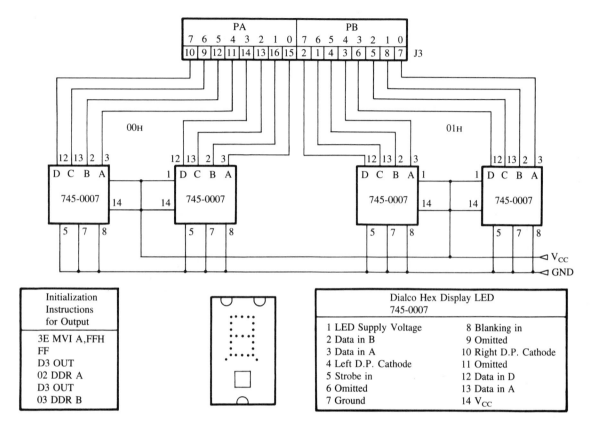

Initialization
Instructions
for Output

| 3E MVI A,FFH |
| FF |
| D3 OUT |
| 02 DDR A |
| D3 OUT |
| 03 DDR B |

Dialco Hex Display LED
745-0007

1 LED Supply Voltage	8 Blanking in
2 Data in B	9 Omitted
3 Data in A	10 Right D.P. Cathode
4 Left D.P. Cathode	11 Omitted
5 Strobe in	12 Data in D
6 Omitted	13 Data in A
7 Ground	14 V_{CC}

FIGURE B.2
Hex Display Ports

200C	D3	OUT 00H	;Display result at port 00H
200D	00		
200E	76	HLT	

In the above program, the first six machine codes from memory location 2000H to 2005H are initialization instructions for the programmable ports of the 8355 (Figure B.2). These instructions should be included with every program when the LEDs shown in Figure B.2 are used as output displays. The remaining program is essentially the same as it was earlier, except that it includes the OUT instruction. This procedure suggests that the user program should begin at location 2006; however, the execution of this program should begin at 2000H. Inclusion of the initialization instructions at 2000H will require changes in the memory addresses of the illustrative programs in Chapters 7, 8, and 9, if the user wishes to execute these programs. An alternative procedure is suggested below.

The initialization instructions can be written in high memory locations, such as 2090H to 2095H, followed by the Jump instruction to location 2000H as shown below.

```
2090          Initialization
  |           Instructions
  ↓
2095
2096          C3            JMP 2000H            ;Go to user program
2097          00
2098          20
```

The execution of this program should begin at 2090H.

B.26   How to Use Single Step

The Single Step allows the user to execute one instruction at a time.

a. To use the Single Step execution, press

| SINGLE |, Memory, | NEXT | and continue with | NEXT |
| STEP | Address

At each NEXT key, the first memory address of an instruction and its contents will be displayed. The display does not show each byte.

b. To terminate the Single Step, press

| EXEC | or | RESET |

c. To resume the execution with system's clock, press

| EXEC |, | GO | Memory, | EXEC |
                  Address

The execution will begin from the address specified.

B.27   How to Use Examine Register

The | EXAM | key allows the user to examine and modify the contents of the 8085 registers.
    | REG |

a. To examine register contents, press

Step 1. | EXAM |, Register Key (See Register Display Key Code — Table B.3)
           | REG |

This will display the name of the register and its contents.

Step 2. | NEXT | will store the contents of the register shown in Step 1, and display the next register (see Register Code) and its contents.

Subsequent NEXT keys will display the register contents in sequence until (PCL) is displayed, then Examine Register function is terminated.

Step 3. EXEC: will terminate Examine Register function after any register key.

    b. To modify register contents, press

                 | EXAM REG |, Register key, New Byte, | NEXT | or | EXEC |

To use the Examine Register function at the end of the program, the HLT instruction should be replaced by RST 1 (Code CF). To terminate the HLT instruction, RESET is necessary, which will modify the contents of the registers. After the RESET, the Examine Register function cannot provide accurate information.

B.28 How to Debug a Program by Setting Breakpoints

Assume that a program is stored from 2000H to 2050H. To check the segment of the program up to location 2015H, you can insert RST 1 (Code CF) at location 2016H and execute the program. When the 8085 executes the RST 1 instruction, it returns to the monitor program. Now the Examine Register function can be used to check the contents of the registers.

    To resume execution of the program, press

                 | GO |: The address 2017H will be displayed.
                 | EXEC |: will continue the execution.

More breakpoints can be set in the program. Furthermore, the Single Step function can also be used in conjunction with the breakpoint function.

TABLE B.3
Register Display Key Code

Keys	Register
A	Accumulator
B	Register B
C	Register C
D	Register D
E	Register E
F	Flags
I	Interrupt Mask
H	Register H
L	Register L
SPH	Stack Pointer High Byte
SPL	Stack Pointer Low Byte
PCH	Program Counter High Byte
PCL	Program Counter Low Byte

B.29 How to Use the Vector Interrupt

The VECT | INTR | key interrupts the 8085; this is RST 7.5 interrupt.

The program control is transferred to location 003CH in the monitor. The JMP instruction is written at location 003CH to transfer the program in the R/W memory at 20CEH. This key is used primarily to demonstrate an interrupt.

Preferred
Logic Symbols

THE OR GATE AS THE NEGATIVE NAND GATE

The OR gate is normally represented as shown in Figure C.1(a). The truth table in Figure C.1(c) shows that when any one of the inputs is high, the output is high; and when both inputs are low, the output is low. In applications where the output required is active high, the symbol in Figure C.1(a) accurately represents the signal states. However, in some applications, the output required is *active low* when both inputs are low. For example, in Figure 3.5, the control signal $\overline{\text{MEMW}}$ is generated when both inputs $\text{IO}/\overline{\text{M}}$ and $\overline{\text{WR}}$ are low. Therefore, it is preferable to represent the active states by the Negative

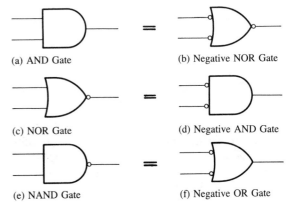

| Inputs | | Output |
A	B	X
High	High	High
High	Low	High
Low	High	High
Low	Low	Low

(a) OR Gate   (b) Negative NAND Gate   (c) Truth Table for Two-Input OR Gate

FIGURE C.1
OR Gate Logic Symbols and Truth Table

NAND gate as shown in Figure C.1(b). Physically, the gate in Figure C.1(a) is the same as the gate in C.1(b); both are OR gates. However, they will be interpreted differently. In Figure C.1(a), the gate function should be read as follows: when input A *or* input B is high, the output goes high. In Figure C.1(b), the gate function should be read as follows: when input A *and* input B are low, the output goes low.

THE AND GATE AS THE NEGATIVE NOR GATE

The AND gate shown in Figure C.2(a) should be read as follows: when input A *and* input B are high, the output goes high. However, the equivalent gate shown in Figure C.2(b) should be read as follows: when input A *or* input B is low, the output goes low. Figure 11.30 is a typical application of the Negative NOR representation of the AND gate. In Figure 11.30, the 3-to-8 decoder is enabled whenever one or the other control signal is asserted.

THE NOR GATE AS THE NEGATIVE AND GATE

The NOR gate in Figure C.2(c) should be read as follows: when input A *or* input B is high, the output goes low. However, its equivalent gate shown in Figure C.2(d) should be

FIGURE C.2
Logic Gates and Their
Equivalent Symbols

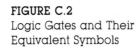

(a) AND Gate   (b) Negative NOR Gate

(c) NOR Gate   (d) Negative AND Gate

(e) NAND Gate   (f) Negative OR Gate

read as follows: when input A *and* input B are low, the output goes high. Figure 11.8 shows the NOR gate (74LS02) connected as the Negative AND gate. It suggests that when the signal I/O write ($\overline{\text{IOW}}$) and the decoded address pulse are low, the output goes high and enables the flip-flop.

THE NAND GATE AS THE NEGATIVE OR GATE

Figure C.2(e) shows the normal representation of the NAND gate and Figure C.2(f) shows its equivalent as the Negative OR gate.

INVERTERS AND BUBBLE MATCHING

When the inverter is represented by its symbol, the bubble can be shown either in the front or in the back depending upon the active level of the input signal. For example, in Figure 2.5 the inverters to the 8-input NAND gate are shown with bubbles at the back. The bubble suggests that address lines A_{15}–A_8 should be at logic 0 to cause the output of the gate to go active low.

SUMMARY

A logic gate can be represented with different symbols. However, the symbol should be selected based on the active level of the signals. If the active level of the signals is represented, it is easy to interpret the gate function and it facilitates troubleshooting.

Specifications and Applications: Programmable Interrupt Controller

Appendix D specifications begin on the next page.

SOURCE: Programmable Interrupt Controller: Intel Corporation, *MCS — 80/85 Family User's Manual* (Santa Clara, Calif.: Author, 1979), pp. 6-132 and 6-136–6-141.

8259A/8259A-2/8259A-8
PROGRAMMABLE INTERRUPT CONTROLLER

- **iAPX 86, iAPX 88 Compatible**
- **MCS-80®, MCS-85® Compatible**
- **Eight-Level Priority Controller**
- **Expandable to 64 Levels**

- **Programmable Interrupt Modes**
- **Individual Request Mask Capability**
- **Single +5V Supply (No Clocks)**
- **28-Pin Dual-In-Line Package**

The Intel® 8259A Programmable Interrupt Controller handles up to eight vectored priority interrupts for the CPU. It is cascadable for up to 64 vectored priority interrupts without additional circuitry. It is packaged in a 28-pin DIP, uses NMOS technology and requires a single +5V supply. Circuitry is static, requiring no clock input.

The 8259A is designed to minimize the software and real time overhead in handling multi-level priority interrupts. It has several modes, permitting optimization for a variety of system requirements.

The 8259A is fully upward compatible with the Intel® 8259. Software originally written for the 8259 will operate the 8259A in all 8259 equivalent modes (MCS-80/85, Non-Buffered, Edge Triggered).

Block Diagram

Pin Configuration

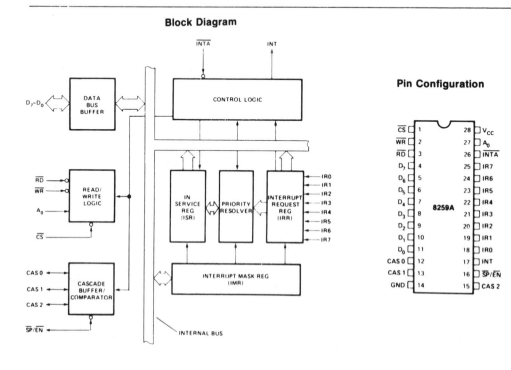

INTERRUPT SEQUENCE OUTPUTS

MCS-80®, MCS-85®

This sequence is timed by three $\overline{\text{INTA}}$ pulses. During the first $\overline{\text{INTA}}$ pulse the CALL opcode is enabled onto the data bus.

**Content of First Interrupt
Vector Byte**

	D7	D6	D5	D4	D3	D2	D1	D0
CALL CODE	1	1	0	0	1	1	0	1

During the second $\overline{\text{INTA}}$ pulse the lower address of the appropriate service routine is enabled onto the data bus. When Interval = 4 bits A_5-A_7 are programmed, while A_0-A_4 are automatically inserted by the 8259A. When Interval = 8 only A_6 and A_7 are programmed, while A_0-A_5 are automatically inserted.

**Content of Second Interrupt
Vector Byte**

IR	Interval = 4							
	D7	D6	D5	D4	D3	D2	D1	D0
7	A7	A6	A5	1	1	1	0	0
6	A7	A6	A5	1	1	0	0	0
5	A7	A6	A5	1	0	1	0	0
4	A7	A6	A5	1	0	0	0	0
3	A7	A6	A5	0	1	1	0	0
2	A7	A6	A5	0	1	0	0	0
1	A7	A6	A5	0	0	1	0	0
0	A7	A6	A5	0	0	0	0	0

IR	Interval = 8							
	D7	D6	D5	D4	D3	D2	D1	D0
7	A7	A6	1	1	1	0	0	0
6	A7	A6	1	1	0	0	0	0
5	A7	A6	1	0	1	0	0	0
4	A7	A6	1	0	0	0	0	0
3	A7	A6	0	1	1	0	0	0
2	A7	A6	0	1	0	0	0	0
1	A7	A6	0	0	1	0	0	0
0	A7	A6	0	0	0	0	0	0

During the third INTA pulse the higher address of the appropriate service routine, which was programmed as byte 2 of the initialization sequence $(A_8 - A_{15})$, is enabled onto the bus.

**Content of Third Interrupt
Vector Byte**

D7	D6	D5	D4	D3	D2	D1	D0
A15	A14	A13	A12	A11	A10	A9	A8

iAPX 86, iAPX 88

iAPX 86 mode is similar to MCS-80 mode except that only two Interrupt Acknowledge cycles are issued by the processor and no CALL opcode is sent to the processor. The first interrupt acknowledge cycle is similar to that of MCS-80, 85 systems in that the 8259A uses it to internally freeze the state of the interrupts for priority resolution and as a master it issues the interrupt code on the cascade lines at the end of the INTA pulse. On this first cycle it does not issue any data to the processor and leaves its data bus buffers disabled. On the second interrupt acknowledge cycle in iAPX 86 mode the master (or slave if so programmed) will send a byte of data to the processor with the acknowledged interrupt code composed as follows (note the state of the ADI mode control is ignored and A_5-A_{11} are unused in iAPX 86 mode):

**Content of Interrupt Vector Byte
for iAPX 86 System Mode**

	D7	D6	D5	D4	D3	D2	D1	D0
IR7	T7	T6	T5	T4	T3	1	1	1
IR6	T7	T6	T5	T4	T3	1	1	0
IR5	T7	T6	T5	T4	T3	1	0	1
IR4	T7	T6	T5	T4	T3	1	0	0
IR3	T7	T6	T5	T4	T3	0	1	1
IR2	T7	T6	T5	T4	T3	0	1	0
IR1	T7	T6	T5	T4	T3	0	0	1
IR0	T7	T6	T5	T4	T3	0	0	0

PROGRAMMING THE 8259A

The 8259A accepts two types of command words generated by the CPU:

1. *Initialization Command Words (ICWs):* Before normal operation can begin, each 8259A in the system must be brought to a starting point — by a sequence of 2 to 4 bytes timed by $\overline{\text{WR}}$ pulses.

2. *Operation Command Words (OCWs):* These are the command words which command the 8259A to operate in various interrupt modes. These modes are:

   a. Fully nested mode
   b. Rotating priority mode
   c. Special mask mode
   d. Polled mode

The OCWs can be written into the 8259A anytime after initialization.

INITIALIZATION COMMAND WORDS (ICWS)

GENERAL

Whenever a command is issued with A0 = 0 and D4 = 1, this is interpreted as Initialization Command Word 1 (ICW1). ICW1 starts the initialization sequence during which the following automatically occur.

a. The edge sense circuit is reset, which means that following initialization, an interrupt request (IR) input must make a low-to-high transition to generate an interrupt.

b. The Interrupt Mask Register is cleared.

c. IR7 input is assigned priority 7.

d. The slave mode address is set to 7.

e. Special Mask Mode is cleared and Status Read is set to IRR.

f. If IC4=0, then all functions selected in ICW4 are set to zero. (Non-Buffered mode*, no Auto-EOI, MCS-80, 85 system).

INITIALIZATION COMMAND WORDS 1 AND 2 (ICW1, ICW2)

A_5-A_{15}: *Page starting address of service routines.* In an MCS 80/85 system, the 8 request levels will generate CALLs to 8 locations equally spaced in memory. These can be programmed to be spaced at intervals of 4 or 8 memory locations, thus the 8 routines will occupy a page of 32 or 64 bytes, respectively.

The address format is 2 bytes long (A_0-A_{15}). When the routine interval is 4, A_0-A_4 are automatically inserted by the 8259A, while A_5-A_{15} are programmed externally. When the routine interval is 8, A_0-A_5 are automatically inserted by the 8259A, while A_6-A_{15} are programmed externally.

The 8-byte interval will maintain compatibility with current software, while the 4-byte interval is best for a compact jump table.

In an iAPX 86 system A_{15}-A_{11} are inserted in the five most significant bits of the vectoring byte and the 8259A sets the three least significant bits according to the interrupt level. A_{10}-A_5 are ignored and ADI (Address interval) has no effect.

LTIM: If LTIM = 1, then the 8259A will operate in the level interrupt mode. Edge detect logic on the interrupt inputs will be disabled.

ADI: CALL address interval. ADI = 1 then interval = 4; ADI = 0 then interval = 8.

SNGL: Single. Means that this is the only 8259A in the system. If SNGL = 1 no ICW3 will be issued.

IC4: If this bit is set — ICW4 has to be read. If ICW4 is not needed, set IC4 = 0.

INITIALIZATION COMMAND WORD 3 (ICW3)

This word is read only when there is more than one 8259A in the system and cascading is used, in which case SNGL = 0. It will load the 8-bit slave register. The functions of this register are:

a. In the master mode (either when SP = 1, or in buffered mode when M/S = 1 in ICW4) a "1" is set for each

slave in the system. The master then will release byte 1 of the call sequence (for MCS-80/85 system) and will enable the corresponding slave to release bytes 2 and 3 (for iAPX 86 only byte 2) through the cascade lines.

b. In the slave mode (either when $\overline{SP}$ = 0, or if BUF = 1 and M/S = 0 in ICW4) bits 2-0 identify the slave. The slave compares its cascade input with these bits and, if they are equal, bytes 2 and 3 of the call sequence (or just byte 2 for iAPX 86 are released by it on the Data Bus.

INITIALIZATION COMMAND WORD 4 (ICW4)

SFNM: If SFNM = 1 the special fully nested mode is programmed.

BUF: If BUF = 1 the buffered mode is programmed. In buffered mode $\overline{SP/EN}$ becomes an enable output and the master/slave determination is by M/S.

M/S: If buffered mode is selected: M/S = 1 means the 8259A is programmed to be a master, M/S = 0 means the 8259A is programmed to be a slave. If BUF = 0, M/S has no function.

AEOI: If AEOI = 1 the automatic end of interrupt mode is programmed.

μPM: Microprocessor mode: μPM = 0 sets the 8259A for MCS-80, 85 system operation, μPM = 1 sets the 8259A for iAPX 86 system operation.

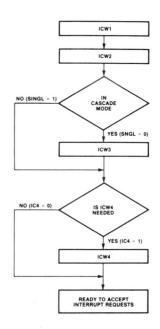

Initialization Sequence

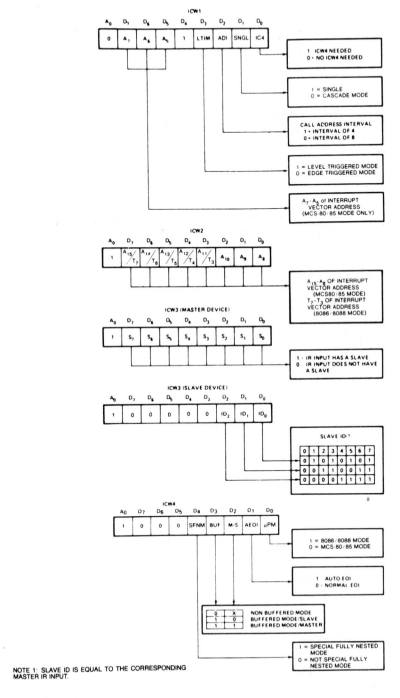

NOTE 1: SLAVE ID IS EQUAL TO THE CORRESPONDING MASTER IR INPUT.

Initialization Command Word Format

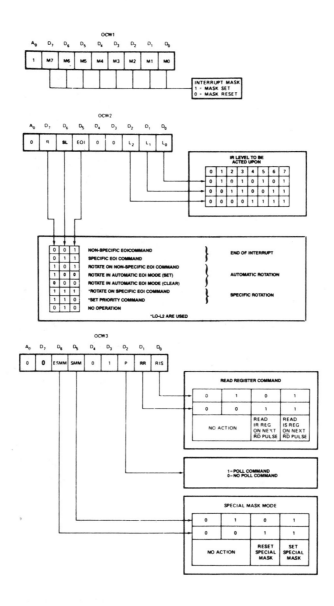

Operation Command Word Format

OPERATION COMMAND WORDS (OCWs)

After the Initialization Command Words (ICWs) are programmed into the 8259A, the chip is ready to accept interrupt requests at its input lines. However, during the 8259A operation, a selection of algorithms can command the 8259A to operate in various modes through the Operation Command Words (OCWs).

OPERATION CONTROL WORDS (OCWs)

OCW1

A0	D7	D6	D5	D4	D3	D2	D1	D0
1	M7	M6	M5	M4	M3	M2	M1	M0

OCW2

A0								
0	R	SL	EOI	0	0	L2	L1	L0

OCW3

A0								
0	0	ESMM	SMM	0	1	P	RR	RIS

OPERATION CONTROL WORD 1 (OCW1)

OCW1 sets and clears the mask bits in the interrupt Mask Register (IMR). $M_7 - M_0$ represent the eight mask bits. $M = 1$ indicates the channel is masked (inhibited), $M = 0$ indicates the channel is enabled.

OPERATION CONTROL WORD 2 (OCW2)

R, SL, EOI — These three bits control the Rotate and End of Interrupt modes and combinations of the two. A chart of these combinations can be found on the Operation Command Word Format.

L_2, L_1, L_0—These bits determine the interrupt level acted upon when the SL bit is active.

OPERATION CONTROL WORD 3 (OCW3)

ESMM — Enable Special Mask Mode. When this bit is set to 1 it enables the SMM bit to set or reset the Special Mask Mode. When ESMM = 0 the SMM bit becomes a "don't care".

SMM — Special Mask Mode. If ESMM = 1 and SMM = 1 the 8259A will enter Special Mask Mode. If ESMM = 1 and SMM = 0 the 8259A will revert to normal mask mode. When ESMM = 0, SMM has no effect.

American Standard Code for Information Interchange: ASCII Codes

	Graphic or Control	ASCII (Hexadecimal)
NUL	Null	00
SOH	Start of Heading	01
STX	Start of Text	02
ETX	End of Text	03
EOT	End of Transmission	04
ENQ	Enquiry	05
ACK	Acknowledge	06
BEL	Bell	07
BS	Backspace	08
HT	Horizontal Tabulation	09
LF	Line Feed	0A
VT	Vertical Tabulation	0B
FF	Form Feed	0C
CR	Carriage Return	0D
SO	Shift Out	0E
SI	Shift In	0F
DLE	Data Link Escape	10
DC1	Device Control 1	11
DC2	Device Control 2	12
DC3	Device Control 3	13
DC4	Device Control 4	14
NAK	Negative Acknowledge	15
SYN	Synchronous Idle	16
ETB	End of Transmission Block	17
CAN	Cancel	18
EM	End of Medium	19
SUB	Substitute	1A
ESC	Escape	1B

	Graphic or Control	ASCII (Hexadecimal)
FS	File Separator	1C
GS	Group Separator	1D
RS	Record Separator	1E
US	Unit Separator	1F
SP	Space	20
!		21
"		22
#		23
$		24
%		25

Graphic or Control	ASCII (Hexadecimal)	Graphic or Control	ASCII (Hexadecimal)
&	26	S	53
'	27	T	54
(	28	U	55
)	29	V	56
*	2A	W	57
+	2B	X	58
,	2C	Y	59
−	2D	Z	5A
.	2E	[	5B
/	2F	\	5C
0	30	]	5D
1	31	∧	5E
2	32	−	5F
3	33	`	60
4	34	a	61
5	35	b	62
6	36	c	63
7	37	d	64
8	38	e	65
9	39	f	66
:	3A	g	67
;	3B	h	68
<	3C	i	69
=	3D	j	6A
>	3E	k	6B
?	3F	l	6C
@	40	m	6D
A	41	n	6E
B	42	o	6F
C	43	p	70
D	44	q	71
E	45	r	72
F	46	s	73
G	47	t	74
H	48	u	75
I	49	v	76
J	4A	w	77
K	4B	x	78
L	4C	y	79
M	4D	z	7A
N	4E	{	7B
O	4F			7C
P	50	}	7D
Q	51	~	7E
R	52	DEL Delete	7F

8085/8080A
Instruction Set

Appendix F describes each instruction fully in terms of its operation and the operand, including details such as number of bytes, machine cycles, T-states, Hex code and affected flags. The instructions appear in alphabetical order and are illustrated with examples. The following abbreviations are used in the description of the instruction set.

Flags

Reg.	= 8080A/8085 Register	*S*	= Sign
Mem.	= Memory Location	*Z*	= Zero

Flags

R	= Register	AC =	Auxiliary Carry
Rs	= Register Source	P =	Parity
Rd	= Register Destination	CY =	Carry
M	= Memory		
( )	= Contents Of		
XX	= Random Information		

ACI: ADD IMMEDIATE TO ACCUMULATOR WITH CARRY

Opcode	Operand	Bytes	M-Cycles	T-States	Hex Code
ACI	8-Bit Data	2	2	7	CE

Description   The 8-bit data (operand) and the Carry flag are added to the contents of the accumulator, and the result is stored in the accumulator.

Flags   All flags are modified to reflect the result of the addition.

Example

Assuming the accumulator contains 26H and the previous operation has set the Carry flag, add byte 57H to the accumulator.

Instruction   ACI 57H   Hex Code: CE 57

Addition

```
    (A): 26H   =  0  0  1  0    0  1  1  0
 (Data): 57H   =  0  1  0  1    0  1  1  1
    CY  1      =                         1
                 _____
         7EH   =  0  1  1  1    1  1  1  0
  Flags:          S = 0   Z = 0   AC = 0
                  P = 1   CY = 0
```

Comments

1. After addition the previous Carry flag is cleared.

2. This instruction is commonly used in 16-bit addition. This instruction should not be used to account for a carry generated by 8-bit numbers.

ADC: ADD REGISTER TO ACCUMULATOR WITH CARRY

Opcode	Operand	Bytes	M-Cycles	T-States	Hex Codes	
					Reg.	**Hex**
ADC	Reg.	1	1	4	B	88
	Mem.		2	7	C	89
					D	8A
					E	8B
					H	8C
					L	8D
					M	8E
					A	8F

Description   The contents of the operand (register or memory) and the Carry flag are added to the contents of the accumulator and the result is placed in the accumulator. The contents of the operand are not altered; however, the previous Carry flag is reset.

Flags   All flags are modified to reflect the result of the addition.

Assume register pair BC contains 2498H and register pair DE contains 54A1H. Add these 16-bit numbers and save the result in BC registers.   *Example*

The steps in adding 16-bit numbers are as follows:

1. Add the contents of registers C and E by placing the contents of one register in the accumulator. This addition generates a Carry. Use instruction ADD (explained on the next page) and save the low order 8-bits in the register C.

```
        98H  =      1 0 0 1   1 0 0 0
        A1H  =      1 0 1 0   0 0 0 1
    1   39H  =  1   0 0 1 1   1 0 0 1   Store in register C
   CY          CY
```

2. Add the contents of the registers B and D by placing the contents of one register in the accumulator. Use instruction ADC.

The result will be as follows.

```
   24H  =  0 0 1 0   0 1 0 0
   54H  =  0 1 0 1   0 1 0 0
    1   =                 1   (Carry from the previous addition)
   79H  =  0 1 1 1   1 0 0 1   Store in register B
```

Comments   This instruction is generally used in 16-bit addition. For example, to add the contents of BC registers to the contents of DE registers this instruction is used to account for the carry generated by low order bytes.

ADD: ADD REGISTER TO ACCUMULATOR

Opcode	Operand	Bytes	M-Cycles	T-States	Hex Codes	
ADD	Reg.	1	1	4	**Reg.**	**Hex**
	Mem.		2	7	B	80
					C	81
					D	82
					E	83
					H	84
					L	85
					M	86
					A	87

Description   The contents of the operand (register or memory) are added to the contents of the accumulator and the result is stored in the accumulator. If the operand is a memory location, that is indicated by the 16-bit address in HL register.

Flags   All flags are modified to reflect the result of the addition.

Example

Register B has 32H and the accumulator has 47H. Add the contents of register B to the contents of the accumulator.

Instruction   ADD B   Hex Code: 80

Register contents
before instruction

Addition

Register contents
after instruction

A	47	X	F	47H	=	0 1 0 0	0 1 1 1	A	98			
B	51	X	C	51H	=	0 1 0 1	0 0 0 1	B	51			

S Z AC P CY

A	98	1 0 0 0 0	F
B	51	X	C

98H = 1 0 0 1   1 0 0 0

S = 1   Z = 0   AC = 0
P = 0   CY = 0

Example

Memory location 2050H has data byte A2H and the accumulator has 76H. Add the contents of the memory location to the contents of the accumulator.

Instruction   ADD M   Hex Code: 86
Before this instruction is executed registers HL should be loaded with data 2050H.

Register contents
before instruction

A	76	X	F
B	X	X	C
D	X	X	E
H	20	50	L

2050 | A2 |

Addition

Register contents
after instruction

S Z AC P CY

(A)	76H	=	0 1 1 1 0 1 1 0
(2050H)ₘₑₘ	A2H	=	1 0 1 0 0 0 1 0
	1/18H	=	1/0 0 0 1 1 0 0 0
	CY		CY

Flags: S = 0, Z = 0, AC = 0,
P = 1, CY = 1

A	18	0,0 0 1 1	F
B	X	X	C
D	X	X	E
H	20	50	L

ADI: ADD IMMEDIATE TO ACCUMULATOR

Opcode	Operand	Bytes	M-Cycles	T-States	Hex Code
ADI	8-Bit Data	2	2	7	C6

Description   The 8-bit data (operand) are added to the contents of the accumulator, and the result is placed in the accumulator.

Flags   All flags are modified to reflect the result of the addition.

The accumulator contains 4AH. Add the data byte 59H to the contents of the accumulator.   Example

Instruction   ADI   59H   Hex Code: C6 59

Addition

(A)	:	4AH	=	0 1 0 0 1 0 1 0
	+			
(Data)	:	59H	=	0 1 0 1 1 0 0 1
		A3H	=	1 0 1 0 0 0 1 1

Flags: S = 1, Z = 0, AC = 1
P = 1, CY = 0

ANA: LOGICAL AND WITH ACCUMULATOR

Opcode	Operand	Bytes	M-Cycles	T-States	Hex Codes	
ADA	Reg.	1	1	4	**Reg.**	**Hex**
	Mem.	1	2	7	B	A0
					C	A1
					D	A2
					E	A3
					H	A4
					L	A5
					M	A6
					A	A7

Description The contents of the accumulator are logically ANDed with the contents of the operand (register or memory), and the result is placed in the accumulator. If the operand is a memory location, its address is specified by the contents of HL registers.

Flags S, Z, P are modified to reflect the result of the operation. CY is reset. In 8085, AC is set and in 8080A AC is the result of ORing bits D3 of the operands.

Example

The contents of the accumulator and the register D are 54H and 82H, respectively. Logically AND the contents of register D with the contents of the accumulator. Show the flags and the contents of each register after ANDing.

Instruction ANA   D   Hex Code: A2

Register contents before instruction

Logical AND

Register contents after instruction

```
                                                             S Z AC P CY
A  54   X   F     54H  =  0  1  0  1     0  1  0  0    A     00      0 1  1  1  0  F
                  AND
D  82   X   E     82H  =  1  0  0  0     0  0  1  0    D     82                E
                         0  0  0  0     0  0  0  0

                  S = 0   Z = 1   P = 1
                  AC = 1   CY = 0  (for 8080A, AC = 0)
```

ANI: AND IMMEDIATE WITH ACCUMULATOR

Opcode	Operand	Bytes	M-Cycles	T-States	Hex Code
ANI	8-Bit Data	2	2	7	E6

Description   The contents of the accumulator are logically ANDed with the 8-bit data (operand) and the results are placed in the accumulator.

Flags   S, Z, P are modified to reflect the results of the operation. CY is reset. In 8085, AC is set, and in 8080A, AC is the result of ORing bits D_3 of the operands.

AND data byte 97H with the contents of the accumulator, which contains A3H.   *Example*

Instruction   ANI   97H   Hex Code: E6 97

Logical AND

(A)	:	A3H	=	1	0	1	0		0	0	1	1								
			AND																

(Data)   :   97H   =   1   0   0   1   0   1   1   1   SZ AC P CY

                        1   0   0   0   0   0   1   1   A   [83   ] |1 0 1 0 0| F

CALL: UNCONDITIONAL SUBROUTINE CALL

Opcode	Operand	Bytes	M-Cycles	T-States	Hex Code
CALL	16-Bit Address	3	5	18 (8085) 17 (8080)	CD

Description   The program sequence is transferred to the address specified by the operand. Before the transfer, the address of the next instruction to CALL (the contents of the program counter) is pushed on the stack. The sequence of events is described in the example below.

Flags   No flags are affected.

Write CALL instruction at memory location 2010H to call a subroutine located at 2050H.   *Example*
Explain the sequence of events when the stack pointer is at location 2099H.

Memory Address	Hex Code	Mnemonics
2010	CD	CALL 2050H
2011	50	
2012	20	

Note   See the difference between writing a 16-bit address as mnemonics and code. In the code, the low-order byte (50) is entered first then the high-order byte (20) is entered. However, in mnemonics the address is shown in the proper sequence. If an assembler is used to obtain the codes, it will automatically reverse the sequence of the mnemonics.

Execution of
CALL

The address in the program counter (2013H) is placed on the stack as follows.

Stack pointer is decremented to 2098H
MSB is stored
Stack pointer is again decremented
LSB is stored
Call address (2050H) is temporarily stored in internal WZ registers
    and placed on the bus for the fetch cycle

2097	13
2098	20

SP → 2099

Comments   The CALL instruction should be accompanied by one of the return (RET or conditional return) instructions in the subroutine.

Conditional Call to Subroutine   **Operand — 16-bit Address**

Op Code	Description	Flag Status	Hex Code	M-Cycles T-States	
CC	Call on Carry	CY = 1	DC	8080 — 3M 11T	If condition is not true.
CNC	Call with No Carry	CY = 0	D4	— 5M 17T	If condition is true.
CP	Call on positive	S = 0	F4	8085 — 2M 9T	If condition is not true.
CM	Call on minus	S = 1	FC	— 5M 18T	If condition is true.
CPE	Call on Parity Even	P = 1	EC	*Note:* If condition is not true it continues	
CPO	Call on Parity Odd	P = 0	E4	the sequence, and thus requires	
CZ	Call on Zero	Z = 1	CC	fewer T-states	
CNZ	Call on No Zero	Z = 0	C4		

Flags: No flags are affected.

If condition is true it calls the subroutine, thus requires more T-states.

CMA: COMPLEMENT ACCUMULATOR

Opcode	Operand	Bytes	M-Cycles	T-States	Hex Code
CMA	None	1	1	4	2F

Description   The contents of the accumulator are complemented.

Flags   No flags are affected.

Example

Complement the accumulator, which has data byte 89H.

Instruction   CMA   Hex Code: 2F

	Before instruction						After instruction			

A $\boxed{1\ 0\ 0\ 0\ 1\ 0\ 0\ 1}$ = 89H   A $\boxed{0\ 1\ 1\ 1\ 0\ 1\ 1\ 0}$ = 76H

CMC: COMPLEMENT CARRY

Opcode	Operand	Bytes	M-Cycles	T-States	Hex Code
CMC	None	1	1	4	3F

Description   The Carry flag is complemented.

Flags   The Carry flag is modified, no other flags are affected.

CMP: COMPARE WITH ACCUMULATOR

Opcode	Operand	Bytes	M-Cycles	T-States	Hex Codes	
					Reg.	Hex
CMP	Reg.	1	1	4	B	B8
	Mem.	1	2	7	C	B9
					D	BA
					E	BB
					H	BC
					L	BD
					M	BE
					A	BF

Description   The contents of the operand (register or memory) are compared with the contents of the accumulator. Both contents are preserved and the comparison is shown by setting the flags as follows:

☐ If (A) < (Reg/Mem): Carry flag is set.
☐ If (A) = (Reg/Mem): Zero flag is set.
☐ If (A) > (Reg/Mem): Carry and Zero flags are reset.

The comparison of two bytes is performed by subtracting the contents of the operand from the contents of the accumulator; however, neither contents are modified.

Flags   S, P, AC are also modified in addition to Z and C to reflect the results of the operation.

Example

Register B contains data byte 62H and the accumulator contains data byte 57H. Compare the contents of register B with that of the accumulator.

Instruction   CMP   B   Hex Code: B8

Before instruction   After instruction
                                                                    CY

A | 57 | XX | F   A | 57 | | 1 | F
B | 62 | XX | C   B | 62 | XX | | C

                                          S = 1, Z = 0, AC = 1
                                          P = 1, CY = 1

Results after executing the instruction

☐ No contents are changed.
☐ Carry flag is set because (A) < (B).
☐ S, Z, P, AC flags will also be modified as listed above.

CPI: COMPARE IMMEDIATE WITH ACCUMULATOR

Opcode	Operand	Bytes	M-Cycles	T-States	Hex Codes
CPI	8-bit	2	2	7	FE

Description   The second byte (8-bit data) is compared with the contents of the accumulator. The values being compared remain unchanged and the results of the comparison are indicated by setting the flags as follows.

☐ If (A) < Data: Carry flag is set.
☐ If (A) = Data: Zero flag is set.
☐ If (A) > Data: Neither Carry nor Zero flag is set.

The comparison of two bytes is performed by subtracting the data byte from the contents of the accumulator; however, neither contents are modified.

Flags   S, P, AC are also modified in addition to Z and C to reflect the result of the operation.

Example

Assume the accumulator contains data byte C2H. Compare 98H with the accumulator contents.

Instruction CPI   98H   Hex Code: FE   98
Results after executing the instruction

☐ The accumulator contents remain unchanged.
☐ Z and CY flags are reset because (A) > Data
☐ Other flags: S = 0, AC = 0, P = 0.

Compare data byte C2H with the contents of the accumulator in the above example.   Example

Instruction CPI   C2H   Hex Code: FE   C2
Results after executing the instruction

☐ The accumulator contents remain unchanged.
☐ Zero flag is set because (A) = Data.
☐ Other flags: S = 0, AC = 1, P = 1, CY = 0.

DAA: DECIMAL ADJUST ACCUMULATOR

Opcode	Operand	Bytes	M-Cycles	T-States	Hex Code
DAA	None	1	1	4	27

Description   The contents of the accumulator are changed from a binary value to two 4-bit binary coded decimal (BCD) digits. This is the only instruction that uses the auxiliary flag (internally) to perform the binary to BCD conversion, and the conversion procedure is described below.

Flags   S, Z, AC, P, CY flags are altered to reflect the results of the operation. Instruction DAA converts the binary contents of the accumulator as follows:

1. If the value of the low-order 4-bits (D_3–D_0) in the accumulator is greater than 9 or if AC flag is set, the instruction adds 6 (06) to the low-order four bits.
2. If the value of the high-order 4-bits (D_7–D_4) in the accumulator is greater than 9 or if the Carry flag is set, the instruction adds 6 (60) to the high-order four bits.

Add decimal 12_{BCD} to the accumulator, which contains 39_{BCD}.   Example

$$
\begin{array}{rcrcccccccc}
(A) & = & 39_{BCD} & = & 0 & 0 & 1 & 1 & 1 & 0 & 0 & 1 \\
& + & 12_{BCD} & = & 0 & 0 & 0 & 1 & 0 & 0 & 1 & 0 \\
\hline
& & 51_{BCD} & = & 0 & 1 & 0 & 0 & 1 & 0 & 1 & 1 \\
& & & & & & 4 & & & B &
\end{array}
$$

The binary sum is 4BH. The value of the low-order four bits is larger than 9. Add 06 to the low-order four bits.

$$
\begin{array}{rcccccccc}
4B & = & 0 & 1 & 0 & 0 & 1 & 0 & 1 & 1 \\
+ 06 & = & 0 & 0 & 0 & 0 & 0 & 1 & 1 & 0 \\
\hline
& & & & & 1 & & 1 & 1 & \\
\hline
51 & = & 0 & 1 & 0 & 1 & 0 & 0 & 0 & 1
\end{array}
$$

Example

Add decimal 68_{BCD} to the accumulator, which contains 85_{BCD}.

$$
\begin{array}{rcclcccccccc}
(A) & = & 85_{BCD} & = & 1 & 0 & 0 & 0 & & 0 & 1 & 0 & 1 \\
& + & 68_{BCD} & = & 0 & 1 & 1 & 0 & & 1 & 0 & 0 & 0 \\
\hline
& & 153_{BCD} & = & 1 & 1 & 1 & 0 & & 1 & 1 & 0 & 1 \\
\end{array}
$$

The binary sum is EDH. The values of both, low-order and high-order, four bits are higher than 9. Add 6 to both.

$$
\begin{array}{rcccccccccc}
= & ED & = & 1 & 1 & 1 & 0 & & 1 & 1 & 0 & 1 \\
+ & 66 & = & 0 & 1 & 1 & 0 & & 0 & 1 & 1 & 0 \\
& & & 1 & 1 & & 1 & & 1 & & & \\
\hline
& \boxed{1}53 & = \boxed{1}0 & & 1 & 0 & 1 & & 0 & 0 & 1 & 1 \\
& CY & CY & & & & & & & & & \\
\end{array}
$$

The accumulator contains 53 and the Carry flag is set to indicate that the sum is larger than eight bits (153). The program should keep track of the Carry; otherwise it may be altered by the subsequent instructions.

DAD: ADD REGISTER PAIR TO H AND L REGISTERS

Opcode	Operand	Bytes	M-Cycles	T-States	Hex Codes	
DAD	Register Pair	1	3	10	**Reg. Pair**	**Hex**
					B	09
					D	19
					H	29
					SP	39

Description   The 16-bit contents of the specified register pair are added to the contents of the HL register and the sum is saved in the HL register. The contents of the source register pair are not altered.

Flags   If the result is larger than sixteen bits the CY flag is set. No other flags are affected.

Example

Assume register pair HL contains 0242H. Multiply the contents by 2.

Instruction   DAD   H   Hex Code: 29

Before instruction	DAD operation	After instruction
	0242	
H	02	42	L	+0242	H	04	84	L
	0484	

Example

Assume register pair HL is cleared. Transfer the stack pointer (register) that points to memory location 2099H to the HL register pair.

Instruction   DAD   SP   Hex Code: 39

Before instruction	DAD operation	After instruction
H $\boxed{00\ \vert\ 00}$ L	0000	H $\boxed{20\ \vert\ 99}$ L
SP $\boxed{2099}$	$+2099$	SP $\boxed{2099}$
	2099	

Note   After the execution of the instruction, the contents of the stack pointer register are not altered.

DCR: DECREMENT SOURCE BY 1

Opcode	Operand	Bytes	M-Cycles	T-States	Hex Codes	
DCR	Reg.	1	1	4 (8085)	**Reg.**	**Hex**
				5 (8080A)	B	05
	Mem.	1	3	10	C	0D
					D	15
					E	1D
					H	25
					L	2D
					M	35
					A	3D

Description   The contents of the designated register/memory is decremented by 1 and the results are stored in the same place. If the operand is a memory location, it is specified by the contents of the HL register pair.

Flags   S, Z, P, AC are modified to reflect the result of the operation. CY is not modified.

Example

Decrement register B, which is cleared, and specify its contents after the decrement.

Instruction   DCR   B   Hex Code: 05

Before instruction

A $\boxed{\ \vert\ XX}$ F
B $\boxed{00\ \vert\ XX}$ C

Decrement Operation

$$(B)\ =\ 0\ 0\ 0\ 0\quad 0\ 0\ 0\ 0$$
$$-01\ =\ 0\ 0\ 0\ 0\quad 0\ 0\ 0\ 1$$

Subtraction is performed in 2's complement

$$(B) = 0 \quad 0 \quad 0 \quad 0 \quad \quad 0 \quad 0 \quad 0 \quad 0$$
$$+$$
$$\text{2's complement of 1} = 1 \quad 1 \quad 1 \quad 1 \quad \quad 1 \quad 1 \quad 1 \quad 1$$
$$(B) = 1 \quad 1 \quad 1 \quad 1 \quad \quad 1 \quad 1 \quad 1 \quad 1$$

After the execution of the DCR instruction register B will contain FFH; however, CY is not set to indicate the results are in 2's complement.

Example

Decrement the contents of memory location 2085, which presently holds A0H. Assume the HL register contains 2085H.

Instruction   DCR   M   Hex Code: 35

Before instruction   **Memory**

H [20 | 85] L   2084
                       2085   A0
                       2086

After instruction

H [20 | 85] L   2084
                       2085   9F
                       2086

DCX: DECREMENT REGISTER PAIR BY 1

Opcode	Operand	Bytes	M-Cycles	T-States	Hex Codes	
DCX	Reg. Pair	1	1	6 (8085)	**Reg.**	
				5 (8080A)	**Pair**	**Hex**
					B	0B
					D	1B
					H	2B
					SP	3B

Description   The contents of the specified register pair are decremented by 1. This instruction views the contents of the two registers as a 16-bit number.

Flags   No flags are affected.

Example

Register pair DE contains 2000H. Specify the contents of the entire register if it is decremented by 1.

Instruction   DCX   D   Hex Code: 1B

After subtracting 1 from the DE register pair the answer is

$$D \quad \boxed{1F} \boxed{FF} \quad E$$

Write instructions to set the Zero flag when a register pair (such as BC) is used as a down counter.

To decrement the register pair instruction DCX is necessary; instruction DCR is used for one register. However, instruction DCX does not set the Zero flag when the register pair goes to 0 and it continues counting indefinitely. The Zero flag can be set by using the following instructions.

For BC Pair

⟶ DCX B	;Decrement register pair BC
MOV A, C	;Load accumulator with the contents of register C
ORA B	;Set Zero flag if B and C are both 0
⟶ JNZ	;If Zero flag is not set, go back and decrement the contents of BC pair

---

DI: DISABLE INTERRUPTS

Opcode	Operand	Bytes	M-Cycles	T-States	Hex Code
DI	None	1	1	4	F3

Description   The Interrupt Enable flip-flop is reset and all the interrupts except the TRAP (8085) are disabled.

Flags   No flags are affected.

Comments   This instruction is commonly used when the execution of a code sequence cannot be interrupted. For example, in critical time delays, this instruction is used at the beginning of the code and the interrupts are enabled at the end of the code. The 8085 TRAP cannot be disabled.

EI: ENABLE INTERRUPTS

Opcode	Operand	Bytes	M-Cycles	T-States	Hex Code
EI	None	1	1	4	FB

Description   The Interrupt Enable flip-flop is set and all interrupts are enabled.

Flags   No flags are affected.

Comments   After a system reset or the acknowledgment of an interrupt, the Interrupt Enable flip-flop is reset, thus disabling the interrupts. This instruction is necessary to reenable the interrupts (except TRAP).

HLT: HALT AND ENTER WAIT STATE

Opcode	Operand	Bytes	M-Cycles	T-States	Hex Code
HLT	None	1	2 or more	5 or more (8085)	
				7 or more (8080A)	76

Description The MPU finishes executing the current instruction and halts any further execution. The MPU enters the Halt Acknowledge machine cycle and Wait states are inserted in every clock period. The address and the data bus are placed in a high impedance state. The contents of the registers are unaffected during the HLT state. An interrupt or reset is necessary to exit from the Halt state.

Flags No flags are affected.

IN: INPUT DATA TO ACCUMULATOR FROM A PORT WITH 8-BIT ADDRESS

Opcode	Operand	Bytes	M-Cycles	T-States	Hex Code
IN	8-Bit Port Address	2	3	10	DB

Description The contents of the input port designated in the operand are read and loaded into the accumulator.

Flags No flags are affected.

Comments The operand is an 8-bit address; therefore, port addresses can range from 00H to FFH. While executing the instruction, a port address is duplicated on low-order (A_7-A_0) and high-order ($A_{15}-A_8$) address buses. Any one of the sets of address lines can be decoded to enable the input port.

INR: INCREMENT CONTENTS OF REGISTER/MEMORY BY 1

Opcode	Operand	Bytes	M-Cycles	T-States	Hex Codes	
INR	Reg.	1	1	4 (8085)	**Reg.**	**Hex**
				5 (8080A)	B	04
	Mem.	1	3	10	C	0C
					D	14
					E	1C
					H	24
					L	2C
					M	34
					A	3C

Description   The contents of the designated register/memory are incremented by 1 and the results are stored in the same place. If the operand is a memory location, it is specified by the contents of HL register pair.

Flags   S, Z, P, AC are modified to reflect the result of the operation. CY is not modified.

Register D contains FF. Specify the contents of the register after the increment.   *Example*

Instruction   INR   D   Hex Code: 14

$$
\begin{array}{rl}
(D) = & 1\ 1\ 1\ 1\quad 1\ 1\ 1\ 1 \\
+1 = & 0\ 0\ 0\ 0\quad 0\ 0\ 0\ 1 \\
\hline
& 1\ 1\ 1\ 1\quad 1\ 1\ 1\quad\ \ \text{Carry} \\
00 = & \boxed{0}\ 0\ 0\ 0\ 0\quad 0\ 0\ 0\ 0 \\
& \text{CY}
\end{array}
$$

After the execution of the INR instruction, register D will contain 00H; however, no Carry flag is set.

Increment the contents of memory location 2075H, which presently holds 7FH. Assume   *Example*
the HL register contains 2075H.

Instruction   INR   M   Hex Code: 34

Before instruction   Memory

H │ 20   75 │ L   2074 ┌──┐
                         2075 │7F│
                         2076 └──┘

After instruction

H │ 20   75 │ L   2074 ┌──┐
                         2075 │80│
                         2076 └──┘

INX: INCREMENT REGISTER PAIR BY 1

Opcode	Operand	Bytes	M-Cycles	T-States	Hex Codes	
INX	Reg. Pair	1	1	6 (8085)	**Reg.**	
				5 (8080A)	**Pair**	**Hex**
					B	03
					D	13
					H	23
					SP	33

Description   The contents of the specified register pair are incremented by 1. The instruction views the contents of the two registers as a 16-bit number.

Flags   No flags are affected.

Example

Register pair HL contains 9FFFH. Specify the contents of the entire register if it is incremented by 1.

Instruction   INX   H   Hex Code: 23
After adding 1 to the contents of the HL pair the answer is

H | A0   00 | L

JMP: JUMP UNCONDITIONALLY

Opcode	Operand	Bytes	M-Cycles	T-States	Hex Code
JMP	16-Bit	3	3	10	C3

Description   The program sequence is transferred to the memory location specified by the 16-bit address. This is a 3-byte instruction, the second byte specifies the low-order byte and the third byte specifies the high-order byte.

Example

Write the instruction at location 2000H to transfer the program sequence to memory location 2050H.

Instruction

Memory Address	Code	Mnemonics
2000	C3	JMP 2050H
2001	50	
2002	20	

Comments   The 16-bit address of the operand is entered in memory in reverse order, the low-order byte first followed by the high-order byte.

JUMP CONDITIONALLY

Operand: 16-bit Address

Op Code	Description	Flag Status	Hex Code	M-Cycles/T-States
JC	Jump on Carry	CY = 1	DA	8080A: 3M/10T

JNC	Jump on No Carry	CY = 0	D2	8085: 2M/7T (if condition
JP	Jump on positive	S = 0	F2	is not true)
JM	Jump on minus	S = 1	FA	: 3M/10T (if condition
JPE	Jump on Parity Even	P = 1	EA	is true)
JPO	Jump on Parity Odd	P = 0	E2	
JZ	Jump on Zero	Z = 1	CA	
JNZ	Jump on No Zero	Z = 0	C2	

Flags No flags are affected.

Comments · The 8085 requires only seven T-states when condition is not true. For example, instruction JZ 2050H will transfer the program sequence to location 2050H when the Zero flag is set (Z = 1) and the execution requires ten T-states. When the Zero flag is reset (Z = 0), the execution sequence will not be changed and this requires seven T-states.

LDA: LOAD ACCUMULATOR DIRECT

Opcode	Operand	Bytes	M-Cycles	T-States	Hex Code
LDA	16-Bit Address	3	4	13	3A

Description The contents of a memory location, specified by a 16-bit address in the operand, are copied to the accumulator. The contents of the source are not altered. This is a 3-byte instruction, the second byte specifies the low-order address and the third byte specifies the high-order address.

Flags No flags are affected.

Assume memory location 2050H contains byte F8H. Load the accumulator with the contents of location 2050H.

Example

Instruction LDA   2050H   Hex Code: 3A   50   20   (Note the reverse order)

A [F8 | X] F   2050 [F8]

LDAX: LOAD ACCUMULATOR INDIRECT

Opcode	Operand	Bytes	M-Cycles	T-States	Hex Code	
LDAX	B/D Reg. Pair	1	2	7	**Reg.**	**Hex**
					BC	0A
					DE	1A

Description   The contents of the designated register pair point to a memory location. This instruction copies the contents of that memory location into the accumulator. The contents of either the register pair or the memory location are not altered.

Flags   No flags are affected.

Assume the contents of register B = 20H, C = 50H, and memory location 2050H = 9FH. Transfer the contents of the memory location 2050H to the accumulator.

Instruction   LDAX   B   Hex Code: 0A

Register contents before instruction		Memory contents	Register contents after instruction	
A	XX	XX	F			A	9F	XX	F
B	20	50	C	⟶	2050	9F	B	20	50	C

LHLD: LOAD H AND L REGISTERS DIRECT

Opcode	Operand	Bytes	M-Cycles	T-States	Hex Code
LHLD	16-Bit Address	3	5	16	2A

Description   The instruction copies the contents of the memory location pointed out by the 16-bit address in register L and copies the contents of the next memory location in register H. The contents of source memory locations are not altered.

Flags   No flags are affected.

Assume memory location 2050H contains 90H and 2051H contains 01H. Transfer memory contents to registers HL.

Instruction   LHLD   2050H   Hex Code: 2A   50   20

Memory contents
before instruction

2050 | 90 |
2051 | 01 |

Register contents
after instruction

H | 01 | 90 | L

LXI: LOAD REGISTER PAIR IMMEDIATE

Opcode	Operand	Bytes	M-Cycles	T-States	Hex Code	
LXI	Reg. Pair, 16-Bit Data	3	3	10	**Reg. Pair**	**Hex**
					B	01
					D	11
					H	21
					SP	31

Description The instruction loads 16-bit data in the register pair designated in the operand. This is a 3-byte instruction, the second byte specifies the low-order byte and the third byte specifies the high-order byte.

Flags No flags are affected.

Load the 16-bit data 2050H in register pair BC. Example

Instruction LXI B, 2050H Hex Code: 01 50 20
This instruction loads 50H in register C and 20H in register B.

Comments Note the reverse order in entering the code of 16-bit data. This is the only instruction that can directly load a 16-bit address in the stack pointer register.

MOV: MOVE—COPY FROM SOURCE TO DESTINATION

Opcode	Operand	Bytes	M-Cycles	T-States	Hex Code
MOV	Rd, Rs	1	1	4 (8085) 5 (8080)	See table below
MOV	M, Rs		2	7	
MOV	Rd, M				

Description This instruction copies the contents of the source register into the destination register, the contents of the source register are not altered. If one of the operands is a memory location, it is specified by the contents of HL registers.

Flags No flags are affected.

Hex Code

	Source Location							
	B	C	D	E	H	L	M	A
B	40	41	42	43	44	45	46	47
C	48	49	4A	4B	4C	4D	4E	4F
D	50	51	52	53	54	55	56	57
E	58	59	5A	5B	5C	5D	5E	5F
H	60	61	62	63	64	65	66	67
L	68	69	6A	6B	6C	6D	6E	6F
M	70	71	72	73	74	75	76	77
A	78	79	7A	7B	7C	7D	7E	7F

Destination Location (rows, leftmost column B–A)

Example

Assume register B contains 72H and register C contains 9FH. Transfer the contents of register C to register B.

Instruction   MOV B,C   Hex Code: 41

Note the first operand B specifies the destination and the second operand C specifies the source.

Register contents   Register contents
before instruction   after instruction

B | 72 | 9F | C   B | 9F | 9F | C

Example

Assume the contents of registers HL are 20H and 50H, respectively. Memory location 2050H contains 9FH. Transfer the contents of the memory location to register B.

Instruction   MOV B,M   Hex Code: 46

Register contents   Memory   Register contents
before instruction   contents   after instruction

B | XX | XX | C   B | 9F | XX | C
D | XX | XX | E   ──────────→   2050 | 9F | D | XX | XX | E
H | 20 | 50 | L ───┘   H | 20 | 50 | L

MVI: MOVE IMMEDIATE 8-BIT

Opcode	Operand	Bytes	M-Cycles	T-States	Hex Code	
					Reg.	Hex
MVI	Reg., Data	2	2	7		
	Mem., Data		3	10	B	06
					C	0E

D	16
E	1E
H	26
L	2E
M	36
A	3E

Description   The 8-bit data is stored in the destination register or memory. If the operand is a memory location, it is specified by the contents of HL registers.

Flags   No flags are affected.

Example

Load 92H in register B.

Instruction   MVI B, 92H   Hex Code: 06   92
This instruction loads 92H in register B.

Example

Assume registers H and L contain 20H and 50H, respectively. Load 3AH in memory location 2050H.

Instruction   MVI M,3AH   Hex Code: 36

Contents before instruction	Contents after instruction

H | 20 50 | L ⟶ 2050 | 3A | H | 20 50 | L

NOP: NO OPERATION

Opcode	Operand	Bytes	M-Cycles	T-States	Hex Code
NOP	None	1	1	4	00

Description   No operation is performed. The instruction is fetched and decoded; however, no operation is executed.

Flags   No flags are affected.

Comments   The instruction is used to fill in time delays or to delete and insert instructions while troubleshooting.

ORA: LOGICALLY OR WITH ACCUMULATOR

Opcode	Operand	Bytes	M-Cycles	T-States	Hex Code	
ORA	Reg.	1	1	4	**Reg.**	**Hex**
	Mem.	1	2	7	B	B0
					C	B1
					D	B2
					E	B3
					H	B4
					L	B5
					M	B6
					A	B7

Description   The contents of the accumulator are logically ORed with the contents of the operand (register or memory), and the results are placed in the accumulator. If the operand is a memory location, its address is specified by the contents of HL registers.

Flags   Z, S, P are modified to reflect the results of the operation. AC and CY are reset.

Example

Assume the accumulator has data byte 03H and register C holds byte 81H. Combine the bits of register C with the accumulator bits.

Instruction   ORA C   Hex Code: B1

Register contents
before instruction   Logical OR

Register contents
after instruction

A	03	XX	F
B	XX	81	C

03H = 0 0 0 0   0 0 1 1
81H = 1 0 0 0   0 0 0 1
83H = 1 0 0 0   0 0 1 1
S = 1, Z = 0, P = 0
CY = 0, AC = 0

S Z AC P CY

A	83	1 0 0 0 0	F
B	XX	81	C

Comments   The instruction is commonly used to

☐ reset the CY flag by ORing the contents of the accumulator with itself.
☐ set the Zero flag when 0 is loaded into the accumulator by ORing the contents of the accumulator with itself.
☐ combine bits from different registers.

ORI: LOGICALLY OR IMMEDIATE

Opcode	Operand	Bytes	M-Cycles	T-States	Hex Code
ORI	8-Bit Data	2	2	7	F6

Description The contents of the accumulator are logically ORed with the 8-bit data in the operand and the results are placed in the accumulator.

Flags S, Z, P are modified to reflect the results of the operation. CY and AC are reset.

OUT: OUTPUT DATA FROM ACCUMULATOR
TO A PORT WITH 8-BIT ADDRESS

Opcode	Operand	Bytes	M-Cycles	T-States	Hex Code
OUT	8-Bit Port Address	2	3	10	D3

Description The contents of the accumulator are copied into the I/O port specified by the operand.

Flags No flags are affected.

Comments The operand is an 8-bit address; therefore, port addresses can range from 00H to FFH. While executing the instruction, a port address is placed on the low-order address bus (A_7–A_0) as well as the high-order address bus (A_{15}–A_8). Any of the sets of address lines can be decoded to enable the output port.

PCHL: LOAD PROGRAM COUNTER WITH HL CONTENTS

Opcode	Operand	Bytes	M-Cycles	T-States	Hex Code
PCHL	None	1	1	6 (8085) 5 (8080A)	E9

Description The contents of registers H and L are copied into the program counter. The contents of H are placed as a high-order byte and of L as a low-order byte.

Flags No flags are affected.

Comments This instruction is equivalent to a 1-byte unconditional Jump instruction. A program sequence can be changed to any location by simply loading the H and L registers with the appropriate address and by using this instruction.

POP: POP OFF STACK TO REGISTER PAIR

Opcode	Operand	Bytes	M-Cycles	T-States	Hex Code	
POP	Reg. Pair	1	3	10	**Reg.**	**Hex**
					B	C1
					D	D1
					H	E1
					PSW	F1

Description   The contents of the memory location pointed out by the stack pointer register are copied to the low-order register (such as C, E, L, and flags) of the operand. The stack pointer is incremented by 1 and the contents of that memory location are copied to the high-order register (B, D, H, A) of the operand. The stack pointer register is again incremented by 1.

Flags   No flags are modified.

Example

Assume the stack pointer register contains 2090H, data byte F5 is stored in memory location 2090H, and data byte 01H is stored in location 2091H. Transfer the contents of the stack to register pair H and L.

Instruction   POP H   Hex Code: E1

Register contents before instruction	Stack contents	Register contents after instruction
H XX XX L	2090 F5	H 01 F5 L
SP 2090	2091 01	SP 2092
	2092	

Comments   Operand PSW (Program Status Word) represents the contents of the accumulator and the flag register, the accumulator is the high-order register and the flags are the low-order register.

Note that the contents of the source, stack locations, are not altered after the POP instruction.

PUSH: PUSH REGISTER PAIR ONTO STACK

Opcode	Operand	Bytes	M-Cycles	T-States	Hex Code	
PUSH	Reg. Pair	1	3	12 (8085)	**Reg.**	**Hex**
				11 (8080A)	B	C5
					D	D5
					H	E5
					PSW	F5

Description   The contents of the register pair designated in the operand are copied into the stack in the following sequence. The stack pointer register is decremented and the contents of the high-order register (B, D, H, A) are copied into that location. The stack pointer register is decremented again and the contents of the low-order register (C, E, L, flags) are copied to that location.

Flags   No flags are modified.

Assume the stack pointer register contains 2099H, register B contains 32H and register C   **Example**
contains 57H. Save the contents of the BC register pair on the stack.

Instruction   PUSH B   Hex Code: C5

Register contents
before instruction

Stack contents
after instruction

Register contents
after instruction

B | 32 | 57 | C

B | 32 | 57 | C

2097	57
2098	32

SP | 2099 |

2099 | XX |

SP | 2097 |

Comments   Operand PSW (Program Status Word) represents the contents of the accumulator and the flag register, the accumulator is the high-order register and the flags are the low-order register.

    Note that the contents of the source registers are not altered after the PUSH instruction.

RAL: ROTATE ACCUMULATOR LEFT THROUGH CARRY

Opcode	Operand	Bytes	M-Cycles	T-States	Hex Code
RAL	None	1	1	4	17

Description   Each binary bit of the accumulator is rotated left by one position through the Carry flag. Bit D_7 is placed in the bit in the Carry flag and the Carry flag is placed in the least significant position D_0.

Flags   CY is modified according to bit D_7. S, Z, AC, P are not affected.

Rotate the contents of the accumulator through Carry, assuming the accumulator has A7H   **Example**
and the Carry flag is reset.

Instruction: RAL   Hex Code: 17

CY
$\boxed{0}$

Accumulator contents
before instruction

D_7	D_6	D_5	D_4	D_3	D_2	D_1	D_0
1	0	1	0	0	1	1	1

CY
$\boxed{1}$

Accumulator contents
after instruction

0	1	0	0	1	1	1	0

Comment   This instruction effectively provides a 9-bit accumulator. The original contents of the accumulator can be restored by using instruction RAR (Rotate Accumulator Right Through Carry). However; the contents will be modified if the instruction RRC (Rotate Accumulator Right) is used to restore the contents.

RAR: ROTATE ACCUMULATOR RIGHT THROUGH CARRY

Opcode	Operand	Bytes	M-Cycles	T-States	Hex Code
RAR	None	1	1	4	1F

Description   Each binary bit of the accumulator is rotated right by one position through the Carry flag. Bit D_0 is placed in the Carry flag and the bit in the Carry flag is placed in the most significant position, D_7.

Flags   CY is modified according to bit D_0. S, Z, P, AC are not affected.

Example

Rotate the contents of the accumulator assuming it contains A7H and the Carry flag is reset to 0.

Instruction   RAR   Hex Code: 1F

CY
$\boxed{0}$

Accumulator contents
before instruction

D_7	D_6	D_5	D_4	D_3	D_2	D_1	D_0
1	0	1	0	0	1	1	1

CY
$\boxed{1}$

Accumulator contents
after instruction

0	1	0	1	0	0	1	1

RLC: ROTATE ACCUMULATOR LEFT

Opcode	Operand	Bytes	M-Cycles	T-States	Hex Code
RLC	None	1	1	4	07

Description   Each binary bit of the accumulator is rotated left by one position. Bit D_7 is placed in the position of D_0 as well as in the Carry flag.

Flags   CY is modified according to bit D_7. S, Z, P, AC are not affected.

Rotate the contents of the accumulator left, assuming it contains A7H and the Carry flag is reset to 0.

Example

Instruction   RLC   Hex Code: 07

CY
[0]

Accumulator contents
before instruction

D_7	D_6	D_5	D_4	D_3	D_2	D_1	D_0
1	0	1	0	0	1	1	1

CY
[1]

Accumulator contents
after instruction

0	1	0	0	1	1	1	1

Comments   The contents of bit D_7 are placed in bit D_0, and the Carry flag is modified accordingly. However, the contents of the Carry are not placed in bit D_0 as in instruction RAL.

RRC: ROTATE ACCUMULATOR RIGHT

Opcode	Operand	Bytes	M-Cycles	T-States	Hex Code
RRC	None	1	1	4	0F

Description   Each binary bit of the accumulator is rotated right by one position. Bit D_0 is placed in the position of D_7 as well as in the Carry flag.

Flags   CY is modified according to bit D_0. S, Z, P, AC are not affected.

Rotate the contents of the accumulator right, if it contains A7H and the Carry flag is reset to 0.

Example

Instruction RRC   Hex Code: 0F

CY

0

Accumulator contents
before instruction

D_7	D_6	D_5	D_4	D_3	D_2	D_1	D_0
1	0	1	0	0	1	1	1

CY

1

Accumulator contents
after instruction

1	1	0	1	0	0	1	1

Comments The contents of bit D_0 are placed in bit D_7, and the Carry flag is modified accordingly. However, the contents of the Carry are not placed in bit D_7, as in the instruction RAR.

RET: RETURN FROM SUBROUTINE UNCONDITIONALLY

Opcode	Operand	Bytes	M-Cycles	T-States	Hex Code
RET	None	1	3	10	C9

Description The program sequence is transferred from the subroutine to the calling program. The two bytes from the top of the stack are copied into the program counter and the program execution begins at the new address. The instruction is equivalent to *POP Program Counter.*

Flags No flags are affected.

Example

Assume the stack pointer is pointing to location 2095H. Explain the effect of the RET instruction if the contents of the stack locations are as follows:

2095 | 50 |

2096 | 20 |

After instruction RET, the program execution is transferred to location 2050H and the stack pointer is shifted to location 2097H.

Comments This instruction is used in conjunction with CALL or conditional call instructions.

RETURN CONDITIONALLY

Op Code	Description	Flag Status	Hex Code	M-Cycles/T-States
RC	Return on Carry	CY = 1	D8	8080 1/5 If condition is not true

RNC	Return with No Carry	CY = 0	D0		3/11 If condition is true
RP	Return on positive	S = 0	F0	8085	1/6 If condition is not true
RM	Return on minus	S = 1	F8		3/12 If condition is true
RPE	Return on Parity Even	P = 1	E8	Note:	If condition is not true, it continues
RPO	Return on Parity Odd	P = 0	E0		the sequence and thus requires
RZ	Return on Zero	Z = 1	C8		fewer T-states
RNZ	Return on No Zero	Z = 0	C0		:If condition is true, it returns to the

calling program and thus requires
more T-states.

Flags No flags are affected.

RIM: READ INTERRUPT MASK (8085 ONLY)

Opcode	**Operand**	**Bytes**	**M-Cycles**	**T-States**	**Hex Code**
RIM	None	1	1	4	20

Description This is a multipurpose instruction used to read the status of interrupts 7.5, 6.5, 5.5 and read serial data input bit. The instruction loads eight bits in the accumulator with the following interpretations:

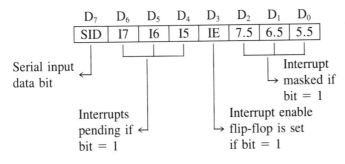

Flags No flags are affected.

After the execution of instruction RIM, the accumulator contained 49H. Explain the accumulator contents. Example

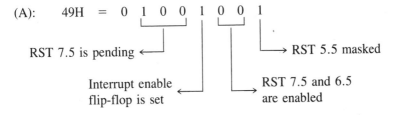

RST: RESTART

	Bytes	M-Cycles	T-States
	1	3	12 (8085)
			11 (8080)

Opcode/Operand	Binary Code	Hex Code	Restart Address (H)
RST 0	1 1 0 0 0 1 1 1	C7	0000
RST 1	1 1 0 0 1 1 1 1	CF	0008
RST 2	1 1 0 1 0 1 1 1	D7	0010
RST 3	1 1 0 1 1 1 1 1	DF	0018
RST 4	1 1 1 0 0 1 1 1	E7	0020
RST 5	1 1 1 0 1 1 1 1	EF	0028
RST 6	1 1 1 1 0 1 1 1	F7	0030
RST 7	1 1 1 1 1 1 1 1	FF	0038

Description   The RST instructions are equivalent to 1-byte call instructions to one of the eight memory locations on page 0. The instructions are generally used in conjunction with interrupts and inserted using external hardware. However, these can be used as software instructions in a program to transfer program execution to one of the eight locations.

Flags   No flags are affected.

Additional 8085 Interrupts   The 8085 has four additional interrupts and these interrupts generate RST instructions internally and thus do not require any external hardware. These instructions and their Restart addresses are as follows:

Interrupts	Restart Address
TRAP	24H
RST 5.5	2CH
RST 6.5	34H
RST 7.5	3CH

SBB: SUBTRACT SOURCE AND BORROW FROM ACCUMULATOR

Opcode	Operand	Bytes	M-Cycles	T-States	Hex Code	
					Reg.	Hex
SBB	Reg.	1	1	4	B	98
	Mem.		2	7	C	99

D	9A
E	9B
H	9C
L	9D
M	9E
A	9F

Description   The contents of the operand (register or memory) and the Borrow flag are subtracted from the contents of the accumulator and the results are placed in the accumulator. The contents of the operand are not altered; however, the previous Borrow flag is reset.

Flags   All flags are altered to reflect the result of the subtraction.

Assume the accumulator contains 37H, register B contains 3FH, and the Borrow flag is already set by the previous operation. Subtract the contents of B with the borrow from the accumulator.

Example

Instruction   SBB   B   Hex Code: 98
The subtraction is performed in 2's complement; however, the borrow needs to be added first to the subtrahend.

| (B): | 3F |
| Borrow: | + 1 |

Subtrahend:	40H	=	0	1	0	0	0	0	0	0		
2's complement of 40H		=	1	1	0	0	0	0	0	0		
(A)		=	0	0	1	1	0	1	1	1		
		0/	1	1	1	1	0	1	1	1	=	F7H
Complement Carry:		1/	1	1	1	1	0	1	1	1		

The Borrow flag is set to indicate the result is in 2's complement. The previous Borrow flag is reset during the subtraction.

SBI: SUBTRACT IMMEDIATE WITH BORROW

Opcode	Operand	Bytes	M-Cycles	T-States	Hex Code
SBI	8-Bit Data	2	2	7	DE

Description   The 8-bit data (operand) and the borrow are subtracted from the contents of the accumulator, and the results are placed in the accumulator.

Flags   All flags are altered to reflect the result of the operation.

Example

Assume the accumulator contains 37H and the Borrow flag is set. Subtract 25H with borrow from the accumulator.

Instruction SBI 25H   Hex Code: DE 25

```
                    (Data):  25H
                 + (Borrow):  1H
                 Subtrahend: 26H  =  0 0 1 0 0 1 1 0
          2's Complement of 26H  =  1 1 0 1 1 0 1 0
                     (A) 37H  =  0 0 1 1 0 1 1 1
                              1/ 0 0 0 1 0 0 0 1  =  11H
           Complement Carry:  0/ 0 0 0 1 0 0 0 1  =  11H
                       Flags:  S = 0, Z = 0, AC = 1
                               P = 1, CY = 0
```

SHLD: STORE H AND L REGISTERS DIRECT

Opcode	Operand	Bytes	M-Cycles	T-States	Hex Code
SHLD	16-Bit Address	3	5	16	22

Description The contents of register L are stored in the memory location specified by the 16-bit address in the operand and the contents of H register are stored in the next memory location by incrementing the operand. The contents of registers HL are not altered. This is a 3-byte instruction, the second byte specifies the low-order address and the third byte specifies the high-order address.

Flags No flags are affected.

Example

Assume the H and L registers contain 01H and FFH, respectively. Store the contents at memory location 2050H and 2051H.

Instruction SHLD 2050H   Hex Code: 22 50 20

Register contents
before instruction

Memory and register contents
after instruction

H `01` `FF` L

2050 `FF`
2051 `01`

H `01` `FF` L

SIM: SET INTERRUPT MASK (FOR 8085 ONLY)

Opcode	Operand	Bytes	M-Cycles	T-States	Hex Code
SIM	None	1	1	4	30

Description   This is a multipurpose instruction and used to implement the 8085 interrupts (RST 7.5, 6.5, and 5.5) and serial data output.

The instruction interprets the accumulator contents as follows:

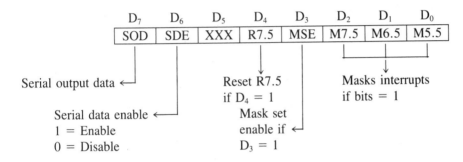

- ☐ SOD — Serial Output Data: Bit D_7 of the accumulator is latched into the SOD output line and made available to a serial peripheral if bit $D_6 = 1$.
- ☐ SDE — Serial Data Enable: If this bit = 1, it enables the serial output. To implement serial output, this bit needs to be enabled.
- ☐ XXX — Don't Care
- ☐ R7.5 — Reset RST 7.5: If this bit = 1, RST 7.5 flip-flop is reset. This is an additional control to reset RST 7.5.
- ☐ MSE — Mask Set Enable: If this bit is high, it enables the functions of bits D_2, D_1, D_0. This is a master control over all the interrupt masking bits. If this bit is low, bits D_2, D_1, and D_0 do not have any effect on the masks.
- ☐ M7.5 — D_2 = 0, RST 7.5 is enabled.
             = 1, RST 7.5 is masked or disabled.
- ☐ M6.5 — D_1 = 0, RST 6.5 is enabled.
             = 1, RST 6.5 is masked or disabled.
- ☐ M5.5 — D_0 = 0, RST 5.5 is enabled.
             = 1, RST 5.5 is masked or disabled.

Write instructions to enable interrupt RST 5.5 and mask other interrupts.   **Example**

Instructions   MVI A,0EH   ;Bits $D_3 = 1$ and $D_0 = 0$
                    SIM   ;Enable RST 5.5

Example   A TTY receiver line is connected to the SOD pin of the 8085. Disable all interrupts and
                 send START bit (logic 0) to TTY without affecting interrupt masks.

                 Instructions   MVI A,40H   ;D_7 = 0, START bit at logic 0
                                                     ;D_6 = 1, Enables serial output bit D_7
                                                     ;D_3 = 0, Does not affect masks

                              SIM   ;Send START bit

                 Comments   This instruction does not affect TRAP interrupt.

SPHL: COPY H AND L REGISTERS TO THE STACK POINTER

Opcode	Operand	Bytes	M-Cycles	T-States	Hex Code
SPHL	None	1	1	6 (8085) 5 (8080)	F9

Description   The instruction loads the contents of the H and L registers into the stack
pointer register, the contents of the H register provide the high-order address and the
contents of the L register provide the low-order address. The contents of the H and L
registers are not altered.

Flags   No flags are affected.

STA: STORE ACCUMULATOR DIRECT

Opcode	Operand	Bytes	M-Cycles	T-States	Hex Code
STA	16-Bit	3	4	13	32

Description   The contents of the accumulator are copied to a memory location specified
by the operand. This is a 3-byte instruction, the second byte specifies the low-order
address and the third byte specifies the high-order address.

Flags   No flags are affected.

Example   Assume the accumulator contains 9FH. Load the accumulator contents into memory
                 location 2050H.

                 Instruction   STA 2050H   Hex Code: 32   50   20

Register contents
before instruction

A | 9F | XX | F

Memory contents
after instruction

2050 | 9F |

STAX: STORE ACCUMULATOR INDIRECT

Opcode	Operand	Bytes	M-Cycles	T-States	Hex Code	
STAX	Reg. Pair	1	2	7	**Reg.**	**Hex**
					B	02
					D	12

Description   The contents of the accumulator are copied into the memory location specified by the contents of the operand (register pair). The contents of the accumulator are not altered.

Flags   No flags are affected.

Assume the contents of the accumulator are F9H and the contents of registers B and C are 20H and 50H, respectively. Store the accumulator contents in memory location 2050H.

Example

Instruction   STAX B   Hex Code: 02

Register contents
before instruction

A | F9 | XX | F
B | 20 | 50 | C

Register and memory contents
after instruction

2050 | F9 |

A | F9 | XX | F
B | 20 | 50 | C

Comments   This instruction performs the same function as MOV A,M except this instruction uses the contents of BC or DE as memory pointers.

STC: SET CARRY

Opcode	Operand	Bytes	M-Cycles	T-States	Hex Code
STC	None	1	1	4	37

Description   The Carry flag is set to 1.

Flags   No other flags are affected.

SUB: SUBTRACT REGISTER OR MEMORY FROM ACCUMULATOR

Opcode	Operand	Bytes	M-Cycles	T-States	Hex Code	
SUB	Reg.	1	1	4	**Reg.**	**Hex**
	Mem.		2	7	B	90
					C	91
					D	92
					E	93
					H	94
					L	95
					M	96
					A	97

Description   The contents of the register or the memory location specified by the operand are subtracted from the contents of the accumulator, and the results are placed in the accumulator. The contents of the source are not altered.

Flags   All flags are affected to reflect the result of the subtraction.

Example

Assume the contents of the accumulator are 37H and the contents of register C are 40H. Subtract the contents of register C from the accumulator.

Instruction   SUB C   Hex Code: 91

(C):	40H	=	0	1	0	0		0	0	0	0	
2's complement (C):		=	1	1	0	0		0	0	0	0	
(A):	37H	=	0	0	1	1		0	1	1	1	

	0/	1	1	1	1		0	1	1	1		
Complement Carry:	1/	1	1	1	1		0	1	1	1	=	F7H

Flags: S = 1, Z = 0, AC = 0
P = 0, CY = 1

The result, as a negative number, will be in 2's complement and thus the Carry (Borrow) flag is set.

SUI: SUBTRACT IMMEDIATE FROM ACCUMULATOR

Opcode	Operand	Bytes	M-Cycles	T-States	Hex Code
SUI	8-Bit Data	2	2	7	D6

Description   The 8-bit data (the operand) is subtracted from the contents of the accumulator and the results are placed in the accumulator.

Flags   All flags are modified to reflect the results of the subtraction.

Assume the accumulator contains 40H. Subtract 37H from the accumulator.   *Example*

Instruction   SUI   37H   Hex Code: D6   37

Subtrahend :37H	=	0 0 1 1	0 1 1 1
2's complement of 37H	=	1 1 0 0	1 0 0 1
	+		
(A) :40H	=	0 1 0 0	0 0 0 0
		1/ 0 0 0 0	1 0 0 1
Complement Carry:		0/ 0 0 0 0	1 0 0 1 = 09H

Flags: S = 0, Z = 0, AC = 0
P = 1, CY = 0

XCHG: EXCHANGE H AND L WITH D AND E

Opcode	Operand	Bytes	M-Cycles	T-States	Hex Code
XCHG	None	1	1	4	EB

Description   The contents of register H are exchanged with the contents of register D, and the contents of register L are exchanged with the contents of register E.

Flags   No flags are affected.

XRA: EXCLUSIVE OR WITH ACCUMULATOR

Opcode	Operand	Bytes	M-Cycles	T-States	Reg.	Hex
XRA	Reg.	1	1	4	B	A8
	Mem.		2	7	C	A9
					D	AA
					E	AB
					H	AC
					L	AD
					M	AE
					A	AF

Description   The contents of the operand (register or memory) are Exclusive ORed with the contents of the accumulator, and the results are placed in the accumulator. The contents of the operand are not altered.

Flags Z, S, P are altered to reflect the results of the operation. CY and AC are reset.

Example

Assume the contents of the accumulator are 77H and of register D are 56H. Exclusive OR the contents of the register D with the accumulator.

Instruction XRA D   Hex Code: AA

(A):	77H	=	0	1	1	1	0	1	1	1
(D):	56H	=	0	1	0	1	0	1	1	0

Exclusive OR: 0 0 1 0   0 0 0 1
    Flags: S = 0, Z = 0, P = 1,
         CY = 0, AC = 0

XRI: EXCLUSIVE OR IMMEDIATE WITH ACCUMULATOR

Opcode	Operand	Bytes	M-Cycles	T-States	Hex Code
XRI	8-Bit Data	2	2	7	EE

Description The 8-bit data (operand) is Exclusive ORed with the contents of the accumulator and the results are placed in the accumulator.

Flags Z, S, P are altered to reflect the results of the operation. CY and AC are reset.

Example

Assume the contents of the accumulator are 8FH. Exclusive OR the contents of the accumulator with A2H.

Instruction XRI A2H   Hex Code: EE A2

(A):	8FH	=	1	0	0	0	1	1	1	1
(Data):	A2H	=	1	0	1	0	0	0	1	0

Exclusive OR: 0 0 1 0   1 1 0 1
    Flags: S = 0, Z = 0, P = 1
         CY = 0, AC = 0

XTHL: EXCHANGE H AND L WITH TOP OF STACK

Opcode	Operand	Bytes	M-Cycles	T-States	Hex Code
XTHL	None	1	5	16 (8085) 18 (8080)	E3

Description   The contents of the L register are exchanged with the stack location pointed out by the contents of the stack pointer register. The contents of the H register are exchanged with the next stack location (SP + 1); however, the contents of the stack pointer register are not altered.

Flags   No flags are affected.

The contents of various registers and stack locations are as shown:

Example

H | A2 , 57 | L   Stacks
SP | 2095 | 2095 | 38
                  2096 | 67

Illustrate the contents of these registers after instruction XTHL

Register contents   H | 67 , 38 | L   Stack
after XTHL   SP | 2095 | 2095 | 57
                                          2096 | A2

8080A/8085 Instruction Set Index

| Instruction | | Code | Bytes | T States | | Machine Cycles |
				8085A	8080A	
ACI	DATA	CE data	2	7	7	F R
ADC	REG	1000 1SSS	1	4	4	F
ADC	M	8E	1	7	7	F R
ADD	REG	1000 0SSS	1	4	4	F
ADD	M	86	1	7	7	F R
ADI	DATA	C6 data	2	7	7	F R
ANA	REG	1010 0SSS	1	4	4	F
ANA	M	A6	1	7	7	F R
ANI	DATA	E6 data	2	7	7	F R
CALL	LABEL	CD addr	3	18	17	S R R W W*
CC	LABEL	DC addr	3	9/18	11/17	S R•/S R R W W*
CM	LABEL	FC addr	3	9/18	11/17	S R•/S R R W W*
CMA		2F	1	4	4	F
CMC		3F	1	4	4	F
CMP	REG	1011 1SSS	1	4	4	F
CMP	M	BE	1	7	7	F R
CNC	LABEL	D4 addr	3	9/18	11/17	S R•/S R R W W*
CNZ	LABEL	C4 addr	3	9/18	11/17	S R•/S R R W W*
CP	LABEL	F4 addr	3	9/18	11/17	S R•/S R R W W*

8080A/8085 Instruction Set Index — *(continued)*

Instruction		Code	Bytes	T States 8085A	T States 8080A	Machine Cycles
CPE	LABEL	EC addr	3	9/18	11/17	S R•/S R R W W*
CPI	DATA	FE data	2	7	7	F R
CPO	LABEL	E4 addr	3	9/18	11/17	S R•/S R R W W*
CZ	LABEL	CC addr	3	9/18	11/17	S R•/S R R W W*
DAA		27	1	4	4	F
DAD	Rp	00Rp 1001	1	10	10	F B B
DCR	REG	00SS S101	1	4	5	F*
DCR	M	35	1	10	10	F R W
DCX	Rp	00Rp 1011	1	6	5	S*
DI		F3	1	4	4	F
EI		FB	1	4	4	F
HLT		76	1	5	7	F B
IN	PORT	DB data	2	10	10	F R I
INR	REG	00SS S100	1	4	5	F*
INR	M	34	1	10	10	F R W
INX	Rp	00Rp 0011	1	6	5	S*
JC	LABEL	DA addr	3	7/10	10	F R/F R R$^+$
JM	LABEL	FA addr	3	7/10	10	F R/F R R$^+$
JMP	LABEL	C3 addr	3	10	10	F R R
JNC	LABEL	D2 addr	3	7/10	10	F R/F R R$^+$
JNZ	LABEL	C2 addr	3	7/10	10	F R/F R R$^+$
JP	LABEL	F2 addr	3	7/10	10	F R/F R R$^+$
JPE	LABEL	EA addr	3	7/10	10	F R/F R R$^+$
JPO	LABEL	E2 addr	3	7/10	10	F R/F R R$^+$
JZ	LABEL	CA addr	3	7/10	10	F R/F R R$^+$
LDA	ADDR	3A addr	3	13	13	F R R R
LDAX	Rp	000X 1010	1	7	7	F R
LHLD	ADDR	2A addr	3	16	16	F R R R R
LXI	Rp,DATA16	00Rp 0001 data16	3	10	10	F R R
MOV	REG, REG	01DD DSSS	1	4	5	F*
MOV	M,REG	0111 0SSS	1	7	7	F W
MOV	REG,M	01DD D110	1	7	7	F R
MVI	REG,DATA	00DD D110 data	2	7	7	F R
MVI	M,DATA	36 data	2	10	10	F R W
NOP		00	1	4	4	F
ORA	REG	1011 0SSS	1	4	4	F
ORA	M	B6	1	7	7	F R
ORI	DATA	F6 data	2	7	7	F R
OUT	PORT	D3 data	2	10	10	F R O
PCHL		E9	1	6	5	S*
POP	Rp	11Rp 0001	1	10	10	F R R
PUSH	Rp	11Rp 0101	1	12	11	S W W*
RAL		17	1	4	4	F
RAR		1F	1	4	4	F

8080A/8085 Instruction Set Index — (continued)

Instruction		Code	Bytes	T States 8085A	T States 8080A	Machine Cycles
RC		D8	1	6/12	5/11	S/S R R*
RET		C9	1	10	10	F R R
RIM (8085 only)		20	1	4	—	F
RLC		07	1	4	4	F
RM		F8	1	6/12	5/11	S/S R R*
RNC		D0	1	6/12	5/11	S/S R R*
RNZ		C0	1	6/12	5/11	S/S R R*
RP		F0	1	6/12	5/11	S/S R R*
RPE		E8	1	6/12	5/11	S/S R R*
RPO		E0	1	6/12	5/11	S/S R R*
RRC		0F	1	4	4	F
RST	N	11XX X111	1	12	11	S W W*
RZ		C8	1	6/12	5/11	S/S R R*
SBB	REG	1001 1SSS	1	4	4	F
SBB	M	9E	1	7	7	F R
SBI	DATA	DE data	2	7	7	F R
SHLD	ADDR	22 addr	3	16	16	F R R W W
SIM (8085 only)		30	1	4	—	F
SPHL		F9	1	6	5	S*
STA	ADDR	32 addr	3	13	13	F R R W
STAX	Rp	000X 0010	1	7	7	F W
STC		37	1	4	4	F
SUB	REG	1001 0SSS	1	4	4	F
SUB	M	96	1	7	7	F R
SUI	DATA	D6 data	2	7	7	F R
XCHG		EB	1	4	4	F
XRA	REG	1010 1SSS	1	4	4	F
XRA	M	AE	1	7	7	F R
XRI	DATA	EE data	2	7	7	F R
XTHL		E3	1	16	18	F R R W W

NOTES: Machine cycle types:
- F   Four clock period instr fetch
- S   Six clock period instr fetch
- R   Memory read
- I   I/O read
- W   Memory write
- O   I/O write
- B   Bus idle
- X   Variable or optional binary digit
- DDD   Binary digits identifying a destination register ⎱ ⎰ B = 000, C = 001, D = 010 Memory = 110
- SSS   Binary digits identifying a source register   ⎰ ⎱ E = 011, H = 100, L = 101 A = 111
- Rp   Register Pair   BC = 00, HL = 10   DE = 01, SP = 11

*Five clock period instruction fetch with 8080A.

†The longer machine cycle sequence applies regardless of condition evaluation with 8080A.

•An extra READ cycle (R) will occur for this condition with 8080A.

SOURCE: Intel Corporation, *MCS — 80/85 Family User's Manual* (Santa Clara, Calif.: Author, 1979), p. 5-19.

8085/8080A Instruction Summary by Functional Groups

DATA TRANSFER (COPY)

Hex	Mnemonic	Hex	Mnemonic	Hex	Mnemonic	Hex	Mnemonic
40	MOV B,B	58	MOV E,B	70	MOV M,B	1A	LDAX D
41	MOV B,C	59	MOV E,C	71	MOV M,C	2A	LHLD
42	MOV B,D	5A	MOV E,D	72	MOV M,D	3A	LDA
43	MOV B,E	5B	MOV E,E	73	MOV M,E	02	STAX B
44	MOV B,H	5C	MOV E,H	74	MOV M,H	12	STAX D
45	MOV B,L	5D	MOV E,L	75	MOV M,L	22	SHLD
46	MOV B,M	5E	MOV E,M	77	MOV M,A	32	STA
47	MOV B,A	5F	MOV E,A	78	MOV A,B	01	LXI B
48	MOV C,B	60	MOV H,B	79	MOV A,C	11	LXI D
49	MOV C,C	61	MOV H,C	7A	MOV A,D	21	LXI H
4A	MOV C,D	62	MOV H,D	7B	MOV A,E	31	LXI SP
4B	MOV C,E	63	MOV H,E	7C	MOV A,H	F9	SPHL
4C	MOV C,H	64	MOV H,H	7D	MOV A,L	E3	XTHL
4D	MOV C,L	65	MOV H,L	7E	MOV A,M	EB	XCHG
4E	MOV C,M	66	MOV H,M	7F	MOV A,A	D3	OUT
4F	MOV C,A	67	MOV H,A	06	MVI B	DB	IN
50	MOV D,B	68	MOV L,B	0E	MVI C	C5	PUSH B
51	MOV D,C	69	MOV L,C	16	MVI D	D5	PUSH D
52	MOV D,D	6A	MOV L,D	1E	MVI E	E5	PUSH H
53	MOV D,E	6B	MOV L,E	26	MVI H	F5	PUSH PSW
54	MOV D,H	60	MOV L,H	2E	MVI L	C1	POP B
55	MOV D,L	6D	MOV L,L	36	MVI M	D1	POP D
56	MOV D,M	6E	MOV L,M	3E	MVI A	E1	POP H
57	MOV D,A	6F	MOV L,A	0A	LDAX B	F1	POP PSW

ARITHMETIC

Hex	Mnemonic	Hex	Mnemonic	Hex	Mnemonic	Hex	Mnemonic
80	ADD B	C6	ADI	9E	SBB M	3C	INR A
81	ADD C	CE	ACI	9F	SBB A	03	INX B
82	ADD D	90	SUB B	D6	SUI	13	INX D
83	ADD E	91	SUB C	DE	SBI	23	INX H
84	ADD H	92	SUB D	09	DAD B	33	INX SP
85	ADD L	93	SUB E	19	DAD D	05	DCR B
86	ADD M	94	SUB H	29	DAD H	0D	DCR C
87	ADD A	95	SUB L	39	DAD SP	15	DCR D
88	ADC B	96	SUB M	27	DAA	1D	DCR E
89	ADC C	97	SUB A	04	INR B	25	DCR H
8A	ADC D	98	SBB B	0C	INR C	2D	DCR L
8B	ADC E	99	SBB C	14	INR D	35	DCR M
8C	ADC H	9A	SBB D	1C	INR E	3D	DCR A
8D	ADC L	9B	SBB E	24	INR H	0B	DCX B
8E	ADC M	9C	SBB H	2C	INR L	1B	DCX D
8F	ADC A	9D	SBB L	34	INR M	2B	DCX H
						3B	DCX SP

LOGICAL

Hex	Mnemonic	Hex	Mnemonic	Hex	Mnemonic	Hex	Mnemonic
37	STC	A9	XRA C	B3	ORA E	BD	CMP L
A0	ANA B	AA	XRA D	B4	ORA H	BE	CMP M
A1	ANA C	AB	XRA E	B5	ORA L	BF	CMP A
A2	ANA D	AC	XRA H	B6	ORA M	FE	CPI
A3	ANA E	AD	XRA L	B7	ORA A	07	RLC
A4	ANA H	AE	XRA M	F6	ORI	0F	RRC
A5	ANA L	AF	XRA A	B8	CMP B	17	RAL
A6	ANA M	EE	XRI	B9	CMP C	1F	RAR
A7	ANA A	B0	ORA B	BA	CMP D	2F	CMA
E6	ANI	B1	ORA C	BB	CMP E	3F	CMC
A8	XRA B	B2	ORA D	BC	CMP H		

BRANCHING

Hex	Mnemonic	Hex	Mnemonic	Hex	Mnemonic
C3	JMP	D7	RST 2	EC	CPE
C2	JNZ	DF	RST 3	F4	CP
CA	JZ	E7	RST 4	FC	CM
D2	JNC	EF	RST 5	C9	RET
DA	JC	F7	RST 6	C0	RNZ
E2	JPO	FF	RST 7	C8	RZ
EA	JPE	CD	CALL	D0	RNC
F2	JP	C4	CNZ	D8	RC
FA	JM	CC	CZ	E0	RPO
E9	PCHL	D4	CNC	E8	RPE
C7	RST 0	DC	CC	F0	RP
CF	RST 1	E4	CPO	F8	RM

CONTROL

Hex	Mnemonic
00	NOP
76	HLT
F3	DI
FB	EI
20	RIM
30	SIM

8085/8080A Instruction Summary: Hexadecimal Order

Hex	Mnemonic		Hex	Mnemonic		Hex	Mnemonic		Hex	Mnemonic	
00	NOP		11	LXI	D	21	LXI	H	31	LXI	SP
01	LXI	B	12	STAX	D	22	SHLD		32	STA	
02	STAX	B	13	INX	D	23	INX	H	33	INX	SP
03	INX	B	14	INR	D	24	INR	H	34	INR	M
04	INR	B	15	DCR	D	25	DCR	H	35	DCR	M
05	DCR	B	16	MVI	D	26	MVI	H	36	MVI	M
06	MVI	B	17	RAL		27	DAA		37	STC	
07	RLC		19	DAD	D	29	DAD	H	39	DAD	SP
09	DAD	B	1A	LDAX	D	2A	LHLD		3A	LDA	
0A	LDAX	B	1B	DCX	D	2B	DCX	H	3B	DCX	SP
0B	DCX	B	1C	INR	E	2C	INR	L	3C	INR	A
0C	INR	C	1D	DCR	E	2D	DCR	L	3D	DCR	A
0D	DCR	C	1E	MVI	E	2E	MVI	L	3E	MVI	A
0E	MVI	C	1F	RAR		2F	CMA		3F	CMC	
0F	RRC		20	RIM		30	SIM		40	MOV	B,B

Hex	Mnemonic	Hex	Mnemonic	Hex	Mnemonic	Hex	Mnemonic
41	MOV B,C	70	MOV M,B	9F	SBB A	CF	RST 1
42	MOV B,D	71	MOV M,C	A0	ANA B	D0	RNC
43	MOV B,E	72	MOV M,D	A1	ANA C	D1	POP D
44	MOV B,H	73	MOV M,E	A2	ANA D	D2	JNC
45	MOV B,L	74	MOV M,H	A3	ANA E	D3	OUT
46	MOV B,M	75	MOV M,L	A4	ANA H	D4	CNC
47	MOV B,A	76	HLT	A5	ANA L	D5	PUSH D
48	MOV C,B	77	MOV M,A	A6	ANA M	D6	SUI
49	MOV C,C	78	MOV A,B	A7	ANA A	D7	RST 2
4A	MOV C,D	79	MOV A,C	A8	XRA B	D8	RC
4B	MOV C,E	7A	MOV A,D	A9	XRA C	DA	JC
4C	MOV C,H	7B	MOV A,E	AA	XRA D	DB	IN
4D	MOV C,L	7C	MOV A,H	AB	XRA E	DC	CC
4E	MOV C,M	7D	MOV A,L	AC	XRA H	DE	SBI
4F	MOV C,A	7E	MOV A,M	AD	XRA L	DF	RST 3
50	MOV D,B	7F	MOV A,A	AE	XRA M	E0	RPO
51	MOV D,C	80	ADD B	AF	XRA A	E1	POP H
52	MOV D,D	81	ADD C	B0	ORA B	E2	JPO
53	MOV D,E	82	ADD D	B1	ORA C	E3	XTHL
54	MOV D,H	83	ADD E	B2	ORA D	E4	CPO
55	MOV D,L	84	ADD H	B3	ORA E	E5	PUSH H
56	MOV D,M	85	ADD L	B4	ORA H	E6	ANI
57	MOV D,A	86	ADD M	B5	ORA L	E7	RST 4
58	MOV E,B	87	ADD A	B6	ORA M	E8	RPE
59	MOV E,C	88	ADC B	B7	ORA A	E9	PCHL
5A	MOV E,D	89	ADC C	B8	CMP B	EA	JPE
5B	MOV E,E	8A	ADC D	B9	CMP C	EB	XCHG
5C	MOV E,H	8B	ADC E	BA	CMP D	EC	CPE
5D	MOV E,L	8C	ADC H	BB	CMP E	EE	XRI
5E	MOV E,M	8D	ADC L	BC	CMP H	EF	RST 5
5F	MOV E,A	8E	ADC M	BD	CMP L	F0	RP
60	MOV H,B	8F	ADC A	BE	CMP M	F1	POP PSW
61	MOV H,C	90	SUB B	BF	CMP A	F2	JP
62	MOV H,D	91	SUB C	C0	RNZ	F3	DI
63	MOV H,E	92	SUB D	C1	POP B	F4	CP
64	MOV H,H	93	SUB E	C2	JNZ	F5	PUSH PSW
65	MOV H,L	94	SUB H	C3	JMP	F6	ORI
66	MOV H,M	95	SUB L	C4	CNZ	F7	RST 6
67	MOV H,A	96	SUB M	C5	PUSH B	F8	RM
68	MOV L,B	97	SUB A	C6	ADI	F9	SPHL
69	MOV L,C	98	SBB B	C7	RST 0	FA	JM
6A	MOV L,D	99	SBB C	C8	RZ	FB	EI
6B	MOV L,E	9A	SBB D	C9	RET	FC	CM
6C	MOV L,H	9B	SBB E	CA	JZ	FE	CPI
6D	MOV L,L	9C	SBB H	CC	CZ	FF	RST 7
6E	MOV L,M	9D	SBB L	CD	CALL		
6F	MOV L,A	9E	SBB M	CE	ACI		

Index